Big Bore
Rifles & Cartridges

Big Bore
Rifles & Cartridges

Wolfe Publishing Co.
ISBN: 1-879356-00-7
Copyright © 1991

February 1991
Wolfe Publishing Co.
6471 Airpark Drive
Prescott, Arizona 86301

CONTENTS

CHAPTER
1

The Big Bores are back

Al Miller

A LITTLE MORE than a century ago, ordnance experts agreed that the day of the heavy large-caliber bullet was over. The invention of smokeless powder had finally cleared the way for high velocities at safe pressures. The experts were confident that within a few years, light sporting rifles would be firing small-caliber bullets weighing a hundred eighty grains or less, at two thousand or perhaps three thousand feet per second — bullets that could reach out to four or five hundred yards and deliver such tremendous blows that the largest animals would drop in their tracks, their nervous systems in complete disarray and their vital organs a shambles.

Maybe crystal balls of the nineteenth century were superior to the current models; at any rate, those old boys were pretty close to the mark with their predictions. Today, high-intensity, small-caliber, flat-shooting cartridges rule the hunting roost and have for years. Not only can any number of big-game car-

tridges propel bullets to well over three thousand feet per second but thousands of sportsmen have demonstrated pretty conclusively that anyone armed with a .300 Weatherby Magnum or its equivalent can tackle the biggest, meanest game in the world without unduly risking his own neck.

Those old-timers were wrong in one respect, however: although high-velocity cartridges get most attention and the heaviest use these days, those with big, slow bullets are still with us. There aren't as many as there used to be, but those that remain show no sign of disappearing. On the contrary: there seems to be a whole new generation of Americans who are fascinated by them, experiment with them and even hunt with them — and this new interest in the big-bores amounts

almost to a resurrection of the old-time favorites.

When the production of sporting arms resumed after World War Two, almost every rifle chambered for a caliber larger than .32 vanished from the catalogs. The exceptions were the .348 Winchester, which hung-on until 1958, and the .375 H&H Magnum, which is still with us and probably always will be.

Each time an announcement was made that one of the large cartridges was to be discontinued by a manufacturer, the response was a flood of protest letters. Nobody who was in a position to do anything about the matter was impressed; evidently, they attributed all the noise to a militant minority, a

While one hunter is more likely to select a .30-06 for its practical virtues, some are fascinated by a cartridge like this .500 Express.

Although caliber .35 doesn't get much publicity these days, many experienced hunters swear by the likes of the .35 Remington, .358 Winchester, and .350 Remington Magnum — shown here with the .270 Winchester for a size comparison.

Two of the most popular big-bores in America are the .375 H&H Magnum and the .458 Winchester Magnum, here flanking the newest .375 — the .375 Winchester.

handful of nostalgic cranks blessed with more *chutzpah* than purchasing power. Then a strange thing happened, although nobody realized its significance at the time: in 1956, Winchester introduced the first of their innovative short, belted magnums, the .458 Winchester Magnum.

Lots of Americans were going on safari in those days, so there was a ready market for a dependable elephant rifle that didn't cost an arm and a leg. Even though the Model 70 African, as Winchester called it, came only in the Super Grade version, its price of three hundred ten dollars made it just a tenth as costly as the least expensive British double rifle chambered for a comparable cartridge. As a result and to nobody's surprise, the first production rifles were snapped-up as quickly as they were distributed.

Then Bill Ruger chambered his Number One for the old .45-70. Before any of his critics could get off so much as one cutting remark, it was obvious that Ruger had another winner. Shooters' response to the big-bore single-shot was beyond good; it was great. So great was it, in fact, that Ruger soon offered the .45-70 chambering in the lower-cost single-shot, the Number Three.

Knowing a good thing when they saw it, several other arms companies added .45-70s to their lines. Today, Marlin and Harrington & Richardson offer them; Navy Arms sells rebarreled Siamese Mausers and newly manufactured rolling-blocks to fans of the .45-70, while hundreds of custom riflemakers and skilled gunsmiths turn-out yet more rifles chambered for the ancient army cartridge.

Taken singly, either of these success stories could qualify as "just one of those things." But *two* of "those things?" That's asking too much of coincidence. The fact is that there's a sizable number of American riflemen who lean toward the large calibers — there always has been. Anyone who isn't convinced of this need only check with his nearest dealer in bullet moulds — or talk with the folks at Barnes, Eagle Cap, or any other custom-bullet outfit. Most of these admit that they are hard-pressed to keep up with the orders that they receive for bullets in such oddball calibers as .366, .405, .416, .423, .475, and .50. And if their testimony isn't convincing enough, consider the special run of Hornady .416 solids currently sold by Brass Extrusion Labs: in spite of their price — a *dollar* a bullet — those big bullets sell at a steady pace, I'm told. I know a fellow who bought two hundred of them at one time — to add to the supply that he'd already laid-up.

Add together all of these indicators, and they point to only one conclusion that makes any sense: that the big-bore cult in the United States is still alive, well, and livelier than ever.

That term *big-bore* means different things to different people. Here in the United States, most of us follow the National Rifle Association's practice of lumping under that heading everything from caliber .30 up. The British, with their long-cultivated sense of order, prefer to divide sporting cartridges into four neatly defined categories, each appropriately titled. My own approach is a slight modification of the NRA's: in my book, any rifle cartridge with bullets 0.350 inch or more in diameter and weighing two hundred grains or more qualifies as a big-bore cartridge. I've established those criteria strictly for my own convenience and never carved it into stone. Anyone who favors a different definition, wants to include some of the larger handgun cartridges, or would rather stick with the British system can do whatever he prefers, with my blessing.

Why, in this day and age, would anyone prefer big, slow bullets to ones that are faster, shoot flatter, and are easier to hit with? Quite a number of sportsmen hunt with them because of a conviction that under certain conditions and against some species of game animals, large-caliber bullets offer definite advantages. Traditionally, woods hunters have always subscribed to that thinking. They insist that big, heavy bullets are better able to plow unswervingly through bush and thicket than the lighter, narrower, and more pointed bullets are. Plenty of old hands argue the point still, but a variety of field tests reveal that in the woods, the odds favor the big-bores.

No bullet is immune to deflection, no matter how heavy it is, how it's constructed, or how large its diameter is. Still, if you fire a hundred .30 spitzers and the same number of .45 flat-noses at targets obscured by a screen of brush, the .45s' percentage of hits will be higher.

Although the country where they hunt is quite different now, multitudes of elk hunters also depend upon the heavier calibers like the .35s and the .375s. The big belted cartridges, they insist, put the big deer down much more positively than cartridges like the .270 Winchester, the .30-06, or even the vaunted 7mm Remington Magnum.

Whether all that extra power is really necessary is open to argument. But one acquaintance of mine, who has tagged at least twenty good bulls with his old .375, explains his preference this way: "Sure, an aught-six or a two-seventy will fill a freezer with elk meat, but I've seen lots of bulls hit with those cartridges — hit hard, too — and never give the slightest indication

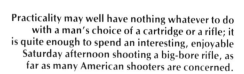

Practicality may well have nothing whatever to do with a man's choice of a cartridge or a rifle; it is quite enough to spend an interesting, enjoyable Saturday afternoon shooting a big-bore rifle, as far as many American shooters are concerned.

If calibers thirty and below are smallbores, then these are certainly big-bore bullets: a 250-grain .338 and a pair of Barnes .416s weighing three hundred and four hundred grains.

Hunters who handload cartridges in caliber .375 can easily match their loads to the game that they hunt, with bullets like the two-twenty-grain Hornady, two-thirty-five Speer, two-seventy Hornady, three-hundred Hornady, and three-hundred Sierra. Many are finding this caliber a good "all-around."

that they'd been touched. Every year, wounded elk get away because the guys who shoot 'em think that they've missed. When I hit an elk with that three-seventy-five, even when the bullet doesn't go *exactly* where I want it to, we both know it. If he doesn't drop, he stumbles or sheers away. There's no doubt that he's hit. And there's always a good blood trail — although I've never had to follow one more than a couple of hundred yards or so. Since I started packing the three-seventy-five, I've never lost an elk — not one." Even if you don't agree with this man's choice of an elk rifle, you have to admit that his rationale has merit.

A new type of big-bore hunter has surfaced over the last four or five years. I'm not referring here to the muzzle-loader hunters — they're a breed apart — but to a distinct class

of sportsmen who rely on the last century's rifles, originals and replicas, to bring their game down. They favor rifles that range from heavy, long-barreled Winchester lever-actions and Remington rolling-blocks to replicas of the Sharps rifles. Their chamberings are just as varied, with .45s and .50s predominating but with a good sprinkling of .38s and .40s. Nearly all of these fellows depend on cast bullets.

How successful are they? One of my acquaintances has taken six better-than-average antelope with a .50-70; another has brought in three excellent mule-deer bucks over the last three seasons with a replica of a Sharps chambered for the .45-90 — and he took them out on the plains, where most shots exceed two hundred fifty yards.

Even those who come home empty-handed seldom complain about their poor luck. The limitations of their rifles, they maintain, force them to put the emphasis where it belongs : on hunting know-how, on the estimation of wind and distance, and on plain old-fashioned marksmanship. Admittedly, that makes everything tougher than needs be, but as one fan of a .40 cartridge put it, "when I do bring home some venison — and I've succeeded only once in three tries — I really feel like I've done something!"

For every big-bore rifle carried afield, there must be a couple of dozen that never get farther from home than the nearest rifle range. Most clubs, I'm told, have their share of regulars who shoot nothing but vintage arms. The range that I use has its share of these fellows; one who is out there quite a bit has a

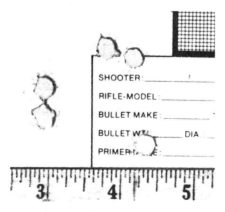

Many shooters who favor big-bore cartridges find that although the trajectory may not be the flattest, accuracy is usually quite good. A bench-supported .458 Winchester Magnum made this inch-and-a-quarter group at a hundred yards, and better accuracy isn't unusual.

Just when a good many American shooters thought that the big-bore was obsolete, the never-quite-dead .45-70 Government started its remarkable come-back, which has been such a success that several ammunition manufacturers now offer flatter-shooting loads for it.

Shooters who favor caliber .35 find a smaller variety of bullets available now than there used to be, but those that are still available are deadly and useful — for example, Sierra and Hornady two-hundred-grains, and Hornady and Speer two-fifty-grains.

The fellows who like caliber .45 have increased in number over the last several years, and the popularity of this caliber has increased the number of bullet available for handloads. A .375 bullet is small alongside the likes of these .45 weighing from three hundred to five hundred grains.

fine collection of Remington rolling-blocks in buffalo calibers. He's a remarkable shot — I've seen him punch-out off-hand targets, with those old charcoal burners, that I'd be proud to call mine.

This burgeoning interest in the rifles of yesteryear has spawned a new industry. Today, a rifleman can indulge his ambition to shoot his grandfather's rifle without risking either his heirloom or his neck. Replica arms of all descriptions are available, based on the patterns of such as the Winchester Model 1873, the Remington rolling-blocks, the trap-door Springfields, the Sharps, the Henry — just about any rifle that figured prominently in our nation's history. Most of these replicas are made well enough and are stronger than the originals.

In addition, there are those who regard gaping muzzles and finger-long cartridge cases as personal challenges. Most of the big-bores have more than enough recoil; even a .45-70 loaded with watered-down factory loads comes back against the shoulder with a fairly noticeable amount of authority. Not everyone can control such healthy kickers; so in some eyes, there's an aura of *machismo* surrounding anyone who totes *and fires* an elephant rifle with any frequency and aplomb.

One local shooter — a short, wiry retired marine — was smart enough to acquire a number of British double rifles fifteen or twenty years ago, when they were still priced within reason. Every week or so, he shows-up on the firing line with one

and proceeds to try some new combination of powder and bullet. He can't weigh more than a hundred fifty pounds, but those heavy rifles are perfectly disciplined in his hands. Despite all the ammunition that Si burns, he has never — to the best of my knowledge — hunted so much as a rabbit. He simply likes to shoot elephant rifles.

Like shooting muzzle-loaders, shooting big-bore rifles can be addictive. A month or so back, I was trying-out some new cast-bullet loads in a .458 Winchester Magnum. A couple of benches down the line, another shooter was keeping an eye on my progress. Noting his interest, I offered him the last five rounds. He put the first two an inch and a half apart on the hundred-yard target, then turned to the gong — a chunk of armor plate about eight inches square, hanging on the end of a wire out at two hundred sixty yards. Each of the last three 350-grains made that gong clang merrily and dance a wild jig. He looked up and in an awed whisper said, "I got to get me one of these." Two weeks later, he came to the range with a Ruger Model 77 in .458 Winchester Magnum and has been trying to wear it out ever since.

To the dedicated handloader, the most attractive trait of a big-bore is its high accuracy potential. Everyone who has ever said or written anything of consequence about the renowned .375 H&H Magnum has included a few remarks about its superb grouping. The same is true of most large-caliber cartridges. The

obsolete .38-55 wasn't *accidentally* the choice of so many target shooters of the late nineteenth century; and its modern descendent, the .375 Winchester, shows the same natural inclination to cut tight groups. Even the more ferocious .458 Winchester Magnum prints close to an inch when a shooter who can control it shoots it from a bench.

There are, no doubt, other reasons for American shooters' fascination for the big-bores. I'm convinced that most reasons fall under the classification of recreational shooting — shooting for the pure pleasure of shooting rather than in hunting or competing. Perhaps that's what fooled so many experts for so many years: then tend to judge sporting cartridges by their utilitarian value, forgetting that there's more to a rifleman's life than medals and antlers.

A hunter's choice of cartridge usually depends upon what he is accustomed to or what is popular among his comrades. Technological advantages, genuine or imaginary, exercise much less influence on sales than you might suppose. That's one of the reasons that the popularity of the .30-30 endures. It also helps to explain the existence of so many big-bore hold-outs.

Big-bore cartridges and rifles are anything but endangered. As long as there are woods hunters and those who shoot buffalo guns, elephant cartridges, and antiques simply for the fun of it, long cases behind large-caliber bullets will abound. ●

CHAPTER
2

Loading the Big Bores

Al Miller

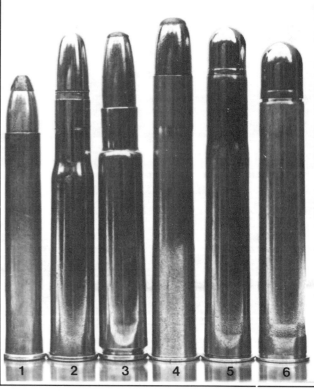

Handloading components are readily available for these and other near-extinc African cartridges: (1) .405 Winchester, (2) .450/400 N.E., (3) .416 Rigby, (4 .450 N.E., (5) .470 N.E. and (6) .500 N.E.

HANDLOADING foreign cartridges, especially the British proprietary rounds, used to be a real chore. Factory brass was almost impossible to find and locating the proper primers and bullets was not only a challenge to the imagination but a test of character as well. Fortunately, the days of rim-turning, cutting new extractor grooves and machining belts away are long gone. First, Jim Bell began manufacturing a few of the more popular, Boxer-primed Basic cases, then custom bullet makers got into the act. Later, foreign firms, sniffing a burgeoning market for their wares, joined in. Today, anyone desiring to assemble ammunition for antique rifles or arms chambered for British or metric calibers will find all the ingredients at his disposal, from dies to completely formed cases made to accept Boxer primers. In addition, Berdan primers of all sizes are available for those lucky enough to have a stock of original British or metric brass.

Although not absolutely necessary, it's a good idea to know exactly what you're dealing with when reloading a foreign-made firearm. Slugging bores and making chamber casts before attempting to develop handloads can save a great deal of frustration and grief later on. Worn bores, eroded throats, eccentric or pitted chambers are easier to cope with when you know they exist.

Along the same lines, a chronograph is a great help. Not only will it register the velocities a load actually develops but it will give the shooter a better feel for powder burning rates, load unifor-

mity, the effect of switching primers, crimping, seating depth adjustments and detecting pressure aberrations. It's like having a small, portable laboratory at your beck and call. There are any number on the market now, ranging in price from $100 to $500, depending on quality, complexity and the amount of data they compute. Some even come equipped with printers — not necessary but nice to have. A chronograph can take most of the guesswork out of load development.

No data for any of the old black powder rounds or "Nitro for Black" loads (those created by Kynoch and others to be fired in rifles originally chambered for black powder cartridges) are covered here.

Why not?

Because many of those arms are more than 100 years old. Neither metal nor wood become stronger with age. Since the performance of, say, a .450 Black Powder Express (BPE) can be duplicated with modern black powder or Pyrodex, why should anyone chance ruining a fine antique and possibly sustaining injuries experimenting with modern smokeless powders? Granted, a bore fouled by smokeless powder is easier to clean than one littered with black powder residue, but a 450-grain cast bullet launched around 1,750 fps

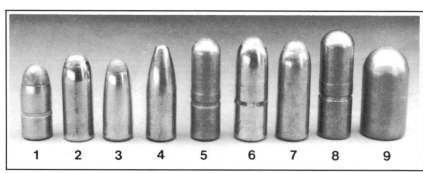

These are just some of the jacketed bullets available to the African cartridge handloader: (1) 300-grain .412 custom, (2) 350-grain .412 Barnes, (3) 300-grain .416 Hawk, (4) 350-grain .416 Barnes-X, (5) 400-grain .416 A-Square, (6) 500-grain .458 Hornady, (7) 500-grain .458 Woodleigh, (8) 460-grain .457 A-Square and (9) 850-grain .622 custom.

8

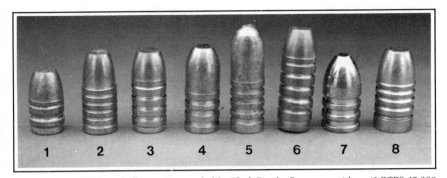

Here are a few of the cast bullets recommended for Black Powder Express cartridges: (*1*) RCBS 45-300 FN, (*2*) 390-grain Hoch, (*3*) RCBS 45-405 FN, (*4*) Lyman 457193, (*5*) Lyman 457125, (*6*) RCBS 45-500 FN, (*7*) Lyman 515141 and (*8*) Lyman 515142.

from a .500 BPE is no less deadly because it's propelled by GOEX FFg instead of cordite or IMR-4831. Besides, if cleaning bores and cartridge cases is the primary objection, switch to Pyrodex. It's much cleaner burning.

To sum up: Rifles that are proofed for black powder should never be exposed to smokeless powder pressures.

Owners of black powder doubles, however, will find it worthwhile to experiment with different grades of black and Pyrodex. Although a given rifle may have been regulated for a charge of 142 grains of (black) powder, probabilities are that the burning characteristics of the original British or Continental powder were markedly different from those of their modern equivalents. Their grades weren't the same, either. Consequently, the burning rate of GOEX FFg probably won't duplicate that of Curtis & Harvey's No. 6. Considering the relative inefficiency of black powders as compared to smokeless, a slight discrepancy like that isn't enough to lose sleep over, but it might have a decidedly adverse effect on the grouping ability of an old double rifle.

A .500 three-inch BPE double in my rack is a case in point. Specifications of the original load called for either a 340 or a 380-grain patched alloy bullet seated over 136 grains of black powder (grade unspecified). After trying every combination of components I could think of, best accuracy was achieved with 100 grains of RS-grade Pyrodex plus a tuft of Dacron filler behind Lyman's 509134, which weighed 354 grains. Velocity, 10 feet from the muzzles, averaged 1,750 fps, some 150 fps slower than the published ballistics claimed. On the other hand, that load let both barrels put all their bullets in 2.5 inches at 100 yards, right where the

sights pointed. Any time I can get that kind of accuracy with open sights, I'm more than happy to settle for it. When cases were filled with a full charge of Fg, the best those same bullets would do was four to six inches at the same range, and point of impact was four inches above the aiming point.

Of course, critics will point out that

the accuracy load didn't pack the punch the full load did. That's true, but none of the deer hit by any of those Pyrodex-launched bullets seemed to notice.

Black powder loads always benefit from a hot primer. RWS primers can be substituted for British Berdan primers in Kynoch cases. If Boxer-primed cases are employed, try any Large Rifle Magnum primers. Their hotter spark improves combustion and, consequently, reduces variations in velocities from one round to the next.

A wad between the powder and the bullet's base also reduces velocity variations, or the extreme spread, as many prefer. As a rule, the more uniform the ammunition's performance, the better its accuracy. It doesn't always work that way, unfortunately. Rifles, double rifles in particular, are highly individualistic. That's why experimentation often pays unexpected dividends to anyone shooting black powder or Pyrodex.

Sources of Boxer-Primed Cartridge Cases

New Cases Can Be Obtained

caliber	from loaded ammunition sold by	or formed from
.450/.400-3″ Nitro	2,4	.450-3¼″ Basic brass
.450/.400-3¼″ Magnum	2,4	.450-3¼″ Basic brass
.416 Remington	local dealers*	
.416 Rigby	2,3	
.416 Weatherby	local dealers*	
.404 Jeffery (10.75x73)	5	
10.75x68	5	
.425 Westley Richards	1,2	.425 Basic brass
.500/.450 Magnum NE-3¼″	1	.500-3¼″ Basic brass
.450 No. 2 NE-3½″	1,2,5	
.450 NE-3¼″	1,2,4	.450-3¼″ Basic brass
.458 Winchester Magnum	local dealers*	
.460 Weatherby Magnum	local dealers*	
.500/.465 NE	1,2,4,5	.500-3¼″ Basic brass
.470 NE	1,2,3,4,5,6	.500-3¼″ Basic brass
.475 NE		.475-3¼″ Basic brass
.475 No. 2 NE	1,2	.475-3¼″ Basic brass
.475 No. 2 Jeffery		.475-3¼″ Basic brass
.476 NE Westley Richards	1	.500-3¼″ Basic brass
.500 NE-3″	1,2	.500-3¼″ Basic brass
.500 Rimless Jeffery	none known	must be machined from brass stock
.505 Gibbs	1,2,3	.505 Gibbs Basic brass
.577-2¾″		.577-3″ Basic brass
.577 NE-3″	1,2	.577-3″ Basic brass
.600 NE	1,5,6	

*Unprimed cases also available

1. Afsco Ammunition, Box L, Owen WI 54460
2. A-Square, One Industrial Park, Bedford KY 40006
3. Federal Cartridge Company, 900 Ehlen Dr., Anoka MN 55303
4. Huntington, Box 991, Oroville CA 95965
5. The Old Western Scrounger, 12924 Hwy. A-12, Montague CA 06064
6. PMC-Eldorado Cartridge Corp., Box 308, Boulder City NV 89005-0308

The same is true of those substituting American smokeless powders for cordite or one of the German flake powders. Since the burning characteristics of our propellants aren't identical to those of the foreign powders, chances are that barrel vibrations will be slightly different, too. That may not have any noticeable effect on a bolt action rifle's accuracy, but it probably will in a double rifle's. To put it another way: Simply duplicating the ballistics of a foreign cartridge may or may not result in an accurate round or a cartridge whose bullets will go where a double rifle's sights indicate they should.

A few decades back, it was common practice among American handloaders to substitute IMR-3031, grain for grain, for cordite when developing a load for British cartridges. The result was a safe starting load, with pressures and velocities a bit lower than the round's original ballistics called for. By working up slowly and carefully, adding half a grain at a time, it was possible to duplicate the cartridge's original velocities at safe pressure levels. As time passed and more experience was accumulated with British ammunition, the consensus changed. Today, it is generally agreed by most experienced handloaders that the best powder is the one which fills at least 90 percent of the case and delivers the specified muzzle velocities at reasonable pressure levels.

Currently, IMR-4831 is the powder of choice. For a starting load, simply multiply the original cordite charge by 1.333. The result is the substitute charge of IMR-4831. Some prefer to play it safer by depending on Hodgdon's H-4831 because it's a bit slower burning and consequently, fills even more of the case. IMR-7828 is another slow powder worth considering. So is Hodgdon's new H-1000. Whichever propellant is selected, everyone agrees it should be ignited by

Load Data

caliber	bullet weight (grains)	bullet diameter (inches)	handloads original charge (grains)	charge (grains)	powder	velocity (fps)	remarks
.450/.400-3" Nitro	400	.408-.411	60*	79	IMR-4831	2,125	26-inch barrel
.450/.400-3¼" Magnum Nitro	400	.408-.411	60*	79	IMR-4831	2,130	26-inch barrels
.416 Remington	350	.416	–	81	W-748	2,535	24-inch barrel
	400		–	82	IMR-4350	2,345	
			–	87	H-414	2,366	
			–	75	IMR-4320	2,374	
.416 Rigby	300	.416	–	105	AAC-3100	2,681	
			–	105	IMR-4350	2,957	
	350		–	105	H-4831	2,578	
			–	114	H-870	2,272	
	400		–	100	Scot 4351	2,718	
			–	105	H-450	2,428	
			–	100	IMR-4350	2,613	
			–	106	H-4831	2,422	
			–	107	IMR-7828	2,422	
.416 Weatherby	300		–	127	RL-22	3,035	24¼-inch barrel
			–	116	IMR-4350	3,045	
	350		–	118	IMR-4831	2,892	
			–	109	RL-19	2,567	
	400		–	108	IMR-4350	2,706	
			–	120	H-1000	2,401	
.404 Jeffery (10.75x73)	400		60*	65	IMR-3031	2,150	
			60*	79	IMR-4831	2,125	
10.75x68	347		–	59	IMR-3031	2,260	
.425 Westley Richards	410	.435	–	80	IMR-4895	2,410	
.500/.450 NE-3¼" Magnum	480	.455-.458	75*	99	IMR-4831	2,175	estimated
			75*	95	IMR-4831	2,050	26-inch barrels
.450 No. 2 NE-3½"	480	.455	80*	106	IMR-4831	2,175	estimated
.450 NE-3¼"	480	.458	70*	93	IMR-4831	2,150	estimated
.458 Winchester Magnum	350	.458	–	73	IMR-3031	2,209	compressed load
			–	72	RL-7	2,194	22-inch barrel
	400		–	75	IMR-4064	2,136	compressed load
			–	76	H-335	2,260	24-inch barrel
	500		–	74	H-335	2,114	22-inch barrel
			–	73.5	IMR-3031	2,116	
.460 Weatherby	350	.458	–	114	IMR-4064	3,007	26-inch barrel
			–	122	H-380	2,872	
	500		–	120	IMR-4831	2,549	
			–	119	W-760	2,455	
	600		–	112	IMR-4350	2,351	
			–	118	H-4831	2,258	

Federal's 215 Magnum primer. Not only does the hotter spark guarantee ignition but it improves combustion, adds a few feet per second to the muzzle velocity and, again, reduces the extreme velocity spread between successive rounds.

Slow-burning powders tend to burn more uniformly when slightly compressed. If there is no compaction — or worse still, if there is space between the top of the charge and the bullet's base — ignition may suffer. Sometimes the charge ignites and burns exactly as it's supposed to; sometimes it doesn't. Every now and then the powder shifts

Load Data
Black Powder Express Cartridges

caliber	powder charge (grains)	bullet diameter (inches)	bullet weight (grains)	velocity (fps)	barrel length (inches)	suggested bullet mould
.450/.400 2⅜"	80	.407	250	1,750	27	NEI 4644, (.408) 245 grains
.450/.400 Magnum 3¼"	110	.405	253	1,900	27	Same as above
.450-3¼"	120	.458	365	1,700	28	Lyman 457483, 378 grains
.500/.450 Magnum 3¼"	140	.455	365	1,875	28	Same as above
.500-3"	136	.510	380	1,850	28	NEI 4649 (.511), 350 grains
.500-3¼"	142	.510	480	1,700	28	Lyman 515141 450 grains
.577/.500 2¹³⁄₁₆"	130	.510	380	1,775	28	NEI 4649 (.511), 350 grains
.577/.500 3⅛"	164	.510	480	1,800	28	Lyman 515142, 515 grains
.577-2¾"	160	.584	560	1,650	28	
.577-3"	167	.584	610	1,650	28	

Be alert — Publisher cannot accept responsibility for errors in published load data.

caliber	bullet weight (grains)	bullet diameter (inches)	original charge (grains)	handloads charge (grains)	powder	velocity (fps)	remarks
.500/465 NE	480	.468	73*	97	IMR-4831	2,150	estimated
	480		–	102	IMR-4831	2,045	26-inch barrels
.470 NE		.475	75*	99	IMR-4831	2,125	estimated
	500		–	107	IMR-4831	2,062	23¾-inch barrel
			–	111	IMR-4831	2,166	
			–	107	AAC-3100	2,152	
			–	98	IMR-4350	2,133	
			–	113	RL-22	2,137	
			–	118	IMR-7828	2,152	
			–	125	H-1000	2,063	
.475 NE	480	.475-.476	75*	99	IMR-4831	2,175	estimated
.475 No. 2 NE	480	.483	85*	113	IMR-4831	2,200	estimated
	500		–	110	IMR-4831	2,179	filler employed
			–	118	IMR-4831	2,277	filler employed
			–	84	IMR-3031	1,988	
.475 No. 2 Jeffery	500	.489	85*	113	IMR-4831	2,120	estimated
.476 Westley Richards	520	.476	75*	99	IMR-4831	2,100	estimated
			–	100	IMR-4350	NR	accurate
.500 NE-3"	570	.510	80*	106	IMR-4831	2,150	estimated
			–	105	IMR-4350	2,190	28-inch barrels
			–	80	IMR-4320	2,150	
.500 NE-3¼"	570	.510	80*	106	IMR-4831	2,125	estimated
.500 Jeffery	535	.510	95*	126	IMR-4831	2,200	estimated
			–	100	IMR-3031	2,400	
			–	120	IMR-4350	2,236	
.505 Gibbs	525	.505	90*	119	IMR-4831	2,100	estimated
			–	130	IMR-4831	2,273	24-inch barrel
			–	100	IMR-4064	2,060	
.577 NE-2¾"	650	.584	90*	119	IMR-4831	1,875	estimated
.577 NE-3"	650	.584	90*	119	IMR-4831	1,800	estimated
	750		–	110	IMR-3031	2,131	.25-inch cork wad and .125-inch polyethylene wad
			–	130	H-4831	1,899	26-inch barrel
			–	134	IMR-4831	1,908	
.600 NE	900	.620	110*	133	IMR-4831	1,780	estimated

*Cordite

Caution: Different primers, case lots and brands of bullets can boost pressures unexpectedly. Reduce all listed loads at least 10 percent before trying them in your rifle.

Be alert — Publisher cannot accept responsibility for errors in published load data.

forward, away from the primer. When the latter ignites and its hot flame squirts through the flash hole, the powder doesn't always catch properly. Occasionally the grains spark and fizzle before they begin to burn; once in a while, nothing happens at all and the shooter is left wondering.

On a rifle range, a hangfire or misfire can be frustrating but if such an incident was to take place a few yards from several tons of enraged buffalo homing in on the rifleman, the consequences would be far more memorable. Instant, reliable ignition is a must in any handload; that's why every effort should be made to keep the powder charge back where it belongs: against the flash hole.

A full charge, one which fills the case to the bullet's base, is the simplest way to guarantee that. If 100 percent density isn't practical, the gap between the top of the powder and the bullet can be closed by adding wads or fillers.

Over-powder wads can be made of cardboard, cork or felt. They are formed by the use of a punch and should be slightly oversized so they will make a tight fit when forced down inside the case. When employed, wads should fill the space between powder and bullet completely, otherwise, the wad may become a projectile and the bullet above it an obstruction.

One theory floating around speculates that ringed (bulged) chambers may be explained by cartridges assembled with space left between the over-powder wads and the bullets' bases. When the powder is ignited, the wad is propelled forward, compressing the air imprisoned between it and the bullet. All of this takes place so suddenly, the bullet doesn't have a chance to break away from the case neck's grip before the compressed air forces the brass case to swell outward against the chamber. In turn, the steel in that area gives way before the surging pressure, bulging outward, leaving the chamber wall circumscribed with a permanent, shallow groove.

Inert fillers like cornmeal, Cream of Wheat, Dacron fiber, kapok and toilet tissue have been blamed for the same phenomenon and because of that, have fallen into disrepute. They are also suspected of boosting pressures to dangerous levels. That may be so. Over

the years, I've tried all of them at one time or another and have never experienced any problems. Others have, apparently, so it's prudent to keep all risks, theoretical or otherwise, in mind when assembling any load.

If anyone decides to depend on an inert filler, let me recommend Super Grex. It is a powdered polyethylene used by Winchester as a buffer in their shotshells. Almost weightless, the dust-sized granules compress easily, and because the stuff is so light, it won't raise pressures very much as long as it occupies one third or less of the case.

Despite their minuscule size, those tiny, rough-edged specks of plastic tend to scour the bore as they jet toward the muzzle. If cast bullets are fired, using Super Grex almost guarantees a lead-free bore. It also tends to tighten groups.

When employing Super Grex as a filler, pour enough into the case to ensure that it will be slightly compressed when the bullet is seated. That eliminates all air space in the case and precludes any movement of the powder column, even under recoil.

If a filler is to be part of a load, it should be used from the very beginning. As usual, a conservative approach is safest: Select an initial load which is obviously too low, add the filler and try it on the range. As powder charges are increased, decrease the amount of filler added, keeping the height of the powder/filler column the same.

Super Grex can be weighed or dispensed from a powder measure but the simplest approach is to measure it by volume with the aid of an adjustable black powder measure. They are inexpensive tools, easy to adjust and accurate enough for the purpose. Slight variations in filler weight will have no measurable effect on velocities or accuracy.

Handloaders who still have Berdan-primed British or metric cases in their inventories will find the RCBS decapping tool quick and efficient to use. Those with a more progressive state of mind will appreciate a hydraulic decapping tool offered by a British firm, the Prime Reloading Company (30 Chiswick End, Maldreth, Royston, Hertfordshire, SGB 6LZ, England). Depending on a single drop of water for its power, the unit directs a tiny but

powerful jet against the flash holes, popping the Berdan primers out of their seats with a single tap of a leather mallet. A cleverly designed tool, it does the job without drenching either loading bench or handloader.

Eley primers are no longer available but RWS primer No. 6507 was designed to replace the Eley No. 172 which was standard in most of the large British proprietary calibers. The Old Western Scrounger (12924 Hwy. A-12, Montague CA 96064) stocks them, together with the rest of the Dynamit Nobel line.

Although jacketed bullets of the proper weights and diameters are now available for Nitro Express and metric African cartridges, owners of Black Powder Expresses aren't so fortunate. Those rounds developed their impact energies by mating relatively light, paper-patched alloy bullets with stiff charges of black powder and driving them upward of 2,000 fps, exceptionally high velocities 100 years ago. Slugs for the .450 BPE, for example, weighed 270, 310, 325 and 365 grains. Their muzzle velocities ranged from a claimed 1,700 to 1,975 fps. To my knowledge, no firm in the U.S. makes bullet moulds which will cast bullets of the same weights and diameters, although several come close.

The same is true of the .400, .500 and .577 BPEs. Outfits like RCBS (Blount Industries, Box 856, Lewiston ID 83501) and NEI/Tooldyne (9330 NE Halsey, Portland OR 97220) will make custom moulds but there's an extra charge for the service. Still, the few extra bucks might be worth it, especially to the owner of a veteran double. Regulating one of those persnickety rifles is a lot easier if bullets matching the original specifications are used.

Why all the concern about cast bullets? The steels employed in last century's black powder rifles, although strong enough, are noticeably softer than those found in modern arms. Moreover, many bores were rifled with deeper than usual grooves so that powder residue could accumulate without degrading accuracy — at least, that was the philosophy. A steady diet of jacketed bullets will not only accelerate bore wear but if those slugs don't fill the extra-deep grooves completely, expanding propellant gases will outflank the bullets' bases, eroding the grooves and adding to the wear and tear. Anyone interested in putting a Black Powder Express back in service should stick to black powder or Pyrodex and cast bullets. They're easier on both rifles and shooter.

Double rifles, especially the older models, pose unusual problems to a handloader. In all probability, one barrel — usually the right one — will show more wear than the other. In such cases, it's a good idea to do most of the load development with the least-worn tube. Once that barrel is shooting to the sights, the other barrel can be brought to play.

Although most Express rifles were designed to accept paper patched bullets, modern lubricants permit unpatched cast bullets to be driven at Express velocities with no fear of leading, as long as the bullets obturate to fill the grooves completely and seal off the expanding gases. Because of that, the simplest procedure is to start with as-cast bullets. Leave them unsized, lubricate them by hand and see how they shoot. Next, size them a couple of thousandths larger than groove diameter and find out if accuracy improves or degenerates. Whichever approach delivers the best, most consistent groups is the one to follow for that cartridge and rifle.

Handloaders who don't want to cast bullets, or who can't, for one reason or another, should consider purchasing them. Commercial bullets can be found in most localities. If there are none nearby, check the advertisements in the *Shotgun News* or contact one of the mould-making firms, they can probably give you the name and address of someone who can supply you with the bullets you need.

Jacketed-bullet shooters face a different problem: trying to decide which brand to choose. Leaders in the field, such as A-Square, Bitterroot, Barnes, Woodleigh et al, are complemented by a growing army of clever, conscientious custom makers, much too numerous to identify individually. Anyone who has a particular feature or jacket design in mind can learn who makes or will make such bullets by contacting Dave Corbin (PO Box 2659, White City OR 97503). He manufactures most of the dies, presses and other bullet-making tools used by custom makers around the world.

A-Square (One Industrial Park, Bedford KY 40006) markets a pair of extremely interesting bullets, the Monolithic Solid and Dead Tough softpoint. Not too long ago, I conducted a lengthy series of tests with a .416 Rigby and found both types were capable of sub-MOA performance. Friends who have depended on them against African game have nothing but praise for their performance. The Monolithic Solid is almost indestructible. I watched one hunter prepare for a Botswana safari by shooting offhand at a bullseye painted on an old water tank made of half-inch steel plate. From his .375 H&H, the 300-grain A-Square solids punched neat round holes through the heavy plate. Later, we found some of the slugs buried in a dirt bank behind the tank. All bore faint traces of the rifling but were undistorted and could have been loaded and fired again. A-Square's catalog lists various designs and weights in the following diameters: .409, .416, .423, .458, .468, .475, .488, .505, .510 and .585 inch.

Launched from a receiver-sighted Ruger .458, Woodleigh 500-grain softnoses clocked 2,150 fps and consistently huddled in one inch, center-to-center, at 50 yards from a rest. Field reports indicate their performance on African game is just as impressive. Alaskan hunters are free with their praise, too. They are available in the following diameters: .411, .416, .423, .435, .458, .474, .476, .483, .505, .510, .585 and .620 inch. Woodleigh bullets are made in all appropriate weights, too.

One of the more intriguing designs to hit the market in recent years is embodied in Barnes' X-Bullets (Box 215, American Fork UT 84003). Made of solid copper, their unusual hollow points encourage near-classic expansion but due to their homogenous construction, their reputation for deep penetration in tough animals is outstanding.

One acquaintance took part in a culling operation Down Under last year which required him to drop a great number of water buffalo. Although not as aggressive as the Cape variety, Australian buffalo often run larger and can be difficult to put down at times. X-Bullets were used exclusively and every animal was taken with one shot.

Barnes also offers designs of more conventional construction. Their bullets are available in .411, .416, .430, .435, .458, .468, .475, .488, .510, .577 and .620-inch diameters.

RWS solids in .423 are obtainable from several sources. Two weights are imported: 347 and 401 grains.

Unprimed, formed brass for almost all of the old African calibers can be purchased from several firms. The handful which aren't available can be obtained in one of two ways: either as loaded ammunition, which features new, Boxer-primed cases; or as unformed Basic cases, hulls whose dimensions permit them to be converted to different calibers in the same family with a minimal amount of shaping and trimming.

For instance, Eldorado's (Box 308, Boulder City NV 89005-0308) .450-3½-inch Nitro Express Basic case is offered with either a standard .040-inch thick rim or the .060-inch Jeffery rim. Those two versions serve as the basis for the .333 Rimmed Jeffery .360 No. 2, .369 Purdey, .450/400 BPE, .450/400 three inch, .450/400 Magnum 3¼ and .450 Nitro Express 3¼. The same firm's .500 Nitro Express 3¼-inch Basic case can be made into .500 three and 3¼-inch Nitro Expresses, .476 Nitro Express, .470 NE, .500/465 NE and .500/450 3¼.

Of course, reshaping Basic cases may require purchasing extra dies to change their profiles in stages. In addition, an outside neck-turning tool or an inside neck reamer may be needed if the Basic hull is necked down very much. Then too, the modified cases probably will need to have their new necks annealed. Considering the additional time, effort and expense involved in converting one case to another, it might be cheaper in the long run to depend on loaded ammunition as a source for reloadable brass. Each handloader must decide that for himself.

Ordinarily, I avoid resizing bottlenecked cases full length. That habit can't be blamed on any false sense of economy but I would rather let the location of the cases' shoulders be decided by a rifle's chamber rather than a die's dimensions. Cartridges destined to be used against dangerous game, however, are subject to a slightly different set of priorities than those assembled with match work or deer hunting in mind. Absolute reliability tops the list. Nipping at its heels are ease of chambering and extraction.

When dealing with animals that bite back, those characteristics take precedence over all others. If a handloader is in doubt about the best way to go, let the rifle decide.

Determine if a case fired in its chamber can be rechambered before being resized. If it slips home with ease, neck-sizing should be all that's necessary. On the other hand, if a case chambers reluctantly, if it has to be forced, even slightly, or simply refuses to seat unless it's properly oriented in the chamber, the latter may be slightly out of round and full-length resizing will be required.

Fired cases should extract effortlessly, too. That is especially important if a double rifle is involved because its camming power has limitations. A fired case which drags or balks at a critical moment is the last thing an African hunter needs.

Each of those cautions emphasizes the continuing need to keep cases properly trimmed and filled with charges which generate moderate pressures. Safe loads and longevity go hand in hand, both the case's and the shooter's.

Safety, in fact, should be a basic ingredient in every load development program, so keep that loading bench free of clutter, never allow more than one can of powder to be in reach at any time, check-weigh powder charges periodically and always treat primers with the respect normally reserved for hand grenades.

There are old handloaders and there are bold handloaders. ●

CHAPTER
3

A Worthwhile Wildcat

the 8mm-06

By DON ZUTZ

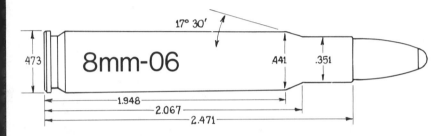

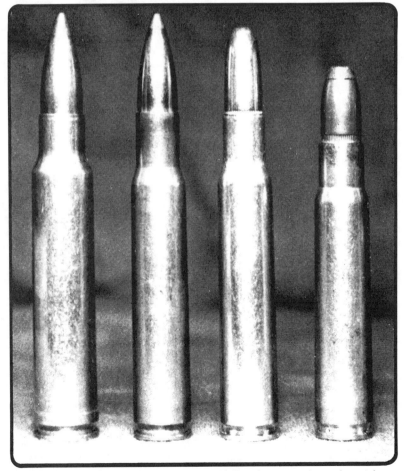

Some of the cartridges mentioned in this article, for comparison: from left, a .338 Winchester Magnum, the 8mm-06, .30-06 and 8x57JS.

HEN HITLER'S fabled "Thousand Year Reich" went *kaput* somewhat prematurely in 1945, thousands of American GI's came marching home with "liberated" 98 Mausers. Chambered for the 8x57 JS cartridge, these rifles had been the standard shoulder arm of the *Wermacht*, and not a few GI's looked forward to substantial shooting with them. Plans for sporterizing the Mausers and taking hunting trips were no doubt conjured up on many crowded, homeward bound troop ships.

But with hundreds of thousands of GI's finishing a modern odyssey within the short space of a year, the demand for 8x57 brass far exceeded the stateside supply. Americans had never been gung-ho over the 8mm in any version; consequently, there were no sizeable inventories of pre-war 8mm Mauser cases awaiting disposal. Moreover, brass of that size had not been drawn during World War II in the United States in deference to .30-06 and M1 Carbine cases, and, as history would prove, it took considerable time for this nation's industry to convert to full peacetime pursuits and satiate the demand for recreational goods. In the meantime, ex-GI's from the European theatre sat under the apple tree with girl friends and polished but empty 98 Mausers, wishing they had spent more time abroad picking up spent 8x57 brass and less time picking up *mesdemoiselles*.

The shortage of 8x57 JS cases was overcome in the 1940's: some enterprising individuals trimmed and re-

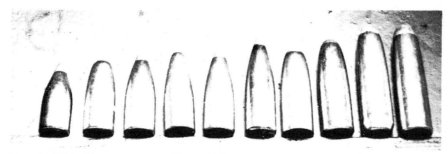

Though .323 bullets aren't as plentiful as .308's, there is no shortage. From left, are the 125-grain Speer, 150 Hornady, 150 Speer, 150 Herter, 150 Sierra, 175 Sierra, 180 Herter, 196 Norma, 226 Norma and 236 Herter.

formed overly abundant .30-06 brass to fit 8x57 JS chambers, which was perfectly legitimate since the cartridges have virtually identical head dimensions.

As the story goes, however, there were many who were not inclined to all that whittling and fiddling at a reloading bench. They wanted to shoot their souvenir rifles, not engage a handicraft project. More appealing to this segment was the simple expedient of rechambering 8mm Mausers to accept the .30-06 case full length, thus creating an instant wildcat known as the 8mm-06. Indeed, merely necking up a .30-06 case to 8mm is less bother than converting naught-six stuff to the lesser capacity 8mm container. The late Vernor Gipson is often credited with fathering the 8mm-06, but it is quite possible that other practical-minded gunsmiths came up with this rather obvious move about the same time Gipson did.

Knowledgeable gun buffs often suspect that the pre-war .333 OKH wildcat, which was the .30-06 necked up to .333-inch, led to the 8mm-06. Perhaps the success of the .35 Whelen also justified a try at the 8mm-06. But we will be making a grave mistake if we interpret the 8mm-06's burst of popu-

larity as being inspired by anything but expediency; for it was the shortage of 8x57 JS brass in the late 1940's that carried this 'cat to its heights; theoretical considerations were secondary to the masses.

But regardless of when and why the 8mm-06 was developed, and regardless of who first cut chambers for it, the 8mm-06 has become one of the few truly worthwhile wildcats in today's line of big game cartridges. For although most wildcats now parallel or duplicate the ballistics of an existing factory round, the 8mm-06 still offers a performance advantage over handloaded 8x57 ammo and the notoriously underloaded Remington-Peters and Winchester-Western 8mm Mauser stuff. Using a 170-grain bullet, for example, a top handload in the 8x57 will do about 2,750 to 2,775 fps at the muzzle, whereas Winchester and Remington commercial loads with the same bullet weight clock a mere 2,570 fps. The 8mm-06, on the other hand, can move a 170-grain bullet at 2,950 to 2,984 fps (*Speer Manual No. 7*), which represents a 200 fps advantage over the best 8x57 reloads and a whopping 350-400 fps over domestic factory fodder.

In all fairness, though, it must be noted that Norma and Speer-DWM ammunition are loaded to higher velocities than R-P and W-W products of the same persuasion. Apparently European ballisticians have more faith in the quality of rifles chambered for the 8x57 than Americans do, or else R-P and W-W have placed 8mm Mauser loading decisions in the hands of the same crew that performed so brilliantly with the .257 Roberts. In either case, recent catalogs show that Norma and Speer-DWM loads for the 8x57 JS are available in the styles and speeds listed in the Factory Load Table.

If one takes a purely handloading approach, however, there is really no

Because the 8mm-06 is a wildcat of expedience, it will be found in a variety of forms, from left, an unaltered J.P. Sauer Model 98 Mauser, a restocked, "sporterized" 8mm-06, and a Schoops custom version.

cause for prolonged discussion regarding the relative merits of the 8mm-06 as compared to the standard 8x57. The water capacity of a .30-06 case is about 61.0 grains to the base of the neck; that of an 8x57 is approximately 53.5 grains. Thus, the greater powder capacity of an 8mm-06 over that of the 8x57 tells the complete story, because neither case is "overbore" for the 8mm tube, and each increase of a proper powder still runs up velocities consistent with safe pressures. As I already mentioned above, this velocity differential between maximum loads in the 8mm-06 and 8x57 will roughly approach 200 fps. With that established, any further elaboration is about as useless as a hot stove session comparing the New York Yankees of DiMaggio's day with the ill-fated Mudville Nine. They're not in the same league.

Thus, since there is no longer a shortage of 8x57 brass, a more interesting and pertinent discussion stacks the 8mm-06 against the .30-06 Springfield. Indeed, the man who sinks time and

Factory 8mm Velocities

Bullet Style	Muzzle Velocity
● **Norma**	
123-gr. Semi-Pointed	2,888
159-gr. Round Nose	2,724
165-gr. Semi-Pointed Boattail	2,855
196-gr. Round Nose	2,526
196-gr. "Dual-Core"	2,526
227-gr. Round Nose	2,329
● **Speer-DWM**	
123-gr. Soft Point	2,968
198-gr. Brenneke	2,731

money into a custom rifle today might well ask, "What can an 8mm-06 do that a standard .30-06 can't?"

And, in large measure, his query would be perfectly legitimate. Both have the same powder capacity; both basically employ the same bullet weights. Physically speaking, the only difference between the pair lies in bullet diameter. The .30-06, of course, has a .308-inch diameter, while the 8mm-06 is built upon a .323-inch bore. By separating the wheat from the chaff, then, our analysis pivots upon one important question: what is the significance of the .015-inch bore diameter difference?

The first conclusion one is likely to jump at is that the wider bullet of an 8mm would automatically register a lower ballistic coefficient than a similar weight .30-caliber projectile. In turn, the 8mm should, theoretically, run behind the .30-06 in matters of long range riflery. And, given identical bullet weights, shapes, and muzzle velocities, this assumption is true. After covering only 100 yards, the better shape of a .30-caliber bullet would allow it to begin edging ahead of an 8mm slug of basically the same weight and design if muzzle velocities were identical.

But drawing a conclusion on the basis of bullet width alone would, in this case, be a mistake. For the 8mm-06 is a more efficient cartridge than the .30-06 because of its better expansion ratio. The wider bore gives powder gases more bullet base upon which to push, and, as a result, the 8mm-06 can outrace the .30-06 by approximately 100 fps at the muzzle with big game bullets and slightly more with the lighter varmint-type pills in the 125-grain category. Thus, the greater velocity attainable with the 8mm-06 negates the .30's form advantage over practical hunting ranges, and it is not until bullets have traveled 500 yards or more that the b.c. advantages of the .30-06 begins to show.

To clarify this point, let's take two Hornady Spire Point bullets of 150 grains. One is the .30-caliber with .308-inch diameter; the other is an 8mm of .323-inch. Ballistic coefficients for the pair are .359 and .332 respectively. If we start the .30 caliber at 3,000 fps (which is very near maximum for a standard .30-06 with 24-inch barrel), and if we push the 8mm at 3,100 fps (which is really somewhat less than maximum for an 8mm-06

sporting a 24-inch tube), the 8mm entry will show slightly superior ballistics at 300 yards. At that range, the .30-caliber Spire Point, according to the Hornady ballistic tables, will be moving at 2,230 fps and carrying 1,656 foot pounds of energy, whereas the 8mm bullet will be toting 1,701 foot pounds of energy at 2,260 fps. Zeroed for 200 yards, the .30-caliber Spire Point would be 7.38 inches low at 300, with the 8mm pointy job a mite flatter at only 6.91 inches below the line of sight.

Granted that there is nothing earth-shaking in this comparison of down-range data, the facts clearly indicate that the increased velocity potential of the 8mm-06 offsets the form advantage of .30-caliber bullets over practical hunting ranges. In other words, the 8mm-06 is not inferior to the .30-06 because of the former's bullet girth, for despite the efforts of sundry long range propagandists, 300 yards *is* a far poke

These recovered 8mm bullets show excellent expansion and weight retention. From left are a 170-grain Remington CoreLokt, recovered from a moose killed at 200 yards, with 159 grains of retained weight; another 170-grain CoreLokt, recovered from a caribou at 100 yards and weighing 132.5 grains; and a 175-grain Sierra, recovered from a mule deer at 100 yards and retaining 153 grains weight.

Handload Data for the 8mm-06
Shooter: Captain B. Frits

(Note: All accuracy information is *not* based upon the same powder charge as that used in chronographing for this table. When there is a discrepancy the powder charge will be shown in parentheses directly below the group size.)

Bullet	Powder	Velocity 24" Barrel	Velocity 29" barrel	Accuracy at 100 Yards
● 125-gr. Speer (3.000" OAL)	59.0/3031	3,379	3,408	3 1/4" (57.0/3031)
125-gr. Speer	60.0/4064	3,298	3,315	1 7/8" (58.0/4064)
125-gr. Speer	63.0/4320	3,280	3,305	2" (61.0/4320)
● 150-gr. Hornady (3.020" OAL)	57.0/3031	3,184	3,214	3" (55.0/3031)
150-gr. Hornady	59.0/4064	3,066	3,104	2 1/8" (57.0/4064)
150-gr. Hornady	61.0/4320	3,080	3,128	2 1/2" (59.0/4320)
● 150-gr. Sierra (3.225" OAL)	57.0/3031	3,190	3,227	2 1/2" (55.0/3031)
● 175-gr. Sierra (3.235" OAL)	57.5/4064	2,984	2,995	2 1/4" (55.0/4064)
175-gr. Sierra	58.0/4320	2,950	2,976	1 5/8" (56.0/4320)
175-gr. Sierra	63.0/4350	2,884	2,914	1 5/8"
● 180-gr. Herter (3.135" OAL)	57.0/4064	2,893	2,909	1 1/2" (55.0/4064)
180-gr. Herter	63.0/4350	2,862	2,881	2 1/8" (62.5/4350)
● 196-gr. Norma (3.200" OAL)	62.0/4350	Not Chronographed		1 3/4"
196-gr. Norma	64.0/4831	2,590	2,628	2" (62.0/4831)
● 226-gr. Norma (3.300" OAL)	59.0/4350	2,544	2,687	7/8"
226-gr. Norma	63.0/4831	2,564	2,700	1 1/8"
● 236-gr. Herter (3.350" OAL)	63.0/4831	2,576	2,604	2 1/2" (61.0/4831)

The above loads are test reports only, not recommendations. Any shooter interested in using the above data should use normal precautions when working toward loads listed herein.

for the average hunter. And if the 150-grain bullet from a .30-06 can drop pronghorns at 300 yards, we can rest assured that an 8mm spitzer or Spire Point won't bounce off the prairie sprinter.

With bullets of 175 to 225 grains, the 8mm-06 is still a stride beyond the .30-06 insofar as muzzle velocity is concerned, thanks again to the 8mm's wider and more efficient bore. And although .30-caliber spitzers of 180 to 200 grains hold form and sectional density advantages over 8mm slugs for extreme distances, the fatter 8mm bullets of spitzer or semi-spitzer design can still lug plenty "stuff" downrange because of reasonably high ballistic coefficients. For example, Sierra's 175-grain 8mm spitzer rates a .465 b.c., and even Speer's 225-grain round nose is listed at .395. Compared with the .387 b.c. of a 150-grain Speer .30-caliber spitzer or the .535 b.c. of a Sierra 180-grain flat base .308 spitzer, 8mm longies hardly seem lacking in practical punch potential for most hunting requirements.

Hunters who have used the 8mm-06 on deer-sized game report a high percentage of one-shot kills, especially when the 150-grain bullet is used. The reasons for this success may be threefold. First, the 8mm-06 has a slightly higher muzzle velocity than the .30-06 and this may contribute to greater shock over short whitetail distances in my home state of Wisconsin. Second, when bullets are of equal weight and construction, the wider item will generally expand more rapidly and release energy sooner and more completely than the one of greater sectional density. This might be considered insignificant when there is only a .015-inch difference between an 8mm and .30-caliber bullet, but on thin-skinned, deer sized game it might be a marginal factor.

A third point, and one which has gotten its share of "ink" lately, is that of twist. Since most 8mm-06's are built on 98 Mausers of World War II vintage, they have rifling twists of 1 turn in 9¼ inches, which, aided by greater velocity, produces a greater rotational velocity than the 1-10 spin used in most .30-06's or the 1-12 pitch of some .308 WCF's. Some argue that a quick twist gives better bullet action on target (due to centrifugal force aiding expansion) than does a slower spin with the same bullet weight and type; and, if this belief is correct — as field observations imply it is — the chance combination of good velocity, wide bullets, and utilization of centrifugal force may indeed be the reason for a high percentage of one-shot, instantaneous kills on deer-sized animals with the 8mm-06's based on military barrels.

Because the 8mm-06 is primarily a big game round without serious varmint or target aspirations, we need not worry about optimum accuracy. Two-inch groups will handle most field requirements to 300 or 350 yards on those critters having a heart/lung area approximately one foot square. One-inch clusters are so much gravy.

Can *Wermacht* Mausers rechambered for the 8mm-06 deliver 2-inch hunting accuracy? Test data supplied *The Rifle* by airline Captain B. Frits certainly indicates they can, as illustrated in the accompanying table.

Before perusing Captain Frits' data, however, the reader must understand that his group sizes were not the result of standard bench rest trials. Being realistic, he determined that game seldom stood around motionless for warming shots or group efforts. Therefore, Captain Frits lists groups fired under simulated field conditions. The first shot comes from a cold, lightly oiled barrel; the second slug follows as quickly as the action can be worked and accurate sighting accomplished. Frits reports that 3-shot groups are handled in the same manner, and overall size is virtually the same as 2-holers. All shooting was done with scope adjusted for center to get that cold tube attempt into the "X."

As one scans the accuracy results, it seems that the desirable 150-grain bullets do not respond well to the 1-9¼ spiral. However, this could be mainly a matter of individual rifles, as the writer knows of converted 8mm military Mausers that do very well with 150-grainers, printing nearly 1.5 MOA on average. Load development work with the 8mm-06 will generally uncover at least one concoction capable of 2 MOA or better at 100 yards with the 150-grain spitzers, although optimum stabilization apparently begins with 175-grain bullets in an 8mm with 1-9¼ pitch.

Handloading for the 8mm-06 is a straight away procedure akin to that of the .30-06 except for necking up cases, which is easily handled by the expander plug of an 8mm-06 sizing die. If case necks stretch during necking up operations, they should be trimmed after the grand opening in either a trim die or trimmer with 8mm pilot. The proper case length is identical to that of the .30-06.

Although the 8mm bore is not very popular in the U.S., there are enough bullets available for it to enable one to load for all occasions. Speer, Norma, Hornady, Herter, and Sierra sources combine to provide various designs in weights of 123, 125, 150, 170, 175, 180, 196, 200, 227, and 236 grains. The 175-grain Sierra is the heaviest spitzer type, after which stylings become semi-spitzer or roundnosed.

The 227-grain Norma and 236-grain Herter slugs present some special considerations for the handloader. Seated to the base of the neck, they generally will not function through a standard magazine. Worked down to an overall length that will fit the magazine infringes upon powder capacity and necessitates a load reduction with its concomitant velocity loss. Thus, the use of these heavyweights would hardly be justified in the 8mm-06 except on the heaviest game at close ranges.

But there is more to bullet selection for an 8mm rifle than just nose and weight considerations, for there are two different bullet diameters bearing the 8mm label. When the 8mm Mauser was first adopted by the German military in 1888, it had a .318-inch diameter. Sporting arms of this bore size were also made in both a rimmed version of the 8x57 case, known as the 8x57 JR, and in the rimless form of the military round, which was called the 8x57 J. Then, in 1905, the bullet and bore size was increased to .323-inch and has remained so ever since. The new and wider bullet has been designated the "S" size, the German military cartridge thus becoming the 8x57 JS instead of the old 8x57 J.

Practically all 8mm bullets now made in the United States have the larger .323-inch diameter. I note, however, that Colorado Custom Bullets of Montrose, Colorado, will size down 8mm slugs to .318-inch while retaining a .320-inch jacket thickness at the cost of one dollar more per hundred. And, at last count, Norma was shipping at least four styles of the .318-inch item into this country. Therefore, despite the preponderance of the larger diameter bullets, 8mm projectiles of both sizes are making it to dealers' shelves, and we must apply the classical economist's admonition, "*caveat emptor*."

The same word of caution must be applied when selecting a military rifle for conversion to 8mm-06. The tremendous influx of 98 Mausers makes them readily available at very reasonable prices, but some of the "bargains" are in extremely poor condition, beset with substandard workmanship, excess headspace, improper hardening at critical areas, and pitting at various places due to lengthy storage. Captain Frits, who has had experience converting 98 Mausers, recommends that Model 93 and 95 Mausers never be used for this wildcat, and he personally looks for JP Sauers, Spandaus, and Oberndorf models of the 98, concentrating upon those receivers dated in the earliest war years and retaining matched bolt-barrel-receiver serial numbers.

If there is the slightest doubt regarding a given rifle's condition, it should be checked out by a *competent* gunsmith who knows *exactly* which critical points to check for hardness. Interesting reading regarding the value and technique of hardness testing can be found on page 65 of Parker O. Ackley's *Handbook for Shooters & Reloaders, Volume II.*

There have been some "Improved" versions of the 8mm-06, and these have been deemed especially good choices for use with the heavier 8mm bullets of 170 grains or more. The 8mm-06 Improved is more efficient than the various "Improved" .30-06's because of the larger bore diameter, and with the bigger bullets it closely approaches the .338 Winchester Magnum in effectiveness on game. Working up loads for an 8mm-06 Improved involves approximately a 4 to 5 percent increase in powder with an accompanying velocity rise.

Some authorities have opined that, because the 8mm-06 is purely a handloading situation anyway, the Improved chamber is a better choice than the basic 8mm-06. However, the 8mm-06 was an expedient developed for men who just wanted to start shooting war souvenirs with a minimum of fuss, and fireforming cases in an improved chamber was, to impatient chaps not of the gun buff and handloader fraternity, an unnecessary extra step. Thus, the 8mm-06 Improved remains a virtual unknown despite a potential that could lead it to stardom.

In conclusion, then, it bears repeating that the 8mm-06 and 8mm-06 Improved are a pair of valuable wildcats amidst our current plethora of factory rounds. It is doubtful whether many men will build a custom 8mm wildcat from scratch while the very versatile .30-06 is still popular, but converting an existing 8x57, whether it be a sporter or military piece, will provide the hunter with much better performance than a handloaded 8x57 can approach with safety. And for the man who has a shot out .30-06 barrel on his rack, reboring to 8mm and chambering for either the 8mm-06 or 8mm-06 Improved would hardly be a mistake. ●

CHAPTER
4

8mm Remington Magnum

Remington's new 8mm Magnum in the Model 700 BDL will make an excellent choice for an all-around rifle/cartridge combination for hunting all mountain game. With the right loads behind the right bullets it will handle all hunting situations on all kinds of game found in North America.

By BOB HAGEL

CARTRIDGES USING 8mm bullets have had a rather unusual history here in the United States. As far as I know, no American commercial rifle manufacturing firm had chambered rifles in that bore until the advent of the new 8mm Remington Magnum. But foreign-made rifles chambered for 8mm cartridges of one designation or another have been floating around this country as far back as I can remember. Most of these rifles were of military persuasion, but a few fine sporting rifles also found their way to these shores— many of them "liberated" during World War II.

For many years American ammunition companies have made ammunition for the 8x57 Mauser, but they did not chamber their own rifles for the cartridge. This seems a little strange when you consider that a number of American companies chambered for the 7x57 Mauser cartridge, and Remington once chambered the Model 30 for the 9x57 Mauser, which was also chambered in the Winchester Model 54.

Sales of 8x57 ammunition undoubtedly reached an all-time high shortly after World War II, and most of the bullet-making companies produced bullets in that diameter, that is, .323-inch, which is the correct diameter for the 1898 Mauser rifles or any other rifle chambered for the 8x57S cartridge. Some companies also made bullets in .318 diameter for the 1888 rifles that had arrived here many years before. The .323 bullet diameter also fits a number of other military and 8mm sporting cartridges of recent manufacture. There are at least 25 military and sporting cartridges listed under the 8mm heading, and many of them have become very popular as hunting cartridges throughout the world. But while most gun buffs know that there were two actual bore sizes, few are aware that some cartridges used bullets as small as .316-inch, while others went to as much as .329, and one number, the 8.15x46, is listed at .337-inch.

It appears that the 8mm cartridges date back to about 1885 when the Portuguese adopted the 8x60R Guedes. The 8x57 appeared in 1888 for the Mauser rifle of that model, and perhaps some others, with the .318 diameter bullet, but the bullet diameter was beefed up to the present .323 size about 1905.

While all of this furnishes a little background for the 8mm cartridges, it also makes one wonder why such a world-popular bore size has so long been ignored by American rifle makers. American custom rifle makers have chambered few rifles for the 8x57 cartridge, or few other 8mm's for that matter, and the ever prevalent American wildcatter has shown little interest in cartridges necked to handle 8mm bullets, either large or small. Of the few wildcat 8mm cartridges dreamed up, only the 8mm/06 gained any popularity, and that one didn't set any records.

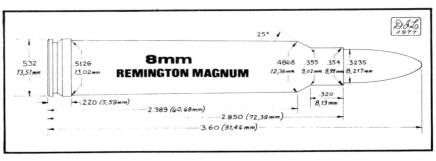

8mm REMINGTON MAGNUM

.532 (13,51mm) .5126 (13,02mm) 25° .4868 (12,36mm) .355 (9,02mm) .354 (8,99mm) .3235 (8,217mm) .320 (8,13mm) .220 (5,59mm) 2.389 (60,68mm) 2.850 (72,39mm) 3.60 (91,44mm)

Probably the best comparison for the 8mm Remington, left photo center cartridge, can be made with the .338 Winchester, left, and the .340 Weatherby. It will be noted that the 8mm Remington and the .340 Weatherby are similar in size, but in spite of the fact that the Remington case appears to be slightly larger in the body, the Weatherby case has a tad more powder capacity due to a large diameter shoulder and lighter case weight. The Remington 8mm Magnum, right photo, is flanked by the 8x57 Mauser, left, and the 8mm-06, right. The 8x57 and the new Remington are the only 8mm cartridges commercially loaded in the U.S.

with other cases in 8mm and other similar calibers like the .338.

Aside from a few wildcats based on belted magnum brass formed from .300 or .375 H&H brass, the 8x68 Magnum is not only the closest in capacity to the 8mm Remington Magnum, but the only other 8mm magnum cartridge of commercial manufacture. While I have never tested loads in either commercial or handloaded form for the 8x68 case, I strongly suspect that factory claims for velocity are somewhat optimistic in sporter rifles with 24-inch barrels. Fact is, I don't have an 8x68 case to check capacity against the new Remington, but according to the dimensional specs it does not have as much boiler room as the Remington case. This is why I doubt the factory quoted velocity, which is higher than is possible to obtain with the 8mm Remington Magnum at reasonable pressures.

While some have compared the 8mm Remington with the .300 Winchester Magnum and the .338 Winchester Magnum, neither case has anything like the powder capacity of the Remington. For all practical purposes, if there is a valid comparison between cartridges with different diameter bullets, the Remington 8mm Magnum is more closely related to the .340 Weatherby Magnum in case capacity. Using full length resized cases for both cartridges so that chamber dimensions do not affect capacity, and

Actually, the answer to the wildcat situation is simple. The great majority of wildcat cartridges are made with one of three things in mind: a super-accurate target round; an accurate, high-performance varmint cartridge; or a big game cartridge that excels for some special type of hunting and/or class of game. The first and most important consideration is bullets that deliver top efficiency for whatever use the cartridge is designed. The rub is that few .323 bullets have ever been made in this country that were outstanding for any of these tasks. I know of no domestic 8mm target bullets; it certainly can't be considered a varmint caliber; and 8mm American made hunting bullets are not only designed with the underloaded factory 8x57 cartridge in mind, they perform well only on the lighter game in the deer class even when handloaded to top velocity in that rather low velocity cartridge. And most of the imported 8mm bullets are no better if you load them in a potent wildcat at the magnum velocity level. I'm not guessing at this, I've seen too many poor performances from most of them. The best bullet I ever saw used in the 8x57 was the 225-grain Speer for game in the class of elk and moose. But even that bullet was designed with the 8x57 in mind, and it is very doubtful if it would hold up under the impact velocity of a big wildcat, the 8x68 Magnum of German origin, or the new 8mm Remington Magnum. It may seem a little odd that the 8x68 Magnum did not become popular here in this day of the magnum, but when the factory ammunition problem, and the lack of suitable bullets for handloading such a high velocity number are considered, it is not hard to understand. And the mention of the 8x68 Magnum brings us to the new Remington offering and a comparison

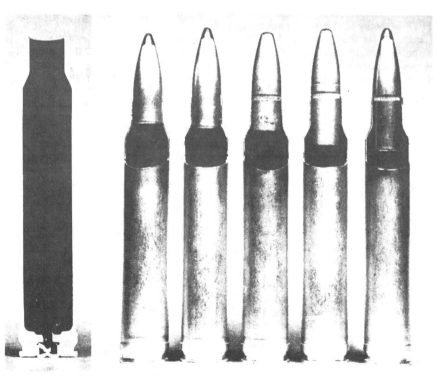

The 8mm Remington Magnum case is of strong construction with a heavy web section found in other R-P belted cases, and handles high pressures very well. The seating depth of the various bullets used in Hagel's tests are shown here. Bullets were seated to function through the magazine and/or chamber throat. From left is the 150-grain Sierra seated to give full neck support, 175-grain Sierra, 185 Remington Core-Lokt, 220 Remington Core-Lokt, and 220 Hornady.

The bullets above were fired into Hagel's recovery box at approximately 100-yard velocity delivered from the 8mm Remington Magnum. From left is the 150-grain Sierra, 175 Sierra, 185 Remington Core-Lokt, 220 Remington Core-Lokt, and 220 Hornady. The right photo illustrates the construction of these bullets. The small remaining amount of core in all fired bullets was loose and would probably have left the jacket if fired into game and heavy bone was struck. Notice the difference in the color of the core of the 175 and 150-grain Sierra bullets. [The core of the 175-grain is probably alloyed for additional hardness.] Also, note the thinner forward jacket of the 185-grain Core Lokt as compared to the 220-grain Core Lokt.

with Winchester 785 sifted slowly through a long drop tube, then tapped down with the flat base of a smaller caliber bullet to fill the case exactly to the base of the neck, the 8mm Remington holds 95 grains while the .340 Weatherby takes 97.5 grains. The .340 case was formed from W-W 375 H&H brass and is somewhat heavier than the Weatherby case, so the difference in powder capacity would be greater if Weatherby factory cases were used. At first glance, the Remington case would appear to hold more powder because the body is longer, but the .340 case has less taper, which gives it slightly more powder capacity. There is actually very little difference in case length, the Remington case being listed at 2.850, or the same as the .375 H&H, and the Weatherby at 2.820. The neck of the 8mm Remington is a bit shorter at .320-inch, while the .340 measures .344. This leaves the body of the Remington 8mm Magnum from head to shoulder base .102-inch longer than the .340 Weatherby Magnum, but not enough to make up for the difference of less taper in the Weatherby case. For all practical purposes, however, the two cases have about the same capacity.

While we are discussing the dimensions of the new Remington offering, there will be those with a technical turn of mind who will measure the case and question the validity of the drawing and dimensions by Art Director Dave LeGate. Let me say that these come direct from Remington as maximum for the cartridge, but do not go along with actual measurements taken from new factory ammunition. While these measurements are listed as maximum for the cartridge, it appears there is more difference between them and the actual cartridge measurements than is desirable. This shows up mostly in the head area. As will be noted from the cartridge spec drawing, the belt and rim are listed at .532-inch, but my lots of factory ammunition in 185 and 220-grain loadings average only .524 on the belt, and .526 on the rim. This is a little unusual, because on most belted cases the rim is slightly smaller than the belt. I did find a good deal of variation in the rim diameter, and some cases miked

8mm Remington Magnum Penetration

Penetration tests with the 8mm Remington Magnum in recovery box at approximately 100 yard striking velocity with loads given in load data chart.

Bullet	Penetration, Inches	Remaining weight, Grains	Average frontal area diameter, Inches
150 Sierra	12	48.5 (32.3%)	0.800
175 Sierra	16	80.0 (45.7%)	0.675
185 Remington CL	12	78.0 (42.1%)	0.720
220 Remington CL	22	127.0 (57.7%)	0.810
220 Hornady	23	114.0 (51.8%)	0.710

8mm Remington Magnum Load Data

8mm Remington Magnum M-700 24-inch barrel.
R-P cases, 260 grains.
Remington 9½M primers.
Oehler 31/50 chronograph.
Velocity instrumental at 15 feet converted to MV. Temperature - 70°.

Bullet	Powder	Charge	Velocity	Remarks
220 factory	- - - -	74.8	2,735	
185 factory	- - - -	80.4	3,007	
220 Remington Core-Lokt	H-4831	84	2,983	
220 Remington Core-Lokt	MRP	83	3,015	
220 Remington Core-Lokt	W-W 785*	82	2,947	Erratic with 220-grain bullets.
220 Remington Core-Lokt	H-205	78	2,985	
220 Remington Core-Lokt	IMR-4831	80	2,928	
220 Remington Core-Lokt	IMR-4350	78	2,935	
220 Hornady	H-4831	84	3,024	Pressure may be a little
220 Hornady	MRP	83	3,022	higher with this bullet.
185 Remington Core-Lokt	H-4831	86	3,170	
185 Remington Core-Lokt	MRP	87	3,228	
185 Remington Core-Lokt	W-W 785	87	3,184	
185 Remington Core-Lokt	IMR-4831	84	3,215	
185 Remington Core-Lokt	H-205	83	3,225	
185 Remington Core-Lokt	IMR-4350	81	3,168	
175 Sierra	H-4831	87	3,274	Good hunting accuracy with
175 Sierra	MRP	88	3,363	all loads.
175 Sierra	W-W 785	88	3,253	
175 Sierra	IMR-4831	85	3,331	
175 Sierra	H-205	85	3,330	
175 Sierra	IMR-4350	83	3,308	
150 Sierra	MRP	91	3,487	This bullet gave best accuracy
150 Sierra	IMR-4831	88	3,473	of any bullet tried.
150 Sierra	H-205	87	3,452	
150 Sierra	IMR-4350	87	3,522	
150 Sierra	N-204	86	3,473	

*Winchester 785 became very touchy at maximum pressures with 220-grain bullets, but did not show this problem with other bullet weights tried.

These loads were all maximum trouble-free hunting loads in the test rifle with the components used. Test loads with two grains more powder were fired with all bullets and powders. Cases fired 10-12 times with no failures, but loads should not be used in any other rifle without working up from three to four grains below.

only .523. Body base diameter just forward of the belt is a little nearer to the specs, and averages .506, and is listed at .5126. In my test rifle cases expand to .5135-inch to fill the chamber, which gives the case body just forward of the belt an expansion of .0075. This makes for a pretty sloppy chamber, but resulted in no problems in repeatedly reloading the cases with heavy handloads.

As indicated, body taper is somewhat more than for the .340 Weatherby case, but is still quite straight. Shoulder is the same 25° angle that is found on most modern commercial belted cartridges.

To the average big game hunter — and this cartridge was certainly designed with big game hunting in mind — the greatest interest will center around the ballistics of the new cartridge. First, it is loaded at the present time with just two bullet weights, a 185 and 220-grain. Both bullets are of the good Remington Core-Lokt hunting bullet design. They have rather flat points that do not, however, add anything to the ballistic shape for long range shooting. The 185 has a ballistic coefficient of .300, and the 220-grain, .366. For comparison, Hornady is producing a new 220-grain pointed soft point bullet especially for the 8mm Remington, which has a B.C. of .448. The sectional density of the 185 is .253 and .301 for the 220.

Remington factory-quoted velocity for the 185-grain is 3,080 fps muzzle velocity, and 2,830 fps for the 220. These figures apparently came from test barrels, and fell short of this in my Model 700 test rifle with its 24-inch barrel. Velocity taken at 15 feet and converted to MV at 70°, gave the 185 R-P factory load 3,007 fps, and the 220-grain load 2,735 fps. Factory ammunition was loaded with what appeared to be IMR-4831 powder; 80.4 grains average behind the 185, and 74.8 grains with the 220. There was a charge variation of .9-grain in the 220-grain load and .7-grain for the 185-grain load for 10 rounds of each. I say the powder appears to be IMR-4831 bcause duplicate loads of that powder came out quite close. One writer has already mentioned that he thought the factory load contained IMR-4350, but the equivalent of the factory charge of that powder gives much higher velocity.

Having done a great deal of reloading for a number of cartridges in calibers on both sides of the 8mm, cartridges like the .300 Winchester Magnum and .300 Weatherby, and the .338 Winchester and .340 Weatherby, I was convinced that the 8mm Remington Magnum had a lot more potential in the velocity department than factory loads gave it. It was also obvious from this experience that only the slower powders would bring out the full ability of the cartridge to deliver the velocity of which it should be capable.

In starting the load development work the greatest problem was in obtaining bullets suitable for the big cartridge. Sure, there are a number of bullets made in 8mm in this country, but, as already pointed out, they were designed with the low velocity of the 8x57 Mauser cartridge in mind. Also, except for the Barnes line, which were not available during the tests, and the old Speer 225-grain, which has been dropped, all of the domestic bullets made for the 8mm are of light weight for the .323 diameter. I can't see a thin-skinned 150-170-grain bullet as being anything except an antelope/deer bullet in the 8mm Magnum — I've seen too many of them come apart even on deer when fired from the 8x57. Remington had promised their 185 and 220-grain bullets for load test work, but they were unavailable for several months after the rifle and factory ammo arrived.

In the meantime, it was decided to do test work with some of the bullets that were already available in 8mm size, so the 150 and 175-grain Sierra spitzers were chosen. While these light bullets didn't give the information I really wanted for the big case, they did show what velocity it was capable of as compared to other big magnums. Starting with the 175-grain, which has only slightly more sectional density than the 150-grain .30-caliber, gave some information as to what powders could be expected to give the best results with other bullet weights.

One thing that was obvious from the start was that this cartridge would digest a lot of the slower powders, and that velocities were up where any experienced reloader would expect them to be, and not down in the class of the wildcat 8mm/06. With that bullet weight, the old magnum cartridge standby H-4831 proved to be a

Supplemental Selected Loads

bullet (grains)	powder	suggested starting load (grains)	suggested maximum (grains)	velocity (fps)
8mm Remington Magnum				
Sierra Data				
150 Sierra	RL-19	80.0	88.0	3,400
	AAC-3100	79.9	88.9	3,400
	RL-22	81.5	91.4	3,450
	IMR-7828	84.5	90.5	3,300
175 Sierra	RL-19	73.1	82.3	3,100
	AAC-3100	73.8	83.3	3,100
	RL-22	77.6	86.3	3,200
	IMR-7828	82.2	88.3	3,100
220-Sierra	RL-19	67.0	76.0	2,800
	AAC-3100	67.0	77.3	2,850
	RL-22	72.6	80.2	2,900
	IMR-7828	74.8	83.2	2,900
Hodgdon Data				
150	H-870	90.0	93.0	3,029
	H-4831	83.0	85.0	3,290
	H-450	82.0	85.0	3,270
	H-414	77.0	79.0	3,320
170 to 175	H-4831	80.0	82.0	3,144
	H-450	80.0	82.0	3,103
	H-414	72.0	75.0	3,076
180 to 185	H-870	88.0	91.0	2,939
	H-450	77.0	79.0	2,987
200	H-870	87.0	90.0	2,914
	H-4831	75.0	79.0	2,932
	H-4350	69.0	73.0	2,919
220 to 225	H-870	87.0	90.0	2,856
	H-4831	74.0	78.0	2,871
	H-450	74.0	76.0	2,822
250	H-870	84.0	86.0	2,764
	H-4831	72.0	76.0	2,776

Be alert — Publisher cannot accept responsibility for errors in published load data.

little on the slow side, but still developed a respectable 3,274 fps at the muzzle. At similar pressure MRP gave the highest velocity, 3,363 fps, which was no surprise. The fastest powder used with the 175-grain Sierra was 4350, which gave 3,308 fps — neither the fastest nor the slowest velocity.

This indicated that it might give the highest velocity with the 150-grain Sierra, which proved to be true. A charge of 87 grains showed 3,522 fps, a load that would not have to take a back seat for any cartridge for long range plains or mountain shooting on the smaller species of big game like antelope and sheep. Remember, though, that this bullet only has a sectional density of .205 and is thin-skinned — definitely not a heavy game bullet where deep penetration may be necessary. All other powders used delivered over 3,450 fps.

When the Remington Core-Lokt bullets did arrive, it was found that MRP, IMR-4831 and H-205 all started the 185-grain at over 3,200 fps, and the other powders used were not too far behind. The 220-grain could be boosted along at better than 3,000 fps with MRP, and near that velocity with some other powders. The 220-grain Hornady developed slightly more pressure for a little higher velocity. It might be well to cut all charges for the 220-grain Remington CL by one grain when using the Hornady bullet.

Accuracy is the next consideration a hunter will be interested in, but will, of course, vary from rifle to rifle, and with various loads within those individual rifles. I did not attempt to tune the test rifle in any way, and it is quite possible that accuracy could be improved somewhat, even though it proved acceptable for hunting under most conditions with most bullets and loads. I was somewhat surprised to find that it delivered better groups with the lighter bullets than the heavy ones; especially considering its 1-10 twist. In fact, the 150-grain Sierra produced the best groups by far with all powders and loads. Some of these groups ran well under 1-inch for three shots, and averaged very little over that when loaded for maximum hunting loads. Accuracy fell off when charges were reduced.

The 175-grain Sierra did almost as well and shot some very tight groups, averaging about 1 1/4-inch for 100 yards with the loads listed in the chart. The

185-grain Remington CL fell a bit short of the 175-grain Sierra accuracy, and was a bit finicky as to what powders it liked best, but averaged near 1 1/2-inch with the better loads. The 220 Remington CL seldom shot a tight group, and some were pretty sour at around three inches. No load tried would average out at better than two inches on the 100-yard range.

This situation was even more pronounced with the 220-grain Hornady in the test rifle. That bullet would not average much under three inches with even the best loads. I tried backing charges of various powders off from the top in an attempt to find better accuracy with both 220-grain bullets, but group size did not improve. Maximum loads were as accurate as any others. This might seem to indicate that the 10-inch twist is too slow for the 220-grain bullets, but this is highly unlikely. The 220-grain 8mm bullet has exactly the same sectional density as the 200-grain .30 caliber, and I never experienced any problem whatever in accuracy with either 1-10 or 1-12 twists with any .30 caliber rifle, even with the 220-grain which has an SD of .332. Neither have I experienced accuracy problems with any .338 caliber with 250, 275 or 300-grain bullets which show much higher sectional densities than the 220-grain 8mm, and they were all fired from 1-10 twist barrels.

While there has been no opportunity to test the 8mm Remington Magnum on game because no seasons have been open since rifles were available, it is no great problem to evaluate it from the ballistics and the bullet weights and designs available. First, as mentioned earlier, all bullets made in this country are made with the velocity of the 8x57 in mind, and the imported bullets I have seen used on elk perform no better, and that includes the famous German H-Mantle, the Norma offerings, and those from DWM and RWS. At the present time this leaves us with the new Hornady 220-grain and the Remington 185 and 220 designed for the big cartridge.

The first thing I did was to section the bullets used in these tests to check jacket thickness and structure. The results are shown in the photo. The next step was to test penetration in the recovery box for the same bullets. To do this they were loaded to approximately 100-yard velocity to simulate action at close game ranges. The results of that test are given in the

chart, and visual proof in the photo of the expanded bullets.

From these tests it seems that the 185-grain Core-Lokt will be at its best on game up to caribou except at very long range, and its ballistic coefficient of .300 does not make it an ideal long range bullet in this cartridge. The other lightweight bullets will fit into the same level of performance, except that the 175-grain Sierra will shoot a good deal flatter at long ranges with its B.C. of .465.

Both the 220-grain Hornady and Remington CL are much better for heavier game from elk up, and both gave good penetration of 22-23 inches in the recovery box, but retained weight was not particularly good. What little core remained in the jacket was loose and would certainly be lost much earlier along the line of penetration when heavy bone was encountered on game animals.

As a form of comparison, 210-grain Nosler bullets gave 28 inches of penetration at muzzle velocity impact of 3,200 fps from a .340 Weatherby, and the 250-grain Nosler drove in 30 inches at a striking velocity of over 2,900 fps. This does not mean the .340 Weatherby will give that much more penetration if bullet design is the same. I feel sure that a 220-grain Nosler 8mm bullet from the 8mm Remington will give equal penetration to the .338 bullets, especially if made in pointed form as it should be for that cartridge.

There is little doubt that the new 8mm Remington Magnum is an outstanding big game cartridge for all classes and sizes of American big game, and for most big game found anywhere in the world, for that matter. It will do quite well for most North American game, as well as African plains game, with either the Hornady 220 grain or the Remington Core-Lokt bullets, but I feel that either of these bullets would do even better in the penetration department if the jacket thickness were beefed up considerably from about one third of the jacket length back. For the ultimate results on the heavier game from elk up under all hunting conditions where penetration angles are long, and where a lot of heavy muscle and bone must be smashed and penetrated along the way, the cartridge would have greater usefulness with a controlled expansion bullet like the Nosler. ●

CHAPTER
5

Wilf Pyle

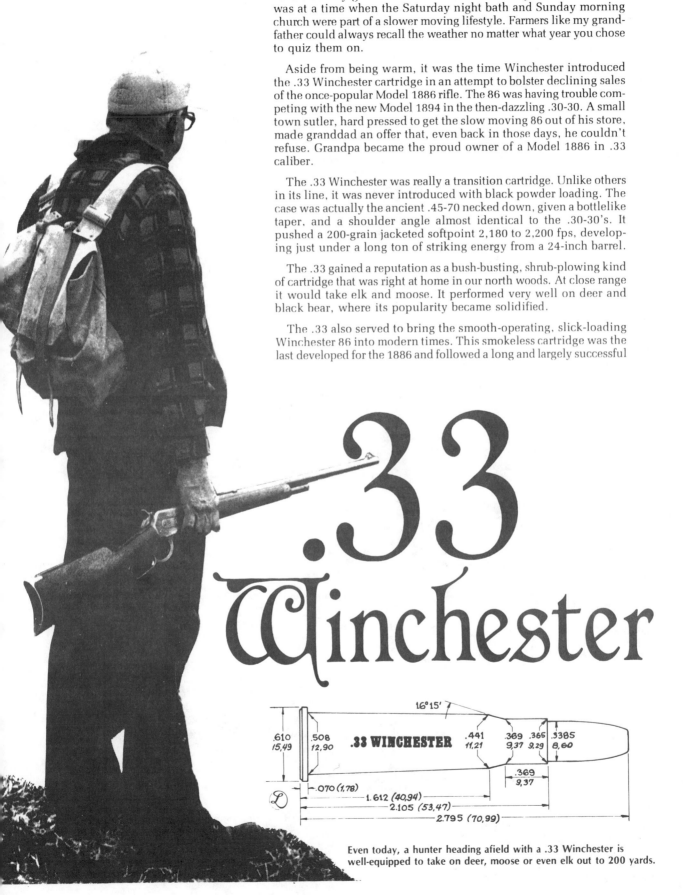

WHERE WERE YOU in August of 1902? I sure wasn't around, but my grandfather told me it was a very warm summer. It was at a time when the Saturday night bath and Sunday morning church were part of a slower moving lifestyle. Farmers like my grandfather could always recall the weather no matter what year you chose to quiz them on.

Aside from being warm, it was the time Winchester introduced the .33 Winchester cartridge in an attempt to bolster declining sales of the once-popular Model 1886 rifle. The 86 was having trouble competing with the new Model 1894 in the then-dazzling .30-30. A small town sutler, hard pressed to get the slow moving 86 out of his store, made granddad an offer that, even back in those days, he couldn't refuse. Grandpa became the proud owner of a Model 1886 in .33 caliber.

The .33 Winchester was really a transition cartridge. Unlike others in its line, it was never introduced with black powder loading. The case was actually the ancient .45-70 necked down, given a bottlelike taper, and a shoulder angle almost identical to the .30-30's. It pushed a 200-grain jacketed softpoint 2,180 to 2,200 fps, developing just under a long ton of striking energy from a 24-inch barrel.

The .33 gained a reputation as a bush-busting, shrub-plowing kind of cartridge that was right at home in our north woods. At close range it would take elk and moose. It performed very well on deer and black bear, where its popularity became solidified.

The .33 also served to bring the smooth-operating, slick-loading Winchester 86 into modern times. This smokeless cartridge was the last developed for the 1886 and followed a long and largely successful

.33 Winchester

.33 WINCHESTER

16°15'

.610 / 15,49   .508 / 12,90   .441 / 11,21   .369 / 9,37   .365 / 9,29   .5385 / 8,60

.369 / 9,37

.070 (1,78)
1.612 (40,94)
2.105 (53,47)
2.795 (70,99)

Even today, a hunter heading afield with a .33 Winchester is well-equipped to take on deer, moose or even elk out to 200 yards.

line of black powder rounds variously available at different times. In addition, the 86 had undergone several re-stylings to make it a lighter, faster handling rifle along the same lines as the Model 1894.

The combination of cartridge and gun seems to have been well chosen. Beginning in 1920 and carrying on until almost the last year of production, 1936, all 86s were in .33 caliber.

From 1903 until 1920, nearly 28,000 Model 86s were manufactured. If half were in .33 caliber, as many collectors insist, the total number of Winchester 86s in that caliber must be around 16,000 units. That is a fair number, considering the slow moving economy back then and the competition from not only other Winchester models but the Marlin 95 as well.

Unlike some cartridges, the firearms media treated the .33 very well indeed. In the book *Sporting Firearms* (MacMillan, 1923), Horace Kepart, at that time a virtual guru on outdoor matters, considered the .33 a very useful medium-powered round. The then-acknowledged expert on big game hunting, Charles Askins, *Rifles and Rifle Shooting* (MacMillan, 1936), wrote that the cartridge was one of the best all-round types available in America at that time. He particularly liked the shape of the bullet and diameter which he felt would allow for the full expenditure of energy upon any game. In more recent writings, Jack O'Connor said that those who used the cartridge reported it was far superior to the .30-30.

It is hard to argue that the .33 is much more than a super .30-30. Comparisons of advertised performance data of the .33 Winchester, .35 Remington and .30-30 Winchester show few really great differences. When sighted in to print three inches high at 100 yards the .33 will be dead on at 180, two inches low at 200 yards and eight inches low at 250.

The .35 Remington with a 200-grain bullet, when sighted the same way, will be on the money at 165 yards, 3½ inches low at 200 yards and over a foot low at 250.

The venerable .30-30 is right on at 175 yards, two inches low at 200 yards and 10 low at 250. All three cartridges would be producing just over 2,000 fps muzzle velocity.

Comparing the .33 to a .348 Winchester, the cartridge which replaced it, the .348 yields a trajectory remarkably close to those of the older round. With a three-inch high hold and 200-grain

The .33's reputation among hunters was probably due as much to the slick-actioned 86 Winchester that chambered it as it was to its ballistics.

Magazine springs of later model 86s were very strong. That, and a fairly hefty recoil, calls for a hard crimp when seating .33 bullets.

At one time, the top-ejecting Model 86 Winchester was the most powerful lever action available.

bullet travelling at 2,500 fps, this grand old classical bush round is on the nose at 190 yards and in the following 10 yards drops one inch. It is seven inches low at 250 yards compared to the .33's eight.

Other less popular cartridges of the day shared similar ballistics but did not gain the following of the .33 Winchester. Included in this list would have to be the 165-grain .32-40, which produced a muzzle velocity of only 1,440 fps. It was more or less considered a target cartridge and disappeared from the shooting scene about the time the .33 was peaking in popularity.

There was also the .32 Winchester, available in the Model 94, and designed with the idea of offering a round that could be easily reloaded with black powder. Unfortunately this idea did not work out all that well, for the Model 94 had a slow twist of one turn in 14 inches. In addition, corrosive primers soon made the barrels woefully rough and inaccurate.

Two other minor contenders were the .30 Remington and its slightly larger counterpart — the .32. Both produced ballistics which equalled those of the Winchester rounds. None of those cartridges were ever able to garner a following anything like that enjoyed by the .33 Winchester.

In today's market, only two cartridges could be considered carryovers from the .33. These are the .444 Marlin, introduced in 1965, and the more recent .375 Winchester, brought out in August 1978. Both cartridges have operating pressures far in excess of the old .33 so it is not really fair to compare them. However, their advertised performance figures are very similar to the older round's. The .444 Marlin, when sighted in to print three inches high at 100 yards, is right on at 175 yards and 6½ inches low at 200 yards. Its poor downrange performance is blamed on the poor sectional density of the stubby 240-grain bullet. It starts out at 2,300 fps but at 100 yards, has shed slightly over 20 percent of its initial velocity.

The .375 Winchester develops such pressure that the Model 94 had to have its receiver redesigned. At the muzzle it produces only 2,115 fps in the 20-inch carbine barrel with a 200-grain bullet. For all its pressure, it ends up with external ballistics no better than those of the .33. (See Table II.)

The fact that the .444 has survived and carved itself a niche in the gun market, and that the .375 was introduced, simply points out that there are still a lot of guides and woodsmen out there who prefer heavy bullets travelling at moderate velocities in lightweight arms. The theory of bushbucking bullets is still alive and well, and lives on to such an extent that one becomes suspicious of gun writers who tell us that all bullets buck brush the same way. Can those guides and woodsmen be wrong?

The robust case of the .33 is excellent for reloading. It is a good idea to check case length after each firing and trim as necessary. Correct case length is 2.105 inches. Since the cartridge will, in most cases, be fired from a tubular magazine rifle, length is important for proper crimping. Crimping is, of course, necessary to prevent the bullets from seating deeper into the case due to recoil and the recurring jolts they suffer while lying within the magazine. Magazine spring pressure can also force bullets deeper into the case.

Cases were made by several companies. My collection has three Winchester head stamps and three Remington, as well as one from Dominion Cartridge Company, the once prominent

Wilf found no significant difference in volume between six different makes of .33 cases.

Be alert — Publisher cannot accept responsibility for errors in published load data.

The Hornady 200-grain flatnose is the only commercial bullet available for the .33 Winchester. It was designed specifically for the .33's velocities and is probably superior to the original factory bullets.

Table I						

.33 Winchester

Bullet - 200-grain Hornady Flatnose

charge (grains)	powder (IMR)	muzzle velocity (fps)	variation	energy (ft/lbs)	free recoil (ft/lbs)	comments
43	4320	2,303	37	2,348	15.7	least variation
45	4320	2,355	72	2,452	16.6	very accurate
40	3031	2,024	135	1,812	12.5	too much variation, mild
43	3031	2,327	49	2,390	16.0	accurate
45	4064	2,216	59	2,168	15.3	good
47	4064	2,467	73	2,688	18.3	maximum
45	4895	2,471	128	2,710	17.9	not recommended
34	4198	2,091	44	1,940	12.1	5-inch groups
35	4198	2,091	40	1,940	12.3	5-inch groups

Canadian ammunition maker. Their volumes were all virtually the same.

The .33 case is capable of holding a lot of powder. As an experiment, I was able to cram 59 grains of FF black powder into an old Winchester case. Using 49 grains of IMR-4064, it was possible to seat the bullet without compressing the load. *That, by the way, is not a recommended load.*

In the life of the .33 it seems there was only the one commercial load. It consisted of a 200-grain bullet with a muzzle velocity of 2,200 fps. Handloaders are also limited in their choice of bullets; Hornady is the only firm I know which produces one suitable for the .33 Winchester, their 200-grain flatnose.

The sectional density of a .338 200-grain bullet is .250, slightly better than the .236 assigned the same weight in .348 caliber and only a smidgen poorer than the .256 value of the 170-grain .308 bullet used in the .30-30. That probably accounts for the deep penetration and dependable results on game reported by that long gone coterie of woodsmen and guides who favored the .33.

In the overall scheme of things, the .33 was probably shortchanged by not having a choice of bullet weights. A 150-grain bullet would have made an excellent "express" load, and might have given the .30-30 a run for its money. Indeed, that was recognized later when the .348 was brought out with a 150-grain loading, although the

The .33 Winchester (left) compared with its successor, the .348 (right). The .33 can be safely handloaded to match the more modern round's performance.

lighter bullets had poor sectional density and shed velocity quickly. Perhaps a 180 or 190-grain bullet would have been a better compromise.

Table I shows the loads used in testing this cartridge. IMR-4064 is, as usual, a good performer with the 200-grain Hornady bullet.

No pressure signs were seen with any of the IMR-4064 loads, but it must be pointed out that the top load is well above any recommended in other reloading literature. It worked well in the test rifle, but anyone duplicating this load should work up slowly from at least 10 to 15 percent below.

Any powder that nearly fills the case and does not produce pressure signs will be suitable in this old bottleneck cartridge. IMR-4895 with 45 grains is about as hot a load as the old Model 86 could handle. Accuracy was good. Muzzle velocity reached 2,400 fps which

puts this cartridge right up with the .348, .444 and .375 Winchester.

The same remarks apply to IMR-4320. Although 100 fps slower than IMR-4064, it showed the least shot-to-shot variation among the powders. It was also the most accurate, producing 3½-inch groups at 100 yards. In short, it was the best overall handload giving sufficient velocity, good downrange energy, and no pressure signs.

Anyone wanting to hunt with either a Marlin or Winchester in .33 caliber is going afield well outfitted for deer and black bear. At 2,400 fps, the muzzle energy is a whopping 2,600 ft/lbs. With the Hornady bullet, which is made to standards unattainable back in the early 1900s, there is adequate power for moose and elk out to 200 yards. The limitation of this cartridge, and many of the others in its class, is the distance at which game, in particular elk, has to be taken. Beyond 200 yards, trajectory and bullet velocity become problems.

Grandfather's .33 Winchester accounted for a lot of game over the two decades he owned it. Hard economic times and more mouths to feed (one of course, was my father's), caused the .33 to be traded for a wagon load of seed barley. My own .33s were years later in coming and they have only accounted for two deer, both taken just over the 150-yard mark. At that range, and on those animals, performance could not be faulted. Like my granddad, I can see the value of that nice, big cartridge and heavy bullet. It really does not part the bush magically, the way Moses separated the Red Sea, but somehow those slugs make it through almost every time.

Table II
.33 Winchester and Other Factory Calibers Compared

cartridge	bullet	velocity (fps)			energy (ft/lbs)		
		muzzle	100	200	muzzle	100	200
.30-30	150	2,390	2,018	1,684	1,902	1,356	944
	170	2,200	1,895	1,619	1,827	1,355	989
.33 Winchester	200	2,200	1,818	1,484	2,150	1,468	978
.348 Winchester	150	2,890	2,428	2,100	2,780	1,965	1,470
	200	2,520	2,215	1,931	2,820	2,178	1,656
.35 Remington	180	2,150	1,733	1,416	1,959	1,334	890
	200	2,020	1,647	1,337	1,812	1,206	791
.375 Winchester	200	2,200	1,814	1,526	2,150	1,506	1,034
	250	1,900	1,647	1,424	2,005	1,506	1,126
.32 Winchester	170	2,280	1,876	1,534	1,827	1,328	955
.444 Marlin	240	2,350	1,815	1,377	2,942	1,755	1,010
	265	2,120	1,733	1,405	2,644	1,768	1,162

CHAPTER
6

by **Ken Waters**

The .338-303 British

THIS IS another of my creations which came into being to meet a specific need.

Around 25 years ago, I acquired a much-used rifle that had been liberated during the bloody Mau Mau uprising in Africa. It was a Mauser-actioned sporter in .303 British with most of the rifling shot out of its bore and seemingly little to recommend it. A closer inspection revealed it was a product of the great Rigby factory with the relatively uncommon slanted magazine to handle rimmed (or as the British say, flanged) cartridges, and a perfectly sound classic stock requiring only moderate refinishing.

Initial test firing quickly confirmed that nothing more in the way of accuracy could be expected from this gallant old hunter which had, no doubt, accounted for innumerable heads of game in the hands of some outback settler. If it was to be of any use to me, it would have to be given a new bore.

Rebarreling was only considered briefly. I didn't want to lose its uniquely different Cape-style rear sight, nor part with the Rigby inscription along its surface. I'd had previous experience with the excellent reboring service offered by J.W. Van Patten (PO Box 145, Foster Hill Road, Milford PA 18337), so I turned the barreled action over to him with instructions to rebore the old barrel to a groove diameter of .338 inch, and rechamber it for the .303 British Improved case with neck opened up to hold .338-inch bullets.

The old barrel was straight and I felt this was the most practicable way to restore it, as I would then have a new bore without losing any of the desirable original features.

Mr. Van Patten did as requested with his usual accurate workmanship, and the rifle returned with a shining new bore and sharp cut-rifling. The rimmed .303 British cases made fireforming relatively easy and safe after first expanding their necks to hold .338-inch bullets.

Fireformed cases have the same 2.22-inch length as the .303 British, but case bodies have the reduced taper and larger, steeper shoulder common to Improved cases. Major case dimensions, in inches, are:

Diameter of rim: .538-.540
  (varies slightly with brass make)
Diameter of base: .455 (same as .303)
Diameter at shoulder: .443
Length, base to shoulder: 1.85
Length of neck: .300
Length of case: 2.22

Internal capacity of the blown-out cases is increased. That factor, augmented by the greater expansion ratio created by the larger bore diameter, requires the use of heavier powder charges than a standard .303 British round. At the same time, heavier bullets can be used — a 200-grain .338 instead of a 180-grain .303 (actually .311 inch), and a 250-grain .338 as against a 215-grain .303.

Due to the heavier bullets, no substantive gains in velocity have been achieved, but 200-grain .338-inch bullets can be driven around 2,350 fps in the strong Mauser action for a muzzle energy close to 2,450 foot-pounds. With a bullet of this weight and diameter, that's enough to down any game animal in the original 48 states. With a 210 grain Nosler Partition bullet, it would be even deadlier on the larger, tougher species. As a brush and timber cartridge for deer and black bear with the more frangible 200-grain softpoints, it is highly effective!

Accuracy has been good with both 200-grain Speer spitzers and 250-grain Sierras. So far, only the original Rigby open iron sights have been used, giving five-shot, 100-yard groups of 1¾ to 2½ inches. The stock has been rubbed down by hand, preserving the original checkering with rewarding results.

As successful as the restoration and change of caliber has been — and I *do* consider the effort to have been eminently worthwhile — I wish it understood that the wildcat cartridge which resulted is not a record-breaker in any sense of the word, nor was it intended to be. Far from revolutionizing anything, its ballistics have been what might have been expected — no more and no less — and I *don't* anticipate it will ever become even minutely popular!

What then has been accomplished? Why precisely that which should, in my estimation, be considered the No. 1 justification for a wildcat's creation: To perform a specific function or meet a specified need. That it *has* done and, I believe, done well.

As with most any development one cares to name, there are some precautions I feel should be observed. Whereas either the Mauser or a Pattern 14 Enfield action is adequately strong for this conversion, if applied to a Lee-Enfield, I wouldn't try for maximum velocities. Frankly, I don't know what pressures this cartridge is generating, probably no more than the smaller .303 British cartridge with its tapered case, but I don't intend taking senseless chances to achieve insignificant gains in velocity.

Some .303 British rifles may also be found with oversized chambers, particularly toward the rear where the case expansion ring forms. Should that part of the chamber's dimensions be too generous, re-chambering to the Improved case won't help because no steel will be removed from that section of the chamber.

If only slightly oversized however, .30-40 Krag *cases* can successfully be substituted for .303 British when forming this wildcat as (in some makes, at least) they have a base diameter .002 to .003 inch larger than that of .303 British hulls. When that substitution is made, case length must remain the same, hence .30-40 cases must be shortened to 2.22 inches.

One final point: new brass forms with a loss of fewer cases than does brass previously fired in .303 British or .30-40 rifles, so it's best to start with factory-fresh cases.

●

CHAPTER
7

Wildcat Pump for the Alaskan Hunter

Jay Turner

WHEN I WAS a youngster I didn't know too much about guns, but I did enjoy going along on some of my father's hunts and I couldn't wait until I was old enough to have a real gun (i.e., not a BB gun). It was a high point of my young life the day my father presented me with an old but well-preserved Remington pump action .22 rimfire rifle. That little rifle spent a lot of time with me over the next few years, but as I grew older my tastes in firearms changed and eventually the old Remington was set aside for more exciting lever, bolt and semiautomatic rifles of both centerfire and rimfire persuasion.

After high school I was again exposed to a pump rifle owned by a hunting buddy. That Model 760 Remington was chambered in .270 Winchester and its owner and I spent lots of time chasing deer and rabbits in Nevada and California, and caribou and black bear in Alaska. As I recall we had much better success with the jacks, but anyway I was impressed with my friend's rifle. It would supply 2 MOA groups on demand with his handloads, which were put together with the old Lee Loader tool, and furnished all the accuracy and power he needed. He still hunts with it occasionally and the last time out it felled a bull moose with one shot.

Since the mid-1970s, bolt-action and single-shot guns have been the mainstays of my rifle arsenal, although a semiauto or two has seen some use. Nearly two decades of hunting in Alaska have enlightened me as to the needs for that state's average hunter, although my personal choices generally have steered away from the popular 7mm and .300 magnums. In spite of what many non-Alaskans think, few local hunters seriously hunt 11-foot brown bear or 70-inch moose. The local hunter is not under pressure to make a choice between taking a chancy shot or losing a trophy on a $10,000 guided hunt, so he can usually take the time to get closer or obtain a better firing angle. Thus, the resident Alaskan hunter seldom requires a big magnum and except for the extremely rare need to stop a charging grizzly, he is well-served by the .30-06; indeed, local gun dealers report an increase in recent years in .30-06 sales and a decline in the number of 7mm magnums sold.

Many hunters, myself included, feel more comfortable with something a little more potent than an '06, but we don't want to be burdened with a magnum-class rifle with its higher weight and longer barrel. I hunt deer on Kodiak Island yearly, and Kodiak in the fall is chock-full of brown bear. While I've had several close encounters, I've never had to defend

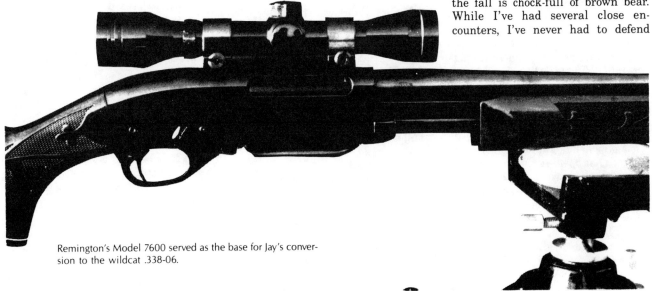

Remington's Model 7600 served as the base for Jay's conversion to the wildcat .338-06.

The barrel and attached extension are trapped between the receiver and the tightened tube. The barrel removal wrench is shown with one of the four holes in the action tube.

myself. If I did, the scenario would probably go like this: It's overcast or rainy, the alders are thick and the bear appears at under 20 yards. He (or more probably a she with cubs) gets within 15 yards before I decide he's coming all the way. A running brownie is a large but difficult target, and typically a well-hit bear will go down but be back up immediately. In this instance a potent repeater with good pointing ability is required. A bolt rifle can be cycled quite rapidly by an experienced shooter, but in spite of what some may claim, a pump or automatic can deliver a faster aimed second or third shot. Autos can be sensitive to ammunition and are sometimes difficult to clear when jammed, but a pump will function with almost any load which gets the bullet out of the barrel and it supplies sufficient leverage to clear a jam.

The Remington Model 7600 was available in several chamberings. The .30-06 that I purchased packed the most punch. Examining the rifle, it appeared that opening the bolt face to a magnum head size would be difficult and there would be no way to predict if the larger case would feed dependably. Reliability was of course a major factor in the project, so I decided that an '06-based wildcat such as the .338-06, .35 Whelen or .375 Whelen would suffice. All three cartridges outperform the .30-06, with muzzle

energies generally between 3,400 and 3,500 foot-pounds.

As the project got underway Remington announced the Model 7600 in .35 Whelen, but I had already decided against this old wildcat. I have had experience with .35-caliber cartridges, and have two friends who own rebored Model 760s in .35 Whelen, so I was aware of the scarcity of stoutly constructed, ballistically efficient .358-inch bullets. Since I also enjoy shooting something a bit different, the factory .35 had little appeal.

My first choice was the .375 Whelen. There are plenty of readily available bullets that are designed for the faster .375 H&H which will expand less and penetrate deeper when pushed more slowly out of the Whelen; it has the maximum practical bullet diameter for the '06 case and it holds the ".375" mystique. With readily available bullets down to 200 grains, it's not just a short-range smasher either.

Close examination of the Model 7600's barrel, however, caused a change in plans. Its .308-caliber barrel was amply thick for reboring to .375 inch, but the boys at the Remington plant got a little carried away when they drilled the holes for the front and rear sights. With the barrel opened up to .375 inch, less than .06 inch of steel

would remain between the bottoms of the holes and the bore — too little to guarantee safety, particularly under the rear sight holes near the chamber. Fitting a new custom barrel was not practical due to the 7600's design. The factory barrel is welded to a barrel extension into which the bolt locks up. Refitting a custom tube would require cutting off the old barrel at the extension and welding on the new one. No gunsmith in my neck of the woods wished to undertake that work.

A local smith, however, could have the barrel rebored. After discussing the project with Bob Rehm of The Gun Nutt (4859 Kupreanof St., Anchorage AK 99507) agreed that taking the bore out to .375 inch was risky. After a little more research, I decided that the .338-06 was a good second choice and Bob shipped the barrel off to Dick Nickel's Ridgetop Sporting Goods of Eatonville, Washington, for reboring. Nickel's shop offers the Obermeyer style of rifling in addition to conventional lands and he was authorized to use this rifling head.

Actually, the .338-06 is probably a better choice than the ⅜ inch Whelen anyway, as .338-inch diameter bullets feature superior ballistic coefficients and sectional densities for their weight. Muzzle energies are nearly the same for both cartridges, but downrange the .338 holds up a bit better. The only real disadvantage to the .338-06 is the smaller hole it makes. Although I believe this to be important, the other advantages outweigh it and I have been very pleased with the way things turned out.

Others have described the Model 7600 as a pump-operated bolt action rifle, and that description is not inaccurate. The rifle's basic design, however, is from the famous Model 870 shotgun and the rifle retains that weapon's smoothness of operation and fine pointing characteristics. Because both hands remain on the stock in their firing positions, follow-up shots can be taken the instant the rifle comes down out of recoil. Bolt action fans are often amazed at the rapidity of effective fire that a pump rifle or shotgun can deliver.

By designing the bolt to lock up into the barrel extension, Remington has inadvertently designed a factory switch-barrel rifle. A threaded stud on the forward face of the receiver slides through a hole in the barrel extension.

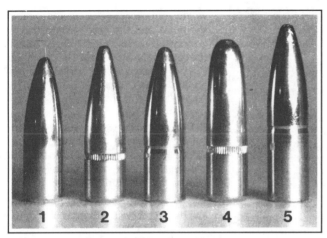

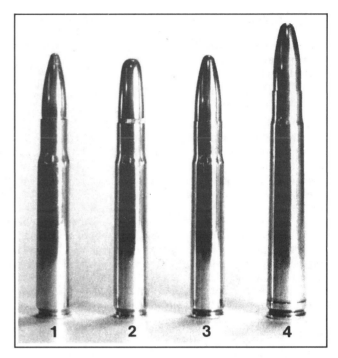

Above, test bullets included the (1) 200-grain Speer spitzer, (2) 200-grain Hornady Spire Point, (3) 210-grain Nosler Partition, (4) 250-grain Hornady roundnose and (5) 250-grain Nosler Partition. Right, Potent big game cartridges for North America include the (1) .338-06, (2) .35 Whelen and (3) .375 Whelen alongside the (4) .375 H&H Magnum.

This extension is secured to the receiver by screwing the threaded forend guide tube onto the stud, trapping the barrel. I made a barrel removal tool by gluing a length of ³⁄₁₆-inch rod into a six-inch long wooden handle; the rod fits into holes in the guide tube and can tighten or loosen the tube for barrel attachment or removal. The bolt and action bars come away with the barrel, but by rotating the bar assembly 90 degrees the barrel is freed by itself. Theoretically, only another fitted barrel/extension assembly is required to switch calibers with this rifle. I do not know Remington's policy on supplying additional barrels, although the rifle's manual lists barrels as factory-fitted parts. A .243 Winchester, .270 Winchester and .338-06 barrel set would meet the rifle needs of most hunters at somewhat less cost than a custom switch-barrel bolt rifle.

Subsequent testing has shown that the rifle's point of impact changes little when the barrel is removed and reinstalled. As long as the guide tube was securely tightened the center of the group moved less than two inches at 100 yards, and barrel loosening has not been a problem.

The Model 7600 feeds from a four-shot detachable clip, allowing rapid reloading compared to most action types. With the clip inserted and the action closed, the receiver is well-sealed

from the elements; even the ejection port is protected by a sliding cover. In freezing rain or snow only the action bars remain vulnerable and a good coating of oil or metal protectant would help guard these from ice formation and freeze-up.

While the barrel was away for reboring and chambering I went to work on the rifle's trigger. By pushing out two spring-retained pins, the complete trigger assembly can be removed from the bottom of the receiver. When new, the factory trigger broke at about five pounds with lots of creep and overtravel, although the creep was quite smooth. Clipping a coil from the sear return spring dropped the pull to under four pounds, but the creep remained. I eventually cut down the hammer engagement notch by about half, stoned the mating surfaces to improve smoothness and cut a little more off the sear spring to bring the pull down to 2½ pounds with just a trace of creep. The trigger is now superior to that of most new factory bolt action rifles.

I drilled and tapped the rear of the trigger guard for a small Allen screw and after careful adjustment to ensure minimum trigger overtravel I applied Loc-Tite to secure it. I must stress that because of the trigger assembly's design, where the safety secures the trigger and not the hammer, all creep or takeup cannot be removed if a safe trigger is to be retained. I suggest that

a spare hammer and spare sear spring be obtained before starting any trigger modifications. Although trigger action, and thus practical accuracy, can be markedly improved, it is the shooter's responsibility to ensure the safety of his firearm. Anyone not sure of his own gunsmithing abilities should contact a competent gunsmith for this work.

Regardless of who modifies your trigger, check it for safety by striking the cocked but unloaded rifle smartly on the butt with a padded hammer, both with the safety on and off. If the hammer falls, the gun is not safe and factory spec parts must be reinstalled. The simplest modification is merely clipping one coil off the sear return spring. This results in a modest improvement in pull while retaining a safe trigger.

The rifle's action was a little stiff at first. Removing all of the packing grease helped some, and cycling the action a few dozen times smoothed things up as well. While I had the barrel off, though, I took a fine, hard Arkansas stone and lightly touched up the edges of the operating bars where they run through the grooves in the receiver walls. Significant metal removal was not the goal here, only the reduction of any slight burrs. Removing metal would only increase the existing tolerances, inviting binding. My purpose was to simulate the wear which would take place by cycling the action many hundreds of times. After reassembling the rifle and lightly lubricating it with Break-Free, the action operation was significantly improved and felt smoother than that old Model 760 whose parts had been lapped by many years of use.

One of the most attractive features of the Remington pumps is their fine natural pointing tendency, hardly surprising considering their shotgun heritage. Unlike some bolt action rifles, the 7600 is stocked well for the factory iron sights. Adding a high-mounted scope raises the sighting plane and degrades the rifle's pointing ability, so I searched for the lowest scope mounting possible, a Weaver one-piece base and a set of low Weaver rings. This setup gave a line of sight only slightly above that of the factory sights and the scope aligns perfectly with my eye when the rifle is mounted rapidly. I'm not sure if this mount would allow a large-objective scope to clear the barrel, but then I consider such optics ill-suited to this type of firearm.

In keeping with the light, quick-handling design of this rifle, I chose to use a small lightweight scope. I happened to have an unmounted Tasco 4x Compact sight on hand, so I elected to give it a try; so far it has performed flawlessly. For use exclusively on larger game or in thick cover, the wider field of view of a 2½x or 3x scope might be preferred, but for all-around use I chose

the 4x. As currently set up my Model 7600 tips the scales at under eight pounds with scope and sling.

The rifle is well-balanced and easy to carry, but any hunter who spends much time walking in the field recognizes the advantages of a sling. The pump presents a problem for swivel attachment, however, since it's a poor idea to mount one on the forend. Swivel suppliers like Uncle Mike's solved the problem by offering a barrel band to hold the front swivel. Mounted at least two inches in front of the forend, it allows a comfortable sling carry. Due to the direct barrel mounting, the sling cannot be used as a shooting aid, since a tight sling would pull the barrel somewhat.

Once the barrel came back from reboring and Bob had rechambered it for the standard .338-06, I began load development. Each bullet I wanted to use was inserted into a test case whose neck I had carefully split with a fine saw. The dummy round was chambered, and the leade pushed the bullet back into the case giving a maximum cartridge overall length with the bullet seated to the leade. It happened that the magazine was the limiting factor and 3.30 inches is a practical maximum overall length; this length did not cause binding or scuffing of the bullet tips on the front of the clip. Seated out to about 3.30 inches put the bullets .023 to .078 inch off the lands.

The Redding custom dies came equipped with a tapered expander for necking .30-06 cases up to .338. With a light coating of graphite inside the case necks the dies opened up new Federal cases perfectly with no rejects. A light trimming squared up case mouths.

Sifting through my library of old shooting magazines produced four articles giving .338-06 loading data and two more with loads for the ancestral .333 OKH. The OKH data used significantly larger powder charges than most of those listed for the .338-06, probably because the older round was usually throated for the very long 300-grain Kynoch bullets. Starting five grains below the lowest maximums listed for the .338 version, I fired one round of one powder charge behind each bullet, carefully noting the expansion ring diameter and extraction characteristics of each load as the charges were increased one grain at a time. This method quickly provided approximate maximum load levels, giving me an idea of how my own rifle and components compared with the other authors' bolt guns. Happily, I found that the 7600 would digest loads at least as heavy as most of the bolt guns could, giving comparable velocities without signs of excessive case stress. Since reliability was an important aspect of this project, no loads listed exhibited the least bit of extraction difficulty in my rifle.

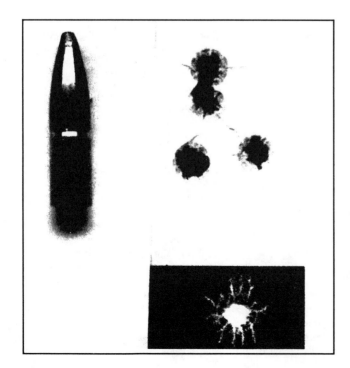

The typical group with the .338-06, a four-shot cluster and one flyer that Jay attributes to variation in his shooting technique. For comparison, the 250-grain Nosler Partition bullet is 1.35 inches long. Far right, the case on the left shows slight cratering and brass extrusion into the ejector hole; this was considered over maximum when compared to loads listed in the tables. The enlarged primer pocket in the case on the right could have resulted from a pressure excursion but the Model 7600 took it in stride.

In fact, most loads which approached maximum levels actually unlocked the bolt without any manual effort. Apparently the higher recoil levels accelerate the bolt, carrier and forend assembly rearward along with the rest of the gun, and while my shoulder stops the rifle's rearward movement, the momentum of the forend and bolt assembly carries them rearward to unlock and retract the bolt about one-half inch. Of course, this happens only after chamber pressures have dropped to zero so no danger is presented by the phenomenon. Instead this helps to increase the rifle's rate of fire since the shooter's arm has only to continue cycling the action open with no extra effort required to unlock it. At first I was concerned that this self-unlocking characteristic was due to a defect in the rifle as the box of .30-06 shells fired before reboring had not caused the bolt to withdraw. I stopped worrying after checking with a friend who has used a Model 760 in .35 Whelen for years and whose rifle exhibits the same characteristic. I'm certain that the higher recoil levels are responsible, because light .338-06 loads leave the bolt locked up tight. Whatever the cause, the result is judged an asset rather than a liability.

Expected uses dictated bullet selection. Alaskan game such as deer, black bear, caribou and sheep are not overly difficult to kill and often require shots at 200 to 300 yards. The various 200-grain bullets were deemed best for these animals, since their relatively light construction would result in quicker kills and velocities of over 2,700 fps provided the flat trajectory required for long-range shots. Of the two 200-grain bullets tested, those by Hornady and Speer, the latter gave somewhat better accuracy, with the best load grouping five shots right at one MOA. I suspect that the Speer bullet showed better accuracy due to its ogive shape; when loaded to the same overall length the more pointed Hornady had about twice as much jump before reaching the lands.

Both bullets have good reputations when used in .338 magnums on deer-sized game; at velocities 200 to 300 fps below magnum levels they behave like tougher bullets, giving less expansion and deeper penetration. Their high ballistic coefficients flatten the bullet

Table I

Ballistics Comparison Chart

cartridge	bullet (grains)	muzzle velocity (fps)	muzzle energy (ft/lb)	300-yard energy (ft/lb)	300-yard drop* (inches)
.338-06	210	2,750	3,526	2,027	−8.5
.338-06	250	2,450	3,332	2,126	−10.5
.30-06	180	2,800	3,133	1,933	−8.0
.338 Mag FL	200	2,900	3,734	2,347	−7.5

*Based on a 200-yard zero.

Table II

Wildcat Cartridges Based on the .30-06 Case

cartridge	bullet (grains)	muzzle velocity (fps)	muzzle energy (ft/lb)	300-yard energy (ft/lb)
.338-06	210	2,750	3,526	2,027
	250	2,450	3,332	2,125
.35 Whelen	200	2,700	3,237	1,545
	250	2,500	3,469	2,111
.375 Whelen	235	2,550	3,393	1,671
	270	2,400	3,453	1,917

The above velocities are average maximums from at least two different sources rounded to the nearest 50 fps. The average muzzle energy for these three '06-based wildcats is 3,402 foot-pounds.

Table III

.338-06 Load Chart

bullet (grains)	powder	charge (grains)	velocity (fps)	remarks
200 Hornady	IMR-4320	53.0	2,632	very mild
		54.0	2,656	
		55.0	2,714	moderate
		56.0	2,724	near maximum
		57.0	2,840	max in cool temps
	W-748	54.0	2,501	1.6 MOA
		56.0	2,554	mild
	IMR-4064	55.0	2,598	3 MOA
200 Speer	IMR-4320	55.0	2,688	warm
		56.0	2,736	maximum
	W-748	59.0	2,753	extremely accurate
		60.0	2,784	1.4 MOA
210 Nosler	IMR-4320	54.0	2,631	moderate
		55.5	2,712	maximum—1.4 MOA
	W-748	58.0	2,701	warm
		59.0	2,742	maximum—1.5 MOA
250 Hornady	IMR-4320	51.0	2,415	12 fps spread
	W-748	50.0	2,210	very mild
		53.0	2,350	moderate
	IMR-4350	55.0	2,341	mild
		57.0	2,384	moderate—1.5 MOA
250 Nosler	IMR-4350	55.0	2,354	1.5 MOA
		57.0	2,405	2.1 MOA
		58.0	2,447	maximum
	H-414	56.0	2,228	very mild
		57.0	2,277	1.9 MOA

Test rifle was a Remington Model 7600 rebored to .338-06 with a 1-in-10-inch twist, 22-inch barrel. All loads were chronographed on an Oehler Model 33 Chronotach with a SkyScreen III system. Instrumental velocities corrected to muzzle velocities at 45 to 55 degrees Fahrenheit. All groups fired in five-shot strings at 100 yards. Federal cases and 210 primers used in all loads.

Be alert — Publisher cannot accept responsibility for errors in published load data.

path, resulting in a trajectory to 300 yards that is virtually identical to that of a good .30-06 180-grain handload. Clearly this .338 rifle is at least as effective as a bolt action .30-06 at long range, with the best loads producing MOA accuracy while delivering a heavier, larger diameter bullet.

For use on moose or the big bears, where higher penetration is often needed, I prefer the 250-grain bullets. The Hornady roundnose, with its Interlock construction, is a good short range bullet, although it would not be my first choice due to its excessive velocity loss at long range. A friend has a jar full of them recovered from elk, each a perfect mushroom, so its performance can't be faulted. At first I encountered a high rate of feeding failures with this bullet. When seated to an overall length to fit the clip and place the ogive about .05 inch off the lands most rounds would strike the flat face of the barrel and hang up. By seating these blunt bullets .06 inch deeper, however, feeding problems disappeared.

My own choice in this bullet weight is the 250-grain Nosler. In recent years Nosler has redesigned this bullet from a semi-spitzer to a full spitzer, thus raising its ballistic coefficient from .364 to .491. The resulting increase in retained energy is welcome, making long range shots more effective. This is probably the heaviest practical bullet weight for the .338-06. Bob Hagel and others have reported that the stoutly constructed Nosler penetrates deeper than do the heavier 275 and 300-grain slugs with their higher sectional densities. In this case superior construction overcomes any mathematical advantages. With higher velocity and superior ranging qualities the Nosler is definitely the better choice for the largest game.

In truth, I seldom hunt grizzly or brown bear, so the bulk of my shooting could be accomplished with the aforementioned 200-grain bullets. The problem here is that although I might not be looking for grizzly, I have accidentally found them — up close to boot. To date, I haven't had to defend myself, but the remote possibility exists and would require accurate, deeply penetrating hits and probably more than one shot. Under these circumstances I do not trust the conventional 200-grain bullets to hold together and penetrate well if heavy bone is hit. On the other hand I don't care to be limited by the heavier recoil and less flat trajectory of the 250 Noslers when hunting lesser game. Thus, for most of my hunting I use the Nosler 210-grain bullet. Its performance makes it perhaps the best all-around bullet for the .338-06 and I would not hesitate to use it on moose or bear if it was the only bullet I had in the gun at the time.

Other shooters have shown IMR-4320 to be the most popular powder for the lighter .338 bullets in this cartridge and I was able to obtain good velocities with it. My top load was 57.0 grains of IMR-4320 under the 200-grain Hornady for 2,840 fps and 3,582 foot-pounds of energy — a potent load indeed, but probably too hot for extended use. Winchester-Olin 748 had performed well at velocities near 2,600 fps with less case expansion than top loads with IMR-4320, so judicious charge increases were made. Fifty-nine grains of W-748 produce 2,753 fps with the Speer bullet at moderate pressures and MOA accuracy. It has become my favorite load for this bullet.

Along with Nosler's 210-grain bullet, W-748 also proved superior for high speeds with sane pressures. IMR-4320 produced maximum acceptable pressures at 2,703 fps, while W-748 gave lower pressure signs at 2,701 fps. I considered 59 grains of W-748 as maximum, giving 2,742 fps with 3,506 foot-pounds of energy; accuracy levels averaged 1.5 MOA for five-shot groups.

DuPont's IMR-4350 is popular with the 250-grain bullets and it did give good performance. Compressed loads, however, were required to reach maximum pressures and I personally don't like to excessively compress any powder. The increased densities of the Ball powders seemed to offer a solution, so I tried W-748 along with H-414.

Beginning with W-748 and the Nosler bullet, I filled up five case lots with 53, 54 and 55 grains and headed to the range. Fifty-three grains gave mild pressure signs and the 54-grain load showed warm but not high pressures. After firing the first of the 55-grain loads, however, I had trouble opening the action. Examining the rifle more closely I noticed smoke seeping out of the covered ejection port. As I was unable to open the action more than one-half inch at the range, the rifle was put in the case and taken home. There I removed the wooden forend and lightly tapped on the action tube with a padded mallet and succeeded in opening the action. I was not too surprised to find the case firmly stuck in the bolt face. After completely disassembling the rifle the case was removed and examined. The case head was swollen to .490 inch and the primer pocket was greatly expanded from what was obviously an extreme overload. Breaking down the remaining four cartridges showed that they each contained the correct powder charge. I can only conclude that for some reason W-748 demonstrates extreme pressure excursions when using this bullet at near 100 percent loading densities (the subject load, however, was not compressed). For obvious reasons I will not use it with heavy bullets in this case at near-maximum charges.

This incident caused me to have much-increased faith in the 7600. After cleaning up the soot and brass shavings and reassembling the rifle, everything functioned perfectly. No broken or damaged parts were found and the rifle was immediately put back into service. It should be noted that the only indication I had that a case had blown was difficulty in opening the action; no gases or fragments whatever exited the receiver to endanger the shooter. A similar occurrence with most bolt guns might have resulted in gas and particles being vented out of the action. While I would much rather not have had the experience, I cannot help but be impressed with the strength and safety of the 7600.

Attempts with H-414 and the 250-grain projectiles resulted in rather low velocities, although maximum pressure loads were never tried. At charge levels offering 100 percent loading density, velocities would probably rival those obtained with IMR-4350.

It is often said that bolt action rifles are required for any hunting except "woods or timber hunting" if the shooter wants to hit his target. It is implied that other action types are too inaccurate for "serious" hunters. This type of snobbery appears to be based on limited or nonexistent personal experience; apparently it is perpetuated because it is "common knowledge." I enjoy shooting and hunting with bolt action rifles and always will, but if the truth be known, not many factory-fresh rifles will consistently group five shots much under 1.5 to two MOA without some modification. I've shot with hunters who sneered at my semiauto which regularly grouped at one inch while their bolt guns were struggling to deliver two to three MOA. Old prejudices die hard, even in the face of hard evidence.

The first few dozen groups with the rifle seldom broke out of the two to three MOA range, but as more bullets were put through the barrel its accuracy began to improve. Inspecting the last four inches of the barrel's interior with a hand lens, I could see the initial roughness of the bore slightly improve as more rounds were fired. I should mention that after reboring my barrel was slightly rough with minute gouges and grooves when compared to the mirror-smooth Remington factory

bore. This observation is not a criticism of Dick's work; I have one rifle rebored by P.O. Ackley in the early 1970s which is equally rough yet it shoots beautifully. Remington factory barrels are hammer-forged over a mandrel which work-hardens the steel, but when that barrel is rebored small hard spots will cause the rifling head to tear tiny gouges in the metal. While these flaws would be unacceptable in a benchrest barrel, they do not appear to impair the accuracy of my rebored hunting rifles. Manufacturers of new barrels have the luxury of using virgin steel and they can discard barrels with slight flaws — an option not open to a reboring firm.

Recoil from the bench with this light rifle is rather stout, certainly above '06 levels with the heavier loads and the effect on the shooter was occasionally painful. I have a bony shoulder and if the rifle's butt was not positioned correctly the hard plastic buttplate pinched badly. After taking as much of this fun as I could stand I decided to try one of the new "high-tech" recoil pads and had Bob install a Pachmayr Decelerator. The result was a dramatic reduction in discomfort. The rifle still recoils fully, but any shoulder pain is eliminated, even when the butt is poorly positioned. Now long sessions at the bench are pleasant rather than dreaded, and I'm certain that groups improved due to reduced shooter error (read: flinch).

After spending some months with the rifle I am very satisfied with its performance. Power and accuracy levels have met expectations and handling, reliability and even safety have been flawless. Some might question whether the rebore job resulted in a meaningful power increase. Serious hunters of large game have written that it takes an increase of at least 500 foot-pounds of striking energy to make a noticeable increase in killing power. Wanting to know how much better this wildcat was than the parent .30-06, actual

chronographed velocities of 16 factory loads fired in 22-inch barrels were compiled to determine the average muzzle energy of factory '06 cartridges. This average came to 2,836 foot-pounds. With top loads reaching 3,500 foot-pounds the .338-06 delivers a substantial energy increase and given good bullets, can be a noticeably better killer on large game. Compared with '06 handloads the margin narrows of course, as most top .30-06 handloads approach 3,100 foot-pounds, but I believe the difference in favor of the .338-inch bore is still meaningful. While I doubt that a hunter would notice a difference on deer-sized game, elk, moose and the big bears are dispatched more cleanly with the larger caliber. It's this extra margin on large game that prompted this project in the first place.

Attempting to obtain accuracy levels below 1.5 MOA with a rifle intended for large game might seem ludicrous, but the fact that I occasionally succeeded proves that modern pump action rifles are capable of good accuracy. Actually, 1.5 MOA is about the average most .338-06 shooters report from bolt guns.

Future work with this rifle will probably center on an attempt to fit a barrel in .375 Whelen. If I can obtain a new factory .30-06 barrel without sights it will be a simple matter to open it up to ¾ inch. An alternative could be to ask the Remington Custom Shop to supply a new .375-inch barrel with the extension to be rechambered to the Whelen case and cut back to 18.5 inches. The resulting rifle would be somewhat more specialized than the .338-06, but for hunting the larger bears its greater diameter and heavier bullets could be an advantage. Until that time I'll be more than happy to hunt with my .338-06, secure in the knowledge that I can hit a small target at long range if I have to, yet still clobber a large one up close. ●

CHAPTER
8

The .338 Winchester, A Versatile Heavy Game Cartridge

By BOB HAGEL

THERE ARE A couple of points I'd like to make clear regarding the .338 Winchester cartridge right at the start: First, while I am a strong disciple of the .33 bore, I do not claim there is anything mystic connected with that bore size, and there is no magic potion mixed with the powder or smeared on the bullet that gives it phenomenal killing power possessed by no other cartridge. Good as it is, I can't quite agree with my old friend Elmer Keith that nothing less than a 250-grain bullet of .33 caliber is adequate for elk and larger North American game — although he does have a point for shooting some game under certain adverse hunting conditions.

The second point is a simple fact: The .338 recoil does set some hunters on their tail ends and they just can't shoot it accurately. And no matter how potent it is, if you can't hit 'em, you can't kill 'em. So if you have a yen for a .338 caliber cartridge, you might give these things some thought before you buy a rifle chambered for it.

It is quite possible that the .33 Winchester was the first .33 caliber cartridge loaded commercially anywhere in the world. At least I know of none made before the 1902 date that the .33 Winchester was unveiled. The .333 Jeffery dates back to about 1911, along with some other .33 caliber British cartridges. The little known .33 Newton based on the .30 Newton case probably did not appear for some time after the .30

Newton made its debut in 1913. I have never seen a .33 Newton cartridge and am not at all certain it was ever in production.

For a good many years after the .33 Winchester appeared, the .33 caliber lay fairly dormant; even the prolific American wildcatters seemed to shun it. However, the .333 Jeffery gained an enviable reputation in Africa as a medium bore cartridge for plains game, and a number of hunters used it to clobber lions, buffalo and even elephant with good success.

No telling how many wildcatters experimented with the .33 caliber down through the years or what they came up with, but the first one to gain any amount of attention was Charlie O'Neil when he cooked up the .333 OKH. Elmer Keith did a lot of field test work with that cartridge and Don Hopkins did a great deal of the first big game hunting with it. This cartridge, along with the .285 and .334 OKH, led to the partnership of O'Neil, Keith and Hopkins. I got into the act in hunting tests with the .333 OKH when Charlie made me a rifle on the 1917 Enfield action in 1939. There were a number of other cartridges by various wildcatters of .333 bore — those by Luft Brothers and Fred Barnes — but they came later. (Before some gun buff takes me to task for omitting someone's wildcat cartridge from the .333-.338 lineup, let me say that this is not intended as an historical wringout of .33 wildcats and wildcatters. The mention of wildcat .33 cartridges is used only for background that led up to the development of the commercial .338 cartridges — the .338 Winchester and .340 Weatherby.)

For those not familiar with the various .33 calibers, the .333 Jeffery and the .333

The .338 Winchester chambered in this Ruger Model 77 makes a fine mountain rifle for hunting heavy game from the size of elk up. With a 24-inch barrel it weighs under 8 1/2 pounds complete with Leupold scope and Brownell Latigo sling as shown.

45

OKH cartridges were of true .333 bullet diameter, while the .33 Winchester, .338 Winchester and the .340 Weatherby take .338 diameter bullets — not interchangeable, of course. There were no suitable .338 bullets available at the time the Jeffery and OKH cartridges were developed. The .33 Winchester was loaded with a single bullet weight of 200 grains and, as a lever action cartridge, the bullet was flat-pointed and designed for use in the tubular magazine of the Model 1886 Winchester. This was the only bullet made in .338 caliber at the time and it had a thin jacket designed for the relatively slow 2,200 fps muzzle velocity delivered by the .33 Winchester cartridge in a lever action.

The .333 OKH was developed for bullets of high sectional densities and deep penetration. (This was before John Nosler came along with positive controlled expansion bullets.) Bullets in .333 caliber were then available and could be imported from England. They came in weights of 250 and 300 grains and were supposedly designed with .333 Jeffery velocities in mind. However, these bullets were expensive and had certain failings; both were very fragile for one thing, and the 300-grainer was about as streamlined as a boxcar. They were hardly ideal for wildcats capable of long-range shooting.

As soon as the .333 OKH got well under way, the new OKH firm prevailed on bullet maker Fred Barnes to make a spitzer 250-grain for long-range shooting, and a round nose 300-grain for heavier game and near-in work. Speer also came out later with a well-shaped 275-grain of semi-pointed configuration.

The first Barnes bullets were made from jacket cups and were, if I remember correctly, .032-inch in thickness. I used hundreds of these in both the .333 OKH and the .333 OKH Belted cartridges on everything from coyotes to elk. They worked very well in the original .333 OKH which was an expanded .30-06 case and which gave the 250-grain a MV of nearly 2,600 fps from the 25-inch barrel. These jackets proved too fragile for the .334 OKH (based on the full-length .375 H&H case) and also for the later .333 OKH Belted (that was about the same length as the .338 Winchester but with the H&H body taper.) The .333 OKH Belted would, however, give the 250-grain over 2,700 fps with full-throttle loads, but

proved too much for the thin jacket — coming apart on elk at anything less than 200 yards. Barnes then came along with the .049-inch jacket made from copper tubing. These held up very well but there was an expansion problem. The jacket was not thinned at the point, and as it thickened in the swaging process the hole left under the extruded lead was only pin-size. I hollow-pointed many of these and they then worked quite well at long range.

Several .333 fans tried to get John Nosler to make bullets in this diameter for wildcat cartridges, but it was not until the .338 Winchester appeared that he decided to make bullets for that cartridge. I decided at that point to change over to the .338. Otherwise I'd probably be using the .333 Belted cartridge today. It is so similar to the .338 Winchester that there is little doubt in my mind that it led to the development of the latter.

Anyway, by the time the .338 Winchester came along, I had killed more big game with .33 caliber cartridges than most people have since with the .338. And anything I did with the .333 OKH Belted, the .338 Winchester will do just as well, and with Nosler bullets in either 210 or 250-grain weights it will perform better than any of the .33 wildcats.

The .338 Winchester Magnum gained a reputation as an outstanding killer of large game and attained sudden and lasting popularity. It actually supplanted the time-proven .375 H&H for a great deal of hunting in various parts of the hunting world. It became very popular with Alaskan hunters for grizzly and moose, and many brown bear guides

adopted it as a back-up rifle for use when the going got rough — after some client had let a wounded brownie get into the alders.

Most of the reputation built up by the .338 is well deserved, and regardless of what .375 H&H fans believe, it does offer several advantages over that enormously successful big game cartridge. One is that it is considerably shorter and can be used in any action with a magazine long enough to handle the .270 or .30-06. Recoil is a little less than the .375, but actually not enough to matter much.

The main advantage lies with the sectional density of the .338 bullets, and their better shape. The 250-grain .338 has a sectional density of .313, while the 270-grain .375 has only .274 and the 300-grain rates at .305. Even the 210-grain Nosler .338 packs .263, and if you really want sectional density, the 300-grain .338 has it at near .370 (I didn't take time to calculate it to the last point). Everything else being equal, and disregarding a controlled expanding bullet like Nosler, sectional density is what governs penetration. So it isn't hard to see that a 250-grain .338 bullet will give as much or more penetration than a 300-grain .375, and far outstrip the 270-grain in that caliber.

Hornady makes the only bullet in .375 with a favorable long-range ballistic coefficient — the 270-grain. But there are many for the .338 with good shape, ranging from the spitzer 200-grain up through the Nosler 210, the Hornady 225 and some pointed 250-grainers — like the Colorado Custom Bullets and the Sierra boat-tail. These bullets can all be driven

These are some of the wildcat and commercial .333 and .338 cartridges that have been used for hunting all over the world for nearly all classes of game. From left are the [1] .333 OKH with 250-grain Barnes; [2] .338-06, 210 Nosler; [3] .333 OKH Belted, 250 Barnes; [4] .334 OKH, 250 Barnes; [5] .338-300 Hagel, .275 Speer; [6] .338 Winchester, .250 Silvertip; [7] .340 Weatherby, 250 Nosler.

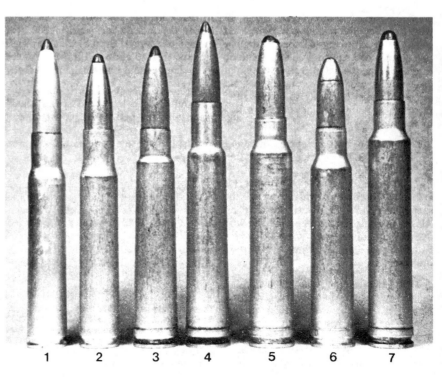

1   2   3   4   5   6   7

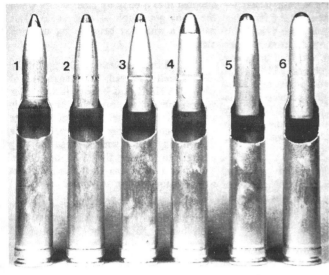

The sectioned cases immediately above illustrate seating depth of the various 250-grain bullets used in the velocity comparison tests in the Ruger M-77 rifle. The different seating depths may have some bearing on velocity variation between various bullet makes. The cases at left show the seating depths of bullets used in the Ruger M-77 seated so that they will barely function through the magazine. From left is the [1] 200-grain Speer [200-grain W-W was used in velocity tests]; [2] 210-grain Nosler, [3] 225 Hornady, [4] 250 W-W Silvertip, [5] 275 Speer, [6] 300 Colorado Custom.

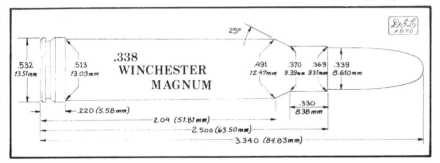

at high velocity for flattened trajectory curves at long range.

I have never felt that the 200-grain bullet was a good weight for the .338. This is especially true where most makes in this weight have fragile jackets that rip apart and give inadequate penetration on the larger game. They work well on deer-size game but are pretty tough on steaks if they don't land just right. Of course, they are designed for the lighter game and to expand reliably at long range, but my personal feeling is that if you want a .338 you probably do not intend to use it primarily as a deer rifle; there are so many cartridges better suited to that use.

I remember reading about a hunter using the .338 Winchester when it first came out. He made the statement that the 200-grain bullet was *the* bullet for everything in that cartridge, yet in the same story he told about shooting an Alaska brownie five times before the bear decided to quit. From what he said I gathered he was having penetration problems, so. . .

There is one exception to this bullet weight rule, and that is the 210-grain Nosler. It can be loaded to a muzzle velocity of 3,000 fps without any great pressure problems, and I've surpassed that in some rifles. It has a sectional density of .263 and a ballistic coefficient

of .386. These bullets shoot very flat over the longest big game ranges and retain a lot of velocity and energy on the far side of a wide canyon. And they do pack a lot of punch — like a muzzle energy of 4,200 foot pounds at 3,000 fps. I haven't killed a lot of game with 210 Noslers in the .338 Winchester, but I've shot assorted animals with them in the .340 Weatherby. In that cartridge my load clocked 3,215 fps at the muzzle for nearly 4,800 foot pounds of energy! Even at that very high velocity, the 210-grain will leave exit holes in the far side of a bull elk on most shots.

For most .338 shooting, I suspect the 210-grain Nosler loaded to around 3,000 fps may be the best bullet on the market today. The 225-grain Hornady has excellent shape for long range and can

easily be loaded to near 2,900 fps for trouble-free hunting loads, but it will not hold together on the heavy bone and muscle of big animals as well as some other bullets. If all shots were over the 200-yard range it would be ideal, but, unfortunately, range is something the hunter can't often control, and the closer you are the less penetration that type of bullet structure will give.

Bitterroot Bullet Co. made a very good hollow point 225-grain .338 bullet that has good ballistic coefficient and stays in one piece under the roughest conditions, but these are unavailable today with no assurance that more will be made. I have also used the BBC (Bitterroot Bonded Core) in 250-grain weight in several .338 caliber cartridges on everything from mule deer to Alaska brown bears with outstanding results, but they too are unavailable.

After killing a great many game animals in all shapes, sizes and colors with various .33 caliber cartridges, I have concluded that the 250-grain bullet weight is about the optimum for velocity, energy and deep penetration in expanding form. This bullet can be pushed to near 2,800 fps at the muzzle with several good powders in the .338 Winchester case,

These bullets are all .333 and .338 and taken from heavy game. From left is the 210-grain Nosler from a bull elk, .340 Weatherby; 250-grain Barnes .032 cup jacket from bull elk, .333 OKH; 250 Bitterroot Bonded Core from Alaska brown bear, .340 Weatherby; and 300-grain Kynoch from bull elk, .333 OKH Belted. All bullets except the 300-grain .333 gave deep penetration of heavy bone and muscle. That one didn't even exit on broadside shot at five point bull elk, indicating a lack of penetration.

47

.338 Winchester Velocity Variation

Variation of velocity with different makes and styles of 250-grain bullets with the same load using W-W cases and CCI No. 250 primers. Overall loaded length, 3.30 inches.

Bullet	Powder	Charge, Grains	Muzzle Velocity, fps	Remarks
250 W-W Silvertip	W-W 785	78	2,772	All velocities instrumental
250 Nosler RN SP	W-W 785	78	2,718	at 15 feet.
250 Hornady RN SP	W-W 785	78	2,752	Group size for three shots,
250 Bitterroot Ptd. HP	W-W 785	78	2,768	average for all bullets —
250 Sierra spitzer SP BT	W-W 785	78	2,714	2 inches.

Variation in diameter and length of bearing surface were probably the major causes of velocity variation. All were fired at the same time in the same five cases so as to eliminate possible variation. Point of impact varied as much as two inches with different bullets. Thus all goes to prove that every 250-grain bullet should be sighted in before going hunting.

.338 Winchester Magnum Load Data

.338 Winchester Model 77 Ruger, 24-inch barrel
W-W cases, weight — 240 grains primed
CCI No. 250 primers
Oehler 31-50
Velocity at 15 feet converted to MV, temperature — 70°

Bullet	Powder	Charge, Grains	Muzzle Velocity, fps	Remarks
Factory 250-grain ST W-W	- - - -	- - - -	2,639	2 1/2 inches, mild.
200 W-W Power-Point	H-4831	81*	2,941	3/4, mild.
200 W-W Power-Point	MRP	81	3,008	1 5/8, Max trouble-free load.
200 W-W Power-Point	IMR-4831	80*	3,068	2, Max trouble-free load.
200 W-W Power-Point	W-W 785	85*	3,041	2 1/4, Max trouble-free load.
200 W-W Power-Point	H-205	79	3,014	1 5/8, Max trouble-free load.
200 W-W Power-Point	IMR-4350	77	3,024	1 3/8, Max trouble-free load.
210 Nosler	MRP	80	2,961	1 3/4, Max trouble-free load.
210 Nosler	W-W 785	83*	2,971	1 5/8, Max trouble-free load.
210 Nosler	IMR-4831	79*	2,985	1, Max trouble-free load.
210 Nosler	H-205	78	2,992	2 1/8, Max trouble-free load.
210 Nosler	N-204	75	2,953	1 1/4, Max trouble-free load.
210 Nosler	IMR-4350	76	2,965	2 1/2, Max trouble-free load.
225 Hornady	MRP	78	2,894	All Max trouble-free loads.
225 Hornady	W-W 785	82*	2,874	All groups average 3 1/2
225 Hornady	IMR-4831	77*	2,897	inches with all powders.
225 Hornady	H-205	76	2,889	
225 Hornady	IMR-4350	75	2,894	
250 W-W Silvertip	H-4831	77*	2,717	2 inches, mild.
250 W-W Silvertip	MRP	75	2,759	1 7/8, Max trouble-free load.
250 W-W Silvertip	W-W 785	79	2,789	2 3/4, Max trouble-free load.
250 W-W Silvertip	IMR-4831	75	2,783	2 1/2, Max trouble-free load.
250 W-W Silvertip	H-205	73	2,775	3 1/2, Max trouble-free load.
250 W-W Silvertip	IMR-4350	71	2,707	1 1/8, Max trouble-free load.
275 Speer	H-4831	76*	2,566	3/4, mild.
275 Speer	MRP	74	2,593	7/8, Max trouble-free load.
275 Speer	W-W 785	78	2,649	2 1/8, Max trouble-free load.
275 Speer	IMR-4831	73	2,602	1 3/8, Max trouble-free load.
275 Speer	H-205	72	2,606	1 3/8, Max trouble-free load.
275 Speer	IMR-4350	70	2,576	5/8, Max trouble-free load.
300 Colorado Custom	H-4831	75*	2,490	15/16, mild.
300 Colorado Custom	MRP	73	2,494	1 3/4, Max trouble-free load.
300 Colorado Custom	W-W 785	76	2,544	1 1/2, Max trouble-free load.
300 Colorado Custom	IMR-4831	71	2,479	2 3/16, Max trouble-free load.
300 Colorado Custom	H-205	70	2,494	1 5/16, Max trouble-free load.
300 Colorado Custom	IMR-4350	69	2,485	1 1/2, Max trouble-free load.

*A bullet can be seated over these charges in full-length resized cases. All bullets were tried with two grains more powder, so these loads could be used in the test rifle in the hottest weather. All charges should be worked up from two grains below in any other rifle.

which gives it a muzzle energy of about 4,360 fp. This proved to be about the top velocity in the Ruger M-77 rifle used for the data in the accompanying chart, but I have had other rifles that would beat the 2,800-foot mark a bit from a 24-inch barrel without going overboard in pressures. For long range work, the 250-grain Sierra soft point boat-tail stands in a class by itself; but for deep penetration the Nosler is first with the BBC running a close second.

Going up the weight ladder, there is the excellent 275-grain Speer which has good ballistic shape (a listed BC of .470), and can be boosted along at around 2,650 fps from the .338 case. This bullet has a good reputation for killing heavy game and deep penetration, but I haven't had a great deal of experience with it. It is, however, a good choice for heavy game at shorter ranges.

The 300-grain bullet has been highly touted by some writers for use in the .338 bore with all case sizes, but I can't go along with this, except perhaps in steel-jacket solid form for brain shots on elephant. While I've shot many Colorado Custom 300-grain bullets, I have never killed anything with one, but I did down some game with the 300-grain British steel-jacket Kynoch expanding bullet in the .333 OKH Belted cartridge. I don't recall ever having one make exit on a broadside bull elk if a shoulder was hit. The thin steel jacket came apart like confetti clear to the heel. Which proves that just because a bullet is heavy it does not necessarily give deep penetration — even when showing the great sectional density of the .333 300-grain at .376!

Even if Nosler did make a 300-grain .338 bullet, it would be less than ideal in the .338 Winchester case for several reasons. First, I have found only one powder that will give it 2,500 fps MV without higher pressure than is desirable in a hunting load. Couple this rather low velocity with the round-nose shape necessary with this weight to hold down overall length, and the combination is not good for flat shooting over the longer

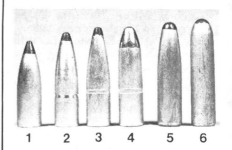

These are some of the most popular .338 bullets. From left are the: [1] 200-grain Speer, [2] 210 Nosler, [3] 225 Hornady, [4] 250 W-W Silvertip, [5] 275 Speer, [6] 300 Colorado Custom.

ranges. It has been said that these heavy bullets soon catch up to shorter, lighter pointed bullets even though they start slower, in both drop and velocity. Don't believe it; they never catch up! I've disproved this theory with many drop tests out to 500 yards. Also, the 300-grainers do not kick up as much energy at the muzzle or down-range as the 250-grain. Loaded to 2,500 fps, the 300-grain shows only about 4,160 fp of muzzle energy as compared to 4,360 for the 250. The 300-grain .338 bullet might pay off on thin skinned game *if* it were of controlled expanding type like Nosler, and then used only for short-range work.

As for the best powders in the .338 Winchester case, a great many will do quite well, but the slower numbers give the best results. For many years H-4831 and IMR-4350 have been considered *the* powders for all bullet weights in the .338 Winchester, but this isn't true considering some of the newer powders. For one thing, H-4831 is too bulky with the lighter bullets, and the .338 case is short on capacity for that slow burning powder, especially with short-magazine rifles like the M-77 Ruger. In that rifle an overall cartridge length of 3.30 inches is the limit. You just can't get enough H-4831 in the case and seat a bullet over it, even when using a funnel with a long drop tube, to build up full working pressures with anything except the heaviest bullets. IMR-4350 is just a little on the fast side for *best* results with any bullet, even though it is good.

The more dense powders like Norma 205 and the later MRP, H-205 and W-W/785 are the best choices with all bullet weights. And regardless of what we have been led to believe, any of these powders do as well with standard primers as with magnums in the .338 case. For use in actions with true magnum-length magazines, and where chamber throats can be let out for longer bullet seating, H-4831 shows up better. However, the rather short neck of the .338 case does not lend itself to long throating, except for a specific bullet weight and style. I have long-throated the chamber of a .338 M-70 to take the very long 275-grain Speer with its base seated to the base of the neck. Only with that bullet, or bullets of equal

Supplemental Selected Loads

bullet (grains)	powder	suggested starting load (grains)	suggested maximum (grains)	velocity (fps)
.338 Winchester Magnum				
Hodgdon Data				
200	H-4831	73.0	79.0	2,998
	H-4350	68.0	71.0	2,949
	H-414	66.0	71.0	2,954
210	H-4831	72.0	78.0	2,951
	H-4350	67.0	70.0	2,907
	H-414	66.0	70.0	2,911
250	H-4831	70.0	76.0	2,724
	H-4350	64.0	67.0	2,660
	H-414	63.0	68.0	2,651
275	H-4831	67.0	73.0	2,660
Sierra Data				
250 Spitzer BT	760	56.3	64.4	2,600
	H-450	68.4	74.0	2,600
	H-4831	67.1	74.8	2,700
	IMR-7828	70.1	74.9	2,600
	MRP	67.8	73.0	2,700

Be alert — Publisher cannot accept responsibility for errors in published load data.

length and bearing surface, was some velocity gained. Lighter, short bullets actually lost velocity because with powders of suitable burning rate, the case ran short of room before pressures were built up.

While on the throating subject, we should mention that the .338 Ruger M-77 has a very long throat of a quarter-inch from case mouth to the lands. This, coupled with a rather large chamber, is probably the reason why the charges used in this rifle were heavier than those shown in most reloading manuals, but they produced no more velocity in most instances. This means that it takes more powder to build up pressure enough to overcome the freebore effect and slight extra chamber expansion.

As mentioned earlier, of the present bullet weights available for the .338, the 250-grain seems to be the optimum for most hunting conditions on heavy American game. However, it must be remembered that there are many makes and styles of 250-grain .338 bullets. These range in shape from the Hornady round

nose with its ballistic coefficient of .280, to the 250-grain Sierra boat-tail that shows the extremely high BC of .570! Some of these 250-grain bullets give extremely deep penetration coupled with adequate expansion for fast, sure kills; some have pretty thin shells and are inclined to expand too soon and too much.

There is yet another condition that few reloaders recognize — the variation in velocity and pressures these various bullets will give with the same case, powder, charge and primer. The accompanying chart shows this variation with W-W/785 reduced one grain below the load considered a safe trouble-free hunting load in the M-77 Ruger test rifle. It is worth studying before changing 250-grain bullets, loading up a batch and heading for the hunting country.

Everything considered, the .338 Winchester is, in my mind, a more versatile light to heavy big game cartridge than the .375 H&H. No one will ever go wrong on any cartridge if it can lay claim to that distinction! ●

CHAPTER
9

THERE HAVE probably been more wildcat cartridges developed to take 0.308-inch-diameter bullets than any other caliber, with .284 running a close second. But if we lump together the wildcats that handle bullets measuring approximately a third of an inch, their numbers will be very near the top of the list. And in considering

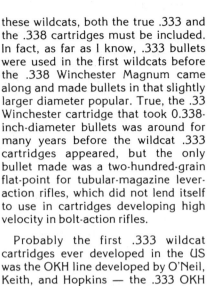

.338-74 Keith

Bob Hagel

these wildcats, both the true .333 and the .338 cartridges must be included. In fact, as far as I know, .333 bullets were used in the first wildcats before the .338 Winchester Magnum came along and made bullets in that slightly larger diameter popular. True, the .33 Winchester cartridge that took 0.338-inch-diameter bullets was around for many years before the wildcat .333 cartridges appeared, but the only bullet made was a two-hundred-grain flat-point for tubular-magazine lever-action rifles, which did not lend itself to use in cartridges developing high velocity in bolt-action rifles.

Probably the first .333 wildcat cartridges ever developed in the US was the OKH line developed by O'Neil, Keith, and Hopkins — the .333 OKH based on the .30-06 case simply necked up to .333, the .334 OKH based on the .375 H&H Magnum case, and the later .333 OKH Belted, a short magnum on the .300 or .375 H&H case. The first .333 bullets used in these cartridges were imported from England, but Fred Barnes was soon persuaded to produce bullets in that diameter in a spitzer 250-grain, and Speer followed a few years later with a 275-grain semispitzer.

How many wildcat cartridges sprouted up to shoot .333 bullets is hard to say, but there was a short magnum by Luft Brothers; Fred Barnes developed at least two on belted cases; and Parker Ackley also made a long and a short magnum version. There was a short magnum on the 7x61mm S&H case, and I once did some shooting with a rifle made by Jack Ashurst using .333 bullets in the .300 Savage case.

When Winchester finally decided that if they necked the .458 Winchester Magnum cartridge down to take bullets in the one-third-inch range it would be a winner for hunting big game anywhere in the world, they elected to go with the 0.338-inch diameter of their old .33 Winchester rather than the 0.333-inch diameter of the British cartridges. With the .338 Winchester Magnum an instant success, all of the bullet companies started producing bullets of various weights and types in that diameter,

With the long throat in the chamber of the .338-74 Keith on the Ruger Number One action, bullets of all weights and styles can be seated with their bases flush with the base of the neck, for the same powder capacity for all loads. Bullet jump, of course, is another matter. Here, the 200-grain Speer (1), 210-grain Nosler (2), 225-grain Hornady (3), 250-grain Nosler (4), and 275-grain Speer (5) have been seated to the base of each case neck.

The .338-74 Keith (left) towers over the .338-.378 Weatherby (right) not to mention the short .338 Winchester Magnum and the somewhat longer .340 Weatherby Magnum. This comparison, however, is misleading — the .338 Winchester Magnum has 3.8 percent more water capacity with bullets seated as shown here in both cases.

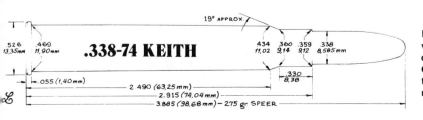

Base dimensions have been converted from the metric figures listed on cartridge drawings from the German authority, R Triebel, the others from direct measurement of a cartridge.

and .333 wildcats gave way to .338 versions.

Apparently, there are about as many wildcat cases floating around that take .338 bullets as there were for the .333 bullets. The .338-06 replaced the .333 OKH, and there seems to be no end to the wildcat .338s based on standard belted cases, the big .378 Weatherby case, and a number of foreign offerings of various sizes.

Along with several others, I expanded the neck of the .300 Winchester Magnum to fit .338 bullets. There are a number of wildcats based on the .375 H&H Magnum case necked-down and blown-out, mostly before the .340 Weatherby came along. And the .340 Weatherby originally started as an experimental cartridge made by necking down the .378 Weatherby to .338 with no other change. But finding that the huge case was far over bore capacity for existing powders, Weatherby used the .300 case by simply expanding the neck to form his .340 Weatherby.

There have also been a number of .338 wildcats made from the .378 Weatherby case cut off to hold the powder capacity to a level better suited to available powders. Elmer Keith and Bob Thompson came up with the .338-.378 K-T, and Gil Van Horn developed the .338 Van Horn. Walt Abe cut the .404 Jeffery case to 2.550 inches and blew out the body for the .338 A&H (Abe & Harris) cartridge. He later used the .404 case nearly full-length at 2.765 inches with a blown-out body and twenty-five-degree shoulder for the .338 Abe Express.

These cartridges give the gun buff who hankers for a big wildcat .338 a choice of belted or rimless cases and a velocity range from the level of the .338 Winchester to well above that of the .340 Weatherby. All of these cartridges were designed for use in bolt-action magazine rifles, and while they *can* be used in single-shot actions, they were not developed with that kind of rifle in mind. Elmer

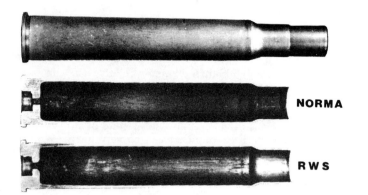

NORMA

RWS

Iver Henriksen's chamber in the Ruger test rifle has a long throat, 0.420 inch from the end of a trimmed case to the beginning of the lands. Sectioned cases show why the Norma case, with thinner walls, weighs an average of thirty-two grains less than the thicker-walled RWS case. This means that their net powder capacities are different, with resulting effects on muzzle velocity and chamber pressure if the same charge is used in both cases.

.338-74 Keith

bullet	powder	charge (gr)	velocity (fps)	
275 Speer	H-4831	73	2,610	compressed charge
	MRP	72	2,562	
	WW-785	74	2,572	
	IMR-4831	70	2,607	
	H-205	68	2,537	
	IMR-4350	67	2,558	
250 Nosler	H-4831	74	2,700	compressed charge
	MRP	73	2,648	
	WW-785	75	2,713	
	H-205	71	2,738	
	IMR-4350	68	2,661	
225 Hornady	MRP	75	2,759	
	WW-785	77	2,715	
	IMR-4831	73	2,866	compressed charge
	H-205	73	2,818	
	IMR-4350	72	2,878	
210 Nosler	MRP	77	2,849	
	WW-785	79	2,780	compressed charge
	IMR-4831	75	2,936	compressed charge
	H-205	75	2,942	
	IMR-4350	74	2,982	compressed charge
200 Speer	H-205	77	3,046	compressed charge
	IMR-4350	75	3,040	compressed charge
	N-204	75	3,044	
	WW-760	75	2,931	high velocity variation, not suitable for this cartridge

RWS cases, CCI 250 primers, 26-3/8-inch barrel. Velocities recorded at fifteen feet from muzzle, converted to muzzle velocities. Temperature seventy degrees Fahrenheit.

These loads were all near maximum for trouble-free working pressures *in the test rifle.* They should not be used in any other rifle without starting at least three grains lower and working up gradually as pressure signs indicate that it is safe to increase powder charges.

Bob tested the .338-74 Keith in Ralph Graham's Ruger Number One with a barrel blank made by Shilen, machined octagon by Ralph Carter, chambered and fitted by Iver Henriksen. This barrel has an integral quarter rib dovetailed for an open rear sight, milled to accept Ruger scope rings, and drilled and tapped to accept conventional mount bases like the Buehler shown here. The integral lug under the barrel just ahead of the forearm accepts detachable sling swivels.

Keith, a major contributor to the development of the OKH .333 cartridges, believed that a .338 cartridge especially designed for use in the stronger single-shot actions was in order, and that it should be rimmed. With no rimmed case being produced in this country that was ideal for the purpose, he turned to the German 9.3x74R cartridge. The 9.3x74R has been used in Europe for many, many years in single-shot, double, and combination guns, and has proved quite effective as it is, but the 0.365-inch-diameter bullet is available here only if imported, or from Barnes Bullets, which limits its usefulness somewhat. Necking the case to .338 solved the bullet problem, and efficiency is certainly not damaged.

The 9.3x74R is a very long, slim case, with a length of 2.93 inches and a body diameter immediately forward of the rim of only 0.465 inch, and the diameter of its slight shoulder is only 0.414 inch. The original .338-74 Keith cartridge used the same body taper as the 9.3x74R, but it was later decided that a little extra powder capacity would not go amiss, so Clymer made a reamer that reduced the body taper to give a shoulder diameter of 0.437 inch and an angle of twenty-five degrees. As the cartridge is designed for use in a single-shot action, there is no limit on overall cartridge length. And with a neck length of about 0.333 inch, it is possible to seat all bullets with the bases just flush with the base of the neck. The test rifle — and presumably all others chambered to the Clymer reamer specs — has a very long throat that measures 0.420 inch from the end of the trimmed case neck to the land leade when a bullet is reversed and seated in the chamber. This adds a little more to the powder capacity of the case over standard throating for the .338 Winchester cartridge.

To make certain where the long rimmed wildcat fit in with other .338 wildcats and commercial rounds, I checked it for water capacity with bullets seated to the base of the neck in RWS cases. At first glance, it appears that it has more capacity than the .338 Winchester Magnum, because of its much greater length, but this is an optical illusion. The .338-74 holds 77.7 grains of water with the above seating, and the .338 Winchester loaded with the same 250-grain Nosler — seated to just function through standard .338 rifle magazines and chamber throats — holds 81.5 grains for a difference of roughly 3.8 percent in favor of the .338 Winchester. If Norma 9.3x74R cases are used, the powder capacity goes up slightly, as the Norma case weighs only 198 grains as opposed to 230 grains for the RWS cases. However, the Norma cases that I have sampled mike 0.003 inch smaller at the base than the RWS cases, so they are less desirable for reloading for chambers cut to fit the RWS case.

After doing experimental work and load development for many .333 and .338 wildcat cartridges since the days when the .333 OKH arrived on the scene back in the late 1930s, I was instantly interested when my friend Ralph Graham suggested that I chronograph some of his loads for his .338-74 Keith rifle, and I struck up a deal to retain that rifle long enough to develop my own loads for it.

Ralph's rifle is a custom-barrel job on the Ruger Number One action. In fact, the barrel is about as custom as you can get it. The barrel blank came from Ed Shilen of Ennis, Texas, was converted to octagon form by Ralph Carter of Penrose, Colorado, and was chambered by Iver Henriksen of Missoula, Montana!

The length is 26-3/8 inches from the muzzle to the face of the breechblock. Muzzle diameter across the octagon flat sides is 0.590 inch, and the barrel has a straight taper back to about two inches forward of the receiver ring, where it has a graceful concave flare to the full diameter of 1.130 inches at 1.20 inches forward of the receiver ring. An integral ramp is grooved lengthwise to accommodate the front-sight blade. There is also an integral base for the front sling swivel that is drilled for European-type swivels three inches forward of the fore-end tip. A 0.450-inch-wide quarter rib extends ten inches forward of the receiver ring. It has a dovetail slot for an open rear sight, is milled to fit Ruger mount bases, and is tapped and drilled for conventional scope-mount bases. This particular rifle was mounted with a Weaver K6 scope in Buehler mounts.

Except for the barrel, the rifle is a standard Ruger Number One, with a very attractive piece of wood that is normal for most Ruger Number One rifles.

From my talks with Elmer Keith, it appears that Hodgdon did much of the original load development with the .338-74 Keith cartridge. Exact velocity figures were not available for those loads in time to enter here, but Elmer was interested in only the loads for bullet weights from 250 grains up, and his favorite is the 250-grain Sierra BT backed by seventy-five grains of H-4831. Whether this was tested in the Norma or RWS case by Hodgdon is not clear, but I found it nearly impossible to seat that bullet in the RWS case over that powder charge with the tail of the bullet below the base of the neck to give full support to the bullet in the neck, even by using a long funnel tube and tapping the case to settle the powder fully. Pressure was also pretty stiff with the RWS case with the lots of powder, bullets, and primers that I used, so I settled on seventy-four grains in the RWS case. I did chronograph some of Ralph Graham's loads using the 250-grain Sierra BT and seventy-five grains of H-4831, at 2,738 feet per second in Norma cases. This compares to an even 2,700 feet per second for seventy-four grains of H-4831 behind the 250-grain Nosler with the powder, primer, and bullet lots that I used in the RWS cases. Pressure is possibly a tad higher in the Norma case with the heavier charge, but not enough to matter at the pressure levels used in these tests.

And while we're speaking of pressures, the rimmed cartridge and Ruger Number One action combine to create some special aspects of pressure estimation that are not encountered by the majority of handloaders.

In working up to pressures that give a maximum trouble-free load for both the case and action for all shooting situations, I prefer to measure the solid web of the case just forward of the rim. Any load that shows expansion of the case head at this point that continues to grow when the same load is fired in that case again, eventually expands the primer pocket and renders the case unusable. When this point is reached, the charge must be backed-off a couple of grains or so — depending on the case capacity and burning rate of the powder — to give long case life and safe and efficient performance. With the standard micrometer caliper, this is difficult because the spindle and anvil do not fit between the rim and the pressure ring where the case body expands just forward of the solid web to fill the chamber. This calls for either a special mike to fit the small area or a dial vernier caliper, which is more difficult to read and less accurate for readings under 0.001 inch.

As far as the Ruger Number One action is concerned, it is very strong but is far different from a bolt action. To start with, the face of the breechblock is smooth with no ejector hole, so if the reloader happens to load a hot one, there is no indication of excessive pressure by the ejector mark on the case head. Also, the breechblock is polished and moves like glass over its abutment shoulders in the receiver, which makes the lever open easily even when great back-pressure is exerted on it by the cartridge head.

With wildcat cartridges and custom

barrels and chambers, there is no pressure data to tell the handloader what pressures to expect from any load with his components in his rifle. The only way he can work-up a load to the full potential of the cartridge that will give good case life and full power is to start low and increase the powder charge in one-grain steps while checking for head expansion after each shot.

With the .338-74 Keith in the Ruger test rifle, all loads listed in the chart were worked-up to the point where the head diameter just forward of the rim gave an average expansion of 0.0003 inch, then backed off by one grain when tested at seventy to seventy-five degrees. Repeated firing of the same case up to ten times gave no head expansion at all, primer pockets remained tight, and the full-length-resized cases still functioned perfectly through the action. Experimenting with slightly heavier charges indicated that somewhat higher velocities can be squeezed from the cartridge, but with a single-shot action with limited extraction power, I prefer holding pressures below where any problem may crop up under any likely shooting condition.

Apparently, Keith had not experimented with any other powder except H-4831, and Graham had used only that powder with the 250-grain bullets and IMR-4350 with the lighter ones. I wanted to include most of the suitable powders, as well as to develop load data for bullet weights from 200 to 275 grains — the 300-grain bullet was not tested, mostly because that weight is no longer available from Winchester, leaving Barnes Bullets as the only source, with none available when the work was in progress.

After doing so much load development with .338 cartridges with case capacities similar to the .338-74 Keith, I suspected that H-4831 was slow for any bullet weight below 250 grains, because it would prove impossible to crowd enough of it into the case to bring pressures up to the desired

working level. This proved to be completely true, and only with the 275-grain Speer bullet did H-4831 give slightly higher velocity than any other powder used. With that bullet, a charge of seventy-three grains was at the same pressure levels as the other powders and delivered a muzzle velocity of 2,610 feet per second, but seventy grains of IMR-4831 averaged 2,607 feet per second, and MRP and WW-785 were close behind.

With the 250-grain Nosler bullet, H-4831 was compressed about to the limit with seventy-four grains and delivered 2,700 feet per second. Both WW-785 and H-205 beat that figure a little with a seventy-one-grain charge.

With the 225-grain Hornady bullet, it is impossible to get enough H-4831 in the case to bring pressure up to the level used for faster or denser powders. With that bullet, top honors went to IMR-4350, with IMR-4831 following close behind.

DuPont's IMR-4350 also held the velocity edge slightly with the 210-grain Nosler bullet but had to be compressed, as did WW-785 and IMR-4831.

With the 200-grain Speer bullet, IMR-4831 had to be dropped because case capacity ran short, and, strangely enough, with H-205, IMR-4350, and Norma 204, velocity difference came out at only six feet per second. Winchester 760 was tried with this bullet, but velocity fell more than one hundred feet per second below the other powders used, and it was the only powder I tried that gave a high velocity spread in any test string. The first three shots fired to check accuracy gave an extreme velocity spread of 127 feet per second, so no more work was done with it.

Nearly any .338 cartridge yields very uniform velocities if the right powders are used. This is especially true with the heavier bullets in the larger cases. The .338-74 followed the same pattern, with exceptionally uniform velocity readings. Most test strings were fired with three shots to hold barrel temperature down, but when

they were often repeated so that six shots were averaged on the chronograph computer, they remained almost identical. Mostly, they ran in the teens and twenties, with few going over thirty. To give average variation figures with all loads, the strings were averaged with all bullet weights and powders at 27.4 feet per second. Few cartridges do better.

As for reloading the .338-74 Keith cartridge, like most other wildcats, it takes some extra time to form cases. After necking to .338, the body must be fire-formed by any of the normal methods. Reloading dies are not available over the counter but are available on special order from Huntington; PO Box 991; Oroville, California 95965. Unprimed 9.3x74R cases are available from Dynamit Nobel; 105 Stonehurst Court; Northvale, New Jersey 07647, made by RWS for Boxer primers. Which brings up a point worth noting: the lot of test cases that I used for these tests had very tight primer pockets. In fact, they were so tight that the Lee automatic priming tool did not have leverage enough to fully seat the primers, and a good deal of pressure was required on the handle of an old Pacific Super C tool to do the job. This may be peculiar to the particular lot of cases, as I have not noted it with other RWS cases I've used.

The .338-74 Keith is an excellent cartridge for use in single-shot rifles. It does not have quite as much powder capacity as the .338 Winchester Magnum, so it gives slightly less velocity with the same barrel length at the same pressures. But with the short single-shot actions, like the Ruger Number One, that are made of modern steels, and barrels twenty-six inches or longer possible with those actions while retaining a fairly short, light rifle for hunting, it about equals the .338 for performance from a twenty-four-inch barrel.

For those who like single-shot rifles for hunting big game and feel that a rimmed cartridge is best for those actions, the .338-74 Keith cartridge answers their purpose very well. ●

CHAPTER
10

The .338-378 Weatherby

Bigger Really Is Better

Donnelly's .338-378 Weatherby features a Brown Kelvar stock, a Mark X Type C action, a 26.8-inch Douglas stainless steel barrel and a Leupold Vari-X II 1.5-5x scope.

Joseph R. Donnelly

ASK A DOZEN shooters to nominate a cartridge for the ideal long-range, big-game rifle and you'll probably get 12 different opinions. Mine, after years of soul-searching and experimenting, has boiled down to the potent .338-378 Weatherby.

I wanted a round which offered first-class accuracy, a trajectory as flat as a 7mm Magnum's and enough impact energy at 400 yards-plus to floor animals the size of moose and elk. The .33 caliber has always appealed to me. There are plenty of good .338-inch bullets available in a decent range of weights that are blessed with excellent ballistic coefficients and high sectional densities. To drive those long, heavy bullets at the speeds I had in mind would demand a sturdy case with plenty of room for big charges of slow-burning powders. The big .378 Weatherby hull seemed a natural choice for the job.

Roy Weatherby may have been the first to neck the .378 case to .338 when he was trying to decide which hull to base his .340, on the .378 or the .300 Weatherby. With the relatively fast powders he had to work with then, the larger case offered no real advantage so the .338-378 was allowed to die on the vine — for a while. Later experimenters, including Bob Hagel, demonstrated that when that big case was stuffed with a real slow-burner,

like H-870, very impressive velocities could be achieved.

The .338-378 is made simply by necking the Weatherby hull to .338 — no trimming, no special dies, no fireforming needed. It is much less troublesome to make than the slightly smaller .338-378 KT (Keith-Thompson). The KT version is based on a shortened .378 case. Its reduced volume allows the use of H-4831 or IMR-7828 but the necessary case-forming dies are expensive and the process of shortening the case and moving the shoulder back is

time-consuming. I saw no advantage in going that route.

Since I already had a spare Mark X action, I set out to make it fit. I couldn't believe that big Weatherby action was really necessary. A review of Otteson's *The Bolt Action* indicated that other actions possessed similar locking lug bearing surfaces and adequate lug shear areas to handle the massive .378 Weatherby case. In addition, the bolt diameters of most actions (Mauser, Remington, Winchester, etc.) were adequate.

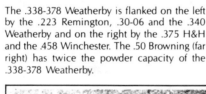

The .338-378 Weatherby is flanked on the left by the .223 Remington, .30-06 and the .340 Weatherby and on the right by the .375 H&H and the .458 Winchester. The .50 Browning (far right) has twice the powder capacity of the .338-378 Weatherby.

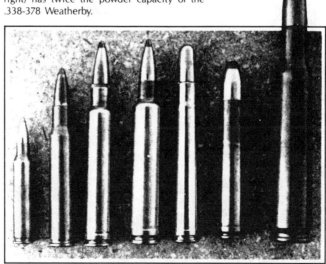

In the interests of accuracy, a Douglas No. 5 magnum barrel in stainless steel was selected. Not only would it be almost impervious to rust but it should also resist the erosion caused by those huge charges of slow-burning powder.

A Brown Kevlar stock was chosen for strength and moderate weight. The width of the stock's butt was flared slightly to 1.83 inches so it would accommodate a Pachmayr decelerator pad. (The original stock was 1.65 inches wide.) The extra contact area between butt and shoulder was meant to make the rifle's recoil more tolerable.

Assembly of the rifle was relatively straightforward, except for the action. The Brown stock, with its graphite reinforcement and extra Kevlar, was one ounce heavier than their standard fiberglass model. They will provide such extra reinforcement on request and recommend it when stocking an action chambered for a cartridge with the recoil potential of the .338-378.

The barreled action was bedded in Brownells' Acraglas gel, with stainless steel powder added to recoil areas. Crossbolts were mounted behind the action and barrel recoil lugs. The latter was soldered and screwed to the barrel six inches in front of the action lug.

The 26.8-inch Douglas barrel is rifled with one turn in 10 inches. Its chamber was cut with a Clymer reamer made to their standard specifications for this wildcat, except that zero freebore was requested. That provided a .75-inch tapered throat.

A Leupold matte-finished Vari-X III 1.5-5x scope was mounted in Leupold

Above, popular .338 bullets include: (1) 200-grain Speer, (2) 210-grain Barnes, (3) 225-grain Hornady, (4) 250-grain Barnes Super Solid, (5) 250-grain Barnes, (6) 250-grain Hornady, (7) 250-grain Nosler, (8) 250-grain Sierra, (9) 275-grain Speer and (10) 300-grain Barnes. Right, the (c) .338-378 is formed by running the .378 Weatherby case through (a) a .338-378 forming die and (b) fireforming it. The (d) well-used case on the end shows imminent signs of separation forward of the belt.

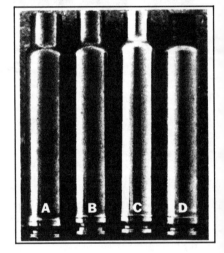

medium-height rings on Redfield bases. The base screws were secured with blue Loctite. The gripping areas of the stock were coated with Acraglas and sand was sprinkled on with a salt shaker. Gray automotive acrylic lacquer with extra flattening agent produced a non-glare finish. An Uncle Mike's Ultra Sling with Super Swivels completed the package. Total weight is under nine pounds. A weight of 8 pounds, 10 ounces was achieved without the sling. After a day of shooting, I'm not sure that is heavy enough!

Cliff Snider (Box 67, Bristol, FL 32321) cut the bolt face with a carbide

tool to fit the larger .378 head, a simple operation. He also chambered and fitted the barrel to .001-inch headspace, installed a barrel recoil lug and blued the action and scope mounts. Barrel, action and scope mounts were sandblasted, producing a pleasing overall effect.

The action was an Interarms Yugoslav Mark X Type C, designed to

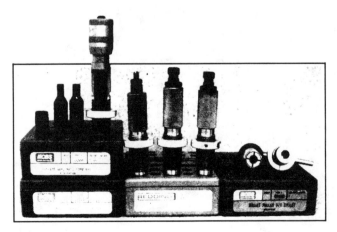

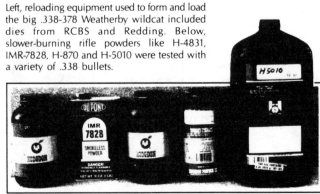

Left, reloading equipment used to form and load the big .338-378 Weatherby wildcat included dies from RCBS and Redding. Below, slower-burning rifle powders like H-4831, IMR-7828, H-870 and H-5010 were tested with a variety of .338 bullets.

Table I

Recoil Energy Comparison

cartridge	bullet (grains)	powder charge (grains)	velocity (fps)	rifle weight (pounds)	recoil (ft/lb)
.30-06	180	56.0	2,800	8.25	23
.375 H&H	300	82.0	2,600	10.0	43
.338-.378	200	111.0	3,528	8.62	56
.340 Wby.	250	83.0	2,880	9.1	43

Table II

.338-378 Weatherby
powder charges (*grains*) and velocities (*fps*)

bullet	mild charge	mild velocity	medium charge	medium velocity	maximum charge	maximum velocity
T-5020 powder*						
250 Sierra	124.0	3,088	125.0	3,109	127.0	3,152
275 Speer	122.0	2,998	124.0	3,078	126.0	3,088
300 Barnes	120.0	2,930	122.0	2,969	124.0	2,998
T-5070 powder*						
250 Sierra	118.0	3,078	122.0	3,131	124.0	3,163
275 Speer	112.0	2,870	114.0	2,931	116.0	2,998
300 Barnes	110.0	2,771	112.0	2,805	114.0	2,857
H-4831 powder						
200 Speer	—	—	107.0	3,360	108.0	3,435
250 Hornady	—	—	102.0	3,037	103.0	3,027
IMR-7828 powder						
200 Speer	109.0	3,435	110.0	3,474	111.0	3,528
210 Barnes	107.0	3,347	108.0	3,372	109.0	3,436
225 Hornady	107.0	3,264	108.0	3,312	109.0	3,323
250 Barnes**	100.0	3,007	101.0	3,068	102.0	3,099
250 Nosler	101.0	3,109	102.0	3,131	103.0	3,141
250 Sierra	102.0	3,067	103.0	3,098	104.0	3,141
250 Sierra**	103.0	3,082	104.0	3,120	105.0	3,163
250 Hornady	105.0	3,130	106.0	3,152	107.0	3,162
275 Speer	94.0	2,788	95.0	2,814	96.0	2,849
300 Barnes	94.0	2,763**	95.0	2,771	96.0	2,805
H-870 powder						
250 Barnes	114.0	2,998	116.0	3,027	118.0	3,099
250 Hornady	120.0	3,047	121.0	3,120	123.0	3,174
250 Nosler	115.0	3,068	117.0	3,078	118.0	3,099
250 Sierra	120.0	3,088	121.0	3,110	122.0	3,152
275 Speer	108.0	2,822	111.0	2,866	112.0	2,875
300 Barnes	106.0	2,722	108.0	2,779	111.0	2,849
H-5010 powder						
250 Barnes	114.0	3,037	116.0	3,068	118.0	3,141
250 Hornady	118.0	3,088	120.0	3,131	121.0	3,174
250 Nosler	113.0	3,057	114.0	3,120	115.0	3,152
250 Sierra	114.0	3,027	116.0	3,078	118.0	3,120
275 Speer	108.0	2,849	110.0	2,912	112.0	2,921
300 Barnes	108.0	2,805	109.0	2,857	110.0	2,866

* T-prefixed powder types are Ball powders from Thunderbird Cartridge Co.
** Indicates powder from a 1987 lot.

Velocities are instrumental at 10 feet from the muzzle. Test temperature, 50 to 55 degrees Fahrenheit.

Be alert — Publisher cannot accept responsibility for errors in published load data.

accept magnum cartridges. It turned out to be an ideal choice for the oversized .378 case. I opened the feed rails with a file. It was easy to open the front to .580 inch and taper the rails to .620 inch at the rear. The lower lug abutment/feed ramp was shortened, like the D-Type actions used with the .375 H&H cartridge. I removed only .06 inch with a carbide burr. The only blown-up Mark X I ever examined personally was a Type D and the lower abutment had been pushed back .22 inch. I therefore preferred to start with the standard action and leave more meat there.

The front wall of the magazine box was heated and bent forward to match the .06-inch cut. The factory rear wall has a tongue extending upward, wasting the rearmost .19 inch of magazine opening in the action. If one removes the rear wall of the magazine box and repositions a new wall rearward, the entire magazine opening of the action can be utilized. With the .060-inch cut at the feed ramp, an overall cartridge length of 3.67 inches is possible.

In order to eject loaded rounds reliably, a cut .1 inch deep was made in the receiver ring on the right side. Cutting the bolt stop back .05 inch with a file and trimming the ejector tip .03 inch allowed the bolt to retract beyond the rearmost point of the magazine cut in the action.

Changes needed for smooth functioning included trimming the extractor for the larger and thicker .378-inch rim. The magazine follower was recontoured for the fatter round and the front of the bridge was trimmed with a carbide burr to lengthen the ejection port from 3.03 to 3.14 inches. The upper right bolt guide inside the bridge was chamfered to assist in clearing spent cases, similar to the approach Remington takes on the Model 700.

Weatherby brass is strong. When a case stuck inside the sizing die due to insufficient lube, the sturdy rim pulled the lip off the shellholder.

Although the changes sound time-consuming, complex and costly for the non-handyman, they were much easier to perform than to describe and any competent gunsmith should be able to include them at moderate cost.

The result was an inexpensive action, well heat-treated and resistant to locking lug setback, that provided positive cartridge feeding and ejection.

It might be worthwhile to lap the locking lugs, in deference to the substantial backthrust produced by the .378 Weatherby case. For reference, at 48,000 CUP or so, the .378 produces as much backthrust as a standard belted magnum churning up 62,000 CUP. For that reason, wiping the chamber with lacquer thinner after cleaning became routine to maximize the ability of the case to grip the chamber walls. Working pressures for the .338-378 wildcat should not exceed 54,000 to 55,000 CUP.

Final details included use of a Timney trigger with a military Mauser striker-blocking safety modified for scope usage, including the shorter striker fall introduced by the Mark X in the early 1980s with a 30-pound Wolff Blitzschnell striker spring. Lock time is about 2.9 milliseconds, competitive with modern commercial actions.

Cartridges feed very smoothly. They are levered into place on the bolt face by the chamber and the top of the feed ramp. On the other hand, the magazine well is rather narrow for the fat case and when a second round is loaded, they don't want to stay in place because the rails bear on such a small segment of their diameter. If a recess for a sheet metal magazine was machined in the action, it would permit the utilization of a magazine box with custom-bent auxiliary feed rails.

All powder charges were metered, then weighed. As might be expected, H-870 metered well through the Redding match-grade powder measure. Two throws, however, were needed to deliver the large amount of powder required. DuPont's IMR-7828 metered satisfactorily, but not as smoothly as some smaller-grained tubular, single-based powders. Occasional bridging occurred and required tapping the metering handle to drop the remaining powder. H-5010 is coarse-grained (.053x.086 inch) and frequently bridged in the measure. Both H-870 and H-5010 were sifted slowly into the case to allow full charges without excessive compression. Full charges of H-4831 and IMR-7828 left about ¼ inch of

space below the case neck. By the way, if you make a mistake, don't reach for your Quinetics inertia puller, it won't accept the fat .378 Weatherby cases. You will need a collet-type puller such as those produced by RCBS.

It is also a mistake not to use enough case lube. No, you won't necessarily pull off the case rim. The big, thick rim is very strong. I succeeded in pulling off the lip of a shellholder while only slightly distorting the .378 rim. The RCBS No. 14 shellholder seemed to be the strongest and best fitting. (I was able to extract the stuck case noted above with an RCBS shellholder.) The Lee No. 8, for their Auto-Prime with .45-70 cases, fit loosely. I ground the bottom off an RCBS No. 14 and enlarged the hole with a carbide burr. It was also necessary to enlarge the slot of the Auto-Prime to accept the .378 case.

Both Redding and RCBS make dies for the .338-378 Weatherby wildcat. The RCBS sizing die has a spit-hole at shoulder level, lessening the possibility of dented cases. The RCBS competition seater die works very nicely if you drill out the bullet guide to ¹¹⁄₃₂ inch (top), and ⅜ inch (bottom), and use a .30-caliber bullet seating plug. Huntington Die Specialties can supply both the plug and guide in .338. While their .338 bullet guide worked well, the tapered hole in their seater plug was too large to fit the bullet ogives properly so I ended up using a .30-caliber seater plug.

Data for the accompanying load table were obtained with a Custom Chronograph. Velocity readings were within .5 percent of those obtained with two Oehler Model 33 units. The moderately priced Custom Chronograph performed well. Additionally, it was very easy to set up and required only one battery. Readings were taken 10 feet from the muzzle and were not corrected to muzzle velocities or temperature.

The maximum cartridge length that would feed from the test rifle's magazine was 3.67 inches, so no loads exceeded that. The 210 and 250-grain Barnes bullets and the 200 and 275-grain Speers required lengths shorter than 3.67 inches to achieve a nominal .06 inch from the rifling.

Best case life resulted from loads rated "mild." Those combinations produced case expansion that measured .5825 inch on the pressure ring in front of the belt. Loads labeled maximum produced a measurement of .5828 inch.

The medium loads produced .5826 to .5827-inch measurements. Stiff extraction and brass flow into the ejector slot occurred with pressure ring measurements of .5830 inch. That required two or more grains of powder beyond the loads listed as maximum.

Most loads were remarkably uniform, repeatedly producing velocities within 10 fps of the average. Raising the ambient temperature by 20 degrees Fahrenheit and a warm barrel increased pressures somewhat — about .0001 inch more expansion at the pressure ring with a proportional velocity increase. Initial loads for other rifles or warmer temperatures should be reduced by 5 percent or so from those listed as mild.

Most data for IMR-7828 were compiled with a powder lot produced in 1986. A 1987 lot tested subsequently was about 1 percent slower.

Three lots of H-5010 were provided by Hodgdon. All the lots performed similarly; each was within 1 to 2 percent of the others when charge weights versus velocities were compared. J.B. Hodgdon advised me that their batch of 5010 is relatively fast, close to H-870 and the now-obsolete H-570. Most batches of 5010 would be slower than H-870 so it would probably be the best for the .338-378 in barrels of the 26 to 28-inch range. Government testing showed that 32 to 34-inch barrels produced worthwhile velocity gains with 5010 that was generally used for the .50 Browning machine gun round. Bruce Hodgdon noted that H-870 is still used by the Lake City Arsenal for 20mm cannon ammunition.

In the .338-378, H-4831 heated the barrel near the chamber first but IMR-7828 heated the barrel uniformly throughout its length. Hodgdon's 870 and 5010 left the chamber end relatively cool while rendering the muzzle hot to the touch, suggesting that a longer barrel would produce significant velocity gains with both powders. With over 100 grains of powder per round, the barrel heated rather quickly. Fouling was not a problem with H-870 during the tests, possibly because pressures of 50,000 CUP and above increased combustion efficiency.

The Mark X action showed no signs of stress or locking lug setback as a result of the tests, even though some loads (not reported here) made brass flow into the ejector slot of the bolt face.

A new powder, H-1000, has a burning rate between IMR-7828 and H-870. Unfortunately, I was unable to obtain any for testing but J.B. Hodgdon said that response has been outstanding. It may be the ideal powder for the .338-378 Weatherby.

Many handloaders prefer not to crimp cases and a case full of powder is used to prevent recoil from setting the bullet back while the cartridge is in the magazine. Maximum loads of H-4831 and IMR-7828, however, did not fill the case.

Top loads with H-870 and H-5010 filled the case to a level just below the neck. Some were moderately compressed and it was possible to develop excessive pressures even with these very slow-burning powders due to the large charges used.

IMR-7828 was the best powder for bullets weighing less than 250 grains and a good choice for 250-grain bullets. Heavier bullets achieved higher velocities with H-870 and H-5010. The 275-grain Speer and 300-grain Barnes have long bearing surfaces and their velocities were similar, lagging well behind the 250-grain bullets. Many loads delivered close to MOA accuracy if the shooter did his part — a non-trivial contribution. Best accuracy was obtained with mild and medium loads. Maximum powder charges for 250-grain bullets appeared to be dependent on variations in bearing surface. Bruce Hodgdon mentioned that Ball powders extend barrel life three to four times when compared to single-based powders so H-870 might be a good choice for shooters who use maximum loads on a regular basis.

While H-4831 is probably ideal for the .340 Weatherby, it is too fast for optimum results in the .338-378 Weatherby. Test results suggest that IMR-7828 would probably produce optimum velocities in the shorter .338-378 KT case.

Case life was good unless they were subjected to excessive pressures. A single pass through the full-length .338 sizing die, after chamfering and lubricating the case necks, formed the cases. If the seater die is not smooth (mine wasn't), the case shoulder may collapse. Since the one-step case forming process seemed to require a lot of pressure, the RCBS form die was used to size the necks down first. After that, full-length sizing proved effortless.

The Forster case trimmer, with a No. 4 collet and the modified collet housing, was used to trim cases to 2.89 inches. The MTM 20-gauge shotshell tray provided a suitable loading block for the fat cases. I have not found a suitable ammo box but the MTM Case Gard can be used without the insert.

Weatherby strongly recommends Federal's 215 primer with the .378 case, since unreliable ignition may occur with milder primers. The only other primer I tested was the CCI-250. It is about .0005 inch larger in diameter so it may be used in cases which had expanded slightly or those with worn primer pockets. Comparisons, however, indicate that at moderate temperatures, CCI's 250 primer was satisfactory.

Since it soon became obvious that the .338-378 could deliver all the recoil I paid for, I felt it would be informative to make numerical comparisons with some popular cartridges. Using the *Lyman Reloading Handbook* formula, the figures listed in Table I were obtained for typical powder charges, bullet weights, rifles and muzzle velocities. The results suggest why the .340 Weatherby still has an important place in this world — it is relatively efficient and produces good velocities with significantly lower recoil. The larger .338-378 generates about the same recoil energy as a .458 Winchester magnum. A lot of people buy and presumably shoot .458s so the .338-378 might be considered a viable compromise between the larger bullet diameter and momentum of the .458 at short ranges for the flatter trajectory and higher downrange energies with a wide selection of moderately priced .338 bullets.

This wildcat is a fine choice for the experienced rifleman who is accustomed to that level of recoil. For minimum recoil and good performance, select IMR-7828. A 250-grain bullet requires about 15 more grains of H-870 or H-5010 to achieve similar velocity and they produce about 1 percent more recoil.

Near the end of this project, two spherical powders, T-5070 and T-5020, from Thunderbird Cartridge Co. Inc. (TCCI, 7215 W. Southern Ave., Phoenix AZ 85041), were tested. These slow-burning powders performed well with the 250-grain Sierra bullet, about on a par with H-5010 and H-870. T-5020 was outstanding with the 275-grain Speer and 300-grain Barnes, producing velocities that were 100 to 150 fps higher than other powders produced. At 2,998 fps, the 300-grain Barnes generated 83 foot-pounds of recoil energy after the rifle's weight was reduced ¼ pound with an aluminum trigger guard/floorplate and sheet-steel magazine box. That was quite sufficient for my needs.

The .338-378 Weatherby met all my criteria. The various bullets tested delivered high velocity with acceptable accuracy and recoil was manageable in a rifle of moderate weight. Case forming and loading were straightforward and costs were reasonable, using a barrel and action commonly employed in custom rifles chambered for more conventional cartridges.

While the costs per round were higher than customary, it could be considered trivial compared to the expense of a big game hunt. The extra retained energy and flat trajectory, resulting from high velocity coupled with excellent ballistic coefficients, allowed the rifle to be zeroed at 300 to 350 yards. The trajectory was as flat or flatter than any 7mm or .300 magnum's when bullets of similar sectional densities are fired. With about 5,300 foot-pounds of muzzle energy, retained energy at 400 yards is greater than the 2,800 foot-pounds often recommended for elk, moose and the big bears. ●

CHAPTER
11

APPARENTLY, THE first cartridge to use .338 bullets originated here in the United States in the form of the .33 Winchester in about 1902. The short rimmed cartridge, chambered in the famous Winchester Model 1886, used a 200-grain bullet that was started at a claimed twenty-two hundred feet per second. The .33 Winchester never gained any great popularity, even though it killed most American big game quite well within its effective range. This effective range was quite limited because of the low velocity and the short flatnose bullet that had neither good sectional density nor ballistic coefficient. It actually was neither fish nor foul, was inferior to the .35 and .405 Winchester offerings for use on the heaviest game, and was badly outclassed in the flat-trajectory

department by the older .30-40 and the soon-to-arrive .30-03 and .30-06, along with several others.

Shortly after the advent of the .33 Winchester, the British came along with the .333 Jeffery, in 1911, in both rimless and rimmed persuasions of the same case capacity. It was undoubtedly the .333 Jeffery cartridge that eventually led to more wildcat experimenting with the .33 bore here in America. The .333 Jeffery used bullets of exactly that diameter, while the .33 Winchester bullet diameter was .338, or the same as today's .338 Winchester and .340 Weatherby. Even though the .333 Jeffery used a slightly smaller-diameter bullet than the .33 Winchester, it was loaded with bullets of much heavier weight and better

design for all-around big-game shooting. The pointed 250-grain bullet at twenty-five hundred feet per second gave flat trajectory coupled with high energy output at long range, as well as good penetration on medium-weight African game, and the 300-grain roundnose was effective for close work where deeper penetration was needed. With the 300-grain solid, it also proved quite effective on elephant for brain shots, delivering extreme penetration.

It was the outstanding performance of the .333 Jeffery that led O'Neil, Keith, and Hopkins to start development of their .333 OKH line of cartridges in 1937. These cartridges all took the .333 bullet, with the first bullets imported from England but later made here by Fred Barnes, father of the present

Few cartridges are better adapted to shooting the heaviest American big game like this Alaskan moose . . .

by **Bob Hagel**

.340 Weatherby Magnum

Barnes Bullets. For the record, chronograph records from Charlie O'Neil and Don Hopkins, as well as later records I have from other sources, show the .333 OKH (the .30-06 case necked up) giving the 250-grain bullet a muzzle velocity of 2,550 to 2,600 feet per second; the .333 Belted OKH (on the shortened .300 H&H case) developed 2,700 to 2,750 feet per second with the same bullet, and the .334 OKH (the full-length .375 H&H case) gave the 250-grain nearly twenty-nine hundred feet per second, all from 25 to 26-inch barrels.

These .333 cartridges perhaps became more popular than any of the other wildcat .333 cartridges that followed by other wildcatters. Not because they were necessarily better performers, but because they were the first, and also received more publicity. For one thing, Don Hopkins was using them for both North American and African hunting with great success, and word of this got spread around. Elmer

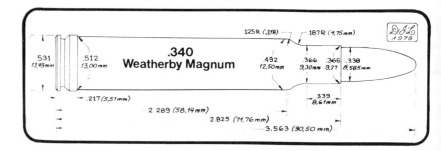

Keith was promoting them in his various writings, and this writer also did a lot of hunting and writing on the OKH cartridges of various calibers, especially the .33s.

Even though there was an attempt by O'Neil, Keith, and Hopkins to interest the big American arms manufacturers in a potent .33 cartridge, they were not successful, and it was not until 1958 that Winchester finally brought out the .338 Winchester Magnum that was the earlier .458 Winchester case necked down to take the same .338 bullet as used in the old .33 Winchester. The .338 Winchester Magnum was an immediate success, and while it did not rival some of the smaller-caliber cartridges in rifle and ammunition sales, it still sells very well and is chambered by most other riflemakers, both commercial and custom.

After the .338 Winchester Magnum appeared on the scene, it seemed logical that Roy Weatherby, who usually set the pace for the development of magnum cartridges, would come up with a .338 cartridge. In 1962, he did. Most gun writers were aware that such a cartridge was in the wind but not certain of the form it would take. The truth is that Roy

wasn't either, and he experimented with the big .378 case necked down to .338 with no other change. These experiments were not overly successful with existing powders, and Weatherby settled on the .300 case as giving optimum performance with bullets of 200 to 250 grains. (I did some load development with the original .340 Weatherby experimental rifle chambered for the .340-.378 Weatherby case; see *Rifle* 53.) When the Weatherby cartridge did appear, it was dubbed the .340 Weatherby Magnum but used standard .338 bullets.

Back in 1967 and 1968, I did some experimenting with the .338 Winchester Magnum, a .338 wildcat on the .300 Winchester Magnum case, and the .340 Weatherby. This experimental load work brought to light the fact that with the Norma-Weatherby brass available for the .340 Weatherby at that time, the velocity could not be pushed very far beyond that delivered by the .338 Winchester Magnum case without excessive head expansion that led to very short case life (See *Handloader* 16). I did find, however, that velocity could be increased to what the big case should deliver by using the harder Winchester-Western .375 H&H cases formed to .340 Weatherby. This load work was done in my personal .340 Weatherby custom rifle with a 23-1/2-inch Hobaugh barrel chambered without freebore, so I recently decided

The .340 Weatherby Magnum, left, is based on the much older .375 Holland & Holland Magnum case, right, but has greater powder capacity. It is essentially the equal of the .375 H&H in killing power but is more versatile — thus better suited to hunting American big game.

To work up loads for this article, Bob used this .340 Weatherby Mark V, with the new Leupold Compact 4x scope in a Leupold mount. This particular Mark V has a rather unusual piece of wood in the stock — very dark in the butt, quite light from the grip forward.

to do some load development work with a standard Weatherby Mark V with the standard 26-inch barrel with its 3/8-inch freebore that Roy prefers to call long throating. The load data also needed to be updated by using some powders that were not in existence ten years ago. Norma had also hardened the brass in their cases since that time, which should also make considerable difference in the amount of pressure the case would stand without head expansion.

The test rifle was furnished with Weatherby factory ammunition in both 200 and 250-grain bullet weights, which is loaded by Norma with Hornady bullets. A breakdown of ten cartridges, with both bullet weights, showed that the 200-grain load consisted of an average of 92.8 grains of what appeared to be Norma MRP, and giving a muzzle velocity of 3,191 feet per second. The 250-grain load contained a charge of 86.8 grains of the same powder, and delivered 2,860 feet per second at the muzzle. Several three-shot groups were averaged, and the 200-grain bullets averaged 1 1/4 inch at one hundred yards, while the 250-grain load averaged only 2 3/8 inches. These velocities are very close to Weatherby's quoted velocities of 3,210 feet per second for the 200-grain bullet and 2,850 feet per second for the 250-grain. A refreshing development! They are, however, a couple of grains heavier than the charges of MRP given in the Weatherby load data for the same velocities as factory ammunition. This is probably because of adjustment of the charge for the powder lot used.

These factory loads expanded the rear of the belt 0.0005 to 0.0007 inch, which is normal for full-power factory loads in most belted cases. When I started handloading, I discovered that with a new case, expansion of the rear of the belt could be taken up to 0.001 inch, where it would not increase until two to three grains of most powders were added. When the charge was increased until expansion started the second time, it continued to expand with the same charge, which eventually leads to loose primer pockets and shortened case life, so all loads fired for recording in the chart were cut to at least one grain below this point of continued expansion. It should be pointed out to those who will bring up the fact that the loads and velocities given in the chart are higher than those found in most reloading manuals, that it took about two grains more of most of the powders used before the mark of the ejector hole in the bolt face appeared even faintly on the case head, and that even that charge did not cause sticky bolt lift. Also, the test cases were fired over a dozen times with the loads listed and still have tight primer pockets.

You'll note that I mentioned miking the case on the *rear* of the belt, and there are two reasons for this. First, the front edge of the belt often becomes rough during reloading and chambering, which causes the diameter to change and give a false reading. Second, even though this new Norma-Weatherby brass is harder than in the past and of excellent quality, the case still has a thin web that does not fully support the forward end of the belt. This allows that section of the belt to expand with the case-body wall at far less pressure than required to expand the rear that is part of the solid web section. Only when the solid head of any case — belted, rimless or rimmed — expands does the primer pocket become loose and cause trouble.

Most of the data compiled in the various reloading manuals for the .340 Weatherby were almost certainly taken with the older cases with softer brass, so loads were held down to avoid the possibility of loose primer pockets, which is as it should be. But with the cases used in my own tests, the charges and velocities found in most manuals are somewhat unrealistic suggestions of what the big cartridge is capable of. While my test rifle has an excellent chamber and bore, it apparently handles much heavier powder charges

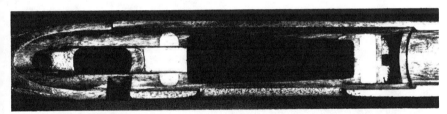

Newer Weatherby stocks have inserts of epoxy bedding compound behind recoil-lug and magazine mortises. Roy Weatherby says there is a steel crossbolt imbedded in the action area for added strength — also a steel rod through the wrist or grip, running from the action inletting through the grip and under the nose of the comb. This is an excellent idea.

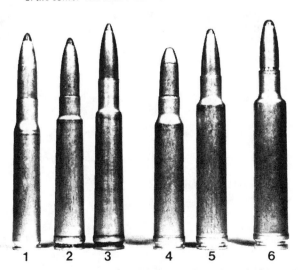

1   2   3   4   5   6

Perhaps the first .33 cartridges to become popular in the United States were the .333 OKH (1), the .333 Belted OKH (2), and the .334 OKH (3). These OKH wildcats surely had some influence on the births and popularity of later commercial .33 cartridges like the .338 Winchester Magnum (4) and the .340 Weatherby (5). The oversize belted cartridge (6) is the .378 Weatherby necked to take .338 bullets; this was the original experimental cartridge that led to the .340 Weatherby.

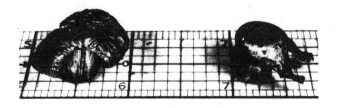

Well designed .338 bullets penetrate well, with a large frontal area. Bullet at left is a 250-grain Bitterroot that penetrated fourteen inches of neck bone in a bull elk, after passing through the neck muscle, then lodged between the shoulder blades. Righthand bullet is a 210-grain Nosler that ranged from the flank up through a foot of spine to rest in the hide at the top of the shoulder. Both bulls were shot at about eighty yards.

than the rifles used to compile the data for most manuals even for the same velocity, and a heavier charge usually delivers higher velocity if the pressure level is the same. Also, the various manuals do not agree on either charge or velocity, nor do Weatherby's figures go along with any of them, but come nearer to my own velocity figures. With some powders and bullet weights, I could not achieve Weatherby velocity at the pressures I did not wish to exceed; with others I could exceed it somewhat.

In load development for several rifles chambered for the .338 Winchester Magnum cartridge, pressures were not excessive at velocities of 2,750 to 2,800 feet per second with the 250-grain bullet. All Speer reloading manuals up to number 9 show loads producing over twenty-six hundred feet per second with their 275-grain bullet, and over twenty-seven hundred feet per second with Norma 205. Considering this, it doesn't seem logical that the .340 Weatherby Magnum cartridge can do no better than twenty-seven hundred feet per second with the 250-grain bullet, as listed in a couple of recent manuals; especially since it burns some seven grains more of the same powders with the same bullet weights.

I knew about what I could expect in the way of velocity with some powders from the .340 case with good Winchester-Western brass, and was not surprised when the Weatherby Mark V showed the velocity capability it should have with the new Norma-Weatherby cases.

Being a little curious regarding the performance of the very slow H-870 spherical powder with heavy bullets, and noting that Hodgdon figures show slightly higher velocity with that powder behind the 275-grain bullet than with H-4831, I started with that powder and the 275-grain Speer bullet. The Hodgdon load of ninety grains proved very mild in my rifle, so the charge was increased to ninety-nine grains, was still giving no belt expansion, but was compressed to the limit, and delivered only 2,662 feet per second as compared to 2,594 feet per second listed by Hodgdon with the ninety-grain charge from the same 26-inch barrel. This is only an increase of sixty-eight feet per second in velocity for a charge increase of nine grains. Try figuring that one out, and you'll learn something about why velocity and charge figures from different sources do not always agree.

There was no need to do further work with that powder with any of the lighter bullets, as all other powder except IMR-

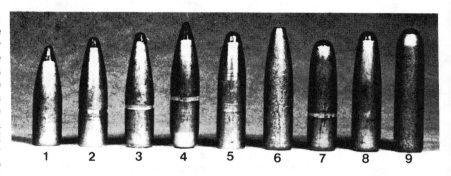

Suitable bullets for the .340 Weatherby are made in many brands, weights, styles, and structure designs, making this cartridge reloadable for hunting any kind of big game anywhere with the right bullet. These are 200-grain Speer (1), 210-grain Nosler (2), 225-grain Hornady (3), 250-grain Sierra (4), 250-grain Nosler, old style (5), 250-grain Bitterroot (6), 250-grain Hornady (7), 275-grain Speer (8), and 300-grain Barnes (9). There are others, also suitable.

.340 Weatherby Magnum Load Data

.340 Weatherby Magnum Mark V, 26-inch barrel
Weatherby cases, 227 grain
CCI 250 primers
Oehler M34/M50 chronograph system
Velocity instrumental at 15 feet converted to muzzle velocity

Bullet	Powder	Charge	Velocity	
Weatherby 250 Factory		86.8	2,860	
Weatherby 200 Factory		92.8	3,191	
300 Barnes	H-4831	82	2,629	
	MRP	82	2,591	
275 Speer	H-870	99*	2,662	
	H-4831	84	2,788	Uniform velocity and
	MRP	85	2,751	good accuracy
	785	83	2,785	
	IMR-4831	80	2,712	
	IMR-4350	77	2,665	
	H-205	83	2,769	
250 Speer Grand Slam	H-4831	87	2,916	
	MRP	89	2,928	Uniform velocity and
	785	90	2,932	best accuracy of all
	IMR-4831	83	2,883	bullets used
	IMR-4350	80	2,822	
	H-205	85	2,927	
225 Hornady	H-4831	90	3,071	
	MRP	92	3,090	Uniform, fair accuracy
	785	92	3,034	
	IMR-4831	86	3,086	
	IMR-4350	82	2,991	
	H-205	87	3,089	
210 Nosler	H-4831	93	3,205	
	MRP	93	3,175	Good accuracy and
	785	92	3,100	fair uniformity
	IMR-4831	86	3,098	
	IMR-4350	82	2,975	
	H-205	87	3,138	
200 Winchester Western	H-4831	94	3,219	
	MRP	94	3,218	Good accuracy and
	H-205	88	3,187	fair uniformity

*Compressed to limit

While all of these loads were below maximum in the test rifle, they are not suggested for use in any other rifle and should be approached from three to four grains below. Loads for chambers without the standard Weatherby throating should be reduced even more to start.

66

4350 gave over twenty-seven hundred feet per second with the 275-grain bullet. In fact, H-4831 and Winchester-Western 785 ran very close to twenty-eight hundred feet per second. It is possible that H-870 would show up better with the heavier 300-grain Barnes bullet, but I had only a few on hand and no more available at the time.

In trying all of the new powders that did not exist at the time I first load-tested the .340 Weatherby, I soon found that H-4831 still was as good as any other suitable powder. The first testing was, of course, done with surplus 4831, while the new tests were run with the new H-4831 made for Hodgdon in Scotland. But I find that there is no more difference between the newly manufactured H-4831 and the older surplus powder than there is between various lots of either. When using the new powder with data taken with the old, I simply start two or three grains low and work up, and usually come out at about the same charge with similar velocity. This is a good idea when switching lot numbers of any powder.

As might be expected, Norma MRP ran very close to H-4831, both in charge weight and velocity. Some bullet weights take a grain or two more of MRP than H-4831, some the same charge, but velocity is quite close with all bullet weights.

I was a little surprised at how well Winchester 785 did with all bullet weights from 275 down to 210 grains. Velocity is right at the top, and so is velocity uniformity, with accuracy at the same level as with other powders. Another powder that did better than expected in this cartridge was H-205. I have found this powder to lag behind both H-4831 and MRP quite badly in the .300 Weatherby but not in the .340. It ran right along with the best. One point that should be brought out is that H-205 was tried first with the 250-grain bullet, and during that testing it was obvious that I would run short with the lot I was using; so when I changed lots, I did some pressure testing of the new lot before clocking velocity. I found that where eighty-three grains was the top for a velocity of 2,861 feet per second, eighty-five grains of the new lot gave the same belt expansion but delivered 2,927 feet per second. An 83-grain charge of the new lot gave only 2,837 feet per second. These loads were checked and rechecked for accuracy of both pressure and velocity and it appears that not only can the charge of the new lot of H-205 be increased by two grains, but that a difference in burning characteristics makes it more efficient with all bullet weights in the .340 case. This is

another case showing that when powder lots are changed, some serious load checking is in order. And also one reason why velocity figures from different sources do not usually agree even when identical rifles and other loading components are used.

The new Du Pont IMR-4831 does not show up overly well in the .340 case with any weight of bullet, and charges run well below those used with H-4831. The charge-velocity differential between the two 4831 powders is greater in the .340 Weatherby than in any of the many other cases I have tested the two powders in.

The big surprise for many shooters may come with the velocity delivered by IMR-4350 with any weight of bullet. Most of the reloading manuals show IMR-4350 as giving velocity as high as any other powder with all bullet weights, but I have never found this to be true in any .340 rifle, and the Weatherby test rifle was no exception. In tests with all of the bullet weights with which I used IMR-4350, I tried to attain the velocity equal to that given by H-4831, but belt expansion, the ejector-hole mark, and sticky bolt lift prevented using charges that came close to the velocity possible with the slower powders. No, I'm not saying everyone else is wrong and I am right, but try as I might, I can't get the best from the .340 Weatherby case with IMR-4350. If you want to try it, I suggest you sneak up on those loads kinda easylike.

If you buy a .340 Weatherby, you probably do so because you want the most a commercial .338 cartridge will deliver, and if you load it with IMR-4350 powder — and certainly anything faster — you are dropping it back into the class of the .338 Winchester and losing the full potential of the big cartridge.

As stated earlier, any garden-variety rifle chambered for the .338 Winchester Magnum cartridge gives at least 2,750 feet per second with the 250-grain bullets and the right powders with no pressure pains whatever, and the .340 is capable of twenty-nine hundred feet per second with the same bullet with trouble-free hunting loads.

While velocity variation is not given in the chart except as uniform, (with some loads, not enough shots were fired to give a completely accurate sample), they averaged very uniform with nearly all loads. As might be expected, the heavier bullets give less extreme spread in velocity than do the lighter bullets. The average extreme spread for all loads was about thirty feet per second, which is very good.

Also note that accuracy figures are not listed specifically for each load. The reason for this is that to start with, accuracy was outstanding, with many three-shot groups running under an inch at one hundred yards, then started going sour. I found that the stock wood had moved somewhat with changes in atmospheric conditions, and the bedding was out of tune. There was no time to go back and reshoot all groups after rebedding the stock, and I don't usually rebed stocks on rifles I do not intend to keep. However, enough groups were fired with different loads before the problem appeared to know that the barrel is capable of top-drawer accuracy.

As a hunting cartridge for the heavier North American big game and most African species, the .340 Weatherby has few peers if the case is loaded to its full potential and is pushing the right bullet for the work at hand. Loaded with the 210-grain Nosler bullet at full throttle, it is flatter at all ranges than the 7mm magnums with 175-grain bullets, as flat as the big .30s with 180-grain bullets, and much more effective on heavy game than either. And for the heavy game from elk up, where the shots are close and may have to be taken fast at adverse angles, the best 250-grain controlled-expansion bullets, or the 275-grain Speer and 300-grain Barnes give the kind of bone-shattering penetration and killing power needed.

Today, the closest rival of the .340 Weatherby in a commercial cartridge for shooting all of the heavier big game up to African Cape buffalo and elephant, is the time-tested .375 H&H. Little needs to be said about the capability of that cartridge on nearly any game found anywhere, and the .340 Weatherby has it shaded in a number of directions. First, with the 200 to 225-grain bullets, the .340 has flatter trajectory and better retained velocity and energy over longer ranges than anything the .375 has to offer. Second, the 250-grain bullet has greater sectional density than the 300-grain .375 and can be started nearly two hundred feet per second faster with both cartridges loaded to their full potential in barrels of the same length. Given the same form factor, the 250-grain .338 bullet is, of course, much flatter at all ranges than the 300-grain .375. And my penetration tests on both game and in the recovery box with the two bullet weights in Nosler Partition bullets show the 250-grain .338 digs in deeper than the 300-grain .375. If you wish to load the 300-grain bullet in the .340 Weatherby, it will do near twenty-seven hundred feet per second, with the top for the .375 300-grain in the H&H

cartridge being about fifty feet per second more. Energy is, of course, similar at close range, but the sectional density of the 300-grain .338 is about 0.368, compared to 0.305 for the 300-grain .375 bullet. There is no argument over which bullet gives the deepest penetration if both are of identical structure.

Of course, the larger frontal area of the .375 bullets must be taken into consideration where shock and killing power are important; the .375 has the edge there. But everything considered for all-around hunting of most big game from deer up, the .340 Weatherby is a much more versatile cartridge than the .375 H&H. ●

CHAPTER
12

Dave Scovill

.348

The .348 Winchester (right) is longer and has a larger rim diameter than the .45-70 (left).

INTRODUCED IN 1935 as an improved version of the .33 WCF, the .348 Winchester was chambered in the modern equivalent of the 1886 Winchester, the Model 71.

Ballistically, the .348 WCF was a brush busting powerhouse that generated 2,821 foot-pounds (ft-lbs) of muzzle energy with a 200-grain bullet at 2,520 fps from a 24-inch rifle barrel. Another factory load with a 150-grain bullet clocked 2,880 fps, but according to those in the know, it lacked long range potential on larger game. Winchester responded with a 250-grain Silvertip at an advertised muzzle velocity of 2,320 fps and nearly 3,000 ft-lbs of energy from a 24-inch barrel. Most writers today openly doubt those claims and the 250-grain factory load probably produced something like 2,200 fps in a rifle barrel, or 2,150 in the 20-inch carbine barrel. Either way, the .348 WCF was capable of holding its own against anything that walked in the lower 48, Canada and Alaska.

Unfortunately, the .348 WCF and the Model 71 outlived their usefulness and were discontinued in 1958 after a production run of 47,254 rifles and carbines, marking the end of an era for the big-bore lever-actions. Within a few years, the supply of .348-inch bullets

dried up as well and shooters had tough going if they intended to keep their Model 71 in service.

The good news is that there has been a resurgence in the popularity of the .348 WCF, largely due to Browning's introduction of their Limited Edition Model 71 in 1987, and there may be a larger selection of cast and jacketed bullets available than ever before. The bad news is that of the 8,000 Grade 1 rifles, 4,000 Grade 1 carbines and 6,000 High Grade rifles and carbines, only a few remain on dealer shelves and the test carbine was one of a handful left in the inventory at Browning in Morgan, Utah in the summer of 1990.

Availability aside (used guns are always available at gun shows and shops), there will never be a lever action that is as smooth, slick and strong as the Model 71. Unlike the Model 94, with its single vertical locking lug, the Model 71, like the Model 86 and the shorter 92, features twin lugs that slide into recessed mortises on either side of tbe bolt. For whatever reason, possibly because the lugs are a bit further forward than the rear-locking Model 94, the 71 lever closes smartly, with minimal friction and effort.

Lever action fans also will note there is no trigger release on the Model 71. The action must be closed completely, or there will be a noticeable increase in the effort required to pull the trigger, if you can pull it at all. This should never be a problem with factory loads but handloaders should make sure that the bullets are seated deep enough so that the shoulder on cast bullets, or the land-diameter area of the ogive on jacketed bullets, does not butt against the lands when the action is closed on a live round. Any variation in the normal trigger pull from one round to the next is a signal that bullets are seated too far out, preventing the lever from fully locking into firing position against the lower tang.

When the Model 71 arrived I ordered a supply of Hornady 200-grain .348-inch bullets and RCBS forwarded a .348-200 cast bullet mould. From there supplies were pretty slim. By coincidence, one of the influential folks at NEI/Tooldyne (9330 NE Halsey, Portland OR 97220) was working on a new 250-grain .348-inch cast bullet

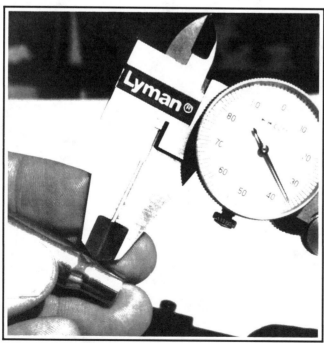

Case necks were sized .035 inch from the shoulder to ensure positive headspace simultaneously on the case rim and shoulder.

70

Winchester

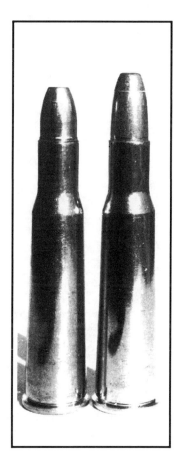

Top, Hornady New Dimension .348 Winchester dies were used to assemble handloads with jacketed bullets, including the (1) 165-grain Hawk, (2) 180-grain Hawk, (3) 200-grain Harris, (4) 200-grain Hawk, (5) 200-grain Hornady, (6) 220-grain Barnes, (7) 250-grain Barnes and (8) 250-grain Hawk. Right, cast bullets included the (1) RCBS .348-200, (2) LBT 250 with the nose and first driving band sized to .339 inch, (3) standard LBT 250, and (4) NEI .348-250. Far right, cast bullets (left) were seated to ensure that the front shoulder on the first driving band did not butt up against the lands when the loaded round was chambered. Jacketed bullets (right) were seated so that the bore diameter section, as indicated by the bright spot on the ogive above the case mouth, was just short of the lands.

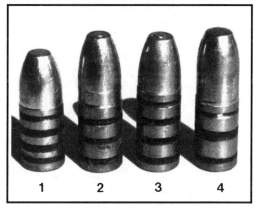

design and offered to forward a mould for testing. About that same time, Veral Smith (LBT, HCR 62, Box 145, Moyie Springs ID 83845) made a 250-grain cast bullet mould for John Kronfeld, and I managed to purloin it as well. That made three cast bullet designs and one jacketed bullet. Pretty slim pickens indeed.

Further efforts uncovered 220 and 250-grain custom bullets from Barnes Bullets Inc. (PO Box 215, American Fork UT 84003) but there was nothing close to the 180 and 150-grain bullets that were listed in some of the older loading manuals.

I was about to abandon further efforts to locate bullets when Bob Fulton, the head honcho at Hawk Laboratories Inc. (Box 112, Station 27, Lakewood CO 80215) started making 200 and 250-grain .348-inch bullets and I suggested that he might consider a 180-grain slug. Better yet, I wanted a

165-grain bullet for deer-sized game. Bob is no fool and he wondered about the practical application of light weight bullets in the .348 Winchester. The big question was whether they would stabilize properly in the Browning barrel with a one-in-12-inch twist that was designed for heavier, 200 to 250-grain, bullets. After some thought, Bob decided to make a run of 165 and 180-grain bullets with .025-inch jackets.

Even though the .348 Winchester was retired nearly 30 years ago, the brass supply does not appear to have dried up, at least not like the bullet supply did. Apparently wildcatters have created a steady demand for .348 WCF cases that are used to produce the .450 Alaskan, .30-348, .40-348, .450-348 Ackley Improved and a host of other wildcats and obsolete cases.

For this project, Winchester forwarded a supply of .348 cases along with a few boxes of factory loads with

200-grain Silvertips. Huntington Die Specialties (PO Box 991, Oroville CA 95965) also has a good supply of .348 WCF brass on hand.

To get things started, a review of older reloading manuals suggested that you can get along just fine with three basic powders: IMR or H-4895, IMR-4350 and IMR or H-4831. Anything else is icing on the cake. For a little variety, I tossed in Reloder 12, 15 and 19 along with AAC-3100 for use with jacketed bullets and broke out a canister of H-4198 for cast bullet loads. Federal 210 primers filled the bill with jacketed loads and CCI 250 caps were used exclusively with alloy slugs.

Since I had a good supply of 200-grain Hornady bullets and H-4831, those were the components of choice for the first go-round. Working up from 61.0 grains of Hodgdon's finest, 67.0 grains pushed the 200-grain bullet out the 20-inch barrel at 2,501 fps.

Somewhere in the series of five-shot groups, which were fired from the Outers Rifle Rest, the Model 71 punched out a .67-inch cluster at 100 yards. The largest group in the series was a shade less than 1.25 inches. Pushing the powder charge to 68.0 grains of H-4831, recoil became a bit rank, velocity jumped to 2,545 fps and groups averaged just over one inch. Although the heavier charge did not produce sticky extraction or excessive case head expansion, I see no purpose in going beyond 67.0 grains of H-4831 with Hornady's bullet in the field. No big game animal is going to notice the difference if the muzzle velocity is 24 or 25 fps less, and variations in ambient temperature might turn the 68.0 grain load into a real barn burner in hot weather.

While I waited for the Hawk bullets to arrive, I made up a batch of the RCBS .348-200 bullets from wheel-weight alloy, sized them to .349 inch and applied LBT Blue lube. Starting at 25.0 grains of IMR-4198, the powder charge was increased one grain at a time until 28.0 grains produced minor leading at the muzzle. Dropping back to 27.0 grains, the PACT Precision Chronograph clocked the RCBS pill at 1,721 fps and 27.5 grains produced 1,798 fps. Groups with both loads were well under two inches, averaging something like 1.25 to 1.5 from one day to the next. On a good day, an occasional group would cluster up inside an inch. Dropping a slightly compressed dose of Super Grex over the 27.5-grain charge, velocity jumped to 1,825 fps while the groups became more consistent, effectively eliminating the occasional flyer. In all, the Model 71 was turning out to be the most accurate sporting rifle I had ever fired, scope or no scope.

Switching to the LBT 250-grain cast bullet, it occurred to me that the long shank and short nose made it necessary to seat the bullet deeper than I might have preferred. Hoping to seat the bullet out further, but still keeping the shoulder of the first driving band off the lands, I sized the nose and the

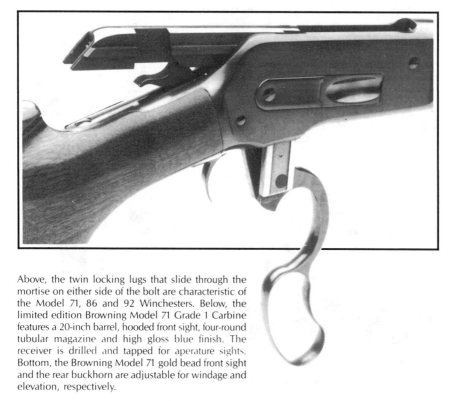

Above, the twin locking lugs that slide through the mortise on either side of the bolt are characteristic of the Model 71, 86 and 92 Winchesters. Below, the limited edition Browning Model 71 Grade 1 Carbine features a 20-inch barrel, hooded front sight, four-round tubular magazine and high gloss blue finish. The receiver is drilled and tapped for aperture sights. Bottom, the Browning Model 71 gold bead front sight and the rear buckhorn are adjustable for windage and elevation, respectively.

first driving band to .339 inch. Seating the bullet over 43.0 grains of H-4895 and 59.0 grains of H-4831, velocities averaged 2,147 and 2,020, respectively. Both loads were capable of dropping five bullets inside 1.5 inches at 100 yards when I did my part with the open sights.

Working with a mixture of six pounds of wheelweights to four pounds of Linotype, the nose on the NEI bullet averaged .340 inch. Since the bore diameter in the Browning barrel miked .338 inch (and the lever will not close smartly on an oversized bullet), the NEI bullets were sized nose-first to .339 inch and the shank was sized .349 inch. Seating the bullet so the gas check was flush with the base of the case neck, 27.0 grains of H-4198 produced 1,672 fps and something close to 1.5 MOA. A standard charge, 43.0 grains of H-4895, generated 2,129 fps and clustered inside two inches.

Also note, 50.0 grains of H-4895 produced 2,218 fps with a 250-grain jacketed bullet while 7.0 grains less powder produced 2,129 fps with a cast bullet of similar weight. I have no idea why, but two chronographs, both from PACT, produced nearly identical velocity readings. Either way, if you happen to use 50.0 grains of H-4895 with a 250-grain cast bullet, you may get a *real* load. Don't do it, at least not until you have started up from a significantly reduced load and have verified that pressure and velocity are within responsible limits.

Switching back to jacketed bullets, slower powders like RL-19, AAC-3100 and H or IMR-4831 failed to produce the kind of velocities I was looking for with the 165-grain Hawk bullet. A review of reloading data and powders on hand suggested that H or IMR-4895, RL-12 or RL-15 were probably more appropriate.

As it turned out, 56.0 grains of IMR-4895 produced 2,753 fps with the 165-grain Hawk bullet and 54.0 grains of RL-15 generated 2,644 fps with their 180-grain slug. Accuracy with either load was perfectly capable of hitting a football-sized target at 200 yards with open sights, which is about as well as I can see anyway.

I should mention too, that most of the loads that were worked up in the Browning Model 71 are listed in one or more reloading manuals. It is by no

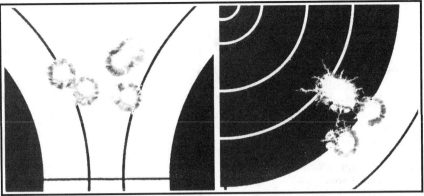

Following a fouling shot from a clean barrel, five-shot groups with the RCBS and LBT bullets over 27.0 grains of H-4198 averaged about one inch or less at 100 yards.

coincidence that my maximum loads echo those in print by various powder manufacturers. The .348 Winchester has been around a long time and standard loads have been pretty well established. For my part, I miked the expansion on the web of the 200-grain Winchester factory loads and compared those measurements with recommended loads from time to time, and most of the maximum loads listed in Table I produced the same expansion as the factory load. I say *most* because Reloder 12, 15 and 19, for example, are not listed for the .348 Winchester in the *Hercules Reloader's Guide* with any bullet weight and none of the manuals list loads for the 165-grain bullet which Bob Fulton made up.

The Winchester factory load is supposed to produce 2,520 fps from a 24-inch barrel, but it developed nearly the same velocity in the 20-inch carbine. My handloads tend to mirror that phenomenon by producing velocities that might be expected from a longer rifle barrel. I have no idea why this occurred, but I pulled a bullet from a Winchester factory load and it contained 53.2 grains of a powder that is similar to H or IMR-4895 and those same factory loads produced velocities that I came to expect from a similar dose of powder from a canister of H or IMR-4895.

I would also caution the reader to work up to my listed maximum loads carefully in the Model 71 Winchester. From all that I have been able to gather from knowledgable shooters, the Winchester rifles had somewhat sloppy chambers and bore diameters when compared to the snug tolerances of the Browning Model 71. For example, the neck diameter of a .348 Win-

chester case with a .348-inch bullet seated averages .368 inch. The chamber neck in my carbine mikes just a shade less than .372 inch. That is a difference of less than .004 inch and is closing in on benchrest chamber tolerances when compared to the .007 to .008 inch difference in most sporting rifles.

Going a step further, the difference between the diameter at the web of a case that is fired with a maximum load and the inside diameter at the base of the Hornady sizing die is a mere .002 inch. In working up to top loads in virgin brass that has been fired two or three times with something less than a maximum load, the Hornady dies did not touch the case body, period. It was not until a maximum load was used that the case body expanded sufficiently for the sizing die to be of any use, except to resize the case neck up to a point .035 inch short of the shoulder, effectively causing the case to headspace on the rim and shoulder, simultaneously.

Loading 65.0 to 66.0 grains of H-4831 with the 200-grain Hornady bullet, the case expanded just enough to form a snug fit in the sizing die and it was possible to use the full-length sizing die to size the neck only. I am also convinced that it was no coincidence that it was those same loads that produced the series of five-shot groups that averaged less than one MOA. It makes you wonder what this carbine could do if it had a scope mounted topside. Even then, if I used virgin cases that were fired one time with a 200-grain jacketed bullet over 66.0 grains of H-4831, and seated a cast bullet that was sized to .349-inch over 27.0 or 27.5 grains of H-4198, the resultant five-

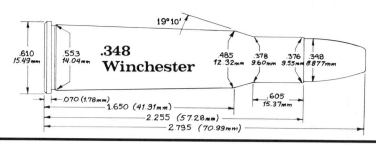

shot groups were usually clustered inside an inch.

The 250-grain softpoints from Hawk Laboratories and Barnes are solid performers. Both bullets would stay inside two inches, and better loads cluster five shots into 1.5 inches or less. There is a good selection of suggested loads for this bullet weight in reloading manuals but 49.0 grains of H-4895 produced 2,156 fps and it would be my first choice, although it is about 1.0 grain below what I would consider a suggested maximum. It is my opinion that the Hawk bullets hold together better, retaining more weight after impact in hard clay, than their jacketed counterparts from Hornady or Barnes. Be that as it may, all the jacketed bullets were capable of shooting inside 1.5 inches at 100 yards with good loads.

After these trials were wrapped up, Harris Enterprises (PO Box 105, Bly OR 97622) forwarded a sample of 200-grain .348-inch bullets. Time precluded testing, but they appear to be well designed.

In the field, I used a variety of cast bullet loads to raise havoc with the local jackrabbit population and the 165-grain Hawk bullet was used with 59.0 grains of H-4895 to take a representative Montana antelope at about 34 paces. Not that such a close-range shot on a relatively light-weight big game animal proved much, but the bullet did the job as effectively as any high velocity bullet from a .30-06 or .270 Winchester might be expected to do under similar circumstances.

The Browning Model 71 is a fine rifle by any standards. Whether the test carbine is an exception to the rule remains moot. Either way, the Japanese (the Model 71 is manufactured by Miroku) have certainly figured out how to hang a forearm on a rifle barrel without disturbing accuracy. My only complaint is that heavy recoil generated by maximum loads with 250-grain bullets would occasionally jar the rear sight ramp hard enough to bounce it back to the lowest notch. If it occurred in the middle of a string of shots, it usually resulted in a bullet hole that was from four to six inches low, depending on which notch the sight was set in. Other than that, if the rest of those Browning Model 71 carbines and rifles shoot like the test carbine, they should have stamped the whole batch "One of 18,000." ●

Table I
.348 Winchester — Browning Model 71
Selected Jacketed Bullet Loads

bullet (grains)	powder	charge (grains)	velocity (fps)
Hawk 165	RL-19	70.0	2,487
	IMR-4895	58.0	2,644
		59.0	2,753
	RL-15	56.0	2,642
	RL-12	54.0	2,612
Hawk 180	RL-19	68.5	2,475
	IMR-4895	57.0	2,575
	RL-15	54.0	2,644
	H-4831	69.0	2,587
		70.0	2,614
	H-4350	65.0	2,606
	RL-12	52.5	2,586
Hawk 200	RL-19	67.0	2,447
	RL-15	53.0	2,429
		54.0	2,453
	H-4831	68.0	2,521
	H-4895	53.5	2,523
Hornady 200	H-4350	59.0	2,226
		61.0	2,339
		63.0	2,401
	AAC-3100	60.5	2,076
		62.5	2,163
	H-4831	61.0	2,010
		63.0	2,122
		65.0	2,408
	RL-15	51.0	2,257
Hawk 250	IMR-4895	50.0	2,218
	H-4831	61.5	2,067

Be alert — Publisher cannot accept responsibility for errors in published load data.

Table II
.348 Winchester — Browning Model 71
Selected Cast Bullet Loads

bullet (grains)	powder	charge (grains)	velocity (fps)
RCBS .348-200	H-4831	60.0	1,911
		63.0*	1,910
	H-4895	43.0	2,196
	H-4198	27.0	1,721
		27.5	1,798
		27.5**	1,825
NEI 250	H-4198	27.0	1,613
		27.5	1,681
		28.0*	1,656
	H-4895	43.0	2,129
LBT-250	H-4198	27.0	1,672
	H-4895	43.0	2,147
	H-4831	59.0	2,020
		60.0	2,050

* Fired at 30 degrees Fahrenheit.
** Super Grex filler.

Be alert — Publisher cannot accept responsibility for errors in published load data.

CHAPTER 13

John Kronfeld

WHILE TESTING cast bullets in the new Browning Model 71 .348 Winchester, the need arose for a throating reamer. Trying to find a gunsmith with this reamer was impossible. The .348 Improved (Ackley) reamer was the closest a few gunsmiths could come to the needed reamer. What were these "good old boys" doing with this uncommon piece of iron?

P.O. Ackley states in his book *Handbook for Shooters and Reloaders*, "The .348 Improved was developed upon request of many hunters with Winchester Model 71 rifles. The original .348 cartridge is poorly designed. Mainly because it had such a steep body taper. The bolt thrust is greater than it should be. Bolt thrust, undesirable as it is, is doubly so in lever actions. The Improved .348 combines minimum body taper and sharp shoulder design and is capable of giving a noticeable increase over the .348 Winchester."

Loading data in his book for the .348 Ackley Improved shows a significant increase in muzzle velocity over the standard .348 Winchester from a 24-inch barrel — 2,530 versus 2,200 fps for 250-grain bullets. That is a big difference.

After finishing the .348 Winchester heavy cast bullet testing, my carbine was sent to Redmans' Gun Shop in Omak, Washington, to be rechambered. Coincidentally, Layne Simpson's Benchtopics column on improved cartridges in *Handloader* No. 134 arrived midway through this project. Simpson felt that improved cartridges are worth the effort if for no other reason than reduced case stretching and trimming, which follows this type of modification. This author's only interest is for the increase in velocities shown in Ackley's book.

If one can get another 200 to 250 fps from their Model 71 and still have good

Ackley stated, there is no more body taper and there is now a very sharp shoulder. Ackley felt that cartridges in the "old" days did not incorporate sharp shoulders because of the difficulties in manufacturing brass in this shape.

New .348 Winchester brass holds 78.4 grains of water to the top of the case mouth; .348 Improved (Ackley) brass holds 90 grains (a 14.8 percent increase in case capacity). From this point the Powley Computer was used to compare loading data for IMR-4350 with listed data in Ackley's book. The computer shows 68 grains as the optimum load for the 250-grain Barnes bullet, producing 2,464 fps in a 20-inch carbine and 2,530 fps for a 24-inch rifle barrel. Ackley shows 66 grains at 2,530 fps for a rifle (it is assumed his data is for a 24-inch barrel since that was the most common barrel length).

The computer reads 46,300 CUP for this load. Since the maximum working pressure for the Model 71 is 44,000

.348 Winchester
Ackley Improved

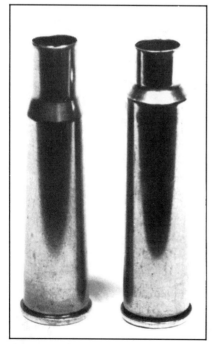

The increased powder capacity of the .348 Improved (right) is evident when compared to the standard .348 Winchester (left).

accuracy, they should be in hog heaven. If not, hope and pray that Browning will rebarrel the rifle to its original .348 Winchester chambering.

Fireforming was used to convert .348 Winchester brass to the Improved shape; it is a very simple process. Load a bullet you would normally use in the .348 Winchester into a case with almost a maximum charge for that bullet weight, then fire the cartridge in the new chamber. The fireforming load of 46 grains of IMR-3031 and a 250-grain LBT cast bullet worked very well. Only new brass was used with three out of 120 cases splitting at the shoulder.

When the first fireformed case was ejected from the new chamber, it was immediately apparent that there is a significant increase in case capacity. As

CUP, new calculations were made with a reduced charge of 65 grains. This brought pressures down to a safe 43,750 CUP and 2,396 fps for my carbine. Starting loads were further reduced to 62 grains and testing began.

Most published data shows the .348 Winchester and the Barnes 250-grain bullet at 2,150 to 2,200 fps from a 24-inch rifle barrel with Winchester brass. Older articles in *Handloader* confirm this. One writer wrote a product review on the Browning carbine with the Barnes bullet being driven at 2,184 fps with 60 grains of H-4831.

Recently tested .348 Winchester 250-grain Silvertip ammunition (no longer manufactured) generated 2,200 fps with a sticky extraction in my carbine. Another author showed velocities for the .348 Winchester rifle with the

Barnes 250-grain bullet at 2,283 fps. The load used Remington brass, which holds more water than Winchester brass but has not been available for years. For realistic velocity improvement, we should be looking at velocities with presently available brass.

Several powders, including IMR-4320, IMR-4064, IMR-3031, H-4831, WW-748, WW-760 and AAC-3100 all showed good accuracy at varying velocity levels. The Barnes bullet with 70 grains of AAC-3100 showed the best overall performance in my carbine putting three shots into .75 inch with 2,412 fps.

It was observed that there is a noticeable increase in barrel heat generated by this cartridge over the .348 Winchester. With the .348 Winchester three, three-shot groups can be fired during a normal 10-minute range session. With the .348 Improved cartridge it was hard to get off two, three-shot groups before the barrel got too hot to shoot. This was remedied by completing the shooting early in the morning in the shade.

Only being interested in bullets weighing 250 grains or more for large game, the lighter 200 and 220-grain

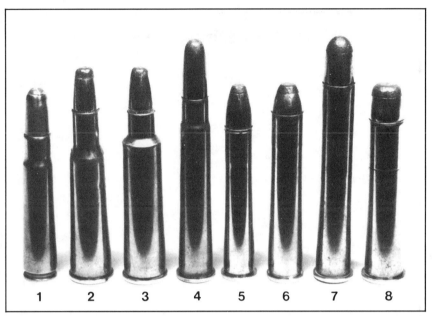

Popular lever action cartridges, past and present, include the (*1*) .35 Remington, (*2*) .348 Winchester, (*3*) .348 Ackley Improved, (*4*) .35 Winchester, (*5*) .375 Winchester, (*6*) .444 Marlin, (*7*) .405 Winchester and the (*8*) .45-70.

.348 bullets from Hornady and Barnes, respectively, were tested with the same powders Ackley used for his data. This would help serve as a further check on Ackley's data. After comparing Ackley's data with mine, it is obvious that there is a strong correlation. The .348 Improved (Ackley) does give the desired increased velocities.

It was my fear that a day would come when the 250-grain Barnes jacketed bullet would be gone, as are many once-available .348 components (this was

predicted by Ken Waters in *Handloader* 15 years ago). This concern resulted in testing high-velocity cast bullets for the .348 Winchester, which led into the .348 Improved (Ackley). It is only fitting, therefore, to test the same lead bullets in the improved chamber. It gives a further check on the increased velocities of the Improved cartridge over its little brother.

As shown in the load data, the Improved version of the .348 Winchester gives a healthy increase over the .348

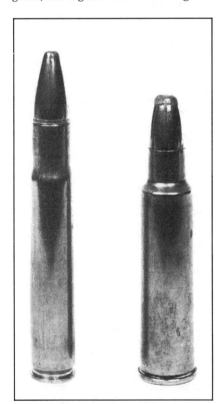

The .35 Whelen (left) is shown next to the .348 Ackley Improved (right) for comparison.

Exterior Ballistic Comparison

bullet (grains)	velocity (fps)	muzzle energy (foot-pounds)	sectional density	recoil (foot-pounds)	100 yards velocity (fps)	energy (foot-pounds)
.348 Winchester						
250 Barnes	2,134	2,541	.295	22.56	1,894	2,001
250 LBT	2,159	2,517	.282	22.72	1,914	1,978
300 Hoch	2,187	3,117	.334	30.25	1,865	2,267
.348 Improved (Ackley)						
250 Barnes	2,412	3,246	.295	30.06	2,143	2,565
250 LBT	2,416	3,257	.295	30.10	2,174	2,637
300 Hoch	2,305	3,557	.334	32.80	1,964	2,583
.35 Whelen						
250 Hornady	2,500	3,470	.279	26.80	2,152	2,571
.444 Marlin						
265 Hornady	2,200	2,894	.205	29.25	1,801	1,910
.45-70						
400 Speer	1,866	3,108	.272	44.03	1,536	2,106

Notes: Weights of cast bullets as tested — LBT – 242 grains, Hoch – 292 grains.

Ackley's Data/Chronographed Data

powder charge (grains)	Ackley's velocity (fps)	chronographed velocity (fps)	
		20-inch	24-inch*
IMR-4350 – 250-grain jacketed			
62.0	2,380	2,332	2,446
64.0	2,470	2,373	2,483
65.0		2,403	
66.0	2,530	2,420	2,530
IMR-4350 – 220-grain jacketed			
63.0	2,410	2,280	2,400
65.0		2,452	
IMR-4350 – 200-grain jacketed			
67.0	2,470	2,482	2,590
68.0	2,500	2,535	2,640
69.0	2,530	2,526	2,685
70.0	2,665		
71.0	2,710		

*Indicates that author's velocity values for 24-inch barrel are calculated. Velocity for the 20-inch barrel are from chronograph.

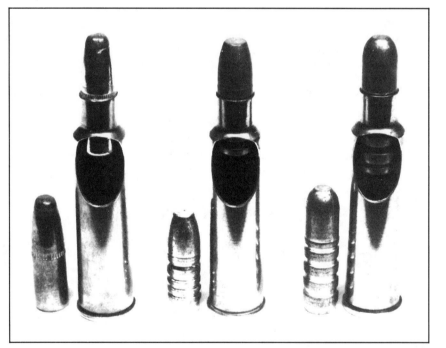

Above, cutaway views show the relative seating depth of the (left) 250-grain Barnes (center), 250-grain LBT and (right) the 300-grain Hoch bullets. Right, recovered bullets show the effect of increased impact velocity offered by the .348 Ackley Improved (bullets on the right in each pair) at 100 yards in comparison to the standard .348 Winchester.

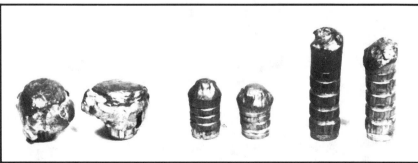

Winchester with cast bullets. With the 300-grain Hoch bullet, 64 grains of IMR-4350 gave one-inch accuracy at 2,305 fps and a muzzle energy of 3,525 foot-pounds.

The sectional density of the 300-grain cast bullet, .340, is higher than the 175-grain 7mm or the .30-caliber 220-grain bullets, .310 and .331, respectively. This high sectional density should ensure superior penetration on large game, especially with long, raking shots. The Improved cartridge with impressive performance from the 300-grain lead bullet now takes on a new light.

The next step was expansion testing into water-soaked newsprint. It was interesting to compare .348 Improved (Ackley) expanded bullets to the same bullets fired in the .348 Winchester. The Barnes 250-grain was fired with a simulated muzzle velocity of 2,400 fps, striking at 2,143 fps and mushrooming perfectly. The expanded bullet measured .762 inch as compared to the .348 Winchester which produced an expanded diameter of .742 inch. Both bullets retained 88 percent of their original weight. The Hoch 300-grain water-quenched Linotype bullet, with a simulated muzzle velocity of 2,300 fps, struck the newsprint at 1,964 fps and expanded at the nose to .432 inch as compared to .396 inch for the .348 Winchester. It weighed 252.4 grains, a few grains more than it weighed when recovered from the .348 Winchester test. The LBT bullet had a simulated muzzle velocity of 2,400 fps and a striking velocity of 2,174 fps. It expanded to .435 inch and had a retained weight of 148 grains as opposed to .385 inch and 150 grains for the .348 Winchester. At the elevated striking velocities in the 1,900 to 2,200 fps range there is only slightly more expansion in the .348 Improved over the .348 Winchester. There also is practically no difference in weight loss in cast or jacketed bullets at these increased velocities.

Improved cases exhibit little stretching; they were trimmed once after initial fireforming. A sectioned case that has been fired nine times does not show any loss of brass forward of the web. When primers start seating too easily after about the eighth or ninth firing, it is a sign that cases have had it. As this occurred, the cases were discarded.

All things being equal, if you start from scratch and buy a Browning Model 71 rifle or carbine, it will cost you about $50 more (the cost of rechambering) to have a cartridge that gives a 28 percent increase in striking energy over the .348 Winchester. Dies, bullets and brass will cost the same no matter which cartridge you choose (RCBS stocks dies for the .348 Improved [Ackley]).

Not to get too far afield, 1988 probably will be remembered in the gun world as the year Remington legitimized the .35 Whelen. It must be quite a cartridge because every shooting magazine has written glowing reports about this bolt-action cartridge. I have one note of interest for all admirers of the .35 Whelen. The .348 Improved (Ackley) and the .35 Whelen are almost ballistic twins.

Recent loading data in many shooting publications for the Whelen shows the 250-grain Speer spitzer bullet from a 22-inch barrel at 2,500 fps and 3,469 foot-pounds of energy. This produces 100-yard striking energies of 2,894 foot-pounds, which is better than the .348 Improved (Ackley) with any bullet weight or barrel length (only flatnose bullets can be used in this lever action rifle, which reduces downrange performance compared to spitzer bullets, which hold their velocities much better). Still most writers feel the roundnose or semi-roundnose is a better bullet for large game at close range. They usually are taken inside 200 yards and with its lower velocities this design will penetrate deeper than a spitzer.

The accompanying graph shows how the Ackley and Whelen cartridges compare at varying ranges with a 250-grain roundnose bullet in the Whelen at 2,500 fps and the 300-grain flatnose lead bullet at 2,300 fps in the .348 Improved (Ackley). The .35

.348 Improved (Ackley) vs. .35 Whelen
(Foot-pounds of energy)

	distance (yds)					
	0	50	100	150	200	250
.348 Improved (Ackley) (300 gr.)	3,469	2,980	2,550	2,175	1,850	1,574
.350 Whelen (250 gr.)	3,470	2,992	2,571	2,201	1,877	1,597

.348 Improved (Ackley)

bullet (grains)	charge (grains)	powder	velocity (fps)	remarks
jacketed bullets				
250 Barnes	IMR-4350	62.0	2,332	good starting load
		65.0	2,403	1 inch
		66.0	2,420	1.5 inches, maximum
	IMR-4895	55.0	2,247	poor accuracy–mild
		58.0	2,382	2 inches
		60.0	2,413	1 inch, maximum
	H-4831	66.0	2,352	2 inches, starting load
		70.0	2,362	1.5 inches
	AAC-3100	66.0	2,353	1 inch
		69.0	2,376	.75 inch
		70.0	2,412	.75 inch, maximum
	IMR-4064	52.0	2,206	2.5 inches, starting load
		54.0	2,367	1 inch
		57.0	2,407	1.5 inches, maximum
200 Hornady	IMR-4350	67.0	2,482	2 inches
		68.0	2,535	1.625 inches
		69.0	2,526	2.5 inches, maximum
220 Barnes	IMR-4350	63.0	2,284	1.5 inches
		65.0	2,452	1.25 inches
cast bullets				
250 LBT	IMR-3031	50.0	2,253	1.25 inches, mild
		52.0	2,289	1.5 inches*
	IMR-4350	63.0	2,300	1.25 inches, mild
		64.0	2,321	1 inch*
	IMR-4895	57.0	2,337	1.25 inches, mild
		58.0	2,376	1.75 inches
		59.0	2,416	1 inch*
	AAC-3100	68.0	2,289	1.25 inches
		69.0	2,296	2 inches
		70.0	2,310	1.25 inches
	IMR-4064	52.0	2,184	1.25 inches
		53.0	2,245	1.25 inches*
300 Hoch	IMR-4350	63.0	2,266	1 inch
		64.0	2,305	1 inch, best hunting load
	AAC-3100	66.0	2,174	.75 inch
		68.0	2,247	1 inch, compressed

* Designates maximum velocity before poor accuracy occurs but is not a maximum load with this bullet.
Notes: CCI-200 Large Rifle primers used in all loads. Cases trimmed to 2.144 inches after fireforming.

Warning: All loads should be approached with caution due to rifles' individual variations in chamber and throat dimensions; case lengths; powder lots; and many other variables and loading techniques. Custom-made bullet moulds will vary as to dimensions and location of crimping grooves.

Be alert — Publisher cannot accept responsibility for errors in published load data.

Whelen jacketed bullets are .358 inch in diameter and the .348 Improved (Ackley) cast bullets are .350 inch.

To determine just how popular the .348 Improved (Ackley) is (or was), Bill Keyes at RCBS was contacted. It was here that my ego suffered a slight setback. Bill informed me that RCBS sold only 12 sets of dies for this cartridge in 1987, 12 in 1988 and nine in 1989. He feels that with the cost of an original Winchester Model 71 being what it is today, very few people want to rechamber the rifle and ruin its collector's value.

Bill said that years back, when the price of a Winchester Model 71 was reasonable, the Improved cartridge enjoyed a fair amount of popularity. He also believes that with Browning putting another 9,000 standard grade Model 71 rifles and carbines on the market, fans of the lever action will again discover the .348 Improved (Ackley). ●

CHAPTER 14

.35

By Maj. George C. Nonte

Are Thirty-Five calibers
BRUSH BUSTERS?

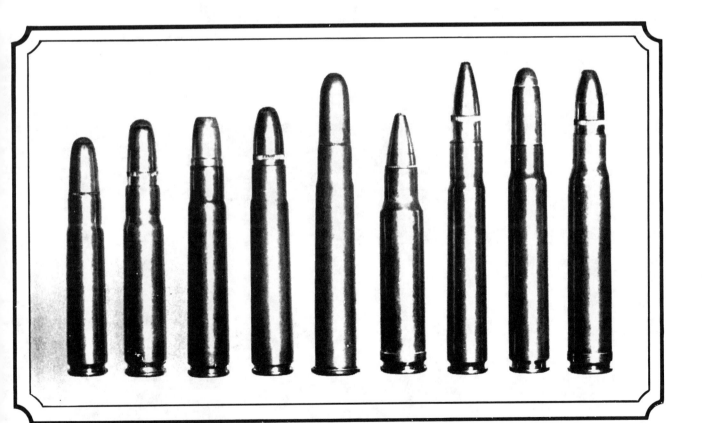

A THIRTY-FIVE CALIBER PORTRAIT

Left to right: .35 Remington, .358 Winchester, 9.3 x 57mm Mauser, 9mm Mannlicher, .35 WCF, .350 Remington Magnum, .35 Whelen, 9.3 x 62mm, and .358 Norma Magnum

THERE'S A LOT TO BE SAID for relatively large, heavy bullets at moderate velocities, regardless of what the lightning-strike boys claim for their 4,000 fps loads. Commonly, calibers in this category are called "brush-busters" because of a much-overrated capability for plowing through all manner of creepers, vines, twigs and even small saplings without being deviated from their original course.

As a group, such cartridges and loads are probably best represented by the .35 calibers that have been developed over the years. Dating back to the long-discontinued Model 1895 Winchester in .35 W.C.F., the many .35's have an excellent reputation for deep penetration, good expansion, and quick one-shot kills on our heaviest game. Guns chambered for them have been of all persuasions; pump, lever, self-loading, bolt, and single shot. Today only levers and bolts are offered as new guns, but there are plenty of the others to be had from used-gun racks all over the country.

To be more specific, new domestic bolt guns are available in .350 Remington Magnum caliber, and Marlin still makes its long-lived M336 in .35 Remington. Only a few years back Winchester quit producing the M70 in .358 Winchester, and some years before that terminated production of the fine old M71 in .348 Winchester caliber. Remington, for a time, chambered both the M740 and M760 series for the .35 Remington.

As a result, fresh factory ammunition is still produced in .358 and .348 Winchester, and .35 and .350 Remington Magnum. One other .35 cartridge, the old .351 Winchester Self-Loading Rifle is also still in production, primarily because of its wide use in M1907 rifles by law enforcement agencies.

Because of its quite low velocity and energy levels, we won't give the .351 much space here. It is, however, easily reloaded to factory-level performance and will do a fair job on medium game at close ranges. A look at the accompanying tables will show clearly why it doesn't come up to scratch with the other .35's.

Among the discontinued .35's we have the .35 Winchester, 9mm Mauser and 9mm Mannlicher, and a host of even earlier black powder numbers we won't even talk about at this time. Ammunition is available only from shops spe-

CAST LOADS FOR THE .35's			
Caliber	Bullet Wt./No.	Powder Wt./No.	Velocity fps
.351 Win	170/350319	19/4227	1,904
.35 Rem.	150/358430	39/3031	2,217
9mm Mann.	247/358318	38/3031	1,950
9mm Mauser	247/358318	38/3031	1,950
.35 Win.	247/358318	48/4320	2,200
.358 Win.	206/358315	40/3031	2,155
.348 Win.	187/350482	37/3031	2,338
.350 Rem. Mag.	206/358315	50/3031	2,298
9.3 x 62mm	282/35318/OS	53/3031	2,400
.358 N. Mag.	247/358318	19/Unique	1,658
9.3 x 64mm	282/35318/OS	56/4064	2,400
.35 Whelen	247/358318	50/3031	2,300

cializing in the obsolete. Cases are easily formed, though, so obtaining the cartridges you need doesn't present any real problems.

Then, of course, we have the bruising .358 Norma Magnum. By all rights it must be included, though neither guns nor ammunition are produced in this country. No less than a half-dozen foreign-made rifles for it are easily obtained here, and Norma's ammunition is widely distributed. It's a popular cartridge, and I might at this point make a cutting remark about domestic manu-

facturers who won't chamber rifles for a cartridge not produced here at home—but I won't.

Among foreign entries the 9.3 x 62mm has a case quite similar to the .30-06/.35 Whelen. The more-potent 9.3 x 64mm holds a lot more powder in a true rimless case whose diameter is about the same as the belted magnums. Both are fine cartridges; ammunition and bolt rifles are produced abroad and are imported here.

Discounting the .351, what do the

Proof that the .35's can be deflected sufficiently to cause a "miss" when shooting in brush country. Even the .50 BMG would be deflected—though slightly.

A handful of different .35's that "missed the mark," deflected by light brush.

.35 LOADING DATA (Jacketed Bullets)				
Caliber	Bullet	Powder	Velocity	Energy
.351 Win. S.L.R.	180 Fact.	19/4227	1,750	1,224
.35 Rem.	150	35/RL-7	2,450	2,000
	200	33/RL-7	2,175	2,100
9mm Mauser	275	46/4064	2,050	2,565
9mm Mannlicher	275	43/3031	2,010	2,466
.35 Win.	200	51/3031	2,465	2,700
	250	49/3031	2,320	2,987
	250	49/3031	2,230	2,987
.358 Win.	200	52/H335	2,530	2,840
	220	48/BL-C(2)	2,460	2,954
	250	44.5/4895	2,250	2,810
.348 Win.	200	53/4895	2,500	2,776
.350 Rem. Mag.	200	60/BL-C(2)	2,800	3,482
	220	56/4895	2,650	3,429
	250	54/4895	2,500	3,470
	275	59/H380	2,350	3,371
.35 Whelen	180 Speer	55/4198	2,950	3,490
	200	59/3031	2,780	3,450
	250	54/3031	2,510	3,500
	275	56/4064	2,370	3,454
	300 Barnes	60/4350	2,300	3,538
9.3 x 62mm	232 Norma	62/4320	2,640	3,550
	286 Norma	53/3031	2,360	3,530
.358 Norma	200	79/4350	2,941	3,838
	250	79/4350	2,825	4,510
	275	68/4350	2,690	4,429
9.3 x 64mm	286 Norma	58/4064	2,400	3,660

.35's have to offer? Well, beginning with the .35 Remington, they run the gamut from 150-grain bullets at 2,400 fps and 1,920 fp energy up to the 9.3 x 64mm's 293-grain ball at 2,790 fps and 4,322 fp energy. Put another way, performance ranges from the level of the .30-30 to beyond that of the .375 H&H Magnum; or, from suitability for small white tail deer to the largest of the world's thin-skinned game.

It is easily seen that except for varmints and small game (the latter need which can easily be handled by reduced cast-bullet loads), the .35's as a group will handle just about anything you might ever want to tackle. However, generally speaking, only at moderate ranges. In weights under 250 grains, that large-diameter bullet doesn't have high enough ballistic coefficient and sectional density to retain velocity very well. It slows down fast, all the more so since most of the bullets available are much closer to round-nose than spitzer form.

Of the present crop, the Speer 250-grain pointed bullet is the best bet for long range work in those cases that have the powder capacity to drive it up around 2,500 fps and more. Speer and Hornady both once furnished nicely-pointed 257-grain .35 bullets which were my personal choice for reaching way out—but they have been discontinued now for some time. Driven at around 2,700 fps in the .358 Norma Magnum, their trajectories were as flat over 300 yards as the factory .30-06 180-grain loads, and were great wind-buckers.

As for powders, the various .35's are quite tolerant. Except for the heaviest bullets in the largest cases, fast-to-medium burning-rate powders such as RL-7, 3031, 4895, and 4064 produce the best pressure-velocity ratios and, in full-charge loads, generally fill the cases very nearly full to the base of the seated bullet. Only the big .358 Norma and the 9.3 x 64mm Brenneke really have the boiler room to take advantage of powders as slow as 4350 and H4831.

Before confusing the issue further, I really should point out that not all the cartridges listed run *true* .35 caliber As any handloader worth a busted cap knows full well, a true .35 has a nominal barrel bore diameter of .350, with a barrel groove and bullet diameter of .357-.358-inch. Four cartridges on our list don't quite fit that specification, but they come so close that we must in all fairness include them. The .351 Winchester S.L.R. is actually .34½ caliber, with a bullet and groove diameter of .350-.351; the .348 Winchester is .34 caliber, with a bore of .340 and groove and bullet diameter of .348-.349; while the two 9.3mm rounds are actually .36 caliber with bullets and grooves measuring .366-.367.

As would be expected, there is no dearth of readily available bullets for the true .35's. The .351, though, is limited to the single factory type (180 grains) turned out by each of the major ammo producers. The .348 is in exactly the same position, since demand isn't sufficient for the independent bullet maker to give it much attention. Only Hornady makes one, and it's in the same 200-grain weight as the factory loads. In 9.3mm, you'll be restricted to the products of Norma and Speer/DWM, which isn't at all bad, since both offer bullets of the proper weight and construction to duplicate those hot factory loads.

All except the largest of the .35's operate at relatively low velocities—low enough that in many instances they can be equalled or approached with good, cast, gas-check lead bullets. This means simply that you can duplicate factory ballistics with cast bullets costing next to nothing, thus avoiding the expense of those seven-cents-each jacketed types. Lyman has offered a wide selection of moulds suitable for all the calibers listed, even under and over-size variations. All manner of weights are available from the very short, light pistol bullets (suitable only for squib loads) on up to the neighborhood of 300 grains. And, believe me, a 300-grain .35 bullet packs a hell of a wallop, even if it is moving only a bit over 2,000 fps. In fact, one of my favorite loads was for many years a linotype metal 300-grain bullet loaded to 2,200 fps in a fine old M1917 Enfield .35 Whelen.

Of course, not just any old cast bullet will do to match factory velocities. First and foremost it must be of the correct weight and of gas check design. Added to that, it must be cast of quite a hard alloy to stand the stress of over 2,000 fps. You can mix all manner of special alloys, but you'll not beat straight linotype metal obtainable from your local printing shop. It has the right hardness just as it is. Naturally bullets must be well cast, and sized concentrically to the correct diameter—

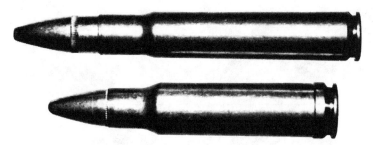

The .35 Whelen, above, and the .35 Remington Magnum can be loaded to near identical performance. The short case suffers in powder capacity with long heavy bullets.

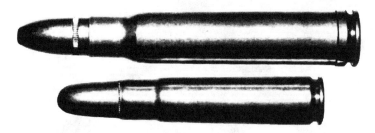

The .358 Norma Magnum, above, and the .35 Remington (with its .30-30 level ballistics) span the .35 caliber performance range.

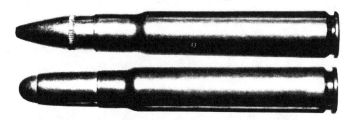

Cases for the .35 Whelen (a necked-up .30-06) and the 9.3 x 62 are similar, as is performance. The Whelen is better to reload due to a longer neck, for better bullet selection.

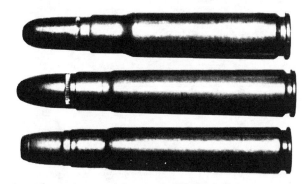

Similar in performance, top to bottom: .358 Winchester, 9mm Mannlicher and 9mm Mauser. The Winchester is a true .35 (of .357-.358 bore) while the 9.3's are .366-.367.

Winchester's .35 rounds, top to bottom: .358 Winchester, .348 Winchester and .35 WCF. None are currently offered in new domestic rifles.

which is usually barrel groove diameter or just a hair over. And the gas checks must fit tightly.

Lubricant can be more important than most people realize. Almost any good grease will keep the bore from leading, but accuracy often won't be too much. It has been rather well proven by now that the Alox-base bullet lubes usually produce the best accuracy, so don't handicap yourself and the rifle by trying wierd concoctions; stick with a proven winner.

We've appended a separate table showing cast-bullet loads which come very close (in *most* instances) to matching factory-load ballistics. The loads shown aren't the only ones that will do that, but they are the ones with which we are familar. And, all of those shown have given good accuracy. A little minor adjustment of powder charge might do a wee mite better in some rifles, but that's something you'll have to check out for yourself. Note that one wildcat, the .35 Whelen, is included. There is a host of others in .35 bore, but none have achieved the wide acceptance and standardization of the Whelen, so aren't mentioned here.

As far as deer-size or smaller game is concerned, a well-placed shot with one of those lead loads shown will kill just as quickly and surely as an expensive jacketed soft-point. This is true primarily because of the large cross-sectional area of the bullet. Even with-out expanding (and some expansion *will* take place) a .35 makes as big a hole as many of the smaller calibers after expansion. And, penetration is usually deeper. After all, our great-grandfathers killed *all* of their game with lead bullets traveling a lot slower than many of the loads listed.

At the beginning of this dissertation we mentioned the muchly overrated "brush busting" ability of this particular class of cartridges. First of all, don't ask me how the story got started that large, heavy, round-nose bullets would plow through all sorts of interference without deviating from their original line of flight. In spite of the fact that many tests which prove otherwise have been publicized over the past couple of decades (including some work done by yours truly), the idea persists. It just won't die. Maybe it's just one of those *apparent* pieces of logic falling back on the "bigger is better" theory subscribed to by so many people in all areas of interest.

The fact is, *any* significant external force applied to a bullet will affect its flight to the extent that it will be turned from its path to *some* degree. The point to which and the angle at which the force is applied has a good bit to do with the effect, as does the degree of stability the bullet possesses at that instant. But, when a bullet strikes an object such as a twig or handful of leaves, it *is* going to be turned from its course a bit. I have personally shot every caliber from .22 Short up through the .50 Browning MG through all manner of brush and *all* were diverted to some degree.

Generally, the faster the bullet is traveling, all other factors being equal, the more it will be deflected by striking brush and the more likely it is to "blow" on the brush. Therein may lie some of the reason for the wide belief that larger calibers cruise through brush well—they usually aren't driven as fast as the smaller calibers. Drive a 275-grain .35 at 2,800 fps and it is just as likely as a .30 at the same speed to go spinning end-over-end off at a 45-degree angle to its original path. *If* you could drive a .35 as fast as a .22-250, it would blow up just as violently. I've seen this proven quite spectacularly with high-velocity 20mm and 25mm cannon whose projectiles were traveling only a hair under 4,000 fps.

So, tradition and old wives' tales notwithstanding, there is no such thing as a caliber or cartridge that will plow through an acre of brush and still be depended upon to hit what you aimed at behind the bushes.

Fine versatile big-game cartridges though they be, the .35's aren't guaranteed brush-buckers. They behave just like any other small arms projectile when they meet something between you, the unerring marksman, and the target. Keep that in mind and they'll serve you long and well. ●

CHAPTER
15

Layne Simpson

To develop *super* .35 Remington loads, Layne used this Model 760 Remington pump with a scope. He developed regular .35 Remington loads in this iron-sighted Model 14-C Remington pump. Both are quick-handling woods rifles.

THE MUSIC of the five Plott hounds was drowned out by the creek that was cascading down the mountain, but I knew that the pack had our quarry at bay by now. The strike dog had led off on a hot trail just after daybreak, and for a little over five hours, I had been hot-footing over hill and dale as fast as the steep terrain and jungle of laurel would let me.

There had been nine other hunters when we started, but age and rough country had taken their toll. I was the youngest, now the only one left with the hounds and — if the size of its track meant anything — one very large black bear. I had long used up a hearty breakfast and by now was one tired fellow, but I figured that the bear was slowing down, too. It had already made a couple of stands, the first battle scene marked by a good-sized piece of ground torn to shreds. The second time that it had turned to face its pursuers, it had cut the odds a bit to its favor — by the extent of one up-and-coming but foolish pup left behind with one side of its rib cage torn away.

I knew the country well and in fact had pulled a few trout from this very stream just a few weeks earlier. If the bear had continued straight on for another quarter of a mile and crossed Green River, it probably would have shaken us from its trail for a while — but it had instead doubled back up Canebrake Creek. But I knew that through the centuries, water had carved a deep channel through the rock, forming steep banks up to twenty feet high on either side of the channel. I also knew that any travel up this creek had to stop about two thirds of the way up — at a roaring waterfall.

When I got there, the bear was on a mossy outcrop of rock, with the hounds a dozen feet or so below. The roar of the waterfall covered all

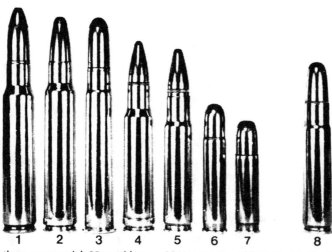

Unlike these commercial .35 cartridges — .35 Newton (1), .358 Norma Magnum (2), .35 Winchester (3), .350 Remington Magnum (4), .358 Winchester (5), .351 Winchester (6), and .35 Winchester Self Loading (7) — the .35 Remington (8) has withstood the passing of time and the ever-changing whims of American hunters.

Remington

sound of my approach. A huge chestnut tree, felled by blight many years before, had slid down the steep creek bank, forming a convenient cover for me. From behind the chestnut, I watched for a minute or two.

Occasionally, a hound got a rise out of the bear by backing off for a running start and leaping up the sheer rock to within inches of the bear. But other than taking a roundhouse swing at the hound and snapping its teeth to intimidate the others, the bear seemed to be bored with its situation. It soon grew restless and occasionally shuffled around and glanced downstream in my direction.

I eased back the hammer on my carbine and aimed high on the bear's shoulder, but just as the hammer began to drop, the bear swung at one of the hounds. My shot went into its lungs. As the bear whirled to face me, I planted another two-hundred-grain Core-Lokt bullet square in the middle of the white patch on its chest. I doubt that the two shots spanned more than three seconds; they certainly took less time than the telling. The bear scattered the hounds one last time as its limp body splashed into the creek.

Back at camp, we combined the use of a cotton scale with estimates of the weight lost in field-dressing and came up with a live weight around four hundred twenty-five pounds. Where I come from, that's a rather hefty black bear.

The .35 Remington cartridge that I used to get that bear should have gone the way of the passenger pigeon and the dodo, if the laws of supply and demand had been operating the way we're taught that they do, through the fifty-four years between its introduction and the day that it ended that chase for me. In spite of its unimpressive paper ballistics, its field performance on that hunt and others since has been right spry for an old-timer. Even now, twenty-one years later, I still use it where the brush is thick, the shots are short, and the game is the size

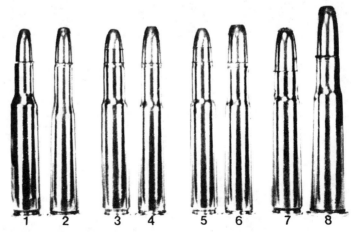

The .25 Remington (*1*) was the rimless rival of the .25-35 Winchester (*2*), just as the .30 Remington (*3*) was the Remington answer to the .30-30 (*4*), the .32 Remington (*5*) competed with the .32 Special (*6*), and the .35 Remington (*7*) was rival to the .35 Winchester (*8*). These rimless cartridges were first offered for the Model 8 rifle.

of deer. And even though a good assortment of belted superzappers are available, that's still .35 Remington country to more than a few hunters besides me.

Late in 1905, the Belgian firm Fabrique Nationale d'Armes de Guerre introduced a recoil-operated autoloading rifle designed and patented by John

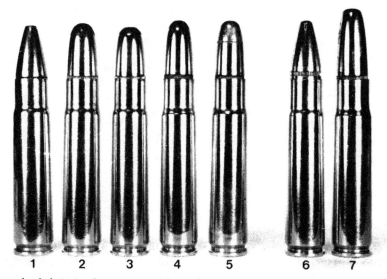

With the 200-grain Hornady bullet seated out for Layne's Model 88 Winchester, the .358 Winchester (3) has only slightly more powder capacity than the .35 Remington with the 250-grain Hornady round-nose (1) or the 200-grain Hornady spire-point (2).

M Browning. Meanwhile, Remington had negotiated the United States manufacturing rights for this design and in 1906 introduced the Remington Model 8 rifle. The two versions were practically identical, but FN's had a solid rib atop the barrel jacket, and the forearm and curved grip were checkered. The Remington had a plain barrel, straight grip, and no checkering.

Three of the four cartridges introduced with the Model 8 — the .25 Remington, .30 Remington, and .32 Remington — were almost identical in performance with Winchester's rimmed .25-35, .30-30, and .32 Special, but Remington's cartridges were rimless for functioning through the autoloader. But there were some larger calibers still popular, among them the .33 and .35 Winchesters. Probably in answer to these, Remington

came up with the .35 Remington. The .35 Winchester was slightly more powerful, but the .33 Winchester and the .35 Remington were essentially identical in performance.

In *Handloader 82*, Charles Suydam mentions similarities between the .35 Remington and the 9x56mm Mannlicher cartridges. After examining an FN autoloader chambered for the 9x56mm, I am left with little doubt about where Remington got the idea for their thirty-five. Whatever their inspiration, they made a good move in introducing this cartridge. Not only has it far outlasted its smaller siblings — the .35 Remington and the .30-30 Winchester are the oldest commercially developed cartridges that continue to be used so much by hunters that they can be considered still popular.

Some may wonder why this little thirty-five has survived the advance of time, the fickle whims of American hunters, and stiff competition from cartridges with more glamor and power. The .358 Winchester and the .350 Remington Magnum are two good examples of cartridges that might have obsoleted the .35 Remington if the multitude of hunters had been in the appropriate mood. On paper and on game, those two great cartridges make the old Remington rimless thirty-five look somewhat like a Nash Rambler toiling around the curves at LeMans. But there are good reasons for its longevity.

First, it was introduced in a firearm that even today is one of the finest and most dependable autoloaders ever used for taking buck, bull, or bruin in the timber. And this rifle became even better in 1936 when Remington beefed-up its forearm, curved its grip, and changed its designation from *Model 8* to *Model 81*. I might add that this opinion comes from something more than mere hearsay or stacks of old gun magazines, since my old Model 81 continues to kill deer as though the gas-operated autoloaders had never come into vogue.

As if to show that if one is good then two are sometimes better, in 1914, Remington added their thirty-five to the choice of chambers for their two-year-old Model 14, a quick and slick pump-action rifle that still does quite well in thick cover. Through the years, there have been other rifles in the history of the .35 Remington, such as the better-forgotten Standard pump-autoloader, the Stevens lever-action and Models 30 and 70 bolt-actions, and most notably the Marlin lever-action. Marlin deserves a good deal of credit for keeping the cartridge popular. I have

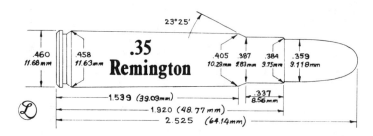

Factory-loaded .35 Remington ammunition with 150-grain (1) and 200-grain Remington (2), Federal (3), and Winchester (4, 5) bullets are about as hot as the weaker rifles can be safely used with, but the stronger front lock-up of the Remington Model 760 allows use of handloads with the 200-grain Remington (6) and 250-grain Hornady (7) at much higher velocities. The dimensions in the cartridge drawing below are from SAAMI specifications.

long thought that Winchester was missing a good thing by neglecting to chamber the Model 94 for it.

In 1950, the .35 Remington lost some ground with the discontinuance of the Remington Model 141 but regained some in the new Model 760 two years later. A crushing blow came in 1954 when the new Model 740 self-loader replaced the Model 81 without including the .35 Remington as one of its options. In 1965, Remington dropped the .35 Remington from even the Model 760, leaving only the Marlin Model 336 available factory-chambered for the cartridge.

Possibly, when the fine little Model 600 carbine was introduced, Remington could have given their thirty-five the same name-change treatment that they have used on their .244

and .280 Remingtons. Factory loads could have been increased somewhat, but they opted for the .350 Remington Magnum — I suppose because of so many older rifles still being used in .35 Remington.

What does the .35 Remington have that enables it to survive in the face of such competition? For one, it has been available mostly in rifles suited for a huge share of the kind of big-game hunting that most of us do: hunting game the size of deer, at close range. Also, the cartridge itself has a few other attributes that almost guarantee that it will be around for quite a while.

Whatever you may hear in hairy-chested hunting-camp yarns, the recoil that the average hunter can tolerate is

The magazine box of the Model 760 is long enough for bullets as long as the 250-grain Hornady to be loaded in the .35 Remington, without even the filler block taken out.

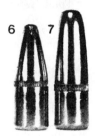

For weaker .35 Remington rifles, the 150-grain Remington (1), 180-grain Speer (2), and 200-grain Remington (3), Sierra (4), and Hornady (5) are the best bullets, while the 200-grain Remington spire-point (6) and 250-grain Hornady (7) can be loaded to higher velocities in such strong rifles as the Model 760 Remington — taking full advantage of spire-point bullets and heavier bullets.

super .35 Remington loads

These loads exceed the 35,000 *cup* SAAMI maximum for this cartridge and are to be used only in strong rifles such as Remington Models 760 and 600 or Winchester Model 70. Even when loading for these rifles, reduce top charges by ten percent for beginning loads.

bullet	type	powder	charge (gr)	velocity (fps)
250 Hornady	round-nose	WW-748	40.0	2,061
		WW-748	39.0	2,008
		IMR-4320	38.0	2,045
		N-202	37.0	2,010
200 Remington	round-nose	N-202	43.5	2,373
		N-202	43.0	2,345
		N-202	42.0	2,308
200 Sierra	round-nose	IMR-4320	44.0	2,366
		IMR-4320	43.0	2,326
		IMR-4320	42.0	2,274
200 Hornady	round-nose	H-335	43.0	2,395
		H-335	42.0	2,339
		H-335	41.0	2,297
200 Hornady	spire-point	WW-748	46.0	2,304
		WW-748	45.0	2,267
		WW-748	44.0	2,256
200 Remington	spire-point	RL-7	37.0	2,380
		RL-7	36.0	2,347
		RL-7	35.0	2,283
180 Speer	flat-nose	RL-7	37.5	2,420
		RL-7	37.0	2,363
150 Remington	spire-point	RL-7	38.5	2,543

Remington Model 760, twenty-two-inch barrel, sixteen-inch twist, Remington 9½ primers, Remington cases, average temperature 88 degrees Fahrenheit, instrumental velocity at fifteen feet corrected to muzzle velocity.

.35 Remington

bullet	type	powder	charge (gr)	velocity (fps)
200 Sierra	round-nose	WW-748	41.5	2,073
		IMR-4064	39.0	2,045
		IMR-4320	38.5	2,069
		IMR-4895	37.5	2,071
		IMR-3031	36.0	2,061
200 Remington	round-nose	N-202	39.0	2,044
		BL-C(2)	39.0	2,051
		H-4895	37.0	2,048
		H-335	37.0	2,051
		RL-7	33.0	2,082
180 Speer	flat-nose	WW-748	42.0	2,144
		N-202	40.0	2,132
		IMR-3031	38.0	2,119
		H-335	38.0	2,168
		RL-7	33.5	2,151
150 Remington	spire-point*	IMR-4320	42.0	2,266

factory loads

bullet				velocity
200 Remington Core-Lokt				1,912
200 Federal Hi-Shok				1,930
200 Winchester Silvertip				1,933
200 Winchester Power-Point				1,876
150 Remington Core-Lokt				2,226

* spire-point bullet single-loaded directly in chamber, *not through tubular magazine*

Remington Model 14, twenty-two-inch barrel, sixteen-inch twist, Remington 9½ primers, Remington cases, average temperature 88 degrees Fahrenheit, instrumental velocity at fifteen feet corrected to muzzle velocity

well below twenty foot-pounds of recoil energy — possibly even below fifteen. This puts a light carbine chambered for the .35 Remington at about the upper limit of acceptable shoulder punishment for the once-a-year deer hunter who wants to use heavier bullets than he can get in a .30-30 or .32 Special.

Cartridges with higher velocities — the .300 Savage, for example — kill deer quicker, but the .35 Remington does the job just as well with the proper bullet placement at woods ranges. Its reliable performance comes in good part from the ammunition manufacturers who have loaded the cartridge with exactly the kind of bullet that help the thirty-five do its best on white-tails — those with generous exposure of lead. I have found that both the Core-Lokt and the Power Point two-hundred-grains have the killing power to perform on game exactly the way that they are supposed to. I have no field experience with Sierra, Hornady, or Federal two-hundreds or the Speer one-eighty, but — according to their performance in my recovery box — they should all be superb on deer, with lung placement.

Many hunters have to consider the economics of their hunting when they choose new rifles, and about the least expensive way to get into white-tail hunting is to buy a rifle chambered for a mild cartridge. Back in the Fifties, I often went to sleep at night mentally watching myself drop all manner of big game with a Model 88 Winchester or a Model 99 Savage. But a Marlin Model 336 sporting carbine and two boxes of thirty-fives just about cleaned out my cache in the old coffee can. Then all of a sudden, four other rifles in my battery — an '03 and a trap-door Springfield, a 7.7mm Arisaka, and a .303 British jungle carbine — sat gathering dust as the leaves turned brown. The little Marlin was exactly what I had been looking for, and for the kind of hunting that was open to me in those days, it filled my needs perfectly.

An indication of exactly what I think of this cartridge is the fact that during more than twenty-five years of hunting deer, I have seen only two seasons pass without my owning a rifle chambered for it. Nowadays, with hunting more crowded in a few of the places where I hunt, I more often choose a cartridge with a bit more stay-down punch that shoots flatter over cultivated fields. But even so, I don't believe that I would be comfortable without a .35 Remington around. This thirty-five has never let me down when I pulled my end of the saw, so I figure that I'd rather have it and not need it than want it and not have it.

Just to be safe in the matter, I have two. One, a C-grade Model 14 Remington, replaces a Model 141 that was longer, heavier, and less trim. It is easy and handy to carry, and it comes to the shoulder with the pointing of a fine shotgun when I have to hurry a shot. The other is a Model 760 that Remington turned out (in this chambering, in limited numbers) in 1979, evidently to test the market one more time. I assume that the response from deer hunters fell too far short of a stampede to gun shops, since the thirty-five was once more dropped.

Few cartridges of such an age have made it so far without having established some sort of reputation. As far as I know, the .35 Remington's is a good one, at least among those of us who have used it for the purpose that it was meant to be used for. But there are some fallacies about this cartridge floating around.

I'll dispel one with a statement that might have caused a great gnashing of teeth, some years back, from the Adirondacks to the Everglades — except among those who have some experience with this cartridge and others like it: if any difference in killing power between the 170-grain .30-30 and .32 Special and the .35 Remington were somehow converted into TNT and packed into the nostrils of a chipmunk, it would do a poor job of blowing the little animal's nose.

Although I have never had occasion to prove it, I suspect that at ranges beyond where the bullets from these cartridges expand, the larger thirty-five punches a slightly larger hole. But this is quite academic to me, since few deer are taken with these cartridges past a hundred paces, and most are dropped at half that distance or less.

For this reason, I doubt that many could detect any difference in the wound channels made by any of these three cartridges. If anything, the .30 and .32 bullets (170-grains) would be preferable for deeper penetration on quartering shots because of their higher sectional density. Performance of all these cartridges is in the same class and in the hands of a cool shot who doesn't get rattled in the presence of game, any of the three can be depended on to get the job done. I must also add that as these three are loaded by the factories, they are all greatly overshadowed in killing power by such cartridges as the .300 Savage, .308 Winchester, and .358 Winchester simply because of the differences in their velocities — which gets me down to fallacy number two.

Some who have written about the .35 Remington flatly declare that handloading it is a sinful waste of time,

since the effort produces no advantage over shooting factory loads. With the old, weaker rifles such as the pumps, lever-actions, and autoloaders, this is almost true. Factory loads are generally accurate enough and loaded almost as hot as they need be for these rifles, but beyond this limit, such a statement is dead wrong.

I have been told that in 1955, when gun writers were making loud noises about the effectiveness of Winchester's new .358 cartridge, its performance was old hat to those who had already recognized the potential of the .35 Remington in rifles with locking lugs at the front of the bolt. When the .35 Remington was handloaded to the higher velocites possible with the Model 760 — which had been on the scene for some three years — there wasn't enough difference between the two cartridges to cause an exodus to the local dealers offering the .358 Winchester. Since the Model 760 was also available in .270 Winchester, one of the hottest factory loads, it made sense that the Model 760 made it possible to improve the performance of the .35 Remington.

After my own tests with one of these rifles, I find that indeed it is possible to improve the performance of the .35 Remington, and safely, but it is not possible to make the older thirty-five equal the newer one — not within two hundred feet per second — without raising pressures too high.

Although I have seen moose and elk bagged with cartridges in the .30-30 class, I have never considered them suitable for game this large except under ideal conditions — which, I might add, seem to get scarcer each year. But when it is souped-up, in one of the stronger actions and with the Hornady 250-grain round-nose bullet, the .35 Remington reaches a new level of performance, and it just might work at woods ranges if put to such a task.

Loaded to its full potential in stronger rifles, the .35 Remington can push the 250-grain bullet about as fast as safe loads in the older and weaker rifles permit driving the two-hundred-grain. Such a load with the 250-grain delivers over sixteen hundred foot-pounds of energy at a hundred yards. More important: its sectional density of 0.279 gives the heavier 250-grain much better potential for deep penetration — a distinct asset if moose or elk is on the hunter's list.

There might be a problem lurking in the fact that the 250-grain bullet may not expand well enough, since it was designed for higher impact velocities typical of the larger-cased thirty-fives. Perhaps this potential drawback could be eliminated by drilling about an eighth-inch cavity into the nose and cutting fracture lines through the nose of the jacket with a three-cornered file. It would certainly be interesting to find out how this would work on game.

Still, I have to admit that the days are long gone when a great number of hunters would choose this cartridge for elk or moose. But to those deer hunters who shoulder Model 760s and head into country intermixed with both thick brush and open spaces, let me send this tip: take note of what this cartridge can do with the two-hundred-grain bullet, whether it be the round-nose or the spire-point style.

Sight-in the two-hundred-grain factory load to hit two inches high at a hundred yards, and it's down about ten inches at two hundred with just over six hundred fifty foot-pounds of energy left. Push the same bullet to twenty-three hundred feet per second with handloads, which you can safely do in a strong rifle, and it's down five inches at two hundred yards, with close to a thousand foot-pounds of residual energy. For typical shots at deer at woods ranges — most often fifty yards

or less — this good cartridge is thus transformed into a better one. This load, by the way, packs over nineteen hundred foot-pounds of punch at fifty yards.

But one characteristic that has kept this cartridge from winning the favor of some shooters is its rainbow trajectory at longer ranges. Admittedly, such shots at white-tails are rare in comparison with the close ones, but the white-tail has adapted well to the encroachment of civilization upon its habitat. In this case, *civilization* means pastures and cultivated fields where game is sometimes spotted at a distance. This is where the round-nose bullet drops out of the running.

Switch to the two-hundred-grain spire-points made by Hornady — or Remington's, if you can find any; they're discontinued now — and the old thirty-five moves into the running with that classic deer cartridge, the .300 Savage: three inches high at a hundred yards and an inch low at two hundred, with a point-blank range of about two hundred fifty yards. Hornady's manual lists the residual energy at fourteen hundred foot-

pounds at two hundred yards. Compare that with six hundred sixty foot-pounds for the factory load — and, while we're at it, with fifteen hundred foot-pounds for a .300 Savage with a hundred-fifty-grain spitzer.

A .25-06 it is not and never will be — nor even a .257 Roberts — but one of those spitzer loads in the .35 Remington could save a bit of grief when a big buck steps out of the woods far across yon soybean field a mere five minutes before it's too dark to shoot.

The old warning to handloaders must of course be repeated here: never load spitzer bullets for rifles with tubular magazines, since their tips can fire the cartridges ahead of them in the magazine. Also, don't use any of the loads listed here for the Model 760 Remington in any of the weaker rifles (those with rear-lock-up systems). To do either of these two stunts is to court disaster.

But in a rifle such as the Remington Models 760 and 600 or those few Models 30 and 70 chambered for the .35 Remington, this fine old cartridge with good handloads has only gotten better as it has grown older. ●

CHAPTER
16

AL MILLER

Winchester's latest 94

... in .356

Model 94 XTR Angle Eject (AE). The Weaver scope mounts come with the gun, and keep the scope low. Upper left photo shows the repositioned extractor on the bolt's right side which flips empties to the right, permitting a receiver-mounted scope.

FOR MORE YEARS THAN I've been alive, hunters have been bombarding the folks at Winchester with pleas for more potent chamberings in the 94. Replies from factory reps were always polite, but negative: rear-locking actions had a limited potential; were one to be beefed up to withstand, say, 50,000 psi, the result would be heavy, cumbersome and probably unsaleable; the action was too short to accept any of the modern, high-intensity rounds anyway — and so on. There were always lots of reasons why the slab-sided little actions couldn't be modified or reinforced to accept hotter rounds.

Then, five years ago, the Big Bore 94

was introduced. Chambered for what was basically a souped-up .38-55, operating pressures for the new rifle and round, it was announced, were 50,000 psi. And they said it couldn't be done!

The only external differences between the Big Bore and the standard 94s were a slight thickening of the receiver walls around the locking lugs and the addition of a rubber recoil pad. In addition, the strengthened action was supplemented by the new round's case. The .375 Winchester hulls were markedly thicker than any of the .30-30 family brass. By combining stouter receiver

walls, tougher, modern steels and sturdier cartridge cases, the vintage action was able to accommodate the increased pressures without straining anything. Best of all, none of the characteristics which made the 94 the favorite deer rifle of so many generations were sacrificed. It was just as light, portable and responsive as ever. Not only that, but the new cartridge had considerably more punch than the .30-30 and its cousins. The Big Bore represented some clever and thoughtful engineering.

For 1983, the Big Bore has been replaced by a new, upgraded carbine officially designated the Model 94 XTR Angle Eject. The barrel stamp is simpler. It reads: Model 94AE XTR. Both emphasize what the designers evidently consider the carbine's outstanding feature — its ability to eject empty cases to the right instead of straight up.

The bolt was redesigned by moving the extractor. Instead of its usual position on top, it was shifted 90 degrees to the right. In addition, about a quarter-inch of steel was milled from the receiver beside it, just above the rail, to give fired cases plenty of clearance when they're flipped aside.

It also makes mounting a scope low

.35 caliber rifles and cartridges

cartridge	Winchester rifle	bullet weight (grains)	muzzle velocity (fps)	energy (ft/lb)	barrel length (inches)	rifle weight (pounds)
.35 Winchester	Model 95	250	2,195	2,670	24	8
.348 Winchester	Model 71	200	2,520	2,820	24	8-1/2
		250	2,320	2,980	24	
.358 Winchester	Model 88	200	2,490	2,753	22	7-3/4
		250	2,230	2,500		
.356 Winchester	Model 94AE	200	2,400	2,550	20	7
		250	2,150	2,570		

above the receiver practical. Judging from factory literature, the AE's makers believe this is a giant step forward for the 94. Perhaps. It seems to me, though, that the new chamberings are the real breakthrough. They lift the 94 right out of the deer rifle class. For the first time in their lengthy history, Winchester carbines have been endowed with the kind of range and power their fans have prayed for.

The AE is available in three calibers: .375 Winchester, .307 and .356. The latter two are slightly rimmed versions of the .308 and .358 respectively. Their operating pressures aren't supposed to exceed 50,000 psi, which makes them a shade tamer than their rimless sires — but far more powerful than any of the other rounds chambered by the 94s. The test carbine was in .356 caliber.

The new Winchester's designers must have been convinced that those who buy one will either use a scope or settle for the old fashioned open rear sight, for the receiver is not drilled and tapped for a receiver sight. They are probably right. I guess there are only a handful of diehards, like myself, who prefer a peep sight in the woods.

For those who intend to mount a scope, however, the AE comes completely equipped. There is a set of Weaver bases and quick-detachable rings included in the box. In addition, there's an offset hammer spur which can be installed to extend left or right, as the shooter wishes. That last is a must once a scope is in place. Talk about low! Unless a person has paper thin thumbs, he'll never be able to cock that hammer or release it.

Quick-detachable sling swivels complete the package. When snapped into place, the forward swivel dangles from the tubular magazine a couple of inches in front of the fore-end. The rear swivel is attached to the buttstock.

Had anyone asked me if a Monte

Carlo would look good on a stock without a pistol grip, I would have said "no," and I would have been right. The new carbines look humpbacked and unbalanced. Nevertheless, that big lump in the wood makes an extremely comfortable stock, no matter which shooting position is adopted. It gives the cheek plenty of support and puts the aiming eye right where it should be, whether glass or iron sights are used.

The buttstock's design encourages the carbine to recoil straight backward. Pitch is minimal and the comb slopes forward slightly, letting the wood back away from the cheek

The .356 barrel on the right is markedly thicker and stiffer than the standard .30-30 barrel on the left. Miller says the finish was better on the .356.

.356 Winchesters

bullet (grains)	charge (grains)	powder	velocity (fps)	remarks
250 Hornady RN	35	RL-7	2,066	Mediocre accuracy
250 Speer SP	46	748	2,134	1.5" groups
250 Hornady RN	42	4064	2,029	1-3/4" average
200 Hornady RN	49	748	2,272	1.5" groups; 60 fps extreme spread
200 Sierra RN	45	3031	2,377	Extreme spread 55 fps; 1-5/8" groups
200 Hornady Spirepoint	38	RL-7	2,351	Only fair accuracy
200 Hornady RN	47	4064	2,309	Extreme spread = 8 fps!
180 Speer	39	RL-7	2,465	1-3/4" groups
180 Speer	51	748	2,475	Fair accuracy
180 Speer	45	3031	2,414	2.0" groups
180 Speer Silhouette	40	H-4198	2,468	1-5/8" groups
158 Hornady	46	3031	2,503	2.5" groups
158 Hornady	50	4064	2,550	2.0" groups
158 Hornady	30	3031	1,716	.5 grain Dacron filler added. 1.5" groups; small-game load.
125 Sierra	46	3031	2,402	2.0" groups
125 Sierra	45	RL-7	2,956	2.0" Seating depth = .25"
Winchester factory load				
200 Power Point			2,360	
250 Power Point			2,115	

Velocities represent three-shot averages, measured on an Oehler Model 33 Chronotach, fifteen feet from the muzzle of a Winchester Model 94AE, with a 20-inch barrel. Ambient temperature: 85 degrees F. Winchester cases and Winchester Large Rifle primers used on all loads.

Left to right are the .35 caliber handgun bullets used for testing: 125-grain Sierra; 158-grain Hornady; 180-grain Speer Silhouette; and the 180-grain Speer soft-point.

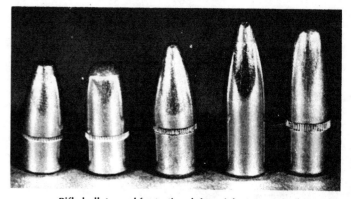

Rifle bullets used for testing, left to right: 180-grain flat-point; 200-grain Sierra round-nose; 200-grain Hornady spire-point; 250-grain Speer spitzer; and 250-grain Hornady round-nose.

instead of slamming into it whenever the hammer drops. Too bad it's not as pleasing to the eye as it is to shoulder and cheek.

The new 94 is about half a pound heavier than the standard model. Some of that heft can be blamed on the larger buttstock and reinforced receiver, but the bulk of it is in the barrel — at least, it is on the .356. The AE's tube is a millimeter thicker, all around, than an average .30-30's. That's a lot more steel than it sounds. Not only does that extra metal add ounces, but it makes a very stiff barrel — and an accurate one.

The carbine doesn't feel like a seven-pound rifle when it's carried, fortunately. Either through luck or clever engineering, those additional eight ounces weren't just tacked on, but distributed evenly over the entire arm. Consequently, this new 94 is just as responsive and quick-handling as any of its lighter ancestors. And although it packs a lot more power, it's just as pleasant to shoot as any .30-30 ever made.

Dimensionally, the only difference between the .356 and the .358 is the former's slightly wider rim (.003 inch, according to my micrometer) and shorter overall length (.1 inch). The rest of the hull's measurements are the same, as is case volume.

Just why the new round was endowed with that smidgen of a rim isn't clear. The test carbine accepted .358 cases as readily as .356s. Whether all the new carbines are that tolerant, I can't say, but every .358 empty was extracted without hesitation — even those which had contained factory-equivalent loads.

Factory .358 ammo wouldn't chamber, though. The Winchester rounds were just a tad too long to function through the action and remained trapped in the magazine. To ensure foolproof feeding, overall length of my handloads was set at 2.5 inches. That limited case volume a bit more than necessary, but it seemed to me that reliability was worth sacrificing thirty feet per second of muzzle velocity.

Reducing overall length that much also meant that most currently available bullets had to be seated with their cannelure below the case mouths. Even so, duplicating performance of factory ammunition with handloads proved perfectly feasible — and without generating excessive pressures, either.

Advertised ballistics for the .356 give the 200-grain Power Point 2,400 fps. The 250-grain PP is listed at 2,150 fps. Chronographed with an Oehler Model 33, fifteen feet from the carbine's muzzle, factory rounds fell about 50 fps short of that, but considering the 94's stubby barrel, that was close enough.

If my calculations are correct, the 200-grain Power Point will register about twenty-two foot-pounds of recoil in the seven-pound carbine. One of the 250-grainers will churn out twenty-three. In comparison, a seven-pound '06, firing 220-grain loads, would deliver 22½ pounds, so the AE should kick like an '06. Maybe it does, but thanks to that well-shaped stock, it sure doesn't feel like it.

At the moment, anyone in the market for .35-caliber round-nosed bullets doesn't have a whole lot to choose from. Sierra markets one weighing 200 grains while Hornady offers both a 200 and a 250-grainer. Tail-ending the list is Speer's 180-grain flat-nose, which has won quite a reputation for itself among whitetail hunters.

For small-game plinking or target practice, .38-caliber pistol slugs make ideal fodder for the .356. The stubby 125-grain flat-noses proved surprisingly accurate, even when pushed close to 3,000 fps. They'd be terribly destructive against flesh and bone, naturally, but one of them would be just the ticket for an annoying crow or a prowling fox with a yen for fresh chicken.

Speer's 180-grain silhouette special, backed by 40 grains of H-4198 might make a very satisfactory turkey load. Certainly it was accurate enough; with most four-shot strings spanning less than two inches at the hundred mark. How that coppery plated bullet would react to feathers and meat I can't predict, but it should be less destructive than the typical soft-nose.

Cast bullets are another option. A few preliminary loads looked very promising, but July is the wrong time to develop good, accurate cast-bullet loads. Barrels heat quickly and refuse to cool. Since hot barrels and cast bullets simply aren't compatible, I decided to wait until fall rolls around. Once temperatures become more reasonable, I'll see what the Angle Eject can do with alloy slugs.

Speaking of hot barrels, it took very few rounds to discover that, like most 94s, the .356 would string its bullets vertically if the barrel became too hot to hold. It's easy enough to remedy that situation, of course, but since the carbine wasn't mine, I thought it best not to file any metal from the barrel bands or try relieving the fore-end. The Winchester crew are pretty understanding, but they probably wouldn't appreciate some ham-handed character, like me, revamping one of their products.

As it turned out, I discovered the carbine would hold for four shots so I settled for that. Cooler air would probably allow five-shot groups without any modifications to the gun at all.

Accuracy was excellent from the beginning. Factory rounds averaged around two inches. Most handloads did better than that, usually punching out from 1.5 to 1.75 inches. Those results were obtained using a Burris 4x compact.

Some might not be impressed with those groups, but considering the 94's basic design was laid down almost a century ago, I found it remarkable. Despite its modernizing, this newest 94 still sports a barrel encircled by steel bands and that same old tubular magazine hangs below. Moreover, the old fashioned hammer is a constant reminder that lock time is nothing to get excited about. Neither was the test gun's trigger pull. It dragged, crept, grated, and worst of all, it resisted. It never improved with use, either. It was just as uncooperative at the end of the range tests as it was when the first round cracked downrange.

Indifferent lock time and the recalcitrant trigger notwithstanding, the Winchester was a very consistent performer. As long as the barrel remained reasonably cool, four-round strings ran from 1.5 to 2 inches, center to center.

Another barrel characteristic was its instant reaction to every change of bullet or powder. Every time a switch was made, the point of impact shifted. For example, 250-grain Winchester factory loads struck some ten inches lower than the factory 200-grainers at one hundred yards. Even bullets of the same weight, but different shapes, landed inches apart. Hornady 200-grain spire-points smacked three inches higher than the same marque's round-nosed 200-grainers when launched at the same muzzle velocities. Light bullets always struck higher than heavy ones. That, no doubt, can be attributed to the heavier than usual barrel.

Shooting spitzers in the 94, by the way, is perfectly feasible as long as no more than two rounds are loaded at a time: one in the chamber, the other in the magazine. Anyone hunting with a .356 in open country needn't hobble himself with aerodynamically inferior round-noses unless he chooses to.

Of the powders tried, WW-748 was the 94's first choice, both for accuracy and velocity. Reloder 7, on the other hand, proved extremely selective. Mated to the light pistol bullets, its accuracy was first class. When employed to back the heavier big-game bullets, its groups were no better than mediocre. The two DuPont powders were their usual dependable selves. IMR-3031 racked up slightly higher velocities, but as far as accuracy was concerned, it was a toss-up.

Hodgdon's H-4198 acted as though it had been made specifically for the 180-grain Speers — or vice versa. The majority of their four-shot groups spanned well under two inches.

Inevitably, the .356 will be compared to its parent, the .358. The elder round, of course, is slightly more potent, but if both were fired from barrels of equal length, any differences between them wouldn't amount to much.

Like its sire, flexibility is the .356's middle name. It can be loaded all the way down to duplicate .38 Special performance, or that of the .357 or the new .357 Maximum — or even the old .35 Remington — take your pick. Jacketed pistol slugs make a deadly pest rifle out of the Angle Eject, too. All it takes is a little imaginative hand-loading and a guy would have a carbine for all seasons.

Uncharacteristically conservative, factory advertising has labeled the .356 a two-hundred yard rifle. In my judgment, that's selling both carbine and cartridge short. A few strings fired at two hundred fifty and three

hundred yards left no doubts in my mind about the new gun's potential. Those 200-grain Power Points zipped out there fast and hit hard. One of those in the boiler room of a scampering mulie, even if he's three hundred yards out, will put him down in short order.

The new chamberings put the 94 Angle Eject head and shoulders above anything in the .30-30 class. Not only does the .356 make a superior woods rifle out of the Winchester carbine, but it turns it into a more-than-adequate open country rig as well. At last, 94 lovers needn't feel undergunned when the trees thin or animals larger than deer are hunted. ●

CHAPTER 17

.358 WINCHESTER

Al Miller

IN SOMETHING of a reversal of the usual routine, the .308 Winchester cartridge was announced by Winchester in 1952, *before* it officially became the military 7.62mm NATO. During the time that the Army was calling it the T-65, folks at the arms factories — according to industry scuttlebutt — were already necking it down and up, to all the standard bullet diameters from .22 to .35. (Which means, of course, that both Remington and Winchester had a 7mm-.308 in their hands 'way back then. *If* the rumor is true.)

But it was the savants in New Haven who announced, in 1955, two factory "wildcats" on the new .308 case: the .243 Winchester and the .358 Winchester. The .243 needs no comment here; it has so well established itself that it seems to have been around

for much longer than only a quarter of a century. Virtually every major centerfire rifle manufactured today is available in this chambering.

The .358 Winchester, altogether as legitimate and virtuous as its smaller sibling, is another matter. It was never chambered in any great variety of rifles, nor by many manufacturers, and even its fathers have abandoned it, leaving just two American arms companies now making rifles so chambered — Browning and Savage.

Efficient and powerful, the .358 was one of the first of the short-case, high-intensity cartridges. Versatile, too. With a bit of imaginative handloading, it can be safely tailored to take on just about anything from grouse to grizzly. But it must lack something, because hunters simply haven't cottoned to it. Just why is a good question, one that has sparked periodic bursts of speculation ever since the cartridge was introduced.

Like most of life's complexities, the .358's lack of popularity stems from a multiplicity of causes. Its originators put a hex on it right at the start: first, the rifles chambered for it were poorly stocked; second, it was the victim of semantic underkill. Remember when your mother (God bless her!) would encourage you to date Mrs. Smith's daughter down the block? After an almost endless list of the girl's attributes, she'd wind up with something like "you'll like her — she's a very *nice* girl."

Nice girl; that did it. The gal had to be bucktoothed, cross-eyed, with all the charm and vivacity of a first sergeant, and most likely a perfect thirty-eight (38-38-38, that is). A similar kiss of death was planted on the .358 Winchester when several of its first reviewers described it as an ideal woods cartridge, a great deer and black-bear round. From that day on, the .358 Winchester was damned, effectively branded by those who had never tried it as just another medium-powered cartridge, okay for ranges up to a hundred and fifty yards or so but pretty useless for any distance beyond that. Early experimenters found it surprisingly similar to the ever-popular .35 Whelen in performance, but the facts were never quite sufficient to lay to rest that initial reputation.

To make matters worse, it was first chambered in Winchester's Model 70 Featherweight. Later, their then-new Model 88 (a few, at least) was chambered for it. So was the little, light Savage 99-F. All three rifles shared several characteristics: each tipped the scale at seven pounds or less; each had a light twenty-two-inch or shorter barrel;

The Savage Model 99-358 is wisely fitted with a longer and much wider forearm than the older version so often found on Model 99 rifles. Al found the Redfield mount thoroughly sturdy, capable of holding a scope such as this Leupold without loosening during a long series of range tests with the hard-kicking, light Savage .358.

and each featured a buttstock right out of the last century, complete with knife-edge comb and excessive drop at the heel. Their stocks aggravated the cartridge's vigorous recoil to painful proportions, and in no time at all, the word was out: the .358 Winchester is a hard kicker! That was the final feather. Who wanted a cartridge with the ballistics of a slightly overgrown .35 Remington and the kick of a .458?

Well, nobody — at least, not very many. Sales dragged from the very start, then deteriorated to a near-stop. Winchester threw in the towel early in the game; they haven't made a .358 Winchester rifle since 1961. Mannlicher turned out a few but eventually gave up. So did Savage. Some years ago, Ruger made a limited run of Model 77s in this caliber, and later on, Browning and Savage took another stab at it. Whether that proves out or not, .358 Winchester owners don't have a thing to worry about. Ammo will be available for years, and because of the collecting mania sweeping the country, the value of their rifles will undoubtedly appreciate 'way out of proportion to their practical worth. That may persuade some to clean, oil, and store their collectibles until someone makes an offer they can't refuse — but I hope not. A good hunting rifle deserves to be used — and a .358 Winchester is a great hunting rifle.

Naturally, there are differences between makes. I've never had the good fortune to try one of Browning's BLRs in .358 Winchester, but of those .358s that have crossed my path, the Savage 99-358 is by far the most comfortable to shoot. Credit for that must be shared by the thick, nicely rounded comb and recoil pad, a standard item on the Savage .358. Pitch of the stock is still a shade abrupt, but thanks to the rest of the stock's proportions, recoil isn't bad at all.

Since my shoulder is not overly sensitive to a rifle's bounce, a comparative firing test was conducted with another Model 99, an A Model chambered for the .308 Winchester. Equipped with iron sights, the bantam A weighs about a pound less than the scope-burdened .358 Winchester. As far as I could tell, recoil of both rifles was identical. Had I been blindfolded at the bench, it's doubtful whether I could have distinguished between them by merely comparing their recoil.

The .358's forearm really captured my fancy. Basically,

it's a slightly modified beavertail, reminiscent of the old 99-R, with the addition of a longitudinal finger groove on either side. Wide, hand-filling, and an arm-stretching 10½ inches long, it makes the rifle much easier to control when swinging or pointing. Most important, it discourages canting. It's the best forearm ever designed for a sporting rifle, bar none! The stock is a decent grade of walnut, but its appearance is cheapened by a plastic coating of some sort that shimmers like shellac. It may offer the wood superior protection, but that harsh showroom glitter has no place in the woods. Except for that, the new Model 99 is certainly an improvement over those turned out a quarter century or so back. There wasn't a hint of creep in the trigger, and although pull seemed a tad heavy, letoff was crisp.

The action seems stronger, too. On most lever-actions, the rear-locking bolt suffers a certain amount of spring, especially when high-pressure rounds like the .243 or .308 Winchester are touched off in front of them. Somehow, Savage has managed to correct that. In both the borrowed 99-358 and my own A Model, fired cases, unsized or merely neck-sized, can be rechambered with

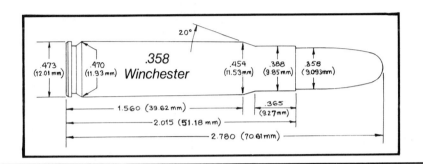

loads for the .358 Winchester

bullet	powder	charge grains	velocity fps	length inches	remarks
Hornady 200-gr spire-point	IMR-3031	48	2,532	2.75	2-1/4 to 2-5/8 in. at 100 yd
Hornady 200-gr spire-point	WW-748	50	2,572	2.75	same as above
Hornady 200-gr spire-point	IMR-4895	48	2,567	2.75	same as above
Speer 250-gr soft-point	IMR-3031	41	2,173	2.75	2 to 2-1/2 in. at 100 yd
Speer 250-gr soft-point	IMR-4895	42	2,202	2.75	same as above
Speer 250-gr soft-point	WW-748	46	2,214	2.75	same as above
RCBS 35-200-FN	IMR-3031	40	2,258	2.75	2-1/2 to 3 in. at 100 yd
Lyman 358315	IMR-3031	35*	2,010	2.75	same as above
Lyman 3589 290 gr	WW-748	42	1,976	2.75	2 to 2-1/2 in. at 100 yd
Lyman 358156 154 gr	IMR-3031	30*	1,701	2-5/16	5/8 to 3/4 in. at 50 yd
Lyman 358156	PB	11*	1,624	2-5/16	same as above
Winchester 200-gr Silvertip	factory load		2,513		2 to 2-5/8 in. at 100 yd

Velocities listed are five-shot averages chronographed fifteen feet from the muzzle with a Tepeco Time Meter. Temperature 55° F. Winchester cases and CCI Large Rifle primers used in all loads. All loads were safe in the test rifle. No wind was blowing during the accuracy tests. Group measurements equal the distance between centers of the two widest holes. Loads marked with asterisks include Dacron filler.

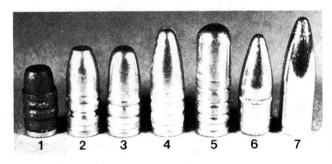

In the lever-action .358 Al tested, the jacketed bullet that outperformed all others was Speer's 250-grain spitzer (7). Hornady's 200-grain (6) grouped well if velocities were mild. Some cast bullets did well, but one simply wouldn't — Al had to retire Lyman mould 35897 (4) but found a winner in Lyman 3589 (5), which required deep seating but was very accurate. Most useful was Lyman 358156 (1), while RCBS 35-200-FN (2) and Lyman 35815 (3) were acceptable but only so-so.

cast-bullet data

bullet	advertised weight grain	actual weight grain	as-cast diameter (inch)	length (inches)	length of body (inch)	proportion-body to length	total bearing surface (inch)	proportion-bearing surface to length OA
Lyman 3589	282	290	0.361	1.33	0.475	0.357	0.99	0.744
RCBS 35-200	200	203	0.358	0.87	0.336	0.374	0.575	0.684
Lyman 358315	200	208	0.360	0.94	0.335	0.345	0.513	0.545
Lyman 35897	232	242	0.355	1.09	0.379	0.345	0.513	0.467

Bullets were cast from eight-year-old wheel-weight metal. When fired, all were equipped with Hornady crimp-on gas checks. Three lubricants were used alternately during the tests: a thirty-percent solution of Bullet Master; Lyman's Deluxe; and Accu-Lube. There was no difference in their effectiveness. None of the bullets leaded the bore, even those pushed more than twenty-five hundred feet per second. On the other hand, changing from one lube to the other had no effect on groups, good or bad.

ease. Try that with one of the older actions, and you'll usually wind up with an almost-chambered hull jamming the works. No two ways about it, today's rifles are far sturdier than those I grew up with.

Cases do stretch, of course, but flowing brass isn't the problem it is with some lever-actions. For instance, twenty factory rounds were fired to check velocity and accuracy levels. Subsequently, they were fired, resized full length, and reloaded twenty-eight more times. They required trimming *twice*. Despite all that wear and tear, there wasn't a single failure, not so much as a split neck. When the shooting stopped, every hull appeared to be in sound condition: primers still met resistance when being seated, and all lengths were within established limits — a pretty impressive record by anyone's standards. Winchester deserves high marks for building so much durability and safety into their brass.

The .358 Winchester demands no special approaches or reloading techniques. Factory ballistics can be duplicated with canister powders without exceeding excessive pressure levels. When the .358 Winchester was introduced back in 1955, it featured two loads: a two-hundred-grain Silvertip at 2,530 feet per second and a 250-grain at 2,250. Sometime during the Seventies, those figures were readjusted down to 2,490 and 2,230 feet per second, respectively. It's interesting to see that the chronographed factory loads of recent manufacture churned up muzzle speeds approximating the original rather than the current loads. Ballistics tables aren't usually conservative.

Because of the hull's limited capacity, medium-burning powders work best. Unexpectedly, none of those tested stood out from the rest. When developing loads for a given cartridge or rifle, I usually find that one or two deliver better accuracy than others. Not so with the .358 Winchester. At any given velocity level, accuracy with a particular bullet, jacketed or cast, remained the same regardless of the powder used.

On the other hand, the Savage barrel made no bones about preferring some bullets to others. Although it rejected only one — Lyman's cast 35897 — none of the rest grouped quite alike. In addition, their points of impact differed, too. Although displacement at one hundred yards wasn't dramatic, it was usually great enough to make sight adjustment worthwhile whenever one type of bullet followed another.

Accuracy with factory ammunition was good but certainly not outstanding. Three five-shot strings of Winchester's two-hundred-grain Silvertips printed 2½, 2, and 2-5/8 inches, in that order. Jacketed bullets, handloaded to match standard ballistics grouped from two to 2½ inches. To achieve the same degree of accuracy, cast-bullet velocities had to be dropped several hundred feet per second below those of their commercial counterparts.

Because of my experience with the Model 99-A, I'd anticipated tighter groups from the 99-358. As the range tests progressed, however, my disappointment was replaced by a growing respect for that barrel. Hot or cold, clean or fouled, it proved itself a stubborn but consistent performer. No matter what the powder or charge, regardless of how the rifle was supported on the bench, groups ranged from that same two to 2½ inches. Even removing the forearm and resting the rifle on its receiver made no difference. Never have I encountered a more dependable performer.

There aren't a whole lot of jacketed bullets to choose from in thirty-five caliber. Hornady produces three, Speer two, and Sierra one. Those selected for testing were chosen because they duplicate factory bullet weights. Speer still offers a 180-grain flat-point for anyone seeking a little more muzzle velocity. Speer's 250-grain spitzer was the 99-358's hands-down favorite. As long as I did my part, those bullets chopped two-inch holes out of the targets every time. For some reason, Hornady's two-hundred-grain spire-points wouldn't print smaller than 2¼ inches unless velocities were reduced to uninspiring levels.

The cast-bullet situation is no better. Together, the current Lyman and RCBS catalogs list a grand total of three moulds in thirty-five caliber — and only two drop bullets worth shooting: Lyman's 358315 and RCBS's 35-200-FN. The RCBS bullet recorded an actual weight of 203 grains. Accuracy was good, averaging 2½ inches until velocities passed 2,250 feet per second. By the time speeds got to twenty-five hundred feet per second, five-shot strings were averaging five inches center to center.

Lyman's 358315 was originally designed for the .35 Remington and enjoys a reputation as a tight grouper in rifles of that caliber. With an average weight of 208 grains, it performed only so-so in the .358 Winchester. At a hundred yards, its point of impact was

always several inches to the right of the RCBS bullets', and at any given velocity, its groups were always larger, too.

A couple of old Lyman moulds were scrounged from Ken Howell's private supply: 35897 and 3589. The former, as mentioned before, simply refused to group — period. Powder, charge weight, moon phase — nothing helped. Eventually, I gave up, cleaned the mould, oiled it, and returned it to its box. Its companion, 3589, too long for the .358's short case, required deep seating, further reducing the hull's already limited powder capacity. Nevertheless, it was the most accurate of the cast bullets. Two-inch groups were common, and none exceeded 2½ inches center to center. At fifty yards, it took very little effort to keep all holes touching.

To those hypnotized by Weatherby velocities, a 290-grain bullet moving out at around two thousand feet per second may sound somewhat unimpressive, but that's a lot of lead, and its muzzle energy approximates that of a 180-grain .30-06 load. Frankly, I'd hate to get in its way, even at three hundred yards. I tried a few check shots at that distance, and those massive bullets plowed into the backstop with unabated fury. Backed by forty-two grains of WW-748, that bullet should be just the ticket for deer in thick cover. Its generous weight, extra length, and blunt, round nose should discourage deflection and ensure an easy-to-follow blood trail when game is hit. I hope Lyman will resume its production one day. A slightly scaled-down version — say around 225 or 250 grains — would be even more helpful.

The most useful bullet of all was Lyman's 358156, a Thompson design and a favorite among those who shoot .357 Magnums and high-speed .38 Specials. Backed by either of the charges listed in the accompanying table, the little semiwadcutter is very pleasant to shoot and extremely accurate. Unsized, lubed with a thirty-percent solution of Bullet Master, and fired without gas checks, those shouldered bullets zapped into one ragged hole at fifty yards. They averaged 1¼ inches at seventy-five and three inches at one hundred yards. They're flat-shooting, too. With the scope set to put the two-hundred-grain Hornadys three inches above point of aim at one hundred yards, the Thompsons smacked the target dead center at fifty, dropped an inch at seventy-five, and two more at one hundred. A magazine filled with them turns the .358 Winchester into a dandy small-game rifle, good for year-'round use. Those loads are deadly on rabbits, great for grouse or turkey, accurate enough for head shots on squirrels past fifty yards, and in addition, pack plenty of punch for an occasional fox or coyote farther out.

Commercial half-jacketed .38 bullets can be driven much harder, but all that extra velocity just makes them more powerful, not more effective. They're terribly destructive when used against small animals. For those who don't cast their own, however, they offer a practical alternative.

All cast bullets were moulded from eight-year-old wheel-weight metal. After various experiments, I found that the tightest groups could be obtained when neither bullets nor cases were sized. Case necks were belled slightly with the aid of an RCBS expanding die. Hornady gas checks were added to all the rifle bullets. Dacron was tamped over all powder charges of forty-five grains or less. Experimental loads fired with and without the synthetic filler left no doubt about its role as a group tightener.

Cast-bullet performance in the .358 Winchester made a fascinating study. What made 3589 group so well? Why was 35897 so completely unreliable? And the two-hundred-grain lookalikes — what gave the RCBS entry such a decided edge over the Lyman design? To puzzle out the answers, I measured the bullets — their dimensions are compared in my little table. Before I review it, a couple of words of explanation are necessary.

The rifle bullets are listed in the order they performed: the best, 3589 is on top; the worst is on the bottom. (For obvious reasons, pistol bullet 358156 was excluded.) Ordinarily, the best-performing bullet would be the one that cut the smallest groups while delivering the highest velocity. Had that criterion been followed, the RCBS bullet would have taken top honors. However, because 3589's velocity was limited only by case capacity rather than expanding groups, I felt that it had earned first place. Had it been possible to cram more powder behind that long bullet, there's no telling how fast it could have been driven before its grouping ability began to suffer.

Bearing surfaces were measured by eye. The measurements are close, but it would take better eyes and more-precise instruments than mine to pinpoint those lengths exactly. Nevertheless, the figures are dependable enough for comparison. It takes no more than one quick glance at the comparison table to spot the obvious correlation between performance and bearing. While the proportion of bearing surface to overall length isn't the only factor involved in determining the accuracy potential of a cast bullet, it's certainly the most decisive. All else being equal, the more support a bullet receives from lands and grooves, the more accurate it is.

But all else is rarely equal. Dimensional aberrations can condemn the best-designed bullets to mediocrity, and as in the case of 35897, if a bullet's proportions are ill drawn to begin with, the added curse of an undersized body completely destroys its grouping ability. At the moment, there aren't any really suitable cast bullets available for the .358 — or for any other .35 cartridge, for that matter. The RCBS design comes close, but what's really needed is a two hundred or 250-grain patterned after those Loverin made so famous, with their long, long bodies covered with lubricant grooves. Bullets so shaped could be sent downrange just as fast and just as accurately as their jacketed relatives.

It will take more than a new cast-bullet design to rejuvenate the dying .358 Winchester, though. From all indications, it's following the same route its predecessor took. Despite what may be said about it today, the older .348 Winchester was never very popular during its lifetime. It always enjoyed a good press, and those who hunted with it liked it very much. Nevertheless, nobody fought to get his hands on a Model 71 until it disappeared from Winchester's lineup. Once it became obsolete, collectors and hunters couldn't say enough good things about the rifle — or pay too much to own one, either. Apparently, the .358 Winchester and its rifles are destined to share the same fate.

If anyone's looking for a general-purpose hunting rifle, one that can fulfill at least ninety percent of his hunting needs, I'd recommend a Savage 99-358. Everyone I know who uses one is more than happy with it — with good reason. ●

CHAPTER
18

.35 WHELEN

Ken Waters

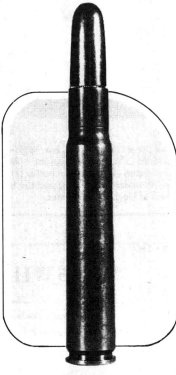

Iver Henriksen built the .35 Whelen test rifle for Alaskan Ken Howell in the mid-Fifties, putting a Buhmiller barrel on a Sauer-made Mauser action. On Alaskan game, owner used just one bullet: the 275-grain Hornady (above). Original scope in this old photograph was a Weaver K-2.5; mount was Buehler with one-piece base and solid rings.

MORE THAN ANY other wildcat cartridge, and indeed more than a great many standard factory cartridges, the .35 Whelen did something for American big-game hunters that has led to its near-immortalization amongst those older shooters who remember the impact of its introduction.

Not only was the cartridge right for its intended use; quite as important was that its timing was right. When the .35 Whelen appeared in 1922-1923, interest in hunting big game in Alaska, the Yukon, and British Columbia was growing, but the stateside hunter looking for a suitable rifle found himself faced with a choice of three options: use the marginally effective — for such game — .30-06; buy a foreign or custom rifle chambered for one of the larger "African" cartridges — at considerable expense, I might add; or turn to a Winchester Model 1895 lever-action rifle chambered for the most powerful standard American cartridge then available, the .405 Winchester.

Quite a few shooters found none of these alternatives appealing. They wanted a more modern cartridge than the .405 Winchester with flatter trajectory, and they wanted it on a standard bolt action such as the Springfield — *not* an expensive magnum Mauser with its long bolt throw. Also, they didn't want cartridges that had to be reloaded with Berdan primers, which had to be imported.

Enter the .35 Whelen on the shooting scene. Picture, if you will, how an Alaska-bound bear hunter might have reacted to the news that now he could have his 1903 Springfield or 1898 Mauser rebarreled — or even rebored and rerifled — to thirty-five caliber, chambered for the familiar old .30-06 case simply necked up to take .35 bullets, and have himself a powerful, flat-shooting, but relatively inexpensive rifle that would handle 250-grain spitzers out to three hundred yards or more, or 275-grain and 300-grain roundnose busters for penetration and emphatic knockdown on heavy animals at close quarters.

That's about the way things stood during the remainder of the Twenties and the depression years of the Thirties. Yes, I'm aware of the fact that the Western Cartridge Company started producing the great .375 H&H Magnum *cartridge* in 1925. But until the Winchester Model 70 *rifle* appeared in 1937, there was no off-the-shelf standard factory rifle to be had in that caliber — only custom jobs such as a Griffin & Howe. And don't forget that for eight of those intervening fourteen years, the country was gripped in a depression that makes our modern recessions look like child's play. There simply wasn't money available for a hunting trip to Alaska or western Canada — or for a new rifle to take along, if you had been able to go.

So the .35 Whelen came along at the right time to arouse the interest of both the actual big-game hunters and those poor unfortunates who would have proved equally dedicated and competent as hunters but were never able to accumulate the time or the money that such trips required. At least they could thereafter enjoy the pleasure of owning a rifle of Alaskan stature. What's more, they could use it on local deer very effectively indeed without any of the alleged trauma of being "overgunned." And handloading the wildcat was downright simple, starting with the plentiful .30-06 cases and utilizing the less expensive .35 Remington bullets — which even in the larger cartridge were still adequate for all but the largest American big game.

How did this cartridge come about? I researched this question, going clear back to some of the original writings on the subject — with what I feel to be some rather significant findings.

The more recent publications appear to have followed one another in claiming that James V. Howe, of the famous gunmaking firm of Griffin & Howe, developed the .35 Whelen and merely named it in honor of Townsend Whelen. Going back thirty to thirty-five years, we find references asserting that it was a joint development by the two men. One source, whose author should have known better, went so far as to declare that the .35 Whelen was "developed by Griffin & Howe."

But myths are poor substitutes for facts, so let's go all the way back to 1922 and 1923. Now we find that (1) at that time, Colonel Townsend Whelen

was the commanding officer of the Frankford Arsenal, and James V. Howe was a toolmaker in the same establishment; (2) the wildcat .400 Whelen came first, and in the old but still interesting pages of a 1923 issue of *The American Rifleman*, Colonel Whelen referred to it as "the first cartridge that I designed" and in that same article stated that "Mr. James V. Howe undertook this work of making dies, reamers, chambering tools, and of chambering the rifles, *all in accordance with my design*" (the emphasis is mine). This pretty well establishes Whelen as the designer, I think, and Howe as the gunsmith. Now let's go on to the second development, the .35 Whelen.

In the very next issue of *The American Rifleman*, Whelen told of his motivations for developing a .35 cartridge on the .30-06 case. While not mentioning Howe by name in this follow-up report, he frequently used the pronoun *we*, evidently in a generous desire to share much of the credit for the new cartridge. Yet in his final paragraph, he said, "I have had lots of pleasure in developing these two cartridges and the rifles for them."

So I think it's pretty clear that Whelen was indeed the designer of the cartridge and Howe the maker of the rifles. As such, each played an important role, but their roles should be kept separate, the credit properly

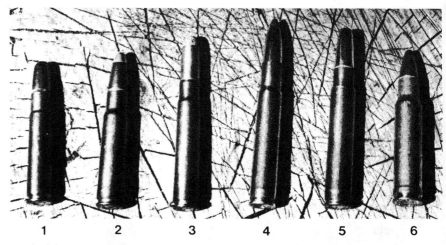

None of these .35 cartridges is a "high-velocity" round; the ancient .350 Griffin & Howe and the modern .358 Norma Magnum — not shown — hold that honor among the .35s. But the .35 Remington (1), .358 Winchester (2), 9x57mm Mauser (3), .35 Whelen (4), Ken's .35-.318 Square-Shoulder wildcat (5), and the belted .350 Remington Magnum (6) are all among the very best of big-game cartridges.

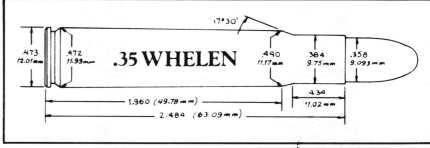

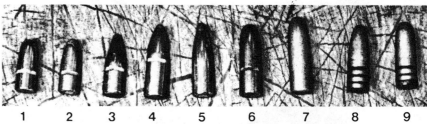

Some of the bullets Ken used in developing a variety of loads for the .35 Whelen were the 200-grain Sierra (1), Remington (2), and Hornady (3); 250-grain Hornady (4) and Speer (5); 275-grain Hornady, discontinued about 1967 (6); 300-grain Barnes with copper-tubing jacket (7); 226-grain Lyman cast bullet 35897 (8); and 252-grain Lyman cast bullet 358318 (9).

assigned. So, to set the record straight: Colonel Townsend Whelen actually designed the .35 Whelen; it wasn't just named for him.

Now about that design. Although the .35 Whelen case is formed from .30-06 brass, some .35 Whelen dimensions are slightly different from corresponding measurements of the .30-06. For example, the case length is 2.484 inches on the Whelen (according to Colonel Whelen's original design) and 2.494 inches on the .30-06. From the base to the point of the shoulder, the Whelen is 1.960 inches, and the .30-06 is 1.948 inches. But the shoulder angle is the same 17.5 degrees, and the all-important base dimensions are the same. Forget any loose talk you may have heard about the .35 Whelen lacking enough shoulder for adequate headspacing. 'Tisn't so; it has plenty of firm bearing in a correctly reamed chamber.

Forming cases for the test rifle was dead easy with the Pacific Durachrome die. The regular full-length-sizing die came with two expander plugs: the standard "ball" or rounded button on the decapping stem and a second expander in the shape of an upside-down truncated cone. The second is the one intended for expanding .30-06 case necks to .35 in a single pass, and it does just that without wrinkling, buckling, or otherwise distorting cases

.35 Whelen

	charge (gr)	powder	velocity (fps)	case	primer	length (in.)	expansion	
jacketed bullets								
180 Speer FNSP	58.0	IMR-4064	2,613	LC 62	CCI 200	3.06	moderate	poor load in test rifle
	56.0	BL-C(2)	2,646	LC 62	CCI 200	3.06	moderate	poor load in test rifle
200 Sierra RNSP	51.0	IMR-3031	2,489	W-W	CCI 200	3.10	normal	fifth most accurate load
	53.0	IMR-3031	2,549	W-W	CCI 200	3.10	normal	third most accurate and best light-bullet load
	56.0	IMR-4895	2,588	W-W	CCI 200	3.10	near max	
200 Win. PP	56.0	IMR-4320	2,569	W-W	CCI 200	3.14	normal	very accurate; excellent
200 Remington RNCL	56.0	IMR-4064	2,500	W-W	CCI 200	3.14	near max	fourth most accurate load
	58.0	IMR-4895	2,658	W-W	CCI 200	3.14	maximum	second highest velocity
200 Hornady RNSP	56.0	H-4895	2,583	LC 62	CCI 200	3.11	normal	
	60.0	IMR-4831	2,279	LC 62	CCI 250	3.11	moderate	powder too slow-burning
200 Hornady Sp-Pt	58.0	IMR-4064	2,601	LC 62	CCI 200	3.23	near max	
	58.0	IMR-4895	2,674	LC 62	CCI 200	3.23	maximum	highest-velocity load tested
220 Speer FNSP	55.0	IMR-4064	2,450	LC 62	CCI 200	3.15	normal	fine load; accurate
	58.5	IMR-4350	2,239	LC 62	CCI 200	3.15	moderate	second most accurate load; best load in alternate rifle
250 Speer spitzer	50.0	IMR-3031	2,344	W-W	CCI 200	3.33	near max	
	52.0	IMR-4064	2,280	W-W	CCI 200	3.33	normal	most accurate load
	54.0	IMR-4064	2,378	W-W	CCI 200	3.33	near max	
	55.0	IMR-4064	2,422	W-W	CCI 200	3.33	near max	good load
	56.0	IMR-4064	2,474	W-W	CCI 200	3.33	maximum	
	56.0	IMR-4320	2,535	W-W	CCI 200	3.33	near max	best all-around load
	57.0	IMR-4320	2,564	W-W	CCI 200	3.33	maximum	highest velocity with 250-grain
	58.0	H-205	2,128	W-W	CCI 200	3.33	normal	accurate but too slow
250 Speer RNSP	52.0	WW-748	2,302	W-W	CCI 200	3.17	normal	
	55.0	WW-760	2,207	W-W	CCI 200	3.17	moderate	
250 Hornady RN	58.0	IMR-4831	2,209	W-W	CCI 250	3.25	moderate	
250 Hornady Sp-Pt	54.0	WW-748	2,405	W-W	W 120	3.30	near max	good load
	55.0	IMR-4320	2,462	LC 63	CCI 200	3.30	normal	
	55.0	IMR-4895	2,479	W-W	CCI 200	3.30	normal	
250 Win. ST	57.0	WW-760	2,112	LC 62	W 120	3.30	moderate	
275 Hornady RNSP	52.0	IMR-4064	2,251	W-W	CCI 200	3.25	normal	
	53.0	IMR-4320	2,307	W-W	CCI 200	3.25	normal	poor load
300 Barnes RNSP	51.0	IMR-4320	2,214	W-W	CCI 200	3.25	maximum	
	58.0	IMR-4350	2,232	W-W	CCI 250	3.28	maximum	compressed load; accurate
cast bullets								
252 Lyman 358318	21.0	IMR-4227	1,525	LC 63	R 9½	3.18	light	most accurate cast load
226 Lyman 35897	26.0	IMR-4198	1,692	LC 63	R 9½	3.18	moderate	accurate
	35.0	IMR-3031	1,883	LC 63	R 9½	3.18	moderate	first three shots grouped 3.8 inches

Test rifle: Henriksen Mauser sporter with twenty-two-inch Buhmiller barrel, M8-4x Leupold scope in Redfield mount. Velocities chronographed with Oehler Model 33 and skyscreens; instrumental velocity at ten feet adjusted to muzzle velocity.

in any way. Just lubricate cases lightly and run them *once* all the way into the sizer die with this expander plug in place. On the way in, necks are expanded, and final forming of the necks occurs on the withdrawal stroke — and cases are ready to load. I didn't lose a single case during this forming process.

Thereafter, I made tests to determine whether this tapered expander plug could be left in the die permanently and thus avoid the necessity of switching back and forth. It worked so well when I was simply resizing cases that I saw no need for putting the regular expander back in — so I left it in and used it whether I was forming cases or just resizing fired hulls.

An interesting finding was that in the forming of .35 Whelen cases from .30-06 brass, the cases shorten to around 2.475 inches, eliminating the need for trimming at this stage. After cases were fire-formed, trimming wasn't necessary until after two to four loadings and firings — depending upon the intensity of the loads used. I should mention here also that re-formed cases emerge from the sizer die with practically perfect headspacing for the chamber of the test rifle, so they require very little fire-forming.

Cases formed from two lots of Winchester Super-Speed and two lots of GI arsenal match brass (LC 62 NM and LC 63 NM) were used in this test series. The fired arsenal brass weighed an average of 197 grains empty, including the fired primer, and held an average of 58.2 grains of water when they were filled to the base of a seated 250-grain bullet.

The commercial Winchester cases

had an average weight of 194 grains and held 58.8 grains — measured the same way. With this small capacity differential of only 0.6 grain of water, there was no detectable difference in either chronographed velocities or case expansion when the same loads were used in both kinds of brass. Still, I kept all cases segregated during the entire test series.

The test rifle I was using has an excellent chamber that held base expansion, even with maximum loads, to a range between 0.4680 and 0.4685 inch, which is as it should be. I dislike chambers that have been reamed so large that they allow cases to expand beyond 0.470 inch, causing a great deal more working of the brass in sizing. This chamber was accordingly easy on cases, and only a couple were lost because of split necks.

Back in the Fifties, there was some trouble with arsenal brass of one or more years, but these 62 NM and 63 NM cases were properly annealed in the shoulder and work-hardened in the base, and they demonstrated a potential for long life with very little stretching. The Winchester brass was likewise tough and trouble-free.

Of course, credit for this sort of case performance must be shared with the rifle. In addition to the matter of chamber dimensions, such considerations as headspacing, bolt lockup, and freedom from springing are of considerable importance in extending case life. For this test series, I used a Mauser sporter with twenty-two-inch Buhmiller barrel and Jaeger trigger belonging to editor Ken Howell, built for him by Iver Henriksen quite some years ago. Despite a total weight of only 8-3/4 pounds, including an M8 Leupold 4x scope in a Redfield two-

piece mount, the rifle has a stiff barrel — it is 0.620 inch in diameter at the muzzle and has no sight cut or dovetail to weaken it. The rifling twist is one turn in sixteen inches.

Although the stock is a plain Bishop sporter, it was well laid-out, with straight grain in the grip and fore-end, and the rifle has been bedded in glass. There is no fore-end screw, and the barrel doesn't move when the front receiver screw is loosened. All of these facts warranted a supposition that this rifle would turn out to be rather more than usually accurate.

Maybe I expected too much, but it wasn't as accurate as I'd thought it would be. My first five-shot hundred-yard groups measured between 2-1/4 and 4 inches, depending upon the load. Believing that the rifle was capable of doing far better than this, I backed off an eighth of a turn on the front receiver screw, and the rifle at once shot better, cutting group sizes down so that they ranged from 1-1/4 to 2 inches. With a little improvement in bedding, groups will shrink still more. *(As I remember, Iver glass-bedded that barrel for the full length of the fore-end — in those days, this was considered the best way to guarantee accuracy. I've simply never gotten around to modifying it to float the barrel. I've never fired this rifle from a bench, strangely enough, but equally strange is the fact that in those long-gone days when the rifle was new, I shot groups that were in the size range of Ken's tighter ones, just mentioned — and I was shooting from prone! Interesting. — Ken Howell)*

Components had to be assembled for the broadest testing program possible that would fit within the time allowed, so to get a jump on things, I started by repeating some of the trials that had given me the best results in two earlier .35 Whelen Mausers. They included loads with Du Pont powders of "medium" burning rates, from IMR-3031 to IMR-4350, including IMR-4064 and IMR-4895. While my range notebook had recorded the accuracy grouping of some of these earlier combinations, no chronograph had been available to me in those days — so I had no idea what velocities those old loads had developed. Now I could find out.

Logic dictated that the .35 Whelen, with less bottleneck than a .30-06, a larger bore, and a greater expansion ratio, would require somewhat faster-burning powders, and this proved to be the case — even more so than I had estimated. For example, consider my earlier experience with IMR-4350 in .35 Whelens. For a good many years, one of my favorite loads in those earlier Whelens consisted of 58.5 grains of

Supplemental Selected Loads

bullet (grains)	powder	suggested starting load (grains)	suggested maximum (grains)	velocity (fps)
.35 Whelen				
Hodgdon Data				
180	H-4831		66.0	2,375
220	H-4831		66.0	2,360
250	H-4831		66.0	2,364
	H-380		61.0	2,564
Sierra Data				
200 Sierra RN	H-335	50.9	55.3	2,650
	AAC-2230	50.5	54.0	2,600
	IMR-4320	53.2	58.6	2,600
225 Sierra BT	AAC-2230	48.7	52.6	2,500
	IMR-4064	50.5	55.5	2,550
	RL-12	52.9	57.0	2,500

Be alert — Publisher cannot accept responsibility for errors in published load data.

IMR-4350 behind Speer's 220-grain flatnose soft-point. It was and is extremely accurate and pleasant to shoot, a load that appeared to be efficient and was certainly effective. If I had been called upon to estimate the velocity of that load, I'd probably have said it was somewhere around twenty-five hundred feet per second. But then came the chronograph, and what an eye-opener it was! Only 2,239 feet per second, average, from a twenty-two-inch barrel, is what the Oehler told me. So from my favorite barrel length of twenty-four inches, I couldn't have been getting more than about twenty-*three* hundred feet per second. And this with a load density of a hundred percent.

Now, don't take me wrong. That's still a fine-shooting load for a .35 Whelen if you can be content with velocities that are two hundred to three hundred feet per second below what they seemingly ought to be. But the chronograph taught me a great deal about loading the .35 Whelen. After reading the old stories and reports on this fabled cartridge, with their guesstimated velocities, I found the revelation of actual velocities — to say the least — disappointing.

One old source, for instance, had claimed top velocities of 2,755 feet per second with 220-grain bullets and up to 2,850 feet per second with 200-grains. Colonel Whelen himself, in that original 1923 report, listed muzzle velocities of 2,834 feet per second with the 200-grain and 2,635 with the 250-grain.

I found such figures unrealistic. Admittedly, this most recent .35 Whelen test rifle has a throat long enough to accept the blunt 300-grain Barnes bullet, but even this fails by a considerable margin to account for the disagreement between claimed and measured velocities. My highest recorded instrumental velocity with 200-grain bullets was 2,661 feet per second, ten feet from the muzzle, which when adjusted to muzzle velocity gave me 2,674 feet per second. And with 250-grain bullets, my highest velocity was 2,564 feet per second.

With the 200-grain bullets, top velocities were obtained with IMR-4895 powder, and IMR-4320 gave the 250-grain bullets their top speeds, effectively demonstrating that for maximum velocities, a faster-burning powder than IMR-4350 is required. This nonmagnum case simply doesn't have the internal capacity to accommodate large-enough charges of coarse, slow-burning stick powders, nor does it have the restrictive case shoulder and bore to burn them well.

On the other hand, there would be a definite limit to how far one could prudently go in the direction of fast-burning powders, or else pressures would rise faster than velocities. Working with the chronograph in conjunction with measurements of case expansion, I eventually established propellant parameters that designated IMR-3031 as the fastest-burning powder practical for use in full-power loads for the .35 Whelen, and IMR-4320 as the slowest — except with 300-grain bullets, with which IMR-4350 proved to be suitable.

By the same token, IMR-3031 is a bit too fast-burning for the best results with bullets that weigh more than two hundred or possibly 220 grains. Amongst the IMR powders, then, IMR-4895, IMR-4064, and IMR-4320 emerged as the most versatile choices, especially with the popular 250-grain bullets.

I tried several ball or spherical powders, including Winchester-Western's WW-748 and WW-760 as well as Hodgdon's BL-C(2). I'd like to have tried H-414, but I found that I'd exhausted my supply and couldn't find any more locally. WW-748 proved to be the best-adapted of the ball powders I used, but with 250-grain bullets, pressures rose faster than velocities did, forcing a halt to increases in charges. WW-760 is just too slow-burning in the .35 Whelen for either the best accuracy or those sought-after velocities. And for some reason I haven't determined, BL-C(2) was erratic in its burning, with fluctuating pressure signs and excessive blast. I went back to using stick powders.

I believe that some of the Norma powders would be well adapted to this cartridge, but readers report having so much difficulty in obtaining any of them that I decided to spend my remaining time working with what could be readily purchased in most areas. Last to be tried was Hodgdon's fine H-205; it gave good accuracy but at too-low velocities.

Judging from my tests so far, high marks for accuracy in this latest .35 Whelen test rifle go to IMR-4064 and IMR-3031, in that order, while the highest velocities resulted from the use of IMR-4895 and IMR-4320. Optimum powders with cast bullets were IMR-4227, IMR-4198, and IMR-3031 — but of course with these bullets, velocities were purposely lower in search of the finest accuracy.

If this .35 Whelen rifle is adamant as to which powders are best-adapted to it, it is quite as pronounced in its acceptance or rejection of the several makes and weights of bullets used in these tests. It absolutely refuses to deliver acceptable accuracy with either

180-grain Speers on the light side or 275-grain Hornadys among the heavyweights. Five-shot groups in each case ranged from 3-1/4 to 4-1/4 inches at a hundred yards. Contrastingly, both 200-grain and 250-grain Hornadys and 250-grain Speers performed ever so much better.

In my earlier Whelens, the 220-grain Speer flatnose soft-point had ranked first in accuracy grouping. Unfortunately, that fine bullet has been discontinued. But I still had some on hand, so I tried them in Ken Howell's rifle with similar results. Speer should restore this bullet production, both because of its accuracy and for its intermediate weight.

Only the 250-grain Speer did better. This beautifully shaped and proportioned bullet is quite likely the best single bullet presently available for the .35 Whelen. With this bullet and fifty-two grains of IMR-4064, I obtained the finest accuracy — and by simply switching to fifty-six grains of IMR-4320, everything else remaining the same, increased velocity by an average of 255 feet per second at a cost of less than three quarters of a minute of angle in reduced accuracy.

This rifle showed an obvious liking for 200-grain roundnose bullets, which I find somewhat surprising in view of its long throat. Either the 200-grain Sierra or 200-grain Remington Core-Lokt groups inside 1-1/2 minutes of angle; so does the no longer available 200-grain Winchester Power-Point. All these are excellent deer loads at twenty-five hundred feet per second. Note this: the short 200-grain bullets should be seated farther out of the case neck than their cannelures indicate. The 250-grain Hornady spire-point, designed for the overly short .350 Remington Magnum, also has its cannelure in the wrong place for this .35 case.

Even more surprising were the results obtained with the long, blunt 300-grain Barnes bullets. After finding it so difficult to reach the upper twenty-four hundreds with 250-grain bullets — and indeed only twenty-one to twenty-two hundred with some loads — I hadn't expected to do much better than twenty-one hundred feet per second with the heavier 300-grain bullets. And I wondered whether the sixteen-inch twist would be enough to stabilize those heavy bullets.

When the chronograph registered over twenty-two hundred feet per second with each of two loads, it was difficult to believe. I can only assume that the greater resistance offered by these bullets with their longer bearing surface produced more nearly complete burning of the powder, partially offsetting the opposite effect of the large bore. Furthermore, bullet holes in the targets showed no sign of tipping, and accuracy was good.

The .35 Whelen owner looking for a single all-purpose load will find it difficult to beat my choice of a good 250-grain bullet — in this instance, the Speer spitzer — driven by fifty-six grains of IMR-4320 for a muzzle velocity of 2,535 feet per second from a twenty-two-inch barrel, or about twenty-six hundred feet per second from a twenty-four-inch barrel. That load packs both accuracy and punch.

Incidentally, the .35 Whelen owner may well be better off if he sticks to one load. Points of impact shift about noticeably with changes in bullet weights. Switching bullet weights in the field could easily cause a complete miss or — worse still — a wounding hit.

Then there's the matter of recoil, for this also changes with changes in bullet weight. My shoulder's built-in "kick estimator" tells me that .35 Whelen recoil with 180-grain and 200-grain bullets feels about the same as that of a .30-06, which is of course understandable. But with 250-grain and heavier bullets, recoil is markedly heavier, though it isn't severe. With full-power loads and 300-grain bullets, this rifle moves up into an entirely different class, with recoil that may be classified as strenuous.

Finally, knowing that many big-bore enthusiasts enjoy shooting cast bullets, I decided to work-in a brief test with them. For these tests, I chose Lyman 35897, a gas-check bullet weighing 226 grains, and Lyman 358318, another gas-check design but with a more blunt nose. Using three powders in which I place the most faith when it comes to shooting cast bullets in rifles, I loaded twenty-one grains of IMR-4227 with 358318 bullets and twenty-six grains of IMR-4198 with 35897 bullets. An alternate to the latter load was thirty-five grains of IMR-3031. These three loads produced average velocities of 1,525, 1,692, and 1,883 feet per second, respectively. Accuracy descended as velocities increased.

When velocity is of no importance and the emphasis is on accuracy alone, IMR-4227 has often given me fine grouping with cast bullets, almost invariably beating out SR-4759, which is the reason I have so much confidence in it. Occasionally, IMR-4198 equals it or beats it, and might have done so this time if I'd used a grain or two less of it. IMR-3031 is a favorite for loads where higher velocities are wanted along with good cast-bullet accuracy.

Colonel Whelen thought that his thirty-five-caliber cartridge was ideal for the hunter who desired a powerful but still accurate cartridge capable of taking the largest American game, with increased long-range hitting capabilities. That, of course, remains true. The .35 Whelen is as good a cartridge today as it ever was. Over the years, experimenters have attempted to improve it by steepening the shoulder angle and straightening out the body taper to an "improved" form, or in the case of the .35 Brown-Whelen, actually moving the shoulder forward to increase powder capacity.

Actually, I suspect that the best way to improve on the .35 Whelen is to neck it down to .338, retaining the same standard .30-06 case and shape but taking advantage of the better sectional density of .338 bullets as compared to .358 bullets, as well as the larger and better selection of available .338 bullets. I wouldn't be a bit surprised to find that powders burn a bit better in the smaller bore as well.

In any case, if I ever have another Whelen rifle built — and I suspect that I shall — it will be a .338 so I can test out my theories. If and when that happens, you'll be sure to hear about it.

●

CHAPTER
19

.35 Whelen
UPDATE

Remington Model 700 Classic chambered for the .35 Whelen. With its 22-inch barrel and a Leupold 4x scope clamped in Weaver mounts, the stylish sporter weighs a handy 7 pounds, 10 ounces.

Ken Waters

LITTLE DID I THINK, when I wrote my first report on the .35 Whelen in 1980, that the day would come when this great old cartridge would be adopted as a standard factory round. After all, it has been 65 years or so since the wildcat .35 was announced. Conventional wisdom would have held that if it were ever going to be commercially adopted, it should have happened before this.

The .35 Whelen's record is clear and almost spotless. I don't recall ever reading an adverse report concerning its performance, only an occasional slighting comment questioning whether it had enough shoulder to provide adequate headspacing.

For the record, it does! Rest assured, Remington would never have adopted the .35 Whelen if it didn't have enough shoulder. The case dimensions verify it with diameters of .441 inch at point-of-shoulder and .385 inch at neck. That's a difference of .056 or .028 per side, which is plenty. Indeed, it has some .015 more shoulder than the .35 Remington — and nobody questions the functioning of that time-tested old round or that of the 9x57mm which has .010 less shoulder than the .35 Whelen.

Those questions probably originated with the .400 Whelen which didn't have an adequate case shoulder. Hopefully, we can put all those misleading old rumors to sleep, once and for all.

Remington's move makes a lot of sense. A need exists for a medium-caliber big game cartridge. Although the .350 Magnum amply met that need, for some reason that capable round hasn't achieved the popularity it deserves, nor has the less potent .358 Winchester. One might logically ask why the .35 Whelen should be expected to gain acceptance?

For starters, the .35 Whelen is based on the ever-popular .30-06 case. Matter of fact, it is the .30-06 case with its neck expanded to hold .358-inch bullets. That simplifies ammunition production for the factory; rifle actions made for the 06 readily accept the Whelen cartridge requiring only a .35-caliber barrel; and the large and growing handloading fraternity can, with little effort, form their own cases from 06 brass if desired.

Finally, there's an alternate type of rifle available in the new caliber, Remington's popular Model 7600 pump-action as well as the Model 700 Classic. It doesn't take a soothsayer to predict that other rifle makers will follow.

Factory ballistics call for a 200-grain pointed softpoint with a muzzle velocity of 2,675 fps (from a 24-inch barrel) developing 3,177 foot-pounds of muzzle energy and a 250-grain tapered round-nose rated at 2,400 fps and 3,197 foot-pounds of muzzle energy. Sighted for 200 yards, the 200-grain PSP strikes only 2.6 inches high at 100 and 4.2 inches low at 250. The 250-grainer, more properly sighted for 150 yards, is 1.6 inches high at 100 and four inches low at 200 yards. Trajectories are comparable to those of factory .30-06 rounds with 180 and 220-grain bullets

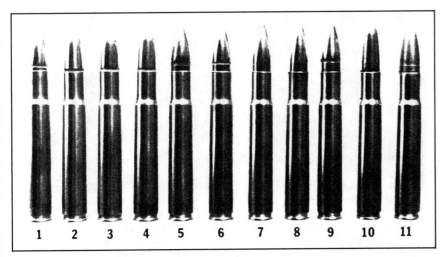

Because of the Remington's long throat, Ken adjusted his seating depths accordingly: (1) 180-grain Speer; (2) 200-grain Remington; (3) 200-grain Sierra; (4) 200-grain Hornady; (5) 200-grain Hornady Spire Point; (6) 220-grain Speer; (7) 225-grain Sierra; (8) 250-grain Speer; (9) 250-grain Hornady Spire Point; (10) 250-grain Hornady; and (11) 226-grain Lyman No. 35897.

The .35 Whelen Redding dies, some typical loaded rounds and some of the targets fired with them: (1) 200-grain Remington factory load; (2) 200-grain Hornady Spire Point over 57 grains of IMR-4895; (3) 220-grain Speer and 56 grains of IMR-4064; (4) 225-grain Sierra and 53 grains of H-4895; (5) 250-grain Hornady and 53 grains of H-4895; and (6) 250-grain Speer and 55 grains of IMR-4064.

Ken made up a few loads with .38 pistol bullets: left, a 158-grain Sierra; center, a 140-grain Sierra; and right, a 140-grain Speer. Because of the bullets' flat faces, rounds loaded with them refused to feed from the magazine. They had to be loaded and fired one by one.

so shooters used to the 06 can feel quite at home with the Whelen.

Retained bullet energies at 200 yards are 1,958 and 1,722 foot-pounds, respectively. The 200-grainer may be thought of as a 250-yard load and the 250-grainer capable of ranges up to 200 yards.

Two of my gun writer friends deplored Remington's selection of a roundnose for their 250-grain bullet, maintaining that it doesn't shoot as flat as a 250-grain spitzer. True, but I'll disagree nonetheless. The 250-grainer was intended for the larger species usually taken inside 200 yards and with its semi-roundnose and lower velocity, it will penetrate deeper than a spitzer. I prefer it to the former 250-grain Remington PSP.

The test rifle was a Model 700 Classic bolt action with a 22-inch barrel, mounting a Leupold 4x Compact scope in a Weaver quick detachable mount. Rifling twist rate is one turn in 16 inches. The entire outfit, including scope and mount, weighs only 7 pounds, 10 ounces, a light rifle for so much power. A thick rubber recoil pad and proper stock dimensions made recoil feel about the same as that of a .30-06 weighing the same and firing 180 to 220-grain bullets.

Accuracy was not adversely affected by this rifle's lightness; factory ammo averaging 1⅛-inch groups (five-shot strings at 100 yards) with 200-grain loads, and 1½-inch groups with 250-grainers, shooting benchrest. The better handloads improved on that.

I can find only a single fault with this splendid big game rifle: It has been throated too long. The 250-grain factory loads have an overall length of 3.24 inches and their bullets must jump some .3 inch of freeboring before entering the rifling.

The 200-grain factory rounds, measuring only 3.12 inches overall, have still farther to go. Whether that was done to hold down pressures or to accommodate bullets longer and heavier than 250 grains, I'm not sure. My guess is, however, that it accounts for the slightly poorer accuracy ob-

tained with the 200-grain loads. While overly long throating causes fewer problems than throating which is too short, I believe a reduction in freeboring would prove beneficial.

Preparing for handload tests, some 14 different bullets, including 10 jacketed, one cast and three handgun slugs were assembled, along with 16 different powders. Cases were a mix of new Remington .35 Whelen brass and necked-up .30-06 arsenal Match hulls. Depended upon to perform the neces-

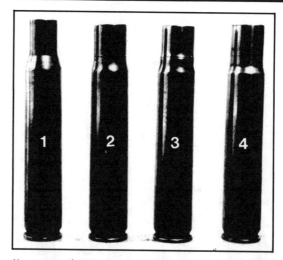

Ken converted .30-06 brass to .35 Whelen in three steps. Beginning with a (1) once-fired 06 case, (2) it was forced into a Redding sizing die with a tapered expander button which opened the case mouth to .35 caliber with one pass. After expanding the necks to .367 in a Belding & Mull die, then partially sizing the neck back to .358, a slight secondary shoulder was left (3) which held the case back against the bolt face while it was fireformed. (4) The final product, after fireforming. At the far right, a case showing evidence of impending separation. Ken found that new Remington cases stretched much more than the old arsenal brass.

sary work was a set of Redding dies containing a tapered expander plug which served to open up 06 case necks to .35 caliber with a single pass.

Case preparation came first. Modern references, including Omark Industries drawing No. 70799, list .35 Whelen case length as 2.494 inches, the same as the parent .30-06. Colonel Whelen's original cartridge drawing, which appeared in the September 15, 1923 issue of *The American Rifleman*, showed case length as 2.484 inches. Unfired R-P factory cases from which the bullets had been pulled, varied from 2.480 to 2.485 inches, verifying the good colonel's dimension. Following first firing however, many factory cases measured 2.490. Because there seemed to be some question as to the correct length, I decided on 2.490 inches as maximum. When cases exceeded that, they were trimmed back to 2.480. Although that was unnecessarily cautious, I experienced no excessive pressures caused by cases too long for the chamber.

Cases formed from 06 brass shorten during the process, so there is no need for trimming except to square-up case mouths which may have become slightly distorted in the expanding procedure.

Of particular importance is to make sure that in forming, case shoulders aren't set back, creating excessive headspace. In that connection, if you have a .35 Whelen rifle that was chambered for the cartridge when it was a wildcat, it should be checked for headspace before using either new factory ammo or formed 06 cases.

My routine practice of first weighing empty cases (including the fired primers), and then again after filling them with water to the base of a seated bullet — in this instance, a 250-grain Hornady roundnose for a 3.25-inch car-

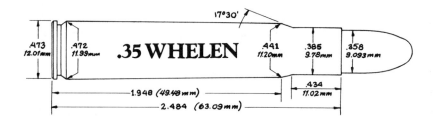

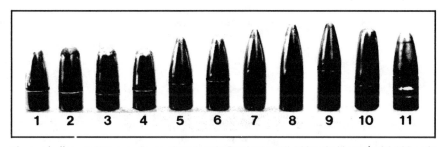

The test bullets: (1) 180-grain Speer, (2) 200-grain Remington, (3) 200-grain Hornady, (4) 200-grain Sierra, (5) 200-grain Hornady Spire Point, (6) 220-grain Speer, (7) 225-grain Sierra, (8) 250-grain Speer, (9) 250-grain Hornady Spire Point, (10) 250-grain Hornady and (11) 226-grain Lyman gas-check bullet No. 35897.

The Remington .35 Whelen

bullet	charge (grains)	powder	muzzle velocity 22-inch barrel (fps)	case	primer	overall cartridge length (inches)	case expansion*	remarks
180 Speer FNSP	47.0	IMR-3031	2,251	R-P	R-9½	3.12	normal	
	50.0	IMR-3031	2,394				normal	
	52.0	IMR-4064	2,377				normal	duplicates .300 Savage-180-grain ballistics
	55.0	IMR-4064	2,494				normal	
	57.0	IMR-4064	2,600				near max	duplicates .308 Winchester 180-grain ballistics
	57.0	IMR-4895	2,752				maximum	highest velocity load
200 Remington roundnose	48.0	RL-7	2,485			3.10	normal	
	52.0	RL-12	2,147				light	duplicates .35 Remington ballistics
	53.0	RL-12	2,225				normal	
	55.0	IMR-4064	2,486				normal	duplicates .358 Winchester ballistics
	57.0	IMR-4064	2,557				near max	second best accuracy
200 Sierra roundnose	52.0	IMR-3031	2,457			3.06	normal	very accurate
	54.0	IMR-3031	2,540				near max	
	55.0	IMR-3031	2,592				maximum	
200 Hornady roundnose	54.0	H-4895	2,415	FA-M		3.11	normal	good load
	56.0	H-4895	2,509	FA-M			maximum	
	56.0	IMR-4895	2,646	R-P			maximum	
200 Hornady Spire Point	57.0	IMR-4895	2,687	FA-M		3.25	maximum	very accurate
	56.0	IMR-4320	2,636	FA-M			near max	
	58.0	IMR-4320	2,707	FA-M			maximum	third best accuracy and highest velocity with 200-grain bullets

bullet	charge (grains)	powder	muzzle velocity 22-inch barrel (fps)	case	primer	overall cartridge length (inches)	case expansion*	remarks
220 Speer FNSP	54.0	IMR-4895	2,504	R-P	R-9½	3.22	near max	
	55.0	IMR-4895	2,583				maximum	
	55.0	IMR-4064	2,465				near max	duplicates .30-06 — 220-grain ballistics
	56.0	IMR-4064	2,516				maximum	very accurate
	56.0	IMR-4320	2,555				near max	
	60.0	IMR-4350	2,299		R-9½M		maximum	compressed load
225 Sierra spitzer boat-tail	50.0	H-335	2,365	LC-M	R-9½	3.30	normal	
	51.0	H-335	2,430	LC-M			near max	accurate
	53.0	H-335	2,549	LC-M			maximum	
	51.0	IMR-3031	2,427	R-P			normal	accurate
	53.0	IMR-3031	2,517				maximum	accurate
	53.0	H-4895	2,440				normal	most accurate load
	55.0	H-4895	2,545				near max	
	55.5	IMR-4064	2,499				near max	
	57.0	IMR-4064	2,568				maximum	fifth best accuracy plus best all-around
	55.0	IMR-4895	2,598	LC-M			maximum	accurate; duplicates .338-06; also, flattest long range trajectory and greatest retained energy at 200 yards
250 Speer spitzer	50.0	RL-15	2,200	FA-M		3.32	maximum	
	53.0	IMR-4895	2,453	R-P			near max	accurate
	54.0	IMR-4895	2,505				maximum	duplicates .350 Rem-Mag ballistics
	54.0	IMR-4064	2,396				near max	accurate
	55.0	IMR-4064	2,434				maximum	very accurate
	57.0	H-414	2,161		R-9½M		near max	
	57.0	W-760	2,163		R-9½M		near max	
	55.0	RL-19	1,946	FA-M	R-9½		light	duplicates .375 Winchester 250-grains
	58.0	RL-19	2,102	FA-M			maximum	fourth best accuracy
250 Hornady roundnose	53.0	H-4895	2,387	R-P		3.25	near max	very accurate
	55.0	H-4895	2,517				maximum	highest velocity w/250-grain bullets
	54.0	W-748	2,300				normal	
	55.0	IMR-4320	2,489				maximum	
250 Hornady Spire Point	53.0	IMR-4064	2,355			3.30	normal	
	54.0	IMR-4320	2,442				near max	
	58.0	IMR-4350	2,238		R-9½M		normal	
	59.0	IMR-4831	2,127		R-9½M		normal	compressed load; accurate

Revolver Bullet Loads

bullet	charge (grains)	powder	muzzle velocity 22-inch barrel (fps)	case	primer	overall cartridge length (inches)	case expansion*	remarks
158 Sierra JHC	30.0	IMR-4198	1,940	R-P	R-9½	2.94	normal	cartridges loaded with revolver bullets won't feed from magazine
	33.0	IMR-4198	2,132				normal	
140 Sierra JHC	33.0	H-4198	2,010			2.90	normal	best accuracy with revolver bullets
	35.0	H-4198	2,152				near max	not as accurate as 33-grain load
140 Speer JHP	42.0	H-322	2,262	LC-M			normal	
	45.0	H-322	2,434	R-P			maximum	favorite load with revolver bullets

Cast Bullet Loads

bullet	charge (grains)	powder	muzzle velocity 22-inch barrel (fps)	case	primer	overall cartridge length (inches)	case expansion*	remarks
226 Lyman #35897GC	22.0	IMR-4227	1,645	FA-M	R-9½	3.24	normal	
	24.0	IMR-4227	1,730				normal	
	28.0	H-4198	1,676				normal	
	27.0	IMR-4198	1,738				normal	best cast bullet load; duplicates power of old .38-55 high velocity load
	30.0	IMR-4198	1,853				near max	not as accurate as 27-grain load

Factory Loads

bullet	charge (grains)	powder	muzzle velocity 22-inch barrel (fps)	case	primer	overall cartridge length (inches)	case expansion*	remarks
200 Remington PCL			2,589	R-P		3.12	normal	
250 Remington roundnose			2,389	R-P		3.24	normal	

* Loads designated "maximum" or "near max" in this table are intended for use in the new commercial Remington rifles. Older custom-chambered rifles may require reduction in loads. The author's rifle also had a somewhat long .3-inch freebore; this may be reduced in later production rifles.

Test rifle was a Remington Model 700-C with 22-inch barrel with 1-in-16-inch twist; Leupold 4x Compact scope. Velocities chronographed with Oehler Model 33 Chronotach have been corrected to muzzle velocity.

Cartridge case code: R-P Remington .35 Whelen factory cases.
FA-M Frankford Arsenal Match .30-06 cases formed to .35 Whelen.
LC-M Lake City Match .30-06 cases formed to .35 Whelen.

Be alert — Publisher cannot accept responsibility for errors in published load data.

tridge length — gave the following weights:

	water (grains)
R-P .35 Whelen cases	59.5
Arsenal 06 Match cases	60.0

It was something of a surprise to find that the commercial Remington cases were heavier than the arsenal brass. The difference in both weight and internal capacity is miniscule and for those cases I used, can be disregarded.

While case capacity of the .35 Whelen comes close to duplicating that of the .350 Remington Magnum, being only about one grain less, the .350 Magnum (at least, my rifle of that caliber) allows somewhat heavier powder charges to be used. Consequently, I don't think it advisable to assume that .350 Magnum load tables, especially those loads close to maximum, should be applied without adjustment to the .35 Whelen.

For some reason, longitudinal case stretching was more pronounced with the new R-P cases than with the older arsenal brass. That is to say, the appearance of the bright ring encircling the cases just forward of their solid head sections, warning of the possibility of an incipient separation, occurred sooner with the commercial cases.

A possible cause: The dial calipers indicate that the diameter of unfired R-P cartridges at point-of-shoulder is only .430 inch. Once-fired factory cases measure .443 there. Case shoulders are visibly sharper on fired cases, too. The RCBS-Omark case drawing shows a shoulder diameter of .441 inch. While fired cases have an obviously adequate shoulder (as previously discussed), can it be that the rounded, less sharply defined shoulder of new unfired .35 Whelen cartridges permits brass to flow forward on first firing?

When excessive stretching occurred initially with the formed 06 cases, I tried expanding necks with a .367-inch expander button in my old Belding & Mull tool, then sized them back down to .358 (inside diameter) part way. That left a secondary shoulder measuring .395 (outside diameter) at the bases of the necks, which served to hold the cases back against the bolt face, letting the bolt close with some resistance. Stretching of cases thus formed slowed immediately and probably accounts for their longer life.

Another approach would be to seat the bullets out far enough to contact the rifling, thereby positioning the cartridge properly in the chamber. Cast bullets can be used to reduce costs.

Now let me be clear about all this. What I've just pointed out should not be taken as indicating insufficient headspacing. Once-fired factory cases, even before resizing, have diameters of .443 inch at their point of shoulder and .389 at their necks. That amounts to a difference of .054 inch or .027 per side, which is plenty of shoulder for headspacing. What I'm talking about here is the comparison between a sharply shaped shoulder and one that's rounded. Once case shoulders have been defined by fireforming, stretching reduces.

One more thing before we leave the subject of cases: As readers of my column know, I measure the base diameter of cases after every firing, noting the amount of expansion that has taken place as an indication of relative chamber pressure — relative, that is, to factory round expansion. It doesn't tell me what actual pressures were; just whether they were higher or lower than those produced by factory ammunition. Remington .35 Whelen loads expanded case bases from .4680 to .4685 inch, which were considered normal for the test rifle. On that basis, expansion measuring .4685 to .4689 inch was rated "Near Max," with .4690 to .4695 inch recorded as "Maximum." With that criteria as a guide, I experienced no case loss due to overexpansion.

Remington primers were used throughout the test series, mostly No. 9½ standard caps, except with the slower-burning powders. IMR-4350, IMR—4831, W-760 and H-414 were paired with No. 9½-M Magnum primers. Actually, the standard 9½s could have been used with all loads.

Let me start my discussion of bullets by going into a bit more detail on the rifle's long throating. Lightly sizing necks of a pair of cases, a 250-grain Hornady roundnose was finger-started in one and a 250-grain Speer spitzer in the other. After placing them, in turn, in the chamber, the bolt was carefully closed. Contact with the rifling seated those bullets to the maximum overall cartridge length allowed by the barrel throat. To my considerable surprise, I found those rounds measuring 3.52 inches with the Speer bullet and 3.55 inches with the Hornady. That is some .20 inch longer than the 3.32-inch length I used with the 250-grain Speers and a whopping .30 inch beyond the 3.25-inch length to which 250-grain Hornadys had been loaded!

Naturally, the freeboring effect would

be even greater with 180 and 200-grain bullets. How much influence the throating has on velocity and accuracy I don't know but I'd like to see it reduced by half.

Load tests were started with 200-grain bullets, commencing with a box of Remington roundnoses I had squirreled away. My best five-shot group at 100 yards cut ⅞ inch and the poorest, two inches. Not a bad beginning. Following that I tried 200-grain Sierras and Hornadys, both roundnoses and pointed. The latter averaged smaller groups, of course. Of the four different 200-grain bullets, the test rifle seems to like the Remington and Hornady Spire Points best.

Of all the full velocity rifle bullets tried, the 180-grain Speer FNSP gave the poorest average accuracy ranging from 1⅞ to 2½ inches, possibly due to that long throating. Of course, that is adequate for short-range deer loads. The highest velocities were recorded with them.

The 220-grain Speer FNSPs came next. I was particularly glad to find that despite their small flat nose, they fed from the magazine and chamber in the test rifle without a hitch, making them highly useful hunting bullets.

The bullet handloaders of .35-caliber bolt rifles have long been waiting for, a 225-grain spitzer boat-tail, was introduced by Sierra in 1988. That is the intermediate weight bullet of high ballistic profile the .35 Whelen needed to compete with the .338-06 and is sure to prove beneficial in the .358 Winchester and .350 Remington Magnum as well. It offers the flattest, long-range trajectory in the Whelen, with the greatest retained energy at 200 yards and beyond. It may prove to be the optimum bullet for all-around use. Accuracy in the test rifle was outstanding and it gave up less than 100 fps to most 200-grain loads.

For the largest game, I'd choose either 250-grain Speer spitzers or Hornady roundnoses of same weight, depending upon the terrain, cover and hunting ranges. A finer .35-caliber bullet than the 250-grain Speer for larger game under varying field conditions would be hard to imagine. The ever-reliable Hornady, with its nicely formed round nose has served me well in other .35-caliber cartridges and makes this a timber rifle par excellence.

Even though Hornady no longer lists any 250-grain Spire Points, I had some left and couldn't resist trying them with several different loads. While they were good bullets offering somewhat flatter trajectories, I confess to a preference for the semi-roundnoses in typical cover.

Bullets heavier than 250 grains weren't tried. All but custom bullets in those weights have been discontinued and too much velocity must be sacrificed, with the attendant possibility of insufficient expansion from this non-magnum cartridge. Better leave the 275 and 300-grain bullets to the magnums.

Since .38 Special bullets have the same .358-inch diameter, our editor suggested that specimens loaded in .35 Whelen cases might offer an inexpensive alternate for small game and practice shooting. Sierra's 158-grain and 140-grain JHCs and Speer 140-grain JHPs were tried, using different powders with each type. Velocities varied from 1,940 to 2,132 fps with the 158-grainers and from 2,010 to 2,434 fps with the 140s. Hundred-yard groups measured from 1½ to 2⅜ inches. Because they won't feed from the magazine without jamming their blunt noses against the barrel's breech face, they must be single-loaded directly into the chamber. With the right loads, they are suitable for pest shooting and plinking, especially the 140-grain Speer and Sierra bullets.

Another budget-saving alternative would be to use cast bullets. That too was tried, employing Lyman mould 35897 — a 226-grain gas check bullet no longer listed. Sized .359 inch and seated to an overall cartridge length of 3.24 inches, those bullets grouped from 1½ to 2¾ inches, depending upon the load.

The powder story of the .35 Whelen trials is soon told. Befitting its caliber and case capacity, powders of medium burning rate are most suitable, ranging from Reloder 7 and IMR-3031 on the fast side to IMR-4064 and 4320 on the slow. The final verdict on the newer Reloder powders isn't in yet. They'll require more testing, as will W-748, but based upon my trials it appears that H-414, W-760, IMR-4350 and IMR-4831 are all too slow-burning, failing to develop velocities comparable to faster burning powders in full power loads.

Unless you are willing to use a drop tube and go to some lengths to settle powders in cases, 59 grains of either IMR-4350 or 4831 is about all you can get in a .35 Whelen case and leave room to seat 250-grain bullets to proper depths. Those are compressed loads, of course.

Of all the powders used in the trials with jacketed rifle bullets from 180 to 250 grains, my choice would be either H-4895 or IMR-4064 as best combining accuracy with high velocity. The most accurate load consisted of Sierra's new 225-grain spitzer boat-tail over 53 grains of H-4895 clocking 2,440 fps. The load with the flattest trajectory over 200 yards saw the same bullet driven by 55 grains of IMR-4895 for 2,598 fps — a maximum load which also possessed the greatest retained energy at 200 yards.

IMR-4064 was the powder giving the second-best accuracy and the load considered best all-around. For third place I'll nominate IMR-4320 as producing both fine accuracy and high velocities. After that comes IMR-4895, the velocity champ, plus IMR-3031 and H-335. Those last two named are best limited to use with bullets of 225 grains and under, however.

Cast bullets responded best to faster burning powders, 27 grains of IMR-4198 ranking first in accuracy among those tried. Duplicating the old .38-55 high velocity load, it is adequate for deer at short range but is otherwise best restricted to practice and informal target shooting.

IMR-4198 and H-4198 performed well with jacketed hollowpoint handgun bullets, 33 grains of H-4198 turning in the smallest groups when paired with Sierra's 140-grain JHCs. Still, H-322 rates as the standout favorite because it allowed velocities to be increased to 2,400+ fps without excessive case expansion or loss of accuracy, using up to 45 grains with 140-grain Speer JHPs.

In the accompanying load table, I've attempted to demonstrate the great versatility of the .35 Whelen cartridge by showing how it can be handloaded to duplicate the ballistics of a number of other cartridges ranging from the .300 Savage, .35 Remington and .358 Winchester to the .350 Remington Magnum. That, of course, is one of the outstanding attributes of the old .30-06 case, making it a prime favorite for necking up (and down) to other bore sizes.

Approached with reasonable expectations (for it is not a magnum), it always seems to work well in calibers from .25 to .35 — and the addition of Sierra's 225-grain Spitzer boat-tail has given the .35 Whelen just what it needed to challenge the .338-06.

Loads designated "Maximum" or "Near Max" in the table are intended for new Remington rifles. Custom-chambered rifles built on other actions may require some reduction in loads.

Care should be exercised by owners of ex-military actions which have been rebarreled to .35 Whelen. The chambering reamers used may have differed and excess headspace may be present. If you have such a rifle, better have it checked out for safety.

The .35 Whelen ranks with the .338-06 and .350 Remington Magnum as one of our most versatile, medium-caliber cartridges. ●

CHAPTER
20

Built by Garrett Accur-Lt. D.F.S. Co. on an FN Mauser action, the author's .35 Whelen Improved features a Burris 1¾-5x scope. The 20-inch barrel averages about 70 fps less velocity than 22-inch barrels.

depends on reduced body taper and a sharpened shoulder angle for increased powder capacity. The Brown-Whelen, probably the second most widely known Whelen improvement, also features a longer body, created at the expense of more laborious forming chores and a shortened neck.

In addition to expanded powder capacity, the improved cartridges provide a certain amount of mechanical advantage over the original Whelen. Reducing body taper diminishes bolt thrust to some degree. The modest shoulder left when .30-06 brass is necked up to .35 caliber is, by all

than I had hoped for in terms of performance and general usefulness.

Wanted was a short, light rifle for hunting in timber, but fully equal to the demands of the occasional shot at longer range — 300 yards or so. A cartridge capable of handling bullets larger than .30 caliber, with good weight and sectional density, was indicated. The general rule of thumb says kinetic energies of 2,000 foot-pounds are the minimum for elk. This may or may not be a meaningful requirement, but it doesn't seem excessive force on 700 or 800 pounds of brute vitality.

My .338 Winchester Magnum would not do. It has the required ballistic qualifications, but weighs 8¼ pounds with scope and sling. Besides, it has the 24-inch barrel usually found on magnum rifles and is therefore too tall for the stated purposes.

When specifications for the rifle

.35 Whelen
Improved Ackley

G. Sitton

ANY CONSIDERATION of the .35 Whelen Improved must begin with a definition. The original cartridge developed by James Howe and Col. Townsend Whelen in the early 1920s has attracted the attentions of numerous more recent wildcatters, all intent on somehow enhancing the archetype. This has to do with the Ackley version. It is the most popular of the lot, I believe.

Each of the improved case designs

reliable accounts, adequate for headspacing purposes as long as sizing dies are adjusted with care. The more pronounced shoulders of the improved versions are better than adequate. Blowing out the case apparently retards the stretch and flow of the brass under firing pressures, too. Cases for my .35 Whelen Improved (Ackley) need trimming far less often than did those for a conventional Whelen I owned some years ago.

I came to the improved Whelen as a compromise cartridge for a specialized elk rifle. It turns out to be rather more

began to evolve in my mind, a magnum of any stripe was eliminated from consideration. As envisioned, the rifle would weigh less than 7½ pounds. For reasons having to do with function and appearance in about equal measure, the fiberglass Mannlicher stock by Garrett Accur-Lt. D.F.S. Co. was selected. This handle dictated a 20-inch barrel. The magnum rounds are not suited to such a brief tube — noise levels go up as velocities go down. Magnum recoil in the trim little rifle would have been overly vigorous, particularly with the heavy bullets I had in mind for most uses.

At the time all this rumination took place — early 1989 — the shooting press was full of notices on Remington's adoption of the standard Whelen cartridge. The original round can be prudently loaded to produce 2,500 fps at the muzzle with 250-grain bullets; this from a 22-inch barrel. A shorter barrel would, of course, give something less than that and residual energy would drop below 2,000 foot-pounds somewhere around 225 yards, according to the Barnes Ballistics program.

The standard Whelen was not enough, but an improved version looked like it might be. The Brown-Whelen was passed over as too much work for too little gain. With factory Whelen brass from Remington, the Ackley looked easy. I like easy. Certainly, the added capacity of the blown-out case would more than compensate for velocity lost to the short barrel. Another turn on the computer projected energies of more than 2,000 foot-pounds all the way out to 300 yards *if* 2,600 fps could be achieved at the muzzle with 250-grain Speer spitzers.

The decision was made. A Model 98 FN Mauser action and a bill of particulars were sent to Mark Phipps at Garrett Accur-Lt. D.F.S. Co. In the fullness of time, a long carton arrived from Fort Collins, Colorado. It was

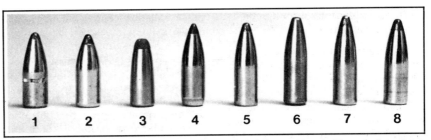

The .358-inch bullets used in the author's testing included the (*1*) 200-grain Hornady Spire Point, (*2*) 200-grain Barnes spitzer, (*3*) 200-grain Hawk (6D ogive), (*4*) 225-grain Sierra spitzer boat-tail, (*5*) 225-grain Nosler Partition, (*6*) 240-grain Trophy Bonded Bear Claw, (*7*) 250-grain Barnes spitzer and (*8*) 250-grain Speer spitzer.

Christmas in the simmering heat of a Tucson summer. The action had been fitted with a No. 2 contour Douglas Premium barrel (one-in-16-inch), a Buehler safety and a Timney trigger. Two-piece bases and rings were from Leupold. With a blind magazine to eliminate the weight of a floorplate, the trigger guard was one of the new steel ADL units from Remington. All of the metal had been bead blasted and blued to a flat finish. With a sling and a Burris 1¾-5x scope in place, the rig weighs just over 7¼ pounds. It measures 41 inches, end to end.

While waiting for the rifle, I had ordered 100 Remington .35 Whelen cases. Using a set of standard Whelen dies, fireforming loads were assembled with 50 grains of IMR-4895, Winchester Large Rifle primers and 250-grain Speer spitzers. The bullets were seated in the lands in order to center the cartridge in the chamber. This tends to improve the concentricity of fireformed cases. It is worth noting that the first lot of brass has served throughout the entire load development program for this rifle. Some are tired and will be retired shortly, but none have failed.

A pleasant morning on the range furnished fully formed cases for the improved cartridge. Fireforming in the chamber of the Garrett rifle increases usable capacity by 6 percent, as measured in grains of water, over that of the factory case. Three samples were sent to Bill Keyes at RCBS for reference in cutting the sizing die. A month or so later, the dies arrived and I was ready to begin work in earnest. The dies were, incidentally, exactly what I have come to expect from 20 years of reliance on RCBS: finely finished and precisely correct.

The factory brass, which measures on average slightly less than 2.484 inches,

is shortened in fireforming by some .010 inch. After trimming to square up their mouths, my cases measured 2.470 inches. I took Ken Waters' maximum case length of 2.490 inches and never encountered any difficulties. Being able to let cases grow .020 inch between trimmings is a real luxury. Since the improved Whelen lengthens very slowly in a closely cut chamber, trimming is needed only after six or seven firings.

Thanks to demand created by Remington's adoption of the standard Whelen, .358 bullet selection is no longer a problem. To date, I have tried, at least briefly, bullets ranging in weight from the 180-grain Speer FNSP to the 300-grain Barnes RNSP. As a practical matter, the useful slugs in the .35 Whelen Improved probably run from 200 to 250 grains. The 180-grain projectiles are meant to operate at .35 Remington velocities and will be seriously overdriven at anything approaching normal velocities in the improved Whelen. On the high end, the 275-grain Barnes spitzer delivered nothing you could call accuracy, perhaps because this very long bullet is not adequately stabilized by the barrel's slow one-in-16-inch twist and the rather sluggish velocities attainable. Likewise, the 300-grain Barnes RNSP, while it shot reasonably well, is simply too much weight for a non-magnum cartridge. When the situation calls for 300 grains, I pull down the .375 H&H Magnum.

I would note before addressing the specifics of bullet choice that my rifle will not win any benchrest matches. It is, however, very steady, delivering more than satisfactory precision with many different component combinations. Accuracy with the best ammunition identified to date varies from just over .9 to 1.2 MOA. Given the violence

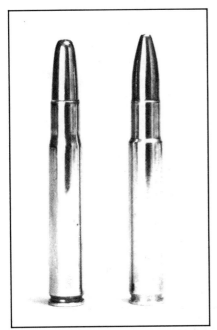

At left is Remington's factory version of the .35 Whelen loaded with the 250-grain RNSP bullet. On the right, the .35 Whelen Improved (Ackley) with a 240-grain Trophy Bonded Bear Claw bullet that was swaged down from a .375 slug.

of full-house loads in such a light rifle, I have no complaints.

In the Garrett rifle, decent handloads give more than ample accuracy with 200-grain bullets. Both the Hornady Spire Point and the Barnes spitzer will go inside 1¼ inches (three shots) at 100 yards with at least one of the loads listed. Either bullet can be loaded to produce lethal hits on deer-size animals without worrying about bullet drop out to about 300 yards.

Since no 200-grain bullet will make a legitimate sniping load in the improved Whelen, I like the slightly more blunt 200-grain Hawk slugs very much. I would pick the .030-inch jacket and six-diameter ogive for a high-velocity deer loading. The two-diameter form and .025 jacket loaded down to about 2,200 fps should make a superb, meat-saving combination in heavy cover. I have used Hawk bullets in five different firearms, from the .300 Winchester Magnum to the .458 Lott, and performance has been uniformly fine.

This cartridge does its best work with projectiles weighing from 225 to 250 grains. Given efficient shapes, bullets in this range provide superior velocity and energy retention at responsible ranges beyond 100 yards. Trajectories are as flat as can be had from a non-magnum .35. We are fortunate to have several options, and more on the way. In addition to the bullets included in my testing, Bill Steigers has a 225-grain Bitterroot, Barnes has a 235-grain X Bullet nearing production and Speer's 250-grain Grand Slam should be on the shelves by the time this sees print. I begged a handful (literally) of the Grand Slams as deadline loomed, shot them into three groups, and got the merest impression that they will serve well on truly large game. Finally, Hornady has introduced a new 250-grain Spire Point; this with a longer, sleeker nose and the can-

.35 Whelen Improved (Ackley)

bullet	powder	charge (grains)	primer	velocity (fps)	O.A.L.	remarks
200 Hornady Spire Point	RL-15	63.0	Fed. 210M	2,841	3.20	choice long range deer load
	S-4065	59.0		2,646		near maximum
	IMR-4064	61.0		2,783		normal
200 Hawk softpoint	IMR-3031	58.0	Fed. 210M	2,824	3.14	
	RL-12	56.5		2,329		deer load for brush, mild
	H-4895	60.5		2,870		accurate with high velocity
200 Barnes spitzer	RL-7	51.0	Fed. 210M	2,639	3.17	moderate
	S-3032	57.0		2,807		good accuracy
225 Nosler Partition	RL-15	61.0	Fed. 210M	2,743	3.30	near maximum
	IMR-4064	61.0		2,747		near maximum
	AAC-2520	62.0	Fed. 215	2,750		excellent all-around load
	IMR-3031	58.0	Fed. 210M	2,603		maximum
225 Sierra spitzer boat-tail	H-4895	60.0	Fed. 210M	2,739	3.27	most accurate load tested
	S-4065	59.0		2,597		
	IMR-4320	61.5		2,805		choice long-range load
	RL-12	58.0		2,523		accurate, near maximum
240 Trophy Bonded Bear Claw	IMR-4320	59.0	Fed. 210M	2,616	3.32	favorite load for large game
	AAC-2520	60.0	Fed. 215	2,645		accurate and fast
250 Speer spitzer	IMR-3031	55.5	Fed. 210M	2,544	3.34	maximum
	H-4895	58.0		2,586		
	S-4065	57.0		2,547		accurate
	IMR-4064	58.5		2,562		near maximum
	IMR-4320	59.0		2,609		accurate-MOA
	AAC-2520	60.5	Fed. 215	2,613		equals IMR-4320 load
	H-380	62.5		2,451		near maximum and poor accuracy
	H-414	65.0		2,435		near maximum
	S-4351	63.0		2,437		compressed load
250 Barnes spitzer	IMR-4320	58.5	Fed. 210M	2,613	3.36	near maximum
	H-4895	57.5		2,542		maximum
	AAC-2520	60.0	Fed. 215	2,621		accurate, near maximum

All loads were safe in the test rifle. Other custom rifles may require substantial reduction in loads. Reduce listed loads by at least 10 percent for starting loads in other rifles. The author and Wolfe Publishing assume no responsibility for the use of these loads by others.

Test rifle was a Garrett Accur-Lt. Mannlicher with 20-inch barrel, one-in-16-inch twist; Burris 1¾-5x scope. Velocities chronographed with Oehler Model 35P and are listed as instrumental at 10 feet. Average temperature: 85 degrees Fahrenheit.

All cartridge cases were formed from Remington .35 Whelen factory cases.

Be alert — Publisher cannot accept responsibility for errors in published load data.

nelure properly located for the .35 Whelen, instead of the .350 Remington Magnum as was the case with the old design.

Nosler's Partition and Sierra's spitzer boat-tail bullets weighing 225 grains will cover most hunting requirements in North America. They afford the greatest long-range potential by a substantial margin. If the possibility exists of an opportunity appearing on the far side of 200 yards, I would pick one or the other over any 200-grain bullet, even for game as small as deer. Out yonder, no matter how you calculate killing effect, the 225s have significantly more of it than the 200s.

The 240-grain Bear Claw from Trophy Bonded Bullets is a particular favorite of mine. Three shots routinely punch into 1⅛ inches at 100 yards. Penetration and weight retention verge on the spectacular. Loaded to full potential, it makes the improved Whelen a genuine 300-yard elk and moose slayer. I took a six-point bull with the Bear Claw in New Mexico last fall; my friend Chris Denham took another in northern Arizona. Both were one-shot kills. Both shots were through-and-through. Everything between entry and exit was ruined.

Great penetration is also the chief benefit of the 250-grain bullets. They are just the thing for our largest game, particularly when ranges are expected to be moderate. They do not, however, give up much in the way of reach to the 225-grain slugs.

Assuming the 10-inch vital zone appropriate to elk, moose and optimum zero, the 225-grain Nosler Partition has a maximum point blank range (PBR) of 330 yards when started at 2,750 fps. For the 250 Speer spitzer at a muzzle velocity of 2,600 fps, the PBR is 314 yards. Three hundred-yard energies for the Nosler and Speer are 2,313 and 2,311 foot-pounds, respectively.

To make the promised point concerning the limitations of the 200-grain bullets, the Hornady Spire Point in that weight has a ballistic coefficient of only .295. Driven to 2,840 fps at the muzzle, its PBR is 297 yards on a vital zone of eight inches (deer-size). Sierra's 225-grain spitzer boat-tail, with a ballistic coefficient of .385, has exactly the same PBR when started 100 fps slower. The Sierra may be preferred because it carries a 24 percent energy advantage at the 300-yard mark. With 1,738 foot-pounds remaining at that distance, the 200-grain bullet is by no means deficient for beasts of medium size; the 225 is just more authoritative. As a general rule, when lighter bullets provide no appreciable extension of hitting ability, I gratefully accept the power bonus of heavier bullets. As long as bullets expand without exploding on impact, you cannot shoot a soft-skinned animal too hard.

Powders for the .35 Whelen Improved are no mystery at all. As these are hunting loads, a balance of precision and speed is the goal. Early work established IMR-4320 as the premier propellant with 225 and 250-grain projectiles. Then, the powder disappeared. Whether we will see it again is unknown at this time. Having six or seven pounds of IMR-4320 on hand consoled me, but a suitable replacement was still required. I have for years been annoyed by writings which tout various discontinued powders as the absolute ultimate for this round or that. There was no need for anxiety. Accurate Arms 2520 is an altogether acceptable substitute for the IMR product, delivering comparable velocities and even shading the older fuel on accuracy with some bullets. For 200-grain bullets, H-4895 stands out, with RL-15 and IMR-4064 running close behind.

One of the alleged virtues of *improved* chamberings is the ability to fire standard, factory ammunition as need may dictate. How much of an advantage this may be in reality is problematical. Remington's 250-grain load gives almost 2,400 fps in standard Whelen rifles with 22-inch barrels. Their 200-grain offering gets along at a bit under 2,600 fps. In my rifle, with its shorter barrel and improved chamber, instrumental velocities 10 feet from the muzzle are 2,321 fps for the big bullet and 2,563 fps for the small one. Obviously, not much lost, though it must be said that chronographing was done in very hot weather. Results at 70 degrees Fahrenheit would likely be less impressive. The 250-grain roundnose load is also nicely accurate. Three-shot groups with the 200-grain load tend to spread across three inches and more.

The .35 Whelen Improved is a good and broadly useful cartridge, adequately powerful and flat-shooting for virtually all North American big game requirements. With good ammunition, it will do out to 300 yards and more. This ranging capability would have sufficed for all but 2 or 3 percent of the animals I have taken in 30 years of more or less fanatical hunting.

As a sworn enemy of the "all-around rifle" — a notion beloved of editors and people who will never hunt widely enough to need one — I am forced to admit that a .35 Whelen Improved could serve reasonably well across the length and breadth of this continent. Provided proper bullets are loaded, the cartridge has ample force for all circumstances except brown bears in the bushes. In a 7¼-pound package, calculated recoil energy with the heaviest loads is 37.5 foot-pounds, or approximately 36 percent greater than would be generated were the same rifling firing 180-grain bullets at top speeds from a .30-06. I do not find this objectionable, but it is near the boundary of things I do for fun.

In all, I like the .35 Whelen Improved so much that I intend to give it to Mike Ray, a young outfitter friend. He has gazed upon it with some longing and I have a slightly refined version of the rifle in mind for Mark Phipps to build. As any hardened rifle crank will understand, settling for a very good thing is simply intolerable. ●

CHAPTER
21

The .35 Newton

Ken Waters

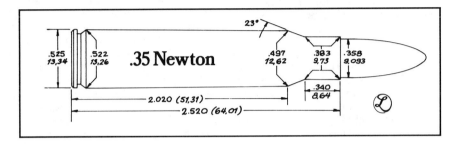

WHEN IS A magnum *not* a magnum? Why, when it's one of the big rimless Newton cartridges. Back in the Wildcat Cartridge section of *Handloader* No. 102, we discussed the .30 Newton, its historical background and designer Charles Newton's efforts to introduce modern high velocity cartridges for his struggling rifle production. This time we'll take up the .30 Newton's big brother — the .35 Newton — most powerful of the Newton cartridges commercially produced.

It was in 1915 that Charles Newton worked up the design for his Big 35, utilizing the same large rimless case he'd previously used for the .30 Newton, but with the neck expanded to hold .35-caliber bullets. Like its predecessor, the .35's large powder capacity and high velocity performance qualified it as a magnum (although never called that), despite the lack of a belt around its case.

Probably due to World War I, production of the new cartridge was slow getting started. Then Major Townsend Whelen in his book, *The American Rifle*, published in October 1918, stated that development of the .35 Newton cartridge had not been completed at that time. Just when production of this ammunition started, or who made it first, I've been unable to track down.

Eventually, the Western Cartridge Company adopted the .35 Newton for commercial production, but that date also eludes me. My old 1925 catalog fails to show it, but Phil Sharpe's 1938 book, *The Rifle in America*, lists it as, ". . . still commercially manufactured." That reference would seem to infer the cartridge had been in production for some time. I found it listed in the Lyman *Ideal Handbook* No. 29 issued in 1929, together with a Western Lubaloy bullet. Based on that, I assume Western Cartridge Company production pre-dated that year.

Newton's ballistics for the .35 called for a 250-grain soft-point bullet with a muzzle velocity of 2,975 fps from a 24-inch barrel, giving the very high muzzle energy rating of 4,925 ft/lbs. Remaining velocities were quoted as being 2,737 fps at 100 yards, 2,512 at 200, 2,297 at 300 and 1,896 fps at 500 yards.

Western factory .35 Newton cartridges were loaded with 250-grain open-point expanding bullets to a more conservative 2,670 fps muzzle velocity, also from 24-inch barrels — a figure that seems more realistic.

Other sources reported 200 and 220-grain bullets in this cartridge reaching 3,000 fps muzzle velocity, claiming 250-grain bullets could be loaded to reach 2,800 fps, and 275 grain slugs to 2,600 fps. Even these assertions might have difficulty standing up if fired over a modern chronograph, but I have trouble accepting the Newton claim of 2,975 fps with a 250-grain bullet.

Working pressure was said to be 50,000 psi and it must have taken all of that to approach those ballistics! Old DuPont tables listed loads of 68 to 78 grains of IMR-3031 with 200-grain bullets giving velocities in the 2,625 to 3,000 fps range, and 62 to 72 grains of IMR-3031 with 250-grain bullets for muzzle velocities of 2,400 to 2,765 fps.

Before the introduction of the IMR-series of powders in the 1930s, the older DuPont powders Nos. 15½ (introduced in 1919), and 17½ (1923), were used in loading the .35 Newton. These were the predecessors of IMR-4064 and IMR-3031 respectively. Still earlier, Newton was said to have used the older DuPont Nos. 10 and 15 powders.

While one source maintained that the .35 Newton's large case was unsuitable for reduced powder charges, another writer of the time, in listing handloads such as 50 grains of IMR-3031 or 57 grains of IMR-4064 with cast lead alloy gas-checked bullets, was saying virtually the opposite.

Experienced handloaders know there are very few cartridges which can't be successfully loaded down, especially those of .375 Magnum size or smaller. It sometimes takes a bit of experimenting, but it is seldom impossible. Newton himself is said to have planned to produce a scaled-down loading for the .35 Newton that would be suitable for deer hunting and target shooting.

Case capacity of the .35 Newton comes close to being ideal for the bore size. Newton rifled his .35-caliber barrels with a 1-in-12-inch twist to stabilize bullets up to 275 grains in weight. Some .35 Newton rifles from custom gunmakers are said to have had 1-in-14-inch rifling twists.

No factory-standard rifles other than the Newtons are known to have been chambered for this cartridge, although it is possible that one or more of the custom gunmakers of the period, such as the Hoffman Arms Company or Niedner Rifle Corporation, *may* have produced a few rifles in .35 Newton caliber.

Newton's rifles, weighing only some 7½ pounds, were too light for such a powerful cartridge. Recoil was definitely on the heavy side, even excessively so in those too-light rifles. Attempting to play down this adverse feature, Newton compared the .35's recoil to that of a 12-gauge shotgun with trap loads, fired at a stationary target. As anyone who has ever fired a lightweight 12 gauge with deliberate aim at a stationary target knows, this is not something to be casually dismissed as unworthy of notice!

Whether considered from the standpoint of ballistic performance or big game killing capability, the .35 Newton, like the .30 Newton, has always been recognized as possessing design excellence ahead of its time. Contemporary writers appear to have especially liked its steep shoulder angle and slight case body taper, both outstanding features in an era of tapered cases and long, low-sloping shoulders.

Why didn't this cartridge gain wider acceptance? Most probably because it was offered only in a single make of rifle — and that one, a short-lived financial failure. Had Winchester or Remington adopted the caliber as a standard chambering, it would likely still be with us. The Western Cartridge Company discontinued production of .35 Newton cartridges around 1938, causing the round to revert to wildcat status.

For a brief time following World War II, the Speer Cartridge Works of Lewiston, Idaho, produced reloadable .35 Newton cases for handloaders. Apparently there wasn't enough demand even for those limited quantities, and production soon ceased.

George Nonte, in his book *Cartridge Conversions*, told how .375 H&H Magnum cases could be converted to .35 Newton by slightly turning down the belt, trimming to 2½ inches, full-length sizing and fireforming. Unfortunately, this method permits some excessive case expansion to take place just forward of the belt, not exactly ideal if full-power loads are to be used.

Now that strong new RWS brass in 8x68S caliber is available, pocketed for American primers, I believe this would be the best case to use for forming to .35 Newton. Like the latter, the 8x68S is a large rimless case without a belt, and comes closest to matching the Newton in size. Trimmed to 2.5 inches and run into a .35 Newton full-length sizing die, simultaneously expanding case necks, 8x68 cases should chamber

in a .35 Newton readily and be ready for fireforming.

The redoubtable big bore authority, Elmer Keith, said that the .35 Newton exceeded the .35 Whelen in power and had a flatter trajectory, making it a good cartridge for elk. Loaded with 275-grain bullets, it was preferable to the .375 Magnum with 270-grain bullets, he felt, because of its greater sectional density.

The .35 Newton even went to Africa in the hands of the renowned Charles Cottar, who used it to stop rhinos. Certainly, it would have proven to be a most excellent cartridge for Alaskan hunting. Any chance it might have had for a comeback, however, has probably been eliminated by the popular .338 Winchester Magnum. Nevertheless, in its day, the .35 Newton was quite a cartridge! ●

CHAPTER
22

The .35 Whelen and .338-06 COMPARED

Layne Simpson

Layne's .35 Whelen was built by E.C. Bishop & Son. Butch Searcy was responsible for all the metal work. With an old but treasured Redfield 1-4x variable, four cartridges and a light sling, the rifle's field weight is right around nine pounds.

THERE'S NO BETTER spring tonic for a rifle lover than a new custom rifle. During the past few months, I have been putting such a rifle through its paces and oh, what joy it doth bring. It's a special rifle because its creation has been a totally new experience.

Now don't misunderstand. I own a few other custom rifles, am proud of them and enjoy them, but most are either pre-1950s vintage, were traded for, or I participated in building them. One exception is a rifle given to me by a close friend.

Until the new rifle arrived, I had never experienced the enjoyment of creating one on paper, exactly the way I wanted it to be, and then let someone else do all the work. About two years ago I decided it was time I did. I placed an order with E.C. Bishop & Son of Warsaw, Missouri.

I also specified that Butch Searcy of Farmington, New Mexico, perform all metal work.

The rifle has a '98 Mauser action with square bridge receiver, dovetailed for Kimber quick-detachable scope rings. Its 22-inch, Apex barrel has a rifling pitch rate of 1 in 16 inches. At the muzzle sits a barrel band front sight. At the rear, a quarter rib holds a simple folding leaf. Between the two is a sling swivel stud mounted under a barrel band. The only things different about the action are a custom bolt handle and a Model 70 type safety on the bolt shroud.

Bishop calls the rifle Masterpiece Grade. Its stock dimensions are mine but the European styling is theirs, from the nicely shaped cheekpiece to the steel grip cap and schnabel forend. The thin recoil pad is a Pachmayr Old English model, brown in color. I specified lightly figured wood with emphasis on proper grain flow through the wrist area. It had to be

133

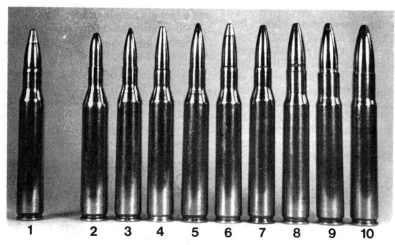

The (1) .30-06 and some of its commercial and wildcat offspring: (2) .22-06, (3) 6mm-06, (4) .25-06, (5) 6.5-06, (6) .270 Winchester, (7) .280 Remington, (8) 8mm-06, (9) .338-06 and (10) .35 Whelen.

relatively light and yet strong. What it all boils down to is a rifle made for *using* instead of *looking* but as a bonus, it looks good too. With an old and treasured Redfield 1 to 4x variable sitting on top, the rifle weighs eight pounds, six ounces. A light sling and four cartridges brings it close to nine pounds.

The rifle is chambered for the .35 Whelen. Not the Brown version, nor even the improved, just the plain-vanilla .35 Whelen. Despite the availability of numerous modern marvels of the wildcatter's art, I chose an ancient old boomer said by some to be so decrepit as to have moss on its back and a creak in every joint.

Does it really? Is a cartridge that smites a 300-yard target with as much energy as the .300 Winchester Magnum really ready

Left, the test rifles: on the far side, the Searcy Alpiner in .338-06 with its electroless, nickel-plated action and 24-inch SGW barrel. On the right, Layne's Bishop-built .35 Whelen.

for Sunnyside Acres Home for the Aged? Does a seven-inch drop at 300 paces relegate the old-timer to the class of forked sticks and strips of rubber? I think not.

Despite its track record and continued popularity among those in the know, the .35 Whelen has reeled from a few blows to its blind side of late. it seems most writers can't praise other '06 wildcats without giving the old .35 Whelen a sharp boot in the ribs for good measure. My good friend Ken Waters didn't exactly break any ribs in *Handloader* No. 87, but he did manage to step on a finger or two in his summary of the .35 Whelen. Steve Timm followed suit with another boot where it hurts in his excellent article in *Handloader* No. 109. Of course, both Ken and Steve were spotlighting the .338-06 wildcat.

I have no quarrel with either Ken or Steve. Both have every right to voice their opinions and I'm glad they did. I enjoyed both articles and thanks to them, was inspired to write this one. In case you missed the two articles, Steve did a fine job of backing up what he said with field experience — which is awfully tough to argue with. Ken — well you know how it is with him — when he speaks, people listen, and for good reason. Ken was working up loads and shooting game with them long before many of us were even born. In other words, he knows a thing or two about what he speaks.

Still, as the patient said to the doctor with the big, long knife, "I think it's time we had a third opinion." With this in mind, here's mine.

I needed a .338-06 in order to make a shoulder-to-shoulder comparison of the two. Butch Searcy filled in the blank with the loan of one of his fine fiberglass-stocked Alpiner rifles. With Redfield 2-7x Tracker scope, one-piece base and rings, the Alpiner weighed 7 pounds, 10 ounces. Only problem was, it arrived with a 24-inch barrel. "Chop off two inches," said Butch, but I just couldn't bring myself to take a hacksaw and mutilate someone else's rifle.

Let's take a look at both wildcats. Cases for either are easily formed by running '06 brass through a full-length resizing die. Case loss with virgin brass is zero during the neck-up process but quite high with cases already work-hardened by several firings. My .35 Whelen dies are Pacific. RCBS made the .338-06 dies. Due to the popularity of these wildcats, dies for them are stock items with both companies. A tapered expander plug is standard equipment with the RCBS dies but must be specified with Pacific, otherwise you'll get a plug too fat to enter '06 necks. Cases formed for both cartridges will need to be squared by trimming to eliminate lopsided mouths.

Now I'll try once and for all to dispel an old wive's tale about the .35 Whelen. *The cartridge has plenty of shoulder for headspacing.* Just to prove it, I fired a round in my rifle and ejected the empty case. I removed the extractor from the bolt so it couldn't resist the firing pin thrust against the case. Next, I deprimed the case with Dick Lee's little punch tool (without resizing the case) and seated a fresh primer.

Placing the primed case back into the chamber, I closed the bolt, pulled the trigger, opened the bolt and pushed the case from the chamber with a cleaning rod from the muzzle. Then I went through the same routine with the same case 10 more times. According to my measurements, firing pin thrust had not pushed back the case's shoulder one iota. Keep in mind now, the '98 Mauser firing pin whacks a primer with the slam of a log sliding down a water chute.

Who started such a silly rumor? Darned if I know. Possibly some chap who set case shoulders back too far with his resizing die. Maybe it was some fellow promoting his version of the .35 Whelen Improved. I could care less who started the rumor because it amounts to no more than stale bologna. The old .35 Whelen headspace fallacy is just that — a fallacy. A problem with the written word is that it often gets carved into granite whether it's true or not, and for this reason the .35 Whelen will always be burdened with an undeserved untruth.

At this point in our race, the .35 Whelen and .338-06 are running neck to neck. Cases are easily formed for both and both have adequate shoulder area. True, the .338-06 has more shoulder area but the .35 Whelen has enough. Where I come from, enough is all you need.

Now let's look at bullets. For shooting game up to deer in size, the Hornady .35-caliber, 200-grain Spire Point will do anything the Speer .338-caliber, 200-grain spitzer will do. However, under most conditions neither cartridge is actually needed for shooting deer. A .30-06 with 150-grain bullet at 3,000 fps is just as effective, shoots flatter and punishes the shoulder less. While I'm on the subject, a .30-06 loaded with a Nosler or

Speer 200-grain spitzer is no slouch in the company of the two larger calibers, when they also are loaded with the same bullet weight.

I have a .30-06 with 24-inch barrel which will push the 200-grain Nosler to 2,700 fps with no sign of excessive chamber pressures. The same bullet exits the muzzles of most 22-inch barrels a bit over 2,600 fps. When chambered in 24-inch barrels, the .338-06 and .35 Whelen will push 200-grain bullets about 2,800 fps.

If we take Nosler, Speer and Hornady ballistic data at face value and compare the three rounds' performance (see Table I), it would appear that the .30-06 is

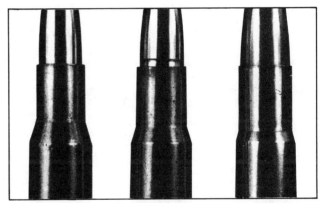

Although both the .30-06 (left) and .338-06 (center) boast more shoulder area, Layne's tests proved the .35 Whelen case (right) had enough.

After .30-06 cases are expanded to .338 or .358, their mouths should be squared by trimming.

When all three rounds are loaded with 200-grain bullets, Layne considers the old '06 the best performer.

Table I
200-grain Bullets — Performance Comparison

caliber	velocity (fps)	sectional density	at 100 yards trajectory	at 100 yards energy	at 200 yards trajectory	at 200 yards energy	at 300 yards trajectory	at 300 yards energy	at 400 yards trajectory	at 400 yards energy
.30-06	2,700	.301	+3.0	2,830	+2.2	2,537	-3.4	2,239	-17.0	1,972
.338-06	2,800	.254	+3.0	2,990	+2.3	2,556	-4.4	2,172	-18.2	1,836
.35 Whelen	2,800	.223	+3.0	2,746	+1.8	2,145	-6.7	1,660	-24.5	1,274

Trajectories in inches, energies in foot-pounds.

superior to both its offspring when the range exceeds 200 yards and when all are loaded with 200-grain bullets. True enough, the .33 and .35-caliber bullets will likely open up to a larger diameter but the .30, with its higher sectional density, will penetrate deeper. If choosing between the three cartridges at this point in my comparison, I'd pick the .30-06 with a 200-grain bullet for elk. Too, I could also load it with lighter bullets for lighter game.

I brought the .30-06 into the argument

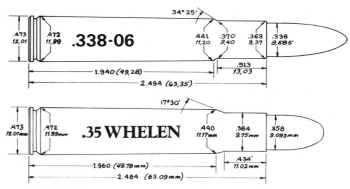

Table II				
.35 Whelen				
bullet	powder	charge (grains)	velocity (fps)	accuracy level
250 Speer SP	N-204	59.0	2,350	C
	N-204	63.0	2,520	A
	N-204	64.0	2,587	C
	N-204	65.0	2,648	A
250 Hornady SP	N-204	63.0	2,517	B
250 Hornady RN	N-204	63.0	2,553	A
250 Norma RN	N-204	63.0	2,590	D
250 Speer RN	N-204	63.0	2,557	A
250 Remington SPCL	N-204	63.0	2,531	C
250 Speer SP	H-414	62.0	2,564	B
	IMR-4350	61.0	2,570	D
	W-760	59.0	2,375	D
	W-760	60.0	2,394	E
	H-380	58.0	2,527	D
	IMR-4320	56.0	2,538	A
	IMR-4895	54.0	2,507	C
	IMR-4064	52.0	2,472	D
	N-202	52.0	2,484	D
	H-335	49.0	2,419	D
220 Speer FN	H-414	65.0	2,526	D
	N-204	65.0	2,559	A
	IMR-4320	58.0	2,679	C
200 Hornady SP	H-414	65.0	2,529	D
	W-760	65.0	2,544	C
	N-204	65.0	2,575	C
	H-380	64.0	2,705	D
	IMR-4320	59.0	2,743	C
	IMR-4064	56.0	2,612	D
	N-202	56.0	2,641	B
	IMR-4895	54.0	2,577	B
	H-335	53.0	2,576	E

Test rifle was Bishop Masterpiece Grade '98 Mauser with 22-inch Apex barrel, 1-in-16-inch twist, Redfield 2-7x scope. Winchester cases and 120 primers. Oehler Model 33 Chronotach with Skyscreen III detectors. Average temperature 85 degrees F.

Accuracy levels of loads shown

A +	under ¾ inch	C	1¼ to 1½ inches
A	¾ to 1 inch	D	1½ to 2 inches
B	1 to 1¼ inches	E	over 2 inches

Table III				
.338-06				
bullet	powder	charge (grains)	velocity (fps)	accuracy level
275 Speer SS	IMR-7828	58.0	2,231	A
	W-785	58.0	2,192	D
	H-450	58.0	2,184	D
	H-4831	58.0	2,304	C
	H-4831	59.0	2,348	A +
	N-MRP	58.0	2,421	A +
	N-MRP	59.0	2,469	A +
	IMR-4831	56.0	2,328	A +
250 Hornady RN	IMR-7828	61.0	2,278	A +
	W-785	61.0	2,232	B
	H-4831	61.0	2,408	D
	N-MRP	65.0	2,532	A
	H-4350	61.0	2,534	A
	IMR-4831	61.0	2,541	B
	N-204	61.0	2,645	A
	W-760	60.0	2,569	A +
	H-414	60.0	2,583	A
	IMR-4350	59.0	2,610	A
250 Nosler P	N-MRP	64.0	2,551	B
	H-4350	60.0	2,569	A +
	N-204	59.0	2,632	C
	W-760	59.0	2,541	B
225 Hornady SP	N-204	62.0	2,723	E
	IMR-4350	61.0	2,710	B
	IMR-4320	54.0	2,681	A
210 Nosler P	N-204	64.0	2,825	E
	H-414	62.0	2,807	C
	IMR-4350	62.0	2,829	E
200 Speer SP	H-4350	61.0	2,610	D
	H-4350	65.0	2,730	C
	IMR-4831	61.0	2,655	D
	IMR-4831	65.0	2,775	C
	W-760	60.0	2,680	C
	W-760	61.0	2,693	E
	N-204	61.0	2,705	D
	N-204	64.0	2,819	D
	H-414	61.0	2,743	E
	H-414	63.0	2,802	D
	IMR-4350	61.0	2,752	E
	IMR-4350	63.0	2,817	D
	IMR-4320	55.0	2,774	E

Test rifle was a Searcy Alpiner with 24-inch SGW barrel, 1-in-10-inch twist, Redfield 2-7x scope. Winchester cases and 120 primers. Oehler Model 33 Chronotach with Skyscreen III detection system. Average temperature, 85 degrees F.

All loads were safe in the test rifle but must be reduced by at least 10 percent for starting loads in other rifles. The author and Wolfe Publishing assume no responsibility for the use of these loads by others.

Be alert — Publisher cannot accept responsibility for errors in published load data.

to make a point: I really don't believe a logical reason exists for choosing the .338-06 or .35 Whelen over their daddy unless bullets heavier than 200 grains are used. Now I'll back up and get on the trail I started down.

As popular opinion seems to go, the .338-06 has an edge over the .35 Whelen in bullet selection. I really can't buy that as a reason for choosing one over the other. A wider selection, yes — but when viewed through a practical eye, I don't see it as being better until we reach game larger than elk and moose.

For the .35 Whelen, we have three bullets exceeding 200 grains in weight: the Speer 220 flatnose and 250 spitzer, plus Hornady's 250 roundnose. For game larger than deer, the 220-grain bullet is out, leaving us with two. For woods hunting the Hornady 250-grain roundnose has a slight edge because its tougher jacket hangs onto more core out to about 100 yards. For shots at longer ranges, the Speer 250-grain spitzer takes the lead because it shoots flatter, resists wind deflection better and packs more punch. The Speer is the best all-round choice. Its penetration at close range is a bit less than that of the Hornady bullet but still adequate for elk-sized game when started at .35 Whelen velocities. Another bullet superior to both in all ways except accuracy is the Remington 250-grain Core-Lokt spitzer, but since it is no longer available, I'll do no more than mention it for the benefit of those who, like me, have hoarded a supply.

When loaded with H-414, N-204 or IMR-4350, the .35 Whelen with its 22-inch barrel will launch the 250-grain Speer bullet at 2,600 fps. According to Speer, when this bullet is zeroed three inches high at 100 yards, it strikes 1.5 inches high at 200 and 7.2 inches low at 300 yards. Residual energy at the three ranges is 3,208, 2,725 and 2,303 foot-pounds. Out at 500 yards (for whatever the information is worth), the bullet is still chugging along with over 1,600 foot-pounds of steam.

Everything including barrel lengths being equal, the .338-06 won't quite match .35 Whelen velocities for the same reason that the .338-06 will push a 200-grain bullet slightly faster than is possible with the .30-06. For sake of comparison, let's say that the .338-06 and .35 Whelen are equal in terms of potential velocity.

In the .338-06's corner I see nine bullets: Nosler 210 and 250-grain spitzers; Speer 200 spitzer, 250 Grand Slam and 275-grain semi-spitzer; Hornady 200-grain flatnose, 225 Spire Point and 250-grain roundnose plus the Sierra 250-grain spitzer boat-tail. Exiting the muzzle at 2,600 fps, the 250 Sierra delivers 3,340, 2,965 and 2,623 foot-

pounds of energy at 100, 200 and 300 yards, respectively. Zeroed three inches high at 100 yards, trajectory reads 1.75 inches high at 200 and six inches low at 300. At 500 yards, 2,023 foot-pounds of energy remains.

At this point in the contest, the .338-06 has surpassed the .35 Whelen in performance — on paper. Trajectories are about the same but the .338-06 packs more punch at long range. However, for shooting game at close to medium range (where both cartridges are probably most often used), the .35 slips by the .33 in real life.

According to my bullet recovery box, the Hornady and Speer .35-caliber bullets are superior in penetration to that of the Sierra .338. When fired into the test medium at 50 yards, the Hornady and Speer bullets retained over 50 percent of their original weight while the Sierra's jacket and core, without fail, went their separate ways. It probably has to do with the boat-tail jacket.

Switching to the Nosler 250-grain Partition bullet (the new spitzer), we see the .338-06 leap ahead in penetration and slightly best the .35 Whelen in residual energy. The heavy Nosler bullet also puts the .338-06 ahead in the bone-smashing department but since one does not intentionally shoot edible, non-dangerous game in areas containing heavy bone, I rate such an advantage as academic. For smashing the shoulders of a brown bear at 14 paces, the .338-06 has an edge but why hunt such game with either of the '06 wildcats when we have the .338 Winchester and .340 Weatherby Magnums available.

For all-round use in the .338-06 on game up to elk in size, my vote is cast for the Nosler 210-grain Partition as the bullet most likely to succeed under all conditions and circumstances. A 24-inch barrel will send it on its way around 2,800 fps but to keep our comparison even-steven with my short-barreled .35 Whelen, I'll use a muzzle velocity of 2,700 fps.

Zeroed three inches high at 100 yards, the 210-grain Nosler will be 1.4 inches high at 200 and 7.4 inches low at 300 yards. Residual energy for the three ranges is rated at 2,829, 2,342 and 1,929 foot-pounds. At this point the .338-06 has lost some ground since it has fallen behind the .35 Whelen's 2,300 foot-pounds at 300 yards. Still, energy alone does not a satisfactory big game cartridge make and to illustrate what I mean, I'll go back to the recovery box.

When fired into my expansion medium, the 210-grain Nosler retained an average of 74 percent or 155 grains of its original weight. The 250-grain .358 Speer hung onto 53 percent of its weight for a net retention of 133 grains while the seemingly tougher Hornady bullet of the same

weight retained 145 grains for 58 percent. The Nosler bullet penetrated an average of two inches deeper than did the Speer and Hornady, probably because of its higher velocity and smaller frontal area.

What we have here is somewhat of a Mexican standoff. The .35 packs more punch but the .33 penetrates a bit deeper. Nosler bullets are constructed for maximum weight retention and penetration with optimum expansion at any reasonable impact velocity. Whether fired from a standard or magnum cartridge, this bullet will open up, yet retain enough of its weight for maximum penetration.

In contrast, Hornady and Speer .35-caliber bullets are designed to operate at standard velocities. When launched from a .338 Magnum, the Nosler bullet will usually retain more weight and penetrate deeper than Speer and Hornady bullets fired from a .358 Magnum. All of this is fine so long as we continue to remember that this particular story is about two standard-velocity cartridges, not two magnums.

Pitting heavier .35-caliber bullets against a lighter .338-caliber may sound like stacking cards in the Whelen's favor but such is not the reason for doing it. My intent is to compare both cartridges when they are loaded with what I consider to be optimum bullets.

You might be wondering about the performance of other bullets in my expansion box. The Hornady 200-grain .358 Spire Point retained a bit more weight than the Speer 200-grain .338 and penetrated a bit deeper into the expansion medium. The Hornady 225-grain .338 retained an average of 12 grains more weight than the Hornady .35-caliber bullet but penetration was practically identical with the two. The Speer 275-grain .338 semi-spitzer retained an average of 14 grains less weight than did the Hornady 250-grain .358 roundnose but penetrated an average of six inches deeper.

Not surprisingly, the Nosler 250-grain .338 bullet retained almost 76 percent of its weight and penetrated 11 inches deeper than any other bullet tested. I had intended to include the Speer 250-grain Grand Slam in my tests but unfortunately, none were available.

Again, our two wildcats appear to be about dead even when used on game no larger than elk and moose. In the .338-06 corner is its milder recoil with the lighter Nosler bullet but there is not as much difference as you might think, given rifles of the same weight. Even so, can it not be said that the .35 Whelen offers more of what increases the pulse rate of big bore fans? If it is, in fact, true that by increasing bullet diameter from .308 to .338 inch, we realize an increase in killing power with the .338-06 over that of the .30-06, does it not also hold true that increasing bullet diameter by an additional .02 gives the .35 Whelen an edge over the .338-06?

The one slight advantage I have uncovered in favor of the .338-06 has nothing to do with performance, but with its lower expansion ratio as compared to that of the .35 Whelen. Top velocities can be reached with a greater variety of propellants. In addition, slower burning powders like IMR-4831 and H-4831 can be used.

In the other corner, when loaded behind the 250-grain bullet, H-414 and IMR-4350 exceed 2,550 fps in my .35 Whelen while a compressed load of N-204 almost makes it to 2,650 fps in the 22-inch barrel, all at safe pressure indications in my rifle. Needless to say, N-204 is the .35 Whelen powder — if it can be found. Since I have taken the liberty of borrowing Ken Waters' method of illustrating which powder and bullet combination produced best results in the two test rifles, I won't dwell on the subject any longer.

The .338-06 and .35 Whelen are both fine cartridges and I wouldn't spit twice for any difference between the two — but let's face it, neither is as flexible as its parent. Moreover, both eat dust from the .338 Magnum by a good hundred yards and neither is as good a choice for large, dangerous game. With either the .338-06 or .35 Whelen, I wouldn't back down from the largest North American game but if it has the capability of eating my young and tender body, I expect my palms would sweat a bit less if wrapped around a .338 Magnum or a .375 H&H. By a similar token, if I had to spend the rest of my days hunting whitetails, mule deer, pronghorn and such with either of the two, I wouldn't complain a great deal but I'd really rather have a .30-06.

Flipping a coin might be the simplest way to choose between the two '06 wildcats. If you enjoy playing around with a number of different bullets, the .338-06 might be the way to go. In the other corner, if settling on one good load and spending the rest of your time doing something else is your cup of tea, then the .35 Whelen will serve your needs just fine. I lean slightly toward the .338-06 because I do enjoy working with a variety of bullets, but that doesn't mean it's one bit better than the .35 Whelen.

If ever I should build a .338-06 or another .35 Whelen, I'm not at all sure I would use the rifling pitch rates which seem to have become standard for both cartridges. I say this because of my belief in the 210-grain Nosler and 250-grain Speer bullets as best for the respective calibers. My .35 Whelen is quite accurate with the Speer bullet but I wonder if maybe it would be more accurate with a 1-in-14-inch twist.

Winchester chose a 1-in-10-inch twist for the .338 Magnum in order to stabilize its long 300-grain bullet (no longer available). Of the few rifles in .338 Winchester Magnum I have tested, all were more accurate with the heavier (and longer) bullets. The .338-06 test rifle indicated the same preference. This leads me to believe that a 1-in-12-inch twist would merit consideration. The slower rate may not stabilize the Sierra bullet or the 275-grain Speer but according to my calculations, all others including the 250-grain Nosler and Speer 250-grain Grand Slam would fly nose-first from a 1-in-12-inch rifling pitch rate. More important, I wouldn't be surprised to see an improvement in accuracy with the 200-grain Speer and 210-grain Nosler. ●

CHAPTER
23

The .350 G&H Magnum

Ken Waters

A S I BELIEVE I remarked once before in these columns, the first test of a wildcat cartridge's worth is whether it meets a specific need. A second criteria — for this writer, at least — concerns case forming. How complicated and/or laborious a process is it? The simpler it is, the higher rating I give it, and not just because it's easier or faster. As a general rule, the fewer and less radical changes a case requires in forming, the longer its expected life will be, and that can be important when each and every case has to be hand-made!

An old wildcat cartridge, seldom mentioned these days, but one that is nevertheless deserving since it met both the cited requirements, is the .350 G&H Magnum, also known as the .35 Griffin & Howe Magnum. Dating back to the mid-1920s, it was developed by the prestigious New York gunsmithing firm of Griffin & Howe in response to a perceived need for a cartridge and rifle of medium caliber suitable for all-around use by American big game hunters going to Africa.

Leslie Simpson, perhaps the most experienced American hunter on African game at that time, had recommended that a most practical rifle would be one chambering a .35-caliber cartridge loaded with a heavy bullet to as high a velocity as permissible within pressure and rifle weight limitations. Specifically, he suggested its ballistics call for a 275-grain bullet with a muzzle velocity of 2,500 fps, but added the caveat that if such a combination produced excessive pressures, velocity, rather than bullet weight, should be reduced.

He was, of course, referring to shooting the many species of African plains game, making it quite clear that for a stopping rifle, he favored a big double-barreled ejector type of at least .450 caliber with 480-grain bullets. He felt the proposed .35-caliber rifle, possibly with a lighter bullet, should also prove useful for North American big game hunting.

Those recommendations made a lot of sense. Griffin & Howe, recognizing the logic, developed just such a cartridge. Exercising the professional gunsmith's sound judgment for which that firm has long been known, they kept its design simple and straightforward by merely necking-down the .375 H&H Magnum case to hold .35-caliber bullets, leaving the case its original full length. Fired .375 Magnum cases could thus be re-formed to .350 G&H Magnum by a single pass through a full-length sizing die. New unfired .375 Magnum brass might simply be neck-sized to .35-caliber — convenient, time-saving and easy on the cases. No shortening, annealing or other high jinks needed!

The G&H cartridge met Simpson's specifications almost to the letter: A 275-grain, .35-caliber bullet with a muzzle velocity of 2,441 fps for African hunting, or one of 220-grains at 2,790 fps for American big game. One source even claimed a muzzle velocity of 2,600 fps for the heavier bullet, though the reference may have been to a 250-grain bullet. Muzzle energy of the 275-grain G&H load was listed as 3,640 foot-pounds — knockdown power rivaling the great .375 H&H Magnum.

Those earliest .350 G&H Magnum cartridges were loaded with either semi-pointed or open-point bullets having thick copper jackets produced by the old Western Tool & Copper Works. Herein lay the first obstacle to the cartridge's success. In those days, the .35 Remington and .35 Winchester with their thinner jacketed 200 and 250-grain bullets were the popular .35 calibers, the big (and infrequently seen) .35 Newton being the only other high velocity cartridge of this bore size. Consequently, the commonly available .35-caliber bullets were too thin-jacketed for the magnums.

At the same time, Elmer Keith reported that although the 275-grain W.T.C. Co. bullet was proving acceptable as to shape and weight, the open point was too small and its jacket *too* thick at the nose for reliable expansion except at short range. In view of that, his proposal for a 300-grain, .35-caliber bullet seems a bit strange. Of course, it was meant for American game, for which the 275-grain bullet was not intended. That hard nose should have been just the ticket for raking shots requiring deep penetration on large game and, with its better nose shape, shoot flatter over longer ranges.

At any rate, the problem of obtaining .35-caliber bullets suitable for American hunting was the first barrier to be overcome. It was not the only one, however. A second obstacle was presented by the .350 G&H cartridge's great overall length: 3.70 inches. That required either a magnum Mauser action or rebarreling one of the long American bolt actions such as the Winchester Model 70 Magnum, Remington Model 30 or Enfield, with their long bolt throws. Magnum Mauser actions were quite costly, even at pre-war prices, and owners of Model 70 rifles in .375 H&H Magnum caliber had little incentive to rebarrel them to .35-caliber, especially in view of the bullet situation then prevailing.

Today, we have better bullets. Hornady makes 250-grain roundnoses intended for .35-caliber magnums. Speer offers a spitzer in the same weight with a ballistic coefficient of .446. Barnes lists a truly splendid selection including a 250-grain spitzer with .032-inch jacket thickness for thin-skinned game, a 275-grain spitzer with .049-inch jacket and a 300-grain roundnose with a choice of .032 or .049 jackets, plus a 300-grain roundnose with full metal jacket for the big, tough stuff. There's no longer any need to downgrade this cartridge because of a lack of good bullets.

Too, there are current, more appropriate powders to be considered. In the big magnum case, IMR-4350, H-4350, Norma-204 and IMR-4831 would all be capable of producing high velocities with lower chamber pressures than the old No. 15½ powder formerly used. It should now be possible to reach 2,600 or 2,700 fps with 275-grain

bullets, and 2,750 fps, or a mite faster with those weighing 250 grains. For smaller big game, reduced loads using powders of medium burning rate, such as H-4895, IMR-4895, 4064 and 4320 would be appropriate when combined with thinner-jacketed bullets.

Old records show the original load of a 275-grain bullet at 2,441 fps as having a mid-range trajectory of only 2½ inches over 200 yards. Even flatter shooting could be expected with modern powders and bullets of higher ballistic coefficients.

Recoil should be quite tolerable for an experienced big bore shooter in rifles of eight to nine pounds, and comparatively moderate in those weighing nine pounds or more, especially if bullets no heavier than 250 grains are used.

In addition to the aforementioned actions capable of conversion, there are at least four others currently available which are listed as being suitable for full-length magnum cartridges, including the .300 and .375 H&H Magnums, and the Weatherby .300 and .340 Magnums. All should be suitable for building a .350 G&H Magnum with overall cartridge length held to 3.60 inches. They are the Sako

A-3 (Magnum), Weatherby Mark V, Kleinguenther K-15 Insta-Fire and Interarms Mark X Magnum. The Mark X has the old, much missed claw extractor. With one of those actions as a basis, there should no longer be a problem of action length.

With the former obstacles eliminated, the old .350 Griffin & Howe Magnum becomes a better as well as a more practical wildcat than it ever was in its heyday. Oh yes, I'm well aware that we now have .35-caliber magnum cartridges of close to standard length, including the fine commercial .358 Norma Magnum, plus such reputable wildcats as the .35 Ackley Magnum and .35 Apex Magnum. For those shooters who place great stress on shorter bolt travel, they are undoubtedly the way to go. There are other shooters however, myself included, who don't find a long bolt throw objectionable, and would therefore exclude this factor from consideration.

On balance, I suppose that with the .375 H&H Magnum and .358 Norma Magnum calibers to choose from, there is little need for the .350 G&H Magnum, but wildcat fanciers don't always have to prove a need for their pets — despite my criteria. ●

CHAPTER
24

9x56mm

John B
Van Marter

Mannlicher-Schoenauer

THE DEVELOPMENT of hand-loads for a new rifle or cartridge is always an enjoyable experience. Recently, I have had the pleasant task of working with a number of rifle-and-cartridge combinations that went beyond my normal handloading requirements. These included Mannlicher-Schoenauers in 6.5x54mm, 8x56mm, and 9x56mm; a Kessler *drilling* in 16-gauge-by-16-gauge over 8x57mm JR (0.318 inch bullet diameter); an 8mm-06 Ackley Improved; and the cream of the crop, an original .416 Rigby. This article deals with two 9x56mm Mannlicher-Schoenauers, their challenges (read *problems*), and the answers that I finally settled on.

Both were Model 1905 carbines with eighteen-inch barrels and double set triggers. One had a 2-7x Leupold scope, the other a 2½x Bushnell, both in Jaeger side mounts. Both rifles had been rebedded in PPG 777 epoxy. The new bedding supports the rear tang and the area from the front of the magazine well to the rear sight on the barrel. The rebedding was necessary because the small recoil lugs had set back in the rifles' original bedding.

The second rifle required a new stock, as the factory stock had been broken through the magazine area and repaired. The choice for replacement was a Fajen classic-style stock, for two reasons — aesthetic appeal and a minimum drop in the butt to help

control recoil. The recoil felt on the face is much less with this new stock than it is with the factory stock on the other rifle.

The designation *Model 1905* indicates the year that the rifle was introduced, which was also the year that a new cartridge was introduced — the 9x56mm. As might be expected, a cartridge with a nine-millimeter bullet (0.354 to 0.356 inch in diameter) at a velocity of twenty-one to twenty-two hundred feet per second would allow the taking of game larger than was normally found in Europe. This combination was recommended for use in both Africa and Asia on thin-skinned animals, normally up to some twelve hundred pounds, which would include some of the larger antelopes. Also, I imagine that in a pinch, it might stop a big cat at short range.

The 9x57mm Mauser was also in use at the same time for the same game, and it was thought to be a better cartridge than the 9x56mm Mannlicher. Its 245-grain bullet had a velocity of twenty-three to twenty-four hundred feet per second and should have produced greater penetration and shock, therefore helping to ensure more reliable kills. The operating pressures for both the 9x56mm Mannlicher-Schoenauer and the 9x57mm Mauser were in the range of thirty-nine to forty thousand pounds per square inch. I suspect that the pressures were kept to this level to

avoid problems that might arise in the high temperatures common in Asia and Africa.

Handloading the 9x56mm Mannlicher-Schoenauer has produced some of the most satisfying results that I have had in my years of handloading — three-quarter-inch to seven-eighth-inch groups with two-fifty-grain Speer spitzers at a hundred yards, from a seven-pound carbine with full-length factory stock.

Development of loads started in a rather unusual way. Mannlicher literature warns against using ammunition other than the 9x56mm Mannlicher-Schoenauer — in other words, don't use 9x57mm Mauser, even though it may chamber. This warning seems to indicate that the headspace or over-all case lengths or diameters, or some combination of these on the 9x57mm Mauser cartridge should not allow it to chamber in a 9x56mm Mannlicher. George Nonte's book on cartridge conversions lists two sets of different dimensions for the two cartridges. Well, both of the 9x56mm Mannlichers that I used accepted 9x57mm Mauser ammunition as if they had been chambered for it.

The owner of the factory-stocked Mannlicher carbine had on hand a supply of Kynoch factory-loaded 9x57mm ammunition. Breaking down a number of rounds revealed an average of forty-eight grains of a flake powder, a 245-grain round-nose bullet, and a Berdan-primed case that weighed a hundred sixty-six grains (more about the weight of the case in a moment).

The factory bullet for the 9x57mm Mauser was oversize for the Mannlicher bores by 0.0015 inch. When this ammo was fired in one Mannlicher, the only sign of high pressure was definite resistance to bolt rotation. The five-

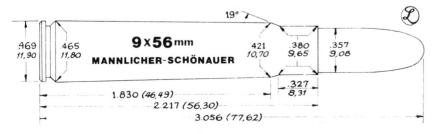

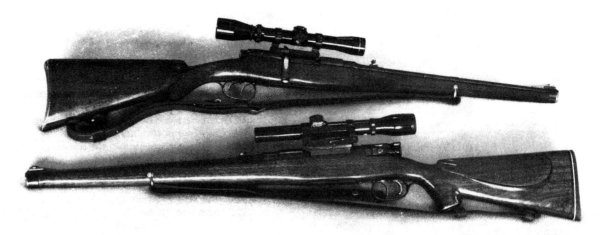

The rifle that Van Marter's friend owns (*top*) is a Mannlicher-Schoenauer with the original stock. Van Marter's own rifle is a similar barrel and action with the stock recently replaced with a Fajen "Classic" blank (*bottom*).

shot group measured two and a half inches — fired at a hundred yards. I broke down three rounds and removed three grains of powder from each charge, then reassembled the three cartridges and fired them. The group size was now an inch and three quarters, and the bolt lift was still sticky, so I reworked three more rounds. I removed six grains of powder from each charge this time, reassembled the cartridges, and fired them. The group was now an inch and seven eighths, but the bolt opened smoothly, so the functioning of the rifle seemed all right.

Back to the matter of the weight of the case: decapped Kynoch cases weighed a hundred sixty grains, and I felt that reworking some .30-06 national-match brass that I had on hand would be worth my while. My rationale was that for a given chamber, light cases and sticky bolt lift indicated either relatively soft, thin case heads or high pressure — or both. Bob Hagel has written on this topic of case design in *Handloader* 90 and 91. Also, having to rework the

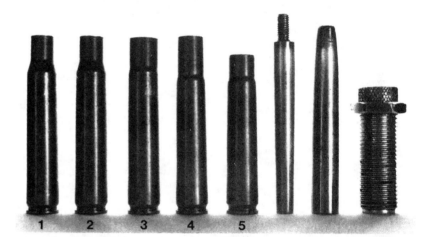

Forming cases for the 9x56mm Mannlicher-Schoenauer (5) from .30-06 brass (1) is easy, particularly with a pair of special tapered pins (6, 7) for the top plug (8) of a Lyman M-2 die. Neck to 8mm (2), then to .375 (3); size neck down to 9mm (4), leaving shoulder in new location, then trim to final case length (5).

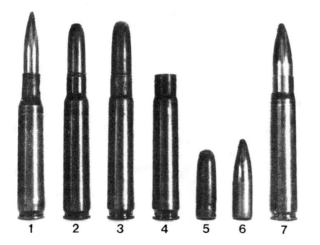

The fifty-seven-millimeter-long Mauser case has known a good many bullet diameters and shoulder locations — for example, the 7x57mm Mauser (1), the 8x56mm Mannlicher-Schoenauer (2), and the 9x57mm Mauser (3, 4). Original 9mm rifle bullets (5) are smaller than the 0.358-inch diameter of Speer .35 bullets (6), requiring that current .35 bullets be swaged down. Van Marter loaded reswaged Speer spitzers in arsenal brass re-formed to 9x56mm (7).

9x56mm Mannlicher-Schoenauer
loads with modern American components

FIRST RIFLE

charge (grains)	powder	velocity (fps)	group size (inch)
45	N-203	1,950	13/16
43	IMR-3031	2,085	1-5/16
44		2,128	2-13/16
45		2,177	1-1/2
46		2,205	1-7/8
44	N-202	1,934	1-1/4
45		1,982	2-5/16
46		2,047	1-11/16
47		2,093	1-5/8

SECOND RIFLE

charge (grains)	powder	velocity (fps)	group size (inch)
44	IMR-3031	1,996	
45		2,077	
46		2,088	

Speer 250-grain spitzers, sized to 0.3542 inch in diameter; LC 64 NM military brass with CCI 200 primers in first rifle. R-P 7x57mm Mauser brass with W-W 120 primers in second rifle; average velocities instrumental at 12.5 feet from muzzle; three-shot groups; all charges weighed. *These loads were near maximum in the two test rifles. Reduce all data at least fifteen percent for beginning loads. The author is responsible for these data and loads in the test rifles only.*

146

factory loads, decapping and repriming Berdan cases, seemed like more effort than should have been necessary.

I made new cases by necking .30-06 brass up to 8mm and then to 9mm, setting the shoulders back, trimming to length (2.20 inches), and deburring the mouths. I removed the two-diameter cast-bullet sizing pins from the plug of a Lyman M-2 neck-expanding die and substituted first one and then a second replacement taper pin. The first or smaller pin tapers from caliber .25 to 8mm, the second or larger from .30 to .41. I overexpanded the necks to about caliber .38 (0.380 inch) to make sure that the 9x56mm sizing die resized the neck diameters correctly and allowed the shoulder to be re-formed for zero headspace. Either 7x57mm or 8x57mm cases can also be used by necking them up to 9mm and resizing them in the 9x56mm Mannlicher-Schoenauer die, trimming them to length, and deburring their mouths.

The Kynoch bullets that were used during the firing of the factory loads were recovered from the soft soil of the hundred-yard berm, and they had come completely apart, with the cores separated from the jackets. Also, the jackets were badly broken up.

I had a swaging die made with a 0.354-inch-diameter bore to reduce both the Kynoch factory bullets and the Speer bullets to produce a better diameter fit to the bore and to help reduce the excessive pressures. Using the larger-diameter bullets with reduced loads merely created extensive copper fouling in the bore, seemingly because of soft jacket material. So problem number one was to make bullets of the proper diameter to fit the bore, and problem number two was to clean the bore of the fouling left by the original firing test.

I tried cleaning the bore the easy way — with Hoppe's solvent, a brush, and patches. No luck at all; so much for the easy way. Then I used J B compound, and after half an hour of scrubbing, I still could not see much progress. Even mercury left in the bore for three days didn't faze the fouling (it works on *lead* fouling, but not on copper). I finally used twenty-eight-percent stronger ammonia in the bore for twenty-four hours. I should have tried this procedure first — it cleaned out all of the fouling, so that was the solution to problem two.

After I had reduced some Speer bullets in diameter, I assembled them in loads with national-match brass using Norma 203 powder and CCI 200

primers. Loading began at forty-two grains of Norma 203 and extended through forty-six grains in one-grain increments. The aforementioned groups of three quarters and seven eighths of an inch showed-up at forty-five grains. Pressure signs — bolt lift and case-head expansion — indicated that this very accurate load was also safe.

The average velocity for the above load was 1,950 feet per second. Bullets recovered from the hundred-yard berm were intact and nicely mushroomed. The only fly in the ointment for this combination came to light when I rechecked the diameters of the bullets. Evidently, the swage die had expanded slightly, as the bullet diameters were over 0.355 inch. A new swage produced bullets 0.3542 inch in diameter, and these worked just fine. The bore was badly fouled again, but this time, I knew how to clean it the first time around. I filled the bore with twenty-eight-percent stronger ammonia, left it for twenty-four hours, and went back to square one with a clean bore and bullets that were of the right diameter.

One comment on this method of cleaning the bore is in order: a long-taper rubber stopper, its large end half an inch in diameter, was inserted into the chamber and then wedged in place by the closing of the bolt. This stopper provided a very effective seal to keep the ammonia from leaking. Also, it is necessary to replace the ammonia that evaporates from the muzzle end of the barrel, to make sure that *all* fouling gets removed. Or you can cover the muzzle with a plastic disc with the ammonia just below the muzzle, to prevent the fumes from attacking the bluing.

The two-fifty-grain Speer spitzer, reduced in diameter to fit the bore, would help, I felt, to extend the effective hunting range of the 9x56mm because of its high ballistic coefficient of 0.423. Also, its high sectional density of 0.279 and heavy jacket should provide good penetration for hunting large game. The rifle should be very useful for close-range shooting at large bear, moose, elk, and the like. The need for trouble-free functioning of the bolt during hunts for this type of game was the reason for my changing to the stronger national-match brass. These cases should be able to handle higher pressures than the Kynoch cases apparently can, making handloading much easier.

So — finally, I had the right-diameter bullet swage, strong cases to load, modern powders, and bullets of the right diameter, and thus had the

situation well in hand. Well, not quite. I had a hundred seventy-five rounds that had to have the bullets pulled and resized, then reseated in charged and primed cases. Then I'd be ready to head for the range, right? Wrong — the diameter of the case necks was now too large, so the bullets that had been resized to a smaller diameter fell into the neck and came to rest atop the powder column. So I had to dump all charges, remove the expanding button and decapping pin from the decapping stem, then resize all of the cases full-length.

After recharging the cases and seating the bullets, I was at last ready to go back to the range to test these cartridges for both accuracy and velocity. I used the same load as before — forty-five grains of Norma 203, two-fifty-grain Speer spitzers, and CCI 200 primers in cases formed from national-match brass — and the first three rounds went into three quarters of an inch at a hundred yards, from the bench. I figured that's just great, but to impress my onlookers still further, I fired two more rounds and blew the whole thing.

I found myself looking at a five-shot group that was two inches across and not at all impressive. But I knew that the first three shots out of a cold barrel would group well and that the problem with fouling was gone. I also knew that the problem of oversize bullets had been solved.

The load of Norma 203, at 1,950 feet per second, produced 2,120 foot-pounds of muzzle energy. I felt that by changing powders, I might get more velocity and energy, because the forty-five grains of Norma 203 came right to the base of the seated bullet. So I next ran tests with IMR-3031 and Norma 202 (Norma 203 having by then been discontinued by Norma). I loaded forty-three to forty-six grains of each and fired them to check for signs of high pressures. Forty-six grains of IMR-3031 produced sticky bolt lift, but the same amount of Norma 202 didn't seem to produce pressures as high as those of IMR-3031. The velocity data reinforce this idea.

Speer lists forty-six grains of IMR-3031 as maximum for the .358 Winchester with a two-fifty-grain bullet *(That was in some of the older manuals — the tenth edition lists forty-two grains of IMR-3031 as the maximum. Ken Howell)*, so I tried with this test to see whether comparable loads in the 9x56mm would create any problem. Apparently, they do not.

Handloading for the 9x56mm Mannlicher-Schoenauer is straight-forward once the correct bullet diameter for the individual rifle has been established. Acceptable pressure levels with modern brass can be determined from the expansion of the case (see Ken Waters' article in this issue) and by resistance to the lifting of the bolt handle, then reducing charges to reduce case expansion. By limiting case expansion and being able to open the bolt with the middle finger of the right hand to gauge resistance, it is easy to extend case life greatly.

To ensure reliable functioning and maximum support of the case in the chamber, it is a good idea to adjust the sizing die to size only the minimum amount and still allow the bolt to close on a dummy round with only slight resistance. The rather small shoulder of this cartridge seems to provide adequate support to resist the impact of the striker.

My restocked rifle has given me no problem other than replacing the broken factory stock; the problems of loading the 9x56mm have all been solved in my work with the first rifle. One disappointment has been that in my rifle, the same loads give me lower velocities than they did in the other rifle. It turns out that the muzzle of my rifle is slightly enlarged along the last two inches of the bore, which may allow some gas loss and thus lower the velocities. Also, my groups are not as small — again a result of the enlarged muzzle — but they are more than adequate for use out to two hundred yards or so.

When you decide to handload for a nonstandard cartridge like the 9x56mm Mannlicher-Schoenauer, data are almost never available. I was able to find factory data in two references,

a Mannlicher sales brochure dated 1937 and a Stoeger catalog dated 1939. The similarity between them is in the weight and type of bullet and the amount and type of powder. The barrel lengths are different, so velocities are, too. For instance, the Mannlicher brochure shows a 245-grain round-nose at 2,160 feet per second out of a twenty-two-inch barrel. The Stoeger catalog lists a 245-grain bullet at 2,160 with the length of the barrel not specified, or 2,100 feet per second from a barrel twenty-two and a half inches long. The Stoeger book also lists a 9x57mm Mauser with 245-grain round-nose at 2,296 feet per second from twenty-two and a half inches of barrel.

Comparison of the velocities from these factory loads and my handloads shows a definite gain over 9x56mm factory loads in 17.1-inch barrels. My loads stay even with those from the longer barrels and approach 9x57mm Mauser velocities, so the effort that was involved in upgrading the 9x56mm was well worth the time. The 9x56mm and the .358 Winchester have cases of very similar capacities, so the minimum loads for the .358 Winchester, minus five percent, should provide good starting points for developing loads for the 9x56mm. I should mention here that it is necessary to seat bullets deep enough in the 9x56mm to allow the cartridges to feed reliably from the rotary Schoenauer magazine. With a spitzer bullet, this means that you have five sixteenths of an inch of bullet travel before it engages the ends of the lands. This built-in freebore should help to keep chamber pressures within reasonable limits. I feel that this is the main reason behind the ability of this rifle to use loads that would otherwise be considered excessive.

The late great Alaskan guide Hal Waugh, holder of Professional Alaskan Guide license number one, wrote that the .358 Winchester should be a wicked combination for short-range work in the alders, and this cartridge was the one recommended for nonhunting workers and travelers in the Alaskan bush by Ken Howell during his years in Alaska. The 9x56mm Mannlicher-Schoenauer with the loads that I've listed should be equally potent. So if you have one, don't put such a classic rifle into storage simply because of a lack of ammunition for it. With good hand-loads using modern components, it can compete on an even footing with the cartridges of today.

Anderson Bakewell, SJ, the owner of the first Mannlicher carbine used by Van Marter, has this to say about it as a hunting rifle: "I carried the rifle in the Mentasta Mountains of Alaska in the early autumn of 1974. In a large, open spruce meadow, Avery Moore and I put up two bull moose that were traveling together, as young bulls often do at that time of year. For some time, we played hide and seek in the timber, the large animals moving with incredible silence. Finally, one bull stood broadside at about sixty yards. I fired immediately, and with the knowledge that the shot had gone properly, emphasized by the sound of the bullet's strike. I turned my attention to the larger bull, now some distance away and disappearing into the timber. My moose lay dead not many yards from where it had been hit. The 245-grain Kynoch soft-nose bullet, propelled by forty-two grains of IMR-3031, had taken him through the lungs, expanded, and then fragmented against the ribs on the far side opposite the point of entrance. ●

CHAPTER
25

IT WAS A very good year, 1965. The shooting industry was eyeball-deep in new rifles, cartridges, and other choice items introduced that year, during the several years before, and even a few that had spilled over from the fruitful Fifties. Bausch & Lomb, who had introduced a variable scope way back in 1949, was still peddling rifle scopes, as was Savage, who also touted their reloading press as a humdinger. A chap with a flat-top haircut and black bow tie extolled the virtues of a certain scattergun, while African professional hunter David Ommanney chased about two continents bumping off big game with an "improved" Model 70 in one hand and a Winchester expense voucher in the other.

One color advertisement that adorned the back covers of many gun magazines during 1965 never failed to catch my eye. A hunter, clad in a red-and-black-checked wool cruiser was kneeling in snow studying, presumably, fresh deer tracks. In his mittened hand was a short rifle that at first glance

appeared to be a Model 600 Remington outfitted with a candy-stripe stock. An inset showed the chap close-up saying, "Show me a carbine with real power and I'll buy it."

Directly below, he was answered with, "Mister, you've just bought yourself the most powerful carbine ever made. You're getting 6½ pounds of bolt-action fury, the first rifle ever chambered for the rip-snortin new .350 Remington Magnum cartridge — up to 3,280 foot pounds of brush-bucking energy that will stop any game in North America."

So read, in part, Remington's announcement to the woods-hunting multitude that third base was now covered.

Let's take a look at the several variations of one of my all-time favorite rifles for Eastern bear and deer hunting, the Model 600 Remington. Introduced in 1964, the Model 600 was a mere design spin-off from the XP-100 bolt-action pistol that first became available in 1962. Eventually cham-

bered in .222 Remington, .243 Winchester, 6mm Remington, .308 Winchester, and .35 Remington, the short little carbine offered a combination of accuracy, power, compactness, and dependability second to no other commercial rifle available before or since.

Accuracy came from its being a son of the rigid Remington Model 700 action, while the .308 Winchester cartridge was its main claim to power. The .35 Remington chambering has also been known to drop bucks and bruins posthaste, especially when handloaded to its full potential, as can be done with the Model 600's strong lock-up.

Lightness is the result of the 18½-inch barrel but not solely because it's short — it is one of the skinniest barrels ever offered on a factory rifle — which gets us around to the Model 600's unique and most criticized feature — that ventilated rib with its queer-looking front sight that gave the barrel the appearance of a whale harpoon. Now, after all these years of

remington
MODEL
600
.350 magnum

explorative speculations, I'll tell you why Remington carried the rib over from the XP-100. This revelation comes from a friend in the industry who is in a position to know such things. The rib was meant to draw attention away from that thin barrel. Take a look at a Model 600 muzzle sometime, especially in .35, and you'll see what I mean.

A less-often-seen variation is the Model 600 Mohawk, which was manufactured by Remington for various chain stores as an economy model that would not compete with the standard Model 600s sold by gun dealers. I suspect that it *did* compete, since it is absolutely equal in quality to the ribbed version. It does differ, though, other than having no rib, as the barrel is much heavier, measuring a fat 0.615 inch at the muzzle. This added about eight ounces to its weight.

Once, in an effort to wean him from an old .44-40, I offered Dad his choice of any rifle in my battery for hunting whitetail deer. It took him about two years of handling, shooting, and killing deer with close to a dozen rifles before eliminating all but a Model 600 Mohawk in .308 Winchester, with a Leupold 1-4x scope. With the 150-grain bullet loaded to twenty seven hundred feet per second, Pop is as deadly as cyanide on whitetails with this carbine and monotonously places any number of bullets under a nickel at one hundred yards, from a benchrest. Now, any time I mention switching rifles (not that I really want him to), he's ready to fight.

Next we have the Model 600 magnum, which still holds the distinction of offering the biggest punch in the smallest and lightest package of any rifle produced by a US manufacturer. Actually, it's nothing more than a frilled-up version of the

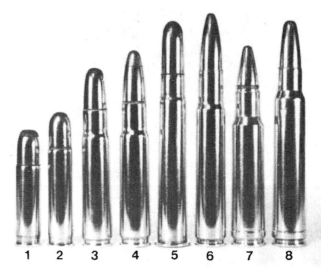

All of these .35 cartridges have seen use by American hunters, but only the .35 Remington (3) is still widely popular. The .35 (1) and .351 (2) Winchester SLR used bullets 0.351 inch in diameter; the .35 Remington (3), .358 Winchester (4), .35 Winchester (5), .35 Whelen (6), .350 Remington Magnum (7), and .358 Norma Magnum (8) all use bullets 0.358 inch in diameter.

standard carbine, except it is chambered in the 6.5mm and .350 Remington Magnum cartridges. The magnum stock consists of two layers of beech sandwiched between three layers of walnut. This laminated construction along with an epoxy-bedded recoil lug is to handle the rather noticeable recoil of the magnum cartridges.

The stock has a recoil pad and is protected from splitting at the wrist by a block of Delrin called a tang support. This little bugger pops out on the floor when the barreled action is removed from the stock, and it drives you crazy figuring out where it came from — unless you try something silly like reading the parts list.

The bolt is magnum-size, naturally, and the barrel has a contour similar to

that of the Model 700 Remington, except of course, it's eighteen and a half inches long. That's it except for the sling and detachable swivels, added-cost options on the standard version. Otherwise, they're much the same, right down to the dog-leg bolt handle, Delrin trigger guard, and a concealed bolt release that has caused many to take up profanity even after buying a pocket knife with a long, slim blade.

Sometime in 1968, the Model 600 was replaced by the Model 660, which had a twenty-inch barrel. Gained, depending on the chambering, was a paltry forty to sixty feet per second (praised by many), but lost were the rib (mourned by nobody) and the pleasingly light barrel contour of the original carbine. Nineteen Seventy-One saw the Model 660's death, but the 6.5mm and .350 Magnum cartridges lived on in the Model 700 until 1974. To my knowledge, the Model 77 Ruger was the only other factory rifle chambered for both cartridges.

Now for the .350 Magnum that Remington designed to squeeze into the short Model 600 action. Take the 7mm Remington Magnum case, shorten it 0.329-inch, open up the neck to .35, and

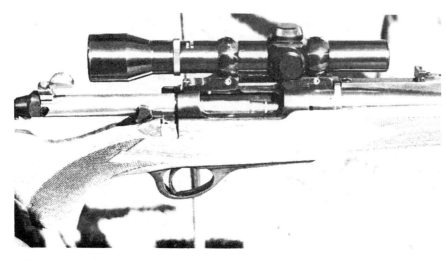

The short, fat .350 Remington Magnum was designed for this short action. For trouble-free feeding through Layne's carbine, loaded cartridges must be no longer than 2.825 inches overall.

Seven bullets designed to expand at velocity of .35 Remington are 150-grain Remington (1), 180 Speer (2), 200 Sierra (3), 200 Hornady (4), 200 Remington (5), 200 Winchester Power Point (6) and Silvertip (7). Fine for magnum velocities are 200-grain Remington spire-point (8), 200 Hornady spire-point (9), 250 Hornady round-nose (10) and soft-point (11), and Speer 250-grain spitzer (12). Winchester 200-grain (13) is not available separately; 250 Speer round-nose (14) has been dropped; 250 Norma (15) is not easy to find.

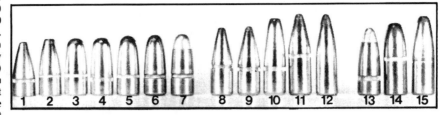

Except for 150-grain Remington handload (1) and Remington 200-grain factory load (3), all bullets in test loads were seated to accommodate the Model 600's magazine and chamber throat. Other bullets are 180 Speer (2), 200 Remington (4), 200 Hornady (5), 250 Hornady (6), 250 Speers (7, 8), and 250 Hornady round-nose (9).

you've got it except for forming the .350's 0.054-inch longer neck. In fact, .350 Magnum cases can easily be formed from several belted cases, including the 7mm Remington and .300 Winchester Magnums. First you run them through a .350 Magnum sizing die with the expander-decapper assembly removed; then trim to 2.170 inches, deburr the case mouths, and run them back through the sizing die, this time with the expander-decapper unit installed. Go easy on the loading-press handle with this last operation, and lube the interior of the necks, or they buckle.

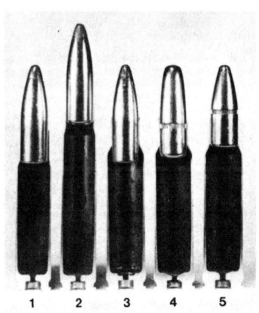

Net usable powder cavity in (1) the .358 Winchester, (2) .35 Whelen, and (3) the .350 Remington Magnum is determined in each case by bullet seating that allows functioning through magazines. With 250-grain Speer spitzer, net capacity of the .350 Magnum is over a fifth more than the .358 Winchester, about equal to the Whelen. Hornady 250 (4) and 250 Remington (5) increase net capacity.

The expander button on my Pacific die is chamfered on its end and glides smoothly through case necks. If yours is not, chuck it in a drill and taper the end with emery cloth, being careful not to reduce its diameter. Should that fail, order a 0.308-to-0.358 expander button from Pacific. Cases formed in this manner require annealing to prevent split necks, and they must be fire-formed with reduced loads to blow out the body taper. Also, watch out for any reduction in powder capacity with some cases, as well as thickening at the shoulder-neck juncture. At the moment, this tip is of limited value, but if you shoot a .350 Magnum, it might be handy to note for future use, since this cartridge will be discontinued one of these days.

Two cartridges often compared with the .350 Magnum are the .358 Winchester and .35 Whelen. Let's see how the three stack up. Filled with water to the bases of their necks,

Cases for the .350 Remington Magnum can be formed from brass for the .300 H&H Magnum (1), .300 Winchester Magnum (2), and 7mm Remington Magnum (3) by first sizing them in a .350 Magnum full-length sizer with the decapping rod removed (4, 5, 6), trimming to 2.170 inches and again sizing with decapper in place (7, 8, 9) and fire-forming with a reduced load to blow shoulder out (10).

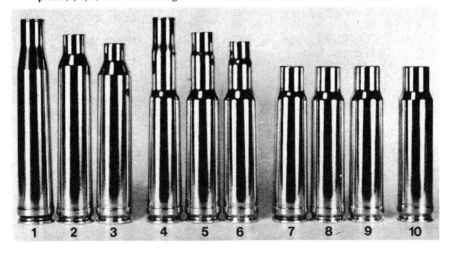

Remington's .350 holds sixty-seven grains as compared to Winchester's .358 and Colonel Whelen's .35 wildcat at an average of fifty-one and sixty-one grains, respectively. But net or usable powder space is what counts, and when the Speer 250-grain spitzer bullet is seated deep enough to feed through magazines, the comparison becomes more valid. They look like this:

rifle	cartridge case	length	net capacity
Model 600	.350 Rem	2.825 inches	63.2 grains
Model 70	.35 Win.	3.325 inches	62.2 grains
Model 88	.358 Win.	2.825 inches	51.0 grains

Load the three cartridges with the 250-grain bullet atop maximum powder charges, and the .358 Winchester, fine cartridge that it is, struggles to reach twenty-three hundred feet per second, while the .350 carbine and .35 Whelen beat that by an easy two hundred feet per second. That little bit of information loses any mystery when powder capacities between the .358 and the two larger cases are compared.

But what about the fact that the .350 Magnum equals the .35 Whelen in velocity with this bullet weight out of five inches less barrel? That one is elementary too, if you ponder it a minute. An '06-size case opened up to .35 yields a relatively high expansion ratio, which should mean that when loaded to equal pressures, the short-barreled .350 lags behind the wildcat by about 125 feet per second. But it doesn't work out that way in practice, because most published .35 Whelen loads run less than fifty thousand cup, while the .350 is more commonly loaded to the SAAMI maximum, fifty three thousand pounds per square inch, and I suspect even higher. Load both cartridges to like pressures in the same barrel lengths, and velocities are as close as the proverbial two peas — rather an academic conclusion when one considers two points. First, and important only to those who prefer short actions, the .350 works in the Model 600, but the .35 Whelen doesn't. Second, at least for now, the .350 is a factory-loaded cartridge, but the .35 Whelen never has been.

Taking it one step further, all things being equal, including chambering the .350 in a rifle that allows seating bullets out of the powder space, and the .350, with its ten percent greater capacity, pulls ahead of the old wildcat by a tad more than one hundred feet per second. When allowed to release its full potential, the .350 Magnum falls just short of midway in performance between the .35 Whelen and .358 Norma Magnum — which is academic too, since the .350 has never been factory-chambered in a rifle that allows it this much room.

Loading the .350 Magnum holds no mystery, and like so many of our big bores, were its pressure curve plotted with suitable powders, it would resemble the profile of a fat watermelon lying on its side. Which is not to say that you can't get into trouble. Load this one with powders too fast to gradually overcome the inertia and bearing-surface resistance of the heavier bullets, and the locking lugs become a bit hard to turn out of their recesses.

It's old news to those who own .350 carbines that this cartridge becomes cramped for powder space when the 250-grain bullets are seated to feed through the magazine. This narrows powder choices down to IMR-3031 on the fast side, with WW-748 and IMR-4320 being the slowest propellants that can be used without extreme compression of the charge.

Though they were compressed to the absolute limit under the 250-grain Speer bullet, WW-760, N-204, and H-380 yielded acceptable hunting accuracy with very moderate pressure indications. But then, it's most difficult to avoid heavy compression in this cartridge, even with many of the faster-burning powders, and I often found it necessary to use a Bonanza drop tube to pack it all in. Of the Winchester powders, WW-748 is an ace in the .350 Magnum behind all bullet weights and would be an excellent choice for those who prefer to stick with one powder for all loads.

IMR-4320 is my choice for top velocities and fine accuracy, but IMR-4895 and IMR-4064 run a very close second. A muzzle flash that has to be seen to be believed erupts from the carbine muzzle when top loads of BL-C(2) are touched off. For this reason, I have scratched it from my list of suitable powders for the stubby barrel. But it might work in longer barrels such as on the Model 700 Remington and Model 77 Ruger. Muzzle flash with H-335 is not as severe, but it's there, so I pick H-4895 as best of the three. Norma's N-202 is another good one in this cartridge, burning quite similar to IMR-4064. It did an excellent job behind the Hornady 250-grain and 200-grain spire-point bullets.

I began the testing using standard primers with all powders but soon switched to magnum primers with the ball powders, for a reduction in velocity spreads of almost fifty percent. Possibly, this is because of the high expansion ratio allowing pressures to peak with these powders a bit too far down the short barrel when the cooler primers are used.

In the beginning, Remington loaded

their .350 with 200 and 250-grain pointed Core-Lokt bullets at advertised velocities of 2,725 and 2,410 feet per second, but only the 200-grain bullet is now available. In fact, the heavier bullet has disappeared from Remington's component lineup as well, which is sad, since the .350 Magnum is at its best on dangerous big game. This type of duty calls for a tough, heavy bullet with high sectional density that can plow through thick hide, tough muscle, and bone. The 250-grain Core-Lokt had few peers in this department, and I would like to see it brought back.

I count thirteen thirty-five bullets presently being turned out by the major manufacturers, six being constructed to perform at the much lower .35 Remington velocities. Of the remaining seven, the Winchester 200-grain Silvertip designed for their .358 deserves little mention here, fine bullet that it is, as it, like all other Winchester bullets, is not available to handloaders. This leaves Remington's 200-grain Core-Lokt spire point, the Speer 250-grain spitzer, and from Hornady a 250-grain round-nose and two spire-points weighing 200 and 250 grains. The latter two are designed especially for loading in the .350 Magnum and have cannelures positioned accordingly — which, I might add, is of little value, as few handloaders crimp cases when loading for bolt-action rifles.

On deer-size game, the 200-grain spire-point bullets from Remington and Hornady are quite deadly. When started at twenty-eight hundred feet per second, they retain seventeen hundred foot-pounds of energy at three hundred yards. They shoot pretty flat, too, dropping six and a half inches at three hundred yards when zeroed three inches high at a hundred. Admittedly not much to brag about in the company of one of the smaller-bore magnums, but as a comparison, a handloaded 180-grain spitzer out of the .30-06 drops about four inches and packs a tad over two thousand foot-pounds at the same range. The thirty-fives in this weight have about the same sectional density as a .30 bullet weighing 150 grains.

But long-range shooting is not what it's all about with this cartridge. It's that sledge-hammer blow in the form of 250-grain bullets from a quick-handling carbine. The late Warren Page often called it smack-down power. I have on various occasions referred to it as stay-down power, while some title it a bunch of baloney. But opinions aside, it's tough to dispute the fact that a heavy, broad-nosed bullet of high sectional density traveling at medium to high velocity makes a lasting impression on big game — so long as the bullet is

154

constructed to hold together during its strenuous trip through hide, meat, and bone. Early in its career, the .350 Magnum quickly established such a reputation, as the 250-grain Core-Lokt bullet was used successfully on all manner of big game, including polar and brown bear, moose, elk, and even cape buffalo. As previously stated, this one is no longer with us, but the three heavy bullets that are readily available should get most any job done.

The Model 600 enjoys a reputation for excellent accuracy, and my .350 is no exception, especially when fed the streamlined Speer 250-grain spitzer bullet. True, it hogs some powder space in this cartridge, but enough remains to boost energy high enough to shiver a bull elk's timbers out to at least three hundred long paces. I put a Weaver 16x scope on the carbine for accuracy-testing, and this bullet cut several three-shot groups at one hundred yards that measured three quarters of an inch. It's a dandy. I also experimented further with this bullet by trimming off the lead tip. This decreased its weight to 244 grains and allowed it to be seated out of the powder space by an additional 0.175 inch. Three more grains of WW-748 brought pressures back to equal those behind the unmodified bullet for a gain in velocity of a mere thirty-five feet per second. Needless to say, it's not worth the time and trouble.

Though the Hornady 250-grain spire-point is not as accurate in my carbine, I suspect that it will hold together a bit better than the Speer bullet if fired into heavy bone. The Hornady bullet's jacket is thicker, and its core seems harder. Perhaps I'm a bit old-fashioned, since most of the hunting world seems to look down on any bullet that does not feature a spitzer or spire point, but my choice for rooting a moose or elk out of thick timber or converting a grizzly into a rug at close range is the round-nose bullet. This calls for something on the order of the Hornady 250-grain bullet of this style, as it is supremely accurate in my carbine. This bullet takes heavier powder charges than any other 250-grain bullet that I tried, and exits the muzzle faster because of its short bearing surface that measures 0.345 inch versus an average of 0.535 inch for the others.

Though the Speer 250-grain round-nose bullet has been discontinued, I still see them on dealers' shelves. For this reason, as well as the fact that I have hoarded a supply, I included them in my tests. I'm not bashful in saying that this is my favorite bullet for woods hunting with the .350 Magnum. It shoots well and hits hard, and as a bonus, the jacket and core cling together like cold molasses in the roof of your mouth.

I also have a few of the Norma 250-grain bullets purchased about ten years ago from a friend who owned a .358 Norma Magnum. My Winchester Model 88 in .358 handles them quite well, but the Model 600 spits them into two-and-a-half-inch groups. During a talk with Greg Pogson of Norma, I learned that most Norma bullets are still available in the States. To put the meat of our conversation in a nutshell, the Swedish bullets do not enjoy the wide distribution as in the past, but Norma continues to make one huge shipment each year to four US distributors. For a list of these distributors, I suggest you contact Greg Pogson at Norma Precision; South Lansing, New York 14882. Anyhow, I managed to round up another box of the 250-grain bullets and ran twenty through the Model 600 at top velocities. Groups immediately shrank to a little under two minutes of angle, yet the only difference between old and new is their diameters. The old batch measured 0.3575 inch in diameter, while the latest model averaged 0.3581 inch. This made sense when I added everything together. The Hornady 250-grain spire-point averaged just under two-inch groups. It too measures under 0.358 inch, 0.3574 to be exact. My carbine prefers the fatter bullets.

When introduced, the standard Model 600 listed for $99.95, while the magnum version sold for forty-five dollars more. As this is written, a Model 600 in .308 Winchester will set you back two hundred bucks. Be prepared to fork out at least four bills if your plans include the addition of a .350 Magnum to the battery. Back in the Sixties, a Model 600 was such a bargain that a bit of successful price haggling left one feeling like quite the horse trader after measuring hundred-yard groups fired from the short little rifle. Now, over fifteen years later, I still get that same feeling — even at today's prices. ●

CHAPTER
26

.358 Norma Magnum

by Jon R. Sundra

Dimensions (on cartridge diagram):

.383
.485
25°
2.205
2.508
2.080
.504
.220
.525

After firing 40 full-power loads with the .358 Norma from the bench, the author "cheated" by placing a third bag between rifle butt and shoulder. The chronograph is the inexpensive, but accurate Oehler Model 10, the ammo box is the MTM "Case-Gard."

*H*OW WOULD YOU LIKE to push a 180-grain bullet at over 3,350 *honest* fps and do it with a mere 22 inches of barrel? If velocity doesn't turn you on, then how about a cartridge that can spit a slug having a ballistic coefficient of .425 and developing 4,500 foot pounds of energy? Add to that a loading versatility that spans a range of bullets from 150 to 300 grains and you have the greatest sleeper ever to come down the well-traveled cartridge pike—the .358 Norma Magnum.

Introduced by Norma in 1959, the .358 made its debut without the usual fanfare that heralds a new domestic cartridge. At that time the relatively new .338 Winchester (introduced only the year before), still had the attention of the gun clan. Besides, the Winchester round was home grown so the major arms companies quickly added the chambering to their lines. The .358 on the other hand, in addition to being a "foreigner," was considered too similar to the .338 to warrant its addition—especially when calibers over .30 comprise only a small fraction of total gun sales.

So to achieve its current modest

Bullets used in testing were, from left, the 250 Hornady, 250 Speer, 250 Norma, discontinued 250 Hornady RN, 250 Speer RN, 220 Speer, 200 Remington, 180 Speer and 158 Hornady.

degree of popularity, the .358 Norma has had to rely strictly on its own merit without the benefit of any of the big arms companies chambering for it with the attendant promotional bally-hoo. I suppose it's simply a matter of not being able to keep a good man—or cartridge—down.

Before the introduction of the Norma round, the nimrod hankering for a potent .35 had to resort to wildcats such as the .35 Ackley or the .35 Whelen. Essentially, the Norma is a legitamatized .35 Ackley Short Magnum. There are some differences in case dimension but they are so minor, says Ackley, that loading data as well as the cartridges themselves are interchange-able. The Whelen, based on the smaller '06 case, cannot match the Norma round in any respect.

The only commercial cartridge to give the .358 any competition at all came about when Remington announced its .350 Magnum in 1964. Because it is based on a *short*, short magnum case having about equal capacity as the '06-based Whelen, performance of the .350 is also in the same class.

But the very existence of the Re-mington cartridge has indirectly helped the .358 Norma. Being a fairly popular number, the .350 has prompted the introduction of some fine bullets that otherwise would not have seen the light of day. Before the .350 Remington made its debut, Speer was the only bullet maker to offer a spitzer bullet in .35 caliber. Now, Remington offers both a 200 and a 250-grain bullet and Hornady has changed his 250-grainer from a round nose to a spire point. These spitzer bullets are the means with which the Big Swede really shows its stuff.

The .358 Norma has a lot going for

it. Take the bore size for example: .358-inch. That big hole in the barrel offers some advantages not found in the smaller calibers. For one, the larger bores seem to suffer less velocity loss with short barrels than do their small-bore brethren. It's not that the .358—or for that matter, any other big bore—has some inherent characteristics which render it less susceptible to the laws of physics. Rather, I think, it's a com-bination of conditions which are nor-mally found in the larger calibers; namely, near optimum case/bore cap-acities and resultant high expansion ratios, along with the ability to use powders with moderate burning rates.

Whether we give a hoot about bore capacity or not, the fact remains that for every caliber there is only so much

powder that can be burned *efficiently*. Once this optimum ratio between case volume and bore size is surpassed, the velocity increase per additional grain of powder drops. Attendant with this condition is the need for long barrels and the slowest burning powders in order to capitalize on what amounts to a relatively small increase in velocity.

To illustrate: the 7mm Remington Magnum requires a case having 21 percent more powder capacity than a .280 Remington to achieve about a nine percent increase in velocity. The .358 Norma on the other hand, has 18 percent greater powder capacity than the .350 Remington Magnum but in-creases velocity by 14 percent. The Big 7, although a great cartridge, is "overbore." The .358 Norma, based

Load Data for the .358 Norma Magnum

Bullet	Load	Velocity*	Best Group**	Remarks
250 Hornady	77.5/4350	2,730	1 1/2	Compressed load
250 Speer	67.5/4895	2,820	1 1/4	Best 250-grain load
250 Norma	77.5/4350	2,720	1 1/2	
250 Hornady	68.5/4320	2,745	2 1/8	
250 Hornady	70.5/N-203	2,790	1 5/8	Norma recommends 70.2
250 Speer	70.0/4350	2,550	1 1/4	Accurate, mild load
250 Hornady	70.5/RL-21	2,785	1 5/8	Compressed load
220 Speer	70.5/4320	2,870	1 3/8	Most accurate 220 load
220 Speer	78.0/4350	2,905	2 1/8	Compressed load
220 Speer	73.5/N-203	2,990	1 7/8	
200 Remington	72.5/4895	3,105	1 1/4	Good long range load
200 Remington	72.0/4320	3,065	1 1/2	
200 Remington	71.0/4064	3,060	1 1/8	
180 Speer RN	75.5/4064	3,305	1	Most accurate load
180 Speer RN	77.5/4064	3,355	1 3/4	Compressed load
180 Speer RN	78.5/4320	3,260	1 7/8	
180 Speer RN	75.0/4350	2,755	1 1/4	Good deer & bear load
158 Hornady	70.0/4350	2,510	1 1/4	Good plinking and varmint load

* All velocities based on five-shot averages taken 12.5 feet from muzzle then rounded to nearest 5 fps. Barrel length for tests was 22 inches. CCI-250 primers used in all loads.
** Five shots at 100 yards.

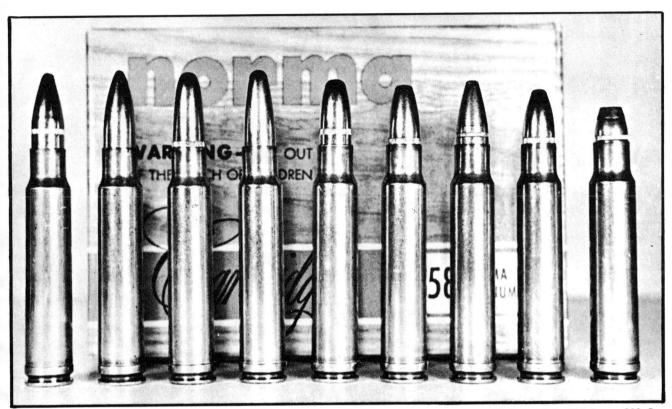

Bullets were seated well forward to provide maximum powder space. From left are the 250 Hornady, 250 Speer, 250 Hornady RN (discontinued), 250 Norma, 250 Speer RN, 220 Speer, 200 Remington. 180 Speer and 158 Hornady pistol bullet.

on the same case, is not.

For the Big 7 you can figure about 35 fps per inch of barrel as you cut back from 26 inches. When I had the barrel on my .358 Norma cut from 24 to 22 inches I lost a grand total of 35 fps; that's 17.5 fps per inch of barrel—truly insignificant when compared to the improved handling qualities of a short barrel.

A commonly held belief which has undoubtedly hurt the .358 is the one which attributes baseball-like trajectories to the big bores. A quick look at the ballistic charts will show this to be largely untrue, but since the Big Swede is only loaded with a 250-grain semi-pointed slug, the full potential of the round is not readily seen.

Looking at the chart we see that Norma lists the MRT at 300 yards to be 6.6 inches. To get some basis for comparison, let's take a 180-grain .30 caliber round-nosed slug which has about the same sectional density, and similar ballistic coefficient, as the 250-grain .35 factory bullet and see what happens. Assuming an optimistic 3,100 fps as furnished by the big .300 Winchester Magnum case, we find the 300 yard MRT to be—low and behold—also 6.6 inches.

"Okay," you say. "So who uses round-nosed bullets in a .300 Winchester Magnum?"

True. So let's switch to spire points. Using any of the 250-grain spitzers offered by Speer, Hornady or Remington, actual 300-yard drop figures based on the easily attainable muzzle velocity of 2,800 fps is 22.9 inches for the Norma case as opposed to 20.8 for the 180-grain pointed bullet of the .300 Winchester Magnum. Translated into MRT the Norma figures out to about six inches while the .30 caliber spire point is 5.3.

A little surprised? Well, there's more. Let's see what happens when we load the 200-grain Remington Pointed Core-Lokt. Based on the very realistic MV of 3,100 fps (which I easily get in my stubby 22-inch barrel with 72.0 of 4895), bullet drop calculated on a ballistic coefficient of .310 is 20.0 inches. Translated, this figures out to a 300 yard MRT of 5.4. Another quick look at the charts shows the famous 130-grain .270 load to be 5.3"! Who says the big bores don't shoot flat?

Thus far I've been talking about those attributes of the .358 Norma which are not readily apparent and have neglected the most obvious commodity this cartridge has to offer—power. Normally, most of my handloading is spent with the smaller calibers trying to extract every last bit of velocity consistent with acceptable pressures and accuracy. But with a cartridge capable of churning up 4,500 foot pounds of energy one's attitude is bound to change. Loading for .358 one soon finds himself not only experimenting with a wider range of bullet weights but also loading down.

As far as handloading is concerned, the .358 is without a doubt one of the most versatile and least demanding cartridges. For example, of the 23 top

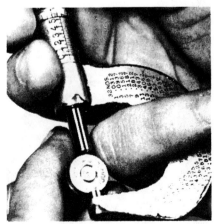

All loads listed were safe in Sundra's rifle. Primer pockets were tight after several reloadings and there was no measurable case head expansion.

loads listed in the Speer, Lyman, and Hornady manuals, 12 of them equal or exceed the rather conservative factory-quoted MV of 2,800 fps. To achieve this, powders ranging from 4895 or 4831 were used. That, my friends, is what I call an easy-going digestive system.

For the most part my own chronography pretty much agreed with published data except with 4350. While this slowest of the IMR series powders furnished the highest velocities listed in most of the reloading manuals and is also the powder recommended by the Powley computer, I found it too slow. Apparently, so did Norma since their data recommends their 203 powder which they say parallels 4320. Norma 204, similar in burning rate to 4350, is not listed as a suitable load.

The reason I say 4350 is too slow is that I just couldn't get enough of it in the case behind the 250-grain bullet to match the velocities furnished by the faster burning powders. Although Speer and Lyman list 79.0 and 79.5 grains respectively as the top loads with 4350, I was compressing powder so severely at 77.5 grains that the big bullets were actually springing back out of the case a full 1/16 inch! Even then loads were mild and velocities ran 2,730 on the average.

In my rifle IMR-4895 proved to be

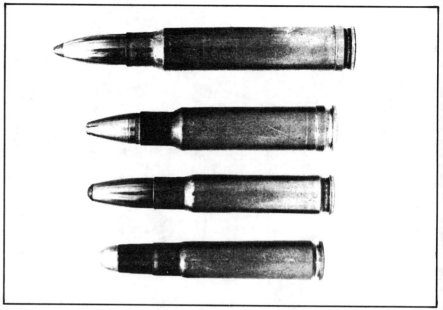

Few calibers can boast such an even progression of power as the .35's—from top, the .358 Norma, .350 Remington Magnum, .358 Winchester and .35 Remington. (Shown about actual size.)

the best powder by not only furnishing the best accuracy but the highest velocities as well. With 67.5 grains of it, the 250-grain Hornady and Speer spire points were sent along at 2,820 fps. The Norma semi-pointed and the now-discontinued 250-grain round-nosed Hornady averaged about 20 fps slower with the same load.

I might mention that all loads discussed as well as those listed in the tables are by all indications not only

within safe pressure parameters but almost mild *in my particular rifle*. In all cases the bolt lift was like a knife through butter; cases literally fell out of the chamber; primers were not excessively flattened; there was no measurable case head expansion; and primer pockets were almost as tight after eight to ten reloadings as when new.

The chamber of my rifle is not freebored; that is, not unless you con-

The most accurate loads from the author's rifle proved to be, from left, the 180 Speer with 75.5/4064, 200 Remington ahead of 72.5/ *4895, and 158 Hornady pistol bullet with 70.0/4350.*

sider 1/8-inch leade "free bore." In any event, gradually work up to any of the loads mentioned in the text.

There's little doubt that the best bullets available for the Big Swede are the 250-grain spitzers. Sailing along at 2,800 to 2,860 fps depending on barrel length, you're playing with upwards of 4,450 foot-pounds of energy. Needless to say, that's more than enough power for anything that walks this continent.

For game that doesn't bite back, you can either load down and/or go to the lighter bullets. Speer's 220-grain flat point at 2,950 fps should be effective on elk or moose but I'd like to see its shape improved. Perhaps one of the bullet makers will fill the large gap between the 200 and the 250-grain spitzers with a 225-grain; it would make an excellent all-around weight.

Next to the 250's I like the 200-grain Remington. At 3,100 fps this excellent game bullet would be my choice for elk and caribou. It shoots flatter than hell and—as is always the case with the .358 Norma—has power to spare.

The 180-grain Speer flat-nosed bullet is very useful. Although it can be pushed along at a fantastic 3,350 fps I can't see any need to do it. Loaded way down with 75.0 grains of 4350 at 2,750 fps it makes an easy shooting but satisfactory combination for whitetail and black bear.

For inexpensive plinking any of the semi-jacketed .357 handgun slugs work very well and give excellent accuracy if loaded to sensible levels. I imagine some really stratospheric velocities could be developed but I quit experimenting when I reached 3,420 fps with Hornady's 158-grain flat point! They were beginning to shed their jackets going through the chronograph's stop screen 17.5 feet away. For really comfortable and accurate plinking, 70.0 grains of 4350 maintains about a 90-percent loading density and sends this fine handgun bullet loafing along at 2,500 fps. I'm getting 1¼-inch groups at 100 yards with this load. And you should see what it does to a groundhog!

There are both heavier and lighter bullets available which can be loaded in the .358 Norma, but I have yet to try them. Frankly, I don't need anything heavier than the 250-grain but there are 275 and 300-grain bullets offered by Hornady and Barnes respectively. There is also a Remington 150-grain spire point available as loaded in the .35 Remington and it should make a great groundhog load. Lyman lists 81.5 grains of 4320 as giving, get this, 3,546 fps!

Incidentally, after my research convinced me that the .358 Norma was the big bore for me, I wanted to build a rifle worthy of its potential. I settled on an L-61 Sako action with a varmint-weight Star premium barrel, distributed through Federal Firearms of Oakdale, Pennsylvania. Normally, this barrel is furnished in a 26-inch length measuring .700 at the muzzle. With that big hole in the barrel, I figured this hefty tube wouldn't really be all that heavy if cut to 24 inches. Later I had it cut to 22.

For the stock I settled on a Fajen all-walnut laminated in the Regent style. Its straight, functional design tames the heaviest recoiling guns and finishes up into a very handsome rifle.

The barrel and action are fully bedded in Brownell Acraglas and the stock has several coats of polyurethane finish *inside* as well as out. The butt is fitted with a Pachmayr rifle recoil pad which subdues the 45 foot pounds of recoil without the rebound one gets from the thicker shotgun-type pads.

Topping the rig is a Leupold 2-7X Variable in Sako mounts. Total weight of the rig ready for hunting is 9 pounds, 14 ounces.

Despite my obvious enthusiasm for the .358 Norma, the cartridge does have limitations. Loading two or three boxes of shells can be an expensive proposition—especially when using the heavy bullets costing over seven bucks per hundred. Then too, depending on the weight of the gun, stock design and loading, recoil can be pretty formidable—up to 50 foot pounds. Using full-power loads on anything but the big beasties is a little ludicrous but loading it down is almost a shame; it's like keeping a Ferrari in first gear so you could use it for shopping and other mundane things equally beneath its dignity.

Nevertheless, the .358 Norma is one of the finest cartridges in the world. It will excel at many jobs and it will do the rest of them extremely well. How can you ask for any more than that?

●

CHAPTER
27

THE FORGOTTEN 9.3x57 MAUSER

— Dieter Sturm

Both these Husqvarna sporters are chambered for the 9.3x57: top, a Model 46; bottom, a Model 146.

THE VERY EXISTENCE of the 9.3x57 Mauser cartridge is ascribed largely to progressive experimentation with the old 8x57 Mauser to produce a large bore hunting round suitable for the largest European big game. The design effort was directed toward a relatively short-range rifle capable of firing a fairly heavy projectile to impart enough knockdown power for moose, yet mild-mannered enough to be handled without discomfort. The 9.3x57 lived up to all those expectations eventually, although it was slow to gain widespread acceptance by hunters who found no fault with their familiar old 8mm's.

Originally designed in Germany around the turn of the century, it remained a supine wildcat in that country just begging to be tested in the field. It was not until Swedish hunters developed an avid interest in the cartridge and Husqvarna began chambering their fine rifles for it around 1927, that the 9.3 gained much of a reputation among big game hunters. For all practical purposes, the 9.3x57 is viewed today as a Scandinavian cartridge because it was there in the vast evergreen forests that it established itself as a reliable game-getter.

The Husqvarna Vapenfabrik in Sweden chambered their models 46, 46A and 146 (until 1941) for the 9.3x57. Slowly it was supplanted by the more capacious 9.3x62. Those who have accepted the 9.3x57 for what it was designed to be have never given it up,

not even for the newer, more glamorous belted magnums which received so much publicity and attention.

The 9.3x57 continues to be used extensively in Scandinavia by experienced professional hunters who refuse to be convinced that the old round is just not enough any more. It has served the serious big game hunter there for decades.

In Sweden, where moose are hunted with the aid of elkhounds, the 9.3x57 is nearly perfect for the job. Shots are usually taken under 100 yards. Custommade for the heavy 286-grain softpoint bullet, it puts down the big moose rather effectively without destroying much edible meat. Moose hunting there is not just for sport alone but is also a business, since the meat is sold to retail stores and restaurants all over Europe. Obviously, nobody pays for blood-shot game meat.

Norma Projectilfabrik in Sweden still produces ammunition and components for this cartridge due to the continued demand. The 9.3x57 Mauser spawned such renowned cartridges as the 9.3x62 and the 9.3x64 Brenneke, as well as several lesser-knowns and a variety of rimless versions. The 9.3x57R appeared

later and was intended to capture the break-open rifle and combination-gun market but it never caught on.

For a short time, RWS produced ammunition for the 9.3x57 but discontinued production at the onset of World War II. Norma and the Swedish Metallverken still market their products in that caliber, as do several other European munitionmakers such as the Hirtenberger Werke and Sellier & Bellot, to name two. At any rate, getting ammunition and reloading components is not a problem if you are willing to look for them in this country. On the other hand, getting a rifle chambered for the 9.3x57 Mauser is.

There are still a few floating around the gun shows, rifles which were apparently brought back by enterprising GI's or imported by visionary dealers who just could not turn down a good deal. If the cartridge/rifle combination appeals to you, grab one before someone gets around to the idea of "improving" the cartridge to a more or less appealing local caliber. There are, however, 9.3 barrels available in the U.S., and several gunsmiths who can chamber for the 9.3x57 Mauser and build an out-of-this-world sporter for the discriminating nimrod.

163

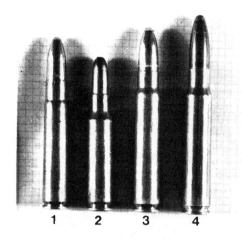

The 9.3 family of sporting rounds includes the *(1)* 9.3x57mm, *(3)* 9.3x62mm and *(4)* 9.3x64mm. The *(2)* .308 was added to the lineup for purposes of comparison.

Critics have called the round puny among other things, yet to the objective observer it will become clear that the 9.3x57 may indeed possess some undefinable and mysterious potential which enshrouds most Mauser cartridges of that length. Like its cousin the 7x57, and its sire the 8x57, the 9.3x57 will surprise you with its performance.

Putting sentiment and implied mysticism aside, I decided to put the old 9.3x57 through a more objective evaluation. The test rifle was a Husqvarna Model 146, based on the FN Model 98 commercial action which was apparently made between 1937 and 1941. It sports a traditional European walnut stock with a tasteful schnabel forend and a pistol grip cap made of trolit as is the buttplate. Trolit, a Swedish tradename, appears to be a hard-rubber material approaching the looks of plastic. The pistol grip is checkered in a coarse, practical pattern. The rifle was tastefully built with utilitarian undertones to make it affordable to those most likely to use it.

As is the case with most rifles which have seen extended use in Europe, the tang section evidenced some hairline cracking, possibly due to age and from standing up in gun cabinets for decades. After the damages were

People always want to compare one cartridge with another; a rather inconclusive attempt to gain instant insight into another round's capability. Well, the 9.3x57 Mauser cannot be fairly compared with anything currently on the market without evoking some bias and preconception. If one absolutely must, the old cartridge could be crammed into an indeterminate space between the .358 Winchester and the .375 Whelen if measured in terms of performance.

Both are classics in their own right. The 9.3x57 Mauser tends to combine the compactness and efficiency of the .358 Winchester with the knockdown power of the Whelen by using a heavier bullet and a proven, efficient case, ideally suited for medium-burning powders. It is a reloader's delight.

The 9.3x57 has a nominal bore diameter of .366 inch, nearly halfway between the .358 and the .375 calibers. Surely an odd caliber by our standards

and if the caliber did not already exist, it would be hard to justify its introduction today. Nevertheless, it has been ignored in this country for over 80 years but refuses to fade away. The 9.3 caliber is firmly established in Europe with a slight glow of interest stirring in this country as well. Not needed and unjustified? Shooters don't need to justify or make excuses for liking a particular cartridge — other than being able to derive some intrinsic pleasure from making it do what they want. I like what stimulates my interest, what provides me with enjoyment, and what challenges and encourages me to further experimentation.

Loading dies for the 9.3x57 are offered by several manufacturers. Bullets for the caliber are more difficult to find but a decent variety is still available — if you know where to look.

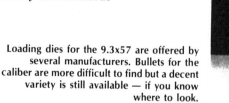

Some representative groups: *(1)* 270-grain Speer, Norma primer and 46.0 grains of H-4895; *(2)* 232-grain Norma roundnose, Winchester 120 primer and 47.0 grains of IMR-4895; *(3)* 270-grain Speer, CCI-200 primer and 44.0 grains of W-748; *(4)* 232-grain Norma HP, Rem 9½ primer, 46.0 grains of IMR-3031 and *(5)* 232-grain Norma Alaskan, Federal 210 primer and 53.0 grains of W-748.

repaired, some modest glass-bedding strengthened the recoil lug area. That proved to be a valuable modification to accuracy, yet unnoticeable to the critical eye.

I secured a brand-new set of RCBS reloading dies, still listed under their special order die column, within a couple of weeks. I was impressed by the fast service. The potential handloader for European cartridges should be forewarned not to seek to purchase dies in Europe; they use imported American brands over there exclusively.

Relatively unprepared, I began gathering brass, bullets and ammo at various gun shows and sporting goods stores. All seemed overjoyed at being able to dump that stuff even at a loss. Bullets in 9.3 caliber are currently made by Speer, Barnes and a number of European manufacturers like Norma and RWS. Speer introduced their 9.3 bullets not too long ago. A welcomed gesture by many, I am sure.

In a bind, cartridge cases for the 9.3x57 can be formed 8x57 brass by simply necking it up to .366 inch. It's a big step if done in one motion. Gradual expansion, using .338 and .358 expander buttons tend to keep neck and shoulder from buckling under pressure. Reformed cases come out a little short but in exchange, offer the questionable advantage of not needing to be trimmed for a while. There are, of course, alternate means of forming brass, something to be left to the reloader's imagination and past experience.

Reloading data for the 9.3x57 is another story. Norma and RWS list several loads in their manuals, all in powders difficult to obtain. While such powders as Rottweil R-902 and R-903 are not available in this country, Norma N-201 is still to be found. Powders can be cross-referenced with suitable domestic propellants such as IMR-4895, IMR-4064, IMR-3031, W-748, H-4895 and H-335. Reloader No. 7 seems a likely choice as well. I did not have any supply of Accurate Arms powder on hand, but am sure that some of their powders would be well suited, too.

It seems that Rottweil R-903 lies somewhere between H-335 and IMR-4064, while Rottweil R-902 is very close to Norma N-201, W-748 and BL-C(2). For those who have RWS reloading manuals, a wide variety of handloads are offered if one is willing to interpolate a little while using prudent judgment.

Working up a load from variables which are unknown is highly speculative and risky. Extreme caution must be exercised in developing handloads when the only gaging mechanisms available are bolt-lift effort, primer cratering, etc.

Factory ammunition made by Norma is of excellent quality. Chamber pressures are quite mild, e.g., in the vicinity of 36,000 CUP while the handloading data recommended by Norma suggests chamber pressures near 47,000 CUP.

Husqvarna rifles chambered for the 9.3x57 are built on commercial actions. Both the Model 98 and Model 96 actions used by Husqvarna tend to be quite robust, inasmuch as Norma makes no distinction as to what rifle or model their factory loads should be fired in. Nevertheless, when we are looking at an old rifle of unknown condition, it is best to have someone competent examine it carefully prior to use.

Test loads showed that W-748, IMR-4895 and H-4895 are best suited for the 9.3x57 when heavy bullets like the Speer 270-grain semispitzer or Norma's 286-grain roundnosed bullets are used. Winchester's 748 proved to be most consistent performer and produced some very impressive groups — as a

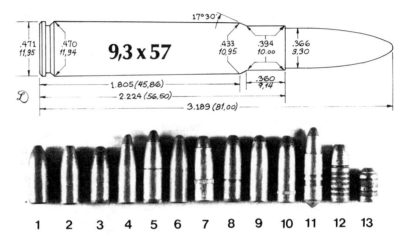

Although some of these bullets are obsolete, most are still available in the U.S.: (1) 232-grain Norma HP, (2) 232-grain Norma Alaskan, (3) 232-grain Norma Dual-Core, (4) 250-grain Barnes, (5) 258-grain RWS Copperpoint, (6) 270-grain Speer, (7) 285-grain RWS, (8) 286-grain Norma, (9) 286-grain Norma Tri-Clad, (10) 286-grain Norma roundnose, (11) 293-grain RWS TUG, (12) 250-grain Lyman 366408 and (13) 130-grain .36-caliber Lyman Maxiball.

9.3x57 loads

bullet	powder	charge (grains)	velocity (fps)	remarks
270 Speer	IMR-4895	46.0	2,145	good hunting load
	IMR-4895	47.0	2,205	maximum
	W-748	46.0	1,985	accurate, mild
	W-748	48.0	2,165	accurate, maximum
	IMR-3031	42.0	2,110	fair
232 Norma	IMR-3031	45.0	2,335	Barnes data
	IMR-3031	48.0	2,485	maximum, but accurate
	N-201	49.0	2,329	Norma data
	N-201	53.0	2,435	warm, accurate
	W-748	54.0	2,450	most accurate
258 RWS	R-902*	46.0	2,115	RWS data
	R-903*	48.0	2,001	RWS data
286 Norma	IMR-3031	40.0	2,000	Barnes data
	N-201	44.6	2,067	Norma data, maximum
293 RWS	R-903*	47.0	2,001	RWS data
232 Norma	factory load		2,330	
286 Norma	factory load		2,070	

* R-prefix powders are Rottweil, not available in the U.S., and are shown for reference only. R-902 is close to Norma 201, W-748 and BL-C(2). R-903 lies between H-335 and IMR-4064.

Test rifle was a Husqvarna Model 146 with 24¾-inch barrel. Loads developed in Norma 9.3x57 brass, using CCI-200, Remington 9½ and RWS-LR primers. Velocities measured on an Oehler Model 12 chronograph with the first screen 10 meters from the muzzle. Ambient temperature averaged 55 degrees Fahrenheit. All loads should be reduced by 10 percent and worked up carefully.

Be alert — Publisher cannot accept responsibility for errors in published load data.

matter of fact, some too small to be believed.

Husqvarna rifles have excessively long barrels for such a cartridge, nearly 25 inches, and a rate of twist designed to stabilize the heavier bullets. To my surprise, the 1-in-14-inch twist stabilized the 232-grain Norma bullets extremely well. These bullets are effective on deer-sized game, while the 286-grain bullets would certainly be adequate for elk and moose in timber.

For the cast-bullet shooter, the old Lyman No. 366408, a 250-grain plain-based bullet, is well-suited for casual shooting and hunting. About 15 grains of Unique groups this bullet quite well. Lyman also makes a .364-inch Maxi ball which, when cast hard, left unsized then dipped in liquid lube, measures about .366 inch in diameter. It is a black-powder rifle bullet, but works in the 9.3x57 quite handsomely and makes a fine plinker when backed with about 10 grains of Unique. I have tried to size the Maxi ball in my 450 sizer, but the lubricant consumption is wasteful.

After a few sessions at the shooting bench, several preferences emerged. The powder which produced the tightest groups was the Winchester's 748 in nearly all bullet weights. The lighter Norma 232-grain Protected Power Cavities shot extremely well, as did the Speer 270-grain semispitzers. The RWS bullets produced excellent groups in all weights but are just a little too expensive for casual shooting. IMR-3031 proved a bit too erratic for my meek disposition in this trial-and-error situation. IMR-4064 never did yield the accuracy obtained by other powders in the test rifle so only a few samples were tried. Both H-4895 and IMR-4895 showed a higher tolerance to my cautious experimentation and therefore received greater attention.

Having had but one chance to try the 9.3x57 Mauser on a Texas whitetail proved inconclusive. Hit behind the shoulder at a range of 50 yards or so, the deer dropped after running another 25 yards. The bullet, a 293-grain Brenneke TUG, went right through the animal without showing much expansion. Obviously, it was better suited to heavier game animals.

The 9.3x57 Mauser may not look great on the drawing board or when fired over a chronograph, but it sure has a lot of Scandinavian moose hunters convinced it possesses some advantage that cannot be described in words. ●

CHAPTER
28

THE INDOMITABLE 9.3x62

Al Miller

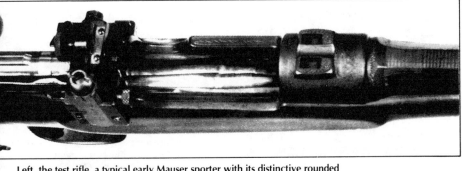

ALTHOUGH INTERNATIONALLY recognized as a premier big game round, the 9.3x62 is still virtually unknown in the United States. A year or so back, Dynamit Nobel sold a grand total of six boxes of RWS ammo in that caliber in the U.S. — six boxes! Even if the folks at Norma figure out how to ship their components over here economically, it's highly unlikely that any 9.3 brass or bullets will be included. Regardless of a caliber's virtues, there is certainly no profit in stocking something that doesn't sell.

Just why so many generations of Americans have ignored the 9.3x62 is hard to explain. It is certainly no late bloomer. It has been around since 1905 and established its reputation as one of Africa's most useful cartridges long before World War I diverted everyone's attention from sporting to military arms and ammunition.

It has been suggested that Americans back then had no particular need for another medium-powered cartridge tossing a heavy bullet out the muzzle around 2,200 fps. After all, they already had the .405 Winchester, didn't they?

Yes, they did — but the .405 wasn't everybody's cup of tea. Witness the birth of the .35 Whelen in 1920. Why James Howe created a wildcat to duplicate an existing round's performance is difficult to fathom at this late date. He and then-Major Whelen couldn't have been unaware of the metric round's existence, yet they certainly acted like it. No matter. What is more important is the .35 Whelen's undying popularity. There are probably as many new rifles being chambered for that round this year as there ever were. Obviously, there are a great many hunters who feel the need for the kind of performance the Whelen offers. Strange that none of them would opt for a factory rifle instead of a custom job. Or factory cartridges which offered the same performance — or better — than the Whelen. As the King of Siam purportedly exclaimed, "Is a puzzlement!"

Some have speculated that its caliber, .366 inch, was just a bit too alien for Yankee tastes. Anything is possible, of course, but why would .366 be any more outworldish than, say, .264, 284 or .323? Nope, that argument doesn't hold much water, either.

It couldn't have been due to lack of performance. The 9.3's original ballistics,

Left, the test rifle, a typical early Mauser sporter with its distinctive rounded pistol grip and side panels. If you look closely, you can just barely see the brass-lined hole on top of the comb about a third of the way back. It served to anchor a stud extending downward from an add-on cheekpiece. Above, almost 18,000 foot-pounds of muzzle energy on tap! A full magazine puts plenty of power at the disposal of anyone toting a 9.3x62.

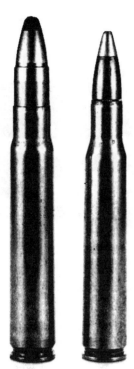

Although many of the 9.3x62's case dimensions (left) resemble those of the .30-06 (right), the metric round is obviously the more potent of the two.

even by today's standards, were nothing to sneeze at. When it first appeared, only one load was offered: a 285-grain bullet, either softnosed or full-patched, with a muzzle velocity of 2,175 fps. Muzzle energy was rated at 3,000 foot-pounds. While that performance level wouldn't justify banner headlines these days, it was a very different story 80 years ago.

The most powerful round in the United States at that time was the .405 Winchester. It featured a chunky 300-grain roundnose launched from the muzzle at 2,200 fps and generating 3,220 foot-pounds of energy. It was a potent cartridge. Best of all, it was chambered in Winchester's Model 95 — the latest and strongest of a distinguished line of lever actions from the famed New Haven plant.

America's love affair with the lever action may have blinded our grandfathers to the 9.3's merits. Developments in foreign bolt actions and their cartridges went largely unnoticed by the Yankee rank and file before World War I but that was no longer true after the troops came home in 1919. Nevertheless, even when firms like Griffin & Howe, Hoffman and other custom gunmakers began offering their rifles in all sorts of metric and British chamberings, the 9.3x62 was seldom mentioned. It was almost as though there was a conspiracy afoot, a sort of gentlemen's agreement not to admit the existence of the round. A decade or so later, when improved powders enabled the Germans to soup the 9.3 up to its present level, nobody turned a hair on this side of the Atlantic.

In Europe — and especially in Africa — the opposite situation prevailed. African

colonists of all nationalities embraced the 9.3x62 at first sight. It was lethal, controllable and chambered in bolt action repeaters they could afford.

There were more powerful cartridges available in Africa then but all were .40 caliber or larger, characterized by long, heavy bullets and fat, finger-length cases. Since they were much too outsized for any of the repeating rifles of the day, they had to be chambered in doubles and single shots, most of which were very heavy and very expensive.

Rifles like that posed no problems for the well-heeled aristocrat heading out on safari for six months to a year or more. Their cost was of no import and as for weight, well, a 15-pound double feels like a feather when somebody else carries it. To a farmer or rancher, whose budget was usually limited and whose personnel roster had no place for a gunbearer or two, rifle choice had to be based on an entirely different set of criteria.

If a census of Africa could have been taken in 1900, observers would have tallied more lions than people in much of the land mass south of the Sahara. Elephants and rhino numbered in the millions. Buffalo had to be counted by the acre and the various species of antelope would have defied a tax collector's ability to inventory them. The continent was a hunter's paradise in those days — but a farmer's nightmare. Not only did the wide-eyed European immigrants find their farms and plantations surrounded by legions of ravenous, crop-eating critters but to their horror, they discovered that many of their four-footed neighbors were meat-eaters and regarded humans as just another potential item on the daily menus! It must have been quite a shock to those men and women to learn that once they left the security of their walls and stockades, they were often the hunted instead of the hunters.

The rifles they brought with them had been effective enough against red stag

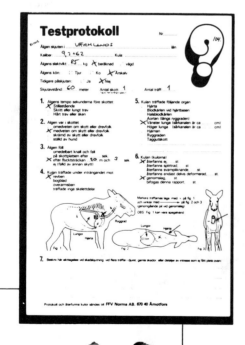

Both Norma and RWS factory loads are imported into the U.S. but at the moment, trying to locate Norma powders is a real problem.

Above, one of the field reports turned in by Swedish moose hunters. Left, an unfired Norma 232-grain PPC and three others which were recovered from Scandinavian moose. Note the classic expansion.

and wild boar at home but were never designed to take on animals which often weighed tons instead of pounds.

What the immigrant landowner wanted was a fairly light, handy rifle; one which would be easy to carry, whether slung over a shoulder or lying across the pommel of a saddle. They wanted a repeater, one chambered for a round which was powerful enough to drop anything they might encounter on their daily rounds, but one which wouldn't separate them from their teeth every time they pulled the trigger.

The 9.3x62 proved to be exactly what they prayed for. Although it is doubtful if Otto Bock, the Berlin gunsmith who sired it, had any of Africa's Big Five in mind during his experiments, it didn't take long for the transplanted Europeans to discover that the new cartridge, in the hands of a cool shot, could take on anything veldt or jungle could throw against it. Continental sportsmen were equally delighted with the round. So were the Scandinavians. The 9.3's performance against polar bear and moose left nothing to be desired.

Although certainly no stranger to Asian game fields, the 9.3x62's reputation as a big game cartridge was won in Africa before World War I. Even the introduction of Holland & Holland's belted .375 Magnum in 1912 did nothing to dim the 9.3's popularity. Although the British round was clearly the more powerful, many experienced hunters preferred the older cartridge. At the close ranges most dangerous animals were taken, the 9.3 was just as deadly, just as dependable as the longer, harder-kicking .375. Then too, most rifles chambered for the 9.3 were lighter and more responsive than those built to accommodate the lengthier H&H hull.

During the twenties and thirties, the 9.3's popularity continued to grow. Although professional hunters and visiting sportsmen leaned toward bigger, more powerful calibers, immigrants who worked and lived in Africa showed a marked preference for the more controllable 9.3. By the time Hitler's panzers rumbled across the Polish boundary in September 1939, the 9.3x62 was one of the most popular — if not *the* most popular — medium-powered caliber in northern Europe and the southern two-thirds of Africa.

By 1945, however, the situation had changed radically. Metric sporting ammunition was impossible to find anywhere in the world. Eventually, trickles of new British and American arms and ammo began seeping through customs at Mombassa and Lourenço Marques. The old Mauser sporters were traded off or stuck away and forgotten. Winchesters and Remingtons took their places on farms and ranches. By the time DWM and RWS were able to resume production, most of their prewar African market belonged to somebody else.

Of late, the old round has been staging something of a comeback. Sales of factory ammo have been gradually increasing the past five or six years, both in southern Africa and northern Europe. What sparked all the renewed interest is anybody's guess but whatever the reason, the 9.3x62 is slowly but surely regaining some of its lost popularity. Not, as noted, here in the good ol' U.S. of A., though.

In this country, owners of 9.3's have always had to load their own. Cases have

never been a problem, of course. Except for that extra millimeter in length, the metric hull's basic dimensions match those of the 06's to an uncanny degree.

Bullets are another story. No American firm has ever manufactured any 9.3 ammunition, consequently slugs of that diameter (.365 or .366 inch, depending on the maker) have always been scarce in the U.S. Every now and then, a custom gunmaker imports a few boxes of factory ammo but it's a rare gunshop that has any on hand.

Back in 1974, Speer produced some 250-grain soft-noses in 9.3. They were extremely slow sellers so two years later, they were unceremoniously dropped from the line. This year, the Lewiston, Idaho, firm made a run of 270-grain semi-spitzers to fill a foreign order. Dave Andrews says there are enough left over to keep homegrown 9.3 fans in business for several years.

Right, Redding's clever tapered expander button took the work out of expanding .30-06 case necks to .366 inch. Expanded necks showed little or no distortion.

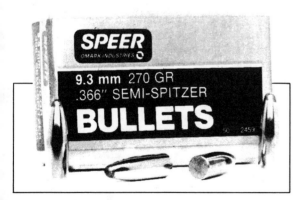

Speer's 270-grain semi-spitzers delivered excellent accuracy from the test rifle.

Norma 9.3mm bullets with a 180-grain .30-caliber Sierra (left) for comparison. In the middle, the 286-grain softnose. At the far right, a 232-grain Protected Power Cavity (PPC) upright and another, pointing toward the camera to give a better view of the unique cavity.

171

Barnes and several other custom makers supply 9.3 bullets of varying designs but the only other source of factory ammo and components is Dave Cumberland, Old Western Scrounger, 12924 Highway A-12, Montague CA 96064. The U.S. distributor for RWS, Dave usually lists all kinds of obsolete, hard-to-get ammo and components in his catalog.

The last word received from Norma was that it did not intend to import any 9.3mm bullets or brass into this country. Mike Bussard, the Swedish firm's American representative, said it might be possible to special-order some but cautioned that both delivery dates and prices would be uncertain. Too bad, because three years ago, Norma came out with a 9.3 bullet which would be ideal for North American game — a 232-grain Protected Power Cavity, usually abbreviated PPC.

The PPC's design is intriguing. Where the ordinary hollowpoint is just that, the PPC's jacket curls over the rim of the orifice in the bullet's nose and extends down into the cavity a tad, lining the inside of the lip, reinforcing it but leaving a small amount of lead showing at the bottom of the hollow. In addition, the bullet's jacket thickens markedly from nose to base. The base itself is solid and a heavy cannelure cinches jacket to core.

The idea behind the PPC's configuration is that the reinforced hollow nose will delay any tendency of the bullet to mushroom until it has had a chance to penetrate a few inches. Once inside the animal's body, expansion takes place with more violence than usual but because of the stout jacket, the soft core peels back instead of wrenching apart. The result should be a bullet with truly controlled expansion, one which will penetrate deeper than most hollowpoints, expand dramatically but hold together and retain more of its weight than hollowpoints usually do.

So much for theory. How well do those bullets work?

Bert Johnsson, Norma's sales manager, supplied me with a collection of hunter's field reports accompanied by dozens of PPC's recovered from the moose they had downed.

In 1981 and 1982, Norma supplied free ammunition to Swedish moose hunters who, in exchange, agreed to report the details of their kills on a field test form provided by the company. One of the reports is shown in an accompanying photo. Each report had a recovered bullet or two taped to it.

Forty-three of the 426 reports collected during the two seasons were submitted by hunters who carried 9.3x62's loaded with the new 232-grain PPC's. Shots were taken at ranges from 18 to 215 meters. The average was 25, pretty close for a

hollowpointed bullet launched at better than 2,600 fps. Nevertheless, the 232-grain PPC's held together beautifully. Recovered specimens revealed they retained about two-thirds their original weight and as you can see by those shown in the photograph, they expanded precisely as they were designed to — and remember, those slugs were pulled out of moose, not recovery boxes.

The 9.3 PPC's are very accurate; the range tests left no doubt about that. A surprising number of five-shot groups were recorded which spanned less than two inches, center to center — pretty good for iron sights and a light-barreled sporter. No group recorded with those bullets exceeded 2½ inches. The majority ranged from 2 to 2¼ inches and ordinarily, I can't do much better than that with any receiver-sighted rifle, no matter how tight-grouping it is.

Barnes bullets were also tested. Both the 250 and 300-grain spitzers grouped well with most of the powders tried. The Speer 270-grain softpoints, on the other hand, were decidedly choosy about the powders they preferred. Backed by a propellant they liked, those long spitzers often gave astonishing results, punching out five-shot groups as small as 1½ inches.

Of course, the rifle itself deserves a share of the credit. Too bad its complete history isn't known. A typical early German sporter, it was built on a Mauser action, sports an octagonal barrel, a rounded pistol grip and old fashioned side panels. Judging from the proof marks, it was put together prior to World War I, then rechambered for the 9.3x62 in 1931. The original chambering is unknown.

When it fell into my possession, most of its blueing was gone and the stock bore a few hairline cracks around tang and trigger guard. It was turned over to the tender mercies of Larry Caudill, the Albuquerque stockmaker, who had the metal bead-blasted then given a subdued matte-blue finish. He also repaired the stock, refinished it and added a neat solid rubber recoil pad, whose cocoa hue complemented the fine old walnut stock. All in all, a very tasteful, professional job.

At one time, the rifle had been fitted with an auxiliary cheekpiece, curved to snug over the top of the comb and joined to it by means of a short metal rod which extended down from the add-on and slid into a vertical hole drilled through the top of the comb. The hole is still there but the cheekpiece was no longer available when I traded for the rifle.

As usual, claw mount bases had been dovetailed into the tops of the receiver's rings. Rather than bother with a high-mounted scope or have the safety modified, the receiver was drilled and tapped for a receiver sight. An old Red-

field model was installed. Too bad they aren't available any more because it has been a very dependable and exceedingly accurate sight.

Like most of its genre, the aging Mauser is light. On a Pitney-Bowes postal scale, it registered an exact seven pounds, empty. With a full magazine (five rounds) its balance point is just about the floorplate's midpoint. Easy to tote, commandably responsive and a natural pointer, it makes an excellent woods rifle. The double set triggers are a great assist for occasional long shots. Were it not for that skimpy forend and its sometimes frivolous behavior on the bench, I'd be hard-pressed to criticize it at all.

When the traditional bench approach was attempted — forend and buttstock on the bags — the rifle torqued to the right and its muzzle tried to vault skyward, sometimes straight up, sometimes swerving to the right as it did so. The solution was to prop the forward bag under the floorplate and clamp the forend in a grip of iron with the left hand while the rear bag was jammed under the stock's toe. So supported, the rifle recoiled straight back every time.

Even so, control was never easy while testing. Any time a seven-pound sporter whomps out 3,000 foot-pounds of energy at the muzzle, it takes everything I've got to make it behave on the bags. Nevertheless, that rifle turned in a great many sub-two-inch groups, too many to be attributed solely to chance.

The barrel's grooves miked .3662 inch and showed traces of very fine pitting, a heritage left by years of shooting ammunition sparked by corrosive primers, no doubt. Land edges were slightly rounded, although the bore was mirror bright. That evidence, plus the well-worn blueing and the nicks and scratches decorating the stock all added up to lots of use but no abuse. It was obviously a hunter's rifle. It must have been carried a lifetime's worth of miles in its day but it had been well maintained, nonetheless.

Before attempting any loads, the first step was to find out what kind of performance the old rifle would turn in with factory ammunition. Norma rounds, with their 286-grain Dual-Core bullets averaged 2,355 fps some 15 feet from the muzzle. That was only five fps short of the published muzzle velocity — not bad.

The RWS 293-grain TUG softnoses clocked 2,325 fps, practically duplicating the Norma round's ballistics but falling short of the advertised 2,430 fps. The latter figure is overly optimistic, I suspect.

Fired cases miked .472 to .474 inch around the pressure belt. Initial accuracy attempts, as mentioned before, were disappointing. Once my bench techniques accommodated the rambunctious old sporter, groups shrank appreciatively and flyers disappeared altogether.

As a glance at the accompanying load data table will indicate, Norma's N-201 is a particularly efficient powder in the 9.3 case. Accuracy with every bullet it was mated with was excellent. Too bad the Swedish powders are so tough to find. Eventually, we're told, their importation will be resumed but in the meantime, anyone who wants some of those red and black cans will have to nose around until they find a dealer who still has a few pounds on his shelves. The only one I know with a half decent inventory is Huntington Die Specialties in Oroville, California.

IMR-3031 and H-4895 were the best choices among the domestic propellants. Both burned clean, developed decent velocities and grouped their bullets reliably, usually around two inches, occasionally less.

DuPont's 4064, W-748, H-380 and W-760 weren't quite as accurate as the faster burners. They weren't inaccurate, mind you, but most of their five-shot strings spanned 2½ to 2¾ inches, markedly larger than the rest. Velocities, however, were right up there.

DuPont's 4350 was a surprise performer. Although it was a shade too slow burning for the 9.3's case, its accuracy was second to none. In fact, two of the tightest groups fired with the 9.3 featured rounds charged with 4350. Both were smaller than 1¾ inches. They may have been flukes — just a series of lucky shots — but regardless, all the loads based on DuPont's 4350 were consistent performers and all, regardless of bullet weight, grouped two inches or less.

Norma cases were used to develop all loads but during the last chronographing session, fireformed military and S&W brass were substituted for the Swedish hulls. Differences in velocities, when bullets, powders and primers were the same, amounted to less than 50 fps.

Reshaping '06 cases to 9.3 is fairly uncomplicated. Most handloaders simply run the .30-caliber case mouths over the 9.3 expander button, trim the case to 62 millimeters, whip up a fireforming load and head for the range. Redding has made the operation even simpler with their special tapered expanding buttons.

The Redding button is shaped like a plumb weight, tapering from less than .308 to .366 inch. Because the case mouth is flared open gradually, the brass expands more uniformly, minimizing distortion. Best of all, it takes about half the effort to stretch a case mouth from .30 to .36 with the taper expander than it does when using just the .366 button.

Once the mouth had been expanded,

NEI bullet 239.366PB, which weighed 232 grains when cast from Linotype, was seated over 10 grains of W-230.

That made a fine fireforming load. The resultant cases were nicely filled out and needed no more attention.

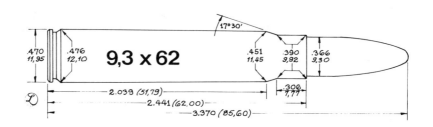

9.3 x 62

bullet	powder	charge (grains)	velocity (fps)	remarks
232 Norma	N-201	58.5	2,563	many sub-two-inch groups. Norma recommends 59.1 grains of N-201 to duplicate factory load
	IMR-4320	56.5	2,476	
	H-4895	58.0	2,439	
	IMR-4064	56.0	2,353	
	H-380	61.5	2,381	
	IMR-3031	54.5	2,442	several 1¾-inch groups
250 Barnes	N-201	56.0	2,444	
	IMR-3031	53.0	2,367	GI Match 06 cases
	H-380	60.0	2,334	
	W-760	62.0	2,337	
	IMR-4350	62.0	2,305	
270 Speer	N-201	55.0	2,371	
	IMR-3031	55.0	2,343	
	IMR-4064	57.5	2,292	
	H-4895	55.0	2,310	
	W-760	64.0	2,225	
	W-748	58.0	2,246	
	H-380	59.0	2,251	cases formed from S&W 06 brass
	IMR-4350	64.0	2,296	
286 Norma	N-201	54.0	2,287	Norma recommends 54.7 grains of N-201 to duplicate factory load
	IMR-3031	52.0	2,301	
	W-748	57.5	2,182	
	IMR-4064	53.5	2,224	extreme spread = 100 fps
	W-760*	59.0	2,157	
	IMR-4350*	59.0	2,123	
300 Barnes	W-748	55.0	2,197	
	W-760	57.0	2,102	
	H-380	57.0	2,140	cases formed from S&W 06 brass
	IMR-4350	57.0	2,103	

* These loads with Remington 9½ primers; all others used CCI standard Large Rifle primers.

Velocities were recorded on an Oehler Model 33 Chronotach and represent five-shot averages measured 15 feet from the muzzle of a 32.5-inch barrel. Ambient temperatures averaged 65 degrees Fahrenheit. Except where noted, all loads were assembled in Norma cases.

Norma Ballistics

	at muzzle		at 100 yards	
bullet	velocity (fps)	energy (ft/lbs)	velocity (fps)	energy (ft/lbs)
232-grain PPC	2,625	3,540	2,307	2,734
286-grain Softpoint	2,360	3,544	2,088	2,769

Be alert — Publisher cannot accept responsibility for errors in published load data.

That load, by the way, proved to be very accurate. All bullets touched at 25 yards. It would make a dandy small game load.

None of the loads in the table were maximum in the test rifle. The majority could be boosted with a few more grains of powder without risking anything — probably. As I grow older, however, I find myself becoming more cautious with rifles that were put together before I was born. Metal doesn't get any stronger with age. If a 270-grain bullet won't do the job at 2,300 fps, it's doubtful if a few more fps would make much difference. On the other hand, those 2,300 fps loads are well below any danger point. Somehow, I find a great deal of comfort in that.

Were that Mauser of more modern vintage, jazzing up some of those charges wouldn't bother me a bit. As it is, there's no great advantage in trying to turn a 9.3 into a .375 H&H. If anyone wants to add more powder to some of the listed loads, however, they have my very best wishes . . .

Some charge that the 9.3x62 is nothing more than a metric .35 Whelen. There's more truth than falsehood in that but it's certainly no criticism. There are no flies on the Whelen. It is a more flexible cartridge than the 9.3 because of the wide variety of bullets available but that's an academic advantage, really. With all the custom bullet makers around, it should be no great problem to get slugs of any weight, shape or construction for a 9.3 these days.

Where can such bullet makers be found? Well, quite a number advertise in these pages. If they can't accommodate you, your best bet is to contact Dave Corbin. He supplies swaging equipment to most of the custom makers in the country and can tell you who is — or who would be willing to — make up just the bullet you're after. His address is: Corbin, Box 2659, White City OR 97503.

Most available 9.3 bullets are too weighty and too heavily constructed for North American animals. Norma's 232-grain PPC would be ideal for most game this side of the Atlantic but as noted, they aren't available and won't be in the foreseeable future.

It seems to me that a 220 to 230-grain spitzer launched at around 2,650 fps, would take care of deer-sized animals nicely out to 300 yards or so. A 250-grain soft-nose, like those made by Barnes, should be just the ticket for elk and moose. So would Speer's 270-grain semi-spitzer — although it's a tad heavier than need be. Those bullets would do well against the big bears, though.

For a real, no-nonsense stopping bullet, any of those adorning the Norma or RWS rounds should be ideal. So should the Barnes 300-grain spitzer, especially when ordered with the tough, .049-inch thick jackets.

The 9.3x62 is certainly no all-purpose cartridge; it was never meant to be. It's a premier big game round, though, and would make an excellent choice for anyone going after the larger species in Canada or Alaska. As for hunting abroad, well, John Taylor's evaluation of the 9.3's merits says it all. In *African Rifles and Cartridges*, he put it this way:

"Having said that it's the most popular and most widely used medium bore in Africa, there isn't a great deal more than one can say about it — that just about covers everything." ●

CHAPTER
29

LOADING THE .38-55

By Christian H. Helbig

Magnum!! today's magic word even for the deer hunter. Seems that without a magnum caliber there's little chance of bagging even a rabbit at twenty paces. If you believe in this trend, then your .30-30 and all the older lever-gun cartridges are less than useless. At the other end of the scale there are those who swear by the old charcoal burners throwing a minimum of 400 grains of lead.

Well, I neither swear at nor by any of these extremes — and I have shot practically all of them. I have, though, found one old-timer that to my thinking is the most useful deer and black bear caliber for *woodland* hunting—the .38-55 with proper handloads.

Here we have an old number which properly handloaded outperforms our country's most popular deer rifle, the .30-30! Please note the reference to woodland hunting, the under-a-hundred-yards situation that actually prevails in over half the nation. A 300-yard cartridge the .38-55 is not.

No one in his right mind would suggest building a .38-55 from scratch, (*don't count on that—ed.*) but there must be thousands of Marlin 93's and Winchester 94's still around in good shooting condition. The owner of one of these in .38-55 has a sleeping tiger

that can really come of age with good handloads.

Before going further, let me state that the loads shown and discussed are *only* for the above 93 and 94 models and *not* for other weaker actions like the Ballard, etc. Here we find the main reason this cartridge lost its popularity; the ammo manufacturers very wisely dropped the loadings way down to be safe in any vintage rifle. This was a necessity because many people paid no attention to warning labels on the boxes.

We are a nation of change, due to progress, but how foolish it is to pay hard cash for a deer rifle if one has a .38-55 in decent shape sitting in the closet. Handloading and tinkering are two hobbies in which most gun enthusiasts indulge, so use these skills with this old cannon and you may have as much fun as I do with my .38-55.

My appreciation of this cartridge started a few years ago when I bought one just because it was priced low. A few rounds of factory ammo were fired, and sounded real sick. Looking at the ballistics table showing the 255-grain bullet at 1,320 fps was quite a letdown. Since I handload for every rifle I own, for pleasure and economy, I decided to see what could be done with this one. Looking at Sharpe's book quickly brightened the outlook. Here is a cartridge that can give up to 30 per cent more muzzle energy, 6 per cent better sectional density and 49 per cent greater bullet area than the famous .30-30.

Sharpe's loads showed over 1,800 fps with the 255-grain pill — enough to persuade me to part with cash for a set of dies and a mould. Working up the loads made this gun seem worth-while, and soon I had it really cracking, and delivering good groups. The .38-55 was always known for its very good accuracy, even in lever actions.

With good (and safe) handloads you can push a 255 or 280-grain bullet to

With .38-55's large bullet diameter, both lead and jacketed bullets should be equally effective on deer.

1,850 fps-plus. These loads give moderate pressures. Since this case has the same base diameter as the .30-30, it can be loaded to the same pressures (in the aforementioned rifles) as the .30-30. Back-thrust or stress on the action will be the same and these rifles are perfectly OK for modern .30-30 loads of 38,000 psi, (factory load pressures).

It will be hard to generate more than 30,000 psi if you use No. 3031 powder. You can't get enough in the case. Hi-Vel No. 2 also cannot be used in enough quantity to get any bad results. Using No. 4198 or RE 7 is quite different—

100-yard group, 1.0 inch, 275-grain hollow-point gas-check bullet, 32.0 grains Reloder 7.

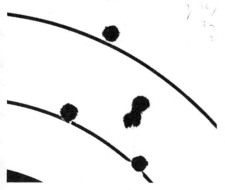

100-yard group, 1.85 inches, 255-grain factory bullet, 32.5 grains No. 3031 powder.

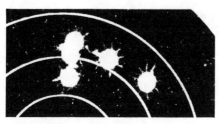

100-yard group, 1.2 inches, 255-grain jacketed bullet, 32.2 grains Reloder 7.

177

To really get the correct impression of the .38-55 we must forget published ballistics and go to the facts. When the standard 170-grain .30-30 factory load is shot in the conventional 20" tube, it comes out at 2,080 fps with a muzzle energy of 1,640 fp. Note this energy well, for it is the true value one gets from the .30-30 and will be used for comparison.

My Marlin .38-55 has a mint barrel, short three-shot magazine and 2¾ power scope. It weighs 7 pounds even — with just the peep sight 6½ lbs. Many rounds have passed through this barrel without any leading, using gas-check cast bullets at 1,850 fps and over. All these were cast quite soft, 1 to 15 for good expansion. Accuracy is good to excellent by lever action standards with all loads staying in two inches and the better ones in 1.2" to 1.5" at 100 yards. This does not require tedious load development.

A few other .38-55 rifles I have checked did about the same when the barrels were in decent condition. The loads in the table were shot and checked in my own Marlin, a Model 336 chosen only because of its pistol grip tang. To this I wedded a new surplus Marlin barrel originally made for the Model 1893 action. Threads are the same, so only a small extractor cut modification is required.

When casting slugs for the .38-55 one should use only Lyman Mould No. 375296 gas check — never 375449, since the latter is only .375" as cast and these barrels mike .377" to .379". I use the solid bullet at 280 grains and the hollow-point at 265 grains. This H.P. is preferred for game shooting, and it is very good on deer and black bear.

I feel this bullet is even better than the factory jacketed one which upsets too much in the barrel if driven over 1,700 fps. I proved this by examining bullets at various velocities fired into soft, wet wood chips. At approximately 1,700 fps, rifling marks began to show ahead of the cannelure, where before firing this portion was under bore diameter. One should not be surprised at this, since it was designed for only 1,320 fps.

they could go beyond sensible pressures if used with a heavy hand. Now that Hi-Vel No. 2 is gone, you can substitute RE 11 but it will not do as good a job. RE 7 and No. 4198 are much better choices.

When using No. 3031, some unburned powder will remain in the barrel; this does not seem to harm the accuracy at all. The fast powders such as No. 2400 and No. 4227 are very accurate and uniform but should be used light to medium, not full powder loads. Even at the top pressure levels these fast powders produce no more than 1,700 fps — not that 1,600 or 1,700 is peanuts. They still make adequate deer loads.

I have found the best powder for the .38-55 is RE 7 with bullets of from 255 to 280 grains, cast or jacketed. This powder burns cleanly and is a joy to put through the powder measure. At no time have I found the .38-55 temperamental in loading; it seems to digest any sensible load with good accuracy.

Bullet				Charge	Powder	M.V.	M.E.
280 Gr.	375296	solid	Gas Check	32.0	Hi-V 2	1854	2130
265 Gr.	375296	Hollow Pt.	Gas Check	32.8	Hi-V 2	1834	1980
265 Gr.	375296	Hollow Pt.	Gas Check	34.0	No. 3031	1863	2050
265 Gr.	375296	Hollow Pt.	Gas Check	29.5	No. 4198	1820	1950
265 Gr.	375296	Hollow Pt.	Gas Check	31.0	No. 4198	1870	2055
255 Gr.	Factory Jacketed Soft Point			32.5	No. 3031	1800	1840
255 Gr.	Factory Jacketed Soft Point			30.0	RE-7	1620	1490
255 Gr.	Factory Jacketed Soft Point			33.0	RE-7	1825	1890
Comparison of Standard Factory 170 Gr. .30-30 load						2080	1640

No cast bullets exhibited this upsetting, even at 1,900 fps. Casting these large-size bullets is easy and fast. I can spend an evening and wind up with 300 to 400 sized and lubricated. It seems moulds smaller than .35 caliber are most temperamental, while the larger ones work well without too much trouble.

My evening's output of 400 cast bullets costs only time and effort. An equal number of the factory jacketed type would cost about $23.00. This amount of loot will buy a good set of dies and a bullet mould. This was one reason I started casting for handloads in the larger calibers. I find these bullets fully as accurate as jacketed ones at a fraction of the cost.

One never needs anything more than cast slugs for most shooting in the .38-55. In fact, I would go as far as to state that jacketed bullets are never needed (in a smooth barrel) even for hunting in this caliber.

Powder charges have never been weighed, always thrown with a Redding measure. Bullets are seated to crimping groove and cases moderately crimped. This crimp is required in tabular magazine lever guns. Part of the accuracy I attribute to an EVEN crimp, which can be accomplished only by trimming cases to uniform length.

The loads in the table have all been personally chronographed in a five counter unit. Each load represents a five-shot average with no temperature correction. On test days it was about +60°F.

These loads show from 20 to 30 per cent more muzzle energy for the .38-55 than the .30-30 — not bad for a cartridge called obsolete. Mid-range trajectory for 100 yards is approximately 1.7", and no one can complain about that. If you sight an inch high at 100 yards, you can forget about any sight correction up to 130 yards — which is way beyond the average deer shot. In load No. 1 you will notice a heavier bullet going slightly faster than a lighter one in load 2, using 0.8 grains less powder. Before anyone yells *foul*, this has been observed in other straight cases and is due to more complete powder combustion when using a bullet of greater sectional density.

Loads 4 and 5 show there is not much point in using over 30.0 grains of No. 4198 in this case with 265-grain bullets — the gain in velocity being negligible. These loads also clearly point out that about 1,850 fps is the most you can coax out of the .38-55 at the 36,000 to 38,000 psi level.

Out at 100 yards where it really counts, the energy figures are still about 30 per cent more than the .30-30. These values have been calculated from Burnside Laboratory charts by Coxe & Beuglass.

All loads were put together with Lyman neck sizing dies, and no sticking of cases occurred. However, I would recommend full length sizing for hunting loads.

Much has been written on finding the right bullet lube combination. Here again, the .38-55 shows its merit. I have used several commercial lubes and my own secret formula with perfect results. You all know my secret lube — lots of odd sticks and beeswax with cylinder oil and general floor sweepings, all melted in a big mess over the kitchen stove.

If your .38-55 is a little rough and pitted, don't despair. Although they are more expensive, you can shoot jacketed bullets and produce groups under three inches at normal hunting ranges. I tried this in another .38-55 that looked horrible inside, but still did three inches.

The brush-cutting concept has been quite overdone but one cannot discount a .377" slug of about .265 sectional density at 1,850 fps. Certainly it will plow through a lot of obstruction without serious deflection, when compared to the 2,800 fps-plus deer cartridges.

If you still think this .38-55 is not potent enough for deer and black bear, just digest the following: out at 100 yards it still has 1,350 foot pounds, compared to the 100-yard energy of 970 fp for the highly touted .44 Rem. Mag. Forty per cent more punch for the old dog over what some say is *the* deer cartridge for brush shooting.

My .38-55s have given me many hours of pleasant shooting at the range and much education at the loading bench. It has accuracy, power and economy and as much energy as the deer and black bear hunter needs. ●

CHAPTER
30

Sam Fadala

.375 WINCHESTER

ABOUT THREE years ago, Winchester announced its new .375 cartridge and a new rifle to chamber it. Probably, we have to amend the words *new* and *rifle* in referring to the Big Bore, especially engineered to handle the .375 Winchester. First, although the arm is remodeled, it is all the same our familiar friend, the Model 94, trusted old lever-action saddle pal of rancher, deer hunter, and movie cowboy. Second, anything with only twenty inches of barrel, plus a compact style that's flat and slim, is going to have to be called a carbine, not a rifle.

The claim of the new .375 Winchester cartridge to fame has been its "ten per cent more energy on target than the popular .30-30 Winchester or the .35 Remington cartridges." While this is a just claim, I think that it is understated — but that's my opinion. I feel that the .375 can be more than ten per

cent above the standard loadings in .30-30 and .35 — in actual effect on big game, that is, not necessarily paper ballistics.

The .375 Winchester and its fine carbine are indeed good for timber and brush, and in the past ten months alone, I have kept track of a dozen queries asked about this cartridge and rifle — it seems that the interest in both that was originally generated by something new in the gun world has been given a secondary boost almost three years after the inception of the combination.

The .375 Winchester is a .375. Sometimes, the names of cartridges don't necessarily describe them, as we know. For America, it seems that the .375 size is somewhat offbeat, but it isn't. True, our minds seize upon the famed .375 H&H Magnum when we think of this caliber. The .375 H&H Magnum

was given to the shooters in 1912 by the London gun firm; and a considerable time later, it came to America. However, America already had a .375, for all practical purposes.

We didn't call it a .375, but it fired .376 bullets, which is close enough. It was the .38-55, an invention of blackpowder days, with a bullet in the 250-grain class (usually a 255), a case about 2.13 inches long, and using about fifty-five grains of black powder, hence the name: *.38* for the approximate caliber, *55* for the load. Today, it's hard to believe that this cartridge was ever important to American shooters, but it was. Now, only a few reloading manuals even refer to it.

Some folks found it superior to the .30-30 class of cartridges, especially in the early days when the .30-30 (.30 WCF) used only thirty grains of black powder, but inferior to the .38-55 in charge and certainly in bullet weight. In the 1930s and 1940s, there were at least two loadings for the .38-55, one the standard 255-grain bullet at

Fadala finds the new Big Bore version of the age-old Model 94 Winchester smoother in operation than the older saddle gun, because of internal improvements not generally given a lot of publicity. The four cartridges in his hand are loads with 250-grain W-W, 220-grain Hornady, 235-grain Speer with modified nose, and 200-grain W-W bullets.

181

factory speeds of 1,590 and 1,320 feet per second. The first was called the *.38-55 WHV,* and I am pretty certain that the initials meant *Winchester High Velocity.*

The .38-55 reminds me of an old-timer we called Lucky. I don't recall his last name, if indeed I ever knew it. He frequented the local gunshop. Back in the 1950s, when I was about fourteen, he must have been seventy-five years old. And he had maintained a love affair with the .38-55 long after the majority of this nation's hunters had forsaken such cartridges for classy bottle-necks. Lucky used to lecture our ears off. Time has erased the exact quotes, but the content is still in my mind.

"If you'd load that .38-55 yourself," he'd say, "it'd better the .30-30 and a lot of them other fancier shells you boys are using, especially you younger men." He was a handloader. I don't know what loads he used, but according to my Lyman manual, he could have been getting as much as eighteen hundred feet per second at the muzzle with the 255-grain bullet. In fact, he probably got more, because his rifle — and I remember the arm as

well as I recall the man — was the twenty-six-inch-barrel version of the Model 94, not the carbine.

When I saw the .375 Winchester, my mind drifted back to that old-time handloader and his .38-55. And when I tested the .375, I thought back on words spoken by a man who had lived in the days before game laws, who had drifted across places where cities are now, and who had shot what he wanted when he felt that he needed it, all with a .38-55; not with factory loads but with handloads, very probably about a 250-grain bullet at about eighteen hundred feet per second.

It's my opinion that the old boy was pretty much right. He used to say that such a ballistic combination would take a deer out right now, if you'd take the time to stalk close, only he didn't put it in those words. I don't recall the exact words, but they went something like this: "Instead of foolin' 'round with them damn high-speed things, what we need is to teach these kids to stalk again (a kid was anyone under fifty-five, to Lucky). Give 'em a beefed-up .38-55, and they'll get the game." Lucky's beefed-up .38-55 is

with us, with two weights of bullets factory-loaded.

One is a 200-grain Power-Point, the other a 250-grain Power-Point. Winchester's data show the 200-grain with a muzzle velocity of twenty-two hundred feet per second, the 250-grain at nineteen hundred. However, this is out of a *twenty-four-inch* test barrel. Therefore, I wanted to chronograph these in the standard Big Bore carbine with its twenty-inch barrel. I fired only five rounds of each type over the screens, with the following velocities:

200-grain	250-grain
2,083 fps	1,789 fps
2,084 fps	1,901 fps
2,031 fps	1,839 fps
2,096 fps	1,843 fps
2,103 fps	1,802 fps

The average velocity for the 200-grain was 2,079 feet per second; for the 250-grain, 1,835 feet per second.

My next test of the factory loads was with the "bullet box," a device that I developed to test the construction of bullets and the reaction of these bullets striking at various retained velocities. The box is simple — merely some water, clay, and catalogues spaced in compartments — but it works. Bullets recovered from game have matched quite closely the performance of the same bullets used on the box.

The distance from the box was only fifty yards. However, a lot of woods and brush shooting can be at close range; therefore, I wanted to see how the bullets would hold up at such a close distance from the muzzle. The 200-grain bullet, perhaps because of its double cannelure, held core and jacket together; but the 250 did not, as a rule. Several rounds were fired and recovered, and performance in each instance was almost identical.

The one and only complaint I had heard from friends who had taken game with the .375 — and I took time to hunt down half a dozen of these — was a bit more tissue disruption than perhaps required; overkill, if you will. Of course, this is a hard problem. If a bullet whistles through, leaving a clean channel but not downing the game, hunters are unhappy. And if the bullet floors game quickly but chews up meat, hunters can be unhappy. Ideally, it seems, a bullet should hang together and penetrate well. Hopefully, core and jacket remain together.

I felt that some handloading was in order. Although I was happy with the ballistic performance of both factory loads, we have become reloaders in America, and a lot of people are going to prepare home-made ammo for their

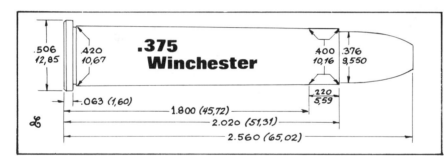

In one way or another, the .375 Winchester (3, 4) is related to these otherwise unlike cartridges. It is a rimmed lever-action cartridge like the .30-30 (1), .38-55 (2), and .444 Marlin (5), and it uses bullets of the same diameter as the .38-55 (2) and .375 H&H Magnum (6). Like any other cartridge for use in tubular magazines, it must be loaded with flat-point bullets for safety.

With sandpaper, Fadala flattened the nose of a 235-grain .375 H&H bullet from Speer (1), removing the rounded lead tip (2). Fadala advises, however, that such an uncannelured bullet should never be loaded in a tubular magazine; the "nose job" is for better terminal ballistics, not magazine safety. Winchester factory loads utilize 250-grain (3) and 200-grain bullets (4). The more familiar Hornady 180-grain .308 bullet (5) is in this line-up just to show the .375 bullets' relative sizes.

The 220-grain Hornady .375 bullet is made for the .375 H&H, with strong cannelure for expansion control — as demonstrated by this bullet fired into a recovery box at fifty yards. This bullet seems excellent for the .375 Winchester despite the lower velocities of the rimmed Winchester carbine cartridge.

.375s. In fact, some might want to cut down the velocity for very close-range work on smaller game, whereas others might want to strain the full *safe* potential from the .375 Winchester. The factory energies, as shown by my own chronographed loads, would be 1,920 foot-pounds for the 200-grain bullet at 2,079 feet per second, and 1,870 foot-pounds for the 250-grain bullet. Naturally, this does not mean that we have a perfect figure to describe "killing power," since kinetic energy does not do that. But it gives an indication.

There were few bullets to choose from when it came time to test the .375 for handloads. I obtained a set of Pacific dies, however, and got busy looking for a bullet. Hornady's 220-grain seemed a superb one to look at. First, I set up the beautiful Pacific dies. These were a pleasure to work with, a three-die set for a straight case that needs crimping.

The instructions with the dies are clear and easy to follow, so there is no point in going into the process here. However, the shooter should be aware that with such a three-die set, the big advantage is realized when the dies are properly set-up in the press. Each die is individually set-up, and then the locknut is turned so that each time the die is put into the press, it works in the same way.

Crimp those bullets in the .375 Winchester! The mouth of the case should fold into the cannelure of the bullet so that the bullet is held firmly in place during recoil. Remember, the Model 94 has a tubular magazine, and bullets are in a line, literally pushing on each other when the gun goes off.

Loose bullets can be shoved back into the case when the rifle is fired.

One final point about reloading. I'd suggest using a hand tool for setting new primers. Primers should be well seated into the primer pocket of the case but not squashed down below the level of the case head. When this condition does exist, the face of the primer is too far forward, and the firing pin may not be able to dent it properly for sure ignition. Hand-fitting the primers ensures that they are placed at just the right depth in the case — deep enough but not too deep.

The Hornady 220 bullet is, I feel, a wonderful compromise choice, a bullet that should do the job on any big game that is matched to the power of the .375 cartridge. Hornady developed the 220 to fit in between the 200 and 250 factory loads. The reason Hornady did this was simple yet important. By using this one bullet, the rifle can be sighted-in (more on that in a moment) and left alone. If the hunter uses both the 200 and the 250, he'd likely have to resight the rifle for whichever one is his choice at the moment.

With the 220, after the rifle was sighted, it could be left that way. Apparently, RL-7 powder was found to be superior with the .375 and its 220-grain Hornady bullet; unfortunately, I could not locate a single kernel of the stuff where I live, so I turned to IMR-4895 for my own tests, and I put together only two loads: thirty-six grains and thirty-eight grains. I felt that thirty-eight grains would be a maximum with the 220-grain Hornady.

For the sake of safety, the shooter should start with thirty-four grains of IMR-4895 and work up carefully to a higher charge with the 220-grain Hornady in the .375 Winchester case and Big Bore rifle. My thirty-six-grain charge gave me a velocity of 1,812 feet per second average at three feet from the first screen, and the thirty-eight-grain charge resulted in 1,910 feet per second, average. The variation in velocity was an extreme of only sixteen feet per second in these loadings, incidentally. The 1,812 feet per second with the 220-grain gives it an energy of 1,604 foot-pounds. The 1,910 feet per second with the 220-grain bullet is worth 1,783 foot-pounds. Frankly, I'd take on any deer in the woods with either one.

However, Hornady — using the same 220-grain .375 bullet in the Big Bore rifle's twenty-inch barrel, a W-W primer (which is what I used), a W-W case (which is what I used) — managed a full twenty-two hundred feet per second with RL-7 powder. Naturally, Hornady can not be responsible for anyone's rifle with any load, since there are so many variables; however, this maximum load was possible in their test arm under their test conditions. To reach twenty-two hundred feet per second, they put thirty-eight grains of RL-7 into the case, and this is a maximum load, with the case plumb full, as they say.

The 220-grain Hornady at twenty-two hundred feet per second gains a muzzle energy of 2,365 foot-pounds. And in my tests, the Hornady bullet at a velocity of 1,910 did not strip its jacket, indicating that a hunter could use this combination on game larger than deer when the range is right. In close hunting, I would not be afraid to use the load on larger game, provided a clear shot was available. It isn't

183

Speer's 235-grain bullet for the .375 H&H Magnum (*left*) shows much less deformation in the recovery box than any other bullet tested by Fadala — which is not surprising, as this bullet was designed to perform well at significantly higher velocities. For the deepest penetration and minimum meat destruction on light game, this would be a good bullet. The 250-grain Winchester factory bullet (*right*) did rather well in expansion, penetration, and weight retention — in a wild boar, not a recovery box. It ranged nearly the full length of a 350-pound boar, yet lost only thirty-one grains.

going to penetrate like a .338 Winchester, but careful hunters would find a lot of punch in the .375 at close range.

I was curious about the use of one other bullet in a handload: the standard 235-grain Speer .375 Magnum bullet. There is no cannelure on this bullet, and a shooter *should not* load this round into the magazine. But for a hunter in love with the .375 Winchester, who lives where game larger than deer is hunted, and who is willing to get close, I could see fitting *one* 235-grain Speer *in the chamber*, followed by flat-point bullets in the magazine. I did, however, cut off the lead tip on the Speer by sanding the exposed lead flat with emery cloth. It leaves the bullet's nose with the same configuration as the factory bullets I tested, touching the primer with the same amount of area. However, I'd still recommend this bullet only in a *chamber* loading.

Why use it? Because it would be a penetrator and quite nondisruptive of tissue. A very dedicated hunter might want to employ this bullet on deer; he had better be aware, however, that exit holes won't be anything like those made by softer bullets. The 235 Speer, which averages 233.3 grains with the lead tip removed, is constructed for .375 H&H Magnum speeds, remember. If a hunter has larger game at close range, he might consider this bullet, too.

A load of thirty-five grains of IMR-4895 produced a velocity of 1,760 feet per second with the 235 Speer (233.3 without lead tip). That is only 1,605 foot-pounds, but I'd bet a new hat that it would go through a mule deer at a hundred yards. With thirty-seven grains of IMR-4895, the velocity was 1,850 feet per second, the energy 1,773 foot-pounds. What would RL-7 do with this bullet? I don't know, not having had any on hand to try. But I'd recommend staying *down* in maximum powder charges, since the thicker jacket could produce higher pressures than desired.

Accuracy with the Big Bore I had on hand was good with all loads I tried, factory and handload. However, I think that the three-inch groups for five shots at a hundred yards (from the bench) could be bettered with better sights. As much as I enjoyed the Big Bore, I did not care for its sights. Open sights need not be so *fat*. I'd want to replace the front sight with a smaller bead, and I think that a clean notch, such as found on the Lyman rear sight so popular these days, would mate fine with a narrow bead up front.

In sighting, I would try to get my group to print about two and a half to

.375 Winchester

bullet	powder	charge (grains)	velocity (fps)	
200	H-4895	39.0	1,893	data from Hodgdon
		41.0	2,044	maximum
	BL-C(2)	42.0	1,825	
		44.0	2,018	maximum
	H-335	41.0	1,846	
		43.0	2,027	maximum
	H-322	38.0	1,896	
		40.0	2,033	maximum
	H-4198	30.0	1,894	
		33.0	2,137	maximum
220	IMR-4198	28.0	1,800	data from Hornady
		30.1	1,900	
		32.2	2,000	maximum
	Reloder 7	31.1	1,800	
		32.8	1,900	
		34.5	2,000	
		36.2	2,100	
		38.0	2,200	case full
	IMR-3031	34.0	1,800	
		35.2	1,900	case full
	H-322	34.8	1,800	
		36.7	1,900	
		38.6	2,000	case full
250	H-4895	35.0	1,713	data from Hodgdon
		37.0	1,845	maximum
	BL-C(2)	38.0	1,693	
		40.0	1,820	maximum
	H-335	38.0	1,706	
		40.0	1,839	maximum
	H-322	34.0	1,729	
		36.0	1,858	maximum
	H-4198	28.0	1,737	
		30.0	1,858	maximum

Hodgdon and Hornady developed these data in their test facilities, under controlled conditions, using .375 Winchester Big Bore 94 carbines in safe condition. Conditions, firearms, and components vary, so approach maximum loads with extreme caution. Each handloader is responsible for his use of these data and the results.

three inches *high* at a hundred yards. This would put the bullet on-target at about 150 yards, and in the area of five or six inches low at two hundred, depending upon the load. I don't think that I could advise shooting at over 175 or maybe two hundred with the .375, because the rifle and the cartridge were made with closer range in mind. If a hunter needs more range, he should look at the bolt-action cartridges made for flatter shooting.

I can see why the Big Bore and its .375 Winchester have caught on. There's plenty of punch in a compact unit with this combination, and enough accuracy to take deer-sized game certainly to 150 yards and a bit more. With a little stalking, the hunter could probably get a hundred-yard shot for sure-fire bullet placement, and the nimrod trucking through the denseness of deep forest or bush would have his shots much closer.

The 220-grain Hornady, it seems to me, would be a fine bear and deer bullet, properly loaded, and both factory offerings are also good, though I like the 200-grain bullet, myself. And if the hunter should insist upon going for game larger than deer, he might consider using a bullet designed for the .375 H&H as long as the nose is blunt and he does *not* load these in the magazine of the rifle. The latter type of bullet is not to be considered for standard work. The factory loads and the 220-grain Hornady bullet would be much better.

If I had a wish for the .375 round, I think that I might like to have it in a rifle pretty much like the one my old acquaintance, Lucky, mentioned earlier. It might have a twenty-four-inch barrel, or even a twenty-six. The Model 94, for the long-armed shooter, seems to have a stock pull that is a good inch or more too short, and the little carbine rears up against the cheekbone. A longer stock and barrel, such as the handsome Model 94 *rifle* had, would no doubt eliminate this problem. It wouldn't be as handy in the brush as the carbine. It wouldn't pack into a corner like a quiet child you didn't even know was there. It wouldn't fit into a saddle scabbard as well, and it wouldn't ride on a rack in the pick-up truck like the carbine. It might not, all things considered, be as practical as the carbine. But next time you get a chance to heft one of those longer-barreled Model 94 rifles, do it, and you'll see what I mean. ●

CHAPTER
31

The purpose of Ken's wildcat cartridge was to give a new life of usefulness to this fine old Westley Richards rifle, using the original barrel with only internal rather than external modification. The high-mounted scope was an expedient, to make the rifle usable with a scope despite the old-style bolt handle, which was to be reshaped later to clear a lower-mounted scope.

IN JULY 1968, I purchased an old Westley Richards "Accelerated Express" rifle, caliber .375-.303, from firearms dealer Gary Herman of Safari Outfitters. It had one of those turn-of-the-century Mauser actions with slanted magazine intended for rimmed cartridges, and judging from its appearance, I'm inclined to the belief that rifle had been on a good many safaris.

Much use with the highly erosive British cordite ammunition had washed out most of the rifling, and cartridges for it were both costly and ancient collector's items, hard to find and unreliable when a very few did turn up. But its strong commercial Mauser action with that uncommon magazine, five-leaf express sight, sound black-walnut stock with genuine horn fore-end tip, and that famous old name on the barrel made it a rifle worth owning and an ideal candidate for reboring to some interesting wildcat cartridge.

The question was, which one? To be sure to remove all traces of the old rifling and erosion roughness, it would have to be bored out to at least .35. The

new case would of necessity (as well as choice) be rimmed, and the overall cartridge length should not exceed that of the original .375-.303 Axite round.

The .38-55 case lacked the powder capacity I sought, and the .45-70's overly large rim and body diameters would have necessitated unwanted alterations to the magazine, bolt face, and extractor. The same objections applied to the .348 case.

The .30-40 Krag case seemed a logical choice until I realized that its body diameter is almost exactly the same as that of the .375-.303, meaning that the old chamber wouldn't be entirely cleaned up by the new reamer, and I didn't want the barrel to be set back, as I wished to put the barreled action back in the original stock. Also, the .30-40's rim diameter is greater, although this was a minor consideration.

This left me with just one more

readily available American-made rimmed case as a basis for forming the new case — the .444 Marlin. I was fortunate in having a good supply of this empty brass on hand; moreover, its dimensions were ideal, with a body diameter some 0.012 inch larger than the .375-.303, ensuring that all of the old chamber walls would be removed, and a rim diameter only 0.009 inch larger would minimize alterations to bolt face and extractor. Body taper of the .444 case is also minimal, and interior powder capacity is slightly larger than that of a .30-40 case trimmed to the same length.

Case length being 0.24 inch shorter than a .375-.303 meant that bullets could be seated to hold the overall loaded cartridge length well below that of the original round, avoiding any problem with the magazine. Furthermore, it has always been my experience that if the neck diameter of a case is to be materially changed, it is easier with

Ken Waters' 'wildcat with a purpose,' the .375 EXPRESS

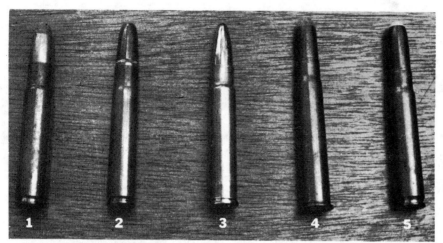

The Waters .375 Express wildcat (3) is closely akin ballistically to these factory-loaded cartridges: the 9.5mm Mannlicher (1), the 9.3x57mm Mauser (2), the .35 Winchester (4), and the 9x56mm Mannlicher-Schoenauer (5). Wildcat design was necessary to use original barrel.

our superb modern sizing dies to neck *down* than to neck up. This was especially true in the early experimental stages before custom dies had been procured, when necking up and necking down brass through a succession of dies in my old reliable Belding & Mull straightline press.

With the decision made to use .444 Marlin brass necked down, the next judgment required was what caliber my wildcat should be. Considering the availability of suitable jacketed soft-point bullets, I was practically limited to a choice of either .35 or .375.

A number of seemingly pretty good reasons pointed to 0.375 inch as the more desirable bullet diameter. Proponents of the .35 are already well served by the .358 Winchester and .350 Remington Magnum amongst factory cartridges, plus the great old wildcat .35 Whelen and discontinued .35 Winchester. But there were at that time no American .375s other than the big .375 belted magnums, the .375 Winchester not having yet appeared.

Overseas, there was the rimless 9.5x57 Mannlicher, or .375 Rimless Nitro Express, as the British called it; also, the .375 Flanged Nitro Express with 2-1/2-inch case; and those cartridges had established good reputations for taking medium to large soft-skinned game but weren't (and aren't) readily available here.

It was this last-named case — the .375 Flanged Nitro Express — which the British had used to neck down and form the .375-.303 Axite, hence the .375 in that cartridge's caliber designation. So why not reverse the process in a sense, taking the caliber back to .375? But by using a case of slightly larger diameter and minimum

body taper, I'd be able to incorporate a shoulder for better powder burning and (hopefully) improved performance. Most of all though, I could use readily obtainable modern brass.

Essentially, this was the decision I made, after which the design of the cartridge was worked out in late 1971, utilizing the .444 Marlin case necked down to hold .375 bullets. Base and rim dimensions were of course left as in the .444, but a twenty-eight-degree shoulder was established with its point 1.840 inches from the rear face of the rim, with body taper of only 0.012 inch and a neck length of 0.325 inch, with outside diameter of 0.399 inch. The original intent was to use 235-grain Speer bullets to attain higher velocities,

my belief being that they would be entirely adequate for any game for which this cartridge is suited.

Accordingly, in February 1972, I asked Bill Atkinson of the old A&M Rifle Company of Prescott, Arizona, whether he would rebore, rechamber, and make the other necessary alterations to my old Westley Richards rifle to handle the new wildcat cartridge, which I had dubbed the .375 Express because of my intention to use the lighter .375 bullets. I provided the following specifications and provided a formed dummy cartridge.

Rebore barrel and rerifle to 0.375 inch groove diameter with 12-inch twist to handle 235 and 270-grain bullets at muzzle velocities of from 2,150 to 2,300 feet per second.

Rechamber for the .444 Marlin case necked down to .375, a dimensioned drawing of which was furnished.

Alter bolt face to accept the .444 Marlin case rim.

Check action for proper cartridge feeding, altering if needed.

Drill and tap receiver for Weaver Q.D. Top Mount blocks.

Alter bolt handle to clear hunting-type scope in Weaver rings.

Mr. Atkinson replied that he could and would do the work, but that I would have to provide him with the necessary chambering reamer, suggesting that I send a dimensioned drawing of the cartridge to Keith Francis of Talent, Oregon, and have him make the reamer.

This was done, and in June, 1972, I furnished Mr. Atkinson with the Francis reamer — a beautifully

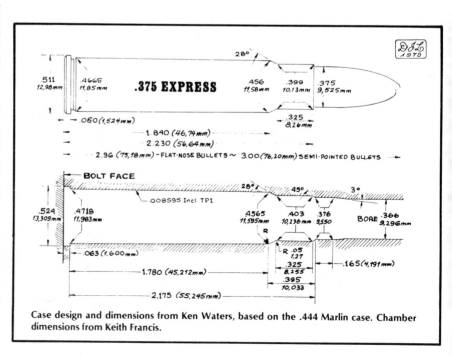

Case design and dimensions from Ken Waters, based on the .444 Marlin case. Chamber dimensions from Keith Francis.

188

executed job of machining — together with the Westley Richards barreled action. Keith Francis had informed me that only a finishing reamer would be required where so little steel was being removed, but that the reamer should be run in slowly.

There followed a long wait while Bill Atkinson bored out and rerifled the barrel, reamed the new chamber, opened up the bolt face for the .444's slightly larger rim, drilled and tapped the receiver for Weaver Q.D. bases, and altered the bolt handle to clear a scope. The barrel was left its original twenty-six inches but with the flat-faced muzzle crowned. All this took the better part of a year, the completed barreled action being received in June 1973.

Back in its stock once more, the next step was to size, load, and fireform a trio of cases to be sent to RCBS for use in making up a set of custom reloading dies. The inimitable Bill Keys did this to perfection, after which it was possible

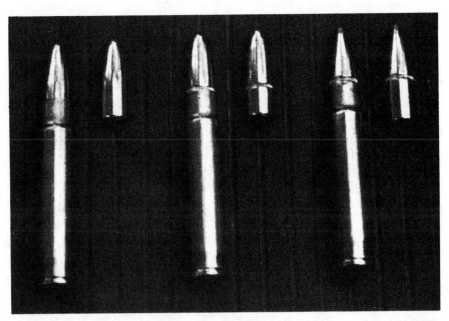

Trials of the rebored, rechambered Westley Richards used these three bullets, seated to the depths shown here: the 235-grain semipointed Speer (left), the 275-grain round-nosed Hornady (center), and the 270-grain spire-pointed Hornady (right). One additional bullet caused jams and was abandoned after a brief trial — the 220-grain flat-nosed Hornady bullet is therefore not shown here. The 270-grain spire-point was the only bullet used that extended below the shoulder of the case.

loads for the .375 Express

bullet	charge	powder	velocity (fps)	length of cartridge (in.)	case expansion*	
235 Speer semispitzer	44.0	IMR-3031	2,166	3.00	0.4665	
	45.0	IMR-3031	2,224	3.00	0.4668	very accurate
	46.0	IMR-3031	2,270	3.00	0.4670	good load; accurate
	47.0	IMR-3031	2,300	3.00	0.4670	
	48.0	IMR-3031	2,321	3.00	0.4672	highest velocity
	45.0	IMR-4895	2,049	3.00	0.4665	very accurate
	46.0	IMR-4895	2,061	3.00	0.4667	
	47.0	IMR-4895	2,112	3.00	0.4668	most accurate load
	48.0	IMR-4895	2,201	3.00	0.4670	
	49.0	IMR-4895	2,257	3.00	0.4672	
	50.0	IMR-4895	2,286	3.00	0.4675	best all-around load; accurate
	37.0	IMR-4198	2,229	3.00	0.4670	
	45.0	H-322	2,165	3.00	0.4668	
	47.0	H-322	2,214	3.00	0.4672	accurate
	48.0	N-201	2,213	3.00	0.4668	
270 Hornady roundnose	45.0	H-4895	1,955	3.00	0.4665	
	43.0	IMR-3031	2,087	3.00	0.4672	poor accuracy
270 Hornady spire-point	44.0	IMR-3031	2,150	3.00	0.4675	
	45.0	IMR-3031	2,212	3.00	0.4678	maximum load
	44.0	IMR-4064	1,980	3.00	0.4665	third most accurate load
	47.0	IMR-4064	2,113	3.00	0.4670	insufficient accuracy
	48.0	IMR-4895	2,154	3.00	0.4675	second most accurate load
	45.0	IMR-4320	2,068	3.00	0.4675	
	45.0	N-201	2,070	3.00	0.4670	very accurate
	45.0	H-322	2,117	3.02	0.4675	poor accuracy
220 Hornady flatnose	45.0	IMR-3031	2,143	2.82	0.4663	poor accuracy
	47.0	IMR-4895	2,113	2.82	0.4670	
	49.0	IMR-4320	2,283	2.82	0.4673	

* Unfired cases miked 0.4665 inch.

All cases formed from R-P .444 Marlin brass. CCI 200 Large Rifle Standard primers used with all loads. Velocities obtained with Oehler Model 33 Chronotach and Skyscreens. Test rifle was a rebored, rechambered Westley-Richards commercial Mauser action with a 26-inch barrel.

to simply run .444 brass, lightly lubricated with RCBS case lube, making a single pass through the .375 Express full-length sizer die, obtaining cases that would chamber ready for fireforming.

Meanwhile, one hitch had developed. It turned out that the bolt handle hadn't been altered enough to clear the ocular housing of a modern one-inch scope, but rather than delay things further I decided — temporarily, at least — to utilize an old Lyman Alaskan 2-1/2x scope with 7/8-inch tube and smaller ocular lens, and this was mounted in a pair of Weaver extension top mounts.

Finally, I was ready to start the lengthy business of load development. I like to proceed slowly and carefully when working up loads, especially when the cartridge is a wildcat lacking data.

The first step was to measure the usable interior capacity of the new case and then try to find another cartridge, factory or wildcat, of close to the same capacity and caliber taking bullets in the 235 to 270-grain weight range, for which at least some loading and ballistic data are available.

Filled with water to the base of the neck, the .375 Express case holds fifty-five grains of water, but because of the relatively short neck, some of this space is occupied by the base of a 270-grain bullet. Amongst commercial cartridges from .35 (9mm) through .375 (9.5mm), those having similar internal capacities include the old .35 Winchester, the 9x57 and 9.3x57 Mausers, and the 9.5 Mannlicher (.375 Rimless). The .358 Winchester has somewhat less capacity. I wasn't able to find any .35 or .375 wildcats that are closely comparable, and I'll save you the trouble of looking up the .35 Whelen and .375-06; they're in an entirely different class, as is the .350 Remington Magnum, having better than six grains more capacity.

The Du Pont *Handloader's Guide* shows the .358 Winchester with 250-grain bullet and forty-two grains of IMR-3031 attaining 2,260 feet per second. The NRA *Handloader's Guide* reported this same load developing 2,204 feet per second from a shorter barrel, while Winchester's *Ball Powder Loading Data* lists 46.2 grains of WW-748 as producing 2,250 feet per second. My .358 Mannlicher-Schoenauer launched the lighter 220-grain bullet at 2,300 feet per second with forty-five grains of IMR-4064, so we can reasonably think of the .358 Winchester as offering from 2,250 to 2,300 feet per second with bullets of comparable weight.

An old Du Pont manual dated 1936

listed maximum loads of fifty grains of IMR-4064, 51.5 grains of IMR-4320, and forty-nine grains of IMR-3031 in the long .35 Winchester case as registering from 2,190 to 2,320 feet per second with 250-grain bullets, or about the same ballistics as the more efficient .358, though I somehow doubt that the old .35 WCF factory loads ever actually reached that higher figure.

Turning to Frank Barnes' most useful book *Cartridges of the World*, we find the 9x57 Mauser with 250-grain bullet and forty-four grains of IMR-3031 at 2,260 feet per second; the 9.3x57 Mauser at 2,330 feet per second with 232-grain bullet and forty-seven grains of IMR-3031, and finally the 9.5 Mannlicher driving a 270-grain bullet at 2,150 feet per second with forty-four grains of IMR-3031.

So my velocity goals were pegged at reaching 2,300 feet per second with the 235-grain bullets and 2,150 feet per second with the 270-grain. Also, in studying those data, it began to look as if IMR-3031 would be the powder most likely to attain those speeds. Apparently too, the optimum loading range with 235-grain bullets — my main area of initial interest — would lie between forty-four and forty-eight grains of that powder.

Accordingly, forty-one grains of IMR-3031 was selected as a starting point, but when this proved unnecessarily conservative, I advanced to forty-three grains. From there, the climb upward was held to a one-grain increase per step. At forty-four grains, 2,166 feet per second was recorded, which increased to 2,224 with 45 grains and 2,270 with forty-six grains. Forty-seven grains of IMR-3031 gave 2,300 feet per second, achieving my goal, and a final step up to forty-eight grains of IMR-3031 registered 2,321 feet per second. At this point, the steady decrease in velocity gained *per grain of powder expended* indicated that the practical maximum load had been reached. Also, pressure indications provided evidence that a halt should be called here if I wished to continue using those cases.

Quite obviously, this sort of ballistic performance doesn't qualify my wildcat as outstanding in the way wildcat cartridges have traditionally been expected to perform, which is to say it hasn't broken any records and isn't a "super" anything. Rather, the .375 Express was designed with two special purposes in mind, the first to provide a practical round with rimmed case and readily available components, for which my old rifle and countless other shot-out .303s and .35s could be rebored or even rebarreled.

And second, my thinking was that

shooters might see in this cartridge an opportunity to re-create the performance characteristics of those grand old medium calibers in a form that bears more than a passing resemblance to a number of memorable rounds.

Other powders were tried, especially those with medium burning rates, such as IMR-4895, Hodgdon's H-322, Norma's N-201, and Winchester-Western's 748 and 760. However, none of those gave as high velocities with 235-grain bullets as IMR-3031, and only IMR-4895 and H-322 approached IMR-3031's average accuracy.

Recalling how the parent .444 case had given maximum results with the faster-burning IMR-4198, I tried this also, finding thirty-seven grains the equal of forty-five grains of IMR-3031, and thirty-eight grains of IMR-4198 giving the 235-grain Speers close to 2,300 feet per second. Accuracy was not as good on the average as with IMR-3031 however, and shot-to-shot velocity variations were more pronounced, because the excess space inside the case allowed the powder charge to assume different positions, depending upon how the rifle was held. When the muzzle was pointed up before firing, to settle the powder back against the flash hole, velocity readings were noticeably higher.

I am accordingly convinced that IMR-3031 is the optimum powder with 235-grain bullets in this cartridge, with IMR-4895, H-322, and N-201 closest competitors but falling behind in velocity. Would this hold true with the heavier 270-grain bullets? I wondered, and knowing there would be shooters wishing to use the heavier slugs, determined to find out.

For this second series of trials, Hornady's 270-grain bullets were chosen, both spire-point and round nose forms, backing off on the powder charges and again working gradually upward.

Forty-one grains of IMR-3031 with 270-grain bullets was under 2,000 feet per second, so the initial advance was to forty-three grains, which gave an average 2,087 feet per second. Forty-four grains attained the target figure of 2,150, and a final increase to forty-five grains registered an impressive 2,212 feet per second. My choice of adjective here stems from the fact that I hadn't expected 270-grain bullets to come so close to equaling the velocities of the 235-grain bullets from this moderate-size case. A loss of 115 feet per second in exchange for an additional thirty-five grains of bullet weight isn't bad, especially when it's done with three grains *less* powder! Note that with equal charges of forty-five grains of IMR-3031, the 235-grain bullets average only twelve feet per second faster than the heavier 270-grain.

This obvious tendency of the necked-down .444 Marlin case to become more efficient as bullet weight is increased was further underscored when experiments were made in the opposite direction. The new (and lighter) 220-grain Hornady flatnose bullets, intended for Winchester's .375 Big Bore, actually recorded *lower* velocities in the .375 Express with that same charge of forty-five grains of IMR-3031 than the 270-grain Hornadys had. Further, because their flat noses caused them to occasionally hang up in feeding from the Mauser's magazine, their use in this rifle was regretfully abandoned.

Returning to the 270-grain bullets, again the chronograph insists that none of the other powders tried — including IMR-4064, IMR-4320, IMR-4895, H-4895, H-322, and N-201 — is the equal of IMR-3031 in producing maximum velocity.

Accuracy grouping with the heavier bullets is another story, however, IMR-4895 and IMR-4064 turning in the smallest groups albeit at lower muzzle speeds, followed by Norma N-201 and H-4895. All things considered, I'd rate IMR-4895 as the optimum powder for use with 270-grain bullets.

An interesting observation emerging from my tests was that while full-power loads could be used in cases that had been die-formed only (that is, hadn't yet been fireformed to fully fit the chamber), the resultant velocities were almost exactly one hundred feet per second lower than those produced by the same loads in cases that had been fireformed. Repeated trials proved this to be so with amazing uniformity.

A real surprise was the finding that when driven hard, the 270-grain Hornady roundnose bullets failed to give as small groups on average as did the 270-grain Hornady spire-points.

Case life gives every indication of being long, and burning only forty-five to forty-eight grains per shot makes a canister of powder last a lot longer than with one of the magnums, yet with proper bullet placement, this cartridge is capable of downing most anything you'll be likely to hunt in the lower forty-eight states and Canada — within two hundred yards, that is. Only the bullets are costly, but they're what gets the game, penetration of the semispitzer and spire-point .375's far exceeding that of the parent .444 Marlin.

Reloading the .375 Express is plumb easy; it just doesn't have any fancy quirks, and most of the case stretching occurs with the first two or three loadings and firings. You won't need magnum primers, because you won't be using slow-burning powders, and at 2,200 to 2,300 feet per second, a barrel should last a long, long time. Recoil seems about like that of a .30-06; in other words, nothing worrisome.

But technicalities aside, the .375 Express is meant for the guy with a shot-out .303 British Enfield who'd like to rebarrel it to a larger caliber taking heavier bullets, or maybe his friend who is building a new single-shot rifle. Or if, like me, you find yourself with a fine old African musket that's fallen on hard times and begs to be restored.

It's not a cartridge that's going to make headlines or induce one of the ammo manufacturers to adopt it. But as a dependable workhorse to take into the Canadian bush for deer or moose *without changing bullet weights or loads*, you'd be hard-pressed to beat it. No more than that is needed to justify this wildcat's existence. ●

CHAPTER
32

Mike Thomas

The .375 Whelen IMPROVED

IN 1951, L.R. "Bob" Wallack developed the .375 Whelen. Mr. Wallack, a gunsmith from Langhorne, Pennsylvania, did specialty work in the area of custom rifles. He was also a contributing member of the *American Rifleman's* panel of experts in the monthly "Dope Bag" feature. Other notable panel members during this era (early 50s) included Elmer Keith and Phil Sharpe. After developing the .375-06, Wallack named it in honor of Colonel Whelen. Whelen himself was more than a little intrigued and enthusiastic about the new wildcat.

The .375-inch diameter, as it turned out, was about as large as the '06 case could be necked and retain enough shoulder to guarantee proper headspacing. Years earlier, the .400 Whelen had been created but proved to be too much of a good thing. Elmer Keith spoke highly of the freight train killing power of the .400, but headspacing created problems. Consequently, the .400 Whelen's popularity was short-lived. Colonel Whelen had his own .400 rebarreled to .35 Whelen because of headspacing difficulties.

It has often been said that the .35 and .375 Whelen lack enough shoulder for correct headspacing. After enjoying a fair amount of experience with the .338-06, the .35 Whelen, the .35 Whelen Improved and the .375 Whelen Improved, I can unequivocally state that such a problem has never arisen. Those headspacing rumors may have been the result of improper chambering jobs.

Some good did come of the headspacing scare: improved, sharper-shouldered versions of the '06 big bores. The more defined shoulder, blown out in the fireforming process, also gave the cartridge cases additional powder capacity, allowing slightly higher velocities.

It is fitting, at this point, to underscore the pragmatic aspects of the .375 Whelen. Bullets as heavy as 300 grains obviously do not transform this '06-based cartridge into a .375 H&H Magnum or a .378 Weatherby Magnum. With all bullet weights, the .375 Whelen is several hundred fps slower than the two magnum .375s. Nevertheless, that certainly does not remove it from the category of cartridges suitable for dangerous game. The .375 Whelen would be more than adequate for the largest of the big bears. If foot-pounds of energy are

The camera angle gives a better idea of the 23-inch (Douglas Contour No. 3) barrel's thickness. Mike credits much of the rifle's grouping ability to the barrel's heft and stiffness.

used as a criterion, the .375 Whelen is in the neighborhood of such factory rounds as the .338 Winchester Magnum and the 8mm Remington Magnum, but it utilizes heavier bullets than either.

Ballistic efficiency is a forte of the .375 Whelen. Figures approaching 3,500 foot-pounds of muzzle energy can be achieved using only the '06 case. Far less powder is required to produce this energy level than is necessary with the magnum hulls.

To obtain a rifle chambered for this wildcat, the custom gunsmith route is the only one to follow. Virtually any sound '06-length action can be used. My .375 Whelen is built on a Mark X Mauser action with a Number 3 contour Douglas barrel, 23 inches long.

After stocking the barreled action, I topped the completed rifle with a 2½x Bushnell Banner scope. RCBS made the custom dies. It is necessary to send RCBS three fired cases and three sample bullets when ordering such dies. This ensures that die dimensions will be compatible with those of the chamber.

I had the rifle chambered for the .375 Whelen Improved rather than the standard version. At the onset of the project, I reasoned that the improved variety would hold slightly more powder and produce a little more velocity with

heavy bullets. The original .375 Whelen has the standard '06 shoulder angle (17 degrees 16 minutes), while the Improved has a blown-out 40-degree shoulder.

When I first began concocting loads for the .375 Whelen Improved, I quickly found out how scarce published loading data was for the cartridge. Some rather limited recipes were found in P.O. Ackley's *Handbook for Shooters and Reloaders, Volume I*, but for all practical purposes, I had to start from scratch. Once the test firing began, the chronograph showed quite a few discrepancies between my rifle's velocities and those published in Mr. Ackley's book.

As an invaluable aid in working up loads for the .375 Whelen Improved (or any other cartridge, for that matter), I used a Powley Computer. The computer allows the reloader to increase his safety margin when working with unknown variables. It saves time, too, because its use takes a great deal of the guesswork out of choosing suitable loads.

First, Remington once-fired '06 hulls were shoved into the .375 Whelen Improved sizing dies equipped with a .35 caliber expander button. Next, a .375 button was installed and the case necks were expanded again. The two-step approach was taken to prevent overwork-

Optical illusion? At first glance the .375 Whelen Improved looks considerably larger than the '06 beside it — even though both are based on the same case.

The .30.06 and some of its descendants: (1) the '06, (2) the .338-06, (3) the .35 Whelen, (4) the .35 Whelen Improved, (5) the .375 Whelen Improved.

ing the brass. With neck sizing completed, fireforming was then necessary. Before assembling handloads, I found it essential to trim all brass slightly to square up case necks. Trim length was 2.44 inches.

Four different bullets were selected for testing. All were jacketed softpoints: The Speer 235-grain semi-spitzer, the Hornady 270-grain Spire Point, the Hornady 300-grain roundnose and the Sierra 300-grain boat-tail spitzer. Bullets heavier than 300 grains were not used as case capacity is simply too limited to obtain practical velocities.

Initially, five different powders were chosen. IMR-3031 was quickly eliminated because of premature high-pressure signs and very erratic chronograph readings. IMR-4350 was found to be unsuitable because not enough of it could be stuffed in the case to obtain decent velocities. This left three powders that provided promising results: IMR-4320, IMR-4895 and IMR-4064. The best performance was turned in by IMR-4064, followed by IMR-4895, then IMR-4320.

I am at a loss to explain the incompatibility of IMR-3031 with the .375 Whelen Improved. Perhaps it is a problem peculiar to my own rifle. Oh well, such surprises keep the game interesting.

When loading unfireformed brass, case capacity is about five percent less than that of fireformed brass. *Do not use top .375 Whelen Improved loads in a standard .375 Whelen case.* The results could prove dangerous to your health.

Examples are in order at this point to illustrate the differences between fireformed loads and those fired in standard .375 Whelen cases. With the 235-grain Speer bullet, 56 grains of IMR-4064 (maximum) produced a muzzle velocity of 2,330 fps, while the same powder charge in the Improved case turned in a reading of only 2,225 fps. With the 300-grain Hornady roundnose bullet, 51 grains of IMR-4895 (maximum) gave a muzzle reading of 2,080 fps before fireforming and only 1,995 afterward.

Some enthusiasts and gun writers advocate using stiff loads for fireforming. While experimenting with this cartridge, I found that very modest loads (giving pressures slightly less than 40,000 psi according to the Powley device) would expand the brass to match chamber dimensions perfectly. Primers extruded slightly during the initial fireforming. No cause to worry,

however, as that condition will be eliminated after the case is blown out and fired again.

Different overall lengths of loaded rounds were mandated by the bullets used. The maximum OAL was 3.35 inches when using the long, 300-grain Sierra BTSP. A longer OAL would not allow a loaded round to feed through the magazine of my rifle.

I was somewhat disappointed at the muzzle velocities recorded with the .375 Whelen Improved. Taken in perspective, however, the cartridge is quite a serviceable one, nevertheless. We are still talking of muzzle energy in the 3,000 to 3,500 foot-pound bracket. The shoulder becomes tender after firing almost 300 rounds during a weekend. The kick seems noticeably less and not as sharp as that generated by a 7mm Magnum or a .300 Magnum, though. The rifle combination is fairly heavy (9½ pounds) and that may account for the tolerable level. Conversely, I feel safe in saying that the .375 Whelen Improved is not a cartridge for a six-pound rifle.

I can't say that the .375 Whelen Improved is inherently accurate, but the groups given by many of the loads tested astonished me. So did the fact that maximum or near-maximum loads produced the best accuracy. Several one-inch groups were recorded at 100 yards.

IMR-4064 powder provided not only

the best accuracy but the highest velocities as well. The 270-grain Hornady, the most accurate bullet tested, represents the best choice for this cartridge. With 57 grains of IMR-4064 behind it, that bullet recorded an average muzzle velocity of 2,340 fps and one-inch groups predominated. The ballistic coefficient of the bullet is relatively high (.485) and when sighted three inches above the point of aim at 100 yards, is on the money at 200 and only 11 inches low at 300. Even at the latter distance, the retained energy amounts to 2,000 foot-pounds.

I cannot testify as to the effectiveness of the .375 Whelen Improved on game, unfortunately. While developing loads, I fired several rounds through water-soaked telephone books. All bullets expanded well except for the 300-grain roundnose Hornady. For any thin-skinned game, the .375 Whelen Improved should be more than adequate. I also bet the big, slow-moving bullets won't leave as much bloodshot tissue surrounding a wound area as would a .270 or 7mm Magnum. I hope to find out positively this fall.

The .375 Whelen Improved is not an all around cartridge, but then neither is anything else. It may not appeal to every enthusiast. For the big bullet fan bent on deriving maximum power and efficiency from the .30-06 case, it has no peers. It uses inexpensive brass, boasts a meager powder appetite and generates no brutal recoil. ●

CHAPTER
33

The .375 H&H ...After 62 Years

By BOB HAGEL

Hagel packs out the head of an Idaho Shiras moose shot with a Sharps Model 78 chambered for the .375 H&H.

THE .375 H&H Magnum, along with the .275 H&H which appeared at about the same time, holds the distinction of being the first belted case. Nearly every belted case to appear since has been based on the original Holland & Holland design and base size. There are only four exceptions that I know of: the 7x73 Vom Hofe Belted that has a belt diameter listed at .533, the two big Weatherby cases in .378 and .460 Weatherby Magnums that have belt diameters of .603, the smaller .240 Weatherby Magnum that has a belt measuring only .473, and the tiny .224 Weatherby that has a belt size of only .429. The .375 H&H case is supposed to be about .530 but, like other cases, varies with the make.

While the .375 H&H is still a large capacity case by today's standards, it was certainly not a big case in either capacity or caliber when it appeared in 1912, for extremely large cases and calibers were then popular. It did deliver impressive ballistics even with the cordite powder used by the British at that time. In fact it

is quite near our own factory figures, the British factory loads using cordite powder being listed at an MV of 2,500 for the 300-grain bullet and 2,650 with the 270-grain, while our own factory loads are given at 2,550 fps and 2,740 fps respectively. What barrel length the British figures may have been taken from I do not know.

The .375 H&H was apparently slightly superior in the velocity department to all the other cartridges of the same caliber of that day, at least with factory loading. The British made at least three other .375 cartridges (although one of them, the .369 Purdey Nitro-Express, was not listed as a .375), and there were three other European cartridges with the 9.5mm designation that were .375 caliber.

None of the other .375 cartridges ever gained a great deal of popularity, or at least nothing that approached the fame of the .375 H&H as a reliable hunting cartridge for game of nearly any size. Perhaps a great deal of this stemmed from the fact that the .375 belted case came along at a time when many hunters were discarding the single shot and double rifles in favor of the magazine gun, and the rimmed cartridges like the

.375 Flanged Magnum were not well suited to bolt action rifle magazines. Holland & Holland did make another .375 belted case known as the .400/.375, but it was not a true .375, using a 270-grain bullet of .371 diameter at a relatively mild 2,175 fps MV. Germany also produced a rimless .375 in the form of the 9.5x73mm Miller-Greiss Magnum that gave ballistics similar to the .375 H&H, but it never gained any popularity.

Back in the period between 1870 and 1900, there were a few American black powder numbers of true .375 caliber and several others that measured from .372-.378 in bullet diameter. These were designated as .38 caliber, none were very potent, and none ever gained a great deal of popularity.

The .375 H&H Magnum wrote a much different story in the pages of hunting cartridge history. Soon after its introduction, its popularity started gaining momentum among African hunters, and it wasn't long until .375 H&H rifles were found in every part of the world's hunting country where medium to heavy game roamed. While there was a difference of opinion as to its effectiveness in stopping the heaviest big game in a tight situation, few hunters disagreed with the opinion that it was one of the finest all-around cartridges for most African hunting ever designed. With good expanding bullets it proved

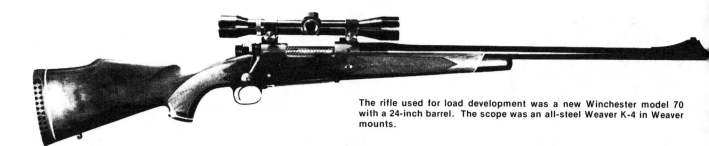

The rifle used for load development was a new Winchester model 70 with a 24-inch barrel. The scope was an all-steel Weaver K-4 in Weaver mounts.

reliable on nearly any class of thin-skinned game, and its fairly high velocity gave it flatness of trajectory for quite long range shooting. With the 300-grain solid, penetration was sufficient for the heaviest game from Cape buffalo to elephant. It proved about ideal for the big cats of Asia and Africa, as well as the big bears of North America.

With all of the publicity given the cartridge and its proven reliability on big game wherever it was found, it was soon being chambered in many makes of rifles, both commercial and custom. Just when the first custom rifles were chambered for it here in the U.S. is hard to say, but Griffin & Howe chambered it in their fine custom rifles back in the mid-'20's, and Western Cartridge Co. introduced it into their cartridge line in 1925. It was not until 1937 that an American commercial rifle was chambered for it when Winchester started chambering the Model 70 for both the .375 and .300 H&H cartridges. Other American manufacturers also chambered for the .375 several years after Winchester proved it had sales appeal. Remington apparently chambered some Model 725 rifles for it, as well as the later M-700 rifles, and Browning furnishes their bolt action rifles in this caliber. I believe that Weatherby also chambered a few rifles for the standard .375 H&H on special order.

There have been many wildcat versions of the .375, most of which have been built on the original .375 H&H case. Most of these have been blown out in the body to give less taper, and most have had sharper shoulder angles than the mild 12-degree 45-minute slope of the original case. These wildcat cases all held more powder and gave somewhat higher velocity, and some of them became fairly popular with wildcat buffs, but only one went commercial. This was the .375 Weatherby Magnum introduced in about 1944 as a commercial number in the

Weatherby Magnum line of cartridges. Even this former wildcat did not gain great popularity, and it was replaced by the huge .378 Weatherby in 1953, and became obsolete as far as commercial chambering is concerned, but Weatherby does still furnish both loaded ammunition and unprimed cases.

There have also been a number of wildcat .375 cartridges built on shortened .375 H&H brass, as well as other short brass in both .30-06 head size and belted cases like the .338 Winchester Magnum necked up. These cases are of course of less powder capacity than the original .375 H&H, and while some impressive velocities have been clocked with them, anyone who has loaded many .375 cases of various powder capacities is well aware of the pressures that exist with these loads. Experience in reloading various capacity .375 cartridges up to the .378 Weatherby indicate that the .375 H&H case is certainly not over-bore capacity

with the powders best suited to the various bullet weights. This experience also indicates that higher velocity with equal pressure results as case capacity is increased.

Many of the wildcat .375's have been chronographed with 26-inch barrels, and most of the work done with the .375 H&H in both commercial and custom rifles has also been done with 25 and 26-inch tubes. Today I know of no American factory rifle chambered for the .375 H&H that has a barrel longer than 24 inches (Remington, Winchester and Browning all have 24-inch barrels), and few imported rifles have longer barrels. Also, much of the reloading data was with the older powders, and it seemed that perhaps some of the newer powders might be better suited to give higher velocities due to their decreased burning rate coupled with greater density. Also, while I had done a good deal of reloading for the old cartridge, none of it had leaned toward

Many .375 caliber cartridges have followed the .375 H&H since it appeared in 1912, but most have been in wildcat form and only two have been made commercially. Here the .375 H&H is shown at left for comparison with the .375 OKH, .375 Weatherby and .378 Weatherby. The .375 OKH is similar in case capacity to the .375-338 wildcat, while the .375 Weatherby is about on par with the full-length, blown-out .375 wildcats.

finding out just how much velocity it would deliver within reasonable hunting load pressure limits.

Using a new Model 70 Winchester with a 24-inch barrel mounted with a Weaver K-4 scope, we decided to do some serious loading to see just how spry the original .375 H&H cartridge was after more than 60 years of beating the brush of big game country all over the world.

The .375 H&H has always had the reputation of giving top-flight accuracy with good bullets and loads, and the new M-70 was no exception considering the fact that it was used untuned in any way, and that all loads tested for accuracy were full-steam hunting loads. When all test shooting was completed and the targets averaged, it was found that with all bullet weights and makes, powders and charges, they averaged out at near 1 1/2 MOA. An occasional load gave much larger groups of up to 2 1/2 inches, but some ran around the 1-inch mark. These are for three shot groups so that the barrel did not heat excessively. The .375 heats a barrel quite rapidly, and too much time is required to let it cool sufficiently between shots for 5 or 10-shot groups when a great deal of testing of different loads is to be done. A great amount of reloading components would also be expended, and target accuracy was not the reason for load testing here. Also, loads that might prove extremely accurate in this rifle might be only mediocre in another.

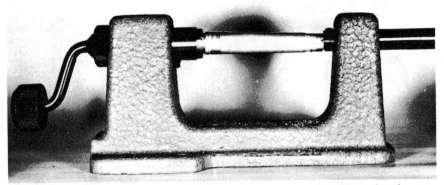

If bullets are to be crimped in the .375 H&H case, the cases must all be trimmed to the same length. If this is not done, slightly longer cases may cause the shoulder to buckle under the pressure of the crimping ring in the seating die. This speedy trimmer is the Redding Master.

As compared to some calibers, the .375 does not afford a large choice of bullet weights or shapes. Actually there are only six bullet weights being offered in this country by either bullet or ammunition makers. Only two of these, the 270 and 300-grain, are being offered by most manufacturers, while Speer makes a 235-grain and Colorado Custom offers a 250 and 350-grain. Speer also made a well shaped 285-grain for some years, but it is no longer available. This 285-grain Speer bullet had good ballistic coefficient and was exceptionally accurate in any rifle I ever used it in, but the jacket was a bit thin for work on heavy game in my experience, which may have contributed to its lack of popularity. Speer also produced this bullet at one time in solid jacket form (FMJ).

Both Remington and Winchester load .375 H&H ammunition with 300-grain solids, and W-W loads both 270 and 300-grain expanding bullet ammo, but R-P today loads only the 270-grain expanding bullet. Hornady also makes a 300-grain solid, as well as a 300-grain expanding bullet, and the only full-spitzer .375 bullet in the form of their 270-grain spire point. Sierra does not to date produce .375 caliber bullets, but Nosler is again in production of their excellent partition jacket 270 and 300-grain soft points. Colorado Custom Bullets (formerly Barnes) makes a solid copper jacketed 300-grain as well as a 300-grain

soft point along with the 250 and 350-grain soft points for the largest weight-design choice of .375 bullets. Their 250 and 300-grain bullets are also in semi-spitzer form which gives the handloader another choice. Bitterroot Bonded Core bullets are made in three weights, 275, 300 and 325 grains and are of hollow point expanding design. I have never used the Bitterroot .375 bullets, but if they perform as well as the other BBC bullets I have used on big game, they should be great medicine for the heaviest thin-skinned game.

When one considers that the .375 H&H, or any other .375 caliber cartridge, is used almost 100 percent for hunting fairly large game, these bullet weights are certainly adequate. In fact, one could get by nicely with only the 300-grain and the addition of the 270-grain is all that one needs for any situation for which the .375 is suited.

From the reloading angle the .375 H&H is pliable and versatile, but there are some points that may not be generally known or considered. For one thing, the size of the case leads to the assumption that capacity is no problem with any suitable powder with any bullet weight. This is far from true, especially with the heavier bullet weights. The large bullet diameter and great expansion ratio make the .375 H&H case lacking in capacity for

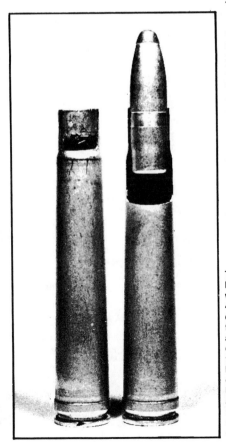

Though the .375 H&H case is quite large, it is still short on powder capacity with the slower powders like 4350 and 4831 with all bullet weights. The fired case at left has not been resized, yet is filled nearly half way up into the neck with a packed charge of 84 grains 4350; this charge fills full-length resized cases nearly to the top of the neck and a 300-grain bullet can't be seated over it in new unfired cases. The case at right shows where the base of a 300-grain Nosler is located after seating to barely function through a standard .375 H&H magazine. The charge of 84/4350 could not be compressed enough to be used with the 300 Nosler.

This 300-grain Nosler .375 bullet penetrated 30 inches of wet sawdust and silt in Hagel's recovery box. The striking velocity was over 2,700 fps.

199

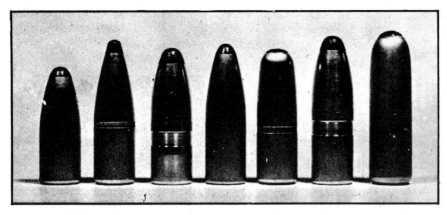

These are some of the more popular .375 bullets. From left they are the 235-grain Speer, 270-grain Hornady Spire point, 270-grain Nosler, 285-grain Speer [no longer made], 300-grain Hornady, 300-grain Nosler and 350-grain Colorado Custom.

bullets of 300 grains and up with coarse grained, slow burning tubular powders like 4350, H-4831 and IMR-4831. In fact, H-4831 is not ideal for this cartridge if maximum velocity is desired from any bullet; there is no way of getting enough of it into the case. This is partially due to the fact that the cartridge is so long that even the longest regularly produced magnum actions require seating bullets from the 270-grain up quite deeply. A second reason is that the bullet is almost as large as the shoulder of the case body, and powders do not compress well under these circumstances. Several of the loads listed in the chart can't be used in new unfired cases because the powder will not compress enough for the bullet to be seated to a depth where the cartridge will function through standard magazines. Even with cases that have been fired and full-length resized, the powder must be poured slowly into a funnel with a long drop tube to settle it down.

This brings up another point that has been mentioned from time to time: whether it is necessary to crimp the bullets in the case with this heavy recoiling cartridge. It has been stated that they will not hold under recoil without driving back into the case. This is true only with certain bullets. When you consider that many .375 bullets do not have crimping cannelures, it becomes obvious that the maker does not believe they require crimping. To prove this point one way or the other, a 300-grain Hornady soft point bullet was loaded into a case full-length resized and with standard expander plug in an RCBS die with no powder in the case. The dummy cartridge was placed in the magazine and left there while some twenty rounds were fired. The nose was battered a bit, but the bullet remained seated in the same spot without crimp. With a full charge of any suitable powder in the case none of the heavier bullet weights can set back due to the pressure exerted by the compressed charge.

I'll modify that statement by saying there is one bullet where this does not hold true, and that is the Hornady 270-grain spire point. This bullet has a rather unusual shank shape, and while it mikes a full .375 on the heel and at the crimping cannelure, it measures only an average of .3742 between those two points. When the heel is forced through the neck in seating it expands it to the .375 heel size, and, being a long bullet, the base is seated below the neck-shoulder junction. This gives the bullet a loose fit in the neck and it will hold without crimping. With fast powders that do not fill the case to the bullet base it will set back, and if you try to compress the slower powders it will pop back up when the cartridge is removed from the seating die. It works fine if you give it a solid crimp. In crimping be sure to trim all cases to the same length, because if this is not done a long neck will buckle the case at the shoulder under the pressure of a good reloading press.

I wrote Joyce Hornady to find out if I had a lot of 270-grain bullets that were off-size. He informed me that all of these

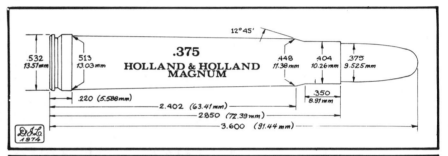

Loads for the .375 H&H

.375 H&H Magnum Winchester M-70 24-inch barrel
W-W Super-Speed cases weighing 251 grains
CCI No. 250 primers
Oehler No. 31 chronotach, No. 50 electronic screens
Velocity instrumental at 15 feet converted to MV

Bullet	Powder	Charge	Velocity	Remarks
350 Colorado Custom	N-205	82	2,460	
300 Hornady SP	H-4831	85	2,559	compressed to seating limit
	N-205	87	2,735	
	IMR-4350	84	2,704	compressed to seating limit
300 Nosler	N-205	87	2,758	
	N-204	83	2,718	
	IMR-4320	71	2,595	
285 Speer SP	N-205	89	2,769	compressed to seating limit
270 Winchester Super-Speed factory load (old lot)			2,680	
270 Nosler	N-205	91	2,872	compressed to seating limit
	IMR-4350	86	2,813	compressed to seating limit
	N-204	87	2,861	
270 Hornady Spire Point*	N-205	91	2,818	compressed to seating limit
	N-203	77	2,757	
	IMR-4064	77	2,787	
235 Speer	IMR-4320	78	2,987	
	N-204	91	3,015	least uniform load tested
	N-203	78	2,977	
	IMR-4064	79	2,960	

* Bullet tightly crimped in case

While all of these loads were loaded to full power they were held below pressures that will give any kind of trouble in big game hunting. They are not recommended for use in any other rifle without starting several grains below and working up.

bullets were made like this and required crimping. He also stated that a new run was being made that would have a full-length shank diameter of .375, which is what the 300-grain Hornady mikes, so that trouble should be eliminated. However, if you don't have a good mike that is correctly zeroed to check this bullet with, I suggest you crimp it in tightly.

For use with 300-grain bullets, 4350 is the best of the domestic slow burning log-type powders in the .375 H&H case. It has to be compressed to the very limit of seating for the load listed in the table with the Hornady RN bullet, and this charge could not be used behind the longer 300-grain Nosler. In the test rifle this charge was certainly not excessive, but a heavier charge could not be tested. The slower but denser Norma 205 proved to give higher velocity and did not require as much compression. Norma 204 gave nearly as much velocity and required even less compression. Both powders gave extremely uniform shot to shot velocity.

Faster powders in the range of 4320, 4064 and 4895 will not deliver nearly as much velocity with the 300-grain, so are not ideal for maximum hunting loads.

Dropping to the 270-grain, N-205 was still out in the lead with N-204 not far behind. With this bullet weight 4350 again ran third with case capacity running short. The faster powders still haven't caught up, but N-203 and 4064 did quite well, producing more velocity than factory ammo by quite a margin.

When the 235-grain Speer bullet was used, even N-205 could not be used in large enough charges to build up maximum pressures. Here N-204 took over the lead with 4320, N-203 and 4064 following in that order.

Norma's 205 seemed the best choice for the long 350-grain CCB soft point bullet, and a near maximum charge of 82 grains delivered 2,460 fps MV.

It would seem that some of the ball powders should be ideal for the .375 H&H but no information listed to date bears this out, at least not if you are looking for the highest velocity with reasonable pressure. According to *Hornady Handbook II,* W-W 760 did very well with the 270-grain but was not a high velocity powder for the 300-grain. Unfortunately, I couldn't obtain any to try.

It will be noted that most of the loads listed in the chart use heavier powder charges than those listed in most reloading manuals. However in the test rifle none of them gave anything like excessive pressures. Whenever enough powder could be crammed into the case a charge two grains above the charge listed was tried, and none of them showed more than .001 belt expansion, no primer pockets were expanded, and even these heavy-charge test cases were fired many times afterward. Also, nearly all of the loads listed were very uniform, most running from 7 fps-20 fps variation, and the highest variation was only 60 fps.

Everything considered, the .375 H&H is an easy cartridge to reload. It is not the least bit touchy when high pressures are reached with proper powders for full power loads. Accuracy is good in most rifles with most powders and suitable charges, and point of impact does not usually vary much between different powders with a given bullet, or between various bullet weights. However, point of impact with different loads will vary from rifle to rifle.

Little need be said about the venerable old-timer as a hunting cartridge; most of it has already been said. It is a flexible cartridge adopted to the great majority of big game hunting situations. Certainly it is needlessly powerful for the smaller species, but it will surely kill them cleanly, and it will reliably lay the big ones on the grass. While the .243 is a better choice for pronghorn and whitetails, I'd much prefer shooting them with a .375 H&H to trying to knock off an elephant with the .243!

On the other side of the coin, some hunters have hoisted the old cartridge to the top of an ivory tower, giving it credit for some kind of mystic killing power that cannot be readily evaluated; killing power that no other cartridge has, including all of the other .375 caliber cartridges. There is nothing mystic about the way a .375 H&H kills except in someone's mind. It is good, but not that good. But any way you cut it, the great old-timer still stands tall beside the best we have to offer today.

●

CHAPTER
34

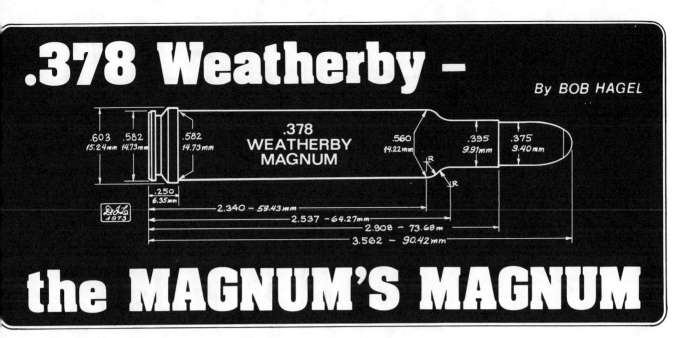

.378 Weatherby –

By BOB HAGEL

.378 WEATHERBY MAGNUM

.603 15.24mm .582 14.73mm .582 14.73mm .560 14.22mm .395 9.91mm .375 9.40mm

.250 6.35mm

2.340 – 59.43mm
2.537 – 64.27mm
2.908 – 73.68m
3.562 – 90.42mm

the MAGNUM'S MAGNUM

MAGNUM CARTRIDGES, in one form or another, have been around a lot longer than most shooters. It seems that the first listed under the magnum title originated some 20 years before this century was born. These were of big bore and of rimmed persuasion, made for use in double-barrel and single shot rifles. Some, like the .450-400 Magnum 3¼-inch, origi-nated as black powder loading. There were also some rimless cases known as magnums, the .425 Westley Richards being an example.

Today we normally associate the name Magnum with the belted case which, as far as I know, first appeared in 1912 as the .375 H&H by Holland and Holland. Nearly every magnum cartridge, regardless of caliber, be it wildcat or commercial, if it is in belted form, is based on the original .375 H&H case. There are, of course, exceptions, and Weatherby has produced most of them; for instance the .224, .240, .378 and .460 Weatherby Magnums — the latter two being built on the same case. The .224 and the .240 are not of es-pecially large capacity for the bullet diameter used, and probably should not be considered as true magnums. The .378 case is a horse of a different color, and is surely a belted magnum's mag-num.

The huge .378 case dwarfs even the .300, .340 and the now-discontinued .375 Weatherby Magnum cases, and it makes the .375 H&H case look like a cayuse compared to a Belgian stud. The big case measures 2.908 in length, is .560 in diameter at the shoulder (the .375 H&H is only .532 on the belt), is .582 on the body just ahead of the belt, has a belt diameter of .603, and the re-bated rim is the same size as the body at .582. These dimensions will vary in actual case measurements, at least in recent lots, with an average of the cases I have going .575 on the rim, .601 on the belt, .580 just ahead of the belt, and .556 at shoulder. So if you find

your new cases do not go along exactly with the specs as given in loading man-uals and elsewhere, it is not a sign of an odd-dimension batch of cases.

The average .375 H&H case will hold 87 grains of 4831 filled completely full and well settled. The mammoth .378 case, unfired, will hold 127-grains of the same powder — 40 grains more! Fired cases will increase this capacity slightly.

The .378 cartridge was developed by Roy Weatherby and first used by him on an African hunt in about 1953. It was designed with the largest and most dangerous game in mind, and there is little doubt that it is well suited to hunting this kind of game. Material put out by Weatherby also indicates that it was designed for the deepest penetration on the heaviest game. While this is certainly true when heavy, solid point bullets are used, it is somewhat misleading where expanding bullets are fired. When one considers that most conventional .375 bullets were designed for the velocities of the .375 H&H Magnum, it is obvious that few will withstand the added velocity delivered by the big .378 Weatherby case. With the exception of a few special purpose bullets like Nosler, Colorado Custom Bullets (formerly Barnes) and Bitterroot Bonded Core, they will expand so vio-lently that they will come apart and actually give less penetration than at .375 H&H velocities. Even these tough, heavy-jacket bullets are expand-ed so rapidly and fully that penetration will be retarded somewhat. In the case of the CCB 350-grain heavyweight, only

The .378 Weatherby Magnum dwarfs the massive .375 H&H, having a bigger shoulder than the .375's belt. It will hold 40 grains more 4831!

the .049 jacket thickness should be used on heavy game.

The rifle the cartridge was designed to be used in, and in which it is chambered by Weatherby, is the Mark V, which is ideally suited to the big cartridge. Most hunters are familiar with the standard Mark V magnum action as used with the standard magnum line of Weatherby cartridges, but few have handled and examined the .378 and/or .460 rifles.

Basically the standard Mark V action and the one used for the .378 and .460 cartridges are the same, with the greatest difference being in the magazine setup for the big cartridges. For all other Weatherby Magnum cartridges the magazine is of the usual Mauser type with the cartridges staggered in the magazine box, and with the follower designed to hold the top cartridge against the side of the magazine box and tight under the receiver rail. For the .378 and .460 cartridges the magazine takes the cartridges in a single column. They are fed off a perfectly flat follower top straight forward between the lips of the magazine box and do not touch the rails of the receiver. The magazine holds only two of the larger rounds as opposed to three for cartridges like the .300.

The receiver ring has a deep notch just right of top center which allows

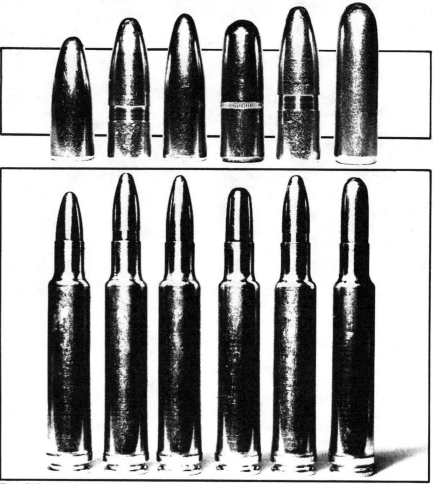

The .378 Weatherby Magnum is shown here loaded with the bullets used in developing load data, pictured in the same sequence above. From left are the 235-grain Speer (seated one diameter deep for an overall length of 3 9/16-inch), 270 Nosler, 285 Speer, 300 Hornady (seated to the crimping cannelure for an overall length of 3 5/8), 300 Nosler, and 350-grain Colorado Custom. All except the two mentioned were seated to just clear the magazine with an overall length of 3 25/32-inch.

Loads for the .378 Weatherby Magnum

.378 Weatherby Magnum, Weatherby Mark V 26" bbl. No. 3, 1-12 twist. Weatherby cases, weight 292 grains. Federal 215 primers. Velocity taken with Oehler M-20 chronograph and Oehler M-50 electronic screens. 10-foot screen spacing for instrumental velocity at 15 feet. All listed velocities converted to muzzle velocity. Temp. 70 degrees.

Bullet	Charge	Powder	Velocity	Energy	Remarks
300-gr. Wby. factory	102	?	2,803	5,232	Max. 2" groups
350-gr. Colorado Custom	106	4831	2,645	5,439	2" seated 3 25/32" O. A.
	101	N205	2,561	5,096	2¼"
	96	4350	2,527	4,959	1½"
	121	H570	2,677	5,565	3" very uniform velocity
	124	H870	2,788	6,037	3" Note Energy
300-gr. Hornady	111	4831	2,924	5,694	2" seated to cannelure
	108	N205	2,891	5,565	2"
	103	4350	2,831	5,340	2¼"
300-gr. Nosler	111	4831	2,944	5,772	2½" seated 3 25/32" O. A.
	132	H870	3,081	6,321	3" Note Energy!
285-gr. Speer	112	N205	2,981	5,620	2¼" seated 3 25/32" O. A.
270-gr. Nosler	116	4831	3,131	5,875	1½" seated 3 25/32" O. A.
	114	N205	3,104	5,772	2"
	106	4350	2,981	5,324	2¼"
235-gr. Speer	119	4831	3,286	5,632	2" seated 3 9/16" O. A.
	116	N205	3,273	5,588	2"
	109	4350	3,179	5,273	2"

All loads are near maximum for trouble-free rifle operation in hunting; should perhaps be reduced by 1-2 grains for hot weather hunting. Charges used with Hornady bullets show slightly higher pressure with Nosler bullets of same weight.

The slow ball powders like H-450 and BR-780 are not listed for two reasons: First, velocity is no better than with 4831 at similar pressures and, second, they leave an undesirable amount of air space in the big case.

unfired cartridges to be ejected. If this notch were not present it would not be possible to eject a loaded cartridge because it is longer than the ejection port of the standard action. Factory .460 cartridges are loaded to 3 3/4 inches overall length, and while factory .378 cartridges are loaded to only 3 9/16-inch and will barely eject from an ungrooved action, most test loads were loaded to 3 25/32, which utilized the groove. The magazine box is 3 13/16 inches in length.

Another feature that presents itself in the magazine of the .378-.460 rifles is that with the single column magazine box you can load from the bottom easier than from the top. In fact, on the test rifle at least, the magazine lips were so stiff that inserting cartridges between them was difficult, even after hand polishing. There is also a distinct advantage in being able to load from the bottom: It is possible to keep one in the chamber while reloading the magazine when dangerous game is wounded by the first or second shot, is not charging, but may come at any second. The chamber need never be empty unless all three rounds are fired.

There is really very little loading data for the .378 Weatherby available. Many loading manuals do not list loads for the cartridge at all, and the ones that do show loading data do not always use the powders that are best adapted to the cartridge for the highest velocities. And if you are going to use the .378 you will want near top velocity, except for possible practice loads, or why did you buy the rifle in the first place? If you don't require the punch the big cartridge is capable of, you would be much better off with a .375 H&H. Rifles cost a lot less, it is cheaper to load for, and recoil is one hell of a lot milder.

And speaking of recoil, this may be one reason why there is so little loading data for the cartridge. Not too many shooters care to sop up the punishment this cartridge dishes out when you have to fire it several hundred times from the bench, which you'll have to do in serious testing for accuracy and in chronographing. I've never been badly upset by recoil, and I normally fire thousands of rounds from various magnums every year, but I'll admit that 25 or 30 rounds of full-throttle test loads are plenty from the bench during any single session! The test rifle weighed only 9½ pounds with scope. And to keep the scope from whacking me over the eye

on some poor-position shot in hunting, I mounted one of the older K4 Weavers (which still had the long eye relief) in Redfield Jr. mounts with front extension ring. It worked beautifully.

Like many other hot cartridges, some pretty giddy ballistic figures have been given for the .375. At least I couldn't duplicate them with my handloads with the powders listed, and the test rifle was a standard new Weatherby Mark V with a 26-inch tube with standard Weatherby free-bore. Some of the ballistics quoted are doubtless honest errors. An example of this being the load data given in *Cartridges of the World*, which shows a charge of 108 grains of 4350 as starting the 270-grain bullet at 3,212 fps, and 103 grains of the same powder as giving the 300-grain bullet an MV of 3,022 fps. Strangely this is exactly 100 fps more than Weatherby lists for the same loads, which leads one to believe it is an error in printing.

In most loading data for the .378 velocity is given as being nearly as high using 4350 as with 4831, with both 270 and 300-grain bullets. However, Weatherby does show that pressures run around 3,000 psi higher for 4350 than 4831 for the same velocity level. I was never able to achieve the velocity listed in Weatherby loading data sheets with 4350 with either bullet weight. My loads were about 100 fps below the Weatherby loads, though they were maximum loads in the test rifle. Using 4831, velocities ran very close to Weatherby velocities, but charges were not always the same (which could be due to different powder and/or bullet lots). I tried 4350 with all bullet weights from 235 to 350 grains, and not in one

instance was velocity as high as with slower powders. With all bullet weights the charge was increased to make certain that maximum working loads were being used with 4350 powder, and an increase of one or two grains expanded heads beyond acceptable levels and primer pockets became too loose to use after a couple of loadings.

This was borne out by the fact that the test ammo that came with the rifle was loaded with 300-grain bullets and 102 grains of what appeared to be 4350 powder. Velocity of this load in my rifle at 65 degrees was 2,804 fps, and that load was pretty hot, leaving the mark of the bolt face ejector hole on most cases. A maximum charge of 103 grains of 4350 gave 2,831 using the same bullets pulled from factory cases.

As far as accuracy goes, I am giving averages of three-shot groups. Several were 1½-inch or less, but were not the rule. If one takes the time to let the barrel cool between shots groups are much tighter. But when you are burning more than 100 grains of powder the light barrel does heat up and it is not always possible to take that kind of time. Accuracy is certainly adequate for the kind of shooting this rifle will be used for. Perhaps there are a few hardy souls who will use the big cartridge for shooting African plains game at longer ranges, but even then an 8-inch group at 400 yards will do the job on most game — it is not ideally suited to shooting American pronghorn or African dik-dik.

The big cartridge is certainly adequately flat for 400-yard shooting with 270 or 300-grain bullets if you can shoot it that well. It would be ex-

<table>
<tr><th colspan="5">Supplemental Selected Loads</th></tr>
<tr><th>bullet (grains)</th><th>powder</th><th>suggested starting load (grains)</th><th>suggested maximum (grains)</th><th>velocity (fps)</th></tr>
<tr><td colspan="5">.378 Weatherby</td></tr>
<tr><td>270</td><td>H-4831</td><td>105.0</td><td>115.0</td><td>3,102</td></tr>
<tr><td></td><td>H-4350</td><td>99.0</td><td>105.0</td><td>3,091</td></tr>
<tr><td>300</td><td>H-4831</td><td>102.0</td><td>112.0</td><td>2,926</td></tr>
<tr><td></td><td>H-4350</td><td>95.0</td><td>100.0</td><td>2,940</td></tr>
<tr><td colspan="5">.378 Weatherby Magnum</td></tr>
<tr><td>Sierra Data
300 Spitzer BT</td><td>IMR-4831</td><td>98.5</td><td>106.8</td><td>2,850</td></tr>
<tr><td></td><td>H-450</td><td>102.4</td><td>112.0</td><td>2,900</td></tr>
<tr><td></td><td>H-4831</td><td>103.0</td><td>111.4</td><td>2,900</td></tr>
<tr><td></td><td>H-870</td><td>119.5</td><td></td><td>2,600</td></tr>
<tr><td colspan="5">*Be alert — Publisher cannot accept responsibility for errors in published load data.*</td></tr>
</table>

tremely flat with the well-shaped 270-grain pointed Hornady bullet, and I'm sure this bullet would work well for thin-skinned game at long range. I doubt that it will hold up on heavy game at close range.

I wish that I could report knocking off countless elephant and cape buffalo, as well as assorted lesser game with the .378, so that I could say just how well it performs on the game it was designed to be used on, but unfortunately, this is not the case. I did take one on a moose hunt on the Alaska Peninsula recently, but a single instance doesn't prove much.

Anyway, for whatever it's worth, I did clobber a pretty husky bull with it and a 270-grain Nosler that started on its way at 3,130 fps. The huge old bull was standing quartering to the gun at what proved to be 175 yards, and had no idea anyone was around. I laid the crosshair on the big shoulder joint and touched the .378 off. The slap of the bullet came back almost as loud as the rifle shot. The bull shuddered from the end of his big nose to the tip of his stubby tail, but he didn't even sag. He just stood there as though he had suddenly frozen solid. I could see that the bullet had landed exactly where it should have gone, so there was no reason to give him another. It took that moose about the usual one minute and 53 seconds to discover he was dead, and he didn't know it then until he tried to take a step.

The Nosler had pulverized the shoulder, passed through the ribs and the full length of the top of the lungs. It had entered the paunch and stopped somewhere inside. I couldn't sort the remainder out of the mess of willow leaves, twigs and water, so do not know how much of it remained. I do know it had penetrated nearly three feet of heavy bone, tough muscle, lung tissue and soggy paunch.

Why didn't the bull drop at the shot after absorbing all of the energy kicked up by the big bullet? A good question. But this is normal moose behavior no matter what you clobber him with unless you break the spine or penetrate the brain. Moose aren't given to fast thinking, and it just takes them a couple of minutes to discover they are on the other side of the Great Divide.

In summing up the .378 Weatherby cartridge and the load data given here, we tried to make this the most complete

tests that have been made so that the prospective owner will know where to start and what powders to use with various bullet weights. We suggest that any load listed in the chart be approached from at least 5 grains below, and that they be cut about 2 grains for use in hot weather, as in African hunting.

Norma 205, which gives outstanding velocities in many big cases and some of the smaller medium bore cases as well, also gives good results in the .378 case. Velocities delivered with N-205 closely approach those produced by 4831 with all bullet weights except the 350-grain CCB. With that heavy bullet, velocity was down more than 80 fps. With all bullet weights the charge of N-205 that gave maximum pressures was below the max charge of 4831; from 2 to 5 grains, depending on the bullet weight.

Using the 235-grain Speer bullet seated approximately one bullet diameter deep for an overall cartridge length of 3 9/16-inch, 4350, N-205 and 4831 gave very nearly the same velocity: N-205 dropped slightly behind 4350, and 4831 still held the lead for a velocity of 3,286. I don't know why anyone would wish to use the 235-grain bullet in the .378, but it was tested just to show what it would do and to make the data complete with readily available .375 bullets.

Using the popular 270-grain bullets the factory ballistics quoted by Weatherby were duplicated almost exactly with 4831. A load of 116 grains delivered 3,131 fps, while Weatherby loading data showed 3,128 with 118 grains. Again, this could have been due to powder lots and the fact that Weatherby used Hornady bullets and I used Noslers, which are again available in .375 caliber in both 270 and 300 grain versions. There is also the difference between the hunting rifle barrel and a pressure barrel to consider. Both their load and mine are considered maximum.

While I know of no loading data for any bullet weight in the .378 with powders slower than 4831, I had a hunch that numbers like H-570 and H-870 might do very well with the 350-grain CCB. Starting with H-570 I worked up to a max load of 121 grains — about all the long 350-grain could be seated over — and muzzle velocity was 2,677 fps. as against 2,645 for 106 grains of 4831.

This indicated that the very dense H-870 ball powder, even though charges would have to be increased, might do even better. A charge of 124 grains proved to be maximum and kicked the big bullet out the muzzle at 2,788 fps. This was 110 fps faster than H-570 and 143 fps more than 4831 would do at the same pressure level. This leaves little doubt that H-870 is *the* powder for this long, heavy bullet in the huge .378 case if velocity is what you want.

H-870 did so well with the 350-grain that it seemed it might also work well with the 300-grain. H-570 is not suitable with the 300-grain because you can't crowd enough in the case to reach maximum pressure. In fact, it is not possible to get enough H-870 in the case and still seat a 300-grain bullet over it to reach case pressure maximum either. A charge of 132-grains was all that could be seated over, although I did manage to seat and fire one round with 133 grains. Neither charge gave readable head expansion, but the 132-grain charge kicked the Nosler 300-grain along at 3,081 fps, which is 137 fps faster than 4831 will do with the same bullet at somewhat higher pressures.

There is, however, one fat worm in the soup where either H-570 or H-870 are concerned, at least in the test rifle. Neither gave accuracy as good as 4831. This rifle averaged around 2-inch groups at 100 yards with nearly all bullets used with 4831, N-205 and 4350, but the big charges of H-570 and H-870 spread groups to a 3-inch average. This doesn't sound so good, but if you want the extra power these powders provide for really heavy game, it will make little difference at the ranges such game as elephant and buffalo are shot.

We did use some bullets like the 235-grain that are not suited to the big cartridge for game shooting except for light game at long range. The 285-grain Speer was also tried even though it is no longer produced, on the off chance some .378 owners may have some on hand. This is why only one load is listed. But from that load the reloader can work up others if he has some of these bullets, and it will give him an idea of the velocity he is getting.

I can see little reason for using the .378 Weatherby for any North American hunting unless you just want to use one of the world's most powerful rifles and be a little different from the masses. For African hunting for the large and dangerous game there is little doubt of its efficiency. And if you can take the recoil and still shoot it well enough, it would serve well as a single rifle for an African hunt. Much better than most of the larger bores.

The .378 Weatherby Magnum was designed with a specific purpose in mind, and I believe anyone thinking of purchasing one should base his decision on whether he has this kind of use for it. ●

CHAPTER
35

Loading the .40-82 Winchester

by

Mike Venturino

W HEN MY friend and coworker Don Stermitz of Gardiner, Montana, suggested we work up an accurate load for his father's 1886 Winchester in caliber .40-82, I eagerly jumped at the chance. Don's passion in life is hunting; mine is handloading projects. Between us, we figured to get the old lever gun shooting again and put it to its intended purpose: bringing home meat.

This fine rifle, which is in very good condition externally and excellent condition internally, was made in 1888, according to a check of its serial number. It has been in the Stermitz family for forty years, but its use has been limited by the scarcity of proper ammo. Over the years, Don has accumulated most of the necessary equipment to load for the old-timer, including RCBS dies, a Lyman bullet mould, and a hundred rounds of brass of the correct length.

Regular .45-70 brass can be necked down in a .40-82 sizing die and fired, but it is a full three tenths of an inch too short. Factory specifications call for .45-70 and .40-82 brass to be 2.1 inches and 2.4 inches long, respectively. Case-head sizes are the same, however, making the .45-70 shellholder correct for the .40-82 also. I did not use any necked-down .45-70 brass in this loading project, so all loads listed are in cases of the correct length.

The bullet mould that Don had acquired was also the correct one. It is Lyman 403169, which Lyman lists as weighing two hundred forty-five grains when cast of their number-two alloy. My bullets as cast of straight wheelweight alloy weighed two hundred fifty-five grains with all grooves full of lubricant. Bullet diameter was 0.407 inch.

Don and I agreed that there was no need to work with jacketed bullets in this rifle. Our plan was to try to duplicate original ballistics and not try to "soup up" such a fine old rifle past the capabilities of cast bullets. Besides, we both feel that a 255-grain cast .40 bullet kills deer well enough.

This collector's piece is also a valued family heirloom that has just been made to shoot again — a Model 1886 Winchester that is in excellent condition inside, good condition outside.

At first, I thought that Don had already done most of the work by rounding up all the scarce tools and components. My assumption was that we would merely assemble some ammo using an appropriate charge of smokeless powder and be in business. We did not want to use black powder in this rifle except as a last resort. It would be a shame to take a chance on pitting that fine bore at this late date, and besides, smokeless powder is so much more convenient.

But our loading project did not turn out to be so simple. Because of my lack of experience with the old blackpowder cartridges, I never dreamed that these older guns could be as finicky about their loads, accuracy-wise, as any modern high-velocity scoped rifle. Ammo could be assembled simply enough, of course, but only about one out of three rounds would hit a two-foot-square target at one hundred yards. Worse than the inaccuracy, however, was the disconcerting number of hangfires and complete misfires we experienced in the beginning.

My experiences exactly parallelled Don's, and that was the reason he asked me to help in the first place. The old girl just didn't want to shoot every time or to the same general area.

Our first move was to slug the Winchester's bore. Most sources give 0.406 inch as the standard diameter for the .40-82 Winchester, but as large variations in bore diameters are not uncommon with older guns, I checked it for myself. Pure lead bullets from Don's mould measured only 0.405 inch, and I was worried that even with a harder alloy containing antimony (which does not shrink as much as pure lead on cooling), the bullets could be too small if the rifle's bore turned out to be oversize. Therefore, I bumped up one of the 0.405-inch pure-lead bullets to 0.412 inch (I squeezed it in a vise) and pounded it down the .40-82's bore. Bore diameter turned out to be 0.407 inch, and bullets from our mould, when cast of straight wheelweight alloy, come out also at 0.407 inch.

I would have preferred that the bullets be a thousandth or two oversize but was relieved that they weren't undersize at all. Bullets and bullet moulds in forty-caliber aren't so common that one can be overly choosy. Luckily, the bullets did not need sizing, for a sizing die to fit my Lyman lubricator-sizer was the one accessory that neither Don nor I possessed.

Dreading the chore of trying to lube

Both the .40-82 Winchester and the .45-70 have the same head dimensions and similar body shapes, but the .40-82 (left) is 0.3 inch longer than the necked-down .45-70 (right).

these .40 bullets by hand, I tried running them through a 0.410-inch-diameter .41 Magnum sizing die. To my surprise, this method applied the lubricant to all grooves quite neatly, without leaking lube all over the place, and yet the bullets remained untouched by the die walls.

The only loading data I could find *anywhere* for this caliber was in Ken Waters' regular "Loading the Old Ones" question-and-answer column in each issue of *Handloader*. Mr. Waters suggested thirty-four to thirty-six grains of IMR-3031. I dumped thirty-five grains in cases primed with CCI 200 primers and seated a bullet so that all grease grooves were covered. A rather light crimp was applied, although I usually prefer a heavier one. However, the RCBS dies could not be turned down far enough to apply a heavy crimp. As it has turned out, the lighter crimp has been adequate.

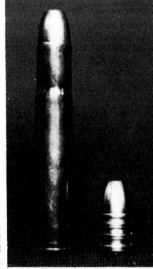

This bullet, cast in Lyman mould 403169, weighs two hundred fifty-five grains when cast of wheelweight alloy, sized to 0.407 inch, and lubricated in all grooves.

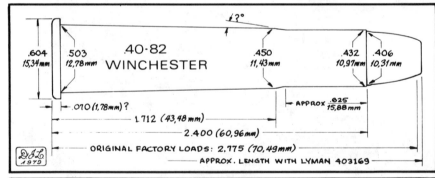

.40-82 WINCHESTER — .604 15,34mm — .503 12,78mm — .450 11,43mm — .432 10,97mm — .406 10,31mm — 1° — .010 (1,78mm)? — APPROX. .625 15,88mm — 1.712 (43,48mm) — 2.400 (60,96mm) — ORIGINAL FACTORY LOADS: 2.775 (70,49mm) — APPROX. LENGTH WITH LYMAN 403169 — DJL 1979

loads for the .40-82 Winchester
with Lyman 255-grain bullet 403169

charge	powder	velocity (fps)	remarks
33.0	IMR-3031	1,450	slightly less than factory ballistics
34.0	IMR-3031	1,480	favorite final load
28.0	IMR-4198	1,530	good load but not quite as accurate as IMR-3031
30.0	Reloder 7	1,580	very accurate
31.0	H-322	1,550	very uniform velocity
55.0	H-4831	1,455	only fair accuracy

All loads except with H-4831 contained cornmeal filler. Load with H-4831 uses CCI Magnum primers. All others use CCI Standard primers. All loads use the Lyman bullet cast of straight wheelweight alloy, lubed with Javelina Alox and left the as-cast diameter of 0.407 inch.

No effort was made to "soup up" these loads as we were trying to equal factory ballistics. Therefore none of the above loads show any signs of excessive pressures.

All of the above loads were fired for group at one hundred yards, and at least three groups were fired with each load. Except with the H-4831 load, no groups measured over four and a half inches.

During the very first shooting session with the half dozen or so cartridges I had prepared, things went smoothly enough. We loaded them singly, and although I noted a couple of slight hangfires, I was not overly disturbed. Accuracy was poor.

"After all," I thought, "This is my first experience with an old big-bore lever gun, and with a little refinement, these loads ought to perk right up." Loading another dozen cartridges with the same load, I next set up the Oehler chronograph to check velocities. The first clocked at around fifteen hundred feet per second, but the second was a definite hangfire and read only about 1,190 feet per second! The third was a slight hangfire and came in just a bit over thirteen hundred feet per second.

With a variation of over three hundred feet per second in only three shots, I could instantly see that we were having erratic ignition. It was not surprising that only two holes appeared on the target. When firing the next three shots over the chronograph screens, I elevated the rifle's muzzle to vertical before each shot. These three rounds ranged in velocity from around fourteen hundred to fifteen hundred feet per second, but the accuracy was only slightly improved — with an eighteen-inch group.

Pressure for this load was obviously low — as expected — with some cases coming out of the chamber smoked, showing they had not expanded enough to seal the chamber. By increasing the powder charge one grain at a time, I worked my way up to thirty-nine grains of IMR-3031. My feeling was that if I increased pressures somewhat, the erratic ignition, hangfires, and poor accuracy would disappear.

The thirty-nine grains of IMR-3031 was giving a velocity of around eighteen hundred feet per second on the average, but if the muzzle was not elevated for each shot, the shot-to-shot variation read in the hundreds of feet per second. With the three-shot groups seldom measuring less than a foot across and usually much more, I would say that accuracy could be called poor.

This rifle could be considered a family heirloom, and the owners basically wanted to duplicate the original factory load that gave only about 1,490 feet per second. Maybe the erratic ignition problems would have abated at higher pressure levels, but I did not consider it worth taking a chance on straining the steel in this nice old gun. I figured there were other ways to make it accurate.

While chronographing the loads already mentioned, I noticed that the first round was always the fastest if the muzzle was not elevated between shots. Because the cartridges were lying horizontally in the tubular magazine, the recoil from the first shot was throwing the powder in the following rounds forward. This I felt was causing most of my problems. Therefore, the next logical step in this loading project was the use of a filler material to hold the powder back against the primer.

For this purpose, I took some Dacron from a worn-out sleeping bag. In use, the Dacron was rolled into little balls with the fingers and pushed on top of the powder with a pencil. Knowing that the Dacron would boost pressures somewhat, I dropped the powder charge back to thirty-five grains of IMR-3031. After chronographing the first three rounds of the fillered load but before checking the target, I had some feelings of success. The variation was down to just fifty feet per second between the three shots, but when I walked to the hundred-yard target, there were only two holes in the paper, about twenty inches apart.

That was the case with every group I fired that day. Some shots were on the paper, some were not. With some three-shot groups, *none* of the bullets put a hole in the target!

Being a bit puzzled at my inability to hit a two-foot-square piece of paper at one hundred yards, I moved my shooting to twenty-five yards. At this range, groups with the Dacron-filled load of thirty-five grains of IMR-3031 ran from four to six inches! Every handgun I own can beat that by a considerable margin. My first instinct in this predicament was to change powders. So I loaded up several three-round sets of cartridges, using every powder type in my stock that is suitable. These included IMR-4198, IMR-4064, IMR-4895, H-322, and Reloder 7. All loads included the Dacron filler, and all were fired for groups at twenty-five yards. Group sizes ranged from about three inches with the IMR-4198 load to an incredible eighteen inches with IMR-4895! Velocities, however, were fairly uniform — never varying more than about seventy-five feet per second between shots in each three-round string.

My suspicions next fell on bullets as the culprits for the inaccuracy. I felt that maybe the 0.407-inch wheelweight bullets were too small after all. The only way I know of to enlarge the bullet's diameter without going to a bigger mould is to use an alloy with more antimony in it. I melted down a bit of my small supply of linotype alloy and cast it in this same Lyman mould.

The cooled bullets did measure a bit larger at about 0.4075 inch, but the weight dropped to about two hundred forty-seven grains.

These bullets were loaded over the same powders and charges as before (including Dacron) and fired for groups at twenty-five yards. The resulting holes in the targets gave me a puzzle that I have yet to figure out. Nearly every bullet hole was either an oblong or showed a complete keyhole — regardless of powder! I was completely dumbfounded, as I have been conditioned to expect excellent results from bullets cast of linotype alloy. That same afternoon, I went home, cast more bullets of wheelweight alloy, loaded them identically as with the linotype bullets, and repeated my group shooting.

Again, the groups were large, *but* with these bullets, there was not the slightest trace of an oblong hole in the target. I can offer no explanation of the strange performance of the lino-alloy bullets, as I have not had the spare time to investigate it. I am only reporting what happened to me.

It would have been nice to have had access to some original .40-82 factory ammo to shoot for a comparison. My efforts to develop accurate hunting loads with this rifle had been completely ineffective to this point, and Don and I were beginning to have doubts about the gun itself, in spite of its excellent condition. My only recourse, as I figured it, was to learn more about loading the older blackpowder cartridges. To satisfy this need, I sat down one evening with my entire collection of *Handloader* magazines and read every word in them about loading for antique rifles.

Something I found very interesting and surprising was the fact that Ken Waters reports one of his most accurate .45-70 loads to be with H-4831 powder (*Handloader* 49). It would never have occurred to me to use such a slow-burning propellant in these old nearly straight-sided cases.

Reasoning that a .40-82 is merely a longer, skinnier .45-70, I thought that maybe H-4831 would make for accurate loads in this rifle. Starting with fifty-two grains and working up to fifty-five, I got groups at twenty-five yards that hovered right at the one-inch mark — give or take a quarter of an inch. Incidentally, primers were switched to CCI magnums with H-4831.

Settling on the fifty-five-grain charge as best, I fired several groups at one hundred yards, and all measured from four to six inches. Now I was satisfied that the rifle itself was OK and that all accuracy problems stemmed from the ammo.

While the loads using H-4831 were probably accurate enough for hunting deer at one hundred to one hundred twenty-five yards, I was not completely satisfied. There was much unburned powder left in the bore, most of which seemed to make its way back into the action, making functioning less than smooth. Knowing that if all else failed, we still had a good-enough hunting load for the .40-82, I decided to keep experimenting with some of the faster powders. To me it seemed that most if not all my accuracy problems came from having so much air space in that old blackpowder case. Air space is inevitable in a cartridge designed to hold eighty-two grains of black powder but in which thirty to forty grains of modern smokeless gives maximum pressures.

I had tried fillers earlier, as I mentioned, but only Dacron and with poor results. In my dim, early gun memories I remembered hearing that the old-timers used to put such things as Cream of Wheat and cornmeal in cases for fillers. I have not heard of anyone doing it recently. Every cast-bullet article I have read in years that mentions a filler material speaks of either Dacron or kapok as the best choice.

Anyway, I dug out my wife's cornmeal and gave it a try. In using it, I dumped the powder charge into the case, then filled the case to the brim with cornmeal and seated a bullet. This compressed the powder and cornmeal so they would not mix with one another. Compressing the powder and cornmeal of course raises pressures, so I dropped my beginning powder charge to thirty-four grains of IMR-3031.

Firing with the first three cornmeal rounds was done at twenty-five yards, and the three holes were touching — cutting a classic cloverleaf group. This was followed by two other very similar groups, none of the three measuring over three quarters of an inch. I rushed home and loaded more of the same load. As calmly as possible after returning to the shooting bench, I touched off three shots at the hundred-yard target.

The group was nicely rounded and measured only three inches! The Oehler chronograph showed my velocities to be exactly where I desired — 1,480 feet per second on the average with only about forty feet per second shot-to-shot variation in a five-shot string.

To date, Don and I have fired more than a dozen groups with the load of thirty-four grains of IMR-3031, and none of them has measured over four and a half inches — most are less than that. I knew that I really couldn't beat what I already had, but just for the fun of it, I tried several other faster powders. These included H-322, IMR-4198, and Reloder 7. Accuracy with all the powders was excellent with Reloder 7 maybe even shading IMR-3031 by a bit. Unfortunately, Reloder 7 is hard to get in this area, so Don and I have stuck to our original load. It's tempting to try to locate more of the Reloder 7 though, because it measures so well.

Anyway, the choice of powder is not that crucial now, as long as the cornmeal filler is used, and I would like to add that the loads giving nearly identical velocity as compared to factory ballistics also shoot to the original sight settings. The sights on this rifle have not been adjusted in over forty years, and it was gratifying to me that it shot dead center for us with the cornmeal loads.

When we started this loading project, Don told me a story about the Winchester. He said that nearly forty years ago, when times were a bit tough for his grandparents, they took this .40-82 to a pawnshop in Livingston, Montana. They were offered only two dollars for it. His father saved it from that fate and kept it for himself. I'm glad he did, because the education that old rifle has given me is worth many, many times that two dollars. ●

CHAPTER
36

THE FORGOTTEN FORTY

By DAVE CORBIN

IF SOMEONE told you that within our lifetimes there would be no .30 caliber rifles or ammunition offered because some other bore would become more popular, what would you think? Impossible? Something of almost the same magnitude has already happened: an entire caliber with not less than 40 different chamberings offered by at least seven major arms and ammo makers has disappeared from the shooting scene!

It wasn't a political plot to disarm citizens that caused this wholesale discontinuance, but a matter of the shooters' own choice. Whether it was a good choice or not deserves some investigation, since the great disappearance is unique in our shooting history. We refer, as you've undoubtedly guessed, to the absence of .40 caliber rifles and ammunition today.

The .45 and the .38 bore, once as popular as the .40, are still around in limited chamberings. But the closest thing to a modern .40 is the 1964-vintage .41 Magnum handgun round. The last .40 caliber factory rifle cartridge was introduced in 1910 and was obsolete by 1936. That was the .401 Winchester Self-Loading, for the old M-10 clip-fed blow-back rifle designed by T.C. Johnson.

Why was the .40 once a popular caliber? Right up to the early 1900's there were dozens of .40 bores used both for target and for game, for the .40 was seen by experts of the day as a multi-purpose caliber. In the late 1800's, most shooters were target shooters, and the sport held such national attention that nearly all factory guns were designed around this purpose. A common complaint in old literature is that manufacturers made their guns too heavy for hunting, since this met with the desires of the larger market of target buffs.

For target work, the .45 caliber was considered best for long range work up to 1,000 yards, and the .38 for both mid-range and close work. The .32 bore was popular but serious shooters still felt that the .38 was about as small as could be used with consistent results with black powder. The .38-55 held the lead in popularity over the .32-40 until Harry

Pope and an improved technology made the latter a famous target combination.

For hunting, few cartridges were more popular than the .38-40, judging from the number of surviving samples we see today, primarily in the Model 1873 Winchester. But at the time the .38-40 (which was a true .40 despite the name) was considered a smallbore rifle cartridge, and owed much of its popularity to the popularity of the 1873 Winchester, as well as to its versatility, since it was also available in the Colt Single Action and other handguns. Despite its usefulness as a general-purpose cartridge (particularly in the West, where ammunition dealers were widely scattered and having a rifle and handgun chambered for the same cartridge solved an important logistics problem) the .38-40 was too light for use on big game.

Winchester solved the problem with the Browning-designed Model 1886, which was light enough for hunting, yet strong enough to handle more-potent cartridges of the type which had been limited, with few exceptions, to single-shot rifles. The .40-70 WCF, .40-82 WCF, .40-60 WCF and .40-65 WCF were all based on the .45-70 case, and can be made from new .45-70 cases today, although the .45-70 case is about 2.105 inches overall and some of the .40 caliber cartridges were a bit longer.

There was quite a bit of confusing designation among the .40 bores. The .40-63 and .40-70 Ballard are the same cartridge with different powder charges, but the .40-75 Bullard of 1887 is the same case as the .40-60 Bullard while the .40-60 Marlin, .40-60 Winchester, and .40-60 Maynard are all different cases. A .40-70 Sharps (Necked) is different from a .40-70 Sharps (Straight) but the same as a .40-70 Remington. And there is a .40-70 Maynard, a .40-70 Peabody, .40-70 Winchester, and the .40-70 Ballard, all slightly or radically different cases.

The largest of the .40 calibers include the .40-110 Winchester Express made for the Winchester M-85 rifle and the .40-90 Sharps, Peabody, Ballard, and a fat bottle-neck .40-90 Bullard. The smallest are in the category of the .401 WSL with its 1.5-inch case and the .40-40 Maynard

This lineup includes a few of the many now-rare .40 bore cartridges. From left: .38-40 WCF, .40-65 Winchester, .40-60 Marlin, .40-72 WCF, and .401 Winchester SL.

215

with a 1 3/4-inch case. They all seem to
have velocity levels of from 1,200 to 1,600
fps, most of them around 1,400 fps,
except for the 2,130 fps .401 WSL and the
2,200 fps .405 Winchester. And that is
one of the reasons these forty-bores aren't
around today — mediocre muzzle velocity
with attendant rainbow trajectories made
worse by short, fat, blunt bullets. But
muzzle velocities can be boosted in
modern rifles with modern propellants.
Why wasn't the .40 given the high velocity
treatment?

One reason was its necessarily large
physical dimensions. The .403 to .406
bore requires a case with at least a .425 to
.430 neck diameter, which means a
commensurately large body. A .30-06 has
a .473 base, but a .40 caliber on the '06
case would have to be headspaced on the
mouth, a system suitable only for
relatively short cases. The solution would
be a rimmed case of fairly large diameter,
requiring a large action, but the
introduction of smokeless powder resulted

The Maynard Improved Mid-Range Target and
Hunting Rifles.

NUMBER 10,

35 or 40 calibre; weight, 8 to 10 lbs.; chambered for 40, 60 or 70 gr. cartridges; elevating graduated Peep Sight; Stock, plain oil finish; the
Barrel is octagon 9 inches at breech.

28, 30 or 32 inch barrel, $34.00
Appendages: Bullet mold, loader, loading block, capper, cap picker, rod, brush,
    rag holder, screw driver, and 10 cartridge cases,   5.00

Extra fancy wood in stock. Checkered stock or change in sights
will be furnished at prices shown in general price-list of parts.

in smaller cases, with commensurately
smaller, lighter actions.

However, suitable cases and actions did
become available, and some powerful .40
wildcats were made, but never captured
the popular fancy. In the 1920's, Newton
Arms Co. listed a .40 Newton, apparently
based on the .525 diameter Newton
rimless case, which produced a muzzle
velocity of 3,042 fps, energy of 6,180 fp,
and 100-yard mid-range trajectory of
slightly over half an inch, but it was never
offered commercially. Some interesting
.40 wildcats have also been made,
including the Ackley .40-348 (Winchester), which produced more than two tons
of muzzle energy. Others worth
mentioning are the .400 Williams, .404
Barnes-Johnson, and .404 Barnes Supreme, made from the sole modern .45
caliber, the powerful .458 Winchester.
Such cartridges are in the same class as
the .400 Jeffery and .416 Rigby, which
have long been popular for African game
at relatively close ranges. But these
British cartridges don't have the flat
trajectories desirable for much North
American hunting, and they have more
power than necessary for American game,
with resultant heavy recoil.

Those are the same reasons why the .40
faded away: the .40 simply doesn't fit
American hunting as well as the smaller
bores. It's a matter of ballistic balance

**A .40 caliber Maynard with its huge
rim is advertised in early Maynard
literature as a "mid-range target and
hunting" rifle, typical of the thinking
about the entire line of .40 caliber
cartridges. The .38 and .32 calibers
were considered shorter-range
calibers and the .45 considered more
effective for long range work.**

**Most of the .40 bores require a .406-inch
bullet for good accuracy, in spite of the
factory published specifications of the day.
However, bullets from .396 to .423-inch
are required for some of them and it is
wise to make a chamber and bore cast or
slug the bore before shooting any bullets
through an unknown .40 caliber barrel.**

between needed energy, needed trajectory
and tolerable recoil.

With the advent of smokeless powder,
the American shooter became enamored
with the benefits, both real and imagined,
of high velocity. The principal real
benefits were flat trajectory and, to a
lesser degree, wind-bucking capability,
combined with high retained energy. A
.30 caliber bullet could be driven at the
velocities necessary to obtain these
benefits with relative ease, and the result
was a balanced load — one with a
relatively flat trajectory, reasonable rifle
weight, reasonable recoil, and with
retained energy in the range needed to
provide reliable kills on typical American
game.

A .40 caliber could be driven to the
same velocities, and with similarly shaped
bullets, could be given the same trajectory
and wind-bucking ability as the .30, but
at the cost of a whopping increase in
recoil. And the resultant load would have
far more initial and retained energy than
is needed for even the largest American
game.

As a matter of curiosity, I did some
calculation to see what kind of load would
be needed to equal the flat trajectory of
one of the earliest commercial .30's, the
.300 Savage. Although any bullet could
have been used, in order to give it good
long range potential, I chose a theoretical
180-grain spitzer bullet with a six-caliber
ogive, at a moderate 2,200 fps. Since two
calibers will have the same trajectory only
with the same velocity and bullets of the

Original bullets for various .40 caliber Winchester, Marlin and Ballard rifles normally used from 0.5 to a maximum of 2-caliber ogives, with flat noses, giving rather poor ballistic coefficients. The single shot rifles available then, or today, could make use of longer-ranged four through six caliber ogive spitzers for vastly superior retained velocity and energy. The .40-72, right, featured a soft point 330-grain bullet with about a one-caliber ogive. These blunt-nosed projectiles shed velocity rather quickly. Note the original "W" stamp on the bullet of this WRA Co. headstamp round.

same ballistic coefficient, it was necessary to calculate a theoretically equal .40 caliber bullet, using the sectional density and ballistic coefficient formulas provided in *Hatcher's Notebook* and other sources.

Both bullets were given the same six-caliber ogive (resulting in the same form factor) and sectional density. As the ballistics tables say, sectional density is the bullet's weight in pounds, divided by its diameter squared. To match the .271 S.D. of a 180-grain .308 bullet, a .403 caliber bullet would have to weigh about .309 grains. With the same form factor, which Hatcher says is .550 for a pointed six-caliber ogive, and the same sectional density, the ballistic coefficient (sectional density divided by form factor), would be .493 for both bullets.

Since 2,200 fps can be obtained with a 180-grain bullet with about 36 grains of a medium-rate IMR powder, according to

both the loading manuals and the Powley Computer, it's a simple matter to plug that information into the Recoil Nomograph which appeared in the March-April 1972 *Rifle* and determine that in an eight-pound rifle, the recoil would be a modest 11 foot-pounds. The hypothetical .40 caliber cartridge, according to the Powley Computer (working backwards from the usual method), could achieve that same 2,200 fps velocity with its 309-grain spitzer using about 60 grains of 4064 in a 70-grain water capacity case. According to the nomograph, that cartridge would belt you with 30 foot-pounds of recoil.

(A cartridge quite similar to the hypothetical .40 already existed when the .300 Savage came into being — the .405 Winchester, introduced in 1904 and the favorite of Teddy Roosevelt for African game.)

While the .30 and .40 would have the same initial velocity, and the same trajectory due to equal ballistic coefficient bullets, the muzzle energy of the .30 would be 1,933 fps — modest by modern standards, but quite adequate for deer-sized game. But the .40 would roar out the muzzle with 3,319 fp energy, equal to some magnums.

But the .300 Savage, except in its earliest days, has never been known as a long-range cartridge, and from the post-World War II years, that's what the American shooter wanted. We were enthralled by a host of wildcat magnum .30's, some of which became factory offerings, such as the .300 Weatherby, .308 Norma and .300 Winchester Magnum. All are capable of driving a well-shaped 180-grain bullet at 3,000 fps, or faster, and they shoot flat.

There would be no great problem in building an equally flat-shooting .40 caliber; cases and actions could be made big enough, but who could handle the recoil? Returning to the Powley computer, a 120-grain charge of 4831 in a .40 caliber case of about 130-grain water capacity (say a .460 Weatherby necked to .40, with shoulder blown slightly forward) would produce the desired velocity of 3,000 fps, thereby achieving trajectories with the 309-grain .493 ballistic coefficient bullet exactly equal to those

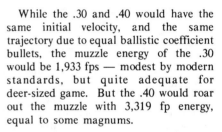

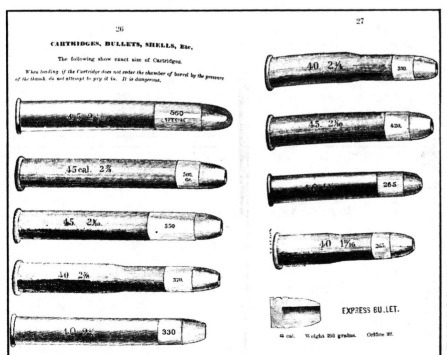

An 1879 Sharps Rifle Company catalog shows two of the .40 Sharps cartridges on the left hand page — both a bottle-neck and a straight version. The .40 caliber 2 1/2-inch cartridge was loaded with 65 to 70 grains of black powder as was the bottleneck. The same guns were offered with either chamber since some shooters didn't like the bottleneck designs and others felt the straight cases were harder to extract.

flat-shooting .30 Magnums. But the muzzle energy would be 6,177 fp, compared to 3,598 for the .30. And while an eight-pound .30 Magnum would jolt you with about 28 fp of recoil energy, the hypothetical .40 Magnum would lay about 85 foot-pounds of recoil energy against your shoulder.

It's now clear why the .40 fell by the wayside, despite its popularity at the turn of the century. At velocities giving reasonable recoil the .40 produced bullet energies compatible with that needed for American game. But when ranges lengthened as game became more scarce, and more hunting was done in the plain and mountain states, flatter trajectories were needed. Those desired trajectories could only be obtained with bullets of better form and greater sectional density, combined with higher velocities. Technically, it could be done with a .40, but the result would have been a cartridge with far more power than needed for the game, and with far more recoil than normal men can tolerate, much less shoot with the precision needed for long range.

Will the popular .30 be abandoned in the future as the .40 was in the past? Not likely. But there is a drift toward smaller calibers, notably the 7mm and .25, both of which have shown a tremendous increase in popularity in the past 15 years. The reasons are precisely the same as those which brought about the demise of the .40. The smaller bores can achieve flatter trajectories, adequate energies, and superior wind-bucking at recoil levels which can be tolerated by shooters who find it difficult to shoot even the .30 magnums with precision.

These smaller bores didn't achieve their popularity earlier for they presented more problems than they solved. In a time when smaller bores were more difficult to cut with precision, when quality bullets were harder to make, when jacket metals were more prone to foul barrels, when slow-burning powders were either non-existent or highly erosive, the .25-06 case form (which has been in existence for better than a half-century) simply couldn't compete with the .30's. But improved technology has made it one of the top sellers.

So who can say that future improvements in technology will not cause the ubiquitous general-purpose .30 to wither and fade away? If this were 1880, how would we have predicted the future for the popular general-purpose .40 caliber? ●

Around the turn of the century, firearms and ammunition catalogs were full of .40 caliber listings — some 40 variations from at least seven major makers. But today not a single U.S. arms or ammo maker offers the caliber which was once as popular as the .30 is now. The .40 didn't die because of a disarmament plot, or even because of the Madison Avenue influence. It died because it didn't fit the American hunting scene. As the table below shows, at velocity levels giving the trajectories needed, or desirable, for western hunting, it produces far more energy than necessary for the game being hunted, and far more recoil than can be tolerated, particularly for accurate long-range shooting. The drawing at bottom shows about what a .40 Magnum would look like alongside a .300 Winchester Magnum.

Equalling .30 Trajectories with a .40

If muzzle velocities are the same, two bullets of different calibers, but with the same ballistic coefficient, will produce equal trajectories and retained velocities at all ranges; however, bullet energy and recoil energy will be different. For this comparison, .30 and .40 caliber bullets with a six-ogive pointed tip (0.55 form factor) and weights of 180 grains and 309 grains, each having sectional densities of .271 and ballistic coefficients of .493 were used. Calculated drop is from line of sight 1.5 inches above the bore with a 100-yard zero. Recoil was calculated on the basis of an eight-pound rifle. Cartridges capable of producing the listed velocities are used to simplify the comparison.

Typical Cartridge	Muzzle Velocity [fps]	Bullet Weight [grains]	Ball. Coef.	Muzzle Energy [fp]	200-Yd. Velocity [fps]	200-Yd. Energy [fp]	200-Yd. Drop [Inches]	Recoil [fp]
.300 Savage	2,200	180	.493	1,933	1,885	1,420	7.3	11
.405 Win.	2,200	309	.493	3,319	1,885	2,438	7.3	30
.300 Win. Mag.	3,000	180	.493	3,598	2,610	2,723	3.0	28
.40 Hypo. Mag.	3,000	309	.493	6,177	2,610	4,675	3.0	85

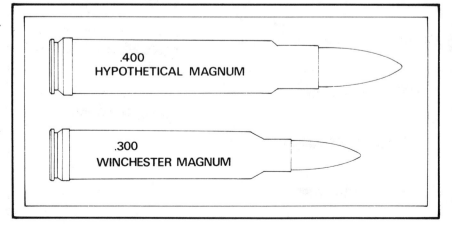

.400 HYPOTHETICAL MAGNUM

.300 WINCHESTER MAGNUM

CHAPTER
37

.400 Brown Whelen

John Kronfeld

"**W**HEN COLONEL Whelen designed the .400 Whelen rifle and cartridge, I believe he created one of the best, if not the best American cartridge for our heavy game such as elk, moose and large bear; especially when shooting is to be done in dense timber." These were the words of Elmer Keith in a 1936 issue of *American Rifleman*.

Three years later Phil Sharpe, premier gun writer of the period, had different words for the .400 Whelen in his *Complete Guide to Handloading*. "The .400 Whelen was designed by Colonel Townsend Whelen, noted author and authority, while he was commanding officer of Frankford Arsenal in the early 1920s. Essentially this is the unnecked Springfield (.30-06) cartridge case necked but very slightly to .40 caliber. It has been widely proclaimed as an excellent cartridge by a number of our so-called authorities throughout the United States, but its designer is only lukewarm concerning its possibilities.

"Only a short time ago, when preparing material for this book, Colonel Whelen suggested that the author warn users of rifles in this caliber to be extremely careful in resizing their cases, and stated that he did not approve of handloading in this caliber because the very faint indication of a neck was inclined to create a serious headspace problem if improperly resized. . . .Properly loaded, however, this cartridge is a very excellent killer for heavy game, at medium and long ranges up to about 400 yards."

Personally, the .400 Whelen has been on my mind for many years for several reasons. Partly because of the later writings of Keith, who claimed 2,300 fps for a 350-grain bullet using 63 grains of DuPont No. 17½ powder. Sharpe shows 2,215 fps for a 350-grain bullet using 62 grains of the same powder. Suffice to say their figures compare favorably; that's roughly 4,100 foot-pounds of muzzle energy from a modified .30-06 case, impressive to say the least.

Remington's removal of the .35 Whelen from wildcat status in 1987, by commercial production, again brought

the .400 Whelen to mind. Also, we have so many popular commercial and wildcat cartridges based on the .30-06 case. They run the gamut from 6mm to .35 caliber; 6mm-06, 6.5-06, .270 Winchester, .280 Remington, 8mm-06, .338-06, .35 Whelen and .375 Whelen, but no .400-06 or .400 Whelen. Why haven't we heard more about this supposedly exceptional cartridge? Apparently, the headspace problem has kept reloaders away.

Discovering Keith's article in January of 1990, at the Rock Island Arsenal technical library, a decision was made to bite the bullet.

Left, the original .400 Whelen (*1*) was manufactured by the Frankford Arsenal in 1923. The Brown Whelen version (*2*) has slightly more powder capacity and a shorter neck. Right, the .35 Whelen (*3*) and the .405 Winchester (*4*) may have inspired the development of the .400 Whelen.

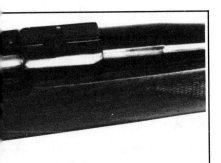

...e extractor on the Ruger Model 77 remains ...hind the case rim until the bolt is turned ...wn, requiring positive headspace on the case ...ulder.

I was not overly concerned with the original .400 Whelen design and its mild shoulder. The purpose of this project was to determine if a .30-06 type case (one could also use a .270 Winchester, .280 Remington or .35 Whelen case) can be modified to some configuration to successfully shoot .411 bullets. Whelen and Keith used these same diameter bullets 70 years ago.

Excepting the previously mentioned authors, I must admit, I have not seen anything written on this cartridge in 42 years of avidly reviewing shooting periodicals. Therefore, the best place to start was with a competent gunsmith like Harry McGowen whose shop rebarrels and chambers thousands of rifles a year to every conceivable caliber — commercial and wildcat.

McGowen (Rt. 3, St. Anne IL 60964) was only temporarily at a loss when asked to build a .411 caliber rifle based on a .30-06 case, a .400 Whelen type rifle. Reamer drawings arrived two weeks later marked ".400 Brown Whelen." They were for a .30-06 type case expanded to .411 caliber incorporating a sharp shoulder in contrast to the long, tapered shoulder of the original .400 Whelen.

The perceived problem with expanding .30-06 case necks to .411 caliber has been the headspace question. Would there be enough shoulder left to provide reliable headspace? If there was, how would I prove this to my satisfaction and hopefully yours? These questions required some soul searching.

I believe these questions were well answered by *not* selecting a bolt action rifle whose extractor engages the extractor groove of the case when the bolt

moves forward, as in the Mauser 98, Winchester Pre-64 and Springfield type actions. This is known as positive, or controlled, feeding. By selecting one of these actions, there might be the question or stigma of Did the cartridge properly headspace on its shoulder? Or, Is the extractor holding the case back against the bolt face?

Discussing the situation with many gunsmiths revealed my theory to be only partially correct. Due to variations in extractor and extractor groove dimension, the extractor may or may not hold the cartridge tight enough against the bolt face to ensure proper primer ignition and eliminate the headspace problem.

Keeping that in mind, a Ruger Model 77 bolt action rifle (a Remington Model 700 or new Winchester Model also could have been used) was sent to McGowen for conversion to .400 Brown Whelen since the extractor did not engage or snap over the rim until the bolt had almost completely closed.

As the bolt strips a cartridge from the magazine and pushes it forward, the case shoulder meets the chamber shoulder, causing the extractor to cam outward and snap around the base of the case and into the extractor groove. I made the assumption that if this could be demonstrated reliably, there would be no headspace problem with the .400 Brown Whelen cartridge.

Two hundred .35 Whelen cases, not .30-06, were purchased. The .35 Whelen case has a thicker neck after expansion to .411 and provides better neck tension. Initially, only 25 cases were expanded to .411 with an RCBS

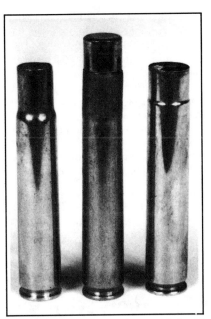

John's fireforming procedure begins with the .35 Whelen case (left) that is necked up to .411 inch (center) and loaded with a .41 caliber handgun bullet that is seated upside down. The base of the bullet engages the lands, holding the case head against the bolt face for fireforming to .400 Brown Whelen (right).

single-stage, neck-up die. (Only 25 cases were formed in order to use as few cases as many times as possible and observe the effect of continued firings on the narrow shoulder.) They were loaded with 48 grains of IMR-3031 behind an inverted Hornady 210-grain .41 Magnum bullet. (Note: It is critical that at least 50,000 CUP be generated when fireforming. This ensures the case is expanded and fully conforms to the chamber dimensions.)

It happened that the overall length

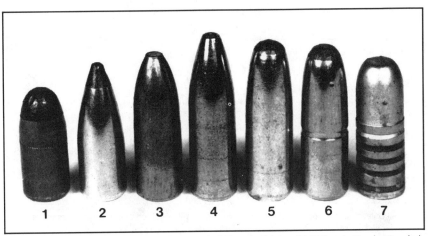

Test bullets include the (1) 300-grain Patriot, (2) 300-grain Barnes, (3) 335-grain Trophy Bonded, (4) 350-grain Barnes, (5) 400-grain Barnes, (6) 400-grain Woodleigh and the (7) 375-grain NEI cast design.

of the case and inverted bullet (when crimped into the cannelure) caused the base of the bullet to rest firmly against the lands when the bolt was closed. It worked very well for fireforming and all 25 cases came out perfectly formed. If the bullet is not inverted, however, the existing shoulder on the .35 Whelen case fails to establish headspace in the .400 Whelen chamber. When the trigger is pulled, the cartridge may, or may not, fire.

RCBS provided the loading dies after a reamer print was sent to Bill Keyes. They must have been watching out for me. When a fired case is inserted into the full length sizing die as far as the shellholder permits, the case shoulder does not touch the die's shoulder. Once the cases are properly fireformed, they can never have their shoulder set back, ensuring proper headspacing for the life of the case.

Availability of .411 inch bullets is surprisingly good. At present .411 bullets are also used in the .411 KDF, .450/.400 Nitro Express, .404 Rimless Nitro and a few Thomspon/Center Contender wildcats.

Original .405 Winchester-style 300-grain roundnose bullets, made by Patriot, came from The Old Western Scrounger (12924-M Highway A-12, Montague CA 96064). They shoot very well up to 2,300 fps, which is a hair faster than the original .405 Winchester factory load that generated 2,230 fps. If one wants to use 300-grain bullets in a scoped rifle the Barnes 300-grain spitzer holds its velocity and trajectory much better, extending the effective range out to 250 yards, while the roundnose design might be restricted to 150 yards or so.

John Taylor's criticism of 300-grain bullets in the .405 Winchester is "the sectional density of its bullet was none too good, with the result that it lacked penetration on all the larger species." By African standards it does have a low sectional density, .254, but for North American hunting it is fine. Our beloved .30-caliber 165-grain bullets are only .248.

The Trophy Bonded 335-grain Bear Claw and Barnes 350-grain X bullets are spitzers that bring out the full potential of this cartridge. Being driven at velocities that generate almost 4,000 foot-pounds of muzzle energy, they can handle anything on the North American continent out to the 275-yard range without too much trouble.

If one wants maximum performance at close range for dangerous game on any continent, the 400-grain roundnose, softpoint or solid bullets from Barnes and Woodleigh (marketed through Huntington's Die Specialties, PO Box 991, Oroville CA 95965) are just the ticket. They can be safely driven to 2,115 fps in my rifle (the Ruger Model 77 has a 22-inch barrel, if it had a 24-inch barrel the velocity would be over 2,150 fps). This is over 4,000 foot-pounds of muzzle energy and equals the .450/.400 Nitro Express and .404 Rimless Nitro Express which John Taylor spoke so well of in his book on African cartridges.

One NEI 375-grain flatnose cast bullet was tested. Cast from wheelweights and 2 percent tin, it is extremely accurate and fully capable of taking all North American game. Bullets were fitted with .41-caliber gas checks, water-tempered to a BHN of 19, sized to .412 and lubed with LBT Blue. When loaded, cases were firmly crimped into the crimping groove. They fed perfectly, as did all loads through the magazine and into the chamber.

Due to the wide variations in ogive dimensions, each bullet is a world unto itself with regard to seating depth and overall loaded length. Roundnose

.400 Brown Whelen Loading Data

bullet (grains)	powder	charge (grains)	velocity (fps)	SD	remarks
Barnes 300 Spitzer	IMR-4198	50.0	2,198	13.7	1.25 inches
		52.0	2,303	40.1	1 inch
		54.0	2,373	11.9	1.5 inches
	IMR-3031	53.0	1,911	25.0	¾ inch
		54.0	1,983	24.8	1 inch
		55.0	2,050	26.0	¾ inch
	RL-7	57.0	2,440	41.5	¾ inch
		58.0	2,546	62.0	1.5 inches
Patriot 300 RN	RL-7	51.0	2,203	27.5	1 inch
		53.0	2,300	45.0	1.5 inches
		55.0	2,345	3.4	1.5 inches
Trophy Bonded 335	IMR-3031	51.0	1,961	26.9	¾ inch, reduce 5 percent
		52.0	2,202	53.1	punctured primers
	IMR-4064	53.0	1,821	39.6	¾ inch
		55.0	1,981	42.8	⅝ inch
	AAC-2520	55.0	2,045	6.2	½ inch
		58.0	2,135	35.0	⅝ inch
		60.0	2,213	6.5	1 inch
		62.0	2,220	10.3	⅜ inch
Barnes "X" 350	AAC-2520	55.0	1,988	11.5	⅝ inch
		57.0	2,067	17.1	1 inch
		59.0	2,130	41.0	1.5 inches
Barnes 400 RN	AAC-2520	54.0	1,997	5.6	1 inch
		56.0	2,205	23.1	¾ inch
		58.0	2,088	6.1	¾ inch
		59.0	2,123	6.7	¾ inch
Woodleigh 400 RN	RL-15	57.0	1,977	33.0	¾ inch
		59.0	2,027	8.3	½ inch
		61.0	2,115	.3	½ inch
NEI 375	AAC-2520	52.0	1,948	56.0	½ inch
		54.0	2,051	26.7	1 inch
		56.0	2,054	8.9	1.25 inches

All primers were Federal 210. Velocities recorded with PACT chronograph with center of screens 10 feet from muzzle. All groups fired at 50 yards. Cast bullets lubricated with LBT Blue.

Be alert — Publisher cannot accept responsibility for errors in published load data.

bullets were seated so their ogive is ⅛ inch back from the rifling. This is to ensure that the cartridge headspaces on the shoulder of the case and not the bullet's ogive.

Initial powder selections were made using the Powley Computer. IMR-4064 was indicated for the heavy bullets. As can be seen from my loading data, however, tests show AAC-2520 and RL-15 are fine choices for the .400 Brown Whelen with heavy bullets.

Ballistics from the .400 Brown Whelen are very close to those, for comparable bullet weights, reported by Keith and Page for the .400 Whelen. Keith's data is from a 24-inch barrel, Page's from a 26-inch barrel and mine from a 22-inch barrel. For all intents and purposes, our velocities agree. That being the case, it is my humble opinion that Keith was correct, at least regarding performance. For a North American hunting cartridge, in his day, the .400 Whelen was an outstanding performer.

Remember that in the early 1920s when the .400 Whelen was conceived, there were not many high-intensity bolt-action cartridges available in the U.S. The .375 H&H Magnum, although introduced in 1912, required an expensive and almost unavailable long action and ammunition was not commercially available until 1926.

It should be noted that when first introduced the .35 Whelen was referred to as the "poor man's .375 H&H Magnum." It could be built on a standard-length action and utilized plentiful .30-06 brass. Unfortunately,

the .400 Whelen has not shared its popularity because of the headspace problem. Hopefully, the .400 Brown Whelen will give new life to those wanting an inexpensive bolt action rifle capable of taking all game on all continents.

After firing the 25 cases, some as many as 12 times (a few necks split after the eighth or ninth firing and this might have been avoided if the cases had been annealed), there was not one failure to properly headspace. After every round was chambered, the bolt was opened and retracted to see if the extractor had engaged the extractor groove. It had, thus indicating that the cartridge is definitely headspacing on its shoulder. The .400 Brown Whelen functioned perfectly.

As a further check for headspace reliability, 100 more .35 Whelen cases were fireformed to .400 Brown Whelen. Each case was reprimed only, 10 times, and fired. There was not one failure of the firing pin to detonate the primer. Hopefully, this should serve as further proof that the .400 Brown Whelen does indeed headspace properly with 100 percent reliability.

Lastly, for those who like the ballistics of this 2½-inch cartridge, but still feel there is a potential for headspace problems, the .240 Weatherby Magnum is often referred to as a belted .30-06. Size the .240 Weatherby Magnum cases like any other belted case. If you should inadvertently push the shoulder back, the belt will establish headspace. Note that the base dimensions of the .30-06 type case and

the .240 Weatherby Magnum are the same. This means that no modification to the extractor or bolt face of your rifle is required.

Shooting this rifle off the bench was a pleasant surprise. Recoil was mild, even at the 4,000-foot-pound level. This can be attributed to the low velocity yielding a push instead of the hard recoil of higher velocity cartridges. I have never worked with a cartridge that consistently gave such small groups with so many bullets over such a wide range of powder weights (this may have been helped by McGowen's installation of a Timney trigger). The Woodleigh never exceeded one inch with any load.

So the reader can fully understand and appreciate the potential of a 400-grain .411 bullet at 2,150 fps, which is what the .450/.400 Nitro Express and the .404 Rimless Nitro Express deliver, note the following excerpts from Taylor's book on African rifle cartridges. Regarding the .450/.400 Nitro Express:

"It is one of the grandest weapons imaginable for all big game hunting. . . .It has ever been one of my favorites. . . .I have used it extensively on all kinds of African game from elephant down with the greatest possible satisfaction . . . no weapon behaved more successfully in my hands. . . .Experience has shown that 4,000 foot-pounds can safely be taken against any animal anywhere." (The .450/.400 was only built as a double barrel or single-shot rifle and the .404 Rimless Nitro was in bolt action.)

●

CHAPTER
38

Mike Venturino

The .40-70 on African Plains Game

Mike and his wife Yvonne with a nyala taken in Natal. Range was around 140 yards. In the foreground, the .40-70 that did the job.

"Iron sights?"
says the guide . . .

Instead of the traditional long tangent sight, Mike installed an old marble tang sight originally designed to fit a Winchester. The target disc was custom made to screw into the sight's hunting aperture.

WHEN THE DECISION was finally made to turn a lifelong dream into reality by booking an African hunt, there was no question about which rifle I would take. Since first buying a Shiloh Sharps in 1981 I have made no secret of my feelings about these well-made, sidehammer single shots.

Most hunters thinking of Africa envision going after the Big Five. For that sort of game, a very powerful rifle capable of a fast second shot is just about a necessity. Dangerous animals were not on my agenda, but the larger species of plains game were. Having successfully hunted elk and deer with Sharps rifles, I felt that hunting with one in Africa would be challenging and memorable.

The Sharps was not the only rifle that went to Africa with me. A Winchester Model 86 in .33 WCF and a .308 Winchester Model 70 Featherweight with a Leupold 2-7x scope made the trip, too. The .40-70 Sharps was to be the main rifle, though.

My hunting Sharps has a 26-inch barrel instead of the more common 30-inch tube. To reduce weight further, the barrel is half round, half octagonal. An aid in reducing the effect of this rifle's recoil is a shotgun-style butt 1.5 inches wide. Since hunting rifles see hard use, the butt is protected by a checkered steel buttplate. All in all, this adds up to a fast-handling rifle that weighs 8½ pounds and is only 42 inches long.

Sights consist of a hooded front globe designed to take interchangeable inserts and a tang aperture rear. The only insert used for hunting was a post .05 inch wide.

The tang peep sight departs from tradition. The various tang sights usual-

ly associated with Sharps often fold forward under recoil and frustrate attempts to reload quickly. In their stead I turned to an old Marble tang sight, originally intended for a lever action Winchester. Its base screw spacing was just right for the Sharps; mounting required only a couple of slightly longer screws. The peep sight was fitted with a fairly large ⅛-inch aperture.

This particular Sharps fits me perfectly. When it jumps to the shoulder, the sights are immediately ready to use, and that particular asset came in very handy in Africa.

In 1983, Shiloh Sharps rifles became available in three traditional .40-caliber chamberings: the .40-50, .40-70 and .40-90 Sharps Bottleneck. Case lengths are 1¹¹⁄₁₆, 2¼ and 2⅝ inches respectively.

One look at the .40-70 told me it would be an ideal smokeless big game cartridge. It has the same case capacity as the famed .45-70 but its bottle-

neck helps smokeless powders burn more consistently.

By reducing the caliber to .40, one can increase ballistic performance without increasing recoil. For instance, a 400-grain .40 caliber bullet has comparable sectional density to a 500-grain .45 caliber roundnose. And a 300-grain .40 caliber flatnose roughly equals one weighing 400 grains in .45 caliber. With bullets of equal weight at equal velocities, a .40-70 should give a flatter trajectory and deeper penetration in large animals.

For two years now I've been experimenting with a variety of Sharps rifles in .40-70 caliber. An entire article would be required to cover all the handloading aspects of that round. However, I would like to touch on a few points. For one, cases are easily formed from any .45 basic case. RCBS can supply the proper forming dies. An alternative for economy-minded shooters is to run standard .45-70 cases into the .40-70 sizing die. The result is a perfectly formed .40-70 case that is .15 inch short. Considering the cost of .45-70 brass as opposed to .45 basic brass, this makes an attractive option. I have used both methods with no problems. The smokeless loads taken to Africa used the full length 2.25-inch cases.

Contrary to what one might think, there are plenty of bullets available in .40 caliber. For the bullet caster, such firms as NEI, Old West, P&C Shooting Specialties, SAECO and C. Sharps Arms offer moulds. Cast bullet weights range from P&C's 270-grain flatnose up to a very long NEI 410-grain roundnose.

Original Sharps rifles in .40-70 caliber had a nominal groove diameter of about .406 inch. The new Shiloh Sharps .40-70 has a groove diameter of .408 inch. To my knowledge, no one offers a cast bullet sizing die for .408 or .409 inch. Fortunately, .410-inch

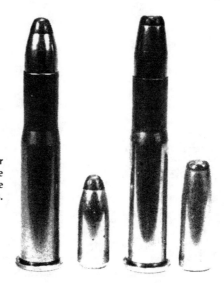

Two loaded .40-70 rounds and their Barnes bullets. The semi-pointed softnose on the left weighs 300 grains; the flatnose on the right, 400 grains.

dies intended for the .41 Magnum work perfectly. Experience taught me the proper as-cast bullet diameter should be at least .410. Some bullets as small as .406 were tested in my rifles but most keyholed and caused severe leading.

Jacketed .40-caliber bullets are not as plentiful. Barnes Bullets caters to those of us involved in odd and unique calibers. The Barnes catalog lists two .40-caliber softnoses: 300 and 400-grain bullets, .408 inch in diameter. Jacket thicknesses of .032 and .049 inch are available. Since working velocities of my .40-70 smokeless loads were still relatively low, my choice was the .032-inch jacket.

Speaking of velocities, it was my intention to boost speeds and pressures of the .40-70 well out of the black powder category. Since 1983, Shiloh Sharps rifles have been fitted with new smaller firing pins better suited to smokeless powder pressures. This greatly aided in developing high velocity .40-70 loads. The Shiloh Sharps are strong rifles, made of modern steels. Nevertheless, the makers don't recommend their products for experimentation.

After extensive handload development, a standard load was settled on for each jacketed bullet weight. With the 300-grain Barnes softpoint, a charge of 57.0 grains of IMR-4320 gives a full 2,195 fps from the 26-inch barrel.

Fifty grains of IMR-4064 behind the 400-grain Barnes chronographs at 1,750 fps. I estimate the pressures of such loads to be relatively mild. Primer pockets are still tight after dozens of firings and fired cases fall from the chamber if the muzzle is elevated. It must be emphasized that such loads are intended only for the modern Shiloh Sharps, not for replica Sharps of any other manufacture and certainly not for antique rifles.

Accuracy with both loads is exceptional considering the test rifles have only iron sights. Three-shot, 100-yard groups of 1 to 1¾ inches are common. Five-shot groups usually cluster under two inches.

Until the advent of the .375 H&H in

Only one of the 400-grain Barnes bullets fired was recovered. The one in the photo lanced through four feet of kudu. Its nose expanded to .56 caliber and it lodged in the off-flank. Range was about 130 yards.

this country, the .405 Winchester was the most powerful American cartridge. Published ballistics called for a 300-grain jacketed bullet at 2,200 fps, about the same as the souped up .40-70. The 400-grain load delivers 2,720 ft/lbs of energy while the 300-grain load generates about 2,940 ft/lbs. Some of my friends have dubbed this cartridge the .400 Sharps Smokeless.

My African hunt consisted of 10 days in the Transvaal (South Africa) and a brief two days in Zululand near the Indian Ocean. My host was Ed Vorster, of 30-30 Hunting Safaris, and the camp was located on his ranch near the Zimbabwe border.

When I uncased my .40-70 and handed it to Ed he asked, "What is it?" I replied proudly, "A newly made Sharps, like the old ones used in the American West."

Ed nearly burst my bubble when he handed the rifle back and said, "Never heard of it. Did you bring anything with a scope?"

That evening at dinner, my apprehensions mounted when Ed informed my professional hunter, Johann Van Rooyen, that I would be hunting with iron sights. Johann glanced at me dubiously but said nothing.

I had heard and read many stories about the abundance of game on the veldt. Some reported that you merely found the herd (of whatever species), then tried to stalk the biggest one. Others told of seeing hundreds, often thousands of animals in one day.

As luck would have it, my trip to the Dark Continent came at the tail end of a record breaking drought in the Transvaal. Animals were neither plentiful nor tame. For example, others who had hunted there previously told of casually shooting wart hogs for camp meat. The camp owner didn't even charge them. In 12 days of hunting I saw one male wart hog — and didn't get a shot at him. Impala are known as the most common of African antelope. Others told of shooting several on their trips. I saw exactly two rams without getting a shot, and we hunted four full days for impala only.

That is why the professionals were

Mike's kudu. Even though the 400-grain Barnes bullet angled from the right front shoulder to the left flank, the big animal ran about 100 yards before collapsing.

concerned about my hunting with an iron-sighted, single shot rifle. They felt I would be further handicapped in an already tough hunting situation. Then too, as they later informed me, most Americans are poor game shots, even with scope-sighted rifles. Since they had never guided a hunter with iron sights, they did not know what to expect.

As it turned out, the scarcity of game did not greatly detract from the enjoyment. We hunted in the true sense. At times we walked for hours from the safari car in hundred-plus degree temperatures. (When we left Montana there was snow on the ground!) That alone gave me an education in carrying a Sharps comfortably.

We rarely had an opportunity for more than one shot at any species so when a chance came, the action was fast and exciting. There was no time to dally, for if an animal escaped, we'd probably never see him again. This is where the quick-handling characteristics of the rifle and the simplicity of the sights were of great benefit.

During the 10 days in the Transvaal, I shot five animals. Three were taken with the .40-70: a wildebeest about 80 yards, a kudu about 130 yards and a zebra about 130 yards. All were one-shot kills made from the kneeling position.

In each instance, I had about five seconds or less to get off an aimed shot. One shot was all too, for the bush was thick and once the animal moved he was lost from sight. Therefore, a single shot rifle was not the least handicap.

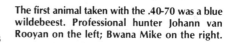

The first animal taken with the .40-70 was a blue wildebeest. Professional hunter Johann van Rooyan on the left; Bwana Mike on the right.

Neither was the peep sight. Ranges were short due to the thickness of the bush. I saw very few spots where shots over 200 yards would have been possible.

Only once did I decline to shoot because the animal was too far away for iron sights. In the last hour of the last day I refused a 200-yard shot at an impala. Not having wounded an animal up to that time, I was not about to attempt any chancy shots. If the hunt had been for record book animals, a scope would have helped judge the horns. I only wanted good heads, not great ones, so never felt the need for a scope.

During the two days in Zululand, Natal, I shot three more animals, two of which fell to the .40-70: a nyala about 140 yards and a reedbuck about 50 yards.

Originally I planned to use both 300 and 400-grain bullets. Upon arriving in the Transvaal, I zeroed the rifle dead on at 100 yards with the 400-grain load. Hunting was difficult and I was shooting pretty well, so the sights were never touched again. After shooting five animals with the 400-grain bullet however, I feel that perhaps the 300-grain might have been best for thin-skinned game.

The wildebeest was shot broadside, through the lungs. The exit hole was slightly larger than the entrance wound, and the animal ran about 75 yards. Next came the kudu. He was standing, quartering with his face toward me. The bullet hit the point of the right shoulder and lodged in the flank on the off side.

It penetrated some four feet of kudu. About a quarter inch of the bullet's nose expanded to .56 caliber. He still ran about 100 yards.

Third was the zebra stallion. He was standing broadside and the bullet took him through the heart. The exit wound was smaller than the entrance hole. He ran about 40 yards and piled up. My rug won't have large unsightly holes, but I would have preferred some bullet expansion.

The nyala, between a deer and elk in size, was the farthest away and the only animal requiring two bullets. The first shot hit a little far back, but still in the chest cavity. He never moved. The guide said not to shoot again; just wait. Those are famous last words. I put another through his shoulders and he dropped on the spot. Neither exit wound showed expansion.

Last was the reedbuck, about the size of a mule deer. He was hit through both shoulders, dropped on the spot, but required a .44-40 bullet from my Colt SAA for a finisher. His wound did not show signs of expansion either.

The problem centers around the moderate velocity of the 400-grain bullets. They will expand if they meet enough resistance but require more speed to be reliable. At 1,750 fps, recoil was stout, though. Both elk and deer have been shot with the 300-grain .40-70 load and expansion was evident, so from now on the 300-grain Barnes softpoint will be my mainstay on thin-skinned game.

When this trip started, I felt my .40-70 was the ultimate hunting Sharps but there is room for an improvement or two.

One would be a sling. Eight and one half pounds is not a great weight; that's about what an average scope-sighted rifle hefts. It's no big deal to carry one over your shoulder. Conversely, try carrying it in your hand hour after hour in 100+ degrees. Pretty soon your fingers start getting numb. After an hour or two, you jiggle it from one hand to the other every five minutes.

After two hours in that heat, I was carrying it by the barrel over my shoulder!

Noted firearms engraver Lynton McKenzie has mounted a sling on his Sharps and I have carried it a few times. His is the only Sharps I have ever seen so equipped. Mine will be the second.

Another needed improvement is the safety. I rarely carry a rifle loaded because I usually hunt on horseback at home. In Africa, the guides wanted me to be ready to shoot in an instant, but they admitted being uncomfortable with only a half cock for a safety. Therefore, I carried the gun with a round in the chamber, but with the breechblock pulled halfway open. The gun could not fire accidentally, but only required a quick move to close the lever and cock the hammer to be ready to shoot. Old English hammer rifles were often equipped with "stalking" safeties — a sliding piece of tool steel that locked into a recess in the hammer. It effectively locked it a half cock; but could be released simply by cocking the hammer. My friend, single shot riflesmith Ed Webber, puts them on his guns. Someday I am going to have him put one on mine.

One factory feature that made some of my shots possible is the double-set trigger. Many shooters don't like set triggers, and they do require some experience before you find yourself comfortable with them. I recall that, while aiming at the kudu from a kneeling position, the .40-70's muzzle began to waver. Taking a deep breath, I raised the barrel slightly and set the rear trigger. As the muzzle lowered and the post front sight showed against his shoulder, I touched the front trigger. A touch was all that was required, and we heard the bullet strike home.

In the end, I did get some satisfaction from my professional hunters. When Johann finished telling Ed about the .40-70's penetration of the kudu and showed him the recovered bullet, Ed looked at my rifle for a moment and said, "You know, that thing would be good enough for cape buffalo."

Someday I hope to find out. ●

CHAPTER
39

.405 Winchester

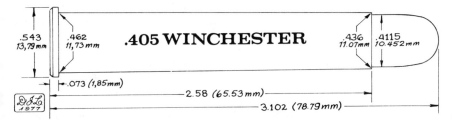

.543
13,79mm

.462
11,73mm

.405 WINCHESTER

.436
11.07mm

.4115
10.452mm

.073 (1,85mm)

2.58 (65.53mm)

3.102 (78.79mm)

DJL
1977

PRIOR TO 1886 American riflemen simply didn't have a truly powerful, long-range repeating (which meant lever-action in these days) rifle. The '76 Winchester was paired with the .45-75 and .50-95 cartridges, but their short, light bullets couldn't match the range and penetration of the .45-70 Government loads; and *that* was what hunters wanted. In 1886 they got it in the Winchester M-1886 and everybody (almost) was happy for a while. Then smokeless powder came along, so they wanted its advantages in a big-bore lever gun. Winchester had the M-1895 lever gun by then, and went to work to develop a powerful big-bore, smokeless cartridge for it. The result was the .405 Winchester, introduced in the M-95 in 1904.

Winchester succeeded better than they knew. Even with the powders of the day, the .405 drove a 300-grain jacketed bullet at 2,260 fps, virtually the same as the new .30-M1903 military cartridge. Muzzle

energy of the .405 was 3,400 fp, and at 100 yards it still struck with 2,250 fp. That put it way ahead of even the very best of the older American big-bores. Its 200-yard mid-range trajectory height of 6.3 inches made hitting at long range ridiculously easy compared to the .45-90 and .50-110 which had reigned supreme until then. Even the big black-powder, single-shot cartridges, like the .45-120-550 Sharps couldn't match the .405's performance near or far — *and*, the .405 came in a five-shot repeater of the traditional type familiar to every American rifleman.

Of course, the M-95 rifle was different from its predecessors, and some objected to its slab-sidedness, to the protruding Lee-type magazine, and to the method of loading. But they couldn't fault the cartridge, and accepted the rifle because of it. A few M-85 Winchester (high wall) single shots were chambered for the .405, as were a very few other-name unsuccessful rifles of the period. A few double

rifles in .405 came out of England and Europe — but, in the main, the M-95 was *the* .405 rifle.

Incidentally, I once ran across a M-98 U.S. Krag rifle with its original barrel rebored and rechambered to the .405. It functioned faultlessly (there may have been magazine alterations); it had a peep sight, the barrel was cut to 20 inches, and the original stock altered nicely to full Mannlicher style. A lovely little brush rifle, and I wish I'd traded for it when I had the chance. Maybe it's still down in east Texas where I ran across it.

The .405 case was rimmed and nearly cylindrical, with just slight body taper. Length was nominally 2.60 inches, and rim thickness was 0.70 inch, virtually the same as the .30-40. Base diameter lay midway between the .30-40, and .30-03, with the result that some call it a lengthened and straightened .30-40, while others call it a rimmed .30-03, straightened and slightly lengthened. Either is possible, but more likely it was simply a smokeless-powder development of the 1895 .40-72 Winchester whose external dimensions are the same. However, the 405 case is much stronger than the thin-walled .40-70.

The .405 bullet was jacketed, weighing 300 grains, and both soft-point and FMJ types were offered. Shape was blunt round-nose, with a diameter of .412-inch. Standard barrel twist was one turn in 14 inches, with groove and bore diameters of .413 inch and about .400-404 inch respectively.

The .405 was certainly adequate for any North American game; probably really too powerful for anything except the three big bears, but too much beats not enough. Quite a few .405, M-95 rifles went to

.405 Winchester Load Data

Bullet	Weight, grains	Powder	Weight grains	Velocity, fps
Lyman 412263	288	2400	20.0	1,430
Lyman 412263	288	Unique	16.0	1,475
Lyman 415175	300	2400	20.0	1,410
Lyman 415175	300	2400	16.0	1,460
Lyman 410214	181	Unique	10.0	- - - -
Lyman 41028	200	Unique	10.0	- - - -
Jacketed Soft Point	300	2400	24.0	1,440
Jacketed Soft Point	300	2400	26.0	1,545
Jacketed Soft Point	300	2400	32.0*	1,840
Jacketed Soft Point	300	3031	52.0	2,040
Jacketed Soft Point	300	3031	54.0	2,120
Jacketed Soft Point	300	3031	57.0*	2,250
Jacketed Soft Point	300	4320	52.0	1,905
Jacketed Soft Point	300	4320	62.0*	2,220

*Loads run over 45,000 c.u.p., which is considered today a bit much for the M-95 Winchester; their use isn't especially recommended for that reason, even though the M-95 was factory-chambered for cartridges (.30-06, etc.) working in the 50,000 c.u.p. range.

The .405 Winchester cartridge shown here is loaded with a Kynoch full metal jacket bullet.

Africa, and Theodore Roosevelt spoke very highly of its performance on lion and other big game there. It was popular enough among Africa-bound British sportsmen that Kynoch loaded the cartridge. It isn't well known, but in the early days of the .405/M-95, there simply wasn't any other that even approached its effectiveness.

U.S. makers dropped the .405 many years ago, and Kynoch did the same, a bit later. Unless you have a hoarded supply of cartridges, shooting depends upon handloading, and that depends upon cases. It still isn't too difficult to find a box of original loads among specialty ammunition dealers, even fired cases, but the price will be a bit steep. I've made many .405 cases from the Norma 9.3x 74R. Trim a bit over correct length, expand to a mouth I.D. of about .410 inch, then trim again to exact length, truing up the mouth in the process. The case *can* be loaded and fired at this point,

but headspace will be excessive; the 9.3mm rim is only about .050 inch thick, as opposed to the .405's .070-.071 inch. Drop the case over a steel rod held tightly in a vise, then peen the outer edge of the rim forward. Do this until the action closes *hard* on the case, and you'll be assured of tight headspace. For hunting use, do that first, *then* clean up the front of the rim so the breech *barely* closes on the case. Alternatively, you can buy .405 cases made by redrawing .30-40 brass to the correct length. Get them from Robert Pomeroy (Morison Avenue, East Corinth, Maine 04427).

Standard Large Rifle primers and several modern powders are suitable, but bullets are another matter. To the best of my knowledge, only Barnes Bullets, formerly Colorado Custom Bullets, (P.O. Box 215, American Fork, Utah 84003) currently offers a proper jacketed bullet for the .405. Order the *thin* jacket, or the

bullet won't expand at .405 velocities. Of course, you can have a set of dies made up and swage your own bullets but that's expensive. Cast bullets are fine, even for hunting. When the bullet is .412-inch in diameter, it does pretty well without expansion — but at 2,000 fps, a 1-10 to 1-16 lead bullet will usually expand at least some. Lyman No. 412263 weighs 288 grains and is intended for the .405; No. 15175 weighs 300 grains and has a flat nose which should do better on game. It can be sized down to .412-.414 inch without damage if a modern tapered die is available. Size bullets to at least groove diameter, but no more than .0015 inch over for best results.

Loading is no sweat — just like any other rimmed, straight-taper case. Use a stiff crimp on the bullet though, to avoid shifting under heavy recoil loads and to achieve consistent powder ignition and combustion. ●

CHAPTER
40

.404 JEFFERY

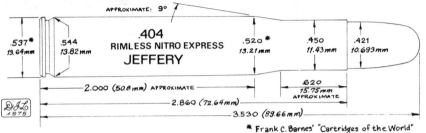

.404
RIMLESS NITRO EXPRESS
JEFFERY

.537* 13.64mm | .544 13.82mm | .520* 13.21mm | .450 11.43mm | .421 10.693mm

APPROXIMATE: 9°

2.000 (50.8mm) APPROXIMATE
.620 75.75mm APPROXIMATE
2.860 (72.64mm)
3.530 (89.66mm)

D.J.L. 1975

* Frank C. Barnes' "Cartridges of the World"

AROUND 1910, the renowned British gunmaking firm of Jeffery introduced a new, rimless, sporting cartridge suitable for the world's heaviest guns. Jeffery's aim was a cartridge equaling the desirable performance of the popular .450/.400 Nitro Express, but suitable for magazine rifles of Mauser type which the rimmed (flanged) .450/.400 was not.

The result was introduced as the .404 Jeffery, also identified as ".404 *Rimless Nitro Express*." Later, when continental ammunition makers produced cartridges to meet the inevitable demand occasioned by its excellent performance, it was given the metric designation "10.75x73mm". In typical metric fashion, this designated, first, the bullet diameter, and second the case length.

The new .404 case was of true rimless form with a base of nominal .544-inch diameter. In practice, the rim often measures as much as .010 inch less than base diameter, though intended to be the same. Length is nominally 2.860 inches. It is moderately bottle-necked with a shoulder diameter of .486-inch and a long neck measuring about .450-inch diameter when loaded. Bullet diameter is .421-inch

in some Kynoch loadings, sometimes as much as .423-inch in European loads.

Originally the .404 was supplied with 300-grain and 400-grain bullets in both solid and soft-point form. The lighter bullet was driven at 2,600 fps by 70 grains of full-length Cordite strands; the 400-grain bullet was pushed at 2,125 fps by 60 grains of Cordite. Primers were, of course, the Berdan type, typical of British big-bore express cartridges, and remained so in all Kynoch ammunition and in European cartridges until just recently.

With the excellent Kynoch solids, the .404 achieved excellent success on elephant, rhino, and buffalo. In fact, it is still widely used by Tanzanian game scouts for elephant control shooting. I saw many .404's (largely on original Magnum Mauser actions) in such use there during 1973. European solid loadings apparently used less-strong bullet jackets and were not highly regarded, though the soft-point loads were considered satisfactory.

Cogswell & Harrison (makers of my .404), Westley Richards, and several European makers produced .404 bolt-action rifles right up until the present. A

few single shots and doubles were reportedly chambered for the .404, but its rimless case caused extractor problems. Anyway, it merely duplicated the *flanged* .450/.400, so it possessed advantages *only* in bolt rifles.

Today, the only source of fresh .404 ammunition and components is Dynamit Nobel (910 17th St., N.W., Washington, D.C. 20006). Recent information indicates both cases and loaded cartridges and *perhaps* bullets are available on a limited scale. Sales are made through designated dealers, not the Dynamit Nobel office above. Incidentally, Dynamit Nobel cases are currently made for standard Large Rifle, Boxer primers, though older DWM, IWK, and RWS (combined under the DN name now) all utilized Berdan caps.

Mechanically, reloading the .404 is the same as for any big, rimless, bottle-neck case. Dies are available from RCBS and other makers on special order. However, components can be a problem. British or European cases require the appropriate Berdan primer and a Berdan decapper or hydraulic decapping. British caps can usually be obtained in small quantities from Oregon Ammunition Service (Box 19341, Portland, Oregon 97291) and European sizes from Godfrey Reloading Service (Box 688, Route 1, Brighton, Ill. 62012).

Keep in mind, though, that early-manufacture cases may contain or have been fired with *mercuric* primers. The result is a brittle, mercury-impregnated case. Such cases may fall apart during resizing, or, surviving that, rupture on firing. Such cases can be identified by squeezing the neck, which will feel abnormally hard and stiff, and probably collapse or shatter under the pressure.

Original cases are perfectly okay for reloading, subject to the above — but your best bet is new, Dynamit Nobel cases. If using old, fired cases, thorough cleaning and moderate neck/shoulder annealing (molten-lead method) are in order after decapping but before resizing to prolong their life.

If cases cannot be obtained from any other source, they can be made from .375 H&H brass. The H&H belt is about .010-inch smaller than the .404 base, while just ahead of the belt it is about .020-inch undersize. Soft, 1/2-inch inside diameter, .010-inch wall thickness brass tube can be pressed over the belt and head, from the front, to eliminate this. Use a 3/8-inch length of tubing, seated flush with the front edge of the extraction groove; then resize, polish off a bit of tube over the belt if necessary, expand case necks, and fire form with a moderate load to establish shoulder location and headspace. It's a lot of trouble, but will produce safe and functional cases if nothing else is available.

Load Data for .404 Jeffery

[.404 RIMLESS NITRO EXPRESS; 10.75x73mm]

	Bullet	Powder	Charge, [grs.]	Velocity, [fps]	Energy, [fp]
1.	Kynoch 300	IMR-3031	76.0	2,575	4,420
2.	Kynoch 400	IMR-3031	65.0	2,150	4,104
3.	Barnes 300	IMR-4895	75.0	2,550	4,332
4.	Lyman 419181 (285-grain lead)	SR-4759	26.0	1,400	1,240
5.	Lead 300	2400	22.0	1,400	1,305
6.	Lead 400*	2400	24.0	1,350	1,616
7.	Lead 400*	IMR-3031	63.0	2,125	4,010

Notes: Loads 4.5.6 should have tissue wad to hold powder against case head.

*Loads 6.7 can be used with Lyman No. 427103 bullet swaged down to .421/.423-inch diameter. cast of type metal.

Bullets are available, but not in a wide variety. Original Kynoch bullets can sometimes be found by diligent searching, and in solid form are preferable to all others, if you're heading for Africa. New, Dynamit Nobel bullets may also be found as previously mentioned. The most reliable source, though, is Colorado Custom Bullets (Route 1, Box 507, Montrose, Colo. 81401). Both solids and soft-points in proper weights and diameter are available in flat-base, round-nose form. They are made from copper-tube jackets available in two thicknesses, depending on jacket strength desired.

Cast lead bullets present a problem. Frank Barnes, in *Cartridges of the World* advises Lyman mould number 419181 of 285 grains weight, which would be heavy enough for targets and deer. Lyman 419180 (200 grains) could also be used for plinking — if you consider the .404 a plinking gun. For a heavier bullet, order Lyman 410219 *oversize,* then have the driving band grooves in the mould cavity bored out to nominal .423 inch diameter. Any *good* lathe operator can do this simply enough with a boring-bar setup. The resulting bullet will weigh about 400 grains and if cast hard enough (straight linotype metal) can be loaded to duplicate the 400-grain, jacketed-bullet, factory-load's performance.

Loading data for the .404 Jeffery is rather limited. Generally speaking, the old Cordite loads can be duplicated by slightly heavier charges of IMR-3031 or 4895. Thus, 65 grains of 3031 approximately duplicates the 60-Cordite/400-grain load's velocity of 2,125 fps. So, one could start with a 3031 charge equal in weight to the Cordite charge and work up carefully until Cordite-load velocity was reached.

In any event, the .404 is an excellent big-game cartridge. It possesses less muzzle energy than the .458 Winchester, but is in the same ballpark as the .375 H&H. Its bigger and heavier bullets, though, make its effects on game more nearly that of the .458 than the .375. If you have one, by all means load for it, and *use* it. ●

CHAPTER
41

.416 RIGBY

Al Miller

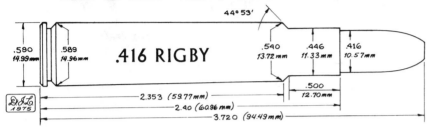

.416 RIGBY

44° 53'

.590 14.99mm | .589 14.96mm | .540 13.72 mm | .446 11.33mm | .416 10.57mm | .500 12.70mm

2.353 (59.77mm)
2.90 (60.96 mm)
3.720 (94.49mm)

DL 1975

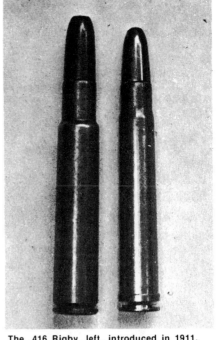

The .416 Rigby, left, introduced in 1911, is compared with the .375 H&H cartridge. As originally loaded with Cordite, the .416 drove a 410-grain bullet at 2,370 fps, producing 5,100 fp of energy at the muzzle; it quickly gained a reputation as an elephant killer.

THE SECOND decade of this century was a busy one for the old-line British gun-makers. London and Birmingham alike hummed with their activity. They were introducing new cartridge developments almost as rapidly as our own big companies did 40 to 60 years later.

Conservative Britain was then the impregnable fortress of big-bore, double express rifles and flanged cartridges, most of which had been born filled with massive charges of the old, reliable black powder. But, conservative or not, the London gun-makers aimed to be competitive with the rest of the shooting world. Smokeless propellants and the Mauser magazine rifle had by then proven themselves, even on the largest game. If modern sportsmen going on safari wanted these new gadgets, forsaking big-muzzled doubles and black powder, the Britishers would bloody well attend to their wishes.

In 1910, Jeffery had introduced his .404 Rimless Nitro Express (see *Handloader* 55); in 1909 Westley Richards had given the sporting world his big .425 Magnum; and Holland & Holland was known to be developing what was to become a perennial favorite and granddaddy of today's belted cases, the wonderful .375 Belted Rimless Magnum Nitro Express. All were for the M-98-type Mauser Magnum action and used the smokeless propellant determined best for tropical use by the British Army — Cordite.

John Rigby, London gun-maker supreme, wasn't about to be outdone by his contemporaries and in 1911 introduced his .416 Rigby. Of course, we may be giving old John a bit too much credit (the other makers as well) for there is evidence that Kynoch did most of the cartridge work. That venerable firm would take anyone's rough specifications and whip out a cartridge in short order, carrying whatever name one wished.

Be that as it may, the .416 Rigby soon earned quite a reputation as an elephant killer, which also meant it would lay out any other beast the world had to offer.

It drove a 410-grain bullet at 2,370 fps, producing 5,100 fp of energy at the muzzle. This performance matched the Westley Richards .425, and exceeded the .404 by a comfortable margin. Apparently because it is so similar to the .404, yet out-performs it substantially, the .416 is described in some references as a "modernized version of the .404". This can hardly be the truth since the two were introduced only one year apart.

Only the one bullet weight, 410 grains, was offered in both solid and soft-point form at equal velocities. Contemporary writers complained that Kynoch solids of

one period would penetrate elephant well without deforming, while those of another period might deform or "rivet" badly and veer off course. In spite of this, the .416 was the *ne plus ultra* of African-bound magazine rifles for many years. It required the magnum-length action. Double rifles are also reported in .416, though until rather recently rimless cases weren't considered suitable for the type.

The .416 case had less taper than its contemporary British brethren, along with a sharper shoulder and shorter neck. In those respects, it closely approached today's high-intensity designs. The case measures nominally .589-inch at the base and rim, with a neck diameter of .445 and a length of 2.90. Shoulder diameter is about .540, and overall loaded length is 3.720, making it the longest of British bolt-gun cartridges.

Differing from its contemporaries, the .416 is named from its actual bullet diameter, .416-inch. It was loaded, of course, with strands of Cordite stacked neatly in the case and topped with a card wad. Final necking of the case was probably done *after* the bundle of Cordite was inserted, as with some other bottle-neck British calibers of the period.

The .416 gained additional notice some years ago when it became evident that Roy Weatherby's .378 and .460 Magnums were essentially the .416 case with an H&H-type belt added.

Today .416 Rigby ammunition is both

Load Data for the .416 Rigby

Bullet	Weight, Grains	Powder	Charge, Grains	Velocity, [fps]	Energy, [fp]
1. Kynoch (Solid)	410	4350	95	2,300	4,813
2. Barnes (SP)	400	4350	95	2,300	4,696
3. Barnes (SP)	400	4895	80	- - - -	- - - -
4. Lead	350	2400	28	- - - -	- - - -
5. Lyman No. 412263	300	4759	25	1,400	1,305

Load four should make a comfortable plinking and small game combination with any hard, lead bullet from 300 to 400 grains weight.

dear and rare. Anyone planning much shooting will be forced into handloading. Mechanically this isn't much of a problem, for several makers can supply the appropriate dies. Components are another matter. Kynoch cases are okay if in good condition but require Berdan primers. The usual suppliers of such can sometimes come up with what you need, but not always. The original primer pocket is too large to alter for our Large Rifle size unless bushed with a section of .30-06 or similar case head.

As an alternative, one can simply turn off the belt and deepen the extractor groove of Weatherby .460 or .378 brass, then resize and trim to length. This makes as fine a case as one could want, and standard Boxer primers may be used in it. This is what I used for my own limited .416 shooting.

Several U.S. powders are suitable for full loads in the .416. The medium-to-slow burning rates are best — IMR-4895 down through IMR-4350.

Bullets can be the biggest problem. No other caliber uses jacketed types of .416-inch diameter. While doubtless other custom makers *could* make them if they chose, only Colorado Custom Bullets, Rt. 1, Box 507-B, Montrose, Colo. 81401 admits to doing so. It may take a while, but .416 bullets of proper weight may be had from that source.

I've never attempted to mould .416 bullets, but there are Lyman moulds for bullets that should be suitable (when properly sized) for the .416 Rigby in light to moderate loads. Frank Barnes (*Cartridges of the World*) recommends Lyman No. 412263, weighing 300 grains. Number 410219 (cast oversize) at 375 grains and 415175 at 300 grains should also be suitable.

If I were serious about lead-bullet shooting in this caliber, I'd get Lyman mould No. 410219, open it up to about .418 diameter and bore out every alternate lube groove to produce more driving band area and bring weight up to a bit over 400 grains. Cast from pure linotype, it should do the job and could be driven to nearly 2,000 fps.

Little tested loading data exists for the .416 Rigby and few rifles exist in this country. The attached data is gleaned from several sources, and is also generated by interpolation. ●

CHAPTER
42

A MODERN ORTY CALIBER: .416-338

By BOB HAGEL

The .416-338, center, is based on the .338/.458 cases. It has the same head to shoulder dimension and angle as the .338 Winchester Magnum at left, but is necked down from the .458 Winchester Magnum case because neck thickness is more uniform when cases are necked down than when expanded.

IT MAY COME as a surprise to many that the .40 caliber was once one of the most popular American cartridges. Most of these were of black powder persuasion; at least 28 different .40 caliber cartridges were chambered at one time or another before smokeless powder took over. Just after the transition to smokeless propellants, two more .40 calibers were developed. The .405 Winchester, introduced around 1904 in the Winchester Model 95 lever action rifle, was not only perhaps the most powerful cartridge ever used in a lever action, it became popular for hunting heavy game both here and in Africa. At the other extreme, Winchester developed the .401 rimless cartridge for use in their Model 10 autoloader. This short, fat round developed poor ballistics which made it one of the classic misfits of all time, and was never popular.

With a total of at least 30 .40 caliber cartridges in one form or another being used by American hunters for the heaviest game, including uncounted thousands of bison, from the mid-1870's until both the .401 and .405 Winchester cartridges became obsolete in 1936, it seems odd that no commercial .40 caliber has been developed on a modern case. It is even stranger in view of the fact that far more Americans are hunting in Africa than ever before — an area where a modern .40 would be quite useful for the larger game.

As for the usefulness of this caliber in Africa, the British developed and used no less than five cartridges in that bore,

including such famous big game numbers as the various .450-.400 rounds, and the potent and much-used .404 Jeffery and .416 Rigby. From Europe, and mostly of German origin, came at least nine more .40 caliber cartridges. Add another three military rounds and you come up with the astounding figure of 47 .40 caliber cartridges that have been used in various parts of the world.

Actually, you can add at least four more American black powder cartridges to this impressive list that are tabulated as .44 calibers but are actually under .43 bullet diameter. And this brings up another confusing point: What bullet diameter can be considered a true .40 caliber? Cartridge designations in this country didn't always run along the same lines as they do today, and those used by the British don't always run in true form either. When going through a list of American .40 cartridges it will be noted that they have bullet diameters ranging from a low of .403 to a high of .423. The British have bullet diameters ranging from .405 to .421. And the .425 Westly Richards, if you wish to consider this a .40 caliber, goes .435. To draw the line somewhere, we seem forced to consider everything from .403 to .430 as a .40 caliber. European 10mm cartridges also mostly run in the same diameter group.

From one angle it seems strange that so many wildcat cartridges have been

developed for the .375 and .45 calibers, yet so little attention has been given the .40 caliber by American gun buffs. But from another angle it is obvious that it may not be a lack of interest in the .40, but the fact that few bullets have been available in this caliber, and still aren't for that matter. The variation in actual bullet diameters among the so-called .40 caliber cartridges also muddied the waters for any wildcatter with aspirations in that direction.

One of the few .40 wildcats developed in this country on a modern case, and the only one that I know of to gain any degree of popularity, was the .424 OKH wildcat line, developed from the mid-1930's to the early '50's. This cartridge was actually made in both a long and short version, but few of the short cartridges were ever used. The long cartridge was used by several hunters in Africa, and Don Hopkins, one of its designers, had great success with it for many species of African game, and his wife Marge used it on several safaris for her "heavy rifle."

The original intent when developing the .424 OKH, was to use the .416 diameter bullet, but at that particular time they were almost impossible to obtain in this country. Bullets for the .404 British Jeffery were available so barrels were cut to fit it. While some sources list the .404 bullet has having a diameter of .421, Fred Barnes later made bullets for the .424

The .416-338 kicks up nearly 70 foot pounds of free recoil in Hagel's 9.5-pound rifle. This photo was taken just after recoil peak; the muzzle does not climb excessively during recoil due to the straight stock and heavy muzzle.

and trying to take the glory. To this I say "horsefeathers!" It is simply a matter of more than one individual working on the same project at the same time without knowing someone else is doing likewise. (*Editor's Note — Similarly, Ken Waters and John Wootters independently have been doing some work along the same lines.*)

Jake wanted a bullet diameter of .408 as a true .40 caliber, but there were no bullets of that diameter available. Colorado Custom Bullets were available in .411 for the .405 Winchester cartridge in 400-grain weight in both .032 and .049 jacket thickness in round nose, soft point design, as well as in full-patch or solid form. However there was some question as to how well the soft copper jackets on the solid bullet would hold up on African buffalo and elephant. There was always the chance that a few Kynoch steel jacket 400-grain .416 bullets for the .416 Rigby could be found, so that barrel diameter was chosen. C.C.B. also produces 400-grain .416 bullets in solid and soft point form with .049 jackets, and a 400-grain round nose and a 300-grain semi-spitzer with .032 jackets.

I had Bill Hobaugh, top-flight barrel maker of Philipsburg, Montana, make up a .416 barrel and chamber it for the .416-338 cartridge, then fit it to a Remington M-700 BDL long action. (Actually, we should call it the .416-458 because we neck down .458 Winchester cases instead of expanding .338 brass, as neck thickness is more uniform this way.) The barrel is 24 inches long and measures .750 at the muzzle with a straight taper from about four inches forward of the receiver ring. This gives enough barrel weight to give a high degree of accuracy and help damp the considerable recoil, yet makes the rifle light enough for hunting — 9½ pounds empty and mounted with a Leupold M-8 3X scope in M-3 mounts.

RCBS made up excellent dies for the cartridge, including form dies to neck the .458 brass. It was found, however, that the full length resizing die did the form job well without the aid of a special form die, when using new .458 W-W brass.

OKH which mike .423 but were used in the original barrels. I don't have a .404 bullet of British manufacture, so can't say what the true diameter is.

Both of the .424 OKH cartridges were made from .375 H&H brass; the long one with the case left full length and blown out in body somewhat, and the short version cut to an overall case length of 2.60 inches. The short case was of about the same body length to the shoulder as the .338 Winchester Magnum case but with a longer neck.

While some wildcatter may have worked with a .40 caliber cartridge in recent years, I was not aware of it until Robert Chatfield-Taylor wrote on his experiments and experience with the .338 Winchester case expanded to take the .416 Rigby bullet, in another gun magazine. Winchester made up that rifle for Taylor, and he used it successfully on an African hunt. While he did give some loading data in the article, he did not go into that aspect to a great extent.

Apparently at about the same time that Taylor was visualizing the .416-338, others were toying with the same idea. My long time friend, hunting companion, and knowledgeable gun buff Carl Jacobson, and I had discussed the merits

of the same cartridge around several campfires more than a year before the Taylor article appeared. Inasmuch as Taylor got around to having a rifle made up before ours was finished, some of his load data was used as a base, then expanded to include other powders and bullets.

This brings to mind something that has always amused and/or disgusted me greatly. As this incident shows, it often happens that two or more wildcatters come up with the same cartridge idea at the same time. Then some of them howl long and loudly that the other fellow stole their design, or were simply copying it

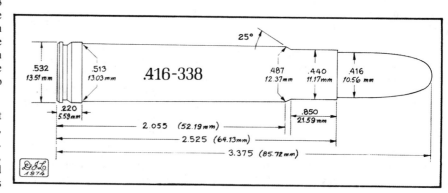

.416-338

.532 13.51mm
.513 13.03mm
25°
.487 12.37mm
.440 11.17mm
.416 10.56mm
.220 5.59mm
.850 21.59mm
2.055 (52.19mm)
2.525 (64.13mm)
3.375 (85.72mm)

D.L. 1974

After stocking the rifle with a good piece of plain but strong French walnut, complete with cross-bolt to eliminate possible splitting of the recoil abutment, and also glass bedding of this area, load testing was started. It was found that the top loads Taylor had used in his Winchester-built rifle were a little hot in this Hobaugh barrel and chamber, so we dropped back and developed our own.

Most cases in this capacity range do well with the faster powders like 3031 with even the heavier bullets, so this powder was tried first. While a maximum load with pressures just below the belt-expanding point gave the 400-grain C.C.B. .049 jacket bullet a velocity of 2,319 fps MV ahead of 68 grains of IMR-3031, accuracy was not outstanding at 2 inches over 100 yards. The charge was cut to 66 grains, which dropped velocity only 43 fps, and groups ran exactly the same size. I had a notion the barrel would do better than that, and a maximum charge of 74 grains of 4320 proved it by dropping group size to 1 3/8-inch.

Wondering what could be done with a slow powder like 4350, it was found that a maximum pressure load could not be used because the case lacked capacity. A charge of 79 grains proved to be all the 400-grain bullet could be seated over, and gave a velocity of only 2,230 fps; this is still a potent load running just over 1-inch groups at 100 yards. This seemed to indicate that a powder of about this burning rate, but dense enough to be loaded in heavier charges, might be the answer, so Norma 204 was tried. It did

The 300-grain semi-spitzer and 400-grain round nose Colorado Custom bullets were tested in the .416-338 wildcat. The 300-grain gave rather poor accuracy in this rifle, but the 400-grain did well with all powders and charges.

quite well in the accuracy department at 1 9/16-inch, and delivered 2,361 fps with 83 grains.

Giving this information a hard look, it was decided that Norma 203 should prove about the ultimate for this case with this bullet. This proved to be a correct assumption, and 76 grains delivered 2,438 fps, with a group size of 1 3/8-inch. This is indeed a potent package that develops almost 5,300 foot pounds of muzzle energy! It also delivers a good helping of energy on the other end with some 70 foot pounds of free recoil from this 9½ pound rifle!

It seemed that under certain conditions, a lighter, faster, flatter-shooting bullet with better ballistic shape might be useful, so loads were worked up for the semi-spitzer Colorado Custom 300-grain bullet. It was obvious that this light bullet would require fairly fast powders for the kind of velocity that would make the 300-grain bullet useful, so both 3031 and 4198 were tried. A charge of 73 grains of 3031 was near maximum and delivered 2,646 fps, but accuracy was pretty sour at 3 1/8 inches. The faster IMR-4198 was not quite as fast with 2,588 fps with 66 grains, but accuracy was somewhat better at 2 1/8 inches. However, if one intended to use the

lighter bullet it would be for smaller animals at longer ranges, and neither the accuracy nor velocity with this short, fat bullet make it especially desirable for this kind of shooting.

As this case is a little larger in shoulder diameter than the short .424 OKH, it probably gives higher velocity due to slightly more powder capacity. It also delivers as much velocity as the long version of the .424 OKH, but may be loaded to higher pressures. While I shot the .424 OKH cartridges a good deal, I did not work up the loads that were chronographed, so do not know what pressure levels they were loaded to. Also, the .458 case has a heavier web section than the older .375 cases, so will likely stand more pressure without showing it if case hardness is equal.

Thinking in terms of factory loaded cartridges, the .416-338 compares favorably with any of the smokeless powder .40's made anywhere in the world. Assuming that the British ballistic dope is correct for the barrel length of the hunting arms in which their cartridges were used, we find that their most

The .416-338, center, is compared to two of its predecessors, left, the .424 OKH Short, and .424 OKH Long. To the right of the .416-338 are the .375 H&H Magnum and the newer .458 Winchester Magnum, two of the most successful commercial cartridges for hunting the world's largest game. The .416-338 delivers almost 5,300 foot pounds of muzzle energy, the .375 gives 4,330 and the .458 churns up 5,100.

The Colorado Custom 400-grain soft point bullet with .049-inch jacket thickness is shown here with two bullets expanded by firing into damp silt and sand packed in a cardboard box. These bullets penetrated about 18 inches of this material. While expansion, retained core and remaining weight may not be the same on bullets taken from game, it does give some idea of what can be expected. The range was 25 feet.

powerful .40 calibers, the .416 Rigby and the .425 Westly Richards, both deliver muzzle energies of 5,100 foot pounds. This is a bit less than the top loads in the .416-338.

From the handloading angle, however, the .416 Rigby is far underloaded by our standards, as one would suspect by the powder capacity of the big case. Knowing that Jack O'Connor had done a good deal of reloading for the .416 Rigby with American powders and bullets, I questioned him about his loads, and he gave me the following information for the 400-grain Barnes (Colorado Custom) bullets: Using H-4831 in the big Rigby case he received 2,450 fps with 105 grains, and a charge of 110 grains gave 2,600 fps. He says pressures were not high even with the heavier charge. The 2,600 fps load would kick up 6,000 foot pounds of muzzle energy!

To compare the .416-338 with other potent cartridges that are considered highly successful for the heaviest of all game, let's take a look at two favorites for African hunting, the venerable .375 H&H and the newer .458 Winchester. The .375 boots a 300-grain bullet along at 2,550 fps for a muzzle energy of 4,330 fp. The .458 starts the 500-grain bullet at 2,150 and churns up 5,040 fp of energy. These are factory quoted ballistics, and in some loads may be boosted a little. But any way you look at it, the .416-338 wildcat rates along with our most powerful commercial numbers, with, of course, the exception of the huge .378 and .460 Weatherby cartridges.

The gap between the .375 and .458 caliber cartridges is the largest in the American cartridge line, which may lead one to wonder when it will be filled with a .40 caliber by one of the big cartridge/rifle manufacturers. Of course the birth of a new commercial cartridge always hinges on its potential sales — and a .40 caliber would not have great appeal to the hunter of American game. You don't need that kind of bullet diameter, penetrating ability with solid bullets, or the power it develops. But it would, I'm sure, carry a lot of appeal for the increasing numbers who hunt the large and dangerous African game.

It may be of interest that one of the big rifle-ammunition makers has had such a cartridge on the drawing board for several years. While I've seen the specs on this cartridge, it is hard to say what form the final cartridge will take if and when it does appear. But I wouldn't be greatly surprised if it closely approximates the .416-338 wildcat, both in appearance and ballistic performance. ●

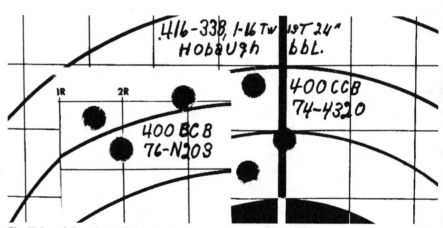

The Hobaugh barrel and Colorado Custom bullets give outstanding accuracy from a cartridge of this power loaded full throttle. These 100-yard groups were fired from the bench; the target grid is laid out in one inch squares. These two three shot groups are about average for the many fired.

.416-338 Load Data

.416-338 Remington M-700 action, Hobaugh 24-inch barrel 1-16 twist.
W-W .458 Winchester cases weighed 228 grains primed. CCI No. 250 primers.
Oehler No. 31 Chronotach, Oehler No. 50 photoelectric screens.
Velocity at 15 feet converted to MV. Temperature 70 degrees.

Bullet	Powder	Charge	Velocity	Energy	Remarks
400-grain C.C.B.	IMR-3031	68	2,319	4,772	2" at 100 yards
round nose — .049	IMR-3031	66	2,276	4,576	2"
jacket thickness	IMR-4320	74	2,373	5,000	1 3/8" extremely uniform
	IMR-4350	79	2,230	4,416	1 1/16" compressed to limit
	N-204	83	2,361	4,948	1 9/16"
	N-203	76	2,438	5,276	1 3/8" uniform 5,300 fp!
300-grain C.C.B.	IMR-3031	73	2,646	4,665	3 1/8"
semi-spitzer — .032	IMR-4198	66	2,588	4,461	2 1/8"
jacket thickness					

Comparison with commercial factory loaded cartridges made famous by successful use on world's largest game.

Cartridge	Velocity	Energy
.375 H&H 300-grain	2,550	4,330 fp
.458 Winchester 500-grain	2,150	5,040 fp
.404 Jeffery 400-grain	2,125	4,020 fp
.416 Rigby 410-grain	2,370	5,100 fp

CHAPTER
43

John Kronfeld

WITH TODAY'S interest in .416 caliber rifles (.416 Rigby, .416 Remington Magnum and .416 Weatherby), the thought of putting together a high power .416 lever action rifle has crossed my mind more than a few times. At the 1990 SHOT Show, Editor Dave Scovill pulled me aside. "John old horse, you've written about the .450 and .50 Alaskan lever action cartridges [cartridges based on a necked up and blown out .348 Winchester case]. With today's interest in the .416s, a high-power .416 lever action is a natural." That did it, with Dave's words in mind, this project was initiated. After the fact, it could best be described as a logistic nightmare.

The Winchester Model 71 used for the .450 and .50 Alaskan projects (*Handloader* Nos. 140 and 143) was returned to Harry McGowen (McGowen Rifle Barrels, Rte. 3, St. Anne IL 60964) for rebarreling and chambering to .416 Alaskan. Since there are no

established dimensions for a .416 Alaskan I coordinated with Clymer Tool Company (1645 W. Hamlin Rd., Rochester Hills MI 48309-3368) through McGowen on dimensions for this new wildcat.

It is important to note that, based on the large .348 Winchester case, a new cartridge can be designed for just about any bullet diameter up to .512. Cartridges may have varying degrees of body taper, neck length and shoulder angle (the cartridge headspaces on its rim). These new dimensions will decide case capacity and in turn velocity and energy.

"Improved" normally connotes a cartridge with minimum body taper, sharper shoulder angle and a shorter case neck, increasing powder capacity 5 to 10 percent over the parent cartridge. Reduced body taper also reduces bolt thrust which is especially undesirable in lever-action rifles. Improved cartridges may require modifications to the feeding system in lever-action rifles. This is due to their

sharp shoulder angles and less body taper.

Keeping the aforementioned in mind led to the new cartridge having more body taper and a longer neck than the .450 Alaskan — slightly less powder capacity. This is opposed to the Improved configuration with maximum case capacity. My reasoning was that the energy levels of the .450 and .50 Alaskan cartridges are more than enough for a brush gun. I was trying to stay at or slightly below their energy levels of 4,000 foot-pounds of muzzle energy.

Now the real fun starts. What do we use for jacketed bullets in a .416 lever-action rifle? Barnes, Jensen, Hornady, A-Square, Swift, Speer and Trophy Bonded all make .416 bullets. They are, with exception of the Trophy Bonded solids, spitzer, semi-spitzer or round-nose. As I have preached before on bullet form in heavy-recoil, lever-action rifles with tubular magazines, anything but a wide, flatnose is suicide.

.416 Alaskan/

The parent .348 Winchester (left) is shown with its offspring, the .416 Alaskan (center) and the .416-348 Improved (right).

Enter the spirit of cooperation. Jack Carter of Trophy Bonded Bullets (PO Box 262348, Houston TX 77207) modified a small run of 400-grain Bear Claw bullets so the meplat is wider than the Large Rifle primer pocket. Tests show this bullet will expand at striking velocities down to 1,700 fps.

Randy Brooks, of Barnes Bullets (PO Box 215, American Fork UT 84003), made a special run of 400-grain, wide, flatnose .416 bullets for this project. With a .032-inch jacket, they will expand very well and, as usual, they are accurate. A-Square Lion Load bullets had their round lead noses machined off just forward of the jacket creating a wide, flatnose bullet.

Most of the jacketed bullets tested did not have a cannelure or have one at the right location. This was remedied by Dave Corbin of Corbin Bullet Swaging Equipment (PO Box 2659, White City OR 97503). Corbin supplied a .416 cannelure wheel and shims for one of his

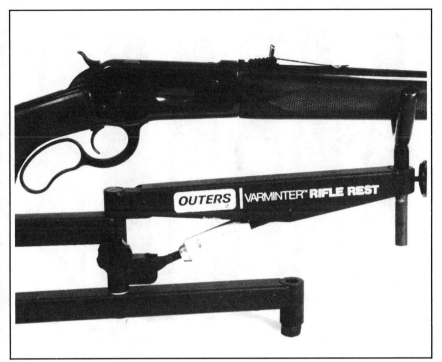

The converted Winchester Model 71 was fired from an Outers Rifle Rest during accuracy trials.

hollow pipe with .75 inch overall diameter over the link.

Bill Keyes of RCBS solved the problem of aligning the oversize gas checks as they enter the small sizing die by cutting a pocket into the top of the die for the .44 gas checks to rest in. As a bullet forces the gas check into the die, they become flush and enter symmetrically. Cast bullet accuracy is excellent with no signs of leading at tested velocities.

Obtaining loading dies was the easiest part of this project. After establishing chambering dimensions, a drawing was sent to RCBS. From this drawing, RCBS made a perfect set of dies. It was easier, faster and less expensive to make dies this way than from a chamber casting.

Because .416 jacketed bullets are so expensive, fireforming proceeded with 360-grain cast bullets over 51 grains of IMR-3031. Cases are trimmed to 2.18 inches and the Powley Computer was used to generate loading data. The

416-348 Improved

PCM-1 Power Cannelure Machine tools that is at my disposal. The machine does an excellent job rolling cannelures in a matter of seconds on each bullet. Shims allow the cannelure to be applied at the desired point on the bullet shaft.

Bullet moulds incorporating gas checks from LBT (360 and 400 grains with wide, flatnose) and Colorado Shooter's Supply (400-grain, two-diameter, wide, flatnose) give excellent results. Guess what? There are no .416 gas checks available at present.

That's OK, .44 caliber gas checks can be swaged down without too much trouble. Put a handful of gas checks in a colander and have at them with a propane torch. Shake the colander around as if you were flipping hotcakes while applying the heat. After all have discolored, let them air cool. You have just annealed the gas checks. Many cast bullet target shooters do this. It will now require less force and reduce

bullet distortion as gas checks are applied to these cast bullets.

There is another problem with swaging .44 gas checks to .417. The magnitude of force required to push a .44 gas check into a .417 sizing die is greater than the handle of the Lyman No. 450 cast bullet sizing tool can take without snapping where it meets the link. This is fixed by sliding an 18-inch

computer (slide rule) does an excellent job, as it did for the .450 Alaskan, selecting IMR-3031 for the 360-grain lead bullet and IMR-4320 for all other tested bullets.

Loading data and performance is shown in the data section. The 360-grain bullet just makes it to 2,060 fps and 400-grain bullets to 1,850 fps from a 20-inch barrel. This is only

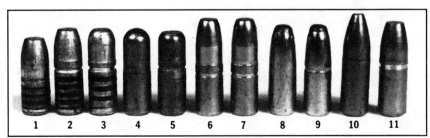

Cast bullets used for load development include the (1) 360-grain LBT, (2) 420-grain LBT and (3) 410-grain Hoch. Jacketed bullets featured the 400-grain A-Square, (4) before and (5) after the lead tip was removed; 400-grain Trophy Bonded Solid, (6) before and (7) after the cannelure was added; the 400-grain Barnes, (8) before and (9) after it was modified by Barnes to function in the tubular magazine; and 400-grain Trophy Bonded (10) before and (11) after manufacturer modification.

3,391/3,039 foot-pounds of muzzle energy, respectively, too far from the .450 Alaskan and .50 Alaskan energies.

As stated earlier, the decision was made to form this cartridge with a conservative Alaskan shape. Recalling the words from the song "Mac the Knife," "could it be our boy's done something wrong." Maybe, just maybe, I was too conservative in selecting the body taper and case neck dimensions. I guess I'm not a very good designer, nor did I ever think velocities and energy levels would be that much lower than the .450 Alaskan.

After the fact, and doing some research, (I should have done a little more homework before I plunged into this project) the cartridge should have had a minimum body taper and shorter neck — an Improved configuration — to approach the 4,000 foot-pound muzzle energy level.

P.O. Ackley shows a similar cartridge in his book of wildcat cartridges, the .400-348 Improved (Ackley) using .411 bullets. It drives a 400-grain bullet at 2,100 fps from a 24-inch barrel giving 3,938 foot-pounds of muzzle energy. Except for the difference in barrel lengths, that was my goal for this cartridge.

The .416 Alaskan rifle was then sent to Redmans' Gun Shop in Omak, Washington, where the chamber was enlarged with a .348 Improved (Ackley) reamer. Simultaneously loading dies for a .348 Improved (Ackley) with .416 neck dimensions were ordered from RCBS. Fortunately, the dimensions of the dies matched the new chamber.

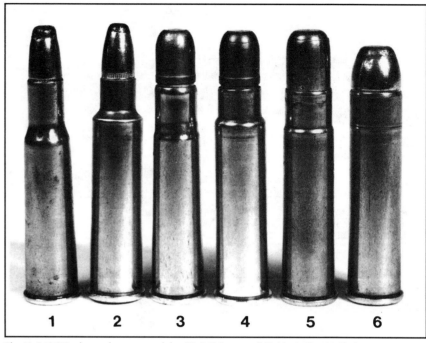

The (1) .348 Winchester has spawned the (2) .348 Improved (Ackley), (3) .416 Alaskan, (4) .416-348 Improved, (5) .450 Alaskan and the (6) .50 Alaskan.

Switching chamber dimensions in midstream only took two weeks.

The .416 Alaskan brass was fireformed again up to .416-348 Improved with the original fireforming load; none of the cases split. It also should be noted that my rifle did not require any modification to the feeding mechanism.

Water capacities of the .416 Alaskan were 84.4 grains to the case mouth. The Improved version holds 91.5 grains (the .348 Winchester case holds 62.2 grains; the .348 Improved (Ackley) and .450 Alaskan both hold 90 grains). This is an 8.5 percent increase in case capacity. Now, the Improved version of my .416 lever action, with 360-grain cast bullets, is in the same 4,000+ foot-pound range as the .450 and .50 Alaskan.

It is difficult to compare the .416 Alaskan and .416-348 Improved to the big .416 bolt-action cartridges that have created such a commotion. They are different concepts for different jobs. The bolt-action cartridges hold twice as much powder as these lever-action cartridges and have working pressures in the 55,000 CUP range. Lever-action cartridges on the Winchester or Browning Model 71 actions have a maximum working pressure of 44,000 CUP. The bolt-action cartridges are also meant for game of far greater proportions with

thick hides that have no equal on this continent. Those considering a .416 lever action must face reality. The performance levels of the .416 bolt-action cartridges is not attainable with the .416 lever-action cartridges.

That's OK; it is my humble opinion that the .416 bolt-action cartridges are best suited for Africa. At 5,100 to 7,500 foot-pounds of muzzle energy, depending on the cartridge and bullet weight, they are pure overkill on this continent (how did we ever get along all these years without the .416s, or have we been doing it wrong all these years?). In close cover you could never recover fast enough for a quick second shot if one is required. It is also my opinion that few people can or want to subject themselves to that magnitude of recoil. As I stated in the .50 Alaskan article, "if you can't do it with 4,000 foot-pounds of muzzle energy, on this continent in close cover, you've got big problems."

Reviewing ballistics and bullet sectional densities leads me to the following conclusions for the .416 lever gun. A 400-grain bullet, with sectional density of .330 also is overkill for North American hunting. Popular North American cartridges like the .300 Winchester Magnum, .338 Winchester Magnum, .35 Whelen and .375 H&H Magnum have sectional densities and

RCBS supplied the bullet sizing and case forming dies for the .416 Alaskan and .416-348 Improved.

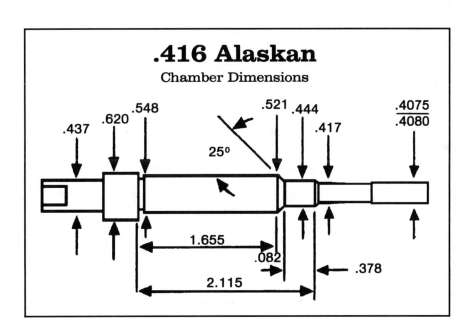

.416 Alaskan
Chamber Dimensions

.437 .620 .548 .521 .444 .417 .4075 / .4080

25°

1.655 .082 .378

2.115

bullet weights of .271/180, .313/250, .279/250, and .305/300, respectively. The .450 Alaskan, which did so well in close cover uses a 400-grain bullet with a sectional density of .272. Therefore, it appears that the .360-grain cast bullet with a sectional density of .295, higher muzzle velocities and energies and flatter trajectory is the best choice.

After weeks of logistic windmills and 850 rounds off the bench, one must ask the critical question, How good is the .416 Alaskan or the .416-348 Improved? And, How good are they next to the .450 and the .50 Alaskans?

On their own, the .416 lever-action cartridges will provide excellent performance on all North American game out to 100 to 125 yards. The .416 Alaskan is superior to other commercial lever-action cartridges like the .348 Winchester, .375 Winchester, .444 Remington and the .45-70 Government.

The .416-348 Improved is in a class by itself. At close range it is as powerful as any of the conventional or wildcat lever-action cartridges and most bolt-action cartridges through the .338 Winchester Magnum. Still, if one is going to go to the trouble of modifying a Model 71 rifle, one must study alternatives such as the .450 and .50

Table I						
Exterior Ballistic Comparison						
	muzzle	muzzle	sectional	100 yards		
cartridge (grains/bullet)	velocity (fps)	energy (ft/lb)	density	velocity (fps)	energy (ft/lb)	recoil (ft/lb)
.348 Winchester 250/Barnes	2,134	2,541	.295	1,894	2,001	22.56
.348 Improved (Ackley) 250/Barnes	2,412	3,246	.295	2,143	2,565	30.06
.35 Whelen 250/Speer	2,400	3,214	.279	2,066	2,369	26.80
.444 Marlin 265/Hornady	2,200	2,894	.205	1,801	1,910	29.25
.45-70 400/Speer	1,866	3,108	.272	1,536	2,106	42.3
.416 Alaskan 360/LBT	2,088	3,484	.297	1,741	2,424	35.12
.416 Alaskan 420/LBT	1,885	3,319	.346	1,605	2,402	38.2
.416- 348 Improved 360/LBT	2,244	4,025	.297	1,877	2,815	39.4
.416- 348 Improved 400/A-Square	2,041	3,699	.330	1,779	2,801	40.0
.450 Alaskan 400/Speer	2,088	3,872	.297	1,744	2,702	41.5
.50 Alaskan 450/Barnes	1,944	3,755	.245	1,684	2,834	44.7

Be alert — Publisher cannot accept responsibility for errors in published load data.

Alaskans. These cartridges have a few more things going for them, diameter and off-the-shelf availability of suitable (flatnose) jacketed bullets.

There is an easy way to make this comparison. Use John Taylor's (famous African hunter) Knockout Factor formula: bullet weight in pounds × muzzle velocity × bullet diameter in inches.

Table II

Knockout Factor

cartridge	bullet weight (grains)	muzzle velocity (fps)	Taylor's Knockout Factor
.348 Winchester	250	2,130	26.47
.416 Alaskan	360	2,060	44.07
.416 Alaskan	400	1,850	43.97
.416 Improved	360	2,244	48.12
.416 Improved	400	2,000	47.54
.450 Alaskan	400	2,100	54.96
.50 Alaskan	485	1,980	70.23

From the figures in Table II, it is obvious that starting from scratch the .50 Alaskan is the way to go. Maybe Harold Johnson, originator of the .50 Alaskan, really did know what he was doing. Yet, for those who can't resist the new aura of the .416s, willing to hunt with cast bullets or modified jacketed bullets, the .416 Alaskan or .416-348 Improved, are excellent cartridges and will serve you well. ●

Table III

Loading Data

powder	charge (grains)	velocity (fps)	sectional density	remarks
.416 Alaskan				
360-grain LBT				
IMR-4895	57	1,965	22.0	2½ inches, starting load
	60	2,036	8.3	1 inch, very accurate, maximum
IMR-4064	57	1,895	28.0	1¾ inches, starting load
	59	2,130	3.6	1¼ inches, best load this bullet
IMR-4320	57	1,809	18.5	2 inches, starting load 60
	60	2,088	21.1	1½ inches, maximum
400-grain Trophy Bonded (modified)				
IMR-4895	52	1,773	27.2	1½ inches, starting load
	54	1,830	42.0	1¾ inches, maximum
420-grain LBT				
IMR-4895	52	1,846	25.0	1¾ inches, start at 50 grains
IMR-4064	53	1,885	17.5	2¼ inches, hot, start at 51 grains
410-grain Hoch				
RL-15	55	1,785	18.2	1¾ inches, starting load
	57	1,873	12.1	1¾ inches, maximum load
.416-348 Improved				
360-grain LBT				
IMR-4064	59	1,960	22.0	2 inches, starting load
	61	2,010	18.6	1¾ inches
	62	2,085	14.0	1¾ inches
	63	2,155	20.0	2 inches
	64	2,202	24.0	2 inches
	65	2,244	21.0	1¾ inches, best hunting load
400-grain Trophy Bonded (modified)				
IMR-4064	57	1,860	9.0	¾ inch, very accurate
	58	1,905	11.0	¾ inch, very accurate
	59	1,961	21.0	¾ inch, very accurate
400-grain Sledgehammer solids				
IMR-4064	57	1,903	41.1	2¼ inches, starting load
	60	1,979	4.2	1 inch, maximum
400-grain A-Square Lion Load (modified)				
IMR-4064	57	1,863	15.7	1½ inches, starting load
	60	2,041	21.0	1¾ inches, maximum
400-grain Barnes flatnose (special order)				
IMR-4064	57	1,890	27.1	1¾ inches, starting load
	60	2,015	29.0	1½ inches, maximum
410-grain Hoch				
IMR-4064	57	1,874	20.0	1¾ inches, starting load
	60	2,035	22.0	1⅝ inches, maximum — hot

Notes:
1. All primers Federal 210 Large Rifle.
2. Velocities with PACT, centerline of screens 10 feet from muzzle.
3. Because of variations in chamber and bullet ogive dimensions, all loading data should be approached with caution and starting loads should be reduced by 5 percent.
4. Velocities are from 20-inch barrel, add 15 fps/inch estimating velocities from longer barrels.

Be alert — Publisher cannot accept responsibility for errors in published load data.

CHAPTER
44

THE .416 TAYLOR WILDCAT IN AFRICA

By JOHN WOOTTERS

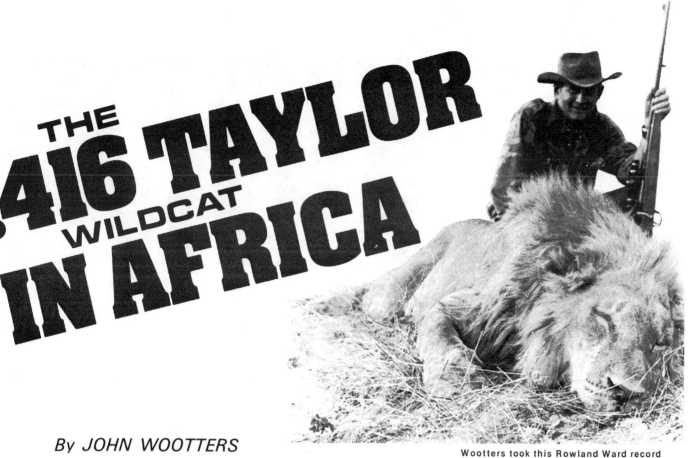

Wootters took this Rowland Ward record
lion in Botswana with the .416 Taylor wildcat.

THE .416 TAYLOR is a wildcat cartridge for heavy game which was originated, to the best of my knowledge, by writer Bob Chatfield-Taylor. He reported on development, loading, and field-testing the cartridge in Africa in a 1973 issue of another firearms magazine.

His article was fascinating, but failed to detail much of the load development work and did little more than state that the cartridge proved effective on dangerous game.

In the March-April 1974 issue of *Rifle*, Bob Hagel reported on his extensive experiments with this same cartridge, but he called it the ".416-338". Loading data with six powders and two different bullet weights were presented, and Hagel's customary thorough, knowledgeable analysis of the potentials of the cartridge shed new light on it.

In the meantime, Ken Waters and I had both been working with rifles chambered to this round, and had exchanged correspondence on our results. In the July-August 1974 issue of *Handloader*, Waters authored a report on the .416 Taylor. As usual, his load development work was comprehensive, embracing just about every propellant which might be suitable

The .416 Taylor proved effective against African elephant, with enough penetration to drive into the brain from any angle.

for such a cartridge, and typically conservative and soundly reasoned.

Both Hagel and Waters commented on the history of .40-caliber cartridges, and I shall not attempt to improve on or repeat their expositions of the background against which Chatfield-Taylor's wildcat must be viewed.

[Editor's Note — There have been several reasons for our devoting so much attention and space to a rare wildcat cartridge. A powerful .40 caliber is the only gap in the line-up of U.S. factory cartridges, and there have been persistent rumors for several years about a commercial .40 or .41. Something quite similar to the .416 Taylor seemed the best bet, for it would require only a different neck on existing case-making equipment. Further, factory-chambered .416 Taylors specially made by both Winchester and Ruger indicated unusual interest. Finally, we've received more reader queries on the feasibility of a .40/.41 wildcat than all other "non-standard" bores combined, so obviously a good many of you readers are interested in this bore size, either for African or North American game. — N.K.]

As a sidelight, some confusion arose about the exact case and chamber dimensions of the cartridge, but each writer stated that he used .458 Winchester Magnum brass, necking it down to .416 caliber in one pass through RCBS sizing dies. This is the technique I use, after which the shoulder is slightly blown out on first firing. Page 49 of the September-October 1974 *Handloader* carried a clarification of these apparent dimensional discrepancies.

To the best of my knowledge, five rifles chambered to .416 Taylor exist. Chatfield-Taylor's is said to have been built in Winchester's custom shop, and is a Model 70. Hagel's is a Remington Model 700 BDL action barreled by Bill Hobaugh. Waters' is one of a pair of Ruger M-77's specially built in the Ruger plant (the other, I think, is in Chatfield-Taylor's possession). Mine has an FFV-Carl Gustaf deluxe magnum action and stock, fitted with a Douglas premium tube by RCBS' gunsmith in Oroville, California.

Only three sets of reamers exist — again, to the best of my knowledge. If I am correct, the two Ruger rifles and Chatfield-Taylor's Winchester were cut with the same set. Hagel's rifle was presumably chambered with another set, and I own the third set. Chatfield-Taylor's reamers and mine were made by Keith Francis, of Talent, Oregon, to identical specifications. I do not know

the source of Hagel's reamers. RCBS has, I believe, constructed all extant sets of reloading dies in .416 Taylor. I presume that my dies and chamber were cut with the same reamers; I know they are closely mated, having been cut in the same plant.

With many wildcats, such extreme variation exists in chambering reamers and techniques that loading data must be treated with suspicion. In the case of the .416 Taylor, however, there is every reason to believe that the five existing rifles all have chambers at least as similar as chambers for any factory standard cartridge in production rifles, and probably more so. I understand that all current .416 rifles except mine have 24-inch barrels; mine was cut to 23 inches. The other writers have not mentioned rifling twist rate; I specified 1 turn to 16 inches, and would be surprised if any of the others is very different.

The appeal of the .416 Taylor cartridge is simple; it modernizes the great .416 Rigby, vintage of 1911, and compresses Rigby performance into a much more

compact package. Ballistics of the two cartridges are identical, for all practical purposes, if .416 Rigby *factory* loads are compared to the Taylor round. And, of course, the Rigby has been highly respected in African and Asian game fields for its effectiveness on Cape buffalo, elephant, rhino, and similar tough and dangerous beasts. In particular, the 400-grain Eley-Kynoch steel-jacketed "solid" with the jacket thickened over the nose earned a great reputation for reliability and penetration on the massive game. If these or equally dependable solids could be had for reloading, the .416 Taylor would give us everything the Rigby version has, in a lighter, shorter, handier rifle with a shorter bolt-throw, with cartridges consisting of the best of

This 45-inch Cape buffalo, shot by Wootters with the .416, is one of the finest ever taken in Botswana by a safari hunter.

Wootters' .416 Taylor rifle features an FFV-Carl Gustaf magnum action and stock, with Douglas premium barrel and Leupold Vari-X III 1.5-5X scope; gunsmithing and dies are by RCBS, Inc.

modern components, readily available.

By contrast, .416 Rigby ammunition is frightfully scarce and expensive. Cases for the handloader can be made by laboriously lathe-turning the belts off .460 Weatherby Magnum brass, but that stuff isn't exactly cheap, either. On the whole, Chatfield-Taylor's idea seemed eminently practical, simple, and intriguing.

Wootters points to a sapling which deflected a 400-grain .416 slug, proof that no cartridge is a reliable brushbucker.

My colleagues, Hagel and Waters, have done so thorough a job of the technical development in the cartridge that they left little for me to say about it — except about my experiences with it on a safari in Botswana in October, 1974. My outfitter was the firm of Safari South Ltd., owned by famous professional hunters John Kingsley-Heath and Lionel Palmer. This was the same firm and the same area in which Bob Chatfield-Taylor had first tested his big wildcat against dangerous game in 1972. It happens that John Kingsley-Heath is one of the few really knowledgeable gunbuffs among African professionals, and he has been intensely interested in the .416 Taylor cartridge since Bob's safari. In fact, he is supposed to have been given a rifle so chambered, and, of course, was curious about my results, loads, etc. Altogether, the FFV-Carl Gustaf was set up to be the star of the safari.

And that is exactly what it proved to be, accounting for no fewer than six Cape buffalo (in my hands and others'), a Rowland Ward-record lion, two wilde-

beeste (as tough as any buffalo, pound for pound), and a big zebra.

Before detailing these results, a few words about my loads. The cartridge is quite simple to form, as mentioned before, with a single easy pass into the FL sizing die. No annealing or reaming was necessary with my lot of brass. The only regular source of bullets in this diameter is Colorado Custom Bullets of Montrose, Colorado, which offers 300-grain semi-spitzer soft-points with .032-inch jackets, 400-grain round-nose softs with the same jacket thickness, 400-grain round-nose softs with .049 jackets, and a 400-grain "solid." This last bullet is interesting, in that the jacket is made of pure copper tubing, swaged closed at each end, over a lead core. Considerable question has arisen as to whether this bullet can be depended upon to perform as a true solid, especially in heavy bone. I corresponded with several well-known writers who have African experience, and found none who had actually fired this CCB solid at dangerous game. All seemed to share my own suspicions that it might act as a soft-point with extremely delayed expansion characteristics. We were afraid that, even if it gave the required penetration, it might deform enough to veer off rather than drive straight through an elephant's skull, for example, to the brain.

I was fortunate enough to trade Jack O'Connor out of 25 Eley-Kynoch steel-cased solids made for the Rigby cartridge, and then to scrounge an additional 80 or so of these bullets, never loaded, from John Kingsley-Heath. I hope this will constitute a lifetime supply, since these have not been made for years and are becoming exceedingly scarce.

Since I could see no particular requirement for a light bullet in this big-game rifle, all my work has been with 400-grain slugs, especially since it's typical of most big bores that bullets of varying weights shoot to hopelessly different points of impact.

My own early development work had contradicted Chatfield-Taylor's opinion that IMR-3031 was the best powder for his .416, and correspondence with Ken Waters supported my suspicion that IMR-4320 was better suited, at least with the 400-grain slugs. Hagel's notes on N-203 didn't help much, since I had none of this propellant and knew of no place to get any more, an all-too-common and sad situation with all reloaders and most Norma rifle powders these days.

In Hagel's rifle, 74 grains of IMR-4320 seems to be a safe maximum, shoving the 400-grain CCB soft-nose out at 2,373 fps. Waters warned that 72 grains of this powder with the same bullet was tops, producing 2,447 fps at the muzzle. My barrel appears to accept heavier charges than Waters', producing quite similar top velocities, however. Compared to Hagel's,

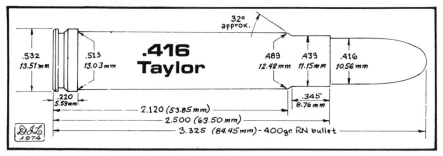

.416 Taylor

.532 (13.51mm)	.513 (13.03mm)
	.489 (12.42mm) .439 (11.15mm) .416 (10.56mm)

32° approx.

.220 (5.59mm)

.345 (8.76mm)

2.120 (53.85mm)
2.500 (63.50mm)
3.325 (84.45mm) - 400gr. RN bullet

DIL 1974

An unfired CCB softpoint, at left, is shown beside an identical slug recovered after being driven through a lion's heart frontally. The center two bullets are the Colorado Custom .416 "solid," showing the pinhole where the copper tubing jacket is closed at the nose and base. At right is the Eley-Kynoch "solid" manufactured for the .416 Rigby cartridge which has a steel jacket thickened over the nose and a hardened core.

mine takes about the same charges but produces slightly higher muzzle speeds. Even so, agreement between the three rifles, cut with three different sets of chambering reamers, is reasonably close. Reference to the loading tables given here will show that the three bullets I took to Africa varied slightly in muzzle velocity with the same charges, even though the bullets all weigh the same. The CCB softs produced highest velocities, while the Kynoch solids were slightly slower.

This perplexed me until I checked the bearing surface of those Kynoch steel-jacketed FMJs, and discovered that they are imperceptibly but distinctly wasp-waisted behind the cannelure, riding on what are in effect full-diameter driving bands at the heel and just behind the cannelure, with the diameter of the shank between these two points a thousandth of an inch smaller. Thus the hardened core and tough jacket don't elevate pressures.

Accuracy with all three bullets — CCB soft and solid, and Kynoch solid — is startlingly good in my barrel. All three *average* around 1¼ inches for three shots at 100 yards from bench rest! The Kynoch seems slightly the most accurate, but the differences are too small to be indicative of anything. Likewise, POI centers for the three bullets are identical at 100 yards when the same charge — 73 grains of IMR-4320 — was used. Nothing about cases or primers indicated anything very close to maximum pressures, and velocities for the three bullets average 2,400 fps, for about 5,100 foot-pounds of muzzle energy. This load duplicates ballistics in the factory-loaded .416 Rigby cartridge. The Taylor wildcat can be loaded hotter, at least in my rifle, but I wanted plenty of margin for safety in the tropics; I can see no reason for risking an excess pressure-stuck case when dealing with dangerous game. The Rigby is undisputably near-perfect for the animals in question, and there is an interesting theory held in some knowledgeable quarters in Africa that, with some bullets, added velocity *decreases* penetration.

The only area of disagreement between me and my gun-writing colleagues about

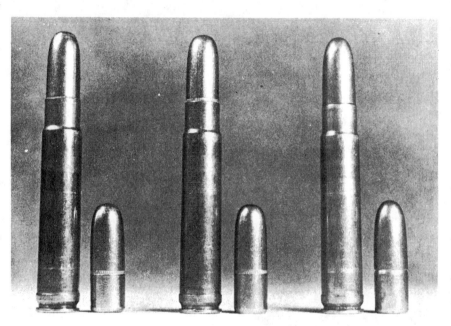

Hunting bullets suited to the .416 are quite limited. The bullets Wootters used in Africa are, from left, the Colorado Custom 400-grain soft nose with .049-inch jacket, Colorado Custom 400-grain copper-jacketed "solid," and Eley-Kynoch 400-grain steel-jacketed "solid." All were loaded to 2,400 fps.

Loads for the .416 Taylor

Powder/Charge	Bullet	MV [fps]	Remarks
70/IMR-4320	400 CCB SP	2,285	mild, 1.85, 1.12-inch groups
70/IMR-4320	400 CCB FJ	2,260	mild, 2.50, .97-inch groups
70/IMR-4320	400 Kynoch FJ	2,265	mild, 1.16, 1.30-inch groups
71/IMR-4320	400 CCB SP	2,295	mild, 1.18-inch groups
72/IMR-4320	400 CCB SP	2,355	moderate, 1.90-inch groups
*73/IMR-4320	400 CCB SP	2,415	not maximum, hunting load, 1.37-inch
74/IMR-4320	400 CCB SP	2,440	safe maximum 2.06, 1.06-inch
*73/IMR-4320	400 CCB FJ	2,390	hunting load, 1.45-inch groups
*73/IMR-4320	400 Kynoch FJ	2,405	hunting load, 1.23, 1.50-inch

Notes: All loads developed in Douglas premium barrel, 23 inches long, rifles 1-16, chambered with Wootter's reamers. Loading data in a wildcat rifle will not necessarily be valid or safe in another rifle. Velocities were taken at 12.5 feet with Oehler M-11 Chronograph with Skyscreens at temperatures ranging from 85 to 95° F., corrected to MV.

All groups are at 100 yards from rest, three shots, with Leupold Vari-X III 1.5-5X scope set at 5X.

Loads marked * were tested on large game in Africa (see text).

this cartridge is recoil. Hagel pegged it at nearly 70 foot-pounds in a 9.5-pound rifle, Waters at about 48.5 foot-pounds (although he expressed his figure as a percentage of .458 Magnum recoil without specifying gun weight) with the 400-grain bullet. The formula I use for calculating recoil yields a *maximum* recoil figure for this cartridge in a 9.5-pound rifle of 44.5 foot-pounds, or only about five foot-pounds more than my Browning .375 H&H Magnum delivers with heavy handloads behind 300-grain bullets. Subjective evaluation of recoil, of course, varies from shooter to shooter, and even from day to day with the same shooter, but the relatively mild recoil sensation (considering the energy being delivered) has been one of the most impressive features of my .416 Taylor rifle from the first. To sum it up, I can detect little, if any, difference in recoil sensation between this rifle and my .375, either from the bench or in offhand shooting, rapid or slow fire, at targets or at game.

John Kingsley-Heath may have made the most cogent remark of all about the recoil of this .416 Taylor when he said, "It's a good elephant rifle for ladies!"

Be that as it may, I can assure you it makes a hell of a buffalo rifle for gentlemen! I'm by no means a veteran Cape buffalo hunter, but I have killed seven of the brutes now, and have been in on the taking of three more. The more I see of Cape buffalo, the more respect I develop for them. No cartridge which can be fired from the shoulder can be depended upon to simply overwhelm a buffalo's life-systems in the way that a .270 can flatten a whitetail even with a less-than-perfect shot.

With a buffalo, the experienced hunter learns to pinpoint his hits as precisely as any varminter, no matter how much power his rifle packs. There is not much room for error, not enough to make up for a first shot I let get away from me on the first bull I tackled with the .416 in Botswana. He was turning as I fired through the tops of high grass, and I'd guess the slug went slightly behind the heart and angled into the guts. It was one of those shots that make you wish you could call the bullet back almost before it leaves the muzzle. In any case, I had two more cracks at the bull and hit him hard both times, but he never went down and managed to limp across a river into a game preserve where we were not permitted to follow. He was recovered by a party of native meat hunters next day, and probably did not live long after we last saw him. I'm not very proud of myself in the whole affair.

About all that could be gleaned from this first trial was that even the mighty .416 Taylor can't make up for poor bullet placement on Cape buffalo.

Another buff shot with the rifle was a cow which had been wounded with a native's .303. She was very sick, and my killing her was an act of mercy and did not count against my license. My first bullet struck on the bridge of her nose from dead ahead and crashed through the massive skull structure below the brain to break her neck. A second shot in the heart at close range served to speed her demise. Neither slug was recovered, although we butchered her for the meat. Conclusions: so far, the .416 wasn't doing anything any .375 wouldn't have done.

The next target was the *piece de resistance* of the entire safari, a record-book male lion. The lion story is a long and exciting one, involving another bad first shot at a running lion (at professional hunter Palmer's urging) which failed to disable him and led us into a hair-raising three hours of tracking the wounded lion through dense brush. Eventually, I had my chance at the beast as he faced me at 30 yards, and drove a 400-grain soft-point straight through his heart. The slug ranged from its entry in the chest diagonally backward to lodge under the hide in one flank. It was recovered, beautifully expanded and retaining about 65 percent of its original weight. It slew the lion, but not before he'd run 100 yards (fortunately, not toward us) and absorbed several more heavy slugs in assorted portions of his anatomy. Our evaluation was still inconclusive, but our post-mortem of the one well-placed shot indicated excellent promise.

When we got back to the buffalo, my shooting and results improved dramatically. A bull with 41-inch-wide horns was taken galloping straight away. I shot for the pelvic structure and the 400-grain Colorado Custom soft drove through the left hip joint and continued along several inches of spine, paralyzing the bull's hindquarters instantly. I then ran to the side and shot the buffalo low in the shoulder, transversely. This bullet perforated the left shoulder blade, ripped through aorta and lungs, and broke the shoulder joint on the far side. This is sensational performance for any soft-nose (except for a Bitterroot), especially since the recovered bullet still retained some of its core. Lionel was very impressed, and so was I.

A day or so later, I shot a zebra of perhaps 700 pounds with the big rifle, deliberately taking the shot from 180 yards in the hope that the striped horse would stop the bullet for recovery. I knew that my loads, which were zeroed for 100 yards, were dropping seven inches at 200, and placed the soft-point exactly where I wanted it. It killed the zebra in seconds, but passed through and was unrecovered. The experience pointed up both the surprisingly flat trajectory of the cartridge and its remarkable penetration ability, a

characteristic for which the .416 Rigby is also famed.

Another big buffalo bull was selected to test the effect of the mysterious Colorado Custom solids, the copper-jacketed ones mentioned earlier. The bull was shot through the lungs broadside, angling forward to penetrate the far shoulder. It exited and was lost, but the buffalo was down and dead within 20 yards. This is the only perfect one-shot kill I have ever witnessed on Cape buffalo, although I've seen a couple of others which were actually killed with a single bullet even though superficially wounded by others.

Terry Palmer, Lionel's 20-year-old son, was with us on this day, and the rear sight on his .458 had developed a wobble, so I loaned him the FFV-Carl Gustaf to fill his buffalo license. He shot one of the most beautiful Cape buffalo bulls I've ever seen, taking the same hip shot as the bull lumbered away that I'd used earlier. His first shot broke one hip joint and his second shattered the other, immobilizing the bull. A tranverse heart shot then added the *coup de grace*. All were with the soft-point bullet, and the two rear-enders were recovered, badly fragmented and having shed their cores, but only after inflicting awesome damage on the equally awesome skeletal structure of this huge buffalo.

As a sidelight, these shots intended to break down a buffalo from behind can hardly be recommended with a .375 unless solids are used. With soft-points in the Holland & Holland cartridge, I wouldn't have taken them. The .416 Taylor handled them perfectly.

The final test of the .416 (a couple of wildebeeste had been knocked over with the big rifle along the way, but had not stopped the slugs) came on the last day of the safari, when we went into the bush after a small herd of buffalo in which we'd glimpsed a couple of good bulls. As we turned a corner in the thicket, we found ourselves face to face with the herd, and standing menacingly before his fellows only 40 yards away was the Cape buffalo bull I've been dreaming of all my life! His boss was like a massive helmet over his beetling brows, and his horns swept into a deep curve and outward to a maximum width that we didn't suspect was as great as it proved to be.

"Gawd!," Lionel Palmer muttered, "Shoot *that* one!" The bellow of the rifle punctuated his command, and as the rifle came down out of recoil and I flung the bolt forward on a fresh round, I knew I'd centered the bull's heart. He bucked and plunged like a cow-pony, whirled, and circled unsteadily away through an open grove of saplings. I drove another bullet at his shoulder as he went, and was sure of that shot, too.

The great bull went perhaps 30 yards and fell. He tried to rise once, twice, and three times, and then threw his great head high and rolled slowly over on his side, uttering the famous death bellow.

His horns spread a full 45 inches, a phenomenal trophy for Botswana, and the finest head Lionel had ever collected for a client in 14 years as a professional hunter. As Palmer put it, this was a real Kenya-type Cape buffalo.

The first shot, with the CCB solid, had destroyed the heart and ranged backward into the grass-filled paunch, penetrating about four feet of buffalo, but we couldn't find it even with an hour of pawing among the fetid contents of the stomach. The second shot turned out to be in the right ham, some five or six feet aft of where I'd aimed it. Refusing to believe that I could have pulled the shot so badly, I went back and examined the grove of saplings through which I'd fired, and sure enough soon discovered a two-inch-thick trunk about 12 yards in front of the buffalo's tracks which the bullet had struck almost center. It ripped out the left half of the wood and deflected from there, and only struck the animal by accident. There's a lesson here for hunters who pin their faith on heavy, blunt bullets of great sectional density and modest velocities for "brush-bucking." Not even a 400-grain,

.41-caliber round-nose at 2,400 fps can be absolutely relied upon to get through the heavy stuff!

My conclusions about the .416 Taylor wildcat, after 22 days in Botswana with it? I think it is a great cartridge, perhaps the single all-round best one-rifle African battery for any trip on which the emphasis will be on dangerous game, and especially if elephant is on the list. The .375 H&H might excel it if much long-range shooting on the plains game were contemplated, but the .416 is distinctly better on Cape buffalo. I developed an enormous amount of confidence in and affection for the rifle. The cartridge is simple to form, easy to load, non-temperamental, extremely accurate, quite flat-shooting, for such a powerhouse, and, for me at least, remarkably easy on the shoulder.

As with all the big African cartridges, there is little real *need* for such a round in American hunting, but the .416 Taylor is at least more flexible than the .458 Magnum for our applications. Faced with a crippled brown bear in the alders and given a choice between the .375 H&H, .458 Magnum, and .416 Taylor, I'd pick up the .416 without a second's hesitation.

Although the CCB "solid" bullet did make two beautiful one-shot kills on buffalo, neither hit much heavy bone, and neither slug could be recovered, so that question remains undecided. The other bullets available in this caliber to handloaders are superb game bullets. It's possible that a die-maker can build a die in which .41 caliber pistol bullets can be bumped-up to .416, making lighter slugs available for plinking and perhaps deer hunting, but this is essentially a cartridge for the biggest of game.

Although rumors have persisted around the firearms industry for years that one of the manufacturers (presumably Winchester) is interested in Chatfield-Taylor's brainchild, I must sadly report that I consider the odds on a commercial version of the .416-458 very low at this moment.

Even more sad is the fact that political and economic developments on the African continent seem to be moving so rapidly downhill (from the hunter's viewpoint) that within a few more years there may be *no* field for a cartridge like the .416 Taylor, anywhere.

It could have been one of the all-time great ones, but I fear it was born about 15 years too late. ●

CHAPTER
45

George bench-tested more than 300 rounds working up loads for the new Remington magnum. The test rifle in the picture was a prototype.

Some Loading Data for the New .416 Remington Magnum

George L. Hoffman

THE .416, like the fabled Phoenix, has risen from the ashes. It just may be that .40 caliber is the best bore size for all types of large and dangerous game. From Alaska to Africa, it has proved to be a most useful tool in the hands of all types of hunters, professional and amateur alike.

If the .416 was so good, why did it die off in the first place?

It wasn't due to poor performance. The .416, together with many of the old standard double-rifle calibers such as the .450, .470 and .500, left the scene when the colonial powers retreated from Africa. Europeans created those heavy calibers and when they lost interest in India and Africa, there was no longer a need for either rifles or ammunition. Many fine old .416 Rigbys

have been rebarreled to other calibers because of ammo supply problems.

In recent years, entrepreneurs like Jim Bell have been turning out new brass for the old-timers. There is a slight resurgence of interest in the .470, but nothing to compare with that lavished on the .416. Paul Roberts, who owns the John Rigby Company, said that most of his orders are now for the .416 Rigby.

The .416, .404 and .425 were among the first large medium-bores to catch on in Africa. The .500 Jeffery and .505 Gibbs came along too late to build up much of a following. The .416 Rigby was really the best of that group and many professional hunters still use theirs when they can come up with some ammo.

The .416 Rigby had some pretty impressive champions: David Blunt, Marcus Daly, John Taylor, "Samaki"

Salmon, Bill Pridham, John Lawrence, Eric Rundgren, Tony Dyer, Harry Selby and Tony Sanchez-Arino, to name a few.

The Remington Arms Company, after years of rumors, has taken the .416 from a wildcat stage (based on a full-length Improved .375 case) and legitimized it. That pleases Yours Truly no end. I have long advocated such a factory offering. I also feel I may have played a small part in its birth.

John Wootters was one of the first to write about the .416. He was, and is, a fan of the wildcat .416 Taylor. It preceded the .416 Hoffman by about five years. I was never impressed with the .458 Winchester with its limited capacity, powder and loading limitations. I considered the Taylor but thought that the same problems would restrict its usefulness. Since there were any number of magnum-length actions available and brass everywhere, why

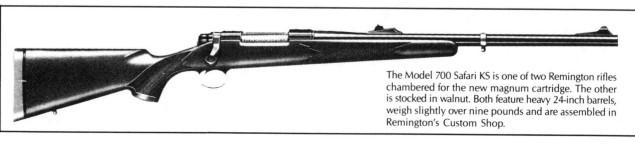

The Model 700 Safari KS is one of two Remington rifles chambered for the new magnum cartridge. The other is stocked in walnut. Both feature heavy 24-inch barrels, weigh slightly over nine pounds and are assembled in Remington's Custom Shop.

Lives Again!

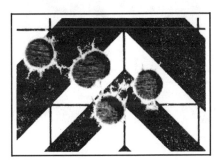

The new Remington magnum is capable of fine accuracy. This 1½-inch group was fired with factory ammo. The target was 100 yards from the bench.

These .416 softnoses were recovered from game: Left, a 400-grain Swift from a Cape buffalo retained 92 percent of its original weight; center, a 400-grain Barnes, also taken from a buffalo, retained 89 percent of its weight; and right, another 400-grain Barnes taken from a lion shot at close range still weighed 340 grains.

not use an Improved .375 case for optimum performance? That's the way the .416 Hoffman saw the light of day.

It seemed to me that Remington had a lot already going for them. The Model 700 Safari grade boasted the right action length and barrel dimensions. All they needed to do was to screw on a .416 barrel. I even suggested they call it the .416 Remington Express. Well, they came close: The new cartridge is called the .416 Remington Magnum.

It differs from the .416 Hoffman somewhat, as they used the 8mm Magnum case instead of the .375 H&H hull as a basis for the new round. There are some other, subtle differences as well. Both the Remington and Hoffman cases are 2.850 inches in length but the Remington has about .008 inch more body taper and is .034 inch shorter. That will give the Remington a slightly longer neck.

As the cited dimensions indicate, the .416 Remington can be chambered in a .416 Hoffman. Since the Hoffman is slightly larger (about 2.4 grains more case volume), pressures should be slightly lower, all else being equal. Nonetheless, neither the Remington Arms Company nor I recommend the practice.

The Remington Model 700 is so well known there is not much left to say about it. It is one of the most accurate and dependable rifles on the market. I am glad to see that Remington kept the 24-inch barrel. I would like to see

a somewhat smaller muzzle diameter, though. It measures approximately .820 inch. A .730 to .750-inch diameter is about ideal for a .416. The sample rifle I tested had a classic stock and it is much better than the standard Safari-grade stock.

When I removed the rifle from its shipping box, I studied the small green and yellow tag that was attached to the trigger guard. My eyes really lighted up when I read that the magazine capacity was five rounds. Sorry to say, it was not true. The magazine will hold only three cartridges. With one in the chamber, that gives a total of four rounds on tap. That should be enough under most circumstances but on several occasions, I have had to use all five in my rifle.

The trigger was the standard factory awful. The trigger gauge only went to

eight pounds but the weight of pull must have been double that. After the barreled action was separated from the stock, the recoil lug area was given the once-over. There is still only one lug but Remington has always had a larger recoil lug than anyone else. The entire lug mortise was glass-bedded, a smart move on the factory's part.

Although the bolt was very smooth, with no hint of binding, the second round from the magazine popped out a couple of times. When the bolt started the round forward, it would jump clear of the magazine and if the rifle was tilted to the right, the cartridge would fall to the ground. The test rifle was a prototype, of course, and I've been informed that problem has been corrected.

The rifle is fitted with Remington's standard open sight, which is adequate.

The recoil lug mortise of the Remington Safari .416 was glass-bedded.

I usually file the rear sight down to form a shallow V so it will work much faster.

The new rifle was quite accurate, right out of the box. At this time, factory loads feature Barnes 400-grain Super Solids and Swift 400-grain, A-Frame bonded softnoses. A very good choice on both counts.

I ran into a very strange thing while testing the solids for penetration. They were fired into ¾-inch plywood squares, stacked back to back, 48 inches deep. There was only an eight-fps-difference between the loads so that was of no consequence but the first test resulted in only 33 inches of penetration for the Barnes Super Solids and 45 inches for the 410-grain Hornadys. I repeated that test three times. Each time the results were the same. Later, Barnes honcho Randy Brooks told me that Remington had requested reshaping the Super Solid's nose so there will be less of a roundball effect. The new bullets should be available by the time you read this.

Although 400-grain bullets represent the best choices for large and dangerous game, not everyone will carry their .416s to Africa. One of the advantages of a .40 caliber is that it will be just as useful in Alaska. In addition, some will consider it the perfect elk rifle. (I wish Elmer Keith were still around.)

The Trophy Bonded Bullet Company

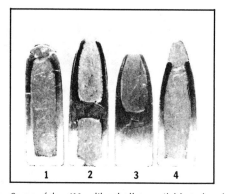
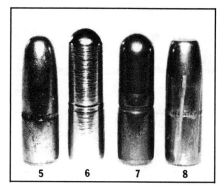

Some of the .416-caliber bullets available to handloaders today: (1) 400-grain Barnes, (2) 400-grain Swift, (3) 335-grain Trophy Bonded, (4) 350-grain Barnes, (5) 410-grain Hornady, (6) 400-grain Super Solid, (7) 400-grain Monolithic Solid and (8) 400-grain Trophy Bonded Sledge Hammer Solid.

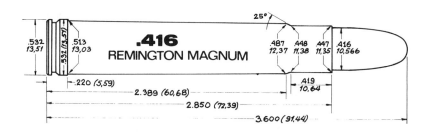

Performance of Trophy Bonded .416 Bullets

Data furnished by Jack Carter of Trophy Bonded Bullet Company

range (yards)	trajectory (inches)	velocity (fps)	energy (ft/lbs)
335-grain bullet, ballistic coefficient 310			
muzzle	0	2,664	5,279
100	+ 2.3	2,382	4,222
150	+ 2.0	2,248	3,760
200	0	2,119	3,338
250	− 4.0	1,993	2,955
300	−10.0	1,871	2,605
400-grain bullet, ballistic coefficient 360			
muzzle	0	2,452	5,340
100	0	2,220	4,377
150	− 1.8	2,109	3,949
200	− 5.6	2,000	3,554
250	−11.4	1,895	3,190
300	−19.8	1,794	2,860

.416 Remington Magnum

bullet	diameter (inch)	powder	charge (grains)	velocity (fps)	extreme spread (fps)	remarks
335 Trophy Bonded	.4162	RL-15	85.0	2,631	35	accurate
			86.0	2,664	20	very accurate
			87.0	2,707	1	maximum load
		IMR-4064	82.0	2,620	61	
350 Barnes Softpoint	.4163	RL-15	86.0	2,653	8	very accurate
400 Barnes Softpoint	.4160	IMR-4320	77.0	2,306	26	
			78.0	2,354	31	
			80.0	2,423	35	maximum load
		IMR-4064	76.0	2,288	62	
			78.0	2,303	26	
			80.0	2,405	6	very accurate
		IMR-4350	87.0	2,379	7	accurate
			88.0	2,402	12	best load for this powder
			89.0	2,424	17	
		RL-15	80.0	2,398	52	may be the best powder
			81.0	2,410	24	for all bullet weights
			82.0	2,422	7	
			83.0	2,452	12	
400 Super Solid	.4143		83.0	2,411	17	accurate
400 Hornady FMJ	.4162		81.0	2,403	10	good load
400 Swift Softpoint	.4162		82.0	2,432	23	OK
Factory Loads						
400 Super Solid	.4143	?	80.0	2,362	85	good grouping
400 Swift Softpoint	.4160	?	80.0	2,385	107	1.5-inch groups

Test rifle was a Remington 700 "Safari" grade with a 24-inch barrel having 14-inch twist. Handloads used Barnes cases and Federal 215 primers; overall cartridge length was 3.6 inches. Not all loads were shot for accuracy due to limited supply of some bullets. Reduce all loads 15% before trying them in your rifle. Velocities were recorded with a PACT chronograph. Mid-screen point was 10 feet from the muzzle.

Be alert — Publisher cannot accept responsibility for errors in published load data.

makes a 335-grain solid base bullet that is a dandy. It retains more than 90 percent of its weight in torture tests and groups very well. Better yet, this bullet printed 2.5 inches high in the Remington when the 400-grain solid was dead-on at 100 yards. That gives an unbeatable combination for the one-rifle man in Africa — or anywhere else for that matter. At 2,664 fps, sighted so it strikes 2.3 inches high at 100 yards, it is only 10 inches low at 300, with a remaining energy of 2,605 foot-pounds. In comparison, a 270-grain bullet from a .375 H&H arrives at the 300-yard mark with 2,228 foot-pounds of energy and its 300-grainer has only 2,141 foot-pounds at the same range.

The .416, with its deep penetration and long, heavy bullets, is going to be a long-range, big game killer. Barnes turns out a 350-grain bullet of conventional design which is accurate and works well. The new .416 X-bullet, with its solid rear half, may offer some promise as well. None were available for my tests, however.

It looks like the .416 is back to stay. Weatherby is planning their own version (400-grain bullet at 2,700 fps) and Ruger will chamber the old .416 Rigby in a new, magnum-length action. My hat is off to Remington for getting in the game first, though. In my judgment, their .416 is going to be the most popular of the breed. ●

CHAPTER
46

Layne Simpson

The .416 Weatherby Magnum

CONSIDERING all the activity in the .416 departments of various rifle and ammunition manufacturers during these past months, the introduction of the new .416 Weatherby Magnum came as no great surprise. It did, however, appear to get spooked from the bushes a bit sooner than many expected. Roy waited four years after the .338 Winchester Magnum was introduced before striking back with his .340 Magnum. And his .460 Magnum came trouncing along in 1958, two years after Winchester gave birth to the less powerful .458 Magnum.

Not so with the new .416 Weatherby Magnum. Within a few months after the first Model 700 .416 Remington Magnum departed Ilion, those busy chaps over in Japan were turning out the first Mark Vs in .416 Weatherby Magnum. Meanwhile, Norma was gearing up to produce the ammunition and once again, the fastest and most powerful factory cartridge of its caliber wears the Weatherby headstamp. It is a pity that Roy isn't still with us to see how fast the new cartridge runs.

The .416 Weatherby Magnum chambering is presently available in four Mark V configurations. Most handsome by far is the Safari Grade with its French walnut stock replete with satin finish, fleur-de-lis checkering, solid rubber recoil pad, ebony forend tip and grip cap, and not a white line spacer in sight. Other refinements include a matte finish on all metal, rear sight sitting atop a quarter rib and a sling swivel eye mounted on a barrel band just forward of the forend.

Moving down quite a few notches in price is the Euromark, my favorite Mark V for the money. Then we have the Lazermark and the Mark V Deluxe, but there is no Fibermark available in .416 caliber at present.

Options available on all Mark V .416

Layne's .416 Weatherby featured a 24¼-inch barrel, muzzle brake and 1.75-5x Weatherby Supreme scope secured in Buehler two-piece mounts.

Weatherby rifles include 24 or 26-inch barrels with or without iron sights and Mag-Na-Port muzzle brake. Also available on either barrel length is a multi-port muzzle brake. The detachable brake on the .416 I've been working with has 30 gas ports arranged in six banks of five. The barrel on the Mark V measured exactly 26 inches with the brake and 24.25 inches without. This would put the 26-inch barrel at 27¾ inches with the brake, a bit unwieldy for some hunting conditions, in my opinion. I ordered a 24-inch barrel.

The rifling on my Mark V is one-turn-in-14 inches. This is two inches faster than the standard for the .416 Rigby, and two inches slower than my preference for .416 calibers.

The Deluxe grade Mark V shipped from Southgate came with no surprises or disappointments. As we have come to expect from Weatherby, quality and workmanship can be described as top-of-the-heap among production rifles. Whoever laid out the walnut blank obviously knew a thing or two about the type of stock needed for a powerful rifle. The buttstock has a considerable amount of contrasting figure on both sides. The grain flows straight through the wrist and has only a trace of fiddle-back around the action area and out through the forearm.

Like all Mark V rifles, the wrist of the .416 Weatherby Magnum is internally reinforced with an aluminum rod. In addition, the .416 has two recoil lugs, one integral with the receiver ring, another attached to the bottom of

the barrel about an inch forward of the receiver ring face. The front recoil lug rests in synthetic bedding material while the web of wood between its mate's mortise and magazine cutout is reinforced with the same material. Farther back, the web between the magazine box and trigger housing cutouts is also reinforced with bedding compound. A pad of wood in the barrel channel exerts light upward pressure on the barrel. With two cartridges in the magazine and one in the chamber, along with a Whelen-type leather sling and a Weatherby Supreme scope secured with two-piece Buehler mount, the rifle weighs precisely 11 pounds, 4 ounces on my postal scale.

The .416 is the third in a line of Weatherby magnums that was inspired by the .416 Rigby case. When Roy began the development of his big .378 Magnum during the early 1950s, he basically necked the Rigby case down, modified the shoulder to a double radius design and added a belt. In 1958, five years after introducing the .378 Weatherby Magnum, Roy opened the neck to .458 and called it the .460 Weatherby Magnum.

The new .416 Magnum is essentially a necked-down .460 Weatherby. In fact, cases in the three boxes of .416 factory ammunition I fired in the Mark V were headstamped "Weatherby 460 Magnum." (The ammunition was from the first lot and in order to ship factory loads with the rifle, the three loads were developed and loaded in Southgate rather than in Sweden.) Headstamps on future lots will bear

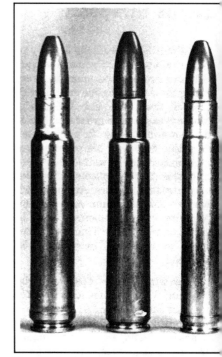

The .416 Weatherby (left) is shown with its major petition, the .416 Rigby (center) and the .416 Remi (right).

the correct designation. I am also told that muzzle velocities for the three loads that Norma will produce for Weatherby will be the same as the factory loads I worked with.

Factory loads are available with the A-Square Monolithic solid, Swift A-Frame softnose spitzer and Hornady roundnose, softnose bullets — all weighing 400 grains. As this is written, I have not received exact velocity ratings for the three loads, but I am told they produce around 2,700 fps in a 26-inch barrel. In the 24¼-inch barrel, two of the factory loads exceeded that velocity by averaging 2,735 and 2,715 fps, respectively, on my Oehler Model 35P. The third factory load missed the mark by 28 fps. Muzzle energy for the 400-grain bullet at 2,735 fps exceeds 6,600 foot-pounds. Variation in point of impact for the three loads was less than 1.5 inches at 100 yards.

For comparison, the two .460 Weatherby magnums I have worked with averaged around 2,600 fps with the 500-grain bullet for a muzzle energy of slightly over 7,500 foot-pounds from a 26-inch barrel. The .378 Weatherby Magnum usually churns up about 5,600 foot-pounds with a

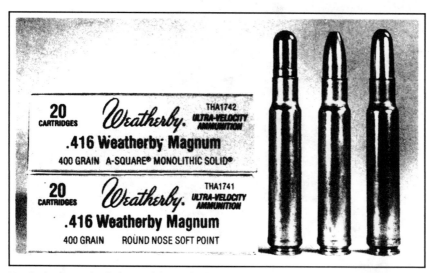

Weatherby factory loads feature, left to right, the 400-grain A-Square Monolithic Solid, 400-grain Swift A-Frame and the 400-grain Hornady roundnose.

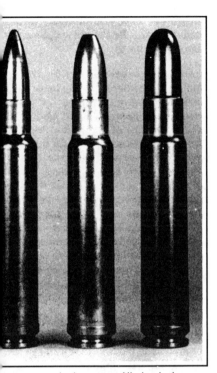

ew .416 Weatherby (center) fills the slot between 78 (left) and the .460 Weatherby (right).

check it out in the .416 Weatherby Magnum. Working up to 116.0 grains of that powder behind the Hornady 400-grain softnose produced an average muzzle velocity of 2,683 fps, about the same velocity the factory load chronographed with the same bullet.

The new Weatherby cartridge is the fastest and most powerful factory-loaded .416 available, something those who prefer factory loads for hunting large and potentially dangerous game will surely appreciate. The .416 Rigby, however, can be handloaded to about the same performance from a modern bolt action rifle when A-Square cases are used. Those who read my report on the .416 Rigby in *Rifle* No. 121 might recall that when it was loaded to maximum safe chamber pressures in a 24-inch barrel, muzzle velocity with H-4350 behind a 400-grain bullet exceeded 2,700 fps. Muzzle velocities with 350 and 300-grain bullets in the .416 Rigby, however, fell about 100 fps short of what I was able to attain with the .416 Weatherby at comparable chamber pressures. Whether this was due to the slightly greater capacity of the Weatherby case or simply a difference in rifles, I can't say.

According to my measurements, gross capacity of Weatherby's .416 Magnum case exceeds that of the A-Square .416 Rigby case by about 3.5 percent. When both are filled to the brim with a fine-grained spherical powder, the Weatherby case holds an average of 145.0 grains versus 140.0 grains for the Rigby case. The larger boiler room is mostly a result of less taper in the slightly longer Weatherby case.

The Weatherby case tapers to .460-inch diameter at the junction of its

body and neck, compared with .440-inch for the Rigby case. Even though the 2.913-inch Weatherby cases I have exceed maximum case length for the Rigby by .013 inch, the necks of my cases average .080 inch shorter than the necks of Rigby cases, or .400 inch versus .440 inch. Rim diameters are .575 inch for the Weatherby and .585 inch for the Rigby. To avoid confusion, these are the actual dimensions of my particular cases and not their SAAMI dimensions.

The .416 Weatherby Magnum case has a gross capacity advantage of about five grains over the .416 Rigby case, but the difference in net capacity is reduced a couple of grains due to a rather deep seating of bullets in the three Weatherby factory loads. The inside length of the Mark V magazine box measures a rather spacious 3.815 inches, but overall length of factory loads with Hornady, A-Square and Swift bullets is 3.725, 3.685 and 3.675 inches, respectively.

The Mark V in .416 Magnum chamber is not freebored but its relatively long throat does require factory-loaded bullets to travel through a great deal of space prior to engaging the rifling. Respective bullet jump with the lots of factory loads I worked with measured .040 inch for the Swift, .065 inch for the Hornady and .185 inch for the A-Square Monolithic solid. Apparently, the bullet freetravel has little, if any, effect on accuracy. A 100-yard, three-shot group fired at the factory indoor range with one of the three loads was included with the rifle; it measured exactly 1.25 inches. My averages for five three-shot groups fired from the 100-yard bench with each of the three factory loads during rather windy range conditions measured 2.11,

300-grain bullet. That positions the new .416 about midway between its two litter mates in terms of punch, bullet weight and diameter.

The three Weatherby factory loads contain a lightly compressed powder charge that averages 116.0 grains of what appears to be Norma MRP. There was no variation in powder charges among five cases from each of the three factory loads. Thanks to the generosity of my pal Lou Palmisano, who graciously sent me his few remaining cans of Norma MRP some months prior to receiving the Mark V, I was able to

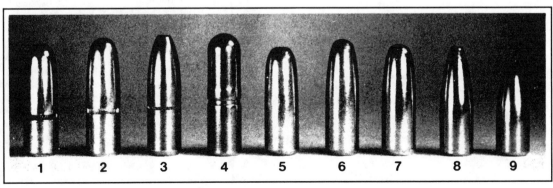

Bullets used to develop handloads are the (1) 400-grain Hornady RN, (2) 400-grain Hornady solid, (3) 400-grain Swift A-Frame, (4) 400-grain A-Square Monolithic solid, (5) 400-grain A-Square Lion Load, (6) 400-grain A-Square Dead Tough, (7) 400-grain Barnes RN softpoint, (8) 350-grain Cor-Bon spitzer and (9) 300-grain Barnes spitzer.

1.74 and 1.62 inches, respectively, for the Swift, Hornady and A-Square bullets. This, I might add, is considerably better than minute-of-Cape buffalo accuracy from a rifle capable of delivering almost three and a half tons of punch each time its trigger is squeezed.

When developing handloads for the .416 Weatherby Magnum, I mostly concentrated on the two new 400-grain bullets from Hornady, mainly because my supply of custom bullets of the same weight had been almost exhausted while working with the .416 Rigby and .416 Remington Magnum. Rather than trying the various 400-grain custom bullets with all powders, I chose to try them with Reloder 22 to determine if chamber pressures would indicate the same maximum charge would be acceptable with all of them.

As it turned out, 114.0 grains of that powder produced factory equivalent velocities at what I considered to be maximum acceptable pressure indications when loaded behind the Swift A-Frame and A-Square Monolithic solid.

That charge had to be increased by two grains to push the two Hornady bullets, the Dead Tough and Lion Load softnose from A-Square and the Barnes softnose to comparable speeds and pressure indications. This would seem to indicate that due to their construction, the A-Frame and Monolithic solid bullets are prone to increase pressure over that generated by the same powder charge behind a bullet of more conventional design. The differences in velocities of the three factory loads also serve to bear this out. Looking at this another way, maximum velocity and pressure can be reached with these two bullets with a bit less powder.

In establishing overall cartridge length, I seated all bullets out for a decrease in jump to .010 inch in lieu of the .040 to .185 inch for factory loads, if their forms allowed doing so and if a minimum of .410 inch of their shank remained in the case neck. This was not possible with the two-diameter Monolithic solid and the Barnes 300-grain (owing to their short bearing surface) and I settled on respective overall lengths of 3.685 and 3.650

inches for those two bullets. Overall loaded lengths for the other bullets are listed in Table II.

A number of powders can be used to duplicate Weatherby factory loads with various 400-grain bullets, but none managed to greatly exceed that level of performance at chamber pressures I consider to be acceptable for hunting potentially dangerous game in tropical climates. With some powders, I was able to push the three bullet weights out the barrel from 50 to 100 fps faster than indicated in my load chart, and although chamber pressures did not appear to exceed what I consider to be an acceptable level for cold weather hunting, they were a bit higher than I would want to subject to a day in the hot African sun.

Of the various powders tried, only one proved to be totally unacceptable for producing maximum velocity in the .416 Weatherby Magnum with any bullet weight — IMR-4320. It is one of my favorite powders for Remington's .416 Magnum and it works fine in the more capacious Weatherby case if midrange loads at .416 Rigby speeds are the objective, but its burning characteristics are totally unsuited for achieving top velocities in the .416 Weatherby Magnum. As charges of all the other powders were gradually increased, corresponding pressure indications were quite uniform. With IMR-4320, an additional grain or two over what appeared to be a relatively mild load caused pressure to suddenly skyrocket.

Another characteristic the .416 Weatherby Magnum seems to share with the .416 Rigby is a willingness to please regardless of what powder it is fed, as long as the burning rates run from medium to slow. Not a single load fired in the Mark V with any powder and bullet combination exceeded 2.5 inches for three shots at 100 yards. The majority of groups measured less than two inches. The single most accurate load proved to be the A-Square Monolithic solid seated over 114.0 grains of RL-22 for three-shot groups that averaged just under 1.26 inches. But several other powders pushed the two Hornady bullets into groups measuring well under 1.50 inches. Truth is, such comparisons are rather moot when we consider how big a target a Cape buffalo's shoulder or a lion's rib cage is at 50 paces.

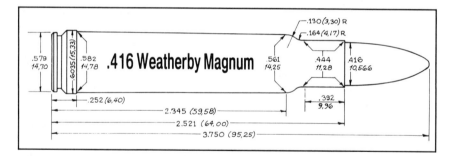

Table I					

.416 Weatherby Magnum Exterior Ballistics

	range (yards)				
	0	100	200	300	400
400-grain Swift					
velocity	2,700	2,465	2,241	2,028	1,828
energy	6,468	5,391	4,456	3,699	2,965
trajectory	—	+3.0	+1.7	−7.5	−23.2
350-grain Cor-Bon					
velocity	2,900	2,685	2,478	2,287	2,090
energy	6,529	5,597	4,767	4,060	3,391
trajectory	—	+3.0	+2.8	−3.3	−16.1
300-grain Barnes					
velocity	3,050	2,803	2,570	2,348	2,135
energy	6,190	5,228	4,395	3,668	3,033
trajectory	—	+3.0	+3.1	−2.4	−14.4

All velocities measured in feet per second; energy measured in foot-pounds; trajectories measured in inches.

Out of curiosity, I tried my favorite .416 Rigby load, 106.0 grains of H-4831 behind a 400-grain bullet, in the Mark V. Accuracy was quite good but velocity fell off by about 100 fps when fired from the slightly more capacious case. Then too, the Mark V was as accurate with the 400-grain bullet reined back to .416 Rigby speed as it was when blasting that bullet out the muzzle some 300 fps faster. A few of the outstanding reduced velocity loads I discovered while working with the Mark V, all producing around 2,400 fps with the 400-grain bullet, are 120.0 grains of H-1000, 114.0 grains of H-450, 110.0 grains of H-4831, 107.0 grains of RL-19 and 101.0 grains of IMR-4831.

Prior to developing load data for the .416 Weatherby Magnum, I had assumed that higher velocities could be reached with the slower powders than with the slightly faster propellants when all were loaded to the same pressures. This did not prove to be true. When all the slow-burners, except for RL-22, are loaded behind the 350 and 300-grain bullets, powder space in the case runs out before top velocities are reached. For these reasons, plus the fact that accuracy was about equal with any of the powders, I consider the medimum burners and their smaller charges to be the best choices for Weatherby's .416 Magnum. Boiling it down to specifics, even though RL-22 does a fine job with all bullet weights, I don't believe the handloader will go wrong by burning a bit less powder for the same performance with RL-19, H-4350, IMR-4350, IMR-4831 or AAC-3100 in the .416 Weatherby Magnum. Two other powders with similar burning rates, W-760 and H-414, are excellent choices for the 300-grain bullet. When loaded behind heavier bullets, however, their load density drops below 90 percent, something I like to avoid when loading Ball or spherical powders.

One thing is certain, my load data for the .416 Weatherby Magnum clearly illustrates the foolishness of making any attempt to assign various powders to specific slots on a burning rate scale or chart. For example, in other cartridges I can usually use similar charges of H-450 or H-4831. When loading my particular lot of H-450 in the .416 Weatherby Magnum, it proved to be second only to H-1000 in burning rate and seemingly, a bit slower than H-4831. After working with H-1000 in

Table II

.416 Weatherby Magnum

bullet	primer	powder	charge (grains)	muzzle velocity (fps)	OAL (inches)
400 Hornady softpoint	Fed. 215	H-450	116.0	2,565	3.780
	Fed. 215		121.0	2,646	
	Fed. 215		124.0	2,711	
	Rem. 9½M		124.0	2,729	
	Win. WLRM		124.0	2,737	
	CCI 250		124.0	2,719	
400 Hornady solid	CCI 250	H-4831	106.0	2,317	3.780
		H-4831	112.0	2,478	
		H-4831	116.0	2,608	
		H-4831	120.0	2,677	
		IMR-7828	120.0	2,703	
		H-1000	116.0	2,331	
		H-1000	120.0	2,401	
		RL-22	112.0	2,591	
		RL-22	116.0	2,716	
400 Hornady softpoint	CCI 250	RL-22	116.0	2,694	3.78
400 Swift A-Frame			114.0	2,732	3.705
400 A-Square solid			114.0	2,726	N/A
400 A-Square LL softpoint			116.0	2,702	3.775
400 A-Square DT softpoint			116.0	2,719	3.78
400 Barnes softpoint			116.0	2,711	3.78
400 Hornady softpoint	Fed. 215	N-MRP	116.0	2,683	3.78
		AAC-3100	115.0	2,706	
		RL-19	108.0	2,549	
		RL-19	112.0	2,653	
		RL-19	115.0	2,737	
		H-4350	110.0	2,687	
		IMR-4831	110.0	2,681	
		IMR-4350	108.0	2,706	
		IMR-4320	95.0	2,459	
		RL-15	88.0	2,618	
350 Cor-Bon softpoint	Rem. 9½M	RL-22	125.0	2,916	3.79
		RL-19	109.0	2,567	
		RL-19	119.0	2,846	
		RL-19	121.0	2,931	
		AAC-3100	114.0	2,697	
		AAC-3100	117.0	2,763	
		AAC-3100	119.0	2,811	
		H-4350	118.0	2,870	
		IMR-4831	118.0	2,892	
		IMR-4350	114.0	2,881	
300 Barnes softpoint	Win. WLRM	RL-22	127.0	3,035	N/A
		RL-19	124.0	3,053	
		H-4350	122.0	3,039	
		IMR-4831	120.0	3,011	
		IMR-4350	116.0	3,045	
		H-414	115.0	3,052	
		W-760	115.0	3,031	

Weatherby factory loads

bullet	primer	powder	charge (grains)	muzzle velocity (fps)	OAL (inches)
400 Swift A-Frame	Fed. 215	N-MRP	116.0	2,735	
400 A-Square solid				2,714	
400 Hornady softpoint				2,672	

The test rifle was a Weatherby Mark V with 24¼-inch barrel and a 1-in-14-inch rifling twist. Weatherby cases were used in developing all load data. Instrumental velocities were clocked 12 feet from the muzzle with an Oehler Model 35P Chronograph and corrected to actual muzzle velocities. Average ambient temperature during velocity readings was 92 degrees Fahrenheit. **Warning:** Maximum loads shown were safe in the author's rifle but may be excessive in others. Maximum powder charges shown should be reduced by 10 percent for starting loads in other rifles.

Be alert — Publisher cannot accept responsibility for errors in published load data.

271

various .264, 7mm or .300 magnums, I was about convinced that its burning rate is similar to IMR-7828, perhaps slightly slower. Comparing velocities with 120.0 grains of both powders behind the 400-grain Hornady solid, my assumption could be correct for some cartridges, but not for the .416 Weatherby Magnum.

Since massive charges of Ball or spherical powders are reputed to be rather difficult to ignite uniformly, I tried four Magnum primers behind 124 grains of H-450 in an effort to determine if one might outperform the others. As it turned out, Winchester's relatively new Magnum primer produced the highest average velocity but it did not represent enough gain in velocity over the Remington 9½M, CCI 250 and Federal 215 primers to make two cents worth of difference on big game animals. Neither could I detect any difference in the accuracy using the four primers.

Prior to the arrival of the .416 Magnum, I talked with a couple of my colleagues who had already put several factory rounds through their rifles. Both opined that recoil, even with the muzzle brake, was quite fearsome.

Perhaps I have been shooting eight pound .375 H&H rifles so long that anything else feels good, but I do not find recoil from the 11-pound Mark V to be at all objectionable when fired off-hand or from the kneeling position. According to my shoulder, the most punishing cartridge from Weatherby is the .378 Magnum, with the .460 Magnum a close second. Despite what paper figures might indicate, the .416 appears to be much kinder to my shoulder without its muzzle brake than the .378 and .460 with muzzle brakes. Neither do I find its recoil to be as uncomfortable as most nine to 10-pound .458 Winchester Magnum rifles.

The muzzle brake does an excellent job of reducing perceived recoil of the .416 Weatherby Magnum down to what feels about like a .338 Winchester Magnum of average weight without a muzzle brake — but muzzle blast seems to be increased by a bushel of decibels. It wasn't so bad out in the open, but the roof over my benchrest seemed to inten-sify the increased blast before concentrating it in my direction at what I quickly decided is an intolerable and downright painful level — even though I wore some of the best ear protection available. Consequently, I removed the brake and tamed recoil from the Mark V to an absolutely painless level with a Bench Wizard from Ultra Light Arms. As a note of possible interest, I filled the Bench Wizard with No. 8 lead shot in lieu of sand. If I were to order a Mark V in .416 Weatherby Magnum tomorrow, I doubt if I would specify a muzzle brake. When shooting the rifle at benchrest, the Bench Wizard or a bag of lead shot makes a brake an unnecessary accessory and after having hunted with cartridges that generate far more recoil, I have concluded that most shooters are unaware of recoil when actually shooting big game anyhow.

I consider the new .416 Magnum to be the most versatile and useful cartridge over .338 caliber that Weatherby has introduced. When loaded with the right bullet, it shoots much flatter than the .460 Magnum, is kinder to the shoulder and enjoys an equal, if not better, bullet selection for handloading. It also shoots about as flat as the .378 Weatherby, delivers a bigger payload up close and strikes a target with about as much punch out to 400 long paces.

Weatherby has definitely covered most of the bases by introducing three factory loads. If there is a better bullet than the A-Square Monolithic solid for punching a straight hole from stem to stern through Cape buffalo without the slightest distortion, I have yet to find it. I have also used the Swift A-Frame bullet, with its core bonded to a thick H-shape jacket, to know that it has few peers among softnose bullets when the job calls for smashing through heavy bone and penetrating vitals. The final slot, thin-skinned game up to the size of zebra and eland, is filled quite well by the 400-grain Hornady factory load.

Handloading the .416 Weatherby Magnum increases its versatility simply because 400-grain bullets are not really required for much of the world's big game. For all the African antelope and possibly lion, as well as North American game such as elk, moose and the big bears, I won't be surprised to see a good 350-grain spitzer eventually prove to be the best all-round choice for Weatherby's .416. It shoots flatter than the slower 400-grain bullet, delivers a mightier blow beyond 100 paces, is a bit kinder to a shooter's shoulder and its sectional density of .279 is plenty for deep penetration on the larger hoofed game. For now, my pick of the bunch for hunting such game with the .416 Weatherby Magnum, or any .416 for that matter, is the Cor-Bon 350-grain spitzer with its soft lead core chemically bonded to a thick copper jacket. I'll bet a .416-inch 350-grain bullet that is designed for controlled expansion which leaves the muzzle at 2,900 fps or so would be some of the finest lion medicine ever created by the hands of mortal man.

The Weatherby Mark V came through several shooting sessions without a hitch. All cartridges, both factory loads and handloads, fired during load development were fed through the magazine without a single bobble. Roundnose and spitzer bullets also fed smooth as silk during my offhand, rapid fire exercise. The guard screws would start to loosen after 30 to 40 rounds had been fired, but this is to be expected from such a powerful rifle. If I were to take the rifle on an extended hunt, I would apply a dab of Loc-Tite to the threads. Interestingly enough, none of the screws in the Buehler two-piece mount required tightening during the firing of several hundred rounds. I suppose that was due to the adhesive that is applied to all screw threads and the inside of the rings at the factory.

The Weatherby Supreme scope also survived a .416-size pounding with flying colors. I consider its magnification range of 1.5-5x to be close to ideal for a dangerous game rifle as you can get. Come to think of it, other than replacing its muzzle brake with a threaded cap and possibly installing open sights and a good quick-detach mount, I can think of no change I would make to the Mark V prior to packing it off to the Dark Continent. ●

CHAPTER 47

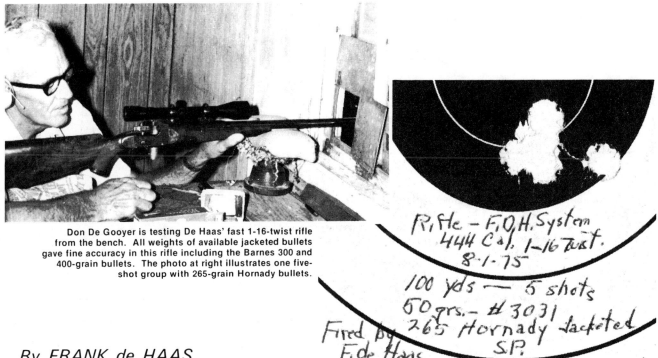

Don De Gooyer is testing De Haas' fast 1-16-twist rifle from the bench. All weights of available jacketed bullets gave fine accuracy in this rifle including the Barnes 300 and 400-grain bullets. The photo at right illustrates one five-shot group with 265-grain Hornady bullets.

Rifle - F.O.H. System 444 Cal, 1-16 Twist.
8-1-75
100 yds — 5 shots
50 grs. - # 3031
265 Hornady Jacketed S.P.
Fired by Fide Haas

By FRANK de HAAS

Handloading Marlin's Own, the .444

THE .444 MARLIN cartridge is an excellent short range big game number — much better than the .44 Magnum. Judging from the fact that there is only one commercial repeating rifle chambered for it, the .444 Marlin cartridge is not very popular now, and in all likelihood will never be. But woodland big game hunters ought to take a good look at it.

The .444 is also a very good single shot rifle cartridge. In a heavy barreled single shot rifle such as the Navy Arms Buffalo

Chambered and threaded .444 Marlin barrels are available from Numrich Arms Corporation, West Hurley, New York, to fit the large Remington or Spanish-made military rolling block actions such as shown here. Numrich .444 barrels have the slow 1-38 rifling twist, and while this barrel won't handle with accuracy bullets over 300 grains in weight, it can be expected to be very accurate with all lighter jacketed bullets.

De Haas' fast twist .444 has a 1-16 twist Douglas Heavy Sporter barrel. This single shot, which De Haas designed and made, proved extremely accurate with jacketed bullets.

Ballistic Comparison

.44 MAGNUM, .444 MARLIN AND .45-70 [405-grain] FACTORY LOADS

Range [Yards]:	Velocity, fps				Energy, fp				Trajectory, Inches (Rifle sighted-in at 100 yards.)			
	MV	100	200	300	MV	100	200	300	50	200	300	Barrel
.444 Marlin	2,400	1,845	1,410	1,125	3,070	1,815	1,060	675	+ 0.6	-9.6	-36.7	24-inch
.44 Magnum	1,750	1,360	1,110	980	1,630	985	655	510	+ 1.4	-17.5	-64.5	18.5-inch
.45-70	1,320	1,160	1,050	990	1,570	1,210	990	880	+ 2.4	-25.1	-81.2	22-inch

rifle, the careful handloader can obtain excellent target accuracy with it. I know, because I have been getting near MOA accuracy from my own two single shot .444 rifles.

The .444 was developed jointly by Remington and Marlin and it, and the first rifle chambering it, the Marlin lever action, was brought out in 1965. So far, the .444 is only loaded by Remington and the cases bear the R-P (Remington-Peters) headstamp. It is a semi-rimmed, straight-bodied cartridge closely resembling the .45-70, and it is factory-loaded only with the 240-grain jacketed soft-point bullet, which is the same bullet that Remington and Peters use in their .44 Magnum soft-point rifle loads. At the present time a box of 20 .444 Marlin cartridges costs $7.95, which is roughly 40 cents per round. This alone is a good inducement to handload it; the single factory bullet is another.

At the present time there are only three commercial rifles available in .444 caliber, the Model .444 Marlin lever action, and two single-shots, the Navy Arms Rolling Block and the Navy Arms Martini.

Numerous .444 single shot rifles have also been built on the large Remington rolling block action using the Numrich Arms .444 conversion kit consisting of a threaded and chambered barrel with sights, and a stock and forearm. The barrels of all of these rifles have the slow one turn in thirty-eight inches (1-38 inches) rifling twist which is standard for this cartridge as well as for caliber .44 Magnum rifles. [*Editor's Note — For more discussion on this slow twist, and the effects of a faster twist, see De Haas' article in the May-June 1976* Rifle.]

The Sporting Arms & Ammunition Manufacturers Institute (SAAMI) standards for the .444 are: bullet diameter, .4305-inch maximum; bore (land) diameter, .424 minimum; groove diameter, .430 minimum.

The .444 cartridge is not just a longer .44 Magnum. Rather, it is based on a special case all of its own, with a base diameter slightly larger than the .44 Magnum case. To give an idea of the differences in powder capacity between the .44 Magnum and .444, the net capacity (grains water) of the .44M is

about 25 grains and the .444 about 54 grains.

The .444 is best compared with the .45-70, which is its closest rival. The .45-70 case holds about 49 grains water. The accompanying ballistic chart shows how the .444 stacks up against the .45-70 and over-shadows the .44M.

In studying the chart and comparing the figures, it must be pointed out that the .44M and the .444 are loaded to the hilt by the factory, and the handloader using the 240-grain bullet cannot expect to improve upon these figures. However, the .45-70 as now factory loaded is loaded moderately and at a much lower breech pressure level than the .44M and .444. In a strong rifle the handloader can get much better ballistic performance from the .45-70 cartridge than shown in the table. Used in equally strong actions and handloaded with the same weight bullets to the same pressure level, there would be no noticeable ballistic separation between the .444 and the .45-70.

Reloading the .44 is best done with a regular reloading press as opposed to a hand-type tool. A 3-die set is required;

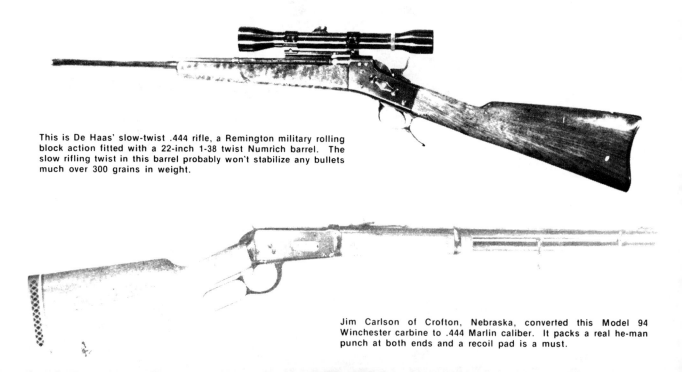

This is De Haas' slow-twist .444 rifle, a Remington military rolling block action fitted with a 22-inch 1-38 twist Numrich barrel. The slow rifling twist in this barrel probably won't stabilize any bullets much over 300 grains in weight.

Jim Carlson of Crofton, Nebraska, converted this Model 94 Winchester carbine to .444 Marlin caliber. It packs a real he-man punch at both ends and a recoil pad is a must.

Handwritten on target:
Rem RB Rifle 444 Cal
55/3031/240 Sierra 100 yds
8-23-75
1-38" Twist

The slow-twist barrel on the rolling block shot respectable groups with lighter 240-grain bullets, as this group illustrates.

De Haas feels that the .444 Marlin cartridge deserves a heavier bullet than it is now factory loaded with, and that rifles in this caliber should have barrels with a faster rifling twist than is now standard. If a faster rifling twist were used, heavier bullets could be utilized, such as the 300 and 400-grain Barnes bullets shown here. The .444 cartridge at left has the bullet seated deep to factory overall length. If maximum velocity is desired with these bullets in a single shot rifle having a barrel with a fast rifling twist, then the chamber should be throated deeper to accept a cartridge as shown at right.

one die to resize the fired cases and expell the spent primer; the second die to expand the neck and bell the case mouth; and the third die to seat the bullet in the case and crimp it in place if necessary. My .444 dies were of C-H manufacture, and I had no problems with them.

I reloaded for two rifles in .444 caliber; both single shots, one built on an old Remington No. 1 military rolling block action using a 1-38-inch twist Numrich barrel, and the other on a falling block I designed and made which was fitted with a Douglas premium grade 1-16 twist barrel. Both were chambered with a Clymer chambering reamer, and I allowed only .001-inch above minimum head-space.

Both had groove diameters of .430-inch. My .444 falling block rifle was much stronger and safer than my rolling block, but even so, that old action took in stride the top loads listed in most of the reloading manuals. I am sure that the Model .444 Marlin, Navy Arms Rolling Block and Navy Arms Martini .444 rifles have actions that are stronger than my rolling block .444, and that any of the loads that I used and list in this article will be well within the safety limits of these actions.

I found the R-P .444 cases to be very durable. In all my shooting I used only 40 cases, 20 for each rifle. They started as factory loads and after reloading the cases many times I have yet to discard one. The minimum headspace in both rifles may partially account for the longevity of my cases, although my discovery that I did not have to completely full-length resize the cases every time they were reloaded may have been the main reason. Even after having fired a heavy load, I found that the sizing die could be backed off two full turns from normal contact with the shellholder and still resize sufficiently to allow them to chamber freely. This practice made case resizing easy, requiring only the slightest trace of lubricant to be used. Actually, only the neck area was worked to any extent.

I also discovered that .444 cases need frequent trimming, not on account of the cases lengthening, but because the case mouths lengthened unevenly or became uneven either by the reloading process or by firing, or both.

I suspect that the unevenness resulted mostly from the neck expansion operation. At any rate, I found that if I kept the mouths even, and all the cases trimmed to the same length, a slight improvement in accuracy resulted. With the mouths trimmed evenly and slightly chamfered, the necks expanded more evenly and more in alignment, with the result that the bullets would also seat more precisely. I preferred to do the trimming prior to the resizing operation. Naturally, with the cases trimmed uniformly, belling and crimping was more even, uniform and precise.

I consider the .444 as a jacketed bullet cartridge, and all of the .44 caliber jacketed bullets made by Sierra, Speer and Hornady have their base edges nicely rounded so that only the slightest mouth belling is required for bullet seating. With full loads behind these jacketed bullets, I found that a tight crimp was not necessary or even desirable. All the "crimp" I employed was just enough to recurve the mouth edge inward as little as needed to leave a smooth juncture between case and bullet. Doing this also stretched case life.

Despite frequent trimming and careful chamfering, I still had the problem of uneven neck expansion. On more than half of the reloaded rounds the neck expanded more on one side than on the other. This unevenness could be felt as well as seen and the effect of such a cartridge in a chamber is probably not unlike a canted bullet in the case, or at least I thought so.

I checked the thickness of the neck metal and found this to be quite uniform in most of my cases, and therefore thought that reaming the necks would not

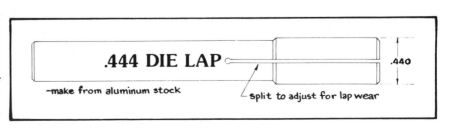

.444 DIE LAP

—make from aluminum stock

split to adjust for lap wear

.440

help much to correct the condition. My C-H .444 Marlin dies were within the dimensions specified by SAAMI, (and so were the chambers in my rifles) but like all commercial dies, the resizing die overdid the job, especially in the neck area. For example, fired in my rifles, the fired cases had an outside neck diameter averaging about .456-inch. Fully resized in my die, the necks were left about .440-inch. The neck expansion operation with the standard .430 expander plug then left the necks approximately .448, and with a .430 bullet seated in the neck, its diameter was .450. This was needless and resulted in excessive neck resizing — around .007 too much. The only correction for this is to lap out the neck area in the reizising die, and this I did.

The lap was lathe-turned from a piece of 1/2-inch round aluminum stock, turning it down as shown in the accompanying drawing. The lapping end was split with a hacksaw so that the split halves could be spread apart as the lap wore and the neck area in the die got larger. I used Carborundum No. AA400-78-WS lapping compound and lapped until the neck of a case resized in it measured .447-inch instead of .440. The result was that neck expansion and bullet seating became much more uniform, with hardly any neck bulging. Less resizing and expansion also means the brass is not worked so much, and this means still longer case life.

Bear in mind, however, that any such die alteration will void the maker's warranty; if you lap it oversize, or egg-shaped, or out of alignment, you can only chunk it in the junk bin.

With the brass worked so little in

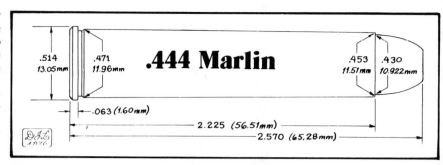

reloading, the .444 R-P cases became "ever-lasting," with almost unlimited life. But more than anything else I hoped this more uniform bullet seating would result in improved accuracy. Up to the time I did this die lapping I had fired 40 5-shot 100-yard groups with my fast-twist rifle. The last eight groups fired just prior to the die lapping averaged 1.4 inches, with the smallest being .80 and the largest 1.825. Using the same load and firing under the same conditions, the next eight groups with reloads from the lapped dies averaged 1.304 inches, with the smallest being .975 and the largest 1.550. My efforts were not entirely wasted. The load was 50/3031/265 Hornady.

The selection of .429-.431 jacketed

bullets suitable for the .444 handloader is limited, and the slow 1-38 rifling twist in most .444 barrels also limits the range of bullet weights than can be used in this cartridge. The soft-point and hollow-point jacketed bullets that work best in the .444 are those that range in weight from 180 to 300 grains. The three big bullet makers, Hornady, Sierra and Speer, make .44 bullets that range in weight from 180 to 265 grains. In my slow-twist Numrich-barreled rifle the 240-grain bullets performed best. My fast-twist Douglas barrel rifle, however, gave the finest accuracy with the 265-grain Hornady bullet.

The heaviest jacketed bullet that I am aware of for handloading the .444 is the

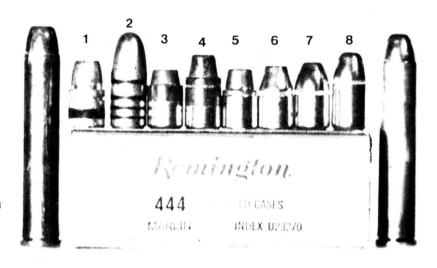

These are some of the bullets De Haas tried in his two .444 Marlin rifles. [1] Lyman Ideal cast bullet, Keith design, 250 grains, [2] Lyman cast bullet No. 439186, 385 grains, sized .433, [3] 240-grain swaged half jacket, [4] 300-grain swaged, [5] 225 Speer, [6] 24 Sierra HP, [7] 265 Hornady SP, [8] 300-grain Barnes jacketed SP. At the far left is the R-P .444 Marlin factory load with 240-grain SP bullet and at the right is a reload with the 300-grain Barnes bullet.

.444 Marlin Jacketed Bullet Loads

[Overall cartridge length for all loads approximately 2.57 inches.]

Bullet	Powder	Charge, Grains	Estimated Velocity	Remarks
180 Sierra HP	IMR-4198	50.0	2.450	High velocity load.
200 Hornady HP	IMR-4198	48.0	2.400	High velocity load.
240 Sierra HP	IMR-3031	55.0	2.275	Near maximum hunting load. Excellent accuracy in both slow and fast-twist rifles.
240 Speer, Hornady, Sierra and Barnes	IMR-3031	50.0	2.050	Moderate load, very accurate in both slow and fast-twist rifles.
240 Hornady or Sierra	IMR-4895	56.0	2.200	Good near maximum hunting load. Good accuracy in slow and fast-twist rifles.
265 Hornady SP	IMR-3031	50.0	2.050	Near maximum powerful hunting load. Excellent accuracy in fast-twist barrel.
265 Hornady SP	IMR-3031	45.0	1.800	Moderate load, excellent accuracy.
300 Barnes SP	IMR-4895	49.0	1.850	Heavy hunting load. Good accuracy in both slow and fast-twist rifles.
400 Barnes SP	W-W 748	42.5	1.500	For fast-twist rifles only.

300-grain Barnes soft-point, made by and available from Colorado Custom Bullets, American Fork, Utah. This big blunt-nosed bullet performed exceptionally well in my fast-twist rifle, and much to my surprise also gave very good accuracy results in my slow-twist rifle. I hadn't expected it to be stabilized, for I had previously tried this bullet in a .44 Magnum rifle and most of the bullets either tipped or keyholed. I had also tried some 300-grain swaged half-jacket bullets in my .444 rifles, and only the fast-twist rifle stabilized them. No doubt the added velocity that the .444 gave the big Barnes bullet is the reason why this bullet is stabilized in the slow-twist .444 rifle, but not in a .44 Magnum rifle with the same twist barrel.

In further tests with my slow-twist rifle I found little difference in the accuracy results with jacketed bullets up to 240 grains, but with a decline in accuracy with the 265 Hornady and 300-grain Barnes. It would be my guess that no 1-38 twist .444 rifle would stabilize bullets heavier than this, probably not even the 300-grain bullet if it had a nose more pointed than the Barnes bullet. However, my fast-twist rifle gave amazing accuracy with all weights of the commercial bullets available, especially the 265-grain Hornady. It handled the 300-grain Barnes bullet almost as well.

But to top this, Bob Brooks of Colorado Custom Bullets made some .430 diameter 400-grain SP bullets for me (they can make and furnish the handloader with almost any caliber and weight jacketed bullet on special order). My fast-twist rifle not only stabilized them, but put them all within a 3-inch circle at 100 yards. The few 400-grain Barnes slugs that I tried in the slow-twist rifle all tumbled and accuracy was terrible. Since both my rifles had standard chambers with short throats for factory 240-grain bullets, it was necessary to seat the 300 and 400-grain Barnes bullets deep into the case, making the handloads the same overall length as the factory cartridge, 2.570 inches. The necessary deep seating with these Barnes bullets in standard chambers reduces the available powder capacity and therefore limits the velocity that can be obtained with them.

Before beginning to reload for my .444 rifles I studied all of the reloading manuals that listed loading data on this cartridge. I found that the data on this cartridge in the Sierra and Hornady manuals were conservative and their top loads with Du Pont powders were considerably below the loads listed in the Du Pont manual. Speer's manual listed a wide variety of .444 loads; some of their top loads with Du Pont powders were the same as Du Pont's loads. Since Du Pont's powders are most readily available, and because I had all of them on hand, and since I wanted to get the maximum from the .444, I used Du Pont's and Speer's top loadings as something to work toward. I was mainly interested in full power loads with the heavier bullets, but accuracy was also a criteria. The accompanying chart lists the loads I found that fullfilled the above stipulattions.

I found 4198 and 3031 to be ideally suited for the .444. In the slow-twist rifle I favored 4198 and the 240-grain Sierra jacketed HP bullet. In the fast-twist rifle, 3031 worked best with either the 240 or 265-grain bullets, and this rifle had a special liking for the latter. I found that 4895 was perhaps the best choice with the 300-grain bullet. By no stretch of anyone's imagination can the .444 cartridge be considered a small game or varmint cartridge. The first two light bulleted loads listed are fun-shooting, target-punching loads only.

The Hornady manual has some data on using Winchester-Western 748 ball powder in the .444, but I found its use in this cartridge unsatisfactory. Even with Hornady's top load of 53.3 grains of this powder behind their 265-grain bullet in my fast-twist rifle, a lot of unburned powder remained in the barrel. Worse yet, powder residue somehow worked back into the chamber and left it sticky; I experienced a similar condition with BL-C(2) powder. However, I must qualify this. In loading the 400-grain Barnes bullet I found that W-W 748 was the best powder of four tried. My trial load with it was 42.5 grains, and the single 5-shot group with it at 100 yards measured 2.5 inches.

My fast-twist .444 rifle was so amazingly accurate with just about any jacketed bullet that it became my favorite bigbore rifle. My most accurate load combination for it was 50 grains of 3031 behind the 265-grain Hornady bullet. Loaded in the lapped-out dies, many of the 5-shot groups fired with this load had four shots clustered in one ragged hole with the fifth shot slightly apart. I am convinced that this particular rifle would be equally as accurate with jacketed bullets ranging up to 400 grains in weight if these bullets were made as uniformly as the 265 Hornady. The 300 and 400-grain Barnes bullets that I tried have jackets made of copper tubing and they were not swaged as uniformly, or so they appeared to me, as the .45-70 bullets made by the big three. However, in spite of this, most of my 5-shot groups at 100 yards with these two big bullets had three shots touching each other. This is mighty good big game hunting accuracy.

As for cast and half-jacketed swaged bullets in the .444 Marlin cartridge, any such bullet made for the .44 Special and .44 Magnum cartridges are suitable for use in the .444.

The Lyman Reloading Handbooks No. 44 and 45, as well as the latest *Lyman Cast Bullet Handbook*, has considerable .444 loading data for use with these bullets. My view of the .444 is that it is an excellent big game cartridge, and for this use only jacketed bullets should be used. For this reason I concentrated my efforts on jacketed bullets only in my .444 shooting. However, I did try various weights of cast and half-jacketed bullets in both of my rifles; their accuracy was so poor, compared to the jacketed bullets, that I soon gave up in disgust. Working up .444 loads with cast and half-jacketed bullets will have to be a separate project. My big fast-twist rifle intrigues me to try some heavy cast bullets in it, and for this I have ordered a couple of custom bullet moulds to cast bullets up to 420 grains in weight. If the project is a success, I will report on it. ●

CHAPTER 48

FOR A SHOOTER smitten with the "big-bore bug," there is no recourse other than to begin shooting big-bore rifles — it is as simple as that. This affliction can take several forms. Some shooters go for the "elephant rifles" such as the .375 H&H Magnum, the .458 Winchester Magnum, or one of the exotics like the .577 Nitro Express. Others get the muzzle-loading fever and end up with rifles having bores of 0.50 inch and larger. Still others get the urge to own and shoot the old-time cartridge guns connected with the American West. As a Western-history buff, I have become a member of this latter group.

This desire to become experienced with obsolete big-bore cartridges became concrete in me after I got involved in a loading project for a vintage 1886 Winchester .40-82 WCF, the results of which I detailed in *Handloader* 84. Loading for that old rifle proved to me that the big-bore cartridge guns originally designed for black powder could give fine accuracy with smokeless powders, as long as the correct loading techniques were used.

Sadly, that very fine 1886 Winchester was a borrowed rifle, and upon returning it to its owner, I told him that I was now in the market for some sort of big-bore rifle — preferably a cartridge gun smacking of the Old West. The field was open as far as I was concerned.

Shortly after that, I attended the second annual SHOT Show in San Francisco. While wandering around there, I turned a corner in the exhibit hall only to come face to face with the extremely attractive display of guns and accessories put up by the C Sharps Arms Company.

After viewing that array of new, reproduction 1874 Sharps rifles ranging from military carbines through sporting rifles to long-range target models, I still wanted a cartridge gun connected with the Old West, but I was not going to be happy with anything but a Shiloh 1874 Sharps reproduction.

Now, that is not to say that I went right out and bought the first Shiloh Sharps that I came across. Life is not as simple as all that. First off, I was full up on projects and wanted to finish a few before diving into something that I had no experience with. Second, it is a rare occasion when you can just go out to the local gun store and buy a Shiloh Sharps across the counter. It is possible, for I have seen a few on gun-store shelves, but they are rare, and invariably they were not in the styles or calibers that interested me.

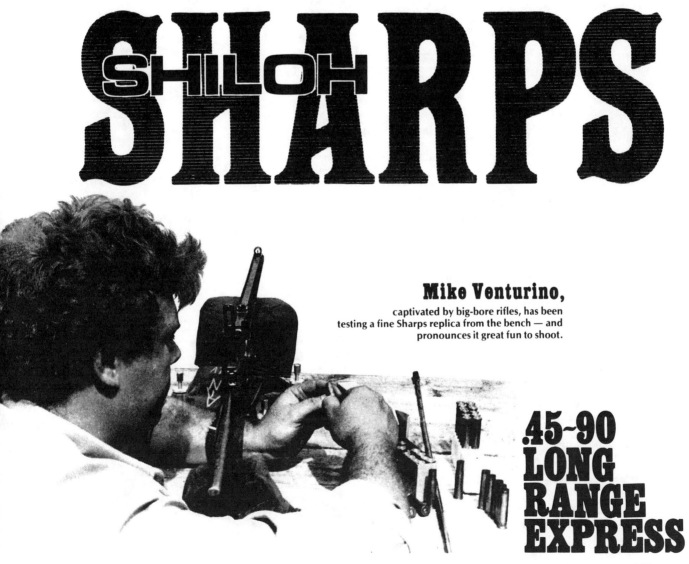

SHILOH SHARPS

Mike Venturino,
captivated by big-bore rifles, has been testing a fine Sharps replica from the bench — and pronounces it great fun to shoot.

.45-90 LONG RANGE EXPRESS

At ten and a half pounds and fifty-one inches long, the Shiloh Long-Range Express rifle is too long and heavy to be handy for hunting. But most buyers of this model want it for shooting rather than for hunting, and its weight can be a benefit for them.

Third, I had to save up a little ready cash. The Shiloh Sharps is not a cheap gun, and rightly so. Anything that has that much workmanship in it can not be inexpensive.

Lady Luck seldom smiles on me — especially in regard to timing — but about a year after that San Francisco SHOT Show, I was ready to make the plunge and called the C Sharps Arms Company at their Washington number. While talking with the boss there, John Schoffstall, I learned that the C Sharps Arms Company would soon be moving to Big Timber, Montana. That is practically in my back yard by Montana standards! I was truly excited. Where is a better place to learn about loading for and shooting these large-bore reproductions than with the people who do it for a living? I bought a Shiloh Sharps then, a number 3 Sporting rifle for the .50 2.5-inch case, but that is another story.

During one of my visits to Big Timber, John asked whether I would like to try working with one of the .45 calibers also. Of course, I said *yes,* and he loaned me a rifle chambered for the .45 2.4-inch cartridge. That rifle, which I have been shooting now for many months, is the top of the standard Shiloh Sharps line. It is the Long Range Express Sporting Rifle.

The first thing that strikes you about the Shiloh Sharps Long Range Express is its length. With a barrel thirty-four inches long, the

Models with the standard rifle-style curved butt are not nearly so comfortable to shoot as the Long-Range Express is; its shotgun-style butt is much easier on the shooter's shoulder.

rifle has an overall length of fifty-one inches. The second impression I had of the gun when John uncased it for the first time was of its wood. The Long Range Express models are fitted with select grades of American black walnut finished in oil. The fanciness of the wood may not equal that of some of the custom stocks, but for a standard production rifle, even a top-of-the-line model, it is exceptional. The butt stock of the Long Range Express is of shotgun styling, about 1.75 inches wide, and carries a large, well defined pistol grip and a medium-sized cheek rest. The fore-end is of matching wood, secured with two screws to the underside of the barrel, and it is of so-called splinter configuration with schnabel tip.

All in all, the wood-to-metal fit of the butt stock to the action is very good but not perfect, which is under-

standable when one takes a close look at the assortment of curves, angles, and straight lines that make up the action and tang of the 1874 Sharps action. It appears to be a stockmaker's nightmare, to me.

My third impression of the Long Range Express was a reinforcement of the very first impression that I had of this line of rifles way back in San Francisco. That is in the workmanship put into them. As sad as it may seem, I am used to picking up a modern American made firearm, be it rifle or handgun, and thinking as I work the action: "Well, it is rough now, but it will smooth up with a little use." Let's face it: the final finish of our standard factory guns could stand some improvement.

However, that is not the case with the Shiloh Sharps. The very first time that I dropped the breech block on this Long Range Express, it felt

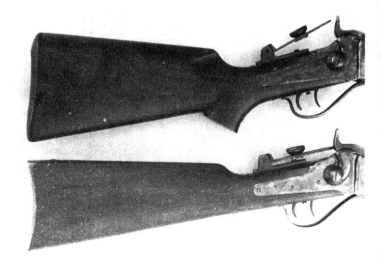

like two pieces of glass sliding together. There was no burr to be worn off, and it did not need to be "broken in." In the past six months, I have put six hundred to eight hundred rounds through it, and it is still as tight as the first day I fired it. It needed no breaking in, and it developed no slop.

The Long Range Express Sporting Rifle is striking in appearance aside from its wood. All metal parts with the exception of the barrel and sights are color case-hardened, and the lower tang is checkered. My only objection to the appearance of the entire rifle is with the rather dull blue of the barrel. I would like to see it a deeply polished black, but that is personal taste and a minor point. As it is, most people whom I have shown this rifle to just say "wow!" when I drag it out.

Something else very noticeable when hefting the Long Range Express for the first time is its weight. My test rifle carried the medium-weight, full-length, octagonal barrel that is 0.925 inch at the muzzle. It has a catalog list

The firing pin and its opening in the breech are large and can be a cause of problems, especially with primers that have soft cups.

Standard on the Long-Range Express is a tang-mounted peep sight, but this wind-gauge spirit-level sight is an extra-cost optional alternative.

weight of 10½ pounds. Optional at slightly extra cost is the heavy tapered octagon barrel, which makes the total rifle weigh about 13½ pounds. The Long Range Express is a beauty to look at, fun to shoot, and interesting to load for, but it is no joy to carry around. Of course, most buyers of the Long Range Express model are buying

Shiloh's Sharps rifles have a certain amount of free-bore and require that bullets be seated forward for the best results.

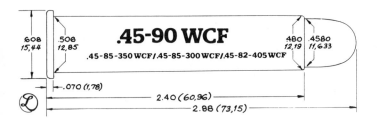

At this late era in its history, the .45-90 cartridge has no single set of official specifications. Dave LeGate's drawing, then, includes dimensions derived from his study of a 1916 Winchester chamber drawing, data from Frank Barnes, and SAAMI specs for the .45-70.

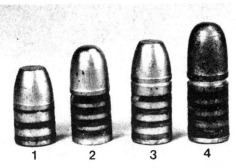

Venturino used four cast bullets in test-firing the Shiloh replica of the Sharps: RCBS 45-300-FN (1), Lyman 457124 (2), RCBS 45-405-FN (3), and Lyman 457406 (4). Only the two in the middle were accurate.

.45 Shiloh Sharps Long-Range Express (.45-90)

bullet	powder	charge (grains)	velocity (fps)	
401-grain Lyman 457124	FFg	85.0	1,525	one cardboard wad
	FFg	75.0		one cardboard wad
	H-322	5.0	1,557	very accurate
	Pyrodex	67.0	1,293	three cardboard wads
	SR-4759	29.0	1,555	Dacron filler best load
	H-322	40.0	1,485	Dacron filler good load
430-grain RCBS 45-405-FN	FFg	85.0	1,462	one cardboard wad
	FFg	75.0		
	H-322	5.0	1,501	one cardboard wad
	Pyrodex	67.0	1,265	one cardboard wad
	SR-4759	28.0	1,486	Dacron filler very good load
	Reloder 7	37.5	1,456	Dacron filler very good load

Over-all length of cartridge 3.00 inches; primer CCI 200 Large Rifle; brass shortened RCBS .45 basic; bullet alloy twenty pounds of wheel-weight alloy and one pound of fifty-fifty solder; Hornady gas checks; bullet diameter 0.457 inch

them for shooting not hunting, so the heavy weight is a benefit there.

Shooters will also find the shotgun-style butt stock of this model a great benefit, as none of the Sharps cartridges give what I would consider to be mild recoil. My personal rifle, the number 3 Sporting Rifle, has the standard rifle butt 1.40 inches wide and capped in steel. When you launch a five-hundred-grain-plus bullet from it while sitting at a benchrest, you feel it! In fact, if you shoot a box or two of loads from it at one sitting, you will continue to feel it for a week!

Conversely, with the 1.75-inch-wide shotgun-style butt of the Long Range Express, I fired forty to fifty rounds a day from the bench with no lasting ill effect. Sure, I may have been a little tender about the shoulder, but I could go right out the next day and do it all over again. To be fair, I should add that the recoil of the .45 2.4-inch cartridge is not as bad as that of the .50 2.5-inch, but it can get noticeable in a day's shooting.

Standard sights for the Long Range Express are a hooded globe front and a tang-mounted peep for the rear. To adjust the rear sight, you first loosen it by turning the whole peep assembly counterclockwise. It is free then to be slid up and down on the scale and locks in place when tightened clockwise. To adjust the sight for windage, loosen the set screw on the rear of the sight, and the whole peep assembly can be moved in the desired direction. Fittingly enough for a rifle that will mostly be used for target shooting, the Long Range Express has no open rear sight.

Also standard for the Long Range Express are adjustable double set triggers. When tested with an Ohaus trigger-pull scale, the front trigger was completely off the scale when tried unset. My scale goes to only 4½ pounds, and I would judge the unset trigger to have about a 5½ to six-pound pull. However, bear in mind that was *unset*. When set by pulling the rear trigger first, that front trigger gave a consistent pull of just four ounces! Group shooting with that set trigger and the peep and globe sights was a joy.

Speaking of shooting: where the original 1874 Sharps are all valuable collectors' items, these Shiloh Sharps reproductions are for the shooter. Besides being enjoyable to shoot, they are capable of a very high degree of accuracy *if* they are loaded correctly. The Long Range Express Sporting Rifle is available in seven chamberings and two bore sizes. These are the .45 2.1-inch (.45-70), .45 2.4-inch (.45-90), .45 2.6-inch (.45-100), .45 2.875-inch (.45-110), .45 3.25-inch (.45-120) .50 2.5-inch (.50-100), and .50 3.25-inch (.50-140). Of these seven, only the .45-70 is available as a factory load, which makes shooting such a rifle pretty much a handloading proposition.

However, I feel that loading for these old buffalo cartridges is a *careful handloader's* proposition. Components can not just be slapped together for these large-volume cases if one expects to get more than a bang from the gun. In fact, if a shooter uses smokeless powders and assembles his ammunition the same as with modern cartridges, he may not even get a bang. I knew better but as an experiment, the very first rounds that I loaded for the Long Range Express were put together by just dumping a suitable charge of Reloder 7 in the case and seating a bullet on top. The first round was a definite hang-fire, and the second was a complete misfire. I will elaborate on this shortly.

As I mentioned, my test rifle was chambered for the .45 2.4-inch case, and the place to start is with the proper brass. To begin with, I trimmed three boxes of RCBS basic .45 brass from its original 3.25 inches to 2.4 inches in an RCBS file-trim die. For those wishing to save on accessories, the brass can also be shortened with a tubing cutter and given a final trimming to 2.4 inches in an ordinary case trimmer. I have used both methods and much prefer the faster file-trim die.

While on the subject of dies, I would like to point out that the RCBS specialty dies for most of the old black-powder cartridges have reached astronomical levels in price. For instance: the dies for my .50 2.5-inch retailed at eighty-five dollars! For this reason, I never bothered to acquire a set of dies for the .45 2.4-inch case. Instead, I merely ran my .45-70 dies a little farther up in the press and neck-sized only. There was never a complication.

If the owner of one of these rifles has the intention of only shooting black powder or Pyrodex in his gun, he will never need reloading dies. The primer can be punched out and a new one inserted by a number of methods, the powder and wads placed in the case, and the bullet placed on top. Reloading dies are handy — just not necessary if a full case of powder is used.

After one has the brass for these guns and the means for making it shootable, the next quest is for bullets. Such big-bore cartridges as the .45 2.4-inch were practically made for cast bullets, but for the noncaster, any jacketed bullet intended for reloading the .45-70 is appropriate. Being a caster, I furnished my own bullets.

This Shiloh Sharps Long Range Express has six lands and grooves with a right-hand twist of one turn in twenty inches. The lands and grooves appear to me to be of equal width, and the grooves are fairly shallow, which I understand was true of the originals. I slugged the bore of this particular rifle at exactly 0.456 inch.

I tried a total of four cast bullets in this rifle, two of which were a waste. Starting at the light end they were RCBS 45-300-FN (323 grains), Lyman 457124 (401 grains), RCBS 45-405-FN (430 grains), and Lyman 457406 (507 grains). Of these, the lightest and the heaviest would never give anything resembling accuracy (twelve-inch groups at a hundred yards!), and I quickly quit wasting lead on them.

Conversely, I was very impressed with the performance given by the two middle-weight bullets and have had some difficulty in deciding which I liked best. The RCBS bullet was perhaps a little more accurate, but the Lyman bullet did not require that I fumble around with gas checks.

For all cast-bullet loads, the lubricant was Javelina Alox, and gas checks (where needed) were from Hornady. I tried both 0.456 and 0.457-inch sizing diameters but could never tell a difference accuracy-wise. Bullet alloy consisted of twenty pounds of straight wheel-weight alloy with the addition of one pound of fifty-fifty bar solder.

These old black-powder cartridges fairly beg the handloader to start experimenting with paper-patched bullets, and I am beginning to get that yearning myself. John Schoffstall tells me that the C Sharps Arms Company is planning to bring out their own moulds for paper-patched bullets, so I am awaiting them.

One last tip in respect to bullets before I move on to other data: the Shiloh Sharps rifles are chambered with a certain amount of freebore and require that the bullets be seated out of the cases and into the leade before giving optimum accuracy. If the new handloader of these cartridges seats his bullets to the traditional crimping groove, accuracy suffers as a result.

Regardless of the propellant to be used — smokeless, Pyrodex, or black powder — these large-volume cases require the handloader to use either wads (with black or Pyrodex) or case fillers (with smokeless). The C Sharps Arms Company brochure warns that loose or unconfined black powder does not give satisfactory performance in these large cases. Believe them! In all loads that I tried using black powder *without* wads, accuracy was very poor. In fact, it was almost nonexistent, because groups measured from six to eighteen inches at a hundred yards. However, when I compressed the black powder with simple cardboard wads, accuracy immediately improved, with groups then measuring from two to four inches for five shots.

Although it may seem a desecration to the purists, I often like to shoot smokeless-powder loads in these Shiloh Sharps rifles. At times, I just do not have the time or inclination for the mandatory clean-up that must follow the use of black powder, and I have found that when loaded correctly, smokeless powder loads give the optimum accuracy these guns are capable of. However, that phrase *when loaded correctly* is important.

The relative light charges of faster-burning smokeless powders that are the optimum choices for loading the older black-powder cases leave excessive air space in those huge cases. That extra air space causes hangfires and misfires, as I have mentioned.

To make a long story short, to get smokeless powders to burn correctly in such large cases requires the use of some sort of case filler. Get that straight! Use a wad with black powder, and a case filler with smokeless. If someone compressed a charge of smokeless with a wad leaving a measure of air space between the wad and the bullet, then the bullet could act the same as a bore obstruction and cause a bulged chamber.

In picking a case filler for smokeless loads, there are two ways to go. One is with one of the cereals such as Cream of Wheat or perhaps corn meal. Another is with a large tuft of some material such as Dacron or kapok. In my load work with the .45 2.4-inch case, I have come to prefer a tuft of Dacron about the size of a four-hundred-grain bullet, although I admit that at times the loads filled with corn meal turned in exceptional accuracy. When seating the Dacron ball in the case, I only press it in with a pencil enough to hold the powder. I do not compress it. All of the loads listed in my chart used such a Dacron filler. If they were to be used with a corn-meal filler instead, I would reduce each powder charge by about three grains.

I have come to rely on only three smokeless powders for loading these Sharps cartridges: SR-4759, Reloder 7, and H-322. Of these, I feel that SR-4759 is the most reliable in regard to both accuracy and velocity variation, but Reloder 7 is a very close second. I might also mention that in loading smokeless in the Sharps cartridges, I am making no attempt to soup them up to velocities that they were not intended for. My only reason for using smokeless is to get by without the mandatory cleaning and to get the best accuracy. In building my loads, I first used black powder to see what velocities it was capable of, and then I tried only to duplicate those velocities with smokeless loads.

One limiting factor in loading these old cartridges in the Shiloh Sharps is inherent in the design of the guns. That is in the sizes of the firing pin and the corresponding firing-pin hole. For some reason, the old boys who engineered the original Sharps felt that a massive firing pin was necessary. When fairly soft primers are used with any type of powder in full-charge loads, the soft primer has a tendency to extrude back into the firing-pin hole. When that happens, you have two ways to go: (1) cock the hammer and dry-fire the rifle, which will reseat the primer, or (2) open the breech block and shear off the extruded part. Since neither of these ways strikes me as satisfactory, I find it easier to just avoid extruded primers by using the relatively hard CCI 200 primers. By using them with the charges I have listed in my chart, there has been no problem in opening the breech block.

Starting approximately with rifles built in 1982, John Schoffstall informed me, the Shiloh Sharps rifles will have the design of their breech blocks changed: all will use a smaller firing pin and firing-pin hole. During a visit, John had one of the prototype breech blocks with him, and we tried it in the Long Range Express. Upon firing some of the loads that had previously given troubles with extruded primers, we found that with the new block, there was no problem at all.

Once I had figured out the correct loading methods for this particular rifle, I have had no problems with accuracy. On one occasion with the listed load of Reloder 7 under the 430-grain RCBS bullet, I fired ten rounds into a 2½-inch group at a hundred yards. Several other times, I was able to put the first three shots into only 1½ inches, again at a hundred yards and again with smokeless powders.

Toward the end of my testing, I moved the targets in to fifty yards so that my aiming would be as precise as possible. At that range, I fired many groups with both black powder and Pyrodex that ran from 1.0 to 1.5 inches for five shots. And several times with loads using SR-4759, I was able to fire five shots into one ragged hole. I admit to not being a good iron-sight shooter, and one of these days I would dearly love to mount a scope on one of these Shiloh Sharps just to see how well I could get it to shoot.

As it is, there are other sighting options available at extra cost. For about 170 dollars, there is a custom vernier tang sight, or at about the same price, there is a windgauge front sight with spirit level that can be fitted with a variety of inserts. The C Sharps Arms Company also has a custom shop offering checkering, engraving, assortments of woods, and different stylings.

All in all, if it sounds as if I am a fan of this type of rifle, it is because I unreservedly am. To my way of thinking, they exhibit top-quality workmanship, impressive good looks, and important to me, they make one be careful and meticulous in his handloading habits. Besides all that, they are fun to shoot.

The Shiloh Sharps Long Range Express Sporting Rifle is not cheap at 749 dollars (at this writing — Jan. 1982). I don't think that I will ever reach the point in my life where that seems like a paltry sum, but when one sees standard, mass-produced, bolt-action sporters going for nearly five hundred dollars, the Long Range Express just doesn't seem that high.   ●

CHAPTER
49

.450 Alaskan

Harold Johnson (insert) test-fired rifles out the back window of his store in Cooper Landing, Alaska.

John Kronfeld

IN 1952, Harold Johnson, a gunsmith and hunting guide living in Cooper Landing, Alaska, developed a wildcat cartridge for the Winchester Model 71 lever action rifle. Based on the .348 Winchester case necked-up and blown out to .458, it was designed to take dangerous game in heavy cover at close range. Johnson appropriately dubbed it the .450 Alaskan.

Harold grew up in North Carolina. By the time he was 12 years old he had a collection of rifles and had read every book on hunting and big game cartridges he could find. It is not surprising then, that when he went to Alaska in 1941, he thought he knew everything necessary about cartridges for the big bears.

On his first attempt at a grizzly, Harold wounded a big bear with his .30-06 using 220-grain roundnose factory ammunition. As he approached the bear to finish him off, the rifle misfired and the bear took the offensive. Harold got the job done but as he said, "It was close."

As a result of that experience, Johnson began to have serious doubts about the effectiveness of the .30-06 on the big bears and he began experimenting with a Winchester Model 86 .45-70. With the barrel cut back to 20 inches, its performance on bear and moose with handloads, using 400-grain Remington tin-jacketed bullets, was excellent.

He also corresponded with Elmer Keith about necking the .348 Winchester up to .45 caliber and blowing it out to increase powder capacity. Elmer concurred that it would make a good cartridge and he encouraged the guide to proceed.

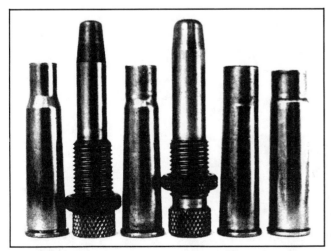

The .450 Alaskan is formed with two tapered expander dies. The first necks the .348 Winchester up to .40 inch; the second expands the neck to .45 prior to fireforming and trimming to 2.145 inches.

287

Cartridge dimensions were drawn and Harold's friend, Bill Fuller, ground the reamers. The famous barrel maker, John Buhmiller, made the 20-inch barrel with a one in 20-inch twist.

Harold's shop began making heavy jacketed bullets that were capable of handling higher velocities by cutting .30-06 cases off an inch or so from their bases, turning them inside and out and finishing with a swaged lead core. This worked but the operation was time-consuming and expensive.

John Buhmiller introduced Harold to Frank Barnes and Frank began to supply his famous bullets, .032-inch thick jackets for Alaska and .049-inch for Africa, with a wide, flat nose for use in tubular magazines. (This style has been discontinued by Barnes.)

Harold began selling his .450 Alaskan to hunters all over the world. The cartridge and the rifle received consistently favorable reviews.

The Johnson Kenai Rifles that were produced in Harold's shop were stamped "JKR" on the barrel. His bear load was 51.5 grains of IMR-4198 under the Barnes 400-grain flatnosed bullet, averaging 2,100 fps at the muzzle for 3,937 foot-pounds of energy. This became the standard load with JKR supplying most of the ammunition; solids were also available.

The first bear to succumb to the .450 Alaskan was a big sow. Harold and his wife were photographing her when the wind shifted. The bear picked up their scent and charged. Harold yelled and waved his arms in an attempt to turn her but as she approached within 30 feet, he was forced to fire, killing her instantly.

My first encounter with a .450 Alaskan was in 1956, when I was given the opportunity to fire one at a range. After being examined by a doctor, I was assured that the recoil had not broken my shoulder!

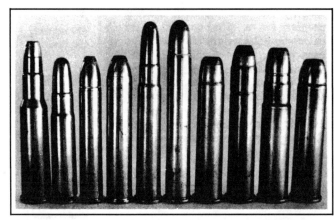

Lever action cartridges, past and present (left to right): .348 Winchester, .35 Remington, .375 Winchester, .444 Marlin, .35 Winchester, .405 Winchester, .45-70 Government, .45-90 Winchester, .45 Alaskan and .50 Alaskan.

I had nearly forgotten that embarrassment, when I found a .450 Alaskan at a Sacramento gun show in 1986. I bought it immediately, complete with RCBS loading and case-forming dies, 90 cases and a magnum recoil pad. The 20-inch round tapered barrel had a one-in-12-twist and measured .7229-inch at the muzzle but lacked the JKR stamp. The rifle weighed eight pounds and its barrel was equipped with an adjustable buckhorn rear sight and a hooded ramp up front. A local gunsmith checked it thoroughly and said the conversion was done well.

The search for loading data centered around currently available bullets. The only information that was close was listed for the .450-348 Improved (Ackley) in P.O. Ackley's *Handbook for Shooters and Reloaders*, Volume 1. I wanted loads developed specifically for the .450 Alaskan.

Ackley also listed a similar cartridge, the .450 Fuller, that had been developed by the same Bill Fuller who ground the original reamers for the .450 Alaskan. I called Cooper Landing, Alaska, and found Mr. Fuller well and still actively shooting. He was able to

provide me with background information on the .450 Alaskan and Mr. Johnson's whereabouts, but he did not have any loading data. (An interesting side note from Mr. Fuller was that a .450 Alaskan had been made for Elmer Keith. He took it to Africa. His guide liked the rifle so much that Elmer left it with him.)

When I contacted Harold Johnson, he told me that he wanted something more powerful than the .45-70 for the big bears. He did not want to give up the lever action rifle, however, because Winchester 86s and 71s handled so well, especially at close range in heavy cover. They could also be reloaded with one round already in the chamber, the hammer cocked and ready to fire. A bolt action, on the other hand, is completely down for a few seconds while being reloaded.

In the meantime Jay Postman of RCBS forwarded a 1962 article on the .450-348 Ackley (Improved). The loads were developed by Homer Powley on his computer and psi calculator. I ordered a set.

These slide rules allow a reloader to

Left: Experimental .45-caliber bullets were fashioned from .30-06 cases that were cut off, turned and filled with swaged lead cores. Right: Bullets tested in the .45 Alaskan: (1) 131-grain Lee RB; (2) 205-grain Rapine; (3) 300-grain Hornady; (4) 400-grain Speer; (5) 400-grain Barnes; (6) 405-grain RCBS; (7) 500-grain RCBS; (8) 500-grain Hornady and (9) 465-grain A-Square.

identify the most efficient DuPont powder for a rifle cartridge. By calculating the weight of water in the case to the base of the bullet and measuring the length of the barrel from the muzzle to the base of the bullet the computer selects conservative starting loads for cartridges in the 40,000 to 50,000-psi range. Chronographed velocities are used to monitor pressure.

The formed cases that came with the rifle were a mixture of old Winchester and Remington hulls with five different headstamps: Rem-UMC, R-P, Super-X, Super Speed, W-W Super. Water capacity varied by as much as 20 grains between some cases and the whole lot was discarded.

I purchased 10 boxes of new Winchester .348 brass with the "W-W Super" headstamp and annealed the entire batch before any of the necks were expanded to .45 caliber. RCBS case lube was used inside the case necks to keep them from collapsing.

The fireforming load was 59 grains of IMR-3031 with a 400-grain cast bullet. After fireforming, cases were trimmed to 2.136 inches.

I needed bullets that were safe to use in a tubular magazine (wide, flat noses), but they had to slip through the loading gate and feed reliably through the action into the chamber.

The 300-grain flatnoses manufactured by Sierra, Hornady and Barnes worked well and are fine for deer and black bear. They lack the sectional density and heavy construction so desirable when the range is short and the animal big and dangerous. Speer's 400-grain flatnose is a better choice for big heavy-muscled targets. It delivered fine accuracy when crimped in the lower cannelure. Speer employees drive those bullets up to 2,400 fps in the .458 Winchester Magnum for elk and suggest muzzle velocities around 1,900 fps for good penetration and expansion at closer ranges. Layne Simpson's article

.450 Alaskan

bullet	powder	charge (grains)	overall length (inches)	velocity (fps)	computed pressure* (psi)	50-yard group (inches)	remarks
300 Hornady	IMR-3031	58.0		1,905		1.0	good deer load
400 Speer		66.7	2.77	2,017	38,000	1.5	
		67.4		2,038	38,760	1.0	
		66.7**		2,050	40,280	.75	
		67.4**		2,123	41,085	1.0	
	RL-7	59.0		1,975		2.25	starting load
		60.5		1,961		1.5	
		61.5		2,088		2.5	maximum load
	H-322	62.0		1,820		1.5	
		65.0		1,934		1.5	
		66.0		1,954		.75	very accurate
	W-748	66.0		1,672		.5	2nd most accurate
		70.0		1,817		.5	very accurate
		72.0		1,926		1.75	maximum load
400 Barnes	IMR-3031	58.8	2.61	1,808	39,000	.5	
		60.0		1,830	40,560	.75	
		60.5		1,862	41,340	1.25	
	W-748	66.0		1,780		.75	starting load
		69.0		1,889		.5	most accurate load
	H-322	62.0		1,876		1.0	starting load
		66.0		2,018		1.25	maximum load
465 A-Square	IMR-3031	61.5	2.97	1,894	37,000	.5	
		62.7		1,927	38,480	.5	
		63.9		1,954	39,960	.75	
		64.6		1,981	40,700	1.25	
		65.8		2,033	42,180	2.5	
	W-748	65.0		1,685		2.0	
		67.0		1,887		1.25	
500 Hornady	IMR-3031	59.5	2.92	1,785	35,000	2.0	
		63.5		1,880	37,800	1.0	

Cast Bullet Loads

bullet	powder	charge (grains)	overall length (inches)	velocity (fps)	computed pressure* (psi)	50-yard group (inches)	remarks
131.7 Lee roundball	Unique	10.6		1,080		2.0	training and practice; no recoil
205 Rapine	2400	17.4	2.38	1,850		1.5	varmint and small game
405 RCBS	IMR-3031	64.0	2.68	1,855	36,200	1.5	
		66.0		2,037	37,000	2.5	
		67.0		2,093	39,562	1.0	
		66.0**		2,085	41,390	2.5	
		67.0**		2,118	41,935	2.0	
	W-748	66.0		1,759		2.0	starting load
		70.0		1,889		.75	good load
		71.5		1,994		2.5	maximum load
	H-322	65.0		1,871		.5	good load
		67.5		1,933		1.0	
		68.5		2,033		1.25	best hunting load
	RL-7	58.5		2,023		1.6	starting load
		61.0		2,086		1.5	2nd best hunting load
		63.0		2,130		4.5	
500 RCBS	W-748	60.0		1,715		2.0	
		63.0		1,820		1.5	heavy recoil
	H-322	54.0		1,719		2.0	
		59.0		1,825		.5	best load this bullet

.450 Alaskan

* Pressures calculated on the Powley Computer.

** Loads with CCI-250 primers; all others used CCI-200 primers. All loads made up in W-W Super .348 Winchester cases. Hornady gas checks used on all cast bullets. 50-yard groups are three shots. Velocities are instrumental at 10 feet with a PACT chronograph.

Be alert — Publisher cannot accept responsibility for errors in published load data.

"Big-Game Bullets in the .45-70" in *Handloader* No. 92 verified those judgments.

The RCBS 405-grain flatnose was cast with a combination of wheel-weights and 50/50 lead-tin. It miked .4587 inch and weighed 414 grains when sized and lubricated with LBT Blue. For powders other than IMR-3031, pure Linotype was used. Bullets dropped from the mould averaged .4592 inch and weighed 400 grains after sizing and lubricating. Hornady gas checks were fitted to all cast bullets.

The bore was slugged and showed a groove diameter of .4585 inch. Some bullets were sized .457; others, .458; still others were pushed through a .459 die which lubricated but didn't size them. As expected, the largest diameter gave the best accuracy and showed no signs of leading in test loads. All bullets were heavily crimped, an absolute must with this cartridge.

Jacketed bullets were crimped in the cannelures. Cast bullets were crimped at the base of the first grease groove rather than in the crimping groove. That gave additional case capacity and still allowed loading through the loading gate and flawless feeding through the action.

The new Barnes 400-grain flatnose functions very well through the loading gate. It gives excellent accuracy up to 2,000 fps but there is one problem in using it in a lever action. It is designated a flatnose but the meplat is not as wide as those on the old Barnes or Speer bullets and the nose rests on the primer in the case ahead of it. As a result, this bullet was used to verify Powley Computer powder selections and velocity computations only.

The Monolithic Solids made by A-Square have long intrigued me, but loads with their 465-grain bullets would not enter the loading gate owing to excessive cartridge length. That is just as well since it is a solid, round-nose bullet which prohibits its use in a tubular magazine.

They are very accurate bullets, however, and shot into 1¼ inches at 50 yards when pushed by 67 grains of IMR-3031. Muzzle velocity was 1,887 fps.

The Hornady 500-grain roundnose has the same dimensional problems as the A-Square but gives excellent accuracy. Backed by 63.5 grains of IMR-3031 (which required a 62-inch drop tube) the calculated muzzle velocity was 1,892 fps. The chronographed velocity was 1,880 fps with three shots going into one hole.

It was suggested by others that the Hornady or A-Square bullet be used as a first shot, with the magazine filled with 400-grain loads in reserve. In theory, that sounded good but I found it inadvisable because of the wide variation in points of impact between the two bullets at normal hunting ranges.

Nevertheless, I still wanted a 500-grain bullet that would function through the magazine. I purchased a 45-500FN RCBS bullet mould. Bullets came from the mould measuring .4592 inch and weighed 489 grains.

Fifty-nine grains of H-322 gave them an average muzzle velocity of 1,825 fps, 3,717 foot-pounds of energy and put three shots into a cloverleaf measuring .5 inch.

Powder selection and weights were determined by the Powley Computer which picked IMR-3031 as the optimal powder for all bullet weights selected.

Calculations for velocity and pressure are affected by several variables, some of which are beyond the reloader's control. Accurate measurement of water capacity and barrel length, however, is up to the reloader and the distance between the bullet and the rifling is a variable that is hard to control in lever actions owing to loading and function requirements.

Jacketed bullets must be crimped in their respective cannelures while cast bullets may be crimped in any of the grease grooves, allowing greater flexibility with overall cartridge length. A jacketed bullet that must be seated out because of its cannelure may not feed through the loading gate. A bullet that is seated deep enough to go through the gate may be seated so deep that it decreases powder capacity and increases the distance to the rifling. Both conditions, either separately or together, may result in a significant velocity and pressure variation.

The Powley Computer was cross-checked with a PACT chronograph on all loads and in most instances, calculated and actual velocities for IMR-3031 were very close.

The Winchester Model 71 in .348 Winchester has a maximum working pressure of 44,000 psi. To maintain a margin of safety, handloads were limited to 42,000 psi.

As an additional control, 10 rounds of factory 250-grain Winchester ammunition were fired in a new Browning Model 71. Case expansion was measured at the pressure ring just ahead of the extractor groove. Similar measurements on the .450 Alaskan cases never exceed the measurements of the .348 brass and at no time did any of the 500 test rounds fail to extract smoothly.

Since the Powley Computer picked IMR-3031 for all bullets, other powders with similar burning rates were tried to see if accuracy and/or velocity could be increased while maintaining safe working pressures. Reloder 7, H-322 and W-748 gave good results and burned clean.

Three-shot groups were used for accuracy testing since I feel that duplicates actual hunting requirements.

It would be a shame to own a classic rifle like this one and restrict its use to Alaska or Africa. It only weighs eight pounds, so there is no reason not to make this an all-round rifle for deer, black bear, elk and plinking.

A review of old Lyman loading manuals shows that roundballs and light bullets were popular in the .45-70 so I bought a Lee .457 double-cavity roundball mould. Linotype balls measured .459 inch at the seam and weighed 131.7 grains. They were crimped over 10.0 grains of Unique for a muzzle velocity of 1,080 fps. Groups hovered around two inches at 50 yards. Recoil and noise were on a par with a .22 rimfire.

Rapine Associates of East Greenville, Pennsylvania, makes a single-cavity 205-grain hollowbase mould for the .45-70. The one I purchased casts perfect bullets measuring .462 inch. They were sized .459 inch and gave 1.5-inch groups with 17.4 grains of Hercules 2400 generating 1,850 fps muzzle velocity. Again, there was almost no recoil. It is an ideal bullet for plinking and small game hunting.

The .450 Alaskan, with bullet weights from 300 to 500 grains, is a versatile rifle. It is accurate, reliable and powerful enough to handle anything on this continent and just about any animal in the world at reasonable ranges. ●

CHAPTER
50

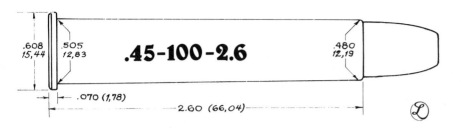

.45-100-2.6

.608 15,44 | .505 12,83 | .480 12,19

.070 (1,78) 2.60 (66,04)

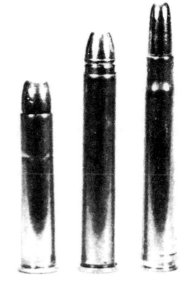

The .45-100 Sharps in the center is compared with two more-popular cartridges, the .45-70 on left and .375 H&H Magnum on the right.

PERHAPS ONE of the least used of the original .45 caliber Sharps cartridges was the one using a 2.6-inch case. As we know it today this is the .45-100 Sharps, and although it is a standard chambering of the Shiloh Sharps rifles distributed by the C. Sharps Arms Company of Big Timber, Montana, it still is relatively obscure. In terms of popularity of the calibers sold by the Shiloh Sharps people, both the .45-70 (2.1-inch case) and the .45-120 (3¼-inch case) outdistance the .45-100. Those shooters desiring ease of loading and inexpensive brass go for the .45-70 while those willing to go to the expense and trouble of loading the longer cases usually opt for the biggest — the .45-120. Therefore, the .45-100 often is bypassed.

The .45-100 — meaning the version using the 2.6-inch case — was first introduced in November 1876, and the standard load used 100 grains of Fg black powder with a 550-grain paper patched bullet. However, the life of the .45-100 was short as it was replaced in June 1877 with the .45

caliber using a 2.4-inch case. In modern parlance the .45 caliber using a 2.4-inch case is referred to as the .45-90, but that was not the term over a century ago. The .45-2.4 in those days was also loaded with 100 grains of Fg black powder and a 550-grain paper patched bullet for a standard load. As a matter of fact, the longest of the .45 caliber cartridges that the original Sharps Rifle Company chambered for was the .45-2-7/8-inch, which was also loaded with 100 grains of Fg black powder. Therefore, by our modern terminology there were three .45-100 Sharps cartridges offered in the 1870s. They all used different case lengths and for practical effect were not interchangeable.

Many modern shooters are unaware that the old-timers who used the Sharps rifle cartridges rarely referred to them with the double set of numbers which we are so fond of today; for example, the .45-70, .45-90, .45-100, etc. Instead, they called their cartridges by the much more specific caliber and case length, such as .45-2.1, .45-2.4, .45-2.6-inch. For confirmation of this look at the caliber designation on original Sharps rifles. They are so marked.

The Shiloh Sharps Company also uses these markings and I compliment them on being so specific.

Another fact little known to many shooters is that the .45-120 (or .45-3-1/4-inch) was never offered by the original Sharps Rifle Company. According to my research only one rifle was chambered by the Sharps Rifle Company for a 3-1/4-inch case and it was made especially for one of the ammunition companies.

Other than length, original .45-2.6-inch Sharps cartridges differed from

Mike Venturino

.45-100 SHARPS

Author's Shiloh Sharps custom Long-Range Express in .45-100 caliber.

The four bullets used in Venturino's testing, from left: RCBS No. 45-405FN; NEI No. 405-458GC; Lyman No. 457406; and the C. Sharps Arms paper-patch. Bullet weights in grains are 424, 440, 494 and 496 respectively. In photo at right the same bullets are shown in loaded form.

standard .45-70 specifications by a few thousandths of an inch in case heads. For example *Cartridges of the World* lists .597 inch as rim diameter on the .45-2.6-inch while the .45-70 is listed as .600. Another difference a century ago was that all Sharps Rifle Company ammunition was loaded with Berdan primers, but ammunition by some other companies had boxer primers. An additional and important difference was that all the various Sharps .45-100 cartridges, regardless of case length, were factory loaded with .451-inch diameter paper patched bullets. At times these same rounds were offered with "grooved" bullets (grease lubricated), but nowhere can I find specifications for their diameters.

To make a confusing situation worse, the bore diameters of the original rifles varied from about .454 to over .460. These are actual measurements of several .45 caliber rifles taken by a collector and passed on to me. I guess the old-timers relied on the soft lead slugs to "bump" up and fill the bore, but now I wonder at the tales of buffalo hunters consistently hitting animals at 500 yards or better!

I am glad to say that all of this is academic to the modern shooter of the .45-2.6-inch Sharps if he is using a Shiloh Sharps rifle and modern components. I have been shooting one of these guns in this particular caliber at least weekly since April 1982. In all, over 3,000 rounds of my handloads have been fired and I feel that I have come to know this rifle and cartridge intimately.

My personal Shiloh Sharps .45-2.6-inch rifle is a version built by the C. Sharps Arms Company's custom shop. It has a 32-inch full octagon barrel .90 inch in diameter, is

checkered on fore-end and pistol grip and the wood is finely figured walnut with a beautifully smooth finish. Perhaps the most important features are its sights. The rear is a tang-mounted custom vernier peep, which the company refers to as the extra long range version. It has a stem about six inches long. The front sight is a custom wind gauge spirit level which accepts a variety of inserts. When using these dual aperture sights on black bullseye targets at 100 yards, it's like using a one-power scope.

This rifle has a groove diameter of .456 with six grooves about .004 inch deep. Twist rate is one turn in 20 inches. Like most current factory-made barrels, the Shiloh Sharps' start out a little rough, but not bad. However, after so much shooting mine is smoothed to a mirror bright finish. The company offers hand lapping as an option on their custom guns.

Brass for the .45-2.6 is easily formed by shortening RCBS 3-1/4-inch basic cases to the correct length. I have done it by using an RCBS file trim die, or by cutting the cases down with a tubing cutter and trimming to final length. The former method is much easier and faster, but these special file-trim dies are becoming quite expensive.

I have loaded over 3,000 rounds of this caliber and I have never touched a set of .45-2.6-inch dies. Instead, I merely turn my standard .45-70 dies out in the press another half inch. When loading for single-shot rifles there is no need to full length size, so I size the cases only enough to hold a bullet. The neck expanding, seating and crimping dies also work as well when properly adjusted.

In my extensive use of this cartridge I have expended a large assortment of

These are the various powders used in Venturino's tests of the .45-100 Shiloh Sharps.

.45-100 (2.6-inch) Sharps

Powder	RCBS No. 45-405FN · 424 grains			NEI No. 405-458GC · 440 grains			Lyman No. 457406 · 494 grains			C. Sharps custom PP · 496 grain		
	charge (grains)	velocity (fps)	group size (inches)	charge (grains)	velocity (fps)	group size (inches)	charge (grains)	velocity (fps)	group size (inches)	charge (grains)	velocity (fps)	group size (inches)
SR-4759	22.0	1,269	3-1/4	23.0	1,304	1-3/4	24.0	1,191	3-1/2	24.0	1,199	4-3/4
	23.0	1,318	3-7/8	24.0	1,338	2-1/4	25.0	1,235	2.0	25.0	1,237	4-1/4
	24.0	1,366	3-3/4	25.0	1,372	4-1/2 (four in 1-1/2)	26.0	1,259	2-1/2	26.0	1,265	4-1/4
	25.0	1,396	2-1/2	26.0	1,411	3-1/2	27.0	1,305	3-5/8	27.0	1,309	4-1/2
	26.0	1,430	3.0	27.0	1,444	5.0	28.0	1,318	3.0	28.0	1,341	3-1/4
IMR-4198	30.0	1,304	3-1/4	30.0	1,325	2-1/4	29.0	1,271	5.0	30.0	1,287	5.0
	31.0	1,356	5-7/8 (four in only 7/8!)	31.0	1,362	1-3/4	30.0	1,295	4-1/2	31.0	1,326	2.0
	32.0	1,419	5-1/4	32.0	1,395	1-3/4	31.0	1,331	5-3/8	32.0	1,358	2-3/16
	33.0	1,457	2-1/2	33.0	1,426	5-7/8	32.0	1,370	3-7/8	33.0	1,388	3-1/2
	34.0	1,490	6-1/4	34.0	1,464	5.0	33.0	1,402	5-1/8	34.0	1,399	2-1/8
Reloder 7	30.0	1,361	2-1/2	29.0	1,299	3-7/8 (four in 2.0)	29.0	1,270	1-3/4	29.0	1,275	4-3/4
	31.0	1,400	2-3/4	30.0	1,331	3.0	30.0	1,305	2-1/2 (four in 1-1/4)	30.0	1,279	3.0
	32.0	1,427	3-1/2	31.0	1,373	2-5/8 (four in 1-3/8)	31.0	1,331	2.0	31.0	1,310	4-7/8
	33.0	1,465	6.0 (four in 2-3/8)	32.0	1,406	3-1/4	32.0	1,366	5-1/8	32.0	1,337	2-3/4
	34.0	1,473	3-3/4 (four in 2-1/2)	33.0	1,439	3-1/8 (four in 1-1/2)	33.0	1,397	4.0	33.0	1,392	4-1/4
H-322	30.0	1,216	3.0	34.0	1,325	3-1/2 (four in 2.0)	35.0	1,255	2-3/4	35.0	1,238	2-5/16
	31.0	1,259	4.0	35.0	1,338	3-1/8	36.0	1,310	3-3/8	36.0	1,283	3-3/16
	32.0	1,288	2-3/8	36.0	1,376	4-3/8	37.0	1,351	3-3/4	37.0	1,296	3-3/8
	33.0	1,303	2-1/2	37.0	1,406	4-3/4	38.0	1,371	5-3/4	38.0	1,321	2-1/8
	34.0	1,359	3-1/4 (four in 1-7/8)	38.0	1,433	4.0	39.0	1,405	3-7/8	39.0	1,363	2.0
W-748	36.0	1,210	3-3/8 (four in 2-1/8)	36.0	1,196	3-1/2	36.0	1,327	2.0	38.0	1,333	3-1/2
	37.0	1,272	2-1/2	37.0	1,236	2.0	37.0	1,366	3.0	39.0	1,361	1-7/16
	38.0	1,268*	2-3/4	38.0	1,281	4-1/2	38.0	1,395	2-11/16	40.0	1,384	1-15/16
	39.0	1,285	2-3/4 (four in 1-1/2)	39.0	1,265*	4-1/4 (four in 2-5/8)	39.0	1,420	2-3/4	41.0	1,425	4-3/8
	40.0	1,307	3-1/4 (four in 2.0)	40.0	1,320	3-1/4 (four in 1-3/4)	40.0	1,458	3.0	42.0	1,440	2-3/4
IMR-4064	39.0	1,286	3-3/4 (four in 2.0)	40.0	1,339	3.0	37.0	1,263	3-7/8	36.0	1,245	3-1/2
	40.0	1,330	4-5/8 (four in 2-3/8)	41.0	1,367	4-3/4	38.0	1,294	3-3/4	37.0	1,268	4-1/4
	41.0	1,359	2-7/8	42.0	1,395	2-1/2	39.0	1,317	4.0	38.0	1,307	4-1/2
	42.0	1,396	2.0	43.0	1,416	4-7/8	40.0	1,353	3-1/4	39.0	1,326	5.0
	43.0	1,428	2-1/4	44.0	1,480	4-3/4	41.0	1,380	3-3/3	40.0	1,354	5-5/8

494-grain Lyman 457406

charge (grains)	powder	velocity (fps)	group (inches)
95.0	Fg black powder	1,366	3-1/4
85.0	Fg black powder	1,511	4-1/8 Duplex
8.0	SR-4759		
75.0	CTG Pyrodex	1,444	5.0

424-grain RCBS 45-405FF

charge (grains)	powder	velocity (fps)	group (inches)
100.0	Fg black powder	1,505	3-1/2
85.0	Fg black powder	1,596	6-1/2 (four in 3-1/2 inches) Duplex
8.0	SR-4759		
75.0	CTG Pyrodex	1,559	2-1/8

All cases were RCBS basic brass shortened to 2.6 inches.
All primers were CCI-200 Large Rifle.
All smokeless loads used a cornmeal filler.
All black powder loads were fired with the bore cleaned for every shot.
All cast bullets were cast of an alloy consisting of 20 pounds wheelweight metal mixed with one pound of 50/50 solder.
Bullets were not weighed individually, but were sized to .457 (except paper-patch) and Lyman gas checks were fitted when needed. Lubricant was NEI Ten-X.
Overall loaded lengths were RCBS 424-grain - 3.16 inches
    NEI 440-grain - 3.26 inches
    Lyman 494-grain — 3.32 inches
    C. Sharps paper-patch - 3.43 inches
All bullets, except the paper-patch version, were crimped slightly.
All groups fired at 100 yards in five-shot strings.
* Note lower velocity with more powder.

powders, primers and bullets -- both cast and jacketed. I have also fired many hundreds of rounds propelled by either black powder or Pyrodex. Those two powders are certainly not my favorites, but I have to admit that once the knack of getting them to shoot accurately is mastered they are fun to play with. On the other hand they are not fun to clean up after!

Although all of us reading this magazine realize that handloading is a variable ridden pastime, loading for an old-timer, such as the .45-2.6-inch Sharps, brings this into full focus. Once you have the components and tools necessary to assemble ammunition for your rifle you are then faced with such questions as: grooved bullets or paper patched? Which grease lubed bullets? Which type of lube? What alloy will shoot best? Plain base or gas check? Which type of gas check? If paper patched bullets are used, what type of paper should they be patched with? or Where exactly on the bullet should the patch be put? The list goes on to include, but is not limited to, powders, primers, bullet seating depth, case fillers for smokeless and wads for black powder or Pyrodex.

In other words, the compulsive experimenter can take just one old-time rifle and spend endless hours trying to select the optimum combination of components.

For many months I got caught in such a trap and for awhile I was determined to try every variation of everything I could think of in my rifle.

After awhile, however, I realized that while such shooting was enjoyable and sometimes maddening, I would never be able to write an article about the .45-2.6-inch Sharps unless I made a few arbitrary decisions on components and tested a variety of loads with some system.

One component was bullet alloys. To my surprise I found that with smokeless powders I could use just about any alloy from very soft to very hard with suitable accuracy. However, for the purposes of this article I stuck with one consisting of twenty pounds of straight wheelweight alloy mixed with one pound of 50/50 bar solder. This alloy is hard, inexpensive and accurate. I used it for both lubed and paper patched bullets.

After my bullets were cast they were given a casual visual inspection during the lubing and sizing operation, or when the paper patch was applied. At no time did I weigh the bullets,

although I am convinced that groups would have been tighter at times if some defective bullets had been culled. However, since I intended to fire 700 to 800 rounds, I simply did not have time to weigh each bullet.

All grease lube bullets were sized to .457 inch, and lubed with NEI Ten-X lubricant. Since all the grease lube bullets were gas check versions, the Lyman brand was applied.

For my final testing I settled on four cast bullets. The most unique of these is the paper patch version cast in a mould sold by the C. Sharps Arms Company.

These moulds are nose pour, adjustable for weight, and drop a bullet with a slightly concave base. I set mine to throw close to 500 grains for this shooting. The paper patches were cut from 100 percent cotton paper sold by the Sharps company and cut with the template supplied with each mould. When applying the patch I set it far enough forward on the bullet so that all the bearing surface was covered and tucked the extension at the base into the concave.

I might add too, that in the beginning I had no hope for my paper-patching ability. However, with a little experience I soon became fairly proficient at this chore and as the charts show, some of my best groups came with paper patched projectiles.

For the other heavyweight I used the round-nose gas check version by Lyman numbered 457406. From my alloy (lubed and gas checked) they weighed in at 494 grains. Although I did get some good groups with this particular bullet, it was generally the least accurate.

My third cast bullet was the RCBS No. 45-405FN. This is another gas check version with flat-nose weighing 424 grains when ready to load. I have come to like this particular bullet in the .45-2.6 and have done some good shooting with it all the way out to 500 yards.

Perhaps the star bullet of all, however, is a relatively new design by NEI. This unorthodox projectile is a spitzer shaped, gas checked version weighing 440 grains from my mould (No. 405-458GC).

At mild velocities with certain powder charges this NEI bullet gave some very small groups and I wonder just what I could get from it if I inspect each and every bullet carefully!

The above four cast bullets are the

only ones I chose to use for this study and jacketed bullets were excluded completely. Most of the bullet-making companies offer jacketed .45s of one type or another, but I consider them as hunting bullets. That is not to say that they are inaccurate, for they are finely accurate. I have tested some of them with very good results, but I just can't see shooting away a large batch of soft-point hunting bullets at paper targets.

I have listed the specific seating depth of all bullets in the load chart, but would like to stress that my chosen seating depth is a compromise. The Shiloh Sharps have chambers with about a half inch of free bore that is intended for the paper patched bullets. Personally, I could do without it. Although I will continue to use paper patched bullets in my gun from time to time, I think the most practical bullets for modern shooters are the grease lube types.

To obtain best accuracy with the grease lubes, they must be seated out in the case slightly to compensate for that free bore. Most rifle shooters and handloaders agree that best accuracy results if the bullet begins its travel near the rifling.

However, if grease lubed bullets are seated out very far there will be exposed grease, which will pick up any sort of dirt or grit. I seat the RCBS and NEI bullets out as far as possible without exposing any grease. With the Lyman bullet I leave the top grease groove empty and seat it exposed. Perhaps, if all the bullets were seated out as far as possible, accuracy could be affected for the better, but I just don't like carrying around cartridges with exposed lube. Some decisions are arbitrary!

At no time during my load work with the 2.6-inch did I attempt to soup it up to modern ballistics. The capacity of the case exceeds that of the .458 Winchester Magnum and might be a source of temptation to some hot rodders. I feel recoil is heavy enough at the old-time velocities and will leave souped up velocities to elephant hunters.

Instead, it is my theory that these old design guns, such as the Shiloh Sharps, are best enjoyed with ammunition that fairly duplicates the velocities of the original loads. For myself, I have loaded and chronographed loads using 100 grains of Fg black powder and then tried to duplicate them with smokeless.

Nearly any of the smokeless

powders from the slower burning handgun types, such as 2400, on up through most rifle powders, can be used safely in the .45-2.6-inch Sharps at proper load levels. The limiting factor is accuracy. Some that were tried gave no promise whatsoever and others were surprisingly good.

Again, some arbitrary decisions were made in picking the powders. I figured that such traditional cast bullet numbers as SR-4759, Reloder 7, and IMR-4198 had to be used. Then I also decided that some nontraditional cast bullet powders of faster burning rates had to be tried, such as H-322 or W-748. In regard to that latter number I am glad it was not left out; it has great potential for these older cartridges.

One powder that was excluded was IMR-3031, which may raise some eyebrows. If any single powder over the years has become identified with smokeless loads in old, big-bore black powder cartridges it is IMR-3031. That is why it was excluded; others have delved into its potential and documented their results. As a replacement, I used IMR-4064, which I have never seen recommended for large-bore, straight-sided cartridges.

With all smokeless powder I use some sort of case filler to hold it back against the primer. For this test session I filled the cases to the brim with cornmeal after the smokeless powder charge was dumped in. This will raise pressures, but at no time were they high; I was working at low pressure levels anyway. A ball of Dacron or kapok can be pressed in on top of the powder, but in my past year's shooting I have found cornmeal gives more consistent results in this particular rifle.

I don't usually list all test loads in my load chart. However, for this article the mode was changed. I wanted to try the half dozen smokeless powders listed to see how accuracy and velocity would be affected by adding one grain at a time. Therefore, I began with a powder charge that I knew would give low velocity and then raised the charge one grain at a time for five grains. By this manner I was able to see how velocities could be changed by small increment powder increases and somewhere along the way I reasoned that some powder charges were going to give better accuracy than others. As is obvious by the load charts, some particular powders and charges were vastly better than others.

I have mentioned accuracy, or the lack of it, but just what are the accuracy standards for a big-bore rifle such as this? In the past few months several people knowing of my work with this rifle have asked if I could get five-shot one-inch groups. On a few occasions I have shot some one-inch groups, but I rule them as flukes. Even with the superb metallic sights, I cannot compete with a high-powered scope for holding ability. As I mentioned, I am shooting cast bullets that have not been weighed so occasional flyers are bound to happen, and I think that asking for one-inch groups from such a rifle is absurd.

My accuracy standards for this .45-2.6-inch are thus: if I can shoot five shots at 100 yards into a 2 to 2½-inch group with unweighed cast bullets I think I have a wonderful load. If the group is 3 to 3¼ inches under the same circumstances the load is still considered adequate and will be more accurate than I can hold. However, if groups are over that, I consider the load not suitable for accuracy.

In my specific tests the best bullets were the NEI spitzer, the RCBS flatnose, the C. Sharps Arms paper patch, and then the Lyman roundnose, in that order. Picking the best powder is a more difficult choice. As my load chart shows, W-748 gave the best groups on the average, but SR-4759, Reloder 7 and IMR-4198 were all good at times.

Two interesting things occurred in regard to powders. First, several gave more velocity with the heavier bullets than with the lighter ones. I feel this was due to the heavier bullets causing the smokeless powders to burn more completely in this large, inefficient case. Second: I switched lots of SR-4759 after shooting the Lyman and paper patched bullets and found that several grains less powder was required to obtain the same velocities. The two lots of powder differed by five years in age.

After all this work with the .45-100 (2.6-inch) Sharps, on one point I am definite. If the shooter intends to use only smokeless powder there is no reason to have any other .45 caliber cartridge than the .45-70. It can be safely loaded to do anything that the .45-100 can do with smokeless, and it will do it without the bother of fillers. The .45-100 looks more impressive than the .45-70, but when using smokeless powders it is not.

Conversely: if you do like the looks of these long, big-bore, black powder rounds and would like to keep the option open of someday loading them with either black powder or Pyrodex, the .45-100 Sharps may be for you. It will give fine accuracy when loaded properly, and even at safe, sane velocities and pressures it will heave a 500-grain bullet a long way out there!●

CHAPTER
51

AT SOME POINT in every dedicated rifleman's life, there comes a time when he simply *must* have a big-bore rifle. Now that term, of course, means different things to different people. To one who is used to popping squirrels from the tops of oak trees with a .22 rimfire, a big bore could be any centerfire cartridge. If one's favorite targets were crows and chucks, the term would probably indicate a rifle of .30 or larger caliber. However, to far-gone riflemen, it means just what it says: *big,* and the bigger the better, dredging up visions of cigar-size English cartridges, accompanied by the heavy double — and later deep-magazined Mauser — rifles that fired them.

Words such as *veldt, mbogo,* and *Kodiak* come to mind, with visions of upturned elephants and ten-foot bear hides. In that context, *big bore* can have only one meaning: a .45 or larger cartridge, of which four make a handful, being fired from a rifle just light enough to be carried by one man, and generating an unspeakable amount of muzzle energy.

So it was that I came to this point; I had to have such a rifle. However, a quick check of the bank balance proved what I had already suspected: there is no way I can *legally* acquire a double rifle. I immediately launched a search for a big English magazine rifle. That didn't turn out to be such a good idea, either — mainly because it took nearly a week and one very good bottle of bourbon to recover from the shock of the asking price.

The obvious answer, of course, is to just go out and buy a factory-made .458 Winchester or .460 Weatherby. While they are at least affordable, these rifles still require a good chunk of cash, considering the premium charged for such cartridges over that of standard magnums. However, as I looked at what that amount of money would buy in a custom rifle, provided one can do some of the work himself, it seemed that was the way to go.

The thought also came to mind as to what cartridges Americans had used before the .458 Winchester was introduced in 1956. A check through Ackley's *Handbook for Shooters and Reloaders* soon proved that not only did cartridges exist but rifles could be made for little more than the cost of rebarreling a surplus military action. These cartridges carry such names as .450 Watts, .450 Ackley Magnum, and .450 Mashburn Magnum. Of course, there are other cartridges, both British and European, for which rifles could be built, but one would run into the same problem that most double-rifle owners now face: a small and necessarily expensive supply of cases and bullets. On the other hand, if one already owns a fine double or big magazine rifle firing one of these cartridges, the purchase of the necessary tools and components to keep it shooting is money well spent. After all, such a rifle is really a physical piece of history — an actual participant in an era in which very few of us lived and, thanks to politics and changing public opinion, is gone forever. An unaltered rifle of this type should be an honored possession, but with uncertain economy of today, it seems wise not to chamber a new rifle for these cartridges, since components may not be available in future years. I definitely want to be able to shoot this thing twenty years from now — assuming I am allowed to shoot anything at all.

The cartridge I finally selected was the .450 Ackley Magnum. It is made from .375 H&H Magnum cases, which should be easily available for as long as sport hunting exists. They are blown out to .45 and what can only be described as minimum body taper, as my fired cases show only a nine and a half thousandths difference in diameter between the body just forward of the belt and the body just behind the shoulder, some two and a quarter inches away. This provides the maximum powder capacity possible from the case without shortening the neck. It is considerably more powerful than the .458 Winchester and doesn't miss field-chronographed .460 Weatherby figures by much.

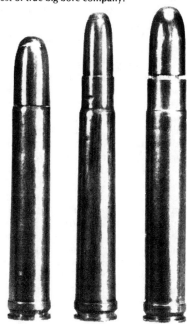

Alongside the universally popular .458 Winchester Magnum (left) and the classic .375 Holland & Holland Magnum (center), the .450 Ackley Magnum (right) is in the best of true big-bore company.

Gil Sengel on the
HANDLOADERS' BIG BORE:

450 ackley magnum

In style reminiscent of early big-bore Mauser sporters, Sengel's dressed-up Enfield has a slight "belly" caused by extension of magazine to hold four of the huge .450 rounds. This particular make of Enfield was chosen in part because its receiver bridge lent itself to a clean-lined and attractive new angular shape.

Being a .45 is also a tremendous advantage. The popularity of the .458 Winchester and new interest in the .45-70 have created many good jacketed bullets in weights from three hundred to five hundred grains. Add to this the availability of several good designs in cast bullets, and a big rifle in this chambering is hard to beat.

Probably the greatest single advantage of selecting this cartridge, however, is the availability of good, cheap actions such as the 1917 Enfield as produced by Remington, Winchester, and Eddystone in .30-06. While that remark about "cheap" actions may be surprising, it is actually becoming more pertinent every year as prices of new actions and factory rifles increase. This does not apply to unaltered, virtually mint military rifles, whose values are also rising, but to the many surplus rifles purchased thirty years ago because they were ridiculously cheap and treated accordingly ever since, and the tens of thousands of kitchen-table conversions so popular at that time. Of course, some modifications are necessary, but none that a serious student of the rifle can't handle. The Enfield action is already long enough — it has the proper bolt throw and magazine cut to accommodate the big cartridge. No work necessary here. As to which of the three manufactures to select, well, I think I would rather stay out of that.

Most controversy centers around the Eddystone action. It seems this action is considered to be everything from "as strong and well made as any" to "unsafe and suitable only for decoy anchors." However, it is a fact that quality custom rifles are virtually always made from either Winchester or Remington actions and carry a much higher resale value, if this is important to you.

Bullets for the .450 Magnum are Lyman cast 457483 (1) and 462560 (2), Hornady 300-grain hollow-point (3), Sierra 300-grain flat-point (4), Hornady 350-grain roundnose (5), Speer 400-grain flat-point (6), and Hornady 500-grain roundnose (7).

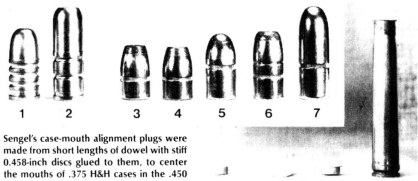

Sengel's case-mouth alignment plugs were made from short lengths of dowel with stiff 0.458-inch discs glued to them, to center the mouths of .375 H&H cases in the .450 Magnum chamber throat. Cases were fire-formed with forming loads of Bullseye powder under tissue wadding and inert fillers. Without alignment plugs, cases would tend to fire-form offcenter in the larger chamber, leaving case walls thinner and necks longer on one side of the formed case.

Also to be considered is that Winchester actions have a large recess milled under the rear sight. It looks like the devil. There is really nothing that can be done with this except make a plug and weld it in place — not a job for an amateur. I have been told that the heat of welding can warp the receiver and cause the thin metal under the plug to bulge down into the bolt raceway. Since this would be enough to make a man take up gardening, I found and purchased a Remington action. It has none of the faults of the other two.

The amount of work done on the action depends upon the individual and just what he thinks a rifle of this type should be like. Following are the major modifications made to my rifle. Not all are necessary to make a satisfactory rifle, but they show what can be done

to make a rather ugly action into a fine heavy rifle.

Let's start at the receiver bridge and the rear sight with its protective ears: this mess has to go. By cutting, grinding, and filing the bridge to a shape resembling a rifle receiver, you can change the look of the whole action. The exact shape and height of the bridge can vary, but if a scope is to be mounted, it would be best to look at the available bases, then shape the bridge to accommodate them. This was no problem on my rifle, as glass sights were never considered, a vintage Redfield receiver sight being used instead. Therefore the bridge was finished flat on top, with the edges being flat also and tapering off at a forty-five-degree angle. These surfaces are easily kept flat and true with the bore by frequent checking with a

The recoil of the .450 Magnum emphasizes the importance of good shooting form for rifles of such great power. The left hand encircles the fore-end, and right elbow is low, making a firm pad of muscles for seating the butt of the stock. This shooter didn't get his face nudged by the comb or his right thumb.

loads for the .450 Ackley Magnum

primer	powder	charge	velocity* (fps)	remarks
300-grain Hornady				
CCI 200	IMR-4198	75	2,768	2-1/8-inch groups
CCI 200	IMR-4198	77	2,812	bullets disintegrating 20 feet from muzzle
CCI 250	IMR-3031	71	2,136	2-1/4-inch groups
CCI 250	IMR-3031	77	2,470	1-7/8-inch groups
CCI 250	IMR-4064	75	2,164	
CCI 250	IMR-4064	80	2,351	2-1/8-inch groups
300-grain Sierra				
CCI 200	IMR-4198	82	2,891	maximum belt expansion
CCI 250	IMR-3031	89	2,789	all case will hold
400-grain Speer				
CCI 200	IMR-3031	75	2,300	1-7/8-inch groups
CCI 250	IMR-3031	81	2,453	jacket peeling off
CCI 250	IMR-3031	83	2,511	maximum belt expansion
CCI 250	IMR-4064	85	2,506	
500-grain Hornady				
CCI 250	IMR-3031	80	2,301	absolute maximum
CCI 250	IMR-3031	81	2,323	too hot!
CCI 250	WW-748	80	2,135	accurate — no belt expansion
CCI 250	WW-748	90	2,273	not gaining much
CCI 250	WW-748	100	2,428	1-1/4-inch groups — 6,549 ft-lb
Lyman 457483 393-grain				
CCI 200	SR-4759	30	1,119	
CCI 200	SR-4759	35	1,522	2-1/2-inch groups
CCI 200	SR-4759	38	1,729	no accuracy — but no leading
CCI 200	IMR-4198	40	1,645	7-1/2-inch groups
CCI 200	IMR-4198	43	1,802	1-7/8-inch groups
CCI 200	IMR-4198	46	1,909	full-choke patterns
CCI 200	IMR-3031	49	1,738	1-1/2-inch groups
CCI 200	IMR-4320	52	1,716	good accuracy
CCI 200	IMR-4895	50	1,659	1-3/4-inch groups
Lyman 462560 520-grain				
CCI 200	IMR-3031	68	2,118	excellent accuracy
CCI 200	IMR-3031	79	2,286	absolute maximum
CCI 200	IMR-4320	84	2,334	maximum belt expansion
CCI 250	WW-748	80	2,130	2-inch groups

* all velocities instrumental at ten feet on Oehler M32 with skyscreens

straight edge that is long enough to reach back to the bridge from the receiver ring, since its surface is parallel to the center of the bolt and bore.

Probably the next most obvious change is the bolt handle. This is best cut off and replaced by welding on a commercially made handle. There are, however, a few differences that could be incorporated in the bolt handle of this rifle, as opposed to one designed for more subdued cartridges. We have probably all read about, or experienced, being rapped on the knuckle by the bolt knob when taking a hasty shot with medium-bore rifles. It can be imagined what would happen with a rifle with the .450's recoil. Also, while never having had any "anxious moments" (as the British term it) with dangerous game, I do know it is not unusual for the bolt knob to slip out of the hand when trying for a quick second shot.

Both of these things are easily taken care of when the new handle is attached. The one on my bolt is styled like a Pre-1964 Model 70 Winchester handle and measures 2 7/8 inches from the bolt body to the end of the knob. It slants rearward at an angle of thirty degrees, while dropping down an inch and a half below the center of the bolt body when the bolt is closed. This allows the knob to clear the knuckle by about an inch and provides a positive grasp for the hand working the bolt.

An optional operation at this point would be the removal of the clip slot by filing back the front and the right side of the receiver bridge. Such work makes for a nicer-looking action, but if you decide to do this, be careful. It will cause the rear of the extractor to clear its lug raceway by about an eighth of an inch when the bolt is closed. This could cause the rear of the extractor to jam against the bridge and prevent the action from opening. If this happens, the rear of the extractor will have to be built up by welding, or its top ground at a slight angle, causing the lug raceway to push the extractor into its proper position as the bolt is drawn back. The welding is a simple operation *if* a heat sink is made to hold the extractor and prevent the heat from ruining its spring action.

Little odds and ends consist of replacing the trigger, a little trigger-guard-magazine work, and the alteration of the action to cock on the opening stroke of the bolt, if this is deemed necessary, by installing one of the commercially available units designed for the purpose. A new stock with forward-sloping Monte Carlo comb may also be greatly appreciated. The trigger-guard alterations are not necessary to make the rifle function, but they add a great deal to its appearance. These include removing the small step directly behind the front guard screw and making a new floorplate. The guard is straightened by measuring the distance between the guard-screw holes, hacksawing out the metal forming the step, again measuring the distance, and clamping and welding the two pieces together.

As concerns the floorplate, it always seemed to me that the Enfield variety had somehow shrunk. It is an eighth of an inch narrower than the bottom of the guard. A new one is easily made from eighth-inch mild steel that is tapered and rounded toward the edges.

Here a peculiarity of hard-recoiling rifles crops up. The so-called quick-release floorplates have the disturbing habit of opening when the rifle is fired — not every time or even often, but frequently enough to provide variety to your shooting, the variety coming from the many directions a follower spring can throw two or three rounds of ammo. Memory brings back times when a rifle I used to own would let go. I'd throw the thing to my shoulder, pull the trigger, and frequently look down at three oblong holes in the snow. If the cartridges happened to fall base-first, they would be hard to find. However, my rifle solved that problem, as the spring and follower generally fell out also, thereby kind of marking the spot to start digging. At first I hid this idiosyncrasy from everyone, especially when it happened with more than one heavy rifle, but as time went on, I found that others had experienced the same thing. Therefore, the floorplates of all my hard-kicking rifles are now pinned shut.

The last of the metalwork involves the magazine box. Quite frankly, a new one has to be made. Three ninety-degree bends are made in a piece of 1/32-inch sheet steel to form a rectangular box 1x3-11/16x7/8 inch inside, with a height of 1 3/8 inches. A 1x1-3/4-inch piece is also cut. This is placed inside, flush with the bottom, and against the rear of the box where the unjoined walls come together. Protruding some five sixteenths of an inch above the sides of the box, this piece fits through the rear of the magazine cut in the action and provides the same function as this piece of metal on the original box. This assembly is then welded or silver-soldered together. The depth of the front of this box must then be reduced to 1-3/16 inches to allow the bottom of the stock to taper upward properly toward the fore-end tip. This yields a magazine with a four-round capacity and creates a slight "belly" in the

magazine area of the stock, as found on the early Mauser sporting rifles chambered for such large cartridges.

The new box is wider than the original. This must be done to allow the larger, belted cases to lie more nearly side by side in the magazine. The rails must then be ground away slightly to accommodate the wider box, make the action feed properly, and keep the cartridges *in* the magazine. Failure to do this results in four rounds flying skyward from the magazine when the bolt is pulled back hard. In other words, making this rifle a single-shot bolt gun with four-round magazine capacity.

Paul Marquart made up one of his superb cut-rifled barrels from 1-3/8-inch stock and turned it to sporter contour, coming out 0.800 inch at the muzzle with a length of twenty-five inches. Twist is one turn in fourteen inches. The reason for starting with 1-3/8-inch stock was to allow an auxiliary recoil lug to be machined integral with the barrel at a point five inches ahead of the receiver ring. The larger blank size allowed this lug to finish up with a 0.163-inch-wide bearing surface running halfway around the barrel. To my way of thinking, a recoil lug on the barrel of a rifle like this is a *must*. Before building this rifle, I had seen two others made up in this caliber. Both had stocks that were cracked and repaired behind the rear tang. Neither rifle had a lug on the barrel, even though one had supposedly had three stocks! Many .458s do the same thing. If one turns up with an uncracked stock, questioning the owner will usually reveal that the rifle has fired few full loads.

Loading for the .450 Ackley turns out to be just as interesting as building the rifle. True, it is a wildcat, but not one with a slap-in-a-factory-round-and-pull-the-trigger case-forming operation. If one researches this cartridge, he finds that at least one source suggests firing factory .375 H&H loads in the Ackley chamber. Since the cartridge headspaces on the belt, there is no doubt this will produce a .450 case. However, a three-hundred-grain Silvertip bouncing from side to side down a custom barrel just does not seem quite right! I never tried it. Another source states the same thing is possible, only this time using .300 H&H ammunition. Forget it. I have seen twenty (yes, twenty!) such experiments, and the cases closely resemble a bunch of aerosol spray cans after a fire.

By far the best method consists of using thirteen grains of Bullseye pistol powder in the .375 H&H case, filling

the remainder with Cream of Wheat. A wad of tissue between powder and cereal, and a quarter-inch-long section of three-eighths-inch diameter dowel with a stiff 0.458-inch-diameter disc glued to its front end keep things properly located until the case (no bullet is used) is chambered and fired (see "Forming Cases by Expansion," *Handloader* 78). This unorthodox load produces a surprisingly loud report, a shower of cereal, and a .450 Ackley case that is ninety-eight percent formed. At a total cost of one cent per round, this is one of the best bargains going.

After some experience with the cartridge, one thing becomes evident — if ever a rifle needed a light practice load, this one does. Actually, the term *light practice load* is somewhat misleading, as a four-hundred-grain bullet at seventeen hundred feet per second is not really light. It produces some 2,550 foot-pounds of muzzle energy. Nevertheless, when one is thinking along these lines, cast bullets automatically come to mind.

With handfuls of good .45 cast-bullet designs available, the choice of two or three can be somewhat of a problem. My rifle seems to like a couple of Lyman designs best — 462560 and 457483. Both are gas-check types. I like the gas checks because they seem to decrease leading and definitely make the bullet easier to seat in the case mouth without excessive belling.

The 457483 bullet is apparently an older-style bullet for the .45-70, as it has a long bearing surface with lots of lube grooves. When it is seated to the base of the neck in the .450, the top lube groove is exposed. This is no big thing, for there is really no need to fill this groove — it seems to make no difference at any velocity. My rifle takes this bullet right up to eighteen hundred feet per second when only the rear two grooves are filled with Alox-base lube. And this when cast of wheel-weight metal.

Strangely enough, the fast-burning powders normally used with cast bullets didn't work well. This includes Du Pont SR-4759. It must be some strange quirk of this rifle, as SR-4759 produces the most accurate cast-bullet load I have ever fired in a .45-70 of mine. Loads are still given for some of the faster numbers in the hope that not all rifles work out this way.

The most accurate — and consistent — load for the little cast bullet yet found is forty-nine grains of IMR-3031. This gives an average of 1,738 feet per second at ten feet, while producing only mild recoil. Also, eighteen hundred feet per second seems to be the maximum for my wheel-weight metal. No semblance of accuracy could be obtained above this velocity.

Taking a different tack, Du Pont IMR-4198 produced the most graphic example of the "individuality" of cast bullets and velocity I have ever seen. Using the previously mentioned bullet, groups would not stay on an 8½x11 target until I used charges of forty grains. At that point, groups were a uniform seven and a half inches. Increasing the charge one grain at a time brought them down to 1 7/8 inches average with forty-three grains of IMR-4198. Going further put them clear off the paper again at forty-six grains. No wonder cast bullets can cause veteran handloaders to bury their bullet moulds.

While there are many choices in the lighter bullets, probably the best design in a heavy cast bullet is Lyman 462560. These weigh in at 520 grains when cast of linotype and can be driven at very near the maximum velocity of which the .450 Ackley is capable. This is a tremendous advantage as it allows practice with full loads without shelling out twenty cents apiece for jacketed bullets. This bullet seems to shoot well with any suitable powder, so long as velocities don't exceed twenty-one-hundred feet per second. Why this should be is puzzling, as smaller calibers use linotype at greater velocities. This same lot of metal has given under-minute-of-angle accuracy at velocities near twenty-five-hundred feet per second in a .338 magnum of mine.

Accuracy is not all that bad, running three to three and a half inches at one hundred yards with velocities of twenty-three-hundred feet per second, but the rifle does much better with the five-hundred-grain jacketed bullets. Perhaps linotype is just not tough enough for a bullet this heavy. As the velocity at which the bullet contacts the lands is increased, the metal may not be able to stand the strain of the lands trying to spin it, and therefore it slips a little before the rifling takes hold. It would be interesting to know whether this is what happens.

When jacketed bullets are considered, there are five choices generally available, a three-hundred-grain flatnose from Sierra, four-hundred-grain flatnose from Speer, and Hornady's three-hundred-grain hollow-point, three-fifty-grain roundnose, and five-hundred-grain roundnose. If you are thinking those light bullets and big belted cases make for an interesting combination, you are exactly right. Fact is, this particular rifle launches those stubby little devils over the chronograph screens at nearly twenty-

nine-hundred feet per second. This however, is largely academic, as the bullets begin disassembling themselves at these speeds — before they reach the target.

The three-hundred-grain bullets, as well as the 350 and even 400, are probably made to work at twelve to fifteen hundred feet per second. At elevated velocities, they become fragile varmint-type bullets — though that word seems a little out of place. One would also naturally expect accuracy to fall off as velocities increased, and this was the case — with one notable exception: the three-hundred-grain Hornady.

Both the Sierra and Hornady shot well with seventy-five grains of IMR-4198, which provides velocities in the range of 2,750 feet per second, or especially seventy-seven grains of IMR-3031 at 2,470 feet per second. Groups averaged right at two inches at a hundred yards with the fast powder and just under with IMR-3031. However, even with a case full of IMR-3031, maximum pressures could not be reached. This was determined by measuring belt expansion on new, unfired Winchester-Western cases, with an average of 0.001 inch considered maximum.

As velocities approached twenty-eight-hundred feet per second, the accuracy of the Sierra fell off until maximum belt expansion was reached at 2,892 feet per second. The Hornady groups, however, just kept getting tighter as speeds went up. Finally at 2,812 feet per second, clusters were in the 1-1/2-inch range, but one in three did not make it to the target, this being indicated by a puff of white mist just past the last chronograph screen. Needless to say, all this power is not really necessary.

The 350-grain Hornady was a disappointment in my rifle, probably because it had to be seated so deep. If the handloader has a tool for rolling his own cannelure about a quarter of an inch behind the factory job, it would help. I do not have such a tool, but when it was seated out like this, accuracy improved, yet crimping in a cannelure is necessary if bullets are to stay in place under recoil.

Speer's four-hundred-grain provides an interesting solution to the cannelure problem by providing two. One is the normal serrated type located for proper seating in the .458 Winchester, and the other is farther forward for the .45-70. This bullet gives excellent performance in the .450 with IMR-3031 and speeds of 2,250 to 2,350 feet per second.

Maximum velocities (and pressures)

are obtained with eighty-three grains of IMR-3031, but here again, the bullet is not designed for such velocities. Groups open up to ten inches, and a very strange thing happens. The jacket starts peeling off at the front cannelure, causing the bullet to take on all the aerodynamic properties of a broken hockey stick. No wonder groups open up. At twenty-three-hundred feet per second, pushed along by seventy-five grains of IMR-3031, the Speer bullet should make a fine load. Accuracy is under two inches, and the bullet does not exhibit the explosive properties of the three-hundred-grain bullets.

Last of all, we must look at the bullet that a cartridge of this type is really intended for, the five-hundred-grain Hornady. Right from the start, accuracy was under two minutes with any load, until eighty grains of IMR-3031 gave an average 0.0012-inch of belt expansion. Velocity from the load was 2,301 feet per second. Very respectable, but I had hoped for better, considering the large volume of the case. Yes, I know that older published data list charges much heavier than this; however, a thousandth of an inch of belt expansion in modern cases is enough for me and offers long case life in a properly chambered rifle. Providing various amounts of freebore would allow charges to be increased, but I doubt that one could ever reach some of those listed in the older references. It is also good to remember that a long jump from case to rifling is disastrous to cast-bullet accuracy. Even at these velocities, the .450 shades the .458 Winchester's newly published 2,040 feet per second by a good margin.

I tried other powders without good results until I discovered WW-748. It may not be the perfect propellant for this cartridge, but it's mighty close. In fact, I don't think I would care to stand behind a rifle that pushes the five-hundred-grain Hornady much faster! If one uses a long soda straw, then begs, pleads, taps, and tamps properly, a hundred grains of this stuff fits under the big Hornady. Slowly firing this load for accuracy and velocity, (believe me, barrel temperature is *not* the reason for firing slowly), I came up with 2,428 feet per second average. That's over sixty-five-hundred foot-pounds of energy! Also, velocity spread did not exceed nineteen feet per second, and belt expansion was only 0.0004 inch.

Accuracy is also excellent, with three-shot groups running an inch and a quarter at one hundred yards. I consider three shots enough, by the way, as the rifle is meant for creatures with teeth, claws, and horns — and if not pacified by three rounds, they will be close enough that sustained accuracy *versus* barrel temperature will not be the foremost question in your mind.

All in all, the .450 Ackley Magnum is a very interesting wildcat for the true big-bore shooter, one from which a serious handloader can learn a great deal. ●

CHAPTER
52

Ken Waters

.458 Winchester Magnum

WHEN WINCHESTER introduced their .458 Magnum cartridge and specially adapted Model 70 rifle chambered for that cartridge in 1956, it was intended to provide big-game hunters going to Africa with an American rifle and cartridge equal in power to the large English Nitro Express cartridges, and at far lower prices.

In doing so, they were breaking new ground, this being the first time ever that a standard American factory cartridge had been developed specifically for African hunting. Pessimists, citing the limited market, occasionally resorted to sarcasm in their estimates as to how the new caliber would or more likely *wouldn't* (they thought) meet with shooter acceptance.

I suspect that more than a few industry people and firearms writers have accordingly been surprised at the demonstrated popularity of the .458 during its first quarter of a century of existence. Not only did it go to Africa, where it quickly chalked up an enviable record; its use soon spread to Alaska and others of the world's big-game-hunting areas. What must have come as the biggest surprise, however, are the numbers purchased that have stayed right here in the United States, with little more than a hope of ever getting to go on safari.

All the more reason therefore, why the subject of handloading the .458 should have received increased attention. The factory loadings with 510-grain soft-points or 500-grain full-metal-jacketed bullets are obviously unsuited to most game animals outside Africa — and even much game there. Yet in twenty-five years of reading a most prestigious firearms publication, I was able to find only a single feature story on the .458, and that was concerned solely with its use in Africa!

Surely there must be riflemen, and especially those of the handloading fraternity, who have looked for more data and commentary on this cartridge than is to be found in the reloading manuals. Particularly, there is a shortage of dope on the assembling and performance of reduced loads and those with cast lead bullets or lighter-than-standard soft-points. What potential do such loads have for stateside hunters?

While not neglecting the preparation of full-power loads of the type suited for the largest game, I was determined to conduct experiments looking to an increased flexibility for the .458 Magnum. Not that it will ever be an all-around cartridge, for that it most assuredly isn't, but rather that it become capable of sensible use by hunters of nondangerous as well as the lighter species of dangerous big game — and yes, even with specialized loads for deer and black bear.

If that strikes you as somewhat extreme (some will say ridiculous), consider the unquestioned success and acceptance of modern high-velocity .45-70 loads. Why then shouldn't a .458 loaded to duplicate or exceed the best .45-70 ballistics — a present-day .45-90, if you will — become a practicable way of extending the usefulness of the .458 Magnum? Theory indicated that it should, so finding out became one of my goals. That my

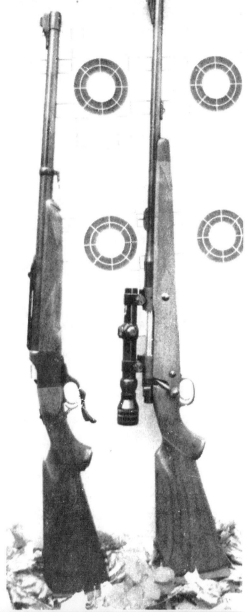

Ken found both of the .458 test rifles too light for the heavy recoil developed by this cartridge, particularly with heavy bullets. Iron-sighted Ruger Number One is a nine-pound rifle. Winchester Model 70 with 1-4x Redfield weighs nine and a half. Ken prefers at least nine and a half pounds without scope — or still better, ten.

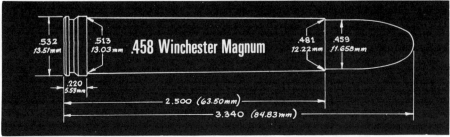

.532 13.51mm — .513 13.03mm — **.458 Winchester Magnum** — .481 12.22mm — .459 11.658mm

.220 5.59mm

2.500 (63.50mm)

3.340 (84.83mm)

tests met with limited success is part of the story I'll be developing as I explain the hows and whys.

First, the .458 Winchester, like all .45 cartridges whether of American or British origin, depends upon bullet diameter and weight rather than high velocity for its game-killing effect. Unlike the monstrous British African rounds, however, the .458 doesn't have an outsize powder capacity, possessing only some twenty-one percent more usable internal space than a .30-06 while it's expected to drive bullets weighing more than twice as much as the heaviest '06 bullets. This proved to be either an advantage or a disadvantage, depending upon the bullets used. In any case, these are factors that must be taken into consideration by handloaders working with the .458 Winchester.

Of course, the .458's comparatively short (2.50 inches) case was no accident, having been deliberately planned to function through standard-length bolt actions. The shorter bolt travel was felt to be an advantage in speeding up manipulation, and perhaps it is, particularly for shooters unfamiliar with the typically longer magnum actions. It may also contribute some to receiver stiffness.

Quoted velocity of factory-loaded 510-grain soft-points, originally listed at 2,130 feet per second, has been reduced to 2,040 feet per second from twenty-four-inch barrels in current tables, but recoil is all that it ever was — every last foot-pound of it — if my shoulder is any judge! With all the thousands of rounds of centerfire shooting with about all calibers from .22 to .45 that I do each year in testing ammunition and rifles, I've become rather inured to recoil and seldom flinch. Compared with other American factory cartridges, however, the .458 with full-power 500 or 510-grain bullets is in a class of its own. Even the great .375 H&H Magnum with 270 and 300-grain bullets pales by comparison. It's just plain vicious when fired from a benchrest!

Now admittedly, part of the blame

for this can be laid to rifle weights in this caliber. My two .458 Magnum test rifles — an iron-sighted Ruger Number One single-shot and a Winchester Model 70 African with Redfield 1-4x variable scope set in Weaver top mounts — weigh only nine and nine and a half pounds, respectively. To my way of thinking, rifles for this cartridge should weigh a minimum of nine and a half pounds *without* scope or mount, and a full ten pounds would be better still.

While I don't wish to overemphasize this business of recoil, it unquestionably limits the popularity of the .458 for nonreloaders who must use only factory rounds. Recognizing the typical American hunter's preference for light rifles, there are only two ways left to go — reduced velocity and lighter bullets.

Heavy-bullet fans who can be satisfied with velocities ranging from fifteen to seventeen hundred feet per second will find that cast bullets weighing five hundred grains or more produce noticeably less recoil, but in doing so must be prepared to accept a big reduction in effectiveness. Duplicating the old Sharps buffalo-

The most accurate load tested in the Winchester, and one of the two best all-around loads, comprised the 350-grain Hornady round-nose and seventy-two grains of Reloder 7. Expansion of case was normal — this was not a max load.

cartridge ballistics, such loads suffer particularly from a more arched trajectory, limiting the useful range.

A far better way to go is to reduce bullet weight to 350 to 400 grains, or even three hundred grains, depending upon the animal being hunted. Good .45 jacketed soft-point expanding bullets such as the 350-grain Hornady and 400-grain Barnes or Speer are adequate for all North American game and can be driven to velocities slightly in excess of factory .458 Winchester loads within acceptable recoil limits. Believe me when I say they're *far* and away more pleasant to shoot.

At the same time, a number of things other than increased weight can be specified, if you're building a custom .458, that will contribute to a reduction in *felt* recoil. One of these is a proper recoil pad of the solid type as found on English big-game rifles as

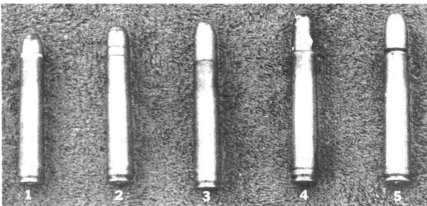

Overall lengths of the loaded .458 cartridge vary with bullets used: *1:* 350 Hornady; *2:* 400 Speer; *3:* 400 Barnes; *4:* 500 Hornady; *5:* 546 Ohaus (cast).

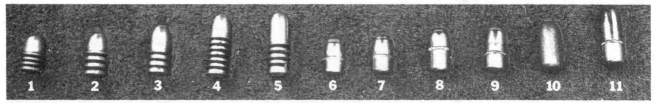

With only the 500-grain Colorado soft-point omitted, these are the test bullets used in this series of loads: *1:* 302 Lyman 457191; *2:* 340 Lyman Gould 457122HP; *3:* 393 Ohaus 45405F; *4:* 502 Saeco-Darr; *5:* 546 Ohaus 45500R; *6:* 300 Sierra HP; *7:* 300 Hornady HP; *8:* 350 Hornady RN; *9:* 400 Speer FNSP; *10:* 400 Barnes RN; *11:* 500 Hornady RN.

.458 Winchester Magnum

bullet	charge (gr)	powder	velocity (fps)	primer	length (in.)	expansion	
300 Sierra HP	58.0	IMR-4198	2,261	F 210	3.00	moderate	poor load in test rifle
	62.0	IMR-4198	2,313	F 210	3.00	normal	
	63.0	IMR-4198	2,367	W 120	3.00	near max	
	63.0	H-4198	2,142	W 120	3.00	moderate	
	65.0	IMR-4320	2,015	W 120	3.00	moderate	velocity from 24-in. barrel (Ruger)
	68.0	Re-7	2,123	W 120	3.00	moderate	good load
300 Hornady HP	68.0	Re-7	2,158	W 120	2.99	moderate	good load
	70.0	Re-7	2,267	W 120	2.99	normal	fifth most accurate load
350 Hornady RN	65.0	IMR-4198	2,358	W 120	3.03	maximum	
	70.0	IMR-3031	2,097	W 120	3.03	moderate	good load
	73.0	IMR-3031	2,209	W 120	3.05	normal	fine load; compressed charge
	72.0	IMR-4064	2,071	W 120	3.04	moderate	
	73.0	IMR-4320	2,132	W 120	3.04	normal	
	69.0	Re-7	2,122	W 120	3.05	moderate	good load
	72.0	Re-7	2,194	W 120	3.05	normal	one of two best all-around loads; most accurate load tested
400 Speer FNSP	64.0	IMR-4198	2,221	W 120	3.14	maximum	poor load in test rifle
	66.0	H-4198	2,126	W 120	3.14	near max	poor load in test rifle
	64.0	IMR-3031	1,943	W 120	3.12	moderate	
	68.0	IMR-3031	2,041	W 120	3.12	moderate	fine load
	70.0	IMR-3031	2,071	W 120	3.12	normal	
	71.0	IMR-3031	2,108	W 120	3.12	normal	
	68.0	Re-7	1,897	W 120	3.12	moderate	
	70.0	Re-7	2,045	W 120	3.12	normal	
400 Barnes RN	71.0	IMR-3031	2,180	W 120	3.25	normal	velocity from 24-in. barrel (Ruger); one of two best all-around loads; fourth most accurate load
	74.0	IMR-3031	2,225	W 120	3.25	maximum	
	75.0	IMR-4064	2,136	W 120	3.25	normal	
	75.0	H-4895	2,149	W 120	3.25	normal	
	75.0	IMR-4320	2,233	W 120	3.25	near max	velocity from 24-in. barrel (Ruger)
	76.0	H-335	2,260	W 120	3.25	maximum	velocity from 24-in. barrel (Ruger)
500 Colorado SP	72.0	IMR-4320	2,017	W 120	3.34	maximum	
	74.0	WW-748	1,908	W 120	3.34	moderate	
	74.0	H-335	2,114	W 120	3.34	maximum	best heavy-bullet load
500 Hornady RN	70.0	IMR-3031	1,990	W 120	3.38	moderate	
	71.5	IMR-3031	2,040	W 120	3.38	normal	good load
	73.5	IMR-3031	2,116	W 120	3.38	maximum	compressed load
	71.0	IMR-4064	1,960	W 120	3.38	moderate	
	73.0	IMR-4064	2,030	W 120	3.38	normal	
	73.0	IMR-4320	2,042	W 120	3.38	normal	duplicates factory load
	76.0	IMR-4320	2,120	W 120	3.38	maximum	
	71.0	H-4895	2,015	W 120	3.38	normal	good load
	74.0	H-4895	2,075	W 120	3.38	near max	
	75.0	WW-748	2,005	W 120	3.38	normal	
	77.0	WW-748	2,060	W 120	3.38	near max	
510 Winchester	factory load		2,035				2,090 fps in Ruger

REDUCED LOADS

bullet	charge (gr)	powder	velocity (fps)	primer	length (in.)	expansion	
300 Sierra HP	50.0	IMR-4198	1,863	F 210	3.00	light	
	54.0	IMR-4198	2,124	F 210	3.00	moderate	
	55.0	Re-7	2,026	W 120	3.00	light	second most accurate load (Ruger)
	60.0	IMR-3031	1,902	W 120	3.00	light	velocity from 24-in barrel (Ruger)
300 Hornady HP	58.0	Re-7	2,062	W 120	2.99	light	good load; velocity from 24-in. barrel
400 Speer FNSP	56.0	IMR-3031	1,564	W 120	3.12	light	accurate low-velocity load
	60.0	IMR-3031	1,766	W 120	3.12	light	
	67.0	IMR-4320	1,915	F 210	3.14	moderate	

CAST-BULLET LOADS

bullet	charge (gr)	powder	velocity (fps)	primer	length (in.)		
302 Lyman	32.0	IMR-4198	1,445	F 210	3.05		excellent accuracy
457191	34.0	IMR-4198	1,550	F 210	3.05		
340 Lyman HP	40.0	IMR-3031	1,395	F 210	3.10		
457122	43.0	IMR-3031	1,495	F 210	3.10		
393 Ohaus FN	33.0	IMR-4198	1,455	F 210	3.10		third most accurate load
45405F	60.0	H-4831	1,144	CCI 250	3.30		unacceptably low velocity
502 Saeco-Darr	58.0	H-4831	1,120	CCI 250	3.34		unacceptably low velocity
	52.0	IMR-3031	1,610	F 210	3.34		accurate
546 Ohaus RN	50.0	IMR-3031	1,550	W 120	3.38		
45500R	57.0	IMR-3031	1,731	W 120	3.38		leaded bore

All loads chronographed from 22-inch barrel (Winchester Model 70) unless otherwise noted. Winchester-Western .458 Magnum cases used for all loads. Chronographed velocities from Oehler Model 33 Chronotach with Skyscreens.

well as the Model 70 African. For heavy-recoiling rifles, the ventilated shotgun-type pad should never be chosen.

Stocks should be relatively straight. Too much drop accentuates recoil. Grip and fore-end should be full in cross-section and checkered to facilitate a firm grip for holding the butt securely back against the shooter's shoulder. Never allow this rifle to get a running start during recoil!

Another thing that I place much emphasis on when working with heavy-recoiling rifles: the front sling swivel should be affixed to the barrel out in front of the fore-end — not on the fore-end, as on many smaller-caliber rifles. A forward hand bruised or cut by the rearward and upward leap of a swivel does nothing good for the shooter's concentration or peace of mind.

Possibly more important than any of those things is the correct choice and mounting of a scope sight. By all means, select a quality scope of low power with long eye relief, and mount it as far forward as possible while still retaining a proper sight picture. The recoil of the .458 is hard on scopes, but if the scope is set too close to the eye, it is even harder on the shooter's face! There's nothing like a cut eyebrow leaking blood to induce flinching and poor shooting.

Assuming that we're now ready to commence loading for this bucking bronc of a cartridge, let's first consider the case we'll be working with: belted rimless, 2.50 inches long with straight tapering sides nominally of 0.513 inch base diameter (in front of the belt) and rim diameter of 0.532 inch, give or take a thousandth. Maximum overall cartridge length is usually listed as 3.34 inches, but my Model 70 African rifle accepts rounds up to 3.38 inches long.

Fired empty W-W .458 brass in my test lots, still containing the spent primers, varied in weight from 225 to 229 grains and held between 73 and 75 grains of *water* when filled to the base of a seated five-hundred grain Hornady bullet, averaging out to 74.3 grains net water capacity.

An early surprise was the discovery that a considerable amount of case stretching was occurring. Since this case isn't bottle-necked — that is, it doesn't have a shoulder for powder gas to impinge on — I hadn't expected any substantial stretching to take place, certainly not so soon. Cases were trimmed to a uniform 2.485 inches long.

Handloaders working with just one bolt-action or single-shot rifle, and starting with new unfired brass, need only to partly resize cases after each firing in the same rifle, simply backing off the full-length-sizing die half a turn from contact with the shell holder, which may help reduce case stretching. While I would normally do this as a more or less standard practice once the pressure characteristics of loads being used were known, I couldn't do it during my test series and still maintain my usual system of checks on pressures by means of case-expansion measurements.

Tests conducted by the H P White Laboratories for the National Rifle Association show Winchester .458 Magnum factory loads developing 2,087 feet per second from a twenty-five-inch pressure barrel with 48,560 pounds per square inch average chamber pressure. Industry maximum is considered to be fifty-three thousand copper units under the current system of designating pressure, but since pressures of some individual rounds usually exceed the average, it would seem prudent not to venture very far beyond factory-load levels.

Powder selection influences chamber pressures in the .458 Winchester quite as much as bullet weight influences recoil. Despite its title of *Magnum*, the combination of a large bore and straight-sided case rules out the use of those slow-burning powders so popular with small-bore magnums. Conversely, too-fast-burning propellants can raise pressures to the point where you suddenly find your bolt hard to open.

Those medium-burning Du Pont powders from IMR-3031 to and including IMR-4320, Hercules Reloder 7, and Hodgdon H-4895 are optimum choices, along with Winchester 748 and Hodgdon H-335 ball powders. To this select group, add IMR-4198 and H-4198 for cast-bullet loads and the lighter jacketed bullets weighing four-hundred grains or less. However, these fast-burning powders should *not* — and I emphasize this — *not* be used with five-hundred grain bullets in full-power loads.

Ballistics comparable to factory ammunition *can* be attained with handloads, but only by a judicious selection of powders. Here's where it becomes important to consider not only the shape of the .458 case but also its capacity limitations. It is both too small for large charges of bulky powders and too large for fast-burning propellants. When you're seeking top velocities, your charges will be

compressed unless you use a ball powder.

With stick powders such as IMR-3031, IMR-4895, and IMR-4064, a drop tube or at least a slow sifting of powder into the funnel while gently tapping the case is necessary to get some of the charges listed in reloading manuals into cases and leave room to seat bullets. Still, maximum loads had to be compressed, which is all right with conventional powders unless done excessively. Ball powders do *not* require compressing, nor should they be compressed, in my judgment.

That would seem to make spherical-grained propellants ideal for the .458, and so those I've listed proved to be. Not all ball powders are suitable, however. Those with burning rates slower than WW-748 are to be avoided, nor with uniformity of ignition in mind would I use *any* ball powder with light or even reduced loads. Some of the sphericals produce an objectionable muzzle flash, but I didn't find this to be true of either WW-748 or H-335 in proper loads with bullets heavy enough to offer sufficient resistance to ensure complete combustion.

Handloads coming close to duplicating factory-cartridge ballistics with five-hundred-grain bullets include 71.5 grains of IMR-3031, seventy-two-grains of H-4895, seventy-three grains of IMR-4320, 72.5 grains of H-335, and seventy-six grains of WW-748.

The load of sixty-five grains of IMR-4198 with five-hundred-grain bullets listed in some reloading manuals proved greatly excessive in my Model 70 test rifle. Pressures were so high that I had difficulty in opening the bolt, cases showed clear signs of excessive pressure, and tests with this load were terminated after just two rounds. Confirming this finding, sixty-four grains of IMR-4198 turned out to be maximum with *four-hundred-grain* bullets. Accordingly, I will not use IMR-4198 in full-power loads with bullets heavier than four-hundred grains.

Now for those civilizing loads I promised, transforming the .458 into an American game-hunting cartridge. Bullets no heavier than four-hundred grains are called for, and if Alaska isn't on your itinerary, three-hundred and 350-grain bullets are sufficient. This reduction in bullet weight is the primary factor in cutting recoil to more manageable levels while simultaneously obtaining bullet performance more suitable for lighter big-game species.

Bullet weight has a real effect on pressure as well. An interesting comparison was found in separate load-test reports that appeared a number of years ago in *The American Rifleman*. In one, a five-hundred-grain Hornady with seventy-five grains of IMR-3031 was listed as producing pressures of better than fifty-one-thousand pounds per square inch, while the other report showed that four-hundred-grain Barnes bullets with that same load of IMR-3031 registered only 35,550 pounds per square inch average and 38,400 pounds per square inch maximum pressures!

Starting at the bottom, modern .45-70 ballistics can be duplicated with either three-hundred-grain Hornady or Sierra bullets and fifty-five grains of IMR-3031 for a velocity of 1,869 feet per second from the Ruger Number One or about eighteen hundred even from the shorter-barreled Model 70. If this isn't enough, fifty-five grains of Reloder-7 raises muzzle velocities to around two thousand feet per second, and for those wanting a real zinger of a load with maximum expansion, I worked up to seventy grains of Reloder 7 with the three-hundred-grain Hornady hollow-point, obtaining an average muzzle velocity of 2,267 feet per second and 1¾-minute groups from the Model 70 test rifle. Although pressure indications were still moderate with this load, I don't believe that any attempt should be made to drive them faster, considering the relatively thin jackets of these bullets.

Stepping up to Hornady's 350-grain round-nose bullets of tougher construction, with deeper penetration for larger game in mind, my favorite load turned out to be seventy-two grains of Reloder-7, which put five shots into 1¼ inches at a hundred yards at just a shade under twenty-two-hundred feet per second muzzle velocity. This should be a good prescription for elk and moose at reasonable ranges.

Next we come to Speer's four-hundred-grain flat-nose soft-point. This bullet should be seated to the *rearmost* cannelure in the .458 case and seemed to prefer IMR-3031, developing an average of 2,041 feet per second with sixty-eight grains in the Model 70. A short-range deer and black-bear load with this bullet at .45-70 ballistics of around sixteen hundred feet per second can be assembled with fifty-six grains of IMR-3031.

Finally, if I were going to Alaska for one of the big bears, I'd turn to Barnes' excellent four-hundred-grain round-nose soft-point and either seventy-one grains of IMR-3031 or seventy-five grains of Hodgdon's

H-4895, either of which drives these tougher, deeper-penetrating bullets at between twenty-one and twenty-two hundred feet per second.

Rounding out the picture for those shooters who feel that they must use five-hundred-grain bullets — and why, outside of Africa, I wouldn't know — I wager that it will come as a surprise to handloaders to learn that my best-performing load proved to be seventy-four grains of H-335, pushing the big five-hundred-grain Hornadys at 2,114 feet per second.

For the benefit of those who may wonder why published ballistics for the .458 sometimes vary substantially between sources, let me point out that in addition to barrel-length differences of as much as three inches, some testing agencies utilized pressure barrels while others worked with actual rifles. Then again, disagreements are found between individual rifles, whether factory or custom.

Still another point undoubtedly having some effect on velocities as well as accuracy with the several bullets is rifling twist. While Winchester, Remington, and Ruger all use a fourteen-inch twist in their .458 Magnum rifles, Mannlicher opted for fifteen inches, and Browning adopted a slower 16½ inches. I'm not certain as to the twist in Colt's Grand African .458, but Sako .458s have a still slower eighteen-inch twist. Theoretically at least, the slower twist should prove advantageous for increased accuracy with the lighter bullets and especially cast bullets up to around four-hundred grains because of the lessened torque.

In my rifles with fourteen-inch twist, I found that considerable experimenting was required to achieve the performance I sought with cast bullets. A virtual balancing act was necessary, attempting to reach acceptable velocities without sacrificing accuracy.

Classic cast-bullet powders in the fast-burning range exemplified by IMR-4198 gave good grouping as long as muzzle speeds were kept below 1,650 feet per second; but above that, plain-base bullets were apparently being damaged by the heat of combustion. Kapok wads weighing ¾-grain, tamped down lightly on the powder, helped materially but proved insufficient to allow any major increase in velocities with those powders. Best loads consisted of 302-grain bullets from Lyman mould 457191 sized to 0.4595 inch with thirty-two grains of IMR-4198, chronographing 1,445 feet per second from the Ruger Number One, and 393-grain Ohaus 45405F flat-nose bullets with thirty-three grains of IMR-4198 at 1,455 feet per second.

Switching to medium-burning powders, represented by IMR-3031, permitted modest increases in velocity, again requiring the addition of kapok wads. Once seventeen hundred feet per second had been reached, however, accuracy went down the drain, so hopefully I turned to Hodgdon's H-4831, recalling how that powder had given good accuracy in the .45-70. For some reason — just why, I can't say for sure, though I suspect that quick-twist rifling — it didn't in the .458 Winchester. Velocities were abysmally low, and accuracy was lacking.

Finally, I tried a pair of heavy-weights — 502-grain flat-nose bullets cast in a custom Saeco-Darr mould and some ponderous round-nose bullets weighing 546 grains from another Ohaus mould. Accuracy grouping improved with the Darr bullets, but velocity fell off drastically, and the big Ohaus bullets failed in both respects.

Despite my best efforts to date, I'm still not satisfied with cast-bullet performance in the .458 Winchester. I intend trying one or more gas-check bullets, also increasing hardness, which should allow velocities approaching two thousand feet per second without leading or major loss of accuracy, but those trials will have to wait until another time.

As for the mechanics of assembling loads, attention should be called to the fact that if you desire to crimp cases on bullets simultaneously with seating in a single die, the seating-stem depth and die-body adjustments must be set with care to ensure that the crimp is turned into the cannelure of jacketed bullets.

Actually, despite the usual advisories, I didn't find crimping necessary as long as bullet bases were in firm contact with the powder charge, as occurs with most full-power loads in the .458, so they can't push back into cases. Indeed, cases can't be crimped on those bullets lacking a crimping cannelure, such as the four-hundred-grain Barnes. A rather tight neck-sizing gave all the friction grip needed to prevent bullet movement from recoil, though of course some .458 sizing dies may not do this. I might note here that my C-H die set performed exactly as intended in every way, a finely machined set, both inside and out.

Another but different sort of accessory that was of great assistance to me throughout this test series was the Williams slip-on shoulder pad that helped in controlling the sometimes fierce recoil of the .458 Magnum. This is a strap-harness affair that can be worn either under or over a jacket and is especially useful when wearing light clothing in summer heat. If you think these rifles kick when you're standing erect, try firing several hundred rounds with full-power loads from a benchrest! The Williams shoulder pad offers a degree of protection without the need for a complete padded shooting jacket.

Not a long-range cartridge despite its power, the .458 Winchester Magnum does rather well in trajectory, considering the size of its bullets. With a 150-yard zero, even five-hundred-grain bullets are down only 5.6 inches at two hundred yards, and with the more usual hundred-yard

sighting, drop is 3.5 inches at 150 and 10.3 inches at two hundred yards. Energy retention is likewise quite good, with 3,547 foot-pounds remaining at a hundred yards and 2,640 at two-hundred yards.

For all its undoubted game-killing power, however, I'm afraid that I must own up to some disappointment with this cartridge. Excessive recoil with full-power heavy-bullet loads pretty effectively cancels out the pleasure of shooting, nor is accuracy with most of the heavier loads all that I could wish for. My .375 H&H Magnums are much superior in all respects, including velocity and trajectory.

The bright spot that the .458 holds for me lies in its potential with the lighter bullets. My experience to date with Reloder 7 in combination with three-hundred and 350-grain bullets is convincing proof that this cartridge *can* be successfully adapted for more general use through a painstaking trial-and-error process of load development.

Whether a slower rifling twist would assist to this end, or perhaps an assembly of components not yet tested, I'm unable to say with certainty. But there are other days and more things to try, and while this remains so, the .458 Winchester Magnum continues to be a challenge. ●

CHAPTER
53

Winchester's Biggest Magnum

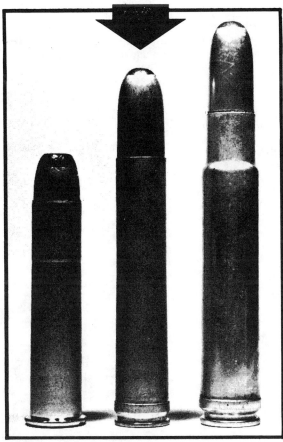

Of the many .45 caliber commercial cartridges that have been chambered in American rifles, these three are the only ones factory loaded and chambered today. From left, they are the .45-70, .458 Winchester Magnum and .460 Weatherby Magnum.

By BOB HAGEL

ACK IN THE days of buffalo and black powder, the .45 was one of the most popular American hunting cartridges. Although exceeded in popularity by both the .40 and .44 caliber cartridges, many of the big black powder .45 cartridges were used by the hide-seeking buffalo hunters. Some of the more powerful numbers like the .45-120 Sharps gave very good long range results when used by sharpshooting hunters of long experience.

When we consider that there were at least sixteen .45 caliber black powder cartridges chambered in commercial American rifles at one time or another, it is a little odd that the .45-70 is the only one to ride out the transition from black to smokeless powders. And even stranger, is the fact that the century-old cartridge is showing a comeback against our modern rounds.

There was a long period of time, however, when the .45 caliber was almost dead. The .45-90 cartridge was discontinued in about 1936, which left only the .45-70 as a .45 commercial round, and no commercial American arm that I know of was chambered for it after the demise of the 1886 Winchester in the same year. This left a period of 20 years without an American commercial rifle being chambered for a .45 caliber cartridge, when in 1956

The Browning Safari grade .458 Winchester Magnum test rifle was mounted with a Leupold M-8 3X scope in Leupold STD mounts. Accuracy was good and functioning perfect.

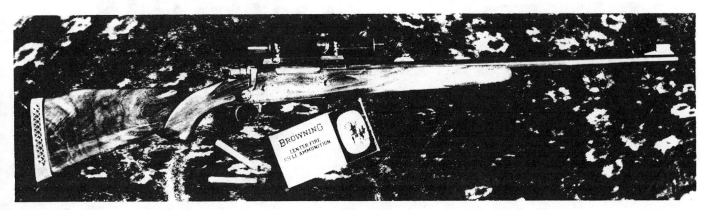

Winchester again entered the field with the .458 Winchester Magnum cartridge chambered in the Model 70 "African."

The reason for this lack of interest in the .45 caliber was the minimal need for such a big bore in American hunting. Also, during the time of the great depression from 1929 until the American involvement in World War II, few American hunters had the wherewithal to make African hunts. Of course there was practically no hunting in Africa during the war years by Americans or any other alien. During the first post-war years the American economy boomed and many hunters who had thought an African hunt was only a dream, found themselves with enough cash to make that dream a reality. The day of the American hunter in Africa had arrived, and with it the need and sales appeal for a big bore American commercial cartridge to fill that need.

Winchester was not blind to the potential a big bore cartridge for African hunting carried in not only American sales appeal, but in the world market. The trend was toward magazine bolt action rifles, and few were available for big cartridges, so the .458 Winchester Magnum was born.

Some work had been done by wildcatters with various cartridge designs, nearly all based on the .300/.375 Holland & Holland case. Most of these were blown out to form less body taper, and most were left near full-length of the original .375 H&H cartridge. Many of these big .45 wildcats gained little or no recognition, but some of the more popular were the .450 Watts, .450 Ackley, .450 Mashburn, .450 Barnes Supreme, and .450 Ashurst. All of these big cartridges would start a 500-grain .458 bullet at 2,400 to 2,500 fps, churning up muzzle

energies of well over 6,000 foot pounds. However, these wildcat .45's were severely handicapped by the lack of suitable solid jacket bullets for heavy African game such as cape buffalo and elephant; even soft point bullets that would hold up under these velocities on lighter game were nonexistent.

At the time Winchester decided to enter the African hunting rifle market, the trend was toward short magnum cartridges, so the .458 Winchester Magnum was made with a short case measuring only 2½ inches long, and having a normal overall loaded length of 3 5/16 inches with the 510-grain soft point and 500-grain solid jacket bullets. This made it possible to use the big cartridge through standard .30-06-length actions, and allowed many actions of this length to be chambered for it, both by custom makers and commercial arms companies.

While the Model 70 .458 didn't set any sales records immediately, it rapidly gained popularity as more and more American hunters appeared in Africa armed with the bolt action .45. Apparently the African white hunters liked the way it performed and it wasn't long until

both rifles and ammunition could be bought there. Today the popularity of the cartridge has gained enough momentum that many foreign-made rifles are chambered for it, and Browning, Remington, Ruger and Winchester all produce .458 rifles. Winchester, Remington and Browning also produce ammunition with both expanding and solid jacket bullets. Besides the factory produced bullets, Hornady makes an excellent solid as well as a soft point bullet, both in 500-grain weight, as well as a 350-grain SP for possible use on thin-skinned, non-dangerous game. Colorado Custom Bullets (formerly Barnes) also make bullets of 400, 500 and 600 grains in soft point, and the 500 and

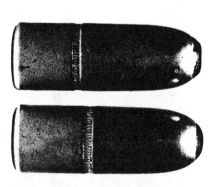

These bullets are both Hornady 500-grain soft points. The upper bullet is from an old lot, the lower one from a recent lot. Note the difference in the location of the crimping cannelure; there is also a slight difference in the exposed lead of the point. Many of the charges listed cannot be used with the newer bullet, seated to the cannelure, because powder will not compress that much in heavy cases like Browning's.

The 510-grain Browning expanding bullet is shown, inset above, before and after firing. The bullet was fired into a recovery box filled with a mixture of damp silt and sawdust at a striking velocity of about 2,120 fps. Penetration was 27 inches, and remaining weight was 425 grains; the cross sectional frontal area was one inch. The sectioned bullets, immediately above, from left, show jacket thickness and design of the Hornady 500-grain SP, Browning 510-grain SP and Browning 500-grain solid. Jacket thickness of the two soft points is about .043-inch, while the solid has a .075-inch jacket.

.532
13.51mm   .513
13.03mm   **.458 Winchester Magnum**   .481
12.22mm   .459
11.658mm

.220
5.59mm

2.500 (63.50mm)

3.340 (84.83mm)

DJL 1974

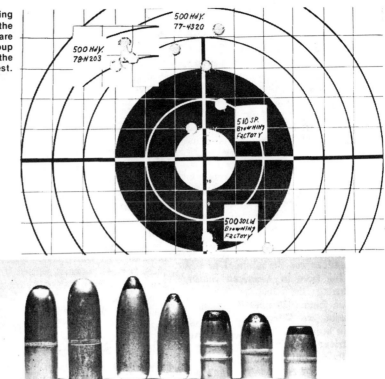

These groups show what the Browning Safari grade .458 will do with some of the 500 and 510-grain loads used. These are about average groups, except for the group fired with Norma 203, which was the smallest.

600-grain in full metal jacket — both with .049-inch jacket thickness. These jackets are made of soft copper in both soft point and solid form and I seriously doubt that the solids are tough enough to stand up under impact with the heavy bone of the heaviest game.

There are also several bullets that have appeared since the revival of the .45-70 that are designed mostly for use in that cartridge, but can also be used in the .458 Winchester if you don't mind having them explode on contact with anything they plow into at .458 velocities. There are the Winchester and Remington 405-grain .45-70 bullets, a 400-grain from Speer and two 300 grainers, one from Hornady and one from Sierra.

It is regrettable that neither Nosler nor Bitterroot make a .458 bullet in the 500-grain class. After killing a good many heavy North American game animals in the class of elk, moose, Alaska brown bears and grizzlies with both makes, I'd expect either of these controlled expansion bullets to be highly effective on cape buffalo in this weight and caliber. John Amber, editor of *Gun Digest*, killed several buffalo with 210 and 250-grain Nosler bullets from a .338 Winchester without difficulty, and I have another friend of considerable African experience who does the same thing regularly with 250-grain Bitterroots of the same caliber. A 500-grain .458 of the same styles should prove even more deadly with a greater insurance factor.

When Winchester brought out the .458, the cartridge was loaded with a 510-grain SP round nose bullet for use where an expanding bullet was indicated, and a 500-grain bullet for the deepest penetration on the heaviest game. Both bullets were loaded to a published velocity of 2,125 fps in early ballistic sheets, but was later revised to 2,130 fps; a change so minor as to be completely inconsequential. Pressure data on the .458 cartridge is scarce, but factory loads seem mild, and the Hodgdon reloading manual lists a load of 77 grains of BL-C(2) as giving 2,117 fps at 43,800 psi. This is unusually mild by today's standards for magnum or standard capacity cartridges, and closely approximates factory quoted ballistics.

What barrel length the Winchester velocity figures were taken with I do not know, but the original .458 rifles had 25-inch barrels, so it seems likely that a barrel of at least that length was used. Model 70 rifles now have 22-inch barrels and velocity figures are quoted at five fps more, so it appears that unless pressures of today's ammo is considerably higher, a

These are some of the .458 bullets used in load development tests. From left are the 500-grain Hornady SP, 500-grain Browning solid, 500-grain Colorado Custom spitzer boat-tail, 400-grain Colorado Custom spitzer boat-tail [both on special order only], 400-grain Speer, 350-grain Hornady and 300-grain Sierra.

.458 Winchester Magnum Load Data

.458 Winchester Magnum Browning Safari 24-inch barrel
Browning cases, 254 grains except where noted
CCI No. 250 primers
Oehler M-31 Chronotach, M-50 photoelectronic screens
Velocity instrumental at 15 feet converted to MV
Five-shot groups at 100 yards

Bullet	Powder	Charge	Velocity	Group Size, Inches
Browning factory 510 SP	- - - - -	71.5	2,132	1 1/4
Browning factory 500 solid	- - - - -	67.0	2,158	2
500 Hornady SP	IMR-4320	77.0	2,208	1 1/2
	N-203	78.0	2,216	5/8
	IMR-4198	64.0	2,133	1 3/4
	IMR-3031	71.0	2,165	2 1/4
	748-BR	80.0	2,216	1 3/4
	IMR-4320	77.0*	2,066	1 1/4
	IMR-4320	79.0*	2,245	15/16
500 CCB PSP BT	IMR-4320	75.0	2,201	2
	IMR-3031	71.0	2,178	2
500 Browning solid	IMR-4320	74.0	2,132	1 1/2
400 CCB PSP BT	IMR-4198	67.0	2,365	2 1/8
	IMR-3031	75.0	2,362	4 1/4
	748-BR	83.0	2,388	2 1/2
400 Speer SP	IMR-4198	67.0	2,330	4
350 Hornady SP	IMR-4198	70.0	2,553	1 3/4
	748-BR	86.0	2,486	15/16
300 Sierra SP	IMR-4198	74.0	2,733	4, printed 14 inches below the 500-grain

*W-W cases weighing 236 grains were used.

With all powders used except 4198 all charges were compressed to the limit of seating with the various bullet weights and styles used in the heavy Browning cases. While these charges gave near maximum pressures in this rifle with the components used, they were limited more by case capacity than by high pressures. They should not be used, however, in other rifles without starting at least two grains below and working up.

There may be some error in muzzle velocities of some bullets due to unknown ballistic coefficient.

few inches in barrel length makes little difference. And with this large bore I suspect this is completely true. There are advantages both ways in barrel lengths for this cartridge. On the side of the 22-inch tube there is the advantage of fast handling in tight places, along with the convenience of carrying the shorter rifle. The longer barrel has less muzzle blast and muzzle jump to upset the hunter, especially for fast second shots.

Seeing that in load testing, speed and carrying qualities hold little advantage to the shooter, and the lack of muzzle blast and jump are certainly desirable assets, a 24-inch barrel has appeal. The Browning Safari grade test rifle has a 24-inch barrel and, while recoil is certainly far from mild, muzzle jump is not at all bad and can be held down even from the bench by using a firm grip on the fore-end just to the rear of the sandbag while exerting down-pressure on the bag. The dimensions of the Browning stock also serve to sop up recoil very well.

Like all Browning guns, the .458 Safari has excellent metal finish, and the wood is of good quality with pleasing figure. During the great deal of testing, the rifle functioned perfectly with all bullet weights and styles. (The only bullets that gave feeding trouble were the experimental 400 and 500-grain Colorado Custom bullets in spitzer form. These had to be chambered rapidly or they jammed on the chamber rim, and sometimes did it anyway.) An M-8 3X Leupold scope in STD Leupold mounts was used because of the longer-than-normal eye relief it affords. Rifle accuracy was good even with this low magnification, and several groups with the best loads went under the one-inch mark for three shots. (Why some of the scope manufacturers do not bring out a 4X scope with about a five-inch eye relief especially for the heavy magnum cartridges, and mounted with extension rings on existing bases, is hard to understand. Such a scope would allow a full field of view without butchering your eyebrows with half moon scars.)

Two boxes of Browning ammunition were provided with the test rifle, one loaded with 510-grain soft point bullets, and one with 500-grain solids. The data on the boxes indicated that both were loaded to 2,130 fps MV, and this is one case where factory quoted ballistics were exceeded slightly. The 510-grain SP ammo clocked 2,132 fps at 70 degrees, while the 500-grain solids did even better at 2,158 fps. When the cartridges were broken down the powder proved to be of spherical form and the 510-grain SP cartridges were loaded with 71.5 grains, while the 500-grain solids were backed by only 67 grains of what appeared to be the same powder. At first glance this appeared odd, but a check of the bullet jackets and bullet length showed why: the

solids have a copper coated steel jacket that is approximately .075-inch thick — almost twice the thickness of the SP — resulting in a longer bullet with more bearing surface, as well as being seated deeper into the case. The soft point bullet is shorter and with what I assume to be a gilding metal jacket of about .043-inch thickness. Later tests showed that the 500-grain Browning solid bullets had to be cut about three grains below the 500-grain Hornady SP to keep pressures near equal when using 4320 powder. Another grain of powder could have been used with the solid 500-grain, but both bullets were seated over all of this powder that could be compressed at 77 and 74 grains respectively.

It was soon found that several suitable powders would give considerably more velocity than factory data shows with 500-grain bullets. Most of these powders, in fact all of them with the exception of 4198, were not limited in charge by pressures, but by case capacity. Even fast-burning 4198 is compressed somewhat with all bullet weights except the 300-grain, and this one gives about 100 percent loading density.

There may be some powder that is of exactly the right burning rate and density to allow pressures to be built up to maximum for hunting loads without undue compression with 500-grain bullets, but if there is I did not find it. With the results obtained with what little Norma 203 I could rake up, I suspect that Norma 201 might come close to being ideal, but, unfortunately, like other Norma powders, none was available.

Neither was any of the new W-W 748 spherical powder available, although I had some of the discontinued 748-BR on hand. Just how much difference there will be in the charges used with these two powders is hard to say, but my load of 80 grains behind the 500-grain Hornady runs near to the maximum load listed in *Hornady Handbook II* with the 500-grain bullet. The difference in velocity was about the same as with other powders and charges for my loads and theirs.

With all 500-grain bullets 4320 is perhaps the best powder as far as both velocity and accuracy goes. It does have to be compressed to the limit for factory overall cartridge length, but so do all of the other powders that will give top velocity. Norma 203 gives extremely good accuracy in this rifle, and slightly higher velocity because at least one grain more can be used due to higher density. But with Norma powders being on the unavailable list anywhere you care to look, using them will depend on whether the reloader happens to have some on hand.

One point that should be considered here is that these loads were worked up in

Browning cases. These cases are very heavy, weighing an average of 254 grains while the lot of W-W cases I had weighed only 236 grains. I did not have R-P cases on hand so do not know their weight. [Ed. Note — *An early lot of R-P cases in the lab weigh just under 240 grains.*] The fact that these loads were worked up in the heavy Browning case allows a margin for both pressure and powder compression over the W-W case. To show what difference can be expected in velocity and allowable powder compression between the two brands of cases, I checked the same load of 77 grains 4320 and 500-grain Hornady in both cases. The velocity in Browning cases stood at 2,208 fps, and in W-W cases 2,066 fps. I found that two grains more powder could be used in the W-W case and still seat the bullet, and velocity increased to 2,245 fps. A charge of 78 grains would about duplicate factory velocity. Pressure was not excessive with even the 79-grain charge in the W-W case.

About the time I was starting to do this work with the .458, Rich Hoch of Colorado Custom Bullets, sent me samples of the experimental batch of both 400 and 500-grain bullets. Believe it or not, in addition to spitzer points, these bullets had boat-tails! Jackets were listed as being .032-inch, so apparently they were designed with long-range shooting at thin-skinned game in mind. I'd personally have to question this line of thinking, but the point here was only to check loads for velocity and accuracy. As might be expected, the 500-grainer is a pretty long number and has to be seated much deeper in the case than the 500-grain Hornady. The charge of 4320 had to be cut from 77 grains to 75 grains, but velocity was nearly the same at 2,201 fps. Charges of 3031 were the same for both bullets, as the longer sticks of that powder were readily compressed by the boat-tail of the CCB bullet. Velocity ran slightly higher with the CCB at 2,178 as against 2,165 with the Hornady. Accuracy was fair in this rifle at two inches with both powders.

With the 400-grain CCB, top velocity was reached with 83 grains of 748-BR at 2,388 fps, while 3031 and 4198 were only slightly below. Accuracy with this bullet was not good for this rifle, running from a low of 2 1/8 inches with 4198 to 4 inches with 3031. However, the rifle didn't seem to like 400-grain bullets in any form. The 400-grain Speer also gave 4-inch groups at 100 yards with the same 67-grain charge of 4198.

While the 300-grain Sierra, like the Speer 400-grain and the several 405-grain bullets, is intended primarily for use in .45-70 rifles, it was tried to see what accuracy and velocity it would give. Of the powders I had on hand, only 4198 seemed suited to this bullet because case capacity ran short with all of the others. A charge of 74 grains gave the 300-grain Sierra 2,733 fps, but groups ran 4 inches and printed 14 inches lower than the 500-grain Hornady at 100 yards.

If one wishes to use a bullet lighter than the 500-grain for thin skinned game, and for flatter trajectories in shooting this kind of game, the 350-grain Hornady seems to be the best choice. While it has a round nose it is much better shaped than any of the 300 or 400/405-grain bullets except the spitzer 400-grain CCB, and can be loaded to good velocity with excellent accuracy. A charge of 70 grains of 4198 gave 2,553 fps with groups running about 1 3/4 inches. Using 748-BR in an 86-grain dose gave 2,486 and proved to be very accurate at just under the one-inch mark at 100 yards. Both loads were compressed to the seating limit without showing high pressures. This indicates a denser, somewhat faster powder might do even better in the velocity department.

One thing that should be brought to the attention of .458 reloaders is that the location of the crimping cannelure on the 500-grain Hornady SP has been changed. Some bullets I have had on hand for some time had the crimp groove located about 1/16-inch nearer the base than on a new lot just received. This will make considerable difference in seating over heavily compressed charges; dense powders do not compress easily under a .458 bullet in a straight-walled case. To keep things the same with both bullets I simply seated the new lot of bullets to the same depth and left the cannelure above the case mouth.

This brings up another question: Will the .458 bullets be held firmly under recoil in the magazine if they are not crimped in place? To find out, I loaded a 500-grain solid in the magazine with no powder in the case and no crimp, then fired the rifle several times. After three firings the bullet had set back about 1/16-inch. This was with full-length resizing and no expander, in RCBS dies (a third die is furnished especially for loading cast bullets that contains an expanding plug which also will bell the mouth of the case for seating softer cast bullets). A case was then loaded with a normal 75/4320 charge under the solid 500-grain with no crimp and placed in the magazine; after a dozen rounds had been fired there was no setback whatever. With the heavily compressed charges used in the .458 with all suitable powders for full-charge loads there is no danger of the bullets setting back in the case.

We will not go into the potential of the cartridge here as to what it will or will not do on heavy game with any of the bullets used. I have not used any of them on game and, therefore, can't say exactly what the results would be. I will speculate that the 500-grain Browning solids will do well for the deepest penetration on the heaviest game due to the .075-inch steel jacket. I would also suspect that the Browning 510-grain expanding bullet will do quite well for that type of bullet, as tests with that bullet fired into a mixture of damp silt and sawdust showed excellent results, with the bullet expanding perfectly with the core remaining in the jacket and retaining 425 of its original 510-grain weight. This is not to say it would not come apart in heavy bone and muscle; only the shooting of heavy game can prove that point.

There is little doubt that the .458 Winchester Magnum is one of the best cartridges for the largest African game if a bullet of correct design is used. For American hunting it would seem there is little use for it unless you happen to be a plain big-bore fan. There are times when it would be comforting to have along in the thick brush of some Alaskan brown bear country, especially for the guide who might have to knock off a wounded brownie at nose-rubbing range, but everything considered, it is far from ideal for American hunting. However, if you like them big from choice or necessity, the foregoing and the chart of loads will show about what to expect from Winchester's biggest cartridge. ●

CHAPTER
54

.460 Van Horn

by BOB HAGEL

More punch than the .458 in the same length action

CARTRIDGE wildcatting isn't as popular today as it was a few years back. There are probably several reasons for this but there are two that have more bearing than the others. First, the commercial cartridge field has pretty well filled all the holes in the caliber line with cases of various capacities and consequent velocities. Second, it has been some time since we've seen a new case on which to base a wildcat.

The fact that few holes are left unfilled by some commercially manufactured cartridge discourages any custom rifle maker who is thinking of working up a wildcat with rifle sales in mind. It is also becoming more difficult to whomp up a wildcat that will outperform some factory number. On the second count the advent of a new cartridge case has always stirred up a frenzy of activity among wildcatters akin to the rush westward to the California gold fields in '49. Like the gleaming bits of gold unearthed by our hearty ancestors from the streams that flow west from the Sierra Nevadas, any new cartridge case brings on cries of pure ecstasy from the true gun buff. He necks it up and he necks it down, he changes the body diameter, the angle and location of the shoulder, and he lengthens or shortens the neck. Case capacity is often changed to the point that it no longer plays in the same ball park with the original case. The company engineers who developed the original cartridge are no doubt often astonished at the results, and the wildcatter may even be a bit astounded himself. But the main thing is he has had fun, and while he is at it he often comes up with a better cartridge than the original. In fact, if it were not for the wildcatter, many of our most efficient cartridges would never have been born. A great many of the cartridges piled on sporting goods store shelves today are the end result of some wildcatter's dream.

Any wildcatter who does his homework well has some special purpose in mind. As strange as it may seem to those outside the fraternity of wildcatters, many wildcat cartridges are not designed with the intent to better the velocity and energy of the factory cartridge on which it is based. The desired result of the wildcatting may well be a cartridge with less power than the original, but one that serves a special purpose in some way. The .460 Van Horn is such a cartridge.

Gil Van Horn, who had worked with a number of big bore wildcat cartridges in the past, and Walt Abe, custom rifle maker, got together and decided to make up a .458 caliber cartridge that would be more powerful than the .458 Winchester, yet function through a standard length action. To do this the case obviously had to have more capacity than the .458 Winchester, but a case based on the .375 H&H case like the .450 Watts or Ackley magnums in a full-length blown out design was out. Also, if the cartridge were to be economical to make, the brass had to be readily available. The logical choice was the .460 Weatherby Magnum case.

Cutting the .460 Weatherby case to

The .460 Van Horn cartridge is flanked by the .458 Winchester Magnum, left, and the .460 Weatherby Magnum. The Van Horn is simply the .460 Weatherby cut off about 3/8-inch, the shoulder pushed back and given a 25-degree angle with no other changes.

2.50 inches in length (the same length as the .458 Win.) would allow functioning through standard .30-06-length magazines. It would also give a good deal more powder capacity than the .458 Winchester, which should boost velocity and energy above the levels of the .458. As it turned out, the powder capacity falls a bit over half way between the .458 Winchester and the .460 Weatherby. A full-length resized .458 Winchester case of

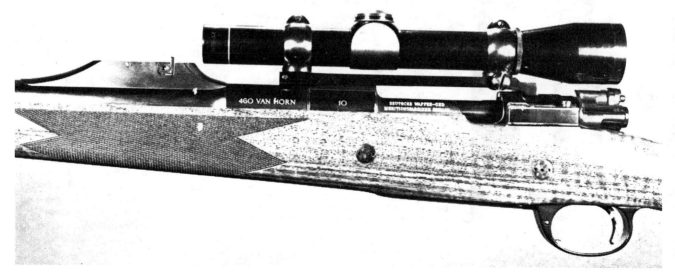

Hagel used a custom rifle built by Walt Abe for the .460 Van Horn load testing. The rifle sports a 21 3/8-inch Atkinson barrel but the integral muzzle brake cuts bore length from the bolt face to 19 1/2 inches.

average weight in W-W brand holds 71 grains of 4320 packed to the base of a 500-grain Hornady soft point bullet seated to factory overall cartridge length. The .460 Van Horn holds 96 grains in a full-length resized case with same bullet seated to the cannelure, and the .460 Weatherby, also full-length resized, takes 117 grains.

Even though the .460 case was cut to

standard length, it posed problems in standard actions, especially the Model 98 Mauser around which most rifles would be built. Even if actions already set up for normal belted cases were used, there would be conversion problems, and the standard action required even more work. Consider that the standard belted case of .375 H&H size has a rim and belt diameter of .532-inch, and a body diameter just forward of the belt of .511-inch; compare this with the .460 Weatherby case, with a rim-belt diameter of .603-inch and a body size of .582-inch, and it is obvious that changes will need to be made in several areas.

The bolt face is no great problem and only needs boring out to accept the larger head size. The extractor also has to be reground a bit, but the Mauser ejector works well with no changes. The

magazine poses the greatest problem. The Weatherby Mark V in both .378 and .460 chambering has a magazine that handles two cartridges, one directly above the other, for straight line feeding. Neither Van Horn nor Abe liked this setup and were determined to use the standard staggered system for a three cartridge magazine capacity. This was accomplished to perfection by widening the magazine box. Where the box of an FN Mauser long action (400 Series) has a rear width of .9-inch and is 11/16-inch in front, the magazine in the M-98 Mauser made up by Abe for the .460 Van Horn and sent to me for testing, has a rear width of 1 1/20 inches and is 9/10-inch in front. Of course a good deal of work had to be done on the action rails, but the result was a rifle that fed the three rounds perfectly. With this arrangement the magazine section of the completed rifle is no more bulky than for any well designed rifle on the Mauser 98 action, and there is a four round capacity — a possible advantage in hunting dangerous game if the first one fails to do the job. I would suspect it could prove to be a real boon to a hunter in elephant control work.

The test rifle was made up for hunting in Africa and was fitted with a short barrel for use in the brush. The total

Walt Abe built the .460 Van Horn rifle on a standard length M-98 action; considerable work was required on the magazine rails for the rifle to properly feed cartridges. There are crossbolts behind both the action recoil lug and magazine well. A Leupold M8-3X in Buehler mounts served as sighting equipment.

barrel length from bolt face to muzzle is 21 3/8 inches. It has an integral muzzle brake with three rectangular ports on each side. This section is counterbored to about .470 ID to a depth of 1 29/32 inches, which leaves the actual bore length from the bolt face at just under 19 1/2 inches. The muzzle diameter is .800-inch, a fairly stiff barrel even in .458 caliber.

There is a sling swivel stud sweated to the barrel about 1 1/2 inches forward of the fore-end tip, or 11 3/4 inches forward of the receiver ring. There is also a second recoil lug sweated to the barrel to help take up the considerable recoil of the big cartridge.

The barrel was made by Bill Atkinson, Prescott, Ariz. and has six lands with a right twist of 1-in-20.

The front sight is a fairly large flat-faced gold bead on a long, graceful, matted ramp. The rear sight is of quarter-rib styling fitted to the barrel with two hex-head screws. It consists of a wide shallow V ideal for fast work at close range, and is adjustable by means of hex-head screws for click adjustment. The test rifle was also fitted with an M8-3X scope in Buehler mounts with a one-piece extension base.

The floor plate is hinged with a release inside the trigger guard, and conventional guard screws have been replaced with hex-head screws. The trigger is a Canjar, and the safety is from Buehler.

The stock is made from an imported

No special forming dies are required for forming Van Horn cases. The .460 Weatherby case is first cut off about 3/8-inch with a tubing cutter. The lubed case is then simply run into the full-length sizing die and trimmed to 2 1/2 inches. Chamber dimensions in Hagel's rifle were such that no neck reaming was necessary. Dies are available on special order from RCBS.

French blank with fairly straight grain. It has good contrasting streaks of dark and light wood and shows a little fiddleback. It's a good piece of wood that I would expect to be very stable. To put strength in the stock where it is needed for heavy recoil, there are cross-bolts behind the action recoil lug and behind the magazine well.

Stock design is of almost classic styling with only a whisper of monte carlo at the rear of the cheekpiece. It is very straight, having a drop from center of bore of 3/4-inch at comb and 7/8-inch at heel. Length of pull is 13 5/8 inches, and the distance from center of trigger to forward edge of pistol grip cap is 3 1/2 inches. The fore-end is nicely rounded and fills the hand well for comfortable holding. The fore-end tip and grip cap appear to be of rosewood. A Pachmayr Old English pad dulls recoil. Weight with scope and no cartridges is an even 10 pounds.

Checkering is of point design, very well done with sharp diamonds, 22 lines per inch. It appears to have been stained somewhat to make the pattern contrast with the finished wood. The finish is of good quality oil, which Abe tells me is Casey's Tru-Oil, and is well done.

The critical areas of the inletting, including both the action and barrel recoil lugs, are bedded in bedding compound. Wood to metal fit has a perfection that shows Walt Abe is a master chaftsman. To complete the job, metal finish is of good quality and nicely

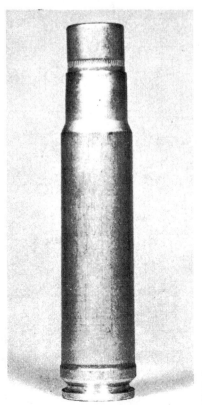

This cartridge with bullet seated base forward was seated by chambering in the Van Horn to illustrate the very long throating of the barrel.

blued — a very nice custom rifle in every respect. Now, to get back to the .460 Van Horn, how to make cases and how it performs.

Actually, making cases isn't at all difficult for anyone who has ever done any case forming. The first step is to cut the .460 Weatherby case off about 3/8-inch. A tubing cutter that can be picked up in any hardware store will do the job nicely, or a cutting wheel in a small grinding tool will do the job even faster. After cutting to length, run the lubed case into the full-length resizing die made by RCBS, then trim to correct length. It is as simple as that! Chamber dimensions in the neck area are made so that no reaming is necessary. There are many wildcats that take a lot more work.

It is always a little difficult to start from scratch with a new wildcat cartridge at the loading bench. There was no load dope whatever for the cartridge aside from a load used for proofing the rifle, which was of no great help. Having done a good deal of work with the .458 Winchester and some other big cartridges of the same class, I knew what powders would probably give the best results, and about what charge to start with. I also had a hunch that later proved to be completely correct, that a number of powders would give the 500-grain Hornady soft point bullet about the same velocity with similar pressures.

It appeared that 4320 should have about the right burning rate and density for this case to give near 100 percent loading density with near top velocity. This hunch also proved to be correct because few powders gave higher velocity, and then exceeded it by very little. Just to

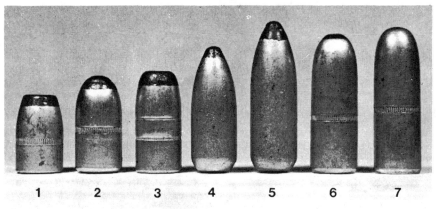

These are some of the .458 bullets that can be used in the Van Horn: 1. 300-grain Sierra; 2. 350-grain Hornady; 3. 400-grain Speer; 4. 400-grain Colorado Custom; 5. 500-grain Colorado Custom [both on special order in pointed form only]; 6. 500-grain Hornady SP; 7. 500-grain Hornady solid. The Sierra and Speer bullets are designed for the .45-70 and although they can be fired in the Van Horn, they are not designed to perform at that high velocity.

be on the safe side a charge of only 80 grains was used as a starting load. Pressure was so mild that the charge was increased by two-grain increments until the belt gave readable expansion. At 87 grains, there was .001 expansion on the rear of the belt (the rather thin web of the Weatherby case does not support the front of the belt so false readings are given if the full belt is miked). An 88-grain charge gave no further expansion, but 89 grains showed .0015, and 90 grains gave .0023 and bolt lift was sticky. Back to the charge of 88 grains for several firings and no indication of excessive pressures, so that load was settled on for a muzzle velocity of 2,280 fps. The same charge of 4064, an old standby that runs neck to neck with 4320 in most instances, and sometimes gives better accuracy, gave almost identical velocity, but seemed a trifle more touchy when another grain or two was added.

Wanting to see how slower powders would do with the 500-grain bullet in the fat case, 4350 was tried. It took a heavily compressed load of 100 grains to come up to pressures equal to the faster powders, and velocity was down to 2,231 fps. Norma 204 is much denser than 4350 and of similar burning rate; the big case swallowed 101 grains before pressure indicated a halt was in order. Velocity was still not up to that received with 4320 and 4064, but not at all bad at 2,264 fps. Norma 203 was slightly better and 93 grains gave 2,283 fps.

So far, no spherical powders had been tried and the case seemed to have about the right capacity for some of the medium to slow numbers. Hodgdon's 414 was the first tried with 103 grains being a top working load; it produced 2,284 fps. Olin's 760 is of similar quickness and a charge of 99 grains gave the highest velocity obtained at 2,299 fps. The faster 748 wasn't nearly as good, with 87 grains starting the 500-grain at only 2,196 fps. I was a little surprised when the top load of 3031 proved to be 84 grains, which delivered 2,260 fps.

Accuracy had not been anything to brag about with most of these loads. The best group came with 748 but shot to shot variation was higher with that powder than any other. The fact that there is a fair amount of air space with this powder may account for the velocity variation, but does not account for better than average groups. Anyway, the best group was just under 2 inches with an average for all powders being about 3 1/2 inches at 100 yards.

Wondering if perhaps the 1-20 twist was a bit slow for the 500-grain bullet, a couple of loads were worked up with the short 350-grain Hornady bullet. It turned out that 3031 is about right for that bullet, and 94 grains started the 350-grain at 2,731 fps. A charge of 97 grains of 4320 didn't do as well but still gave 2,651 fps. However, accuracy ran about the same at three to four inches with this bullet. No 400 or 405-grain .45-70 bullets were tried because they would blow to steam under the velocity of the .460 V.H.

One possibility that might cause the less than excellent accuracy is the fact that the throat is very long at about 3/8-inch from cartridge neck to lands. Some bullets do not shoot well under this free-bore situation. There is no way of knowing without trying a barrel both ways. I'd also like to see the .460 Van Horn chambered in a barrel with a 1-14 or 1-16 twist.

In testing this kind of heavy recoiling

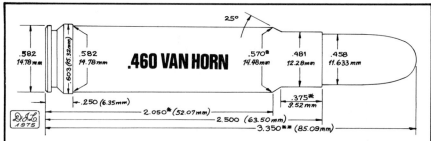

Dimensions marked with an asterisk [*] were obtained by scaling a photograph. Overall length [**] is based on the 500-grain Hornady SP seated to the bullet cannelure.

Load Data for the .460 Van Horn

Custom rifle by Walter Abe on Mauser 98 action, Atkinson barrel with 1-20 twist, length from bolt face to end of bore — 19 15/32 inches
.460 Weatherby cases cut to 2.50 inches
CCI 250 primers

Bullet	Powder	Charge	Velocity	Remarks
500 Hornady SP	IMR-4350	100	2,231	heavily compressed
500 Hornady SP	N-204	101	2,264	slight compression
500 Hornady SP	IMR-4320	88	2,280	
500 Hornady SP	N-204	93	2,283	
500 Hornady SP	H-414	103	2,284	
500 Hornady SP	WW-760	99	2,299	5,900 fp energy
500 Hornady SP	WW-748	87	2,196	
500 Hornady SP	IMR-4064	88	2,279	
500 Hornady SP	IMR-3031	84	2,260	
350 Hornady SP	IMR-4320	97	2,651	
350 Hornady SP	IMR-3031	94	2,731	5,800 fp energy

All of these loads were held to pressures that will be trouble free in hunting. However, this is a wildcat cartridge and all rifles chambered for it will be custom, so there could be a good deal of variation between individual rifles. Starting loads should be dropped by about three grains for all loads given.

cartridge, I always like to find out if the bullet will hold in the case by friction alone. A cartridge loaded without powder so the bullet is free to set back if it lets go of the neck walls was placed in the magazine and left there while several rounds were fired. The bullet started setting back at the third shot. After being crimped in the case it stayed put indefinitely. This situation, of course limits one to the use of cannelured bullets and seating to the depth of that cannelure. I doubt, however, that a bullet seated on compressed charges would move, but to be safe crimp 'em in tight.

Both Abe and Van Horn thought the cartridge would produce at least 2,400 fps with the 500-grain bullet, but I wasn't greatly surprised with the results for several reasons. First, bore travel of the bullet is only 16 inches, which may cut velocity with this hefty powder charge.

Most rifles chambered for the .458 Winchester cartridge have 22 or 24-inch barrels, and the .460 Weatherby has a 26-inch tube. This alone could knock the extra 100 fps off what had been anticipated. Another factor is that the Weatherby .460 case has a thin web section and much of the brass has tested out quite soft, although this lot of .460 brass was not given the Rockwell B test. I strongly suspect that these two points caused pressure pains a bit prematurely because the CCI 250 primers were far from flat. In fact, they looked more like 45,000 psi than the 55,000 such belt expansion would usually indicate. One thing for sure, velocity couldn't be increased very much with any powder tried because another grain or two of all powders caused bolt lift to start to get sticky; loads giving sticky bolt lift are something no one in his right mind would even consider when hunting dangerous game!

But even if the .460 Van Horn did not do all that its designers had in mind, it is still a pretty potent package that will deliver near 5,900 foot pounds of muzzle energy with the 500-grain bullet. Uncounted numbers of the world's biggest and most dangerous game animals have been taken with far less power.

I'd personally like to try a rifle chambered for this cartridge with a 24-inch barrel having a 1-15 twist. I have a hunch it would not only group better but would produce over 2,400 fps with the 500-grain bullet.

In answer to those inevitable questions such as how much a similar rifle would cost, I can't answer because he didn't tell me, but his address is Abe's Gun Shop, 5124 Huntington Drive, Los Angeles, Ca. 90032.   ●

CHAPTER
55

Bob Hagel

.460 weatherby

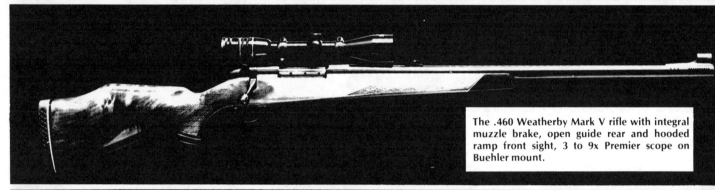

The .460 Weatherby Mark V rifle with integral muzzle brake, open guide rear and hooded ramp front sight, 3 to 9x Premier scope on Buehler mount.

World's Most Powerful Commercial Cartridge

FOR FIFTY-FIVE years the .600 Jeffery held the undisputed title of the world's most powerful commercial cartridge — from 1903 to 1958. This huge cartridge fired a 900-grain bullet with a diameter of .622 at a listed velocity of 1,950 fps and developed 7,600 foot pounds of muzzle energy. Its nearest competitor was the .577 Nitro Express that started a 750-grain bullet at 2,050 fps to deliver 7,010 fp of energy at the muzzle. This cartridge had also held the title of the world's most powerful cartridge from about 1880 until the .600 took over.

In 1958 Roy Weatherby designed and produced a cartridge that made even the mighty .600 seem rather mild where muzzle energy is concerned. The .460 Weatherby, according to Weatherby ballistic data, starts a 500-grain .458 diameter bullet at 2,700 fps and churns up 8,095 fp of muzzle energy! This exceeds the muzzle energy of the .600 Jeffery by 2,095 foot pounds, or nearly as much muzzle energy as the .30-30 with the 170-grain factory load.

There is a significant difference between these two mammoth cartridges designed for slaying elephants: the .600 Jeffery is its own cartridge with no predecessor on the same case, while the .460 Weatherby was not an original case. It sprung from

the .378 Weatherby that was released five years earlier (in 1953) with the case neck simply expanded to take the .458 diameter bullet. From the experimenter's point of view, the .460 could well be considered of wildcat origin, because you can bet the .378 case neck was expanded to .458 and load development done before it became a factory-loaded round.

And speaking of wildcats, like any other basic case, the .378/.460 Weatherby has been wildcatted up and down in neck diameter, as well as shortened and the shoulder angle changed. Examples of the full-length wildcats are the .475 A&M developed by the now defunct firm of Atkinson & Marquart of Prescott, Arizona, and the .510 Wells worked up by Fred Wells, also of Prescott. Fred also developed a .35 cartridge on the full-length .378 case. The .475 and .510 cartridges churn up even more energy than the .460 Weatherby, but are less versatile. Then there are the short wildcat cartridges on the big case, with the .338 K-T (Keith-Thompson) and the .460 Van Horn as examples. While some of these cartridges are more powerful than the .460, they are wildcats not likely to become commercial rounds.

While I did a good deal of test work and load development with the .378 Weatherby several years ago, and even

took it to Alaska to clobber a bull moose, I had shied away from the .460; I felt it had no place in the American hunting scene. But with a little arm-twisting from Tom Hall, who recently assumed the position of Weatherby's sales manager, I reconsidered and decided I'd have to find out just what the big cartridge actually offered.

There are very few bullets of any hunting value for the .460 Weatherby, even though a variety of .458 diameter bullets are being made. Of the domestic bullets, only the 500-grain Hornady soft point and solids and possibly the 350-grain soft point could be recommended, along with the 400, 500 and 600-grain Barnes bullets. All of the Barnes bullets made in .458 caliber have the heavy .049-inch jacket thickness, and all are made in both semi-spitzer and round-nose form. The round-nose FMJ solids are available in both 500 and 600-grain weights. The various 405-grain bullets, the 400-grain Speer and 300-grain Hornady and Sierra bullets should never be considered in the .460 Weatherby for game shooting, because those bullets are designed to expand at .45-70 velocities.

In doing load development for the .460 Weatherby test rifle, I was especially interested to see just what the long 600-grain Barnes would do. There is a good deal of load data available for the .460 with 500-grain bullets and some of the lighter offerings, but I do not recall any loads being published for the 600 Barnes. I wanted to know how much powder the big case would handle with this heavyweight, and which powders would give the highest velocities. It would also be interesting to see how much velocity could be given to the long bullet without going overboard in pressure, as well as what kind of penetration could be expected in my recovery box as compared to the factory loads with their 500-grain Hornady bullets.

There is a considerable amount of load information for the 500-grain bullet, so the 500 Hornady soft-point was used to start the load development. Loads settled on for that bullet are nothing new, except that my charges are not as high as most sources specify and the velocity is somewhat lower. All of the test loads were worked up to a point averaging a couple of grains heavier than the loads listed in the chart, then backed off to where there would be no chance of a problem while hunting.

I measured the expansion of the rear of the belt over the solid web of the case head. The factory ammunition expanded the belt by 0.0014 at that point. And it was found that when handloads reach the same amount of belt expansion, the expansion stopped and remained static until another two grains of powder was added. At that point the belt again started expanding and continued to do so when the same charge was fired again. This would, of course, lead to expanded primer pockets and, considering the cost of the big cases, was undesirable. That

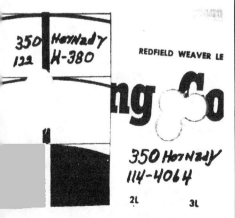

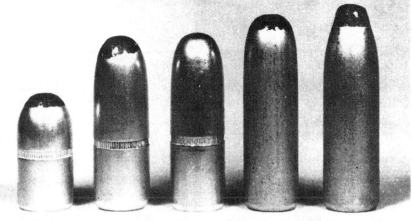

Bullets tested in loads for the .460 Weatherby: No. 1, 350-grain Hornady; No. 2, 500-grain Hornady SP; No. 3, 500-grain Hornady FMJ; No. 4, 600-grain Barnes round-nose; and No. 5, 600-grain Barnes semi-pointed.

The three expanded bullets were fired into the recovery box from the .460 Weatherby at near muzzle velocity. The 350-grain Hornady at left penetrated only 10 inches, the 500-grain factory load penetrated 24 inches, and the 600-grain Barnes round-point penetrated 22 inches. The 500-grain factory FMJ bullet penetrated 64½ inches of dry Douglas fir blocks. (See text and charts for particulars.)

.460 Weatherby

.460 Weatherby Mark V 26-inch barrel
Weatherby cases 313 grains primed
Oehler 34 chronograph & #50 screens
Velocity at 15 feet converted to muzzle velocity
Temperature 70 degrees Fahrenheit

bullet	powder	charge (grains)	velocity (fps)	remarks
500 SP factory ammo	- - - -	120	2,582	
500 FMJ factory ammo	- - - -	120	2,584	
600 Barnes SP RN	H-4831	118 C	2,258	
	IMR-4831	115 C	2,351	
	MRP	118 C	2,296	
	IMR-4350	112 C	2,351	
600 Barnes SP semi-spitzer	MRP	115 C	2,230	
500 Hornady SP	IMR-4831	120 C	2,549	
	IMR-4350	118 C	2,582	
	W-760	119 C	2,455	
	N-204	117 C	2,542	
	IMR-4064	101	2,474	
	IMR-4320	99	2,404	
350 Hornady	W-760	130 C	2,731	
	H-380	122 C	2,872	outstanding accuracy
	IMR-4064	114	3,007	outstanding accuracy
500 Hornady	IMR-4064	85	2,102	roughly .458 Win. velocity
	IMR-3031	80	2,066	roughly .458 Win. velocity
350 Hornady	IMR-4064	85	2,183	poor accuracy
	IMR-3031	80	2,120	good accuracy

These loads were all considered as full-power for hunting any game under all hunting conditions, but should be approached from five percent below in any other rifle.

C — compressed

REDFIELD WEAVER LE

350 Hornady
122 H-380

350 Hornady
114-4064

2L   3L

his is the kind of accuracy the .460 Weatherby ark V rifle is capable of with proper loads. roups were fired from the bench at a hundred rds.

329

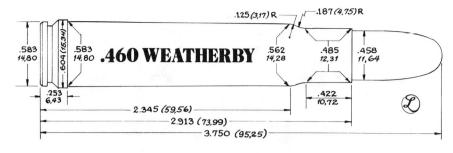

.460 WEATHERBY

kind of head expansion is also not good because anything that might cause pressures to rise, such as a few degrees rise in temperature, will cause the load to become excessive.

For this cartridge, which will certainly be used almost exclusively in Africa on dangerous game, anything approaching excessive pressures cannot be tolerated. Accordingly, all handloads shown in the chart were held to about the same level as factory

If you can't visualize the proportions of the 600-grain Barnes round and semi-spitzer point bullets in .458 caliber, they are compared here with a factory .44 Magnum cartridge loaded with a 250-grain jacketed bullet.

Here are the three .45 caliber commercial rifle cartridges loaded in the U.S. today: the .45-70, .458 Winchester Magnum and the .460 Weatherby Magnum. The cartridge at right is the wildcat .460 Van Horn on the shortened .460 Weatherby case.

loads. It could be that this test rifle is one that shows higher pressure and lower velocity with the same loads than other rifles. But whatever the reason, these loads are as hot as should be considered when hunting dangerous game where temperatures may run twenty or thirty degrees warmer than when the loads were tested.

As will be noted in the chart, factory ammunition gave only 2,582 fps for the soft point 500-grain bullet, and 2,584 fps for the FMJ loads. This is more than a hundred fps less than Weatherby shows for factory ammunition. The only handload I worked up that would equal this was with 118 grains of IMR-4350. The factory load *appeared* to be loaded with Norma 204 with a charge of 120 grains. The top load of that powder in this rifle was 117 grains and gave a muzzle velocity of only 2,542 fps — forty fps less than the factory ammunition. In fact, of the several powders tested, only IMR-4831 and IMR-4350 and N-204 would kick the 500-grain bullet out the muzzle at over 2,500 fps.

With the round-nose 600-grain Barnes bullet, H-4831 does quite well, but is a little slow even with that bullet weight; pressure is on the mild side when the powder is compressed as much as possible and sifted gently through a long funnel tube. IMR-4831 and IMR-4350 proved to be the best powders of those tested for this bullet, with Norma MRP falling behind by more than fifty fps.

The best the 600-grain round-point would do is about 2,350 fps. This load still develops 7,350 foot pounds of energy and, with the FMJ bullet, should give terrific penetration, but none of these bullets were available for testing. Randy Brooks did send along

some 600-grain semi-spitzer bullets, and they were tried with Norma MRP. With this bullet being over a tenth-inch longer than the round-point, it had to be seated that much deeper into the case. This took up enough powder space that the charge had to be cut by three grains of MRP, and the velocity dropped from 2,296 fps for the round-point, to 2,230 fps for the semi-pointed version. It is difficult to see where there is any advantage in using the semi-pointed bullet in a .45 caliber rifle, because at best it is a short range gun and the reduced velocity offsets any gain in ballistic coefficient.

There are a rather large number of powders that do well with the 350-grain Hornady bullet, and equally well with the 400-grain Barnes bullet with its .049 jacket thickness. Only three of these are listed in the chart, but there are a number of powders of similar quickness that will give similar results. Of those tried, 4064 gave the highest velocity with outstanding accuracy, with H-380 coming in a poor second. I might add that both powders gave nothing less than phenomenal accuracy considering that the loads were maximum working loads for this huge cartridge. Three-shot groups made overlapping clover-leaf clusters measuring a half-inch center-to-center! And with 4064 the velocity was over 3,000 fps at the muzzle with 7,400 foot pounds of muzzle energy.

This might cause some hunters and reloaders to assume that the 350-grain Hornady would be the ideal bullet for shooting smaller big game with the .460 Weatherby. But before making that decision it would be well to consider penetration. Fired into my recovery box at near muzzle velocity, all that was left of the bullet was a short piece of jacket mushroomed around the base to form a disc with a smear of lead on the front. It penetrated only ten inches, with a remaining weight of 113 grains. The first cardboard spacer six inches from entrance was almost completely shredded, and the spacer at one foot was pushed three inches back through the medium by the concussion, and was split like cracked glass even though the bullet did not reach it by two inches.

If used on any of the larger game — even elk-size animals — it would most likely cause a shallow surface wound on shoulder shots, and on smaller animals would blow things up much like a good varmint bullet does a chuck when fired from a .22-250. If all shots were at over two hundred yards it might do a bit better, but even then would lack penetration for large game and ruin most of the chops of the smaller animals.

When the factory 500-grain load was fired into the recovery box at the same time, I was impressed with the performance of the Hornady soft point. It penetrated just to the 24-inch spacer, leaving a fist-size hole in the other three. It gave a perfect mushroom with a diameter of .950 and weighed 365 grains, retaining 73 per cent of its original weight. While this is not as much penetration as one might expect from a 500-grain .458 bullet, it did perform perfectly. (Incidentally, a 250-grain Nosler Partition from a .340 Weatherby will average 29 inches of penetration in the same medium but, of course, leaves a much smaller wound channel.)

When the long 600-grain Barnes with its heavy copper tubing jacket was fired into the recovery box, I had visions of at least thirty inches of penetration, but was disappointed. It drove in only 22 inches, or two inches less than the 500-grain. Expansion was tremendous, with a frontal diameter of 1.265, and retained-weight was 440 grains, again 73 per cent of its original weight. The problem with penetration is the very large frontal diameter and the fact that less than half of the remaining weight was in the core — most of it having been blown away. And the portion of the core that remained was held in place only by the forward momentum of the bullet, and fell from the jacket when the bullet was washed before weighing. If the core had been bonded to the jacket so that the remainder of the shank was filled with the core, and with most of the core remaining with the expanded jacket, penetration would be better.

There was no point in firing the factory 500-grain FMJ into the recovery box to test penetration, so

dry blocks of Douglas fir firewood were placed side by side and the solid slug fired into them. It penetrated 64½ inches of that tough wood, with some small knots being hit along the way. That is certainly more than enough penetration for shooting any animal on earth from any position where a vital organ can be hit.

After working out the maximum loads for hunting, I was curious to see what could be done with the 350 and 500-grain Hornady bullets loaded down to around .458 Winchester velocity. It was evident that powders of medium burning rate would be the best bet in the big case to give reasonably good bulk while giving the velocity level desired. It seemed that the long granules of IMR-4064 and IMR-3031 should be ideal, so these powders were tried first, with the results so good that there was little reason to try others. With the 500-grain bullet, 85 grains of 4064 gave a muzzle velocity of 2,102 fps, and 80 grains of 3031 delivered 2,066 fps. This is quite close to factory load velocity for the .458 Winchester with the same bullet weight.

With the 350-grain Hornady, the 85-grain charge of 4064 kicked it along at 2,183 fps, and 80 grains of 3031 gave 2,120 fps. Three-shot accuracy ran 1¾ inches for both 500-grain loads, but was pretty sour with the 4064 and the 350-grain, at four inches. With 80 grains of 3031, three-shot groups dropped to 1 3/8 inches. That load would do quite well on most of the

African plains game and on our own elk and moose if you want to pack around some twelve pounds of rifle, scope and ammo in elk country. I believe, however, the 500-grain bullet with these light loads would be more reliable from all angles.

And looking at accuracy for all of the bullets used, the factory soft-point and solids both averaged about 2½ inches at a hundred yards from the bench, and so did the full-power handloads with the 500-grain Hornady and 600-grain Barnes. Some of the three-shot groups dropped down to an inch and a half, but some were over three inches. There is certainly nothing wrong with that accuracy level for the kind of shooting the big .460 Weatherby will be used for.

I might add here that all shooting for accuracy was done from the bench in the chronograph room over sandbags at one hundred yards, and with a Weaver K2.5 scope in Buehler mounts. I used the Weaver K2.5 scope instead of something with more power because it has the longest eye relief of any scope suited for the big rifle, and I don't need any more scars over my eyebrows. And when the groups fired with the full-power loads with the Hornady 350-grain bullet are considered, it is obvious that it was not a lack of power when groups were on the large side.

This reference to recoil brings up a point always uppermost to anyone who contemplates buying a .460

The Mark V .460 Weatherby rifle has a Pendleton-type muzzle break that effectively dampens upward muzzle jump. In fact, the muzzle jump of the rifle is not nearly as bad as the lighter .458 Winchester Magnum rifles without a break.

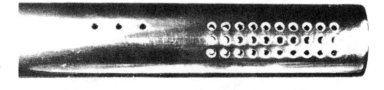

The stock of the Mark V .460 Weatherby has three areas of plastic bedding: around the extra recoil lug on the barrel, behind the action recoil lug, and at the rear of the magazine. These reinforced areas, plus the extra barrel lug, assure that the stock will not split under the heavy recoil of the big cartridge.

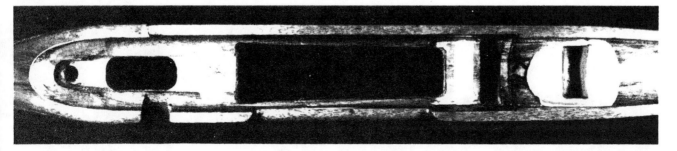

Weatherby. Let us not kid anyone, this gun, which weighs over eleven pounds with scope and mount and minus the two cartridges in the magazine, does set back pretty hard. And regardless of who you are, and whether you are big or little, you don't particularly enjoy shooting it at rockchucks. I shot it offhand and from the kneeling position several times, but mostly it was shot from the bench for serious testing. When shooting in any position except from the bench, I used a 10-X shooting coat with its heavy leather padding. When shooting from the bench I shot in shirt sleeves using a leather shot bag ten inches long, four inches wide and two inches thick, that held fifteen pounds of #8 shot. With that rather thin quilted bag it is not too difficult to see properly through the long eye-relief scope with one end of the bag sitting on the bench top and resting between the rifle butt and the shoulder.

A good deal has been said about the muzzle jump of this rifle, and I wondered if there would be a problem in keeping the muzzle from crashing into the top of the shooting port in the wall between the chronograph and screen rooms. Fortunately, this did not prove to be the case. The Pendelton-type muzzle break does an excellent job of holding the muzzle down, and the only precaution used to hold the barrel down was my left hand holding solidly on the fore-end well back toward the receiver in the normal fashion used for any heavy-recoiling rifle. This gun developed far less muzzle jump than a .458 Winchester without a muzzle break, even though the recoil is much heavier on the shoulder.

There is little to say about the .460 Weatherby in summing up that most knowledgeable gun buffs and hunters do not already know or have guessed. First, the accuracy of the big cartridge and rifle is more than adequate for any game. Second, there is little or no use for the cartridge for North American hunting, or for most African game for that matter. There is little doubt, however, that it would be a distinct comfort to have when a Cape buffalo, rhino or elephant came for you at close range. Third, the recoil of the big, heavy rifle will not shake the fillings from your teeth, bloody your nose (unless your thumb gets in the way), or rear up and tear the ceiling out of the shooting room. A varmint rifle it is not, but neither is it a man-killer on the butt end. ●

CHAPTER
56

.50-70 Government

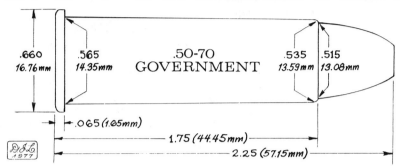

.660 / 16.76mm — .565 / 14.35mm — **.50-70 GOVERNMENT** — .535 / 13.59mm — .515 / 13.08mm

.065 (1.65mm)

1.75 (44.45mm)

2.25 (57.15mm)

DJL 1977

Though other metallic-cartridge arms, even repeating rifles, had been used in the Civil War and shortly thereafter, they and their cartridges were not "standard issue." The first *officially adopted* metallic-cartridge rifle was the breech-loading Allin conversion of .58 rifle muskets. Its cartridge was likewise adopted, identified as the .50 U.S. Gov't., or .50-70. It is probably derived from the .50-60-400 Joslyn rimfire of a few years earlier.

Comprised of a thin, drawn-copper case and a center-fire *inside* primer, it was loaded with 70 grains of powder and a 450-grain, lubricated lead bullet. Its service life was short, lasting only until replaced by the .45-70 in 1873. Even so, many thousands of other rifles were chambered for the .50-70, and it developed into a brass-case, Boxer-primed cartridge that remained in production until just before World War II. There are plenty of reports to indicate that it was a popular cartridge for buffalo and other game on the western plains.

Sharps, Remington, Winchester and other makers chambered fine single-shot rifles for it. In fact, we are told that its popularity prompted development of the .50-110 Winchester in the late 1880s. The .50-70 also spawned longer and more powerful cartridges such as the .50-90 and .50-140 Sharps, and .50-95 Winchester.

The original load used the Benet inside primer, so it *looked like* a rimfire with its smooth head. Seventy grains of black powder propelled a .450-grain lead .515-inch bullet at 1,260-1,275 fps from the long rifle. A shorter-case version was made for the Trapdoor Carbine, with 60 grains of powder and a 400-grain bullet at 1,200 fps. As case and primer design

STUDENTS OF FRONTIER lore will know of the Fetterman Massacre, near Fort Phil Kearny, when Major Fetterman allowed himself to be suckered into a Sioux ambush. The firing of guns could be heard from the post, but by the time relief troops could reach the site, the Sioux were gone and Fetterman and his command had been wiped out.

Fetterman's troops carried muzzle loaders, but not long thereafter, Ft. Kearny received its first shipment of the *new* Trapdoor Springfield, M1866, rifles in .50 caliber. And in due course the Sioux, under White Cloud, again attacked a woodcutting detachment. This time the escort forted up behind its wagon boxes and laid out plenty of ammunition for its new Springfield/Allin .50-70 single-shot "britch loaders." The Sioux came — and died in droves. The second and third waves of warriors didn't realize until too late that they weren't charging slow-loading rifle muskets. White Cloud took his battered forces away, and the blue-clad troopers felt that in at least a small way they had avenged the deaths of Fetterman's command — not to mention having saved their own scalps.

Such was the .50-70 baptism of fire on the western plains — or so it has been told and written many times.

.50-70 Government Load Data

Bullet*	Weight [gr.]	Powder	Weight [gr.]	Velocity
515141	450	FFg	70	1,260
515141	450	FFg	60	- - - -
515141	450	4198	26	1,410
515141	450	3031	36	1,270
518145	350	FFg	70	1,450
518145	350	4198	23	1,350
518144	285	FFg	70	- - - -
518144	285	4198	26	1,430
515142	515	FFg	70	1,200

*Lyman mould number

Modern cases (DGW, Bell) are of much thicker construction than originals and will not hold a full 70 grains of black powder with the 450-grain bullet seated to normal depth. Seat bullet out if the chamber throat or leade will accept it; otherwise, reduce the powder charge to the amount that can be accommodated when it is lightly compressed by the bullet. Pyrodex was not available for load-testing when this article was written, but based on its use in other cartridges, volume-for-volume CTG loads with black powder should be acceptable, although velocities may not be the same.

Shown at left are two inside-primed .50-70s. Cases are drawn copper, of "folded head" construction, the inside priming making them look like rimfires. Next is an old UMC "Solid Head" .50-70 — in modern terminology, a balloon head. These old cartridges should be relegated to a cartridge collection. The two unloaded cases are modern [sturdy solid head construction], for Boxer primers. The short case is Dixie's .50-70; the long case is Bell's ".50 Sharps 3 1/4" which can be cut down to .50-70.

progressed, the Boxer-primed, drawn-brass case had less powder space, but this doesn't appear to have affected the loadings manufactured.

Loading the .50-70 presents no problem if cases are available. While original cases can be found now and then, their use isn't recommended. They are quite old, and usually corroded inside by fouling or deteriorated black powder. They are also a valuable collector's item.

Though not many .50-70 rifles remain in serious use, lots of them are still around. There had apparently been enough demand that Dixie Gun Works arranged for manufacture of new, drawn-brass, solid-head cases which are currently available. DGW also offers a very economical tong-type iron mould for casting .50-70 bullets. The bullet from this mould is intended to be shot without resizing.

Cases may be made without too much trouble from the ".50 Basic" offered by Brass Extrusion Laboratories (800 W. Maple Lane, Bensenville, Illinois 60106). Simply trim cases to 1.75 inches and — in some rifles — ream the neck until it chambers easily with a bullet seated.

Other bullets are also available: Lyman's entire 512 through 518 series (six bullets) may be used, but No. 515141 is standard for the .50-70 and copies the original rather well in both shape and weight.

Loading the .50-70 can be extremely simple. With black powder or Pyrodex propellant, cases, (modern ones) seldom need resizing, so require only washing, decapping and repriming. Fired primers can be poked out with a filed-down nail, and fresh ones seated with a dowel.

Powder can be charge-cupped into the case, and a finger-lubricated bullet seated by hand or a few taps with a stick of wood.

Loading dies are available, though, and more precise loads can be assembled in the usual fashion. If one cares to go to the trouble, paper-patched bullets may be used, though most .50-70 rifles won't really show much appreciation for all that effort.

Smokeless powder can be used in *modern* .50-70 cases, but the real problem lies in the oversize firing pins and their usually loose fit in the breech blocks of those old guns. Primers can extrude or blow, and firing pins can be blown out. We prefer to stick with CTG Pyrodex or FFg black powder, which doesn't cause such things with guns in good mechanical condition. ●

CHAPTER
57

Modern Loads
for the
.50-70

Al Miller

ALTHOUGH IT was our official military round for less than seven years, the .50-70 remained one of the most popular and useful cartridges on the Western frontier right up to the beginning of the present century. In fact, the last military unit armed with .50-70s, a mounted National Guard troop from Wyoming, I believe, were still carrying Sharps carbines when they were called to the colors in 1898.

Among other leading lights of the last century, George Armstrong Custer was a fan of the .50-70. An indefatigable hunter, his personal rifle was an F-grade Remington rolling block in that caliber. He wrote glowing reports about its performance on plains game and was thought to have been carrying it that fatal day at the Little Big Horn.

One of the most famous, William F. Cody, once won a $500 bet by killing more buffalo in eight hours (69) than his rival, Billy Comstock (46). Cody carried his favorite rifle, nicknamed Lucretia Borgia, that day. It was a trapdoor Springfield chambered for the .50-70. What's left of it can be seen today at the Whittier Museum in Cody, Wyoming.

One of the reasons for the round's continuing popularity in the Old West was the ready availability of inexpensive, surplus GI ammunition. Settlements and trading posts were weeks apart in those days and a man packing a rifle or pistol chambered for some rare, hard-to-get cartridge faced aggravation he really didn't need. In the case of the .50-70, the usual supply/demand relationship was reversed:

The Shiloh Sharps 1874 Military Carbine weighs eight pounds with a 22-inch barrel. A new Ideal tang sight was mounted to help shrink groups.

Because ammo for the rifles and carbines was so easy to come by, demand for the arms remained high until the country became more settled and resupply less of a problem.

For some reason, the .50 calibers never benefited from a friendly press. Even though the Big Fifty, the .50-2½, is still honored by historians and became a byword among the plainsmen of the late 1800s, the Sharps Company dropped it and the .50-70 from its line of standard chamberings in 1876 and, like everyone else, began turning out rifles in .45 caliber.

Although its ballistic superiority over the .50-70 is too obvious to be denied, the general impression is that the .45-70 is so much more powerful, so much flatter shooting, there really is no comparison between them. That's not true, at least, not at the ranges most game animals are taken.

Unaccountably, U.S. military authorities in the late 1860s became concerned about long-range accuracy:

500 to 1,000 yards. Just why is puzzling. At that time, Army rifle teams never engaged in long-range matches and even on the vast, featureless western plains, there was seldom a need to shoot beyond 500 yards. Professional buffalo hunters, probably the best marksmen in the nation at that time, rarely took a shot past 350 yards if they could help it. Nonetheless, the Army wanted a long-range cartridge and their tests left no doubt that .45-caliber bullets offered the optimum in flat trajectories and delivered energies at the velocity levels attainable with black powder.

Today, .45 calibers continue to display their superiority at 1,000 yards in black powder matches. At 200 or 300 yards, however, the .45's advantages over the 50s aren't quite so marked. If two hunters headed afield, one armed with a .45-70 and the other with a .50-70, both of which fired bullets of equal weight at the same muzzle

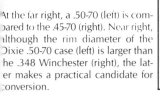

At the far right, a .50-70 (left) is compared to the .45-70 (right). Near right, although the rim diameter of the Dixie .50-70 case (left) is larger than the .348 Winchester (right), the later makes a practical candidate for conversion.

velocities from rifles zeroed at 100 yards, the hunter with the .50-70 would have to aim about eight inches higher than the .45 toter to hit the same target at 300 yards. More specifically, the .50-caliber bullet would drop a whopping 78 inches at the 300 mark while the .45 slug would strike 69 inches low. In other words, the .45's trajectory isn't quite as curved as the .50's, that's all.

Both calibers shared one characteristic: anything either one hit died. Don't be misled by impact energy figures. In what was one of the most famous shots of all time, Billy Dixon knocked an Indian off his horse at a surveyed 1,538 yards with a .50-2¼. Anytime anyone gets an ounce or more of lead moving even a couple of hundred feet per second, anything that gets in its way is in trouble. Launched around 1,350 fps, Dixon's bullet couldn't have had much poop left out

at 1,538 yards but it was enough to ruin one redskin's day.

So the .50-70, for all its modest paper velocities and energies, was something to reckon with a century or so ago. Certainly, nobody, red or white, spoke disparagingly of it or described its performance in condescending terms. When chambered in a replica rolling block or Sharps, the .50-70 will do just about anything a .45-70 can out to 300 yards. Past that distance, the .45 is clearly the better performer.

At this point, it's probably a good idea to emphasize the point that all the loads in the accompanying table are designed to be fired only in modern rifles. If anyone insists on trying any of the combinations listed in an antique rifle, they do so at their own risk. As far as I'm concerned, original black powder arms should be fed a diet of that propellant or Pyrodex only.

Apparently, interest in handloading the .50-70 is increasing because dies, components and accessories are much easier to come by now than they were only 10 years ago. Even so, a handloader won't find anything like the variety enjoyed by those who favor the .45-70.

Dies are available from Lyman and RCBS. Hornady, Lee and Redding do not list them in their catalogs, although the latter firm will make them up on a custom basis.

Unprimed cases are available from Dixie Gun Works (PO Box 130, Union City TN 38261). Basic brass — .50-caliber cases 3½ inches long — can Specialties (601 Oro Dam Boulevard, Oroville CA 95965), the C. Sharps Arms Company (Box 885, Big Timber MT 59011) and the Shiloh Rifle Manufacturing Company, Inc. (Box 279, Industrial Park, Big Timber MT 59011). Both Montana firms can supply Dixie cases, too. In addition, Eldorado Cartridge Company (Box 308, Boulder City NV 89005-0308) reports they will resume production of .50-caliber Basic brass shortly.

There's another source of brass for the .50-70: converted .348 Winchester hulls. True, the rim diameter of the .348 case is only .610 inch, as opposed

Lyman's 51542 and 51541, 520 and 445 grains, respectively, are time-tested and field-proven in the .50-70. Both were accurate and hard-hitting when fired from the test carbine, but the heavier bullet is Al's choice for hunting.

Left, in fireforming, a full-length .348 Winchester (left) is fired in the .50-70 chamber (center) and trimmed to proper length (right). Note that fireforming pressures weren't high enough to expand the rear half of the case, but the rifling impression is slightly visible around the case neck. Below, a trim die, like the one shown on the right, makes life easier when .348 Winchester cases are converted to .50-70, but it isn't absolutely necessary. Everything that needs doing can be done by the three-die set normally used for straight cases.

to the original's .660 inch, but .610 is wide enough for the rifle's extractor to grab if the shooter makes sure the extractor lies in front of the rim while he is loading. Anyone who simply drops a converted .348 case into a .50-70's chamber and snaps the action shut hurriedly will discover that the case rim has managed to sneak ahead of the extractor. When the breechblock locks up, the extractor is forced forward into its mortise, elbowing the head of the case aside as it does so. As a result, after the round is fired and the block dropped, the case will remain in the chamber because the extractor never got a grip on it.

Because of that threat, I never take converted .348 cases afield. My self-discipline is no better than the next man's and if I jumped something which required a quick second shot, it would be just like me to concentrate exclusively on the target, stuff a round in the chamber in a rush and wind up trying to jimmy the empty out of the chamber with the point of a knife blade.

My use of converted cases is limited to load development and testing. Although the Winchester hulls are becoming tougher to find, they're much cheaper than the real thing so I reserve the latter for the field.

Even if you never bother with converted hulls, it's good to keep a box or two around — just in case. You never know when your favorite gunshop may run dry.

It's a simple matter to modify .348 cases to fit a .50-70 and only one extra die, a trim die, is called for. Even that can be ignored if you wish.

Ordinarily, fireforming is the last step in the case-conversion process. In this instance, it will be the first. Charge each .348 hull with 11 grains of Blue Dot, then fill the rest of the case with cornmeal or some other coarse-grained cereal. Case mouths can be stuffed with facial tissue, wax or even a blob of bullet lubricant — anything which will keep the cereal from spilling out. That combination should expand the brass to fill the chamber nicely. If, for some reason, it doesn't, add another grain of Blue Dot and try again.

Just about any shotgun or pistol powder can be used. Simply choose one which requires no more than 15 grains because it's the cereal, not pressures generated by the propellant, which irons the case to its new shape.

Although they are relatively low-pressure loads, be careful where the muzzle is pointed. Those dust-sized grains of cereal act just like fine lead

shot and at close range, could be just as lethal.

One other caution: If you use cornmeal, be sure to shoot outside. Burned cornmeal smells just like singed hair. I made the mistake, one rainy day, of fireforming a couple of boxes of .348s down in the basement, firing into a bullet trap. It took a couple of days before the stench — and my wife's gripes — dissipated.

Fireformed hulls, because of their extra length, look just like a chamber cast, showing the throat and leade as well. If a trim die is used, cut the protruding portion of the brass away. If a trim die isn't available, cut just behind the beginning of the slight shoulder marking the chamber throat. That should give the correct length of 1.75 inches.

Because Winchester brass is thick and very strong, the usable volume of converted .348 cases is three to five grains less than that of Dixie hulls, depending on the density of the propellant. Those cases seem to last forever, though.

Case life with both brands of brass is

excellent. A partial explanation of their longevity may lie in the fact that pressures are low and fired hulls seldom require resizing. Just bell the mouths again (presuming that cast bullets are used, of course), reprime, charge with powder then seat the bullets.

Jacketed bullets offer no particular advantage to the .50-70 shooter. Since they can be obtained only from low-volume custom makers, they are fairly expensive. Worse still, a steady diet of them will shorten the life of the average .50-70 barrel considerably because it is made from relatively soft steel.

Cast bullets, on the other hand, are cheaper to mould or buy; they're easy on barrels; and at the unspectacular velocities generated by the old round, are just as accurate and just as effective against game as any jacketed softnose. Besides, alloy slugs are more in keeping with the black powder era and modernists seldom bother to shoot .50-70s.

Forty years ago, when the Lyman catalog advertised moulds for just about every caliber known to man, a total of nine were listed for the .50 calibers. Designs ranged from a stubby 290-grain hollowpoint to a 515-grain flatnose. Today, only two survive: numbers 515141, the original military bullet, and 515142, a slightly heavier flatnose.

Although the RCBS catalog doesn't list any .50-caliber moulds, the last I heard there were still one or two designs available through their Special Order catalog. Redding also limits their .50-caliber designs to custom moulds. Both NEI/Tooldyne and Old West Bullet Moulds boast relatively wide selections of .50-caliber designs in their catalogs, but don't expect anything like the number offered for more popular calibers like the .308s and .45s.

For the traditionally minded, the two Lyman designs should fulfill all requirements: they cast easily; are natural groupers capable of cutting two

Shiloh Sharps 1874 Military Carbine

Specifications:

Action: Sharps falling block
Capacity: single shot
Barrel: 22 inches
Length of pull: 13⅝ inches
Drop at comb: 2¼ inches
Drop at heel: 3⅞ inches
Pitch: 3 inches
Trigger pull: 2¼-2½ pounds
Length overall: 38¼ inches
Weight: 8 pounds (actual)

inches, sometimes less, at 100 yards; and they hit hard out at 200, even 300 yards.

All test bullets were cast from range scrap. As a result, they dropped from the moulds much harder than necessary. Nonetheless, the alloy filled the moulds beautifully and since the bullets were oversized, there was never any threat of leading, even when the bare-based slugs were driven at .50-90 velocities. They sealed the bore completely.

Load Data .50-70

bullet (grains)	powder	charge (grains)	primer	case	velocity (fps)	overall length (mm)	remarks
445 Lyman 515141	H-4198	31.0	Fed. 215 Magnum	.348	1,187	60.7	Super Grex
	RL-7	32.0	Win. LR		1,247		Super Grex; extreme spread = 164 fps
	IMR-4227	27.0	Rem. 9½		1,238		Super Grex; ES = 23 fps
	AA-2230	40.0	Win. LR	DGW	1,011		
	Scot-4197	31.00	Fed. 215	.348	990		ES = 59 fps; very accurate
	IMR-4350	55.0		DGW	1,345		ES = 43 fps; 3 inches at 100 yards
	IMR-4831	55.0			1,190		ES = 50 fps; 2½-3 inches
	H-4831	55.0			1,155		ES = 28 fps; 2½-3 inches
	AA-3100	55.0			1,136		ES = 41 fps; 2½-3 inches
	RS-Pyrodex	70	CCI LR	.348	1,300		2½-inch average at 100 yards
	P-Pyrodex	75.0	CCI Mag		1,200		2 inches at 100 yards
	RS-Pyrodex	70.0	Fed. 215		1,250		ES = 50 fps
	CTG-Pyrodex	70.0		DGW	1,208		Wad. ES = 39 fps
	Fg	73.0			1,198		ES = 32 fps
	Fg	73.0			1,200		Wad. ES = 21 fps
	FFg	70.0		.348	1,196		Wad ES = 46 fps
	FFFg	70.0			1,232		Wad ES = 43 fps
520 Lyman 515142	H-4198	31.0	Fed. 215	.348	1,134	59.0	Super Grex
	IMR-3031	42.0	CCI LR		1,195		hunting load
	W-680	12.0					
	RS-Pyrodex	60.0			1,367		duplicates .50-90
	P-Pyrodex	70.0	Fed. 215		1,195		2½ inches at 100 yards
	RS-Pyrodex	70.0			1,132		
	FFFg	60.0			1,160	50.0 mm	2½ inches at 100 yards

Velocities are instrumental, chronographed 12 feet from the carbine's 22-inch barrel. Oehler Model 35P and PACT chronographs were employed during tests. Ambient temperatures ranged from 45 to 85 degrees Fahrenheit. All loads were safe in the test carbine but should be reduced at least 10 percent before trying in any other arm.

Be alert — Publisher cannot accept responsibility for errors in published load data.

Number 515141 ranged from .515 to .517 inch in diameter while 515142 varied from .513 to .514. Weighing 445 and 520 grains, respectively, they registered 17 on the Brinell Hardness scale according to the LBT lead hardness tester. For comparison purposes, a batch of 515141s were cast from plumber's lead. Their weight averaged 456.5 grains and they miked .514 inch in diameter.

Since the test carbine's bore miked .512 inch, the bullets were left as cast and hand-lubed. SPG was used for black powder and Pyrodex loads; GAR's Half & Half protected bullets seated over smokeless loads. That last is composed of Alox 2138F and natural beeswax instead of the synthetic type. It was soft and easy to work with during the cold months but didn't run or smear when July temperatures climbed into the high 90s. Good stuff.

Both Lyman bullets grouped equally well. If 515142 averaged two inches with a given powder charge, 515141 would do the same, even though it was driven a few fps faster. The latter's trajectory was a bit flatter out to 200 yards (as far as I ever targeted the .50-70), but the difference in points of impact was measured in inches, not feet — a small advantage at best.

Although the .45-70's ballistics were set in concrete when the one-time military round was introduced back in 1873 (a 405-grain roundnose at 1,330 fps from a 29-inch barrel), the same can't be said for the .50-70. Depending on which reference you believe, the first trapdoor Springfields tossed 425-grain bullets 1,275 fps, a 450-grainer at 1,260 or a 452-grain slug at 1,140.

Part of the confusion may be due to the fact that the Sharps Company offered several loads for the round which featured 425, 457, 473 and 500-grain bullets. In addition, as we know now, bore dimensions of government barrels varied widely and consequently, measured velocities must have, too.

Although everyone agrees that .50-caliber military ammunition consisted of 70 grains of Fg behind a bullet later standardized as Lyman's Number 515141, nobody is sure whether Fg's granulation was exactly the same in 1866 as it is now. When a 456-grain bullet cast from plumber's lead was seated over 70 grains of GOEX Fg and was chronographed 10 feet from the carbine's 22-inch barrel, velocities

averaged 1,145 fps. That combination was ignited by a standard Large Rifle primer and the load was assembled without a wad. Substituting a Magnum Large Rifle primer and adding a cardboard wad .025-inch thick boosted instrumental velocities to an even 1,200 fps.

Fans of the old .50-caliber seem to belong to one of three schools: the traditionalists, who insist on shooting nothing but black powder or Pyrodex; the modernists, who like shooting replicas but hate the mess associated with cleaning black or Pyrodex residue; and last but not least, the nostalgia buffs. They take the middle road: duplex loads. By combining smokeless and less efficient propellants, they create ammunition which sounds and smells like black powder but leaves the bore relatively clean.

Which approach is best? It's strictly a matter of taste. All three can be equally accurate. If a bit more velocity is desired, duplex or smokeless loads offer a greater potential but they should be approached cautiously.

Made from modern steels and held to much closer manufacturing tolerances than were possible 100 years ago, replica .50-70s are strong rifles, capable of accommodating higher pressures than the originals. Even so, their makers won't guarantee them if they are overloaded. Some, in fact, guarantee their rifles for black powder loads only. If smokeless or duplex loads are used, the manufacturer's warranty is automatically void. Anyone who has any doubts about the kinds of loads his rifle or carbine can handle had best check with its maker before developing any handloads for it.

All the loads listed in the accompanying table were safe in the test carbine. None are recommended for antique rifles, not even the black powder loads. Why? Because their pressure levels are higher than those churned up by the original military rounds. Admittedly, they aren't much higher — but they're higher, and those old rolling blocks, Springfields and Sharps aren't as young as they once were. A modern replica should be able to take all those loads in stride but as usual, reduce charges at least 10 percent and work up slowly, just to be sure.

All black powder and Pyrodex loads were measured by volume, not weight.

It's my habit to tap a black powder measure a few times to settle the powder. It's an extra step but charges are more uniform. It also enables me to cram two or three grains more powder in a case, too.

Although adding a cardboard wad above a charge of black powder or Pyrodex reduced the extreme velocity spread and improved accuracy in the test carbine, experiments with other black powder arms indicates that those additions don't always guarantee better accuracy. As usual, it's best to try loads with and without wads to discover what your rifle prefers.

Three different kinds of wads were used in the .50-70 but results on the target were the same with all of them. That being so, I settled for wads made from cardboard milk cartons, .025 inch thick. All wads listed in the Load Data table were that type.

Igniting black powder and Pyrodex charges with Magnum Large Rifle primers also reduced extreme velocity spreads, delivered tighter groups in the test carbine and left the bore cleaner. Several different brands were tried but none proved superior to any of the others. That may or may not prove to be true in other .50-70s.

Which grade of black powder or Pyrodex is best? Historically, Fg and CTG have been recommended by most authorities. Fg was the grade of the original military load and just about everybody since has reaffirmed the Army's choice. In the test carbine, it performed very well, but so did FFFg and P-grade Pyrodex. There was a slight difference in velocities but loads made from either of those three grades could be counted on to cut two inches, benchrest, as long as I did my part. On occasion, the FFFg charges printed smaller than two inches. Moral? Try all grades and see which one your .50 likes best.

Accuracy standards differ but as far as I'm concerned, any combination of powder and lead which punches out 2½ inches at 100 yards is accurate. After all, external hammers, iron sights and laid-back lock time shouldn't be expected to deliver MOA groups. With an open-sighted rifle and good loads, I expect five-shot groups to measure between three and 3½ inches. If the rifle is equipped with a peep sight, groups should range from two to 2½ inches with the same ammunition. If a load is particularly accurate and I'm enjoying one of my better days, groups can shrink below two inches. Sad to say, that doesn't happen as it once did.

A new Ideal tang sight with a target aperture was mounted on the test carbine. Marketed by C. Sharps Arms, the sight offers ⅜ inch of elevation adjustment and ⅛ inch worth of windage. That's more than enough for a .50-70 at normal ranges, say, out to 200 yards. That small peep not only helped squeeze groups down to respectable sizes but the windage adjustment made it easy to compensate for the 520-grain flatnose's tendency to drift a couple of inches right of the 450-grainer's point of impact at 100 yards.

Adding that second rear sight made the carbine easier to use at longer ranges, too. My favorite deer load consists of a 520-grain flatnose backed by 42 grains of 3031 and sparked by a Remington 9½ primer. Velocity, 10 feet from the muzzle, averages 1,195 fps. With the open rear sight at its lowest setting, point of impact is two inches high at 100 yards. The tang sight is zeroed for 200 yards. That combination allows me to use the open sights out to 150 yards with only a slight amount of holdover. If a deer is farther away than that, the tang sight can be flipped up and by holding under or above the animal's heart shots out to 250 yards are feasible.

Grouping was also affected by the bullets' seating depths. The carbine's throat allowed seating them ⅛ inch farther out than usual. That increased the usable case volume, too, but when bullets were extended, groups opened up immediately.

Powders with slower burning rates than IMR-3031's can be used but none I tried were as accurate as the faster numbers. Best choice was 4198, either IMR's or Hodgdon's, closely followed by the new Scot Brigadier 4197 and Accurate Arms' 2230, both of which were slightly slower burning in the big, straight-sided case.

Of course, a handloader can never go wrong with IMR-3031. It delivered dependable accuracy, with groups running from two to 2½ inches, and velocity spreads limited to 50 fps or less.

IMR-4227 didn't come into its own until Super Grex was added as a filler. Used alone, the powder wasn't as accurate as the other fast burners, probably because it occupied so little of the hull's cavernous volume. Once packed back against the primer by the light, dustlike plastic filler, groups averaged a uniform 2¼ inches.

Reloder 7 proved to be the only disappointment among the propellants tried. Whether used by itself or in conjunction with Super Grex, it never delivered acceptable accuracy. Swapping primers didn't help, either. Extreme velocity spreads usually exceeded 100 fps and groups, if you want to call them that, ranged from four to eight inches with the majority six inches or larger.

For all its inefficiency, black powder proved just as accurate as smokeless, especially when touched off by Magnum primers and topped by cardboard wads. The same was true of Pyrodex. As noted, the carbine preferred some grades over others, but there's nothing unusual about that.

To make cleaning less of a chore, I normally pack a few smokeless loads along whenever black or Pyrodex is the primary propellant. After the last smoky load is fired, five or 10 smokeless rounds are sent on their way. Not only do they leave the bore nice and shiny but it can be cleaned as though only smokeless loads had been fired through it.

All the duplex loads listed grouped 2½ inches or less. Although 50 to 65 grains of Pyrodex give a satisfying cloud of smoke, the supplemental smokeless charge was enough to leave the bore amazingly clean.

Properly loaded, a .50-70 can do anything a .45-70 can out to 300 yards. Granted, the .50's trajectory is a bit more rainbowlike and its bullets shed velocity a tad quicker than the .45's but to anything hit by either, the difference in effectiveness is more academic than real.

To anyone thinking of having a .50-caliber rolling block or Sharps made up, I would recommend chambering it for the .50-70 in preference to either the .50-90 or .50-140. Not only are the 1.75-inch cases cheaper and easier to come by than the longer ones, but unless a man intends to depend strictly on black powder or Pyrodex, ballistics of the 2½ and 3½-inch cases can be duplicated without too much trouble in the shorter hull with duplex or smokeless loads. Of greater significance, it is much easier to develop accurate smokeless loads in the short case than it is in either of the larger ones. ●

CHAPTER
58

LOADING FOR THE
TRAPDOOR SPRINGFIELDS
.50-70 • .45-70

THE TRAPDOOR Springfield is one of the most underrated firearms in America. They are often referred to as weak, inaccurate — even poorly made. I have found none of those charges to be true.

To begin with, weak is a relative term. Trapdoors are weak in relation to what? At the approximately 18,000 psi they were built to accommodate, they are perfectly adequate. As far as accuracy is concerned, much depends on the quality of their ammunition. If anyone doubts their quality, just lay a trapdoor down beside a modern firearm, then compare the quality of machine work, fit and finish.

The trapdoor Springfield is one of our most historical guns. Contrary to Hollywood, it was the trapdoor Springfield, in both .50-70 and .45-70, that tamed the West. The list of battles and skirmishes that various types of trapdoors participated in reads like a directory of the Indian Wars. Starting with the Wagon Box Fight in 1867 and continuing through Wounded Knee in 1890, trapdoor Springfields saw service in every Western campaign between the Canadian and Mexican borders. In two calibers, trapdoors were the official service rifle of the U.S. Army for more than 25 years.

It is difficult to understand why trapdoors have not caught the eye of the collecting fraternity to a greater extent. During the past year, I purchased two trapdoor Springfield rifles, one a Model 1873 .45-70; the other, a Model 1870 .50-70 at local gun shows. Both were in good shooting order. The breechblocks were tight with very little lateral play and the lockwork was crisp. The .50-70's bore has some slight pitting but the .45-70's is near perfect. Neither gun has been altered in any way, except that their ramrods are missing. I paid $275 for each.

Now consider some other historical American firearms. At those same gun shows, any Sharps sporting rifle, regardless of condition, was priced over $2,000. Some were 10 times the cost of the Springfields. Shootable lever action Winchester Model 1873's available at the gun shows started at three times

MIKE VENTURINO

The test Springfields: Left, a Model 1870 in .50-70; right, a Model 1873 .45-70 rifle and at the far right, a Model 1878 carbine in .45-70.

Left, the best group the .50-70 fired — pretty good, considering the issue sights and hefty trigger pull. Right, Pyrodex worked beautifully in the .45-70 rifle.

the price of trapdoor Springfields.

A full length article would be required to cover the birth and development of all the trapdoor variations. Let it suffice to say that the .50-70 trapdoor Springfield was made in three basic versions: the Models 1866, 1868 and 1870. All used surplus Civil War musket parts to one extent or another. For instance, my Model 1870's lockplate is marked "1863."

The specifications most pertinent to this article concern the barrels. My research shows that the Model 1870 .50-70 was built with a three-grooved barrel. The grooves start .01-inch deep at the breech and taper to .005 inch at the muzzle. Rifling twist rate is one turn in 42 inches.

I have not been able to find a reference to a nominal bore diameter for the Model 1870 but have slugged two. A friend's measures .512 inch, and mine goes .510 inch as close as I can tell by measuring the three-grooved rifling.

In 1873, the government chose to redesign the trapdoor. The biggest change was the reduction in caliber to .45-70. Starting in 1873, the trapdoor was made with all newly manufactured parts, and it continued as the service rifle in that caliber until 1892.

To a shooter, the most important specs concern the barrels. Model 1873 barrels were made with three-grooved rifling. Twist rate was one turn in 22 inches and grooves were nominally .005 inch deep. Like the Model 1870 .50-70, the Model 1873's barrel length was 32½ inches

in infantry rifle versions, and 22 inches for cavalry carbines. Again, I can find no reference to nominal groove diameter.

As a shooter, I desired to put my two trapdoor rifles into action with accurate handloads. I have owned a Model 1878 trapdoor Springfield carbine for over a decade. Even though its bore has some minor pitting, it had never been tested for accuracy with a variety of handloads. Several months ago, I began a handloading project.

Most of the focus has been on the .45-70's, both rifle and carbine. To that end I have fired over 600 rounds of .45-70 handloads in the two vintage guns. In the past couple of months the .50-70 has been added, and about 200 rounds test-fired in it.

Before delving into the test results, I would like to add a word of caution about shooting

antique rifles. With guns that were manufactured more than 100 years ago, it pays the handloader to be cautious. Before firing any of the three trapdoors, I had them checked by a gunsmith well-versed in antique and obsolete rifles. He pronounced all fit for firing. The .45-70's have now been fired hundreds of rounds with mild smokeless charges and seem to thrive on them. I have been more timid with the .50-70. Only one smokeless powder has been tried, and that for the purposes of comparative testing. I will rely on either black powder or Pyrodex for its ammunition.

Both the .50-70 and .45-70 were originally loaded with a full 70 grains of black powder. The government's .50-caliber bullet weighed 450 grains and was propelled about 1,200 fps (sources vary on exact speeds). Cartridge case length was 1.75 inches, and *Cartridges of the World* lists bullet diameter at .515 inch.

The .45-70 was loaded by the government in three versions. The first consisted of a 405-grain bullet over 70 grains of powder. That load was said to cause too much recoil in the carbines so the powder charge was reduced to 55 grains for cavalry use. An 1874 ordnance manual lists muzzle velocities of 1,350 fps for the former loading in rifles, and 1,100 fps for the latter in carbines. In the 1880's, a second rifle load was introduced using a 500-grain bullet over 70 grains of powder. Various sources list rifle velocities with that one from 1,200 to 1,300 fps.

The .45-70's case is 2.10 inches long and

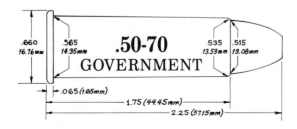

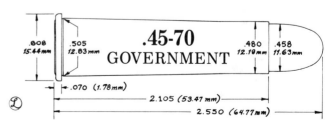

nominal bullet diameter is .457 inch. That latter specification is often a source of irritation for .45-70 trapdoor shooters. The facts are not clear but either loose bores were the norm in trapdoor production or it was impossible for the tolerances to be held closely. Internal dimensions of trapdoor Springfield barrels can vary a tremendous amount. I have read of them ranging from a low of .457 to a high of .464 inch. My own experience with the Model 1873 is probably typical.

After its purchase, I rushed to the range with a small variety of mild cast bullet handloads assembled for a Shiloh Sharps. Bullet diameter was .457 inch. All I succeeded in doing with those rounds was to throw mud on the targets. Every bullet keyholed. I happened to have a few Remington 405-grain loads along and they grouped from 3.00 to 3.50 inches. Back home, I slugged the bore and found it measured between .459 and .460 inch (trying to measure three groove rifling accurately is difficult).

The large bore presented a problem. Most of my .45-caliber rifle bullet moulds drop slugs about .458 inch. Luckily, SAECO mould No. 021 casts a 436-grain semi-pointed, gas check bullet measuring .462 inch. A few were handlubed and loaded over mild charges of SR-4759. To my delight, 100-yard, five-shot groups measured between two and three inches. The moral of the story is simple: Before wasting time, powder and lead shooting a new trapdoor, slug its bore first.

For my trapdoor .45-70 work, I eventually used four cast bullet designs which were chosen for their as-cast diameters. In addition to the SAECO bullet, Lyman's 457483 (.460 inch),

Hoch 460-435 (.460 inch) and NEI 405.458GC (.462 inch) were used. They weighed 396, 454 and 437 grains, respectively. Coincidentally, all four bullets were of gas check design.

Some years back, Ken Waters did an excellent piece on reloading the .50-70 for a modern Shiloh Sharps carbine. One of Ken's problems at that time was trying to locate suitable .50-caliber bullet moulds. Happily, I can report that .50-caliber moulds are no longer scarce. For my .50-70 shooting, a total of six .50-caliber designs were used, including three from NEI, two from Lyman and one by RCBS. The two .50-caliber gas check versions by NEI are my favorites. In this trapdoor and two Shiloh Sharps, they have consistently outshot any other bullet. That serves to reinforce my feeling that gas check bullets are the best choices for obsolete calibers.

The .50-caliber bullets: (*1*) Lyman 515141 (443 grains), (*2*) RCBS 50-450FN (476 grains), (*3*) NEI 440.510GC (461 grains), (*4*) Lyman 515142 (518 grains), (*5*) NEI 500.515 (512 grains) and (*6*) NEI 520.510GC (542 grains).

.50-70 Trapdoor Springfield Loads
32½-inch barrel

bullet	powder	charge (grains)	velocity (fps)	variation (fps)	group (inches)	remarks
443 Lyman 515141	MP-5744	28.0	1,199	41	4⅞	
	Fg Black	60.0	1,113	10	5.00	
	FFg Black	60.0	1,188	35	wild!	
	Pyrodex CTG	48.0	1,150	16	4¾	
461 NEI 440.510GC	MP-5744	28.0	1,175	39	4⅜	
	Fg Black	60.0	1,082	24	4½	
	FFg Black	60.0	1,151	26	4¼	
	Pyrodex CTG	48.0	1,067	55	4½	
476 RCBS 50-450FN	MP-5744	28.0	1,191	56	5.00	(four in 2½")
	Fg Black	60.0	1,090	30	wild!	
	FFg Black	60.0	1,161	34	wild!	
	Pyrodex CTG	48.0	1,087	106	wild!	
512 NEI 500.515	MP-5744	28.0	1,159	66	wild!	
	Fg Black	60.0	1,063	19	wild!	
	FFg Black	60.0	1,126	66	wild!	
	Pyrodex CTG	48.0	1,066	58	wild!	
518 Lyman 515142	MP-5744	28.0	1,199	49	wild!	
	Fg Black	60.0	1,085	16	wild!	
	FFg Black	60.0	1,140	25	3⅜	
	Pyrodex CTG	48.0	1,076	53	4⅛	(four in 1¾")
542 NEI 520.510GC	MP-5744	28.0	1,169	45	3.00	(four in 1½")
	Fg Black	60.0	1,055	20	6.00	
	FFg Black	60.0	1,125	23	4⅞	
	Pyrodex CTG	48.0	1,039	42	3⅝	

All loads made up in Dixie Gun Works cases, with Winchester Large Rifle primers. Bullets using gas-checks used NEI checks. Black and Pyrodex loads were dropped through a 42-inch drop tube. All loads lubed with SPG lube, and lightly crimped. Black and Pyrodex loads not wiped between shots, but cleaned after each five-shot group. Chronograph was an Oehler 33 with Skyscreens III; first screen 5 feet from muzzle.

Be alert — Publisher cannot accept responsibility for errors in published load data.

Incidentally, .50-caliber gas checks are also available from NEI. My .45-caliber bullets were adorned with Hornady gas checks exclusively.

Of course, .45-70 cases are still available but .50-70 brass is limited to that offered by Dixie Gun Works, or to forming it from B.E.L.L. .50 Basic. I have used both but for my recent trapdoor shooting, relied on the former merely because I have a larger quantity of it on hand.

Since firing a large number of rounds in these large bore rifles requires the expenditure of quite a bit of alloy, I tried to be economical. The alloy, therefore, consisted of wheelweights to Linotype in the proportion of four to one. This gave a fairly hard mix that proved accurate, yet it possessed suitable casting characteristics.

Lubricating the bullets was not quite so cut and dried. Those for the .45-70's were not sized. For smokeless powder loads, they were pan-lubed with a homemade lubricant favored by Schuetzen fans. It consisted of one pound of paraffin, one pound of Vaseline and one tablespoon of RCBS case lube. The bullets were placed base-down in a pie plate and the melted lube poured around them. When it set up, the bullets could easily be pushed out with the thumb. The lube is an excellent one for low velocity loads, and the lubing method is quick and easy.

With .45-caliber bullets intended for black powder and Pyrodex plus all the .50-caliber bullets, I used a new bullet lube intended specifically for black powder cartridge shooting. It is called SPG lube and its maker, Steve Garbe, says it is designed to keep black powder fouling soft, a necessary aid to accuracy with black powder cartridge guns.

After firing five black powder loads in either .45-70 or .50-70, I could easily push a clean, dry patch down the bore, which would then appear to be shiny. That would be a difficult chore with the usual black powder fouling. SPG lube does not automatically ensure accuracy but it does free a bore from that hard-caked fouling so that other factors can be tested in the search for accurate loads. My supply of SPG was small so it was applied with the fingers on unsized bullets.

For smokeless loads in the .45-70, I chose SR-4759, MP-5744 and IMR-4198. Previous experience has taught that those three are most apt to give good ignition in large capacity cases without resorting to some sort of case filler. A single charge weight of 28.0 grains of MP-5744

was tried behind each of the six bullets in the .50-70.

The most comprehensive testing was done with smokeless powders in the .45-70 rifle and carbine. In each gun, a total of 39 five-shot groups were fired at 100 yards using four different cast bullets and various charge weights of the three cited powders.

I would like to emphasize just how difficult group-shooting was with the three veteran arms. One problem was caused by the battle sights. All three trapdoors still carried their original sighting equipment. That consisted of an open rear leaf with an age-rounded and brightly worn blade up front. Triggers also offered no help. I would guess those on the .45-70's pulled from six to eight pounds but the .50-70's was a humdinger. It had to go 12 to 14 pounds. There were times when I stopped pulling the trigger and examined the gun to see if something had broken — the trigger was that bad!

Worse still, the .45-70 carbine shot hopelessly high: about 12 to 18 inches, depending on the exact load. The .50-70 shot about that far to the right. With both guns I had to aim at one target to hit a second.

Compared to them, the .45-70 rifle was a beauty. Aiming at a six-inch bullseye put almost every round into the black. When velocities topped 1,250 fps, something snapped in and groups were centered very near the X-ring.

In my study of the Indian Wars, I have read that the average soldier was a terrible shot. After my trapdoor trials, I wonder if part of the blame might better rest on crude sights and horrendous triggers. It cannot be said that the trapdoor Springfields themselves are inherently inaccurate. As an example, 39 groups fired from the .45-70 rifle averaged 3.19 inches. The most accurate bullet was the 435-grain Hoch with an average of 2.90 inches for 11 groups. The least accurate bullet was the 396-grain Lyman at 3.41 inches for nine groups.

The trapdoor carbine was less accurate. Its favorite bullet was the 450-grain SAECO at an average of 3.97 inches for 11 groups. The least accurate projectile was the 405-grain NEI at 6.41 inches for eight groups.

A look at the smokeless powders by average is also illuminating. In the .45-70 rifle, IMR-4198 averaged 2.90 inches for 15 groups while MP-5744 gave 3.62 inches for 13 groups. In the carbine, MP-5744 won with 4.37 inches for 14 groups and SR-4759 came in last at 5.25 inches for 11 groups.

Toward the end of the tests, I acquired a .459-inch sizing die. The SAECO and Hoch bullets sized .459 and loaded over 28.5 grains of IMR-4198 gave $2\frac{3}{16}$ and $2\frac{5}{8}$-inch groups, respectively. Judging from those results, unsized bullets may not be necessary.

In the .45-70, black powder and Pyrodex left me with mixed feelings, especially since I already knew that both carbine and rifle were capable of good accuracy with smokeless powders. Group sizes varied from perfectly acceptable to absolutely wild. Most black powder and Pyrodex groups fired by the carbine were poor. In the rifle, 48.0 grains of Pyrodex under SAECO's 450-grain bullet grouped 2.75 inches. In the carbine, the same load gave a six-inch group. Conversely the very accurate Hoch bullet would seldom group under four inches in the rifle whether Pyrodex or black powder was the propellant.

This unexpectedly erratic behavior was also present in the .50-70. With some bullets, it grouped best with Fg powder; with others, the tightest groups came with FFg. Overall best accuracy was given by Pyrodex in that particular rifle.

At its best, the .50-70 grouped from 3½ to 4¾ inches. Admittedly, that isn't tack-driving accuracy but groups were circular and I cannot help but feel that with better sights, a lighter trigger and additional load refinement, I can cut those group sizes in half.

Modern shooters looking at the velocities delivered by trapdoor Springfields may tend to scoff. A glance at my chart shows that very few loads exceed 1,300 fps from the .45-70 rifle and 1,200 fps from the .45-70 carbine. Not one load broke 1,200 fps from the .50-70 — and don't forget, those rifles have 32½-inch barrels.

That lack of velocity does not bother anyone used to obsolete calibers. When you launch a 400 or 500-grain chunk of lead around 1,200 fps, it takes a lot to slow it down. Once you know the sights, hitting inanimate targets out to 500 meters is quite easy as some trapdoor shooters proved at the first NRA Black Powder Cartridge Silhouette match in Raton, New Mexico.

My trapdoor reloading project left me with a lot of confidence in the old rifles. A gunsmith friend has volunteered trigger jobs and some sight alteration on all three. Some day soon I mean to take him up on that offer. Next season, I intend to do all my elk, deer and pronghorn hunting with .45-70 and .50-70 trapdoor Springfields. I'll bet ahead of time that I don't come home empty-handed.   ●

CHAPTER
59

The .50 Alaskan

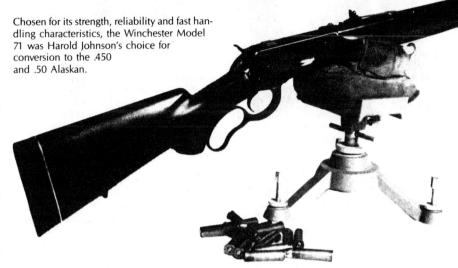

Chosen for its strength, reliability and fast handling characteristics, the Winchester Model 71 was Harold Johnson's choice for conversion to the .450 and .50 Alaskan.

John Kronfeld

SOMETIMES we write about a subject and think when we've finished, that's it. So it was when I finished an article on the .450 Alaskan. Shortly after, however, I had occasion to talk with Fred Huntington, founder and former owner of RCBS. The subject of the .450 Alaskan came up and Fred commented that many years ago he had been good friends with Harold Johnson. "He took me bear hunting one time and we were in the heaviest alders and cover you ever saw; you could hardly see 10 feet in front of you."

My comment to Fred was, "I'll bet you were glad he was carrying his .450 Alaskan." He paused and then replied, "Na, he wasn't carrying that puny thing; he was carrying his big .50 Alaskan."

You could have knocked me over with a feather. I spent almost four months researching my article on the .450 Alaskan and the .50 Alaskan was never mentioned. I had never even heard of the .50 Alaskan.

As it turns out, the .50 Alaskan could probably be construed as Harold Johnson's real bear gun. As he explained in 1988, "I never recovered a slug from a bear or moose no matter what angle the animal was shot at."

The history of the .50 Alaskan began one day in the early fifties when a man walked into Harold's gun shop with a .50 caliber machine-gun barrel that had its throat shot out and had been scrapped. The man wanted to know if Harold had any use for it. He took the barrel and gave it some thought.

His shop was already known worldwide for producing the .450 Alaskan which had made its mark in the hands of men like Keith, Askins and others in Alaska, Africa and Southeast Asia. Harold decided to go the .450 one better and make a .50 Alaskan.

To convert the barrel it was cut off forward of the eroded throat, then threaded and fitted to a Winchester 86 .50-110 that had a worn-out barrel. Reamers were designed and ground by Bill Fuller to use a .348 Winchester case that was blown out with a slight taper to .50 caliber. Bill also made the reamers for the .450 Alaskan.

Bullets were made by cutting off 720-grain .50 caliber boat-tail machine-gun bullets so that the section from the base to the cut weighed 450 grains. They were loaded base forward, with the business end forming a truncated cone. This configuration delivered tremendous shock and cavernous wound channels at close range. Because of the steel core, there is nothing on this continent that could stop or deform them.

I wanted to see for myself what the .50 Alaskan was about so I sent my .450 Alaskan Model 71 Winchester to Harry McGowen of McGowen Rifle Barrels (Rte 3, St. Anne IL 60964) for conversion. I requested a 20-inch barrel with a bore diameter of .50 inch, a groove dimension of .510 and a one-in-12-inch twist.

Not only did he have a reamer for this cartridge, but he told me that for the past 18 months he has received one to two guns a month for this conversion. Most are based on either the Winchester Model 71, the modern version of the old 86, or the new Browning Model 71, a copy of the Winchester 71. He also rechambered a few Siamese Mauser bolt actions.

Waiting for the rifle to be returned, I gathered all the components needed for loading, a three die set from RCBS; various bullet moulds from Lyman, NEI and LBT; a good supply of .348 Winchester brass; a .512-inch RCBS lube size die; and a .50-caliber pilot for my Lyman Auto Case Trimmer. I also ordered a large supply of Barnes 450-grain .510 bullets with jackets .032-inch thick that were designed for the .50-110 Winchester. A-Square 600-grain .50 caliber Monolithic solids completed the list.

The .50-70, .50-70 (1¾), .50-70

The original .50 Alaskan bullets were formed from machine-gun bullets with steel cores. Johnson cut the 720-grain boat-tail in half and seated the lower section upside-down to form a truncated cone-shaped ogive.

Musket (.50 Gov't), and .50-70 (1¾) Sharps (they are all the same) was the first centerfire cartridge adopted by the military from 1866 to 1873, when it was replaced by the .45-70. The centerfire cartridge was chambered in various models and conversions of single-shot Springfield, Remington rifles and the Sharps New Model 1869. The cartridge was popular with buffalo hunters and fired a 450-grain lead bullet at 1,260 fps for 1,488 foot-pounds of energy. By today's standards that is not too impressive. As Ken Waters says in his article in *Handloader* No. 81, however, "Slow, yes, but with that great half-inch-diameter chunk of lead, a fearsome penetrator of bone and tissue."

The Big .50 Sharps of history and legend was introduced in 1872 and is known today as the .50-90 Sharps or .50-90 (2½). Developed to give buffalo hunters more power, it still never achieved the popularity of the .50-70 even though it drove a 473-grain lead bullet 1,350 fps with 1,920 foot-pounds of muzzle energy. In 1876, after a brief four years, the cartridge was dropped from the Sharps line.

Regarding the .50-140 Sharps, Elmer Keith wrote in 1940, "I know if I had to stop a big Alaskan Brownie with just one shot, and my life depended on it, I would rather bust him in the chest with this big gun than with any modern American load. I fired the big .50 at two straight-grain yellow pine blocks 18 inches end to end. The 700-grain slug went through both so I don't know how many it would take to stop it. It is to me one of the most interesting, truly American rifles and loads."

There is a four-year discrepancy about the date this cartridge was introduced; either 1880 or 1884. Since Sharps ceased manufacturing in 1881, the original Sharps shooting this cartridge may have been rechambered .50-90s. The cartridge pushed a 473-grain bullet 1,580 fps and a 700-grain

Left, overall loaded length of the sectioned machine-gun bullet (left) is slightly longer than the 450 Barnes bullet (right). Above, test bullets included the 450-grain Barnes (left), 450-grain custom (center) and 485-grain LBT cast bullet design (right).

bullet 1,355 fps with 2,520 and 2,850 foot-pounds of energy, respectively. Winchester also manufactured a .50-140 for their Model 85 single shot, with duplicate bullet weights and velocities.

Winchester introduced the .50-110 in their Model 86 in 1899. The standard load drove a 300-grain bullet 1,605 fps for 1,720 foot-pounds of energy. A high velocity Express load with the same bullet generated 2,225 fps with 3,298 foot-pounds of energy.

My .50 Alaskan arrived with a single stage expander plug to neck the .348 Winchester brass up to .50 caliber so a bullet can be seated for fireforming. The plug screws directly into a loading press and works very well. Some cases were annealed and some were not, either way the expander did a good job.

A fireforming load used 55 grains of IMR-3031, topped by a 422-grain Lyman cast roundnose. It did a perfect job and the cases literally fell out of the chamber. I called Bill Keyes at RCBS for a trim length and he advised me that RCBS shows an overall case length from 2.00 to 2.10 inches, take your choice. Cases were trimmed to the maximum of 2.1 inches and worked very well.

I erred in the selection of some cast

bullet designs. The NEI bullet has a round nose which allows the tip of one bullet to rest on the primer of the round ahead of it in a tubular magazine. That could be disastrous.

The NEI bullet was used for fireforming, loading one round at a time, and would be fine if restricted to use as a single shot. Since this rifle is to be used as a repeater, however, my choices were the 450-grain Barnes, the Lyman No. 515142 498-grain plain base and the 485-grain LBT gas check bullet. The .50-caliber gas checks are available from NEI. The A-Square bullet is another story and will be discussed later.

The LBT bullet was cast from wheelweights with 2 percent tin added and water-quenched, giving it a 21 BNH 24 hours after casting. It weighed 485 grains after seating the gas checks, sizing and lubing with LBT Blue, measured exactly .512-inch from the mould so the sizing die only served to lubricate. I requested that this bullet be made with a very broad nose. Veral Smith obliged — it measured .410 inch.

No loading data could be found for the .50 Alaskan and the fireforming load was recommended by Harry McGowen; for field loads, I was really starting from scratch. The *Lyman*

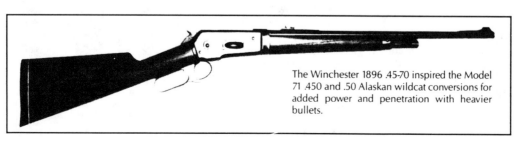

The Winchester 1896 .45-70 inspired the Model 71 .450 and .50 Alaskan wildcat conversions for added power and penetration with heavier bullets.

Reloading Handbook No. 46 shows data for the .50-70, .50-90 and .50-140 but they are very low pressure loads. They are not representative of the 44,000 psi range the Winchester and Browning Model 71 rifles were designed to handle.

The ratio of powder to bullet weight in the .50 Alaskan is so low that it is off the scale on the Powley Computer. Instead of using the slide rule device, I employed the semi-empirical mathematical formulas upon which the computer is based. The formulas are published in the NRA book *Handloading*, which was compiled by William C. Davis, Jr.

The equation for selecting IMR single-based powders is easy to use. Table I lists the formula for determining the relative burning rate of the powder to be used with the bullet and case of choice.

The optimum charge weight will be 86 percent of the water capacity of the case to the base of the bullet if powders slower than IMR-4198 are used. If we end up with a powder selection, from the above formula, with a relative quickness greater than 145, we should be using IMR-4198 or 4227 and it is necessary to recalculate the optimum powder charge by multiplying the water capacity by 80 percent instead of 86 percent.

To determine the water weight to the base of the bullet, weigh an empty primed case, record the weight, fill it to the top, record the weight and subtract the two. This gives the total

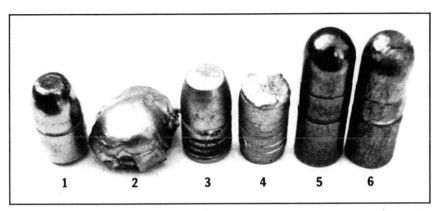

Before and after firing into wet newsprint: (1-2) 450-grain Barnes, (3-4) 485-grain NEI and (5-6) 600-grain A-Square bullets.

weight of water the case holds. Now calculate the amount of water (volume) the bullet will displace from its base to the top of the case neck, multiply that number by 252.89 (the number of grains of water per cubic inch) and subtract that from the total water weight.

Since the .50 Alaskan is a straight-walled case and faster burners are more commonly used in these cases (especially at the 40,000 psi pressure level), I assumed that the powder would be either IMR-4227 or 4198. Water weight to the base of the LBT bullet was 73.34 grains. Multiplying by .80 gives a powder charge of 58.67 grains.

The sectional density of the bullet is .264, the ratio of powder weight to bullet weight is .12 (58.67/485) and the square root of .12 is .346. The formula recommends a powder with a relative quickness of 151. The NRA book shows that IMR-4198 is the powder to use when relative quickness is between 145 and 165.

The formulas for velocity and pressure are a little lengthy but the muzzle velocity worked out to 1,912 fps and chamber pressure is 39,927 psi, well within the maximum working pressure of 44,000 psi for the Model 71 Winchester. I started with 55 grains of IMR-4198.

The first three-shot group with the above load read 1,827 fps on my PACT chronograph. That equates to 3,600 foot-pounds energy and a free recoil of 52 foot-pounds. The shots clustered into 1¾ inches and the cases literally slipped from the chamber. Pressure was monitored by checking case expansion at the pressure ring just forward of the web and comparing those measurements with expansion from .348 Winchester factory ammunition and similar measurements with commonly accepted maximum handloads.

Recoil is not as sharp as it is with high-velocity magnums. Because the muzzle raises quite sharply, however, the back of the fingers on the trigger hand get a good wallop from the lever when shooting from a bench. That was remedied by using a bungee cord to secure a heavy sandbag to the forearm. Firing the rifle offhand is not bad, especially with a good recoil pad and a Pachmayr recoil boot over the butt to add further cushioning.

As loads were increased in one-grain increments accuracy remained good, right up to 59 grains. This put three shots into 1¾ inches for 1,969 fps and 4,197 foot-pounds of energy with no signs of excessive pressure. I enjoyed enough of that from the bench and it was a good time to analyze the data collected from the chronograph.

The only objection to IMR-4198 is the high velocity spread with cast bullets. Thinking the crimps might not be heavy enough, I reshot the whole string using the heaviest crimp possible short of buckling the cases. That did not help reduce the standard deviation until I reached 60 and 61 grains. Velocity with 61 grains went to 2,008 fps and the standard deviation dropped to 11.1, but accuracy fell sharply to 3½ inches.

Results with Hercules Reloder 7 were satisfactory in all aspects. Starting at 53 grains with the LBT bullet, three shots went into a ¾-inch hole with a velocity of 1,711 fps and a standard deviation of 19.3. Low velocity spread

Left to right, an unmodified .348 hull, the special McGowen expanding plug which can be screwed into a standard loading press, an expanded case and a fireformed case trimmed to 2.1 inches.

and good accuracy prevailed up to 59 grains for 1,892 fps. Cases continued to slip easily from the chamber.

The Barnes 450-grain bullet was subjected to the same mathematical formulas and IMR-4198 was again selected, showing 58 grains for 1,960 fps. Starting with 51 grains at 1,712 fps and a 1¾ inch group, 55 grains produced 1,905 fps. At 58.0 grains, accuracy fell off sharply.

Results with Reloder 7 were impressive. Starting at 50 grains and increasing the charge one grain at a time to 59 grains, accuracy was good, rarely exceeding one inch along with a minimal standard deviation. Above 59 grains, accuracy went sour again and I stopped there.

With the cast bullets I'm sure it's the alloy, with the jacketed bullets I feel that a slightly heavier barrel might have helped accuracy. I'm not sure that any more velocity is needed with these bullets, at least on this continent. If you can't do it with this cartridge, you've got big troubles.

The 500-grain Lyman No. 515412 bullet was only peripherally tested with IMR-4198. Plain base bullets were not meant to be driven at these velocities. Accuracy was poor and the barrel was leaded heavily even though the bullets had a BHN of 21.

Because of the location of the cannelure on the 600-grain A-Square bullet, the loaded cartridge will not fit through the loading gate. The bullet was tested only to check the accuracy of the Powley formulas. It should be noted that the formula selected 50.76 grains of IMR-4198 to give 1,632 fps. The chronograph clocked a 51-grain load at 1,677 fps.

The Barnes, A-Square and LBT bullets were fired into water-soaked newsprint at point blank range, with striking velocities to approximate a 50-yard target. The Barnes bullet arrived at 1,825 fps, the LBT at 1,745 fps and the A-Square at 1,695 fps.

At first glance, the recovered Barnes bullet looked like a two-bit piece. It had expanded to .935 inch and weighed 432 grains for 96 percent weight retention.

The LBT bullet, while it did not expand, penetrated almost twice as far as the Barnes offering and weighed 462 grains, retaining 98 percent of its weight.

Table I
Powder Selection Formula
for use with single-base (IMR) powders

$$20 + \frac{12}{SD \times \sqrt{\dfrac{OPW}{BW}}} = RQ$$

SD— sectional density of the bullet
OPW— optimum powder weight
BW— bullet weight, in grains
RQ— relative quickness (burning rate) of powder

See text for additional comments on using this formula

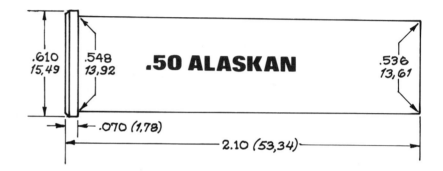

.610 / 15,49   .548 / 13,92   **.50 ALASKAN**   .536 / 13,61
.070 (1,78)   2.10 (53,34)

Table II
.50 Alaskan

bullet	charge (grains)	velocity (fps)	standard deviation	group (inches)
IMR-4198				
485 LBT	55	1,827	56.0	1.75
	57	1,962	52.0	2.0
	58	1,983	90.5	1.25
	59	1,969	19.0	1.75
	60	1,980	11.1	2.75
	61	2,009	13.7	3.25
450 Barnes	51	1,712	29.4	1.75
	53	1,796	6.7	2.0
	55	1,905	25.6	1.63
600 A-Square	51	1,677	13.9	3.0
	52	1,709	3.8	1.75
	53	1,739	8.5	.5*
Reloder 7				
485 LBT	53	1,711	19.3	.75
	56	1,786	.2	1.0
	57	1,820	5.0	1.25
	59	1,892	29.1	1.75
450 Barnes	50	1,683	11.3	1.0
	54	1,823	25.0	1.0
	57	1,847	27.0	.75
	59	1,994	7.4	1.0

All loads used CCI 200 primers. Groups fired at 50 yards with open sights over a PACT chronograph at 10 feet.

* Designates the most accurate load.

Be alert — Publisher cannot accept responsibility for errors in published load data.

The A-Square did not expand or deform. It went through 36 inches of newsprint and was recovered from the dirt backstop.

When loaded and crimped in its cannelure for an overall length of 2.533 inches, the Barnes bullet will just barely feed through the loading gate. Once in the magazine it cycles through the action and chambers perfectly. The LBT bullet is another story.

When loaded to an overall length of 2.5 inches the ogive on the LBT bullet is so short that the cartridge can't make it through the loading gate. All is not lost, however. I removed the magazine plug screw, magazine plug, spring assembly and follower. The rounds were slipped down the magazine and the parts were replaced in reverse order.

All that took about 30 seconds. The lever was cycled and three dummy cartridges went through the action and chambered perfectly. With the chamber empty, the lever can be lowered far enough to place a cartridge in the magazine. It can also be ejected without bringing one of the cartridges from the magazine onto the carrier.

The .50 Alaskan is not the type of cartridge one wants to use on game at a distance of much over 100 yards. Trajectory is not all that great. When sighted in at 50 yards, it will be 1.5 inches low at 100 yards and 6.7 inches low at 150 yards. It also sheds velocity and energy rapidly because of the broad nose configurations of the bullets.

I know our forefathers used the big .50s on buffalo at great distances and with spectacular success; they were using barrels of 30 inches or more with precise peep sights as opposed to open sights and they were aiming at targets much larger than most of us ever get to shoot at. They were also using 12 and 13-pound rifles as opposed to this eight pound carbine. This cartridge is for shooting at close range in heavy cover — use it accordingly.

Lastly, this cartridge is temperamental to variations in case length. If cases are not maintained at 2.1 inches, bullet impact can vary by as much as two inches from point of aim at 50 yards. If you put your best foot forward, you should be happy with the performance of the big .50 Alaskan. ●

CHAPTER
60

.600 Nitro Express

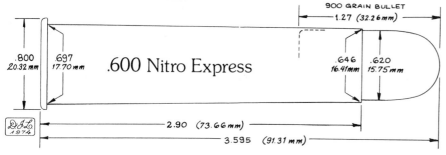

.600 Nitro Express

900 GRAIN BULLET
1.27 (32.26mm)

.800 20.32mm | .697 17.70mm | .646 16.41mm | .620 15.75mm

2.90 (73.66mm)

3.595 (91.31 mm)

DJL 1974

These dimensions were taken from a single specimen of a late Kynoch 110 cordite factory load.

The .600 Nitro Express is shown alongside a .30-06 cartridge for comparison. The 110-grain cordite charge gives the 900-grain bullet 7,600 fp of energy at the muzzle.

BACK IN 1903 the British gunmaking firm of Jeffery introduced what was then, and remains yet today, the largest sporting rifle caliber of all. Developing 7,600 foot pounds of energy at the muzzle, it was not surpassed in power for 55 years, when in 1958 the .460 Weatherby hove on the scene with just under 8,100 foot pounds.

Jeffery called its new number the *.600 Nitro Express*. It consisted of the largest sporting case yet, three inches long, with a base diameter of .695 to .700-inch and a typically British thin rim .805-inch in diameter. This monstrous case approached 12-bore dimensions and has a total capacity of 222 grains of water, reduced to 139 grains when the bullet is seated.

The .600 bullet is by no means a true

.60 caliber, being nominally of .622-inch diameter. In weight the .600 N.E. bullet takes a back seat to no one — it hefts a nice, round, 900 grains — somewhat over two full ounces; over one-eighth of a pound. It was Cordite-loaded, of course, a 100-grain charge producing 1,850 fps, while a 110-grain charge churned up 1,950 fps.

Jeffery's .600 epitomized an era — the era of massive cartridges and side-by-side doubles intended for harvesting ivory in deepest, darkest Africa. The cartridge was intended to offer the professional ivory hunter the massive shocking power of the big 2 and 4-bore muzzle loaders combined with the great penetration of modern (1903) full-jacketed "solid" bullets. It did all that well, and when loaded with strong-jacketed bullets (some

weren't as stout as they should have been) it would punch clear through the massive skull of the biggest rogue bull to be found. Only last year Henk Visser drove down two bull tuskers with his elaborate and priceless Greener .600 double, each with a single shot that passed completely through. The animals never twitched.

Not many .600 rifles were built; the Birmingham Proof House records show less than 300 passed through. Many were single shots, but the classic .600 is a side-by-side double weighing upwards of 18 pounds to soak up the enormous recoil of that two-ounce bullet departing at 1,950 fps. Only professionals bought .600's, aside from Indian princes and maharajahs who had to have one of everything.

Today the .600 isn't used much, and Kynoch quit making ammunition years ago. Not many people have even seen a .600 rifle, but the cartridge has become a legend of its own. Three people we know own .600 rifles, and one of them owns *two* fine doubles so chambered.

Can the .600 Nitro be reloaded? Certainly, once you have cases and bullets. Original cases take the big Kynoch express primer which isn't too difficult to find. However, the No. 172 shouldn't be used, but the No. 40 instead. The 172 is too hot. Original Kynoch bullets are mighty scarce, but a copper-tube Barnes solid of the proper weight and size is available from Colorado Custom Bullets. As for powder, IMR-3031 can be substituted for Cordite in cases such as

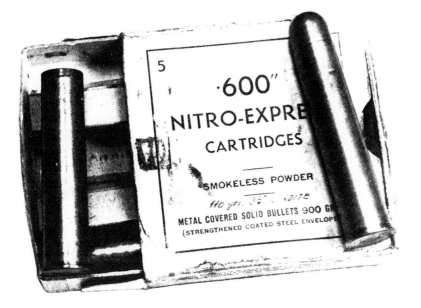

5

·600"
NITRO-EXPRE
CARTRIDGES

SMOKELESS POWDER

110 grs.

METAL COVERED SOLID BULLETS 900 GR
(STRENGTHENED COATED STEEL ENVELOPE)

this on a one-for-one basis, with a slight reduction in velocity from Cordite levels.

Loading dies for the .600 aren't cataloged by any maker, but Hollywood (Whitney Sales, Inc., 6742 Tampa Ave., Reseda, CA, 91335) can supply them on special order, and RCBS can probably do the same.

Cases are the big problem. Original Kynoch brass is fine, but fired cases will benefit from about 1¼ inches of mouth annealing, done in molten lead. New cases can be turned from brass bar stock, and they may also be made by swaging and turning down the head of .50 Browning Machine Gun cases, then trimming to length. In the past a couple of custom gun shops have offered cases made in this fashion — and they proved quite satisfactory. At last report, new .600 (also .577) cases from the .50 BMG can be ordered from East Surrey Firearms Ltd., Gillette House, 55 Basinghall St. London EC2V-5 EA, G.B. These are excellent heavy-duty cases, equal or superior to the originals.

As for loading data, start with 100 grains IMR-3031, Eley-Kynoch No. 40 caps, and 900-grain bullets. From that point, for a single shot rifle, simply work up in small powder increments until the load shoots to point of aim with the original sights. This may require as much as 115-120 grains if the gun was originally regulated for the 110/Cordite load.

With a double rifle, increase charges *only* until the barrels print together. At the starting charge they'll shoot apart, and increasing the charge should move the bullet strikes toward one another. When they are together, stick with that charge, even if elevation is not right on the button. To further increase the charge will cause the barrels to "cross," as well as generate excess pressure.

In the end, the .600 is a unique and impressive member of the 20th Century cartridge family. No matter what you might have been told, it isn't entirely dead — and you *can* handload it with just a bit more effort and expense than usual. Any fine old .600 rifle is well worth the effort to keep it thundering — after all, who knows when a pachyderm might raid your garden. — George Nonte ●